ENGLISH LINGUISTICS, LITERATURE, AND LANGUAGE TEACHING IN A CHANGING ERA

PROCEEDINGS OF THE 1ST INTERNATIONAL CONFERENCE ON ENGLISH LINGUISTICS, LITERATURE, AND LANGUAGE TEACHING (ICE3LT), YOGYAKARTA, INDONESIA 27-28 SEPTEMBER 2018

English Linguistics, Literature, and Language Teaching in a Changing Era

Edited by

Suwarsih Madya
Universitas Negeri Yogyakarta, Indonesia

Willy A. Renandya
Nanyang Technological University, Singapore

Masaki Oda
Tamagawa University, Japan

Didi Sukiyadi
Universitas Pendidikan Indonesia, Indonesia

Anita Triastuti
Universitas Negeri Yogyakarta, Indonesia

Ashadi
Universitas Negeri Yogyakarta, Indonesia

Erna Andriyanti
Universitas Negeri Yogyakarta, Indonesia

Nur Hidayanto P.S.P
Universitas Negeri Yogyakarta, Indonesia

LONDON AND NEW YORK

Routledge is an imprint of the Taylor & Francis Group, an informa business

© 2020 Taylor & Francis Group, London, UK

Typeset by Integra Software Services Pvt. Ltd., Pondicherry, India

All rights reserved. No part of this publication or the information contained herein may be reproduced, stored in a retrieval system, or transmitted in any form or by any means, electronic, mechanical, by photocopying, recording or otherwise, without written prior permission from the publisher.

Although all care is taken to ensure integrity and the quality of this publication and the information herein, no responsibility is assumed by the publishers nor the author for any damage to the property or persons as a result of operation or use of this publication and/or the information contained herein.

Publisher's Note
The publisher has gone to great lengths to ensure the quality of this reprint but points out that some imperfections in the original copies may be apparent.

Published by: CRC Press/Balkema
Schipholweg 107C, 2316XC Leiden, The Netherlands
e-mail: Pub.NL@taylorandfrancis.com
www.crcpress.com – www.taylorandfrancis.com

First issued in paperback 2021

ISBN 13: 978-1-03-224160-9 (pbk)
ISBN 13: 978-0-367-07501-9 (hbk)

DOI: https://doi.org/10.1201/9780429021039

English Linguistics, Literature, and Language Teaching in a Changing Era – Madya et al. (eds)
© 2020 Taylor & Francis Group, London, ISBN 978-1-03-224160-9

Table of contents

Preface	ix
Acknowledgement	xi
Organizing Committee	xiii

Plenary Presentation Papers

Exploring language teacher identity through short story analysis in a disruptive era *Gary Barkhuizen*	3
Literature and literacy in the changing era: Will disruptive bring an end to literature? *Manneke Budiman*	9
Groundless beliefs: Language learners and media discourse *Masaki Oda*	14
Going beyond communicative competence to become literate national and global citizens *Suwarsih Madya*	20

Part I: English Linguistics

Materializing colonial heritage in *Goa* Belanda *Agung Farid & R. Vindy M. Puspa*	37
English and Javanese greeting expressions: A descriptive qualitative study on pragmatics *Ayu T. Andayani & Basikin*	44

Part II: Literature

Ryunosuke Akugatawa's *Kappa:* Warning against the dangers and pitfalls of modernization *Orestis Soidi, Emzir & J. H. Tamboto*	57
Disruptive creativity as represented by Jane Austen & Seth Grahame-Smith's *Pride and Prejudice and Zombies* *Ratna Asmarani*	63
Cultural term translation in *Der Prozess* Novel by Frans Kafka: Analysis of translation methods and ideology *Sulfah Risna & Pratomo Widodo*	69
Digital literacy practices of English language learners: Indonesian context *Westi. H. Utami, Didi Suherdi & Pupung Purnawarman*	76

Part III: English Language Teaching in Changing Era

Teaching critical thinking through reading to Senior High School students *Adnan Zaid & Sri Sarjiyati*	89

Effects of Think Pair Share strategy on Indonesian vocational higher institution students' speaking skills 94
Alfi H. Miqawati & Fitri Wijayanti

Predict, Locate, Add, and Note (PLAN) strategy: An effective way to assist EFL students' reading comprehension in task-based learning 100
Annisa Rizqiana & Anita Triastuti

Professional development challenges for Indonesian English teachers 108
Astri O. Kuncahya & Basikin

Automatic speech recognition to enhance EFL students' pronunciation through Google's Voice Search application 115
Cherlie E. Rayshata & Dyah S. Ciptaningrum

Factors influencing anxiety of non-native ESL teachers in compulsory schooling 123
Cindyra Galuhwardani & Bambang W. Pratolo

A descriptive case study on accommodating Turnitin to optimize the role of portfolio assessment and self-assessment for students' writing process 130
Dewi Cahyaningrum, Hasan Zainnuri & Ngadiso

Foreign language anxiety in relation with students' motivation: What's the matter? 137
Dyta Maykasari & Widyastuti Purbani

The influence of Computer Assisted Language Learning (CALL) to improve English speaking skills 144
Dyah Ratnaningsih, Damoyanto Purba, Daviq Wiratno & Faris Nofandi

Enhancing Indonesian elementary students' engagement in learning English through cooperative learning strategies 150
Emeral, Dyah S. Ciptaningrum, Elsa M. Marahati & Thuthut Kartikarini

The implementation of intercultural language learning in teaching Indonesian as a foreign language to international students 158
Godlove Kiswaga & Anita Triastuti

The implementation of MOOC using Schoology towards students' learning outcomes 165
Hasan Zainnuri, Ngadiso & Dewi Cahyaningrum

The effect of online extensive reading in building the reading fluency of EFL university students 172
Hendriwanto & Utut Kurniati

English Teachers' perception on the implementation of character education in Curriculum 2013 178
Heni P. Lestari & Bambang W. Pratolo

Raising English students' intercultural awareness through cultural texts 187
Indah Permatasari & Erna Andriyanti

Tertiary students' anxiety in speaking English 193
Muamaroh, Nur Hidayat & Sri Lestari

Developing integrated English learning materials of Islamic contents based on instructional analysis: A design-based research 199
Muhammad Saifuddin & Dwi Nurcahyani

An investigation into the English language writing strategies used by Indonesian EFL graduate students 209
Nanik Rahmawati, Endang Fauziati & Sri Marmanto

Let's speak: Encouraging students to speak up in the classroom through project-based learning 214
Nur I. Muslim, Yulia N. Hidayah, Iffah Mayasari & Ashadi

Investigating self-correction strategies for oral grammatical errors and their merit in language acquisition among EFL learners 220
Nurul Marlisa & Ashadi

Proposing literature circle strategy to enhance students' reading comprehension in EFL classroom 227
Nurus Sa'adah & Erna Andriyanti

The representation of cultural elements in the promotion of intercultural communicative competence in senior high school EFL textbooks in Indonesia 235
Oktavia Herawati

The significance of teacher's talent in improving students' engagement in EFL classroom 243
Puspita Wijayati & Erna Andriyanti

English language learning needs of culinary students in vocational school 251
Richa A. Shara & Erna Andriyanti

Narrative story cards for ELT: A report on their development and effectiveness 257
Richard J. Stockton

EFL adult learners' perceptions on language anxiety toward the speaking performance 264
Rini Ardiani & Bambang W. Pratolo

The differentiated types of role play to enhance speaking in contextual learning 271
Sarah M. Azizah & Dyah S. Ciptaningrum

Looking at learner engagement in a digital multimodal-based instruction 276
Siti Kustini

Developing the model of teaching materials for ESP (English for Specific Purposes) 283
Stefhani R. Rahmawati, Emzir & Aceng

The integration of character education in reading classes at the English Education Department 289
Sugirin, Siti Sudartini & Ani Setyaningsih

The implementation of Moodle platform to help teachers develop blended learning in the field of Teaching English as a Foreign Language (TEFL) 300
Tchello Kasse & Anita Triastuti

Administering a need analysis survey to young EFL learners in Yogyakarta 308
Thuthut Kartikarini, Dyah S. Ciptaningrum, Emeral, Elsa M. Marahati & Septiana W. Setyaningrum

Improving speaking skills through role plays for nursing students in Indonesian context 315
Tri W. Floriasti & Indah Permatasari

Developing the students' reflective skills in teaching and learning of reading in disruptive era 320
Umi Rachmawati

Out-of-class language learning activities: A case study of good language learners 328
Wawan Cahyadin & Halijah Koso

Investigating individual's clarity of enunciation with Orai application: implications for L2 assessment 335
Widya R. Kusumaningrum & Rangga Asmara

A need analysis of hearing-impaired students writing materials 341
Wikandari M. Puspasari & Ashadi

L1 and L2 Classroom: Does it truly assist learning? 349
Zefki O. Feri & Ashadi

Author Index 355

English Linguistics, Literature, and Language Teaching in a Changing Era – Madya et al. (eds)
© 2020 Taylor & Francis Group, London, ISBN 978-1-03-224160-9

Preface

This book presents the proceedings of the 1st International Conference on English Linguistics, Literature, and Language Teaching (ICE3LT) held in Yogyakarta, Indonesia, from 27-28 September 2018 hosted by English Language Education Department, Faculty of Languages and Arts, Universitas Negeri Yogyakarta. This conference was organized in response to the impacts of advances in information and communication technology (ICT), which lead to what so called a disruptive era, to English linguistics, literature, and language teaching. The 1st ICE3LT, therefore, aimed to bring together educators, researchers, and practitioners with interests in these three aforementioned areas at all levels. The conference is, accordingly, expected to provide a high quality academic platform for English linguistics, literature, and language teaching communities to promote and strengthen connections between theory and practice, and explore different perspectives on the application of up-to-date research findings in this disruptive era into different practices.

The above aim was realized by promoting the theme *English Linguistics, Literature, and Language Teaching in the Changing Era* from which three subthemes were derived: 1) English Linguistics (psycholinguistic and cognitive explorations, sociolinguistics, language variation and applied linguistics, discourse, corpora and literary analysis, theoretical corpus linguistics, multimodal discourse analysis and linguistics, contrastive linguistics, lexicography and lexicology, rhetoric and stylistics); 2) English Literature (the challenge of literary education in the disruptive era, the opportunity of literature and literary education in the disruptive technology, the role of literature in the disruptive era, the role of literature in establishing literacy in the disruptive era, disruptive era and redefinition of literature and literary education, literature, reading and literacy in the disruptive era, digital literacy and the role of literature); and English Language Teaching (innovation in language teaching and learning, computer assisted language teaching, robot assisted language learning, foreign language teaching and teacher development, teacher evaluation, training and development, learning strategies and learner autonomy, language and education in multilingual settings, language policy evaluation, assessment and testing: testing language skills and sub-skills, discourse and multimodality in text, education technology and language learning, best practices in language teaching, contextual curriculum for language teaching).

The book presents 48 selected papers in the areas of the three subthemes above. These papers were reviewed by the team of internal reviewers and the team of editors. This book consists of three parts, each of which contains papers according to the themes. These three parts are preceded with four plenary presentation papers by the invited guest speakers. The plenary presentation papers represent two themes, English Literature and Language Teaching. Finally, we hope that this book will enlighten the advances of English linguistics, literature, and language teaching in the changing era.

English Linguistics, Literature, and Language Teaching in a Changing Era – Madya et al. (eds)
© 2020 Taylor & Francis Group, London, ISBN 978-1-03-224160-9

Acknowledgement

Sutrisna Wibawa, *Universitas Negeri Yogyakarta, Indonesia*
Margana, *Universitas Negeri Yogyakarta, Indonesia*
Endang Nurhayati, *Universitas Negeri Yogyakarta, Indonesia*
Maman Suryaman, *Universitas Negeri Yogyakarta, Indonesia*
Widyastuti Purbani, *Universitas Negeri Yogyakarta, Indonesia*
Sukarno, *Universitas Negeri Yogyakarta, Indonesia*
Suwarsih Madya, *Universitas Negeri Yogyakarta, Indonesia*
Gary Barkhuizen, *University of Auckland, New Zealand*
Willy A. Renandya, *Nanyang Technological University, Singapore*
Masaki Oda, Tamagawa *University, Japan*
Didi Sukiyadi, *Universitas Pendidikan Indonesia, Indonesia*
Ashadi, *Universitas Negeri Yogyakarta, Indonesia*
Anita Triastuti, *Universitas Negeri Yogyakarta, Indonesia*
Erna Andriyanti, *Universitas Negeri Yogyakarta, Indonesia*
Nur Hidayanto P.S.P, *Universitas Negeri Yogyakarta, Indonesia*
Devi Hermasari, *Universitas Negeri Yogyakarta, Indonesia*
Niken Anggraeni, *Universitas Negeri Yogyakarta, Indonesia*
Ani Sulistyaningsih, *Universitas Negeri Yogyakarta, Indonesia*
Siwi Karmadi, *Universitas Negeri Yogyakarta, Indonesia*
Siti Mahripah, *Universitas Negeri Yogyakarta, Indonesia*
Ella Wulandari, *Universitas Negeri Yogyakarta, Indonesia*
Sari Hidayati, *Universitas Negeri Yogyakarta, Indonesia*
Dyah Setyowati Ciptaningrum, *Universitas Negeri Yogyakarta, Indonesia*
Sudiyono, *Universitas Negeri Yogyakarta, Indonesia*
Suciati, *Universitas Negeri Yogyakarta, Indonesia*
Emy Nur Rokhani, *Universitas Negeri Yogyakarta, Indonesia*
Nila Kurniasari, *Universitas Negeri Yogyakarta, Indonesia*
Yuniar B. Diyanti, *Universitas Negeri Yogyakarta, Indonesia*
Lusi Nur Hayati, *Universitas Negeri Yogyakarta, Indonesia*
Nunik Sugesti, *Universitas Negeri Yogyakarta, Indonesia*

English Linguistics, Literature, and Language Teaching in a Changing Era – Madya et al. (eds)
© 2020 Taylor & Francis Group, London, ISBN 978-1-03-224160-9

ORGANIZING COMMITTEE

PATRON

Sutrisna Wibawa

CHAIR

Ashadi

COMMITTEE

Devi Hermasari
Niken Anggraeni
Ani Sulistyaningsih
Anita Triastuti
Erna Andriyanti
Nur Hidayanto P. S. P.
Ella Wulandari
Sari Hidayati
Siwi Karmadi
Siti Mahripah

Dyah Setyowati Ciptaningrum
Sudiyono
Suciati
Emy Nur Rokhani
Nila Kurniasari
Yuniar B. Diyanti
Lusi Nur Hayati
Nunik Sugesti

Plenary Presentation Papers

English Linguistics, Literature, and Language Teaching in a Changing Era – Madya et al. (eds)
© 2020 Taylor & Francis Group, London, ISBN 978-1-03-224160-9

Exploring language teacher identity through short story analysis in a disruptive era

Gary Barkhuizen
University of Auckland, New Zealand

ABSTRACT: This article explains 'short story analysis', an approach to analysing narrative data, and demonstrates its rationale and methods by drawing on a study that explored the developing identities of a cohort of experienced language teacher educators enrolled in a PhD program at a public university in Colombia, South America. An analysis of an extract from an interview (i.e., a short story) with one of the teacher educators is presented to show how his identity is revealed when telling about how and why he decided on his PhD research topic. This focus teacher challenges what he calls the 'instrumental' language teacher education policies and practices of his country, particularly as they apply to indigenous teachers, and reflects on how he desires in his PhD research to study this situation so he can contribute more effectively in the future in his own English teacher education practices.

Keywords: short story analysis, teacher identity, narrative inquiry

1 INTRODUCTION

The aim of this article is to explain and demonstrate an approach to narrative analysis that I call 'short story analysis' [1]. To do so, I draw on data from a study on language teacher identity that I conducted in a doctoral program at a public university in Colombia, South America. The aim of that study was to explore the complex interrelationships among developing identities of experienced English teachers who had embarked on studying towards a PhD. Seven teachers started the doctoral program together. Besides being experienced teachers, they were also teacher educators with varying degrees of experience. In addition, another identity they shared was that of novice researcher – being PhD students, they were in the early stages of their research careers.

These multiple identities – language teacher, teacher educator, PhD student, researcher – were often in conflict as they lived their busy teaching lives also as PhD students, and they experienced considerable challenges attempting to juggle the identities productively, for themselves and for their language learners and student teachers. Having the ability to deal with conflicts and make sense of the often ambiguous role demands expected of them are symptoms of the disruptive era in which we now live. O'Sullivan [2], writing about young workers in the business world suggests the particular competence they require: "In a fast-disrupting age, what the … business environment needs is young people who are comfortable with ambiguity and can engage and challenge views they find confronting. Not those with closed minds" (p. C2). The same tolerance and agency is probably required for those in the language teaching profession too.

The story I share below is an example of one teacher who desires, through his PhD research, to address the inequity he perceives to be evident in the Colombian education system, particularly in relation to the indigenous population [3]. In other words, he plans to actively work towards managing the disruption he encounters in his working life, and thereby seek some degree of harmony amongst his multiple identities. Identities sometimes do worked together in harmony to promote the desires and needs of teachers, as well as those of their students and institutions [4].

2 NARRATIVE ANALYSIS

Kramp [5] claims that stories "assist humans to make life experiences meaningful. Stories preserve our memories, prompt our reflections, connect us with our past and present, and assist us to envision our future" (p. 107). As such, it makes sense to tap into the stories people tell about their experiences for the purposes of research. Narrative inquiry is all about story – using story to explore a phenomenon such as teacher identity, language learning, or study abroad. Simply, stories in narrative inquiry are those that research participants tell researchers (the data, which is then analyzed), or those that researchers construct from (possibly non-story) data collected from research participants. In the process of *narrative analysis* "some investigators attend to language, form, social context, and audience more than others do" [6]. In other words, there exists a range of analytical methods associate with narrative analysis. Short story analysis, illustrated below, is one of those.

3 THE STUDY: DATA COLLECTION

As stated, the aim of this study was to explore the identity developments of a group of experienced teachers studying towards a PhD at a university in Colombia. The purpose of this article, however, is mainly to describe and illustrate short story analysis using story data from one of the teachers. Two narrative interviews were conducted with each of the seven participants. Interview one took place in June 2017 after their first year of study and lasted approximately one hour. Topics included: their personal biography, language learning and language teaching history, reasons for PhD study, the PhD journey so far, and goals for the future after completing their PhD. Interview two took place four months later in October 2017, and its purpose was to further explore five common themes found during a thematic analysis [7] of the first interview. The second interview was slightly shorter, lasting about 40 minutes. The short story to be analyzed below was extracted from the first interview with Diego.

4 THE PARTICIPANT: DIEGO

Diego is in his 30s, from the city of Bogotá. He completed his BA with a major in languages, and he started teaching English at a private language school while still an undergraduate student. Later he studied for his Master's qualification in applied linguistics, and when he finished he started teaching future English teachers content subjects like linguistics and language pedagogy, thus becoming engaged in teacher education. He is currently head of small English Department (an administrative role and identity) at his university.

Diego decided to do a PhD for a number of reasons, including being envious of a friend who was doing a PhD, "seeing him reading, seeing him writing". He added that he liked learning and studying, saying "I like a personal commitment". He also wants his student teachers to be "very well prepared professionals". Finally, inspired by his research during his Master's studies he explains, "I realised there was a certain area of interest that I wanted to further develop. It was about linguistic identity. I had considered perspectives that are a little outside the norm of what bilingualism is usually considered". Here he signals his commitment to an alternative, political perspective on language education, to become even more evident in the short story.

5 SHORT STORY ANALYSIS

Short stories are excerpts of data extracted from a larger set of data such as conversations, interviews, written narratives, and multimodal digital stories [1]. They can be identified as *stories* in that they narrate experiences, from the past or the imagined future, and include reflective or evaluative [8] commentary on those experiences. They typically also have a temporal dimension, a common characteristic of story, and they show evidence of narrative action; i.e., something happens. Short stories are analyzed *thematically* in detail for both *content* and *context*, an analytical focus typical of narrative inquiry.

In terms of *content*, attention is systematically paid in the analysis to three intersecting dimensions of narrative: *who*, or the characters in the story, their relationships and their positions vis-à-vis each other; *where*, or the places and sequences of places in which the story action takes place; and *when*, or the time in which the action unfolds, past, present and future. The *who, where* and *when* dimensions are familiar in narrative—in literature they are referred to as characters, setting and plot, and in narrative inquiry, Connelly and Clandinin [9] encourage researchers to explore three dimensions or commonplaces relating to sociality, place, and temporality.

The aim in the analysis is to work systematically through the short story text, line by line, and to identify all references, explicit and implicit, to each of the dimensions, focusing on one dimension at a time. On each occasion the following relevant questions are asked: *Who*, and what happened/will happen *together*? *Where*, and what happened/will happen *there*? *When*, and what happened/will happen *then*? The focus on these three dimensions is not particularly innovative in narrative inquiry, but doing so in the way I have suggested requires the analyst to undertake a detailed examination of the story text and thus prevents a cursory scanning of the story in search of (often vague) themes. During this process connections among the *who, where*, and *when* dimensions are made and become thematically meaningful in relation to the topical content of the inquiry.

A focus (only) on content has been critiqued in that it does not pay sufficient attention to the context in which people's stories are lived and narratives are constructed and the form that they take [10; 6]. Context is crucial to an understanding of narratives, and it is uncommon to find narrative studies that do not consider context to some extent. Again, therefore, requiring a close examination of context in short story analysis is not a novel suggestion, but the way I suggest it is done ensures a more rigorous consideration of context, particularly when combined with the three-dimensional analysis of content, as I argue.

I have proposed [11] three interconnected levels of story (or contextual spaces) which not only help guide analysis but also encourage the researcher to look beyond the immediate contexts of face-to-face interactions. These levels are not distinct, of course, but represent an expanding or moving outward of interpretive activity away from a too narrow focus only on the experiences of the individual storyteller, to include a consideration of institutional and community, and then macro-level social structures, discourses and ideologies. These three levels, or what I prefer to call scales of context [12], reflect The Douglas Fir Group's [13] transdisciplinary framework for researching L2 learning.

The first level of *story* (all small letters) is personal and embodies the inner thoughts, emotions, ideas and theories of narrators. It includes the social interactions accomplished using various semiotic resources in the narrators' immediate contexts. Time (*when*) scales are therefore shorter, place (*where*) scales are smaller, and interactions and relationships (*who*) scales are more intimate and personal. In these contexts teachers have more agency and power [14,15] to manipulate and possibly change the social structures they engage with.

The second level of *Story* (with a capital S) spreads outwards to include wider-scale interactions with institutional colleagues and communities. On this scale of *Story*, teachers usually have less agency to construct their practice, their identities, and their stories. Social structures are more rigid and difficult to penetrate and therefore change is less likely to be achieved.

Lastly, *STORY* (in capital letters) refers to the broader ideological structures in which teaching and learning are embedded. Here teachers have even less power to make decisions about conditions which influence their practice and their learners' learning. Examples of *STORIES* include national immigration policies, discourses and values associated with religion, culture, politics, and economics. The use of capital letters to refer to this level of *STORY* merely signifies a wider, macro scale and the power often associated with it, and in no way diminishes the integrity or worth of the narrating teacher' *STORY*. *STORIES* are concerned with context, and they, like *Stories*, are not detached from the experiences of teachers. They are meaningfully connected to what they think, do and feel, and how they enact and negotiate their identities.

The three scales of context (*story, Story, STORY*) and the interconnecting dimensions of the story content (*who, where, when*) interact together to generate a narrative space within which narrators imagine and live their experiences and construct their identities. Short story analysis investigates this space, from two interrelated perspectives: (a) the experience of the narrator—what happens in the story (the narrative action) and the narrator's evaluations of or reflections on that action; and (b) the researcher's interpretations of what is told.

6 THE SHORT STORY: CHOOSING A RESEARCH TOPIC

In order to be accepted onto the PhD program Diego was required to submit with his application a brief research proposal. In the following short story, extracted from his first interview, he tells about how he decided on his research topic. In presenting the short story, I break it down into lines of idea units [16] and number these for ease of reference in the accompanying discussion.

1. he spoke Portuguese
2. he spoke Spanish
3. he spoke English
4. and he became an English language teacher
5. his English was not like standard English
6. I mean, like teachers didn't seem to like him very much
7. I don't know because later on I talked to other teachers
8. who had met him
9. and they didn't like him much
10. I don't know why
11. didn't actually dig him
12. and he also well of course he spoke the Witoto language
13. so then I was like 'this is happening'
14. there's people there are people who are intending to become English language teachers
15. and they have an indigenous background
16. an ethnic background
17. and we need to understand
18. and it was pretty similar to what I had studied before
19. we need to understand the culture and the individual
20. that is behind what is otherwise just normalizing an instrumental purpose of having everybody just learn English
21. so then I felt like that's what I needed to study
    . . .
22. and then I thought like
23. 'well there is something that has always been my passion
24. there is some knowledge that I have already gained by studying that
25. there is a political perspective that I don't want to abandon
26. and there is this guy who was from the university I'm working for and there must be more guys

I find it useful to start the short story analysis by looking for all references to the people in the story (*who*), and how they relate to each other. This immediately gets me into the action of the story. And at the same time I focus on both *where* and *when*, at all times paying careful attention to the three context scales of *story, Story* and *STORY*.

The analysis reveals five main people or groups of people, and they are all intertwined in the story. In line 1 ("He") we are introduced to the "English language teacher" (line 4) who is the focus of Diego's story. This teacher, we learn, has "an indigenous background" (line 15) and we know this because he spoke "the Witoto language" (line 12), a language spoken spoken by a group of people in a particular region (*where*) in Colombia. The second main character, of course, is Diego (*who*), the narrator of the story. And it is the connection between Diego and the indigenous teacher that is the central theme of the story. This is not a 'real' relationship since they do not actually know each other. But it is teachers like him ("there are people", line 14) whom Diego wants to research in his PhD. These 'imagined' teachers (*who*) are the third group of characters in the story.

Diego has noticed that indigenous teachers are discriminated against in the educational system (context at *STORY* level). He had actually met "other teachers" (line 7, and the fourth group of people in the story) who "didn't like him much" (line 9), they "didn't actually dig him" (line 11). This is somewhat ironic considering that the targeted teacher is multilingual, being able to speak Portuguese, Spanish, English and his own indigenous language, Witoto, and would thus probably make a very good language teacher. The first two of these languages represent places (*where*), or countries, that have powerful colonial histories in Latin America (*where*), and have clashed with indigenous populations (*who*). And English (also *where* on a *STORY* level) has done the same through its expansion as a language around the world.

Diego feels that the discrimination suffered by indigenous teachers is unfair, and wishes to expose it in his future research (*when*) (lines 19-20): "we need to understand the culture and the individual/that is behind what is otherwise just normalizing an instrumental purpose of having everybody just learn English". In this comment Diego is resisting the typical instrumental purposes often associate with learning English, such as employment, getting a job, and going abroad. He uses the pronoun "we" (*who*, lines 17 and 19) to include himself and other teachers and researchers working in Colombia. He believes that in addition Colombia should be paying attention to understanding its indigenous teachers and incorporating their beliefs and practices into the English language teaching processes operating in the country.

Diego believes that "I needed to study" (line 21) this topic in the future (*when*) and it is also "my passion" (line 23). In this story, he thus identifies his PhD research topic. He is convinced that it is a worthy topic because he knows of at least one other person ("this guy", line 26) at his university, the fifth main character in the story, who holds similar "political perspectives" (line 25) to his about language education in Colombia, and that "there must be more guys" (line 26). One senses a certain political activism in Diego's story; his past and imagined experiences (*when*) show him, his identity, to be a person who is committed to bringing about change among his future student teachers ("intending to become English language teachers", line 14), his community ("the university I'm working for", line 26), and the education system more broadly ("having everybody just learn English", line 20). Diego's story extends across contexts from micro to macro (*story, Story, STORY*), and in this space his multiple identities, both lived and imagined, are constructed. Most evident among these are language teacher, politically active teacher educator, PhD researcher, and indigenous teacher advocate.

7 CONCLUSIONS

This article has demonstrated short story analysis. Because of space limitations it has done so quite briefly, but I hope it has shown how paying attention to both content (the three *who, where* and *when* dimensions) and context (the three *story, Story, STORY* scales of context) in the process of thematic analysis enables a more detailed analysis of storied textual data. What I have presented in this short article no doubt raises many questions about short story analysis, such as: Which 'short story' extracts should be selected from the data for analysis? How many short stories should be analyzed in any one study or report? How much emphasis should be placed on context versus content? How do analysts make links between the analysis of several short stories? These are important questions, and answering them is beyond the scope of this paper. However, my advice is to try out different approaches, perhaps starting quite small, focusing on only one short story, and then gradually working towards analyzing multiple stories. Working with collaborators is also a good idea – sharing ideas about which stories to select (as well as how to collect them in the first place) and which analytical approaches to use is also good practice.

In this article, short story analysis has shown to be effective for exploring the process of identity construction – both in the living of experiences (as represented in the story told) and in the telling of those experiences (through the storytelling). Diego's story has revealed that he desires for his developing multiple identities to be aligned with his beliefs (and accompanying emotions) about language teacher education and the future of language teaching and learning in Colombia in this disruptive era.

REFERENCES

[1] Barkhuizen, G. (2016). A short story approach to analyzing teacher (imagined) identities over time. *TESOL Quarterly*, *50*(3), 655–683.

[2] O'Sullivan, F. (2018, 11 August). Freedom's just another word for those afraid to think. *New Zealand Herald*, p. C2.

[3] Wilches, J.A.U., Medina, J.M.O., & Gutiérrez, C. (2018). Indigenous students learning English in higher education: Challenges and hopes. *Íkala, Journal of Language and Culture*, *23*(2), 229–254.

[4] Barkhuizen, G. (2017). Language teacher identity research: An introduction. In G. Barkhuizen (Ed.), *Reflections on language teacher identity research* (pp. 1–11). New York: Routledge.

[5] Kramp, M.K. (2004). Exploring life and experience through narrative inquiry. In K. deMarrais & S.D. Lapan (Eds.) *Foundations for research: Methods of inquiry in education and the social sciences* (pp. 103–121). Mahwah, NJ: Erlbaum.

[6] Riessman, C.K. (2008). *Narrative methods for the human sciences*. Los Angeles: Sage.

[7] Barkhuizen, G., Benson, P., & Chik, A. (2014). *Narrative inquiry in language teaching and learning research*. New York: Routledge.

[8] Labov, W. (1997). Some further steps in narrative analysis. *Journal of Narrative and Life History*, *7*, 395–415.

[9] Connelly, F.M., & Clandinin, D.J. (2006). Narrative inquiry. In J.L. Green, G. Camilli, & P.B. Elmore (Eds.), *Complementary methods for research in education* (pp. 477–487). Mahwah, NJ: Lawrence Erlbaum.

[10] Pavlenko, A. (2007). Autobiographic narratives as data in applied linguistics. *Applied Linguistics*, *28*(2), 163–188.

[11] Barkhuizen, G. (2008). A narrative approach to exploring context in language teaching. *English Language Teaching Journal*, *62*(3), 231–239.

[12] Blommaert, J. (2010). *The sociolinguistics of globalization*. Cambridge: Cambridge University Press.

[13] Douglas Fir Group (Supplement 2016). A transdisciplinary framework for SLA in a multilingual world. *The Modern Language Journal*, *100*, 19–47.

[14] Ahearn, L.M. (2001). Language and agency. *Annual Review of Anthropology*, *30*, 109–139.

[15] Darvin, R., & Norton, B. (2015). Identity and a model of investment in applied linguistics. *Annual Review of Applied Linguistics*, *35*, 36–56.

[16] Gee, J. (1986). Units in the production of narrative discourse. *Discourse Processes*, *9*, 391–422.

English Linguistics, Literature, and Language Teaching in a Changing Era – Madya et al. (eds)
© 2020 Taylor & Francis Group, London, ISBN 978-1-03-224160-9

Literature and literacy in the changing era: Will disruption bring an end to literature?

Manneke Budiman
Department of Literature, Faculty of Humanities, Universitas Indonesia, Jakarta, Indonesia

ABSTRACT: The Era of Disruption is at the gate. Many types of skills and jobs are predicted to undergo extinction. Various programs in social sciences and the humanities are deemed to be obsolete and gradually losing their relevance with the coming of the new Age of Disruption as an inevitable effect of the Industrial revolution 4.0. In countries such as the United Kingdom and Japan, education policy's priority is given to the funding and development of STEM (Science, Technology, Engineering, Mathematics), while humanities' programs will be phased out. Facing such an existential situation, studies of literature need to reflect on what role remains for them to play that can enhance human survival in the age of robots and big data. How shall we view literature and its function in our everyday life where the internet of things rapidly and surely takes over many of the chores that we used to do throughout the modern history of humans on Planet Earth? This essay attempts at arguing that not only will literature continue playing an important role in the disruption era, but it will even be more inseparable from our success as human beings in working with the new technologies that begin to be perceived as a serious threat to our autonomy and consciousness as a human subject.

Keywords: disruption era, crisis in humanities, literary studies, industrial revolution, humanity literacy

1 WHAT INDUSTRIAL REVOLUTIONS HAVE DONE TO US

Industrial revolutions have always brought about fundamental changes to an era and changed the face of the era by its far-reaching impact on the society living in that age. The first Industrial Revolution that took place in the late 19th century may have been the most dramatic one compared the other industrial revolutions that came ever since. Initiated by the invention of the steam engine in England, it radically changed the way production was carried out, from a hand-produced process to a manufacturing process, which practically reduced hand-craft goods to a residual status, and at the same time, increased the production capacity enormously.

The second Industrial Revolution happened less than a hundred years after the first one, this time in the United States, which is marked by massive electrification of the manufacturing processes in factories and allowed, for the first time, the introduction of the assembly system to the production line. This is when Ford produced its most successful car, Ford model T, as a mass production. The coming of the digital era in the mid-1990s, or the third Industrial Revolution, happened when manufacturing became widely digitalized, as new technologies fused in the forms of computer software and web-based services. Production became automated and changed from mass production to mass customization to cater for individual customers' preferences [1].

The most recent revolution, the Industrial Revolution 4.0, is not only altering the way we work but also the way we live and interact with one another. The Inrev 4.0 is distinct from the other revolutions that had occurred hitherto in terms of speed, scope, and impact. All kinds of industry across the globe have experienced a large-scale 'disruption', which pushes them toward drastic changes in their production, management, and governance systems. The huge processing power of the latest technologies, as well as their almost unlimited storage capacity and access to knowledge, result in small and handy mobile devices that connect billions of people all over the world faster than the blink of an eye [2].

The boundary between leisure and work that used to be clearly drawn will be blurred. Human beings as predominantly *Homo faber* ('Man the Maker'), who control their life and environment as the result of their success in making and utilizing tools, will quickly and surely transform into *Homo ludens* ('Man of Leisure') or human beings who primarily play, as work and play increasingly become overlapping and simultaneous activities. This is an inevitable impact of industry that experiences 'automation' on a massive scale. Work becomes a kind of leisurely activity, whereas on the other hand leisure becomes a kind of productive activity. Furthermore, productive activities that we call 'work' can be done anywhere in a ubiquitous manner, and physical office space is no longer needed as home and the cyber space can also be work space.

One fine example for such emerging phenomena is online selling and shopping. The last few years have witnessed a growing trend of middle-class women going to high-end shopping malls, not primarily to take part in consumption by spending money for shopping, but to take pictures of new branded fashions from world-celebrity designers exhibited on boutique stores with their latest, sophisticated series of smartphones. When they return home, they would call their personal tailors, show them the pictures, and ask them to produce clothes based on the latest designs found in the malls. Then, they would put the results on display on their personal websites and sell them through online means [3]. These activities are productive activities that contribute to the GDP of their households, yet at the same time are parts of the women's leisurely activities.

Inrev 4.0 certainly has an enormous impact on literacy as well. Already is there a new concept of literacy that involves an integrated approach of three different types of literacy: data literacy, technology literacy, and humanity literacy [4]. These new literacies equip students with competencies and skills in making the optimal use of the internet for identifying key questions, search for information and evaluate it critically, synthesize all of the information for the purpose of answering the key questions, and finally communicate the answers to others [4]. As such, the new literacies actually aim at building critical and intellectual capabilities in understanding how things work in comprehensive ways (data, information, structure) instead of technical abilities to produce things (machines, tools, software).

This is where we can begin envisioning the role that literature plays in the inculcation of the new literacies, since literature and literary studies are basically concerned with reading and understanding (*verstehen*) in a critical sense of the terms, as well as with communication. To be taken into consideration is the fact that our definition and understanding of 'reading' has been undergoing a revolutionary change in this Inrev 4.0 era, and consequently, so has our concept of 'reading habit'. In this paper, I focus my assessment of the relevance of reading and learning literature to the Disruption Era as the result of the advent of the latest stage of industrial revolution.

2 LITERATURE AND THE NEW LITERACIES

Our traditional understanding of learning is one of the immediate 'casualties' of Disruption. Learning today becomes more and more ubiquitous: it can take place anywhere and anytime using any means available at hand. As our mobile devices get smarter and smarter, many more things can be done in a much shorter time, resulting in a constant acceleration of how we experience our everyday life. Thus, "efficiency and pleasure of our personal lives" is the positive quality offered by the new technological devices [2]. In this sense, the Inrev 4.0 and the disruptions it causes not only change how we do things, but our own perception of who we are.

Klauss Schwab argues that the deep integration of technology into our lives may threaten some of our basic human capacities such as "compassion and cooperation" [2]. Only a few days ago a tragedy occurred during a football game in Bandung, when a fan was beaten to death by a group of fans of the opposing team. Throughout the incident, some spectators were passively recording what happened before their eyes using their smartphone's cameras. In a matter of seconds, images and recordings of the tragedy went viral, resulting in widespread criticism on the lack of compassion among those who took the photos and made the videos. The prolonged debate that followed among netizens and sport officials in mass media revolved around whether Indonesians have ceased being a civilized nation.

If the main job of humanities and literary scholars in this era of Inrev 4.0 is to develop a shared insight on how technology affects our lives and reshapes everything around us in order to neutralize the potential danger that the new technologies have to our future. A set of new values that restores our priority of people over machines has to be reinvented. Rereading literature in the context of the present era needs to be performed in such a way that the 'cathartic' effect of a literary work upon its readers may be reactivated. *Catharsis* is generally defined as a feeling of purgation experienced by spectators of a play or readers of a literary work because they are able to share the suffering or shortcoming of the hero in the story, which, in turn, helps them prevent the same unfortunate experience to befall them in their real life.

The most devastating critique on the Aristotelian concept of *catharsis* is that it only gives a false sense of empathy to the spectators of a theatrical art or readers of literature, which will be diminished and gone as soon as they are done watching or reading. They will return home with less guilty feeling for ignoring fellow human beings in real life because they manage to sympathize with the underdog in the story, Nevertheless, this does not automatically make them a better person because the heightened sensitivity resulting from the *catharsis* that makes them feel good about themselves replaces the necessity to perform good deeds in real life. However, the other side of the argument says that the cathartic effect indeed motivates people to translate sympathy into action, and thus becoming a better person.

The endless overflow of information that we receive every day through our electronic gadgets, often via live streaming reporting and video recording of events with strong visual effects does not give us enough time to reflect on what we receive, as we are too absorbed by the daily tsunami of information. Ironically, the more realistic and convincing the images are, the faster we become desensitized, because nothing can be too spectacular or touching anymore to our senses. Nowadays, people do not seem to be bothered taking selfies in front of the ongoing sufferings of others or publish their own outrageous acts on many social media platforms just for the sake of obtaining as many likes and thumbs as possible from other netizens.

Reading literature is not necessarily immune from the same problem. One of the most important modernist visions concerning the role of literature is that it keeps society from losing its 'sanity'. Modern human beings are vulnerable to consumerism, worldly pleasures, and banalities that offer them pleasure through the absence of critical reflection. Good literature offers alternative to the dominant values, and in order to effectively do so, literature has to distance itself from society. Only then will it be able to enlighten its readers and restore their critical minds [5]. Postmodernist critics have pointed out that this modernist vision of literature has already doomed from the start because, by distancing itself from the society it tries to save, literature loses its relevance and is pushed to the margin with no one taking it seriously in time of crises.

Humanities education in the Disruption Era must adapt to society's new demands. If efficiency and compassion are the keywords of the new era, literature still has a place, in fact an important one, that is, to prevent human beings from being 'robotized', as long as it obeys the rule of efficiency at the same time. It means that scholars and teachers of literature can no longer teach literature for literature's sake. The reading skills and analytical ability acquired by students indirectly through the study of literature now need to be transferred to the arena of big data. I say that students obtain reading and analytical skills *indirectly* from studying literature because, in many literary studies programs, literature is taught as part of civilization studies. In this sense, literature serves as a colonial apparatus, as the outcome of the learning process is the adoption of the civilization standards and values of the strong by the weak.

Teachers of literature of the Disruption Era must help students acquire the same types of skills through reading and analyzing data and information originated from the net, evaluate them critically the way we would struggle and wrestle with a literary work in traditional literature classrooms, and communicate the results effectively to others using the same software and web service that provide us with information and data in the first place. The texts that present-day learners are dealing with are not literary texts but may anyway offer similar types of complexity, depths, ambiguity, and multiplicity of meaning the way a literary text does.

They may be false news or hoaxes, misleading information, inaccurate data, unimportant information that need to be weeded out and separated from the important and valid one. The task is especially challenging because the amount of data received is likely to be enormous and does not give us enough time to reflect on it. Such skills are invaluable when jobs begin disappearing, and organizations need far more human resources with analytical and strategic skills than those with technical or specialized skills. However, as the new literacies mentioned earlier in this essay involve more than just data-processing skills, but also require technological skills and humanity skills, literary studies, in its adapted approach, surely cannot work alone. Technology literacy equip students with competencies in using technological devices and software of the purpose of analysis and communication, whereas humanity literacy includes skills such as collaborating and networking.

3   EXPLORING LIBERAL ARTS EDUCATION

Oey-Gardiner et al rightly pointed out that the Disruption Era needs "third-generation" universities that provide the opportunity for learning and research in an interdisciplinary, multidisciplinary, and transdisciplinary environment [6]. The walls of knowledge that compartmentalize knowledge management and growth into separate faculties can no longer hold. Meanwhile, currently our universities are still run and managed based on, first of all, the separation of science, technology and mathematics on the one hand, and social sciences and the humanities on the other.

Secondly, our curriculum setup remains rigid, leaving very little room for flexibility for students to mix and match courses based on what they need. The system does not have enough trust on students' ability to determine what is good for them. Meanwhile, the disruptive era of Inrev 4.0 require graduates who are able to deal with complexities, heterogeneities, and changes. They have to possess strong social responsibility, equally be skilled in both academic and practical knowledge across the disciplinary boundaries and be able to connect well with other people. No department or faculty can deliver all of these qualifications by itself. Today's world's problems have become so complex that no significant solution can be offered without collaboration and synergy. That is why, it does not make any sense to keep the current higher education system going as usual.

Liberal arts education allows the meltdown of boundaries that separate a type of knowledge from another and students to choose what is best for them in terms of courses that they deem relevant with their future professional career. Liberal arts education has little to do with liberalism, or with art education, as many have mistakenly understood. This kind of education prepares students to be generalists who can survive in many different job environments because they have flexibility and agility to adapt with changes. The new literacies, when taken together as an integrated type of literacy, points directly, without mistake, at the liberal arts education system, even when this term hardly appears in the literature about new literacies that currently circulates.

Finally, there is no higher education system anywhere that works successfully in preparing its students and graduate for the complex challenges of the job market if it is heavily intervened and regulated by the state. University autonomy is the key to our success in educating young men and women to survive and succeed in the Disruption Era. At the moment, unfortunately, state intervention in the form of excessive regulations becomes the main hurdle for further progress. In a broader picture, if we fail to equip students with the three areas of competency in an integrated curriculum: information, technology, and humanity competencies, the entire literacy project is in danger of becoming a grand failure as well, and the entire nation will be among the casualties of Disruption.

REFERENCES

[1] *The Economist*. (2012). Manufacturing: The third industrial revolution. 21 April, https://www.economist.com/leaders/2012/04/21/the-third-industrial-revolution.

[2] Schwab, K. (2016). The fourth industrial revolution: What it means, how to respond. *World Economic Forum*, 14 January, https://www.weforum.org/agenda/2016/01/the-fourth-industrial-revolution-what-it-means-and-how-to-respond.

[3] Sinaga, R.T. (2015). Shopping mall, identitas dan politik konsumsi perempuan kelas menengah di Jakarta. Doctoral Dissertation, Postgraduate Program in Literary Studies, Faculty of Humanities Universitas Indonesia. Depok: Universitas Indonesia.

[4] Leu, D.J., Kinzer, C.K., Coiro, J., Cammack, D. (2004). Toward a theory of new literacies emerging from the internet and other ICT. In Ruddell, R. & Unrau, N. (eds). *Theoretical models and processes of reading* (5th ed.). Newark: International Reading Association.

[5] Sarup, M. (1993). *An introductory guide to poststructuralism and postmodernism*. Atlanta: University of Georgia Press.

[6] Oey-Gardiner, M., Rahayu, S.I., Abdullah, M.A., Effendi, S., Darma, Y., Dartanto, T, & Aruan, C. D. (2017). *Era disrupsi: Peluang dan tantangan pendidikan tinggi Indonesia*. Jakarta: Akademi Ilmu Pengetahuan Indonesia (AIPI).

English Linguistics, Literature, and Language Teaching in a Changing Era – Madya et al. (eds)
© 2020 Taylor & Francis Group, London, ISBN 978-1-03-224160-9

Groundless beliefs: Language learners and media discourse

Masaki Oda
Center for English as a Lingua Franca, Tamagawa University, Tokyo, Japan

ABSTRACT: This chapter will discuss the narratives mass media produce which result in supporting the policies. After a brief diachronic review of several major changes in ELT policies in Japan over the past years, I will particular focus on how the narratives are constructed by the mass media and subsequently affect the formation of learners' beliefs about learning English. I will then discuss recent cases from Japanese newspaper articles on the proposal of using commercial standardized tests as a part of university entrance exams, and their possible influences on those readers who may not necessarily have enough backgrounds information to fully evaluate the validity of standardized tests as a supporting evidence. From the analysis of the newspaper article, it was found, as Shohamy [1] suggests, that these standardized tests were powerful enough to demonstrate that policy makers have "serious and meaningful attitude towards education". What language teaching professionals can do is to take more active roles to promote appropriate use of these tests to the general public, by providing them with the optimal use of these standardized tests so that its benefit to the learners be maximized.

Keywords: learner beliefs, mass media, CEFR, language tests

1 INTRODUCTION

Language policies in education "are mostly manifestations of intentions" of policy makers, as suggested by Shohamy [1]. Whenever new policies are planned, the policy makers do their best to implement them without trouble in a limited time. In order to accelerate the process and thus the policies be accepted by the public, they are presented through narratives that are aligned with the policy makers' agenda.

If you were a parent, you have to make various decisions on education of your children at different stages. In early stages of their lives when your children are not old enough to make decisions including which school to go, whether or not to learn a foreign language, when to begin learning the language, and which language to learn, on behalf of your children. Parents are expected to make a sound judgment, often with limited information available to them.

These two elements create a situation in which a road map of language learning by your children has been fixed at an early stage. When they become old enough to make their own decision about learning, many of them are not even aware of various options of foreign language they could choose from.

If the decisions had been right, everybody would have been satisfied, and their language learning would have been successful. As someone who have been involved in language teaching for many years, however, I have heard voices of dissatisfaction from language learners more often than those of satisfaction. This means that there must have been something wrong with their decisions on foreign language learning.

In the past years, I have been working on several different areas of applied linguistics; language policy and planning [2], media discourse [3] and learner beliefs [4]. These areas appear unrelated. However, I have recently realized if there is any way I, as an applied linguist, could take advantage of my knowledge and experience in dealing with these different areas in order to encourage learners to reflect on their foreign language learning, and adjust their road maps if necessary. At the same time, I could also help those who need a direction now.

The main topic of this paper is to discuss the impact of media discourse on decision makings by foreign language learners at different stages of their lives. I will illustrate the significant role media discourse plays in the formation of language learners' beliefs, using the impact of the recent proposal of using commercial standardized tests as a part of university entrance exams by the Japanese National Center for University Entrance Examinations (NCUEE) on the general public. A special attention will be paid to the information of the proposal disseminated by the Japanese mass media to which general public has access. While the cases discussed in this paper are those from the Japanese context, I believe that the discussion can also be applicable to the other contexts in Asia including Indonesia.

2   LEARNER BELIEFS AND THE ROLE OF MASS MEDIA

In my earlier study on learner beliefs [4], I analyzed the results of interviews conducted to three university students. They were asked what they had remembered about their own history of learning foreign languages[s]. The purpose of the study was to investigate the factors influenced on their decisions on whether or not to study foreign language[s] at different stages of their lives, which language[s] to study, and when to begin studying the language[s]. From the series of interviews, I was able to make the following generalizations concerning the factors influenced the decisions.

1) Belief about language learning shifts constantly
2) In the earlier stages, parents' beliefs (derived from their experience) affects the learners
3) In schools, teachers play significant roles in formulating one's beliefs
4) Mass media play significant roles in later stages
5) The more diverse the learner's experience in language learning is, the more options are available to him/her (And thus less chance to give up).

The study mainly talks about different external factors involved in making decisions on foreign language learning. This paper will discuss 4) above, the role of mass media in depth referring to what is happening to foreign language learning in Japan at present. As stated above, the study suggested that the influence of mass-media was more significant as the learners got older. This reflects the fact that the learners had relied on information from their parents (or the parents had made decisions on behalf of them) and then information from their teachers until they became adolescent and tried to become independent. While developing learner autonomy is not necessarily negative, many adolescents including the college students participated in my 2014 study [4] did not realize that they had not been trained to interpret information from mass media critically. As a result, they accepted what was presented to them, and have not been able to realize that there were better choices for them. It is therefore important for those of us who are involved in language teaching profession have to find out the ways to help learners access to relevant information to make decisions as much as possible.

3   ACCESS TO INFORMATION

Following the discussion in the previous section, it is apparent that the pieces of information we are exposed to have already been controlled. We gather information from different sources and cross-check them against our knowledge and experience. However, it is often the case that we are neither given enough backgrounds nor enough time to make decisions about learning foreign languages. Media discourse is a good example.

In our daily life in Japan, we often see advertisements of language schools and/or language learning materials including both visual and textual messages. Whether we pay attention to these advertisements consciously or not, these advertisements are already a part of our daily landscape. On these advertisements, we often see textual messages such as "English is a passport to the world", but we rarely see "Chinese is a passport to the world", even though the speakers of Chinese are far more than those of English [5]. In fact, English is perhaps the only foreign language people talk about, and it is a *de-facto* required language for the Japanese people, despite the fact that it is foreign language not English has been a required subject in Japanese secondary schools for many years.

Moreover, such ideology of learning English as the only foreign language becomes naturalized and further influence the public. This corresponds with what Mirhosseini [6] found in his analysis of advertisements of private language institutes that appeared in a major Iranian newspaper. Moreover, the naturalization of such ideology is further reinforced by statements such as "The earlier, the better. Start now!" and "Forget about grammar. Let's communicate", even though the learners do not necessarily understand what these statements exactly mean. Messages from these statements particularly works well among parents who are pressed to make decisions on behalf of their children. If they could afford to send their children to English language lessons for children, they would make their move as early as possible, even though the children are in the process of their first language.

The process of naturalization of the ideology of learning English in the society proceeds even further by statements such as "In US, even 5 year old kids speak English fluently. Why can't you"?. The statement is apparently superficial as the language required for communication between 5 year old kinds are far less complex than that for communication between adults. In other words, it is hard to imagine a situation in which a 5 year old kid discusses business issues with another five year old kid. Nevertheless, the message from the statement is strong enough for learners and/or parents believe that they have to start learning English immediately.

As van Dijk [7] states, "all forms of printed text, those of mass media are most pervasive, if not most influential, when judged by the power criteria of recipient scope". Therefore, what people read on newspapers, including articles on their websites, are likely to serve as a major source of information for the learners. He continues that "[b]esides the spoken and visual discourses of television, newspaper text play a vital role in public communication" and argues that textual messages on newspapers are usually better recalled and thus has more persuasive influence. This is especially true in the context in which learners have to make a decision in a short time as the amount of information they can gather is limited, and thus they have to rely on what they can recall. Therefore, I believe it worthwhile to analyze the relationship between the discourse of learning English created by newspapers and its influences on learner beliefs, which will trigger decisions the learners make.

4   UNIVERSITY ENTRANCE EXAMINATION REFORM AND MASS MEDIA

In July, 2017, MEXT announced a proposal of new national university entrance examinations which would replace the current examination, National Center Test for University Admissions (NCTUA) administered by the National Center for University Entrance Examinations (NCUEE). A new proposed examination is expected to launch in 2020. The examination includes 'Foreign Language' which is a required subject for upper secondary schools nationwide. Theoretically, a student can select any foreign language available at his/her school. However, English is the only language available at many schools and thus is the *de-facto* foreign language for students. While the current NCTUA still has options of Chinese, French, German, and Korean, only 997 out of 541,335 examinees (0.18%) selected the language other than English in the exam administered in January 2018 according to NCUEE [8].

As we understand at the time of writing, NCUEE has decided to develop foreign language tests replacing the current ones, except English. Instead, it will use 'qualified' standardized tests in place of its own English test. On November 1, 2017, NCUEE issued a call for participation for providers of English standardized tests in the new university entrance examination system. The guidelines issued by the NCUEE [9] list various conditions that the test providers are expected to meet. However, no information has been available to the general public regarding why 'commercial' tests have to be used.

After a several months of evaluation period, NCUEE announced the list of eight standardized tests which had qualified for the new university entrance examination system on March 26, 2018. These tests included The Cambridge English Exam Series, The Test of English as a Foreign Language (TOEFL), The Test of English for International Communication L & R; S & W (TOEIC), The Global Test of English for Communication. (GTEC), The Test of English for Academic Purposes (TEAP), The Test of English for Academic Purposes Computer Based Test (TEAP CBT), *Eiken*, one of the most widely used English tests in Japan and The International English Language Testing System (IELTS). These standardized tests are powerful enough to demonstrate that policy makers have "serious and meaningful attitude towards education" (p.39) as Shohamy pointed out [10].

These tests were approved as replacements of the NCTUA English test, as they are supposed to measure 'four skills' and the test provider has shown the correspondence relationship between the test scores and Common European Framework of Reference for Languages (CEFR). The main problem, however, is that neither the Ministry of Education, Culture, Sports, Science and Technology of Japan (MEXT) nor NCUEE has explained the relevance of 'four skills' and CEFR for this context satisfactorily, and mass media have not questioned their validity either.

Due to the limitation of space, I will introduce a few excerpts of newspaper articles which had been published before the eight commercial tests were approved in March 26, 2018, to illustrate the problem. The articles were originally published in Japanese, but I will provide my own English translation.

> The university entrance examination system which starts in 2020 will utilize commercial standardized test to measure the 'four skills' of English. (*Asahi Shimbun*, February 24, 2018 trans. by the author)

> According to the implementation policy by MEXT, English test will completely have been transferred to Commercial standardized tests in 2024 in order to measure the 'four skills'. (*Yomiuri Shimbun*, March 9, 2018 trans. by the author)

Both of the two excerpts from major Japanese newspapers talk about 'four skills' as the rationale behind using commercial standardized tests in the new university entrance examination system. The idea of the 'four skills' was never criticized in the articles, despite the fact that the validity of four skills in language teaching has been questioned by some scholars for many years. Holliday for example, describes the term as "a long standing cultural icon in English-speaking Western TESOL", and warns that the discourse of 'four skills' is often interpreted "as the natural, default mechanism for solving curriculum problems" [11]. Despite these concerns, however, 'four skills' appears in the articles to represent innovation in language teaching, and thus something desirable to the general public.

Next excerpt talks about CEFR. As Shohamy [12] points out, policy makers "adopt the CEFR, no questions asked, and view it as the ultimate definition of language proficiency".

> Applicants [of universities/colleges] can take a Commercial standardized test twice between April and December. The grade will be given in raw score and a six-point scale grade between 'A1', a basic user, and 'C2', near native proficiency according to CEFR, an international index, and be sent directly to the institutions. (*Mainichi, Shimbun* February 19, 2018 trans. by the author)

CEFR is a framework which "provides a common basis for the elaboration of language syllabuses, curriculum guidelines, examinations, textbooks, etc. across Europe" [13]. As we can see from the excerpt above, mass media describe it as "an international index" and thus it should be the ultimate index for language proficiency without giving the general public what exactly it is for. The next excerpt is from another newspaper article published after the list of the approved standardized tests for university entrance examinations had been announced.

> MEXT produced a table which enables us to compare scores of tests with
> Different objectives including business and study-abroad based on the six

level scale of CEFR, the international standard. However, some questions
its fairness. (*Asahi Shimbun*, March 27, 2018 trans. by the author)

While the writer of this article questions the validity of the approved tests pointing out that these tests were developed for different purposes. However, CEFR is still described as "the standard" without sufficient information. We can assert that the CEFR is in the process of becoming the ultimate definition of language proficiency among the Japanese general public, given its endorsement in the news.

The general public, particularly those students who are going take the new NUCEE entrance examinations as well as their parents, need to understand the theoretical rationale underpinning CEFR, and many of them cannot figure out what A1 or C2 exactly means.

5 CONCLUSION AND IMPLICATIONS

Since the announcements of the list of approved tests, the test providers and various sectors in English language teaching industry have aggressively promote their tests, study aid books, learning materials, preparation courses strategically, by limiting pieces of information they provide the consumers. For the consumers, including upper secondary students and their parents, newspaper articles are their main 'plausible' source of information for the new university entrance examinations. Therefore, they eagerly seek information from the limited news resources available to them, despite the fact that the details of the new examination have not been fully decided at the time of writing.

Van Dijk [7] states that in media encounters, such as the cases discussed in this paper, "the relative position and power of news actors, and journalists usually determine who may have access to whom". Whether the policy maker and/or the mass media is deliberately control the access or not, the information to which the general public has access is already selected. Therefore, it is important for learners (and parents) to realize that they should always interpret the information critically. This is especially important when a new language or educational policy is about to be implemented in a short time as the cases presented in this paper. I believe that this would apply to the contexts in many Asian countries.

Furthermore, ELT professionals can help learners (and parents) avoid making an important series of decisions on language learning based on groundless beliefs prevailed. It is important for us, ELT professionals to constantly reflect what is happening in the profession, and critically examine the issues, so that we can accumulate our knowledge and experience. We always have to make ourselves ready to assist learners by constantly provide them with relevant information accumulated through your reflections so that they will also be able to stop relying on groundless beliefs when they need to make a series of important decisions on language learning.

ACKNOWLEDGEMENT

This work was supported by JSPS KAKENHI Grant Number JP 18K00792

REFERENCES

[1] Shohamy, E. (2006). *Language policy: Hidden agendas and new approaches.* London: Routledge.

[2] Oda, M. (2007). Globalization or world 'in' English?: Is Japan ready to face the waves? *International Multilingual Research Journal. 1*(2), 119–126.

[3] Oda, M (2017). Native-Speakerism and the roles of mass media in ELT. In: Agudo, J.D.M. (Ed.), *Native and non-native teachers in English language classrooms.* (pp.99–115). Berlin: de Gruyter Mouton.

[4] Oda, M. (2014), 'Reconditioning the conditions for second language learning' in K. Sung and B. Spolsky (Eds.), Conditions for English language teaching and learning in Asia. (pp.105–125), New Castle upon Tyne: Cambridge Scholars Publishing.

[5] Graddol, D. (2006), *English next.* London: British Council.

[6] Mirhosseini, S.A. (2014). "Resisting magic waves: ideologies of "English Language Teaching" in Iranian newspaper advertisements" *Discourse: Studies in the Cultural Politics of Education.* 1–16. DOI: 10.1080/01596306.2014.918462.

[7] Van Dijk, T. (2008), *Discourse and power*. Basingstoke: Palgrave McMillan.

[8] NCUEE. (2018a). *Heisei 29 nendo Daigaku Nyushi Sentaa Shiken Jisshi Kekka no Gaiyo* [ASummary of NCTUA in 2017 Academic Year]. Tokyo: The National Center for University Entrance Examinations.http://www.dnc.ac.jp/albums/abm.php?f=abm00009782.pdf&n=2_%E5%AE%9F%E6%96%BD%E7%B5%90%E6%9E%9C%E3%81%AE%E6%A6%82%E8%A6%81.pdf) Retrieved on August 7, 2018.

[9] NCUEE. (2018b) *Daigaku Nyushi Seiseki Teikyo Sisutemu Sanka Yoken* [Requirements for participating in the University Entrance Examination Score Provider System]. Tokyo: The National Center for University Entrance Examinations. https://www.dnc.ac.jp/albums/abm.php?f=abm00011205. pdf&n=1_%E6%88%90%E7%B8%BE%E6%8F%90%E4%BE%9B%E3%82%B7%E3%82%B9%E3%83%86%E3%83%A0%E5%8F%82%E5%8A%A0%E8%A6%81%E4%BB%B6.pdf Retrieved on August 7, 2018.

[10] Shohamy, E. (2001). *The power of tests: A critical perspective on the uses of language tests.* Harlow: Longman.

[11] Holliday, A. (2005). *The struggle to teaching English as an international language.* Oxford: Oxford University Press.

[12] Shohamy, E. (2019). 'Critical language testing and English as a lingua franca: How can one help the other'? In K. Murata (ed.), *English-medium instruction from an English as a lingua franca perspective: Exploring the higher education context.* (pp.271–285), London: Routledge.

[13] Council of Europe. (2001). *Common European framework of reference for languages: Learning, teaching, assessment.* Cambridge: Cambridge University Press.

English Linguistics, Literature, and Language Teaching in a Changing Era – Madya et al. (eds)
© 2020 Taylor & Francis Group, London, ISBN 978-1-03-224160-9

Going beyond communicative competence to become literate national and global citizens

Suwarsih Madya
English Education Department, Yogyakarta State University, Yogyakarta, Indonesia

ABSTRACT: As English plays its role as a global communication means among peoples of different cultures, the ultimate goal of English instruction is in fact the students' mastery of English intercultural communicative competence, which is the ability to effectively communicate in English with different peoples for various purposes in various situations. This can be said to be the visionary outcome of any ELT program. All teachers of English should strive hard to help their students to achieve the highest level of communicative competence. However, the students' mastery of English communicative competence should not be treated as an end in itself. A framework is needed to help students to go beyond communicative competence to become literate national and global citizens, but such a framework has not yet appeared in the literature. This paper will then propose a framework of teaching and learning English to ensure the development of the students' English communicative competence and simultaneously their strong commitment to treating it as a means to an end, which is their fullest personal development to reach an adequate level of literacy as national and global citizens.

Keywords: communicative competence, intercultural competence, personal development, professional development, framework

1 INTRODUCTION

English still plays an important role in this globalized and globalizing world with high information technology despite Graddol's [1] prediction of its decline at the middle of the 21st century. Data of English users from World Internet Stats show that English has the biggest number of users, followed by Chinese, Spanish, Arabic, Portuguese, Indonesian, French, Japan, Russian, and German as the top ten languages used in the internet [2]. In the academic world, in which more and more international conferences and seminars are now held in different countries all over the world, English still remains the working language probably due to practical reasons since it has been in the curriculum for a long time and has now find itself used as the world *lingua franca*. The last emerging status of English as an international language or *lingua franca* has created a new epistemological position [3], in which English belongs to everyone; thus, the end of native speakers' dominance in all aspects of English teaching. In addition, it is well recognized today that everyone has the right to use English without being forced to meet the standards set others [4]. However, it should be noted that the goal of communication will be reached through English if those involved in the communication have the same understanding of the English system used in the communication. In other words, the communication will reach its goal if the English used in it is eligible to everyone involved. It is in this situation that a good understanding of the English communicative competence framework is necessary.

Another important point to consider is the education model in which the teaching of English is carried out. In Indonesia, as in many countries, the teaching of English is carried out within the framework of competency-based education (CBE). This is implied in the formulation the aim of teaching English in secondary schools, which is translated below.

The aim of teaching English in secondary schools is to develop the students' potentials to possess communicative competence realized in interpersonal, transactional, and functional discourses in the form of various English texts, both oral and written, which are coherent, accurate and acceptable, on various knowledge—factual, conceptual, procedural—and instilling noble national character values in the real life context in the family, school, and community environments.

This aim formulation implies the target ability of producing texts, implying the implementation of the genre-based instruction, and the instilment of national character values. Considering the language-culture connection, the teaching of English will certainly bring with it foreign values, which are necessary for opening up the students' perspectives. Without being designed well, however, the teaching of English might cause cultural conflicts, or in Delors' [5] term, the global-local tension. One needs to become a global citizen but he/she needs to preserve his/her identity, meaning that he/she needs to be national and global citizen. To minimize such any cultural conflicts or global-local tension, an intercultural approach is worth considering. The intercultural approach to language learning may have another benefit if the English instruction is designed to support the development of students' commitment to treating English mastery as not an end in itself, but as a means to an end. Levine and Adelman [6] proposed an idea of going beyond language to contribute to the solution for value conflicts between two or more people from different cultures. But the target framework of going further than solving the cultural conflicts to reach further personal and professional development at the adequate level to be national and global citizens who are ready to live together in the global village. Learning to live together is one of the four learning pillars [5]. So the personal and professional development will be achieved through utilizing the mastery of intercultural communicative competence. This will be realized through raising cultural issues when culture is understood in its broadest sense so that students will encounter different discourses which will help improve their literacies in their capacity as national and global citizens. In this case English is a means for literate citizenship development. Now a question rises, "What English instructional framework will be appropriate for facilitating the development of students to be national and global citizens?" It should be noted that in Indonesia the outcomes-based education is now being implemented.

This paper is aimed at providing the answer to this question. In relation to this, the following points will be discussed: OBE framework, the four Cs of the 21st century, the notion of communicative competence, intercultural language learning, the four strands of language teaching, and the proposed framework.

2 CRUCIAL FRAMEWORKS WORTH CONSIDERING

2.1 *Outcomes-based education*

As has been mentioned before, education in Indonesia is within the framework of outcomes-based education (OBE). OBE is an instructional model, which organizes the instructional content and activities to achieve observable mastery of skills, knowledge, or behaviors, which are termed as learning outcomes. It is by no means prescriptive, by offers principles worth considering. The following are the OBE principles:

Clarity of focus: This means that everything teachers do must be clearly focused on what they want students to know, understand and be able to do. In other words, teachers should focus on helping students to develop the knowledge, skills and personalities that will enable them to achieve the intended outcomes that have been clearly articulated.

Designing down: It means that the curriculum design must start with a clear definition of the intended outcomes that students are to achieve by the end of the program. Once this has been done, all instructional decisions are then made to ensure achieve this desired end result.

High expectations: It means that teachers should establish high, challenging standards of performance in order to encourage students to engage deeply in what they are learning.

Helping students to achieve high standards (HOTS) is linked very closely with the idea that successful learning promotes more successful learning.

Expanded opportunities: Teachers must strive to provide expanded opportunities for all students. This principle is based on the idea that not all learners can learn the same thing in the same way and in the same time. However, most students can achieve high standards if they are given appropriate opportunities [7, 8].

OBE has been developed from competency-based education (CBE), which has been developed from mastery-based education (MBE). So all the characteristics of MBE belong to CBE, of which all characteristics belong to OBE but plus reasoning why the mastery of competencies is important (implying critical thinking). The overlapping of these three models of education is summarized in Figure 1.

The critical thinking skill is one the four major skills required of those who want to succeed in this highly technologized era, the so-called disruptive era in which the 4th industrial revolution is undergoing. The other three major skills are creativity, communication, and collaboration. Figure 2 depicts the four skills.

The communication skill as the first C is developed primarily through language teaching and learning with students being the subjects of their own learning. This can be realized through communicative language teaching, encompassing what Littlewood [9] called as an overarching curriculum framework for achieving communicative goals through combining proportionally two types of activities: (1) the non-communicative activities or pre-communicative activities or what Rivers [10] calls skill-getting activities and (2) the communicative activities or what Rivers [10] calls the skill-using activities.

	Mastery-based Education (MBE)	Competency-based Education (CBE)	Outcomes-based Education (OBE)
C H A R A C T E R I S T I C S	Using criteria for measuring the mastery	Using criteria for measuring the mastery	Using criteria for measuring the mastery
	Being adaptive to students' needs	Being adaptive to students' needs	Being adaptive to students' needs
	Providing support for students	Providing support for students	Providing support for students
	Adequate time for reaching mastery	Adequate time for reaching mastery	Adequate time for reaching mastery
		Each student's rate of learning	Each student's rate of learning
			The reason why to reach mastery is important (related to the development of critical thinking skills)

Figure 1. The relationships among mastery-based education, competency-based education, and the outcomes-based education.

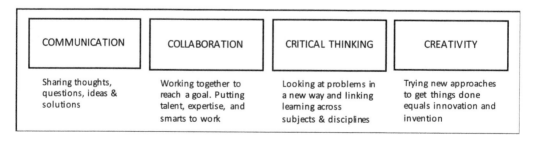

Figure 2. The 4C skills in the 21st century.

2.2 *Communicative competence*

Considering that verbal communication skills are conceptually related to communicative competence, it is important to examine the development of the notion of communicative competence. This will be later taken up again to be related to intercultural competence.

The concept of language ability or competence has developed incrementally, evolutionarily. It was first proposed by Chomsky [11, 12], consisting of purely only the linguistic competence, which was considered as a prerequisite to language performance. That was in response to the overemphasis on language performance in the Audiolingual Method subscribing to Bloomfield's concept of language. The linguistic competence is concerned with the deep structure, whereas the language performance with the surface structure, both being limited to linguistic context at the sentence level. Around a decade later, with the advent of sociolinguistics, the language competence was expanded by Hymes [13, 14] by adding another component, i.e. sociolinguistic competence since the meaning of any expression is believed to be bound to its social context too. With the stronger influence of functional linguistics, the concept was again expanded by adding strategic competence, which is related to the need for a strategy to keep the communication going, and the term linguistic competence was changed into "grammatical competence' by Canale & Swain [15]. Three years later, it was expanded Canale [16] to include "discourse competence" and twelve years later another component, 'actional competence' was added by Celce-Murcia, Dornyei & Farrel [17]. Later Celce-Murcia [18] proposed a revised model by expanding the 1995 model to include the formulaic competence and expanding the actional competence to become the interactional competence, which has three sub-components: actional competence, conversational competence, and non-verbal paralinguistic competence [18]. Four years later, Littlewood [9] revised his 1981 model of communicative competence by including socio-cultural competence. The evolutionary development is summarized in Figure 3 and each component will be described below.

Chomsky (1957, 1965)	Hymes (1967, 1972)	Canale & Swain (1980)	Canale (1983)	Celce-Murcia, Dornyei, &Thurrel (1995)	Celce-Murcia (2007	Littlewood (2011)
Linguistic competence	Linguistic competence	Grammatical Competence	Grammatical Competence	Linguistic Competence	Linguistic Competence	Linguistic competence
		Strategic competence	Strategic competence	Strategic competence	Strategic competence	Pragmatic competence
				Actional Competence	Interactional competence	
					Formulaic competence	
Socio-linguistic competence	Socio-linguistic competence	Socio-linguistic competence	Socio-linguistic competence			Socio-linguistic competence
					Socio-cultural competence	Socio-cultural competence
		Discourse competence	Discourse competence		Discourse competence	Discourse competence

Figure 3. The evolutionary development of communicative competence.
Sources: Combining Celce-Murcia (2007) & Littlewood (2011)

Celce-Murcia's [18] latest framework still maintains the sociocultural competence, i.e. the speaker's pragmatic knowledge (how to express messages appropriately within the overall social and cultural context of communication), which is one component in the previous framework [17]. Of the sociocultural variables, the most crucial ones are the following three variables: (1) social contextual factors (participants' age, gender, status, social distance, and their relations to each other, i.e. power and affect); (2) stylistic appropriateness (strategies of politeness, a sense of genres and registers); and (3) cultural factors (background knowledge of the target language group, major dialects/regional differences, and cross cultural awareness). Four years later, Littlewood [9] extended Canale's [16] framework of communicative competence by adding the fifth component, i.e. sociocultural competence which includes "awareness of the cultural knowledge and assumptions that affect the exchange of meanings and may lead to misunderstandings in intercultural communication". With this, Littlewood separates sociocultural competence from sociolinguistic competence, which "consists primarily of knowledge of how to use language appropriately in social situations, e.g. conveying suitable degrees of formality, directness and so on" [9].

The second component of Celce-Murcia's latest framework is discourse competence, i.e. the selection, sequencing and arrangements of words, structures, and utterances to achieve the unified spoken message. This competence includes (1) cohesion (conventions regarding use of reference (anaphora/cataphora), substitutions/ellipsis, conjunctions, lexical chains, referring to Halliday & Hasan [19]; (2) deixis (situational grounding achieved through the use of pronouns, spatial terms such as *here/there; this/that*), temporal such as *now/then; before/after*), and textual reference such as *the following table, the figure above*; (3) coherence (expressing purpose/intent through appropriate content schemata, managing old and new information, maintaining temporal continuity and other organizational schemata, through conventional recognized means); and (4) generic structure (formal schemata that allow the user to identify an oral discourse segment as conversation, narrative, interview, service encounter, report, lecture, sermon, etc.). This description is obviously more detailed than Littlewood's [9], which seems more operational in terms of terminology. To Littlewood, discourse competence "enables speakers to engage in continuous discourse, e.g. by linking ideas in longer written texts, maintaining longer spoken turns, participating in interaction, opening conversations and closing them" [9].

The third component is linguistic competence. i.e. knowledge about the target language, that includes the following four types of knowledge: (1) phonological competence, including the segmental (vowels, consonants, syllable types) and suprasegmental (prominence/stress, intonation, rhythm); (2) lexical competence, including knowledge of both content words (nouns, adjectives, verbs) and function words (pronouns, determiners, prepositions, verbal auxiliaries, etc.); (3) morphological competence, including parts of speech, grammatical inflections, productive derivational processes; and (4) syntactic competence, including constituent/ phrase structure, word order, basic sentence types, modifications, coordination, subordination, embedding. Again such a description is more detailed than that made by Littlewood [9], who says that linguistic competence includes the knowledge of vocabulary, grammar, semantics and phonology that have been the traditional focus of second language learning.

The fourth component is formulaic competence, i.e. the fixed and prefabricated chunks of language that speakers use heavily in everyday interactions [18]. This component includes: (1) Routines, i.e. fixed phrases like *of course, all of a sudden* and formulaic chunks like *How do you do? I'm fine, thanks, How are you?*; (2) Collocations, including verb-object *spend money, play the piano,* adverb-adjective *statistically significant, substantially important;* adjective-nouns *tall boy, beautiful day, legible handwriting*; (3) Idioms, e.g. *to kick the bucket = to die; to get the ax = to be fired/terminated, be glad to see the back of = be happy when a person leaves; cry over spilt milk = complain about a loss from the past*; and (4) Lexical frames: *I'm looking for ...; See you (later/tomorrow/next week etc.* 17] notes that more acknowledgement is given to the importance of formulaic competence. She cites Hunston [20] who found that "fluent speakers of a language drawn on formulaic knowledge of the target language as frequent as often as they use systematic linguistic knowledge". She admits that formulaic competence has been neglected in language pedagogy so far and this seems to be true since other frameworks, including Littlewood's [9], do not include this competence.

The fifth component is interactional competence, consisting of the following three sub-components: (1) actional competence, i.e. knowledge of how to perform common speech acts and speech act sets in the target language involving interactions such information exchanges, interpersonal exchanges, expressing opinions and feelings, problems (complaining, blaming, regretting, apologizing etc.), future scenario (hopes, goals, promises, predictions etc.; (2) conversational competence, including turn taking systems and other dialogic genres, i.e. how to (a) open and close conversations, (b) establish and change topics, (c) get, hold, and relinquish the floor, (d) interrupt, (e) collaborate, backchannel etc.; and (3) non-verbal paralinguistic competence, including kinesics, proxemics, haptic behavior such as touching, non-linguistic utterance with interactional import such as *ahhh! Uh-oh. Huh?,* the role of silence and pauses [18]. While this framework treats interactional competence as a separate framework, Littlewood's [9] framework accommodates interactional competence in the pragmatic competence, which implicitly also includes strategic competence. To Littlewood, pragmatic competence "enables second language speakers to use their linguistic resources to convey and interpret meanings in real situations, including those where they encounter problems due to gaps in their knowledge" [9].

The sixth component of Celce-Murcia's [18] latest framework is strategic competence, which may involve learning strategies and communication strategies. The latter includes (1) achievement strategies, i.e. strategies of approximation, circumlocution, code-switching, miming, etc.; (2) stalling or time gaining strategies, i.e. using phrases like *Where was I? Could you repeat that?*; (3) self-monitoring, i.e. using phrases that allow for self-repair like *I mean....*; (4) interacting strategies, i.e. strategies that include appeals for help/clarification, involve meaning negotiation, or involve comprehension and confirmation checks, etc.; and (4) social strategies, i.e. strategies that involve seeking out native speakers to practice with, actively looking for opportunities to use the target language.

It is important to note that Littlewood's [9] framework has an element of the ability to prevent communication breakdown in intercultural communication, implying the importance of intercultural communicative competence. Different from Littlewood, Celce-Murcia [18] uses the term cross cultural awareness, which might or not have the same meaning as intercultural awareness. The term 'intercultural communication' seems to be more preferable especially when it is related to the advent of intercultural language learning, in which the foreign language learners become more aware of their own cultural values in comparison with the target culture. This means that they will be able to maintain their identity while respecting others'. This is relevant in this increasingly intensified globalization in which cultural differences among peoples need intercultural competence to ensure that peoples will maintain their identity while developing their perspective of others' cultural identity reflected in their language.

Celce-Murcia's framework is more comprehensive and inclusive because it accommodates the whole aspects of language use and it suits the multicultural situation which necessitates the communication participants to be interculturally competent. Now rises a question, What is intercultural communication competence?

2.3 *Intercultural language learning*

"Intercultural competence is the ability to develop targeted knowledge, skills and attitudes that lead to visible behavior and communication that are both effective and appropriate in intercultural interactions" [21]. Intercultural communication competence (ICC) is one's skill in facilitating successful intercultural communication outcomes in terms of satisfaction and other positive assessments of the interaction and the interaction partner [22]. In other words, a competent intercultural communicator is one who able and skillful to communicate effectively and appropriately in various cultural contexts. The intercultural communication competence development is indicated by the transformation from a monocultural person into a multicultural person. The former tends to be ethnocentric, while the latter has tolerance for differences and respects cultures [22, 23].

In relation to this, Chen [24, 25] identifies four areas of intercultural competence: personality strength, communication skills, psychological adjustment, and cultural awareness. Four areas of skills have been identified by Chen [24, 25]: self-concept (way of viewing self), self-disclosure (willingness to openly and appropriately reveal information about oneself), self-monitoring (using social comparison information to control and modify one's self-presentation, and social relaxations are the personal traits that affect intercultural communication. English intercultural communication skills can be developed through English intercultural language learning.

With English becoming a global *lingua franca* or an international language [26, 4], intercultural learning is rising in importance. Why? It is because two-way and multi-way interactions among peoples from all-over the world is made possible by the internet and face-to-face interactions easier by the advancement of transportation technology. Since the communication is mostly done through language, be it oral or written, and language and culture are naturally connected, the interactions among peoples are likely to arouse cultural value conflicts. Such likeliness will be minimized if the people involved are interculturally competent. The following quotation illustrated how people are influenced through the insertion of new values and norms.

> Members of a particular culture are constantly being influenced by their society's (and/or some of the society's cultural subgroup's) public and cultural representations (with regards to values, norms, traditions etc.), which are changing in the dynamic life of the global world. Such an influence is exerted most prominently through language used by members of the society in communication with other members of the same and different cultural groups. Language as the most important means of communicating, of transmitting information and providing human bonding has therefore an overridingly important position inside any culture. Language is the prime means of an individual's acquiring knowledge of the world, of transmitting mental representations and making them public and inter-subjectively accessible. Language is just the prime instrument of a 'collective knowledge reservoir' to be passed on from generation to generation. But language also acts as a means of categorizing cultural experience, thought, and behavior of its speakers. Language and Culture are therefore most intimately (and obviously) interrelated on the levels of semantics, where the vocabulary of a language reflects the culture shared by its speakers [27].

One component of intercultural learning is the notion of intercultural competence, which consists of knowledge, skills, attitudes, and outcomes. The intercultural knowledge includes cultural self-awareness, culture specific knowledge, sociolinguistic awareness, grasp of global issues and trends. The intercultural skills include skills of listening, observing, evaluating using patience and perseverance, and viewing the word from others' perspectives. The intercultural attitudes are concerned with respects (valuing others' cultures), openness (withholding judgment), curiosity (viewing differences as a learning opportunity), and discovery (tolerance of ambiguity). Outcomes consist of internal outcomes and external outcomes [21]. This is elaborated in Figure 4 below.

Research has shown that intercultural competence cannot be acquired in a short space of time or in one module. It is not a naturally occurring phenomenon but a lifelong process which needs to be addressed explicitly in learning and teaching and staff development. Critical reflection becomes a "powerful tool" on the journey towards achieving it [21].

The requirement to understand cultural differences and communicate across cultural borders has increased exponentially [28]. This implies the importance of interculturally oriented pedagogy. An interculturally oriented pedagogy for language teaching and learning starts from the view that language, culture and learning are fundamentally integrated. Knowledge of intercultural communication, and the ability to use it effectively, can help bridge cultural differences, mitigate problems, and assist in achieving more harmonious, productive relations [29]. This will make it possible to learn and improve together.

Constituent elements of intercultural competence
Knowledge
•Cultural self-awareness: articulating how one's own culture has shaped one's identity and world view •Culture specific knowledge: analyzing and explaining basic information about other cultures (history, values, politics, economics, communication styles, values, beliefs and practices) •Sociolinguistic awareness: acquiring basic local language skills, articulating differences in verbal/ non-verbal communication and adjusting one's speech to accommodate nationals from other cultures • Grasp of global issues and trends: explaining the meaning and implications of globalization and relating local issues to global forces
Skills
•Listening, observing, evaluating: using patience and perseverance to identify and minimize ethnocentrism, seek out cultural clues and meaning •Analysing, interpreting and relating: seeking out linkages, causality and relationships using comparative techniques of analysis •Critical thinking: viewing and interpreting the world from other cultures' point of view and identifying one's own
Attitudes
•Respect: seeking out other cultures' attributes; value cultural diversity; thinking comparatively and without prejudice about cultural differences •Openness: suspending criticism of other cultures; investing in collecting 'evidence' of cultural difference; being disposed to be proven wrong; •Curiosity: seeking out intercultural interactions, viewing difference as a learning opportunity, being aware of one's own ignorance •Discovery: tolerating ambiguity and viewing it as a positive experience; willingness to move beyond one's comfort zone
Outcomes
•The above knowledge, skills and attitudes lead to internal outcomes which refer to an individual who learns to be flexible, adaptable, empathetic and adopts an ethno-relative perspective. •These qualities are reflected in external outcomes which refer to the observable behavior and communication styles of the individual. They are the visible evidence that the individual is, or is learning to be, interculturally competent.

Figure 4.   The constituent elements of intercultural competence.
Source: Deordorff (2006)

So a person's mastery of English intercultural communicative competence (EICC) will enable him/her to benefit in many ways according the potential functions of English as an international language. Referring to Halliday's [29] functions of language, with a good mastery of EICC, we can: (a) Express thoughts, opinions, ideas, feelings etc. in texts both oral and written, both in face-to-face situations and in virtual communication; (b) Establish relationship with other people speaking English for social and economic purposes through face-to-face or virtual communication; (c) Pursue knowledge through self-study in various modes and/or doing further degrees; (d) Write a report representing what we have observe; (e) Influence the environment by causing events to happen; and (f) Assess our own cultures in comparison with other cultures.

All of this leads to the need for intercultural pedagogy. The following are the principles of intercultural pedagogy which can be applied in language teaching and learning:

1. *Active construction*: Learning is understood as involving purposeful, active engagement in interpreting and creating meaning in interaction with others, and continuously reflecting on one's self and others in communication and meaning-making in variable contexts.
2. *Making connections*: Connections are made between existing conceptions and new understandings and between previous experiences and new experiences. Previous knowledge is challenged and this creates new insights through which students connect, reorganize, elaborate and extend their understanding.
3. *Interaction*: Learning and communication are social and interactive; interacting and communicating interculturally means continuously developing one's own understanding of the relationship between one's own framework of language and culture and that of others.
4. *Reflection*: Learning involves becoming aware of how individuals think, know and learn about language, culture, knowing, understanding and the relationship between these, as well as concepts such as diversity, identity, experiences and one's own intercultural thoughts and feelings.
5. *Responsibility*: Learning depends on learner's attitudes, dispositions and values, developed over time [30].

Intercultural literacy, which might be glossed as all the knowledge and skills necessary to the practice of intercultural competences, has become an essential tool for modern life, parallel to the development of information literacy, or media literacy [31, 32]. So it is important for this century's people to attain intercultural competence, of which the requirement includes: (a) Respect ("valuing of others"); (b) Self-awareness/identity ("understanding the lens through which we each view the world"); (c) Seeing from other perspectives/world views ("both how these perspectives are similar and different"); (d) Listening ("engaging in authentic intercultural dialogue"); (e) Adaptation ("being able to shift temporarily into another perspective"); (f) Relationship building (forging lasting cross-cultural personal bonds); and (g) Cultural humility ("combines respect with self-awareness") [32].

Intercultural competence is determined by the presence of cognitive, affective, and behavioral abilities that directly shape communication across cultures. These essential abilities can be broken down into five specific skills that are obtained through education and experience:

1. *Mindfulness*: the ability of being cognitively aware of how the communication and interaction with others is developed. It is important to focus more in the process of the interaction than its outcome while maintaining in perspective the desired communication goals. For example, it would be better to formulate questions such as "What can I say or do to help this process?" rather than "What do they mean?"
2. *Cognitive flexibility*: the ability of creating new categories of information rather than keeping old categories. This skill includes opening to new information, taking more than one perspective, and understanding personal ways of interpreting messages and situations.
3. *Tolerance for ambiguity*: the ability to maintain focus in situations that are not clear rather than becoming anxious and to methodically determine the best approach as the situation evolves. Generally, low-tolerance individuals look for information that supports their believes while high-tolerance individuals look for information that gives an understanding of the situation and others.
4. *Behavioral flexibility*: the ability to adapt and accommodate behaviors to a different culture. Although knowing a second language could be important for this skill, it does not necessarily translate into cultural adaptability. The individual must be willing to assimilate the new culture.
5. *Cross-cultural empathy*: the ability to visualize with the imagination the situation of another person from an intellectual and emotional point of view. Demonstrating empathy includes the abilities of connecting emotionally with people, showing compassion, thinking in more than one perspective, and listening actively Pusch [33].

In addition, what Liddicoat's contention as quoted below is worth considering.

> ...Intercultural language teaching and learning ... does not constitute a language teaching "method". There is no single set of pedagogical practices that can be considered to constitute intercultural language teaching and learning. It is more appropriate to consider what is happening in intercultural language teaching and learning as a "stance" as described by Cochran-Smith and Lytle [32]—that is, as "positions teachers and others ... take toward knowledge and its relationship to practice". [35].

One's intercultural competence may be acquired through the interacting processes of intercultural pedagogy involving a cycle consisting of interacting, noticing, comparing, and reflection. When interacting with people of another culture, most probably through texts, learners notice something which is culturally different/similar. Then they are comparing further the two cultures to find differences and similarities between the home culture and target culture. Then they reflected on the differences and similarities. This cycle repeats as the learning is going on. The processes are illustrated in Figure 5.

Intercultural language teaching and learning is best considered as a set of shared assumptions about the nature of language, culture and learning that shapes an overall understanding of what it means to teach language and to do this in an intercultural way. It is a perspective from which language educators construct practice rather than a set of practices to be adopted.

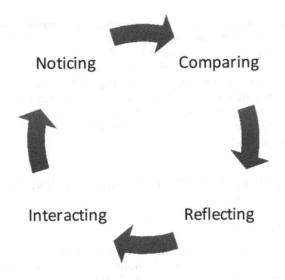

Figure 5. The interacting processes of intercultural pedagogy.
Source: Liddicoat (2011: 841)

In this way, intercultural language teaching may be considered as a "post-methods" pedagogy [36] in that it consists of a theoretical orientation that frames options and principles that are to be adapted by teachers in their own location specific practice. What is a post-method pedagogy then?

2.4 *The post-method pedagogy*

Being founded on the hermeneutic philosophy, which emphasizes meaningfulness, a post-method pedagogy "must be sensitive to a particular group of teachers teaching a particular group of learners pursuing a particular set of goals within a particular set of goals within a particular institutional context embedded in a particular sociocultural milieu [37]. This is the essence of *particularity* parameter, which is the first parameter of the post-method pedagogy.

To bring theory and practice into close connection, teachers "ought to be enabled to theorize from their practice and practice what they theorize" [38]. In relation to this, Edge states that "...the thinking teacher is no longer perceived as someone who applies theories, but someone who theorizes practice" [38]. Through prior and ongoing experience with learning and teaching, teachers gather an unexplained and sometimes unexplainable awareness of what constitutes good teaching [36] or sense of plausibility. This is all the essence of *practicality* the second parameter of the post-method pedagogy.

The third parameter is *possibility,* which: (a) acknowledges and highlights students' and teachers' individual identity; (b) encourage them to question the status quo that keeps them subjugated; and (c) encourages them to develop theories, forms of knowledge, and social practices that *work with* the experiences that people bring to the pedagogical setting" [40]. Working together, talking about ways of seeing new possibility in their classroom practices, teachers and teacher educators see possibilities in their professional lives and later new possibilities in their personal lives [41].

The postmethod pedagogy gives ample room to teachers to meet their students' needs, consider their own styles, and to compromise with the institutional demands. They have responsible freedom to develop their own teaching by considering related variables, from the nearest context to the widest. This pedagogy enables the teacher and students to act locally but think globally. This will enable teachers of English to facilitate their students to go beyond merely achieving the mastery of English communicative competence.

How can they go beyond ECC to ensure so that our students strengthen their own cultural sense of belonging but also appreciate others? This is by developing an instructional framework to ensure that the students will (1) be equipped with communicative discursive skills necessary to reach their communicative goals in collaboration with diverse interlocutors in a wide range of contexts [41]; and (2) be empowered to hold their own in interacting with native culture members in realizing their intentions satisfactorily and in counteracting any self-destructive 'reduction of their personality' [27]. The proposed framework here is the one integrating intercultural English learning into Nation's four strands of language teaching.

3 INTEGRATING INTERCULTURAL ENGLISH LEARNING INTO THE FOUR STRANDS

3.1 *The adoption of the four strands*

To ensure the development of language ability in a more comprehensive way, Nation [42] proposed four strands of language teaching which should be give equal attention in their development. The four strands of language teaching [42]: (1) Learning through meaning-focused input; that is, learning through listening and reading where the learner's attention is on the ideas and messages conveyed by the language; (2) Learning through meaning-focused output; that is, learning through speaking and writing where the learner's attention is on conveying ideas and messages to another person; (3) Learning through deliberate attention to language items and language features; that is, learning through direct vocabulary study, through grammar exercises and explanation, through attention to the sounds and spelling of the language, through attention to discourse features, and through the deliberate learning and practice of language learning and language use strategies; and (4) Developing fluent use of known language items and features over the four skills of listening, speaking, reading and writing; that is, becoming fluent with what is already known. Strand 1 is learning to develop the receptive skills of listening and reading. Strand 2 is learning to develop the productive skills of speaking and writing. Strand 3 is learning the linguistic aspects of the target language, and Strand 4 is practicing what they have learned through listening, speaking, reading, and writing extensively outside the class in various situations on various topics which contains cultural points/values. What is meant by culture here?

3.2 *Elements of culture*

To support the development students' different types of literacies, culture should be understood in its broadest sense. That is, culture has the following elements: (1) social organization: family patterns (matriarchal/patriarchal, social organization, social classes; (2) customs and Traditions: rules of behaviors, holidays, food, clothing, shelter; (3) language, including oral language, written language, local languages, national language, lingua franca; (4) arts and literature, including aesthetic expressions (paintings, literature, music, folktales, sculpture, dancing); (5) Religion or systems of belief, including animism, monotheism, polytheism; (6) government, including levels (unitary system; federal system) and types (democracy, dictatorship, autocracy, monarchy); (7) economic systems, including traditional economy, market economy, command economy, mixed economy; and (8) knowledge and technology. The inclusion of topics on these areas is worth considering. With such a comprehensive understanding of culture, the topics can vary to meet the students' interest.

3.3 *Stages in intercultural competence development*

One's intercultural competence develops through two big stages: the ethnocentric and the ethno relative. The ethnocentric stages are denial, defence, and minimization. The ethno relative stages are acceptance, adaptation, and integration. This is depicted in Figure 8.

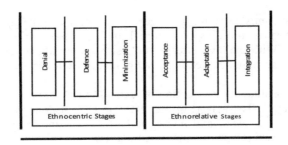

Figure 6. The developmental model of intercultural sensitivity.
Source: Liddicoat(2011:847)

The three ethnocentric stages are described as follows:

- *Denial*: learners have not yet developed a conceptual category of cultural difference.
- *Defence*: learners have gained some ability to notice cultural differences as the result of some form of exposure to other languages and/or cultures.
- *Minimization*: the problems confronted in the defence stage are resolved by assuming a basic similarity among all human beings either in terms of a *physical universalism* or a *transcendent universalism*.

The three ethno relative stages are described as follows:

- *Acceptance*: learners develop an understanding of their own cultural context and so can accept the existence of different cultural contexts.
- *Adaptation*: learners are able to shift their cultural frame of reference and consciously adopt perspectives of other cultural groups.
- *Integration*: at the final stage of development, learners extend their ability to perceive events in a cultural context to their perceptions of their own identity.

Teachers should facilitate the development of learners' intercultural competence through all of the stages by ensuring the processes which include interacting, noticing, comparing, and reflecting (see Figure 6). Learners who have successfully developed his/her intercultural competence will show the following learning outcomes: improved flexibility, adaptability, empathy, and developed ethno relative perspective (internal outcomes), as well as intercultural behavior and communication styles reflecting their intercultural competence (external). The ethno relative perspective is the integration stage which "reflects those individuals who have multiple frames of reference and can identify and move freely within more than one cultural group" [43].

3.4 The proposed model

To ensure the development of intercultural communicative competence realized in the form of texts and commitment to treating English mastery as a means to an end, which is further personal and professional development to reach a high level of different types of literacy, an appropriate instructional framework is proposed here. The framework has been developed by integrating the intercultural pedagogy, elements of culture, and genre-based instruction framework into Nation's four strands of language teaching. The framework is called the intercultural genre-based instruction proposed model (IGBI). The IGBI framework has four stages. Each is described below.

Stage 1 exposes students to some texts of the same genre, of which the topic is on one of culture elements mentioned above. At this stage, students read the texts to understand the contents and notice cultural points. They are then involved in identifying similarities and differences between their own culture and the English cultures. At this stage students are also involved in learning about the key words used in the texts and their expansion.

Stage 2 facilitates students' learning of the generic structure and the grammatical features of the texts. The same texts as those used in Stage 1 are used to learn the generic structure and grammatical features. With the texts already understood, they can concentrate their mind on the text structure and grammatical features. SO grammar exercises are provided to help students learn the system.

Stage 3 facilitates the students' production of texts, be it oral or written, based the results of their reflection in Stage 1. The writing of the texts can be first done in groups and then later individually. Both involve review and revise, both in groups and individually. The intercultural points should be used to review and revise the texts.

Stage 4 encourages students to practice listening, speaking, reading, and writing outside the classroom according to the topics of their interests. To ensure that they do this, their independent performance should be included in the assessment. It is therefore necessary to create an assessment rubric.

At the heart of these four stages are the principles of intercultural pedagogy: Active construction, making connection, interaction, reflection and responsibility. (See the description in Section B3 above). Figure 7 illustrates the proposed **IGBI** framework.

Underlying the proposed intercultural genre-based instruction framework are five principles described below.

Principle 1 : EFL intercultural learning and teaching should be designed and carried out by applying the principles of particularity, practicality, and possibility to facilitate the development of learners to become literate national and global citizens.

Principle 2 : EFL intercultural learning and teaching should provide the students with ample opportunity to gain knowledge of other English speaking people's cultures (the past, the present, and the future), compare them with their own cultures, reflect on the differences and similarities, and derive some important values for development purposes in a cyclic process.

Principle 3 : EFL intercultural learning and teaching should be inclusive in terms of topics, covering all elements of culture

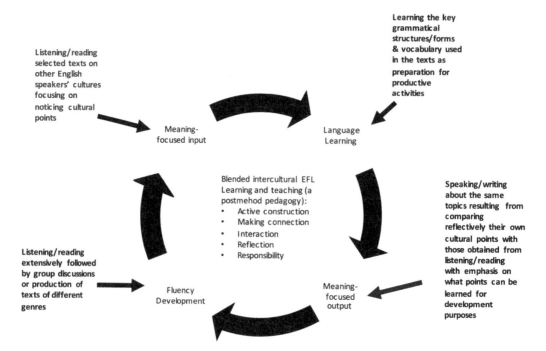

Figure 7. The intercultural genre-based instruction framework.

Principle 4 : The character values dug out from the texts and teaching and learning activities are not limited to these mentioned in the curriculum but also other values.

Principle 5 : The ultimate indicator of students' learning is the texts produced by students.

The above proposed model will ensure that learners will become strongly aware of their own culture and simultaneously more appreciative to others' cultures. In addition, the opportunities they have in dealing comparatively with different types of texts on different cultural topics in their receptive and productive language learning activities will help them in improving their literacies in different areas. The mastery of English intercultural communicative competence will therefore facilitate the students' development into literate national and global citizens of character.

4 CONCLUCIONS

The discussion has so far led to the following conclusions. English still remains to be the top language used in the internet so that one's mastery of English communicative competence and ICT literacy will enable him/her to connect with millions of people all-over the world with their own cultures. This necessitates another type of competence, which will ensure success of intercultural communication, i.e. intercultural competence. This will support the achievement of the mastery of English communicative competence and character formation All of the curricular mandates will be achieved through the proposed framework, i.e. the IGBI framework, which ensure the learning of the English linguistic system, character values, intercultural competence, and commitment to using English as a means to an end, i.e. further personal and later on professional development so as to reach the adequate level of national and global citizenship. Only in this way will the teaching of English contribute to the development of students as national and global citizens.

REFERENCES

[1] Graddol, D. (1997). *The future of English? A guide to forecasting the populatiry of English in the 21st century*. London: The British Council.

[2] Miniwatts Marketing Group (2018). Top ten languages in the internet in millions of users – December 2017. www.internetstats.com/stats7.htm

[3] Kumaravadivelu, B. (2012). Individual identity, cultural globalization, and teaching English as an international language: The case for an epistemological break. In Alsegoff, L., S.L. McKay, Hu, G. and W.A. Renandya (Eds.). *Principles and practices for teaching English as an international language*. New York & London: Routledge.

[4] Widdowson, (2015). Who owns English today?. In *Global Englishes: A resource book for students (Jenkins)*. New York & London: Routledge.

[5] Delors (1996). *Learning: The treasure within*. Paris: UNESCO Publishing.

[6] Levine, D.R. & Adelman, M.B. (1982). Beyond language: *Intercultural communication in second language*. Englewood Cliffs: Prentice Hall Regents.

[7] Killen, R. (2000). Outcomes-based education: principles and possibilities. Retrieved June 2005, via: http://scholar.google.com/

[8] Spady, W.G. (1994). *Outcomes-based education: critical issues and answers*. Arlington, VA: American Association of School Administrators.

[9] Littlewood, A. (2011). Language teaching and learning from an intercultural perspective. In E. Hinkel (Ed.). *Handbook of research and second language teaching and learning*. New York: Routledge.

[10] Rivers, W.M. (1981). *Teaching foreign language skills* (2nd ed.). Chicago: University of Chicago Press.

[11] Chomsky, N. (1957). *Syntactic structures*. Mouton, The Hague.

[12] Chomsky, N. (1965). *Aspects of the theory of syntax*. MIT Press, Cambridge, MA.

[13] Hymes, D. (1967). Models of the interaction of language and social setting. *Journal of Social Issues*, 23(2), 8–38.

[14] Hymes, D. (1972). On communicative competence. In J. Pride & J. Holmes (Eds.), *Sociolinguistics: Selected readings*. Harmondsworth, England: Penguin Books.

[15] Canale, M. & Swain, M. (1980). Theoretical bases of communicative approaches to Second language teaching and testing. *Applied Linguistics, 1*(1), 1–48.

[16] Canale, M. (1983). From communicative competence to communicative language pedagogy. In: Richards J, Schmidt R (Eds.) *Language and communication* (pp. 2–27). Longman, London.

[17] Halliday, M.A.K., & Hasan, R. (1976). *Cohesion in English.* Longman, London.

[18] Celce-Murcia, M., Dörnyei, Z., & Thurrell, S. (1995). A pedagogical framework for communicative competence: A Pedagogically motivated model with content specifications. *Issues in Applied Linguistics 6*(2), 5–35.

[19] Celce-Murcia, M. (2007). Rethinking the role of communicative competence in language teaching. In Soler, E.A. & Jorda, M.P.S. (Eds.). *Intercultural Language Use and Language Learning.* Singapore: Springer.

[20] Hunston, S. (2002). Pattern grammar, language teaching, and linguistic variation. In: Reppen, R., Fitzmaurice, S., Biber, D. (Eds.). *Using corpora to explore linguistic variation* (pp. 167–186). Amsterdam: John Benjamins.

[21] Deardorff, D.K. (2006). Identification and assessment of intercultural competences as a student outcome of internationalization. *Journal of Studies in International Education. 10*, 241–266.

[22] Jandt, F.E. (2013). *An introduction to intercultural communication: identities in a global community.* 7th Ed. Los Angeles: Sage

[23] Chen, Y. & Sarossa, W. (1996). Intercultural communication competence: A synthesis. In B.R. Burleson (Eds.). *Communication Yearbook 19* (pp. 353–383). Thousand Oak, CA: Sage

[24] Chen, G.M. (1989). Relationships of the dimensions of intercultural communication competence. *Communiation quarterly, 37*(2), 118–133.

[25] Chen, G.M. (1990). Intercultural communicative competence.: Some perspectives of research. *Howard Journal of Communciation 2*(3), 243–261.

[26] Alsegoff, L. (2012). Another book on EIL? Heralding the need for new ways of thinking, dong and being. In Alsegoff, L., S.L., McKay, Hu, G. and W.A. Renandya (Eds.). *Principles and practices for teaching English as an international language.* New York & London: Routledge.

[27] House, J. (2007). What is an 'intercultural speaker'? In E. Alcón Soler and M.P. Safont Jordà (Eds.). *Intercultural language use and language learning* (pp. 7–21). Dordrecht, the Netherlands: Springer.

[28] McDaniel, E.R., Samovar, L.A. & Porter, R.E. (2010). Using intercultural communication: The building blocks. In Samovar, L.A., Porter, R.E., & McDaniel, E.R. (Eds.). *Intercultural communication: A reader.* Singapore: Wadsworth Cengage Learning.

[29] Halliday, M.A.K. (1972). *Explorations in the functions of language.* London: Arnold. Blackwell.

[30] Liddicoat, A., Papademetre, L., Scarino, A., & Kohler, M. (2003). *Report on intercultural language learning.* Canberra: Commonwealth of Australia.

[31] Dragićević Šešić, M., & Dragojević, S. (2011). *State of the arts and perspectives on intercultural competencies and skills.* Report prepared for UNESCO Experts Meeting on Intercultural Competences, Paris, France, September 21–22, 2011.

[32] UNESCO. (2013). *Intercultural competences: conceptual and operational framework.* Paris: UNESCO.

[33] Pusch, M.D. (2009). The Interculturally competent global leader. In Deardorff, D.K. (Eds.). *The SAGE handbook of intercultural competence.* Los Angeles: Sage

[34] Cochran-Smith, M., & Lytle, S.L. (1999). Relationship of knowledge and practice: Teacher learningin communities. *Review of Research in Education,24*, 249–305.

[35] Liddicoat, A. (2011). *An introduction to conversation analysis.* London: Continuum.

[36] Kumaravadivelu, B. (2006). *Understanding language teaching: From method to postmethod.* London: Lawrence Erlbaum Associates, Publishers.

[37] Kumaravadivelu, B. (2001). Toward a postmethod pedagogy. *TESOL Quarterly, 35*, 537–560.

[38] Edge, J. (Ed.). (2001). *Action research.* Washington, DC: TESOL.

[39] Giroux, H.A. (1988). *Teachers as intellectuals: Towards a critical pedagogy of learning.* South Hadley, MA: Bergin & Garvey.

[40] Clandinin, D.J., Davies, A., Hogan, P., & Kennard, B. (1993). *Learning to teach, teaching to learn.* New York: Teachers College Press, Columbia University.

[41] House, J. (1993). English as a lingua franca: A threat to multilingualism? In: Coupland, N. (Eds.) Thematic issue on language and globalisation. *Journal of Sociolinguistics 7*, 556–579.

[42] Nation, I.S.P. (2009). *Teaching ESL/EFL reading and writing.* New York & London: Routledge.

[43] Brislin, R., Cushner, K., Cherrie, C. & Yong, M. (1986). *Intercultural interactions: A practical guide.* New York: Sage.

Part I: English Linguistics

English Linguistics, Literature, and Language Teaching in a Changing Era – Madya et al. (eds)
© 2020 Taylor & Francis Group, London, ISBN 978-1-03-224160-9

Materializing colonial heritage of *Goa Belanda*

Agung Farid & R.Vindy M. Puspa
STBA YAPARI-ABA Bandung, Bandung, Indonesia

ABSTRACT: Materializing colonial heritage in *Goa Belanda* is an analysis of material culture within the Systemic Functional Linguistic (SFL) perspective. This study was conducted to identify the experiential, interpersonal and textual function and meaning of a cultural material object and to find out the meaning of colonialism in terms of space and time. This study uses descriptive research and uses a multimodal approach with an SFL perspective as its analytical approach. The purpose of the study is to explain the meaning and interpretation in the form of material, especially buildings. In representing material objects, the results of this study are that the key meaning is in the narrative and the description of the material landscape object itself. The values of meaning and interpretation that arise from material objects are colonial-era romances that are represented byways of communicating relating to the context of time and space. In other words, the colonial heritage was the meaning of the material object.

Keywords: material culture, systemic functional linguistics, the meaning of colonial heritage, Goa Belanda

1 INTRODUCTION

The development of culture and language is closely related to the representation of human thoughts or ideas. To understand the thinking of an individual or group of people, the result of human thought is in the form of material things. The meaning that appears from the material culture is an approach to interpret the material itself. In its development, what is required in the meaning of colonial inheritance are questions such as what the hegemony of colonial inheritance means, and whether there is a change of meaning and identity as time changes? As material objects, colonial inheritance is important objects in studying human history because they provide a concrete basis for ideas and can validate them [1]. Preservation of colonial heritage shows recognition of the importance of the past and the things that tell its story. Maintained objects create a memory and the actuality of objects. The problem in this research is how does a material object of colonial heritage represent its function and meaning. Material culture is simply everything, the environment and the world in which we interact and are surrounded by [2]. In this case, we are creators and created by material culture. However, Prown [3] in his article *Mind in Matter: An Introduction to Material Culture Theory and Methods* explained that the term material culture can be expressed as a study and the subject matter of a study.

In this study, the main topic of research is how to analyze the meaning of semiotic objects. The tools for analyzing semiotic objects include the use of Systemic Functional Linguistic (SFL) analysis [4]. The systemic functional linguistic device aims to investigate the meaning arising from the integrated use of semiotic resources. Based on the view of the SFL above, material objects can represent meaning and function in a multimodal manner. [4]. Therefore, researchers look for historical colonial relics that interpret the material culture. Moreover, the significance of this research theoretically is to make a design or pattern of analysis based on the meaning and function of semantics of landscape in the form of buildings. The significance

Table 1. Modeling of multimodal analysis with a functional linguistic approach [4].

Unit	Experiential/ representational	Interpersonal/interactive	Textual/compositional
1. Building 2. Building components	The user experience of architecture, the functionality of architecture and orientation: 1. The way or layout of architecture in its environment 2. The function of architecture	The relationship between the building and its surrounding buildings, or the building reference that is not around the architectural objects: 1. Relation/role of objects with objects 2. Relation/role of the object with humans	Textual functions, making architectural constructs with other architectures as well as between components of the architecture itself into a coherent one: 1. Components of conjunctions between architectural components 2. Conjunctions between components of architecture with other components

of the practical aspect of this research is to get the information and knowledge for society in understanding the landscape of a building and to try to give a general understanding of social practices and the material culture of a landscape.

This is a qualitative research type with a descriptive method that takes an inductive paradigm [5]. This research approach uses multimodal discourse analysis [6] with SFL analysis [7]. This study takes the perspective of a multimodal method which is basically an analysis of discourse practices with two-dimensional and three-dimensional image objects including visual images and objects or buildings [6]. The tool for analyzing material culture is SFL. This analytical tool attempts to explain semiotic objects into genre analysis [7].

Previous research in material culture came from Fu [8]. In Fu's research, the revival or revitalization of Spanish cultural heritage not only aimed at the aesthetic art aspect but has an ideological purpose where development in the Los Angeles area is based on the ideas of the Anglo-Saxon Protestant elite. Previous studies in the field of multimodal discourse analysis discuss the three-dimensional object of the Sydney Opera House by using SFL analysis [4]. O'Toole, in his research, reveals the meaning of three-dimensional objects using the experiential, interpersonal and textual aspects of the Sydney Opera House and its components, both internally and in relation to its physical and social contexts.

The concept of colonial inheritance is referred to in the concept of cultural heritage. In general, cultural heritage is basically an awareness of the construction of identity, situational, structured and functional knowledge of a society [9]. What is 'cultural heritage'? It is a term that encompasses several major categories of inheritance. Real cultural heritage includes mobile cultural heritage (paintings, sculptures, coins, manuscripts); immovable cultural heritage (monuments, archaeological sites, etc.); submarine cultural heritage (shipwrecks, ruins and an underwater cities); and the cultural heritage of non-objects (oral traditions, performing arts, rituals) [10].

Referring to the previous theoretical foundation, colonial heritage can be interpreted as a cultural heritage of human work, which was produced during the colonial period. The vulnerable time of the Dutch colonial period according to Mujahidin (2017) [11] was for three and a half centuries or 350 years. During that time, the Dutch colonial period also left many historical relics, in the form of buildings, language, and cultural artifacts, and one of the historical relic from the Dutch colonial period is *Goa Belanda* (Dutch Cave) in Bandung City, Indonesia.

Material culture study is a study of social anthropology that uses material culture as an analytical tool [12]. The definition of material culture emphasizes how objects, that are not lifeless in the environment act on people and are followed up by people, for the purpose of showing and explaining social functions, regulating social relations and giving symbolic meaning to human activity [13]. Moreover, material culture is defined as the study of how people have used objects to overcome and interpret their physical world [14].

Besides, material culture can be a study or the subject matter of a social study [3]. Material culture is understood as a study of the value system, beliefs, ideas, behaviors and social assumptions, through serious investigations of artifacts [3]. In other words, material culture is translated as a study of manmade material products, or, as George Kubler (1962) [15] states, 'the history of things'. This study focuses on art and artifacts, as they usually also include the study of the technological processes involved in the production of such objects and the conceptual systems within them that make them appear. Material culture also includes the human construction of the environment as a cultural and economic landscape. With the explanation of the experts above, material culture becomes an interesting research object to be studied by analyzing the relationship between the culture of society and the surrounding environment.

The theoretical approach and language analysis in this study focus primarily on the formal characteristics of the language, which explains, the functions of language. Language is often described as having the following main functions: descriptive function or ideational function, within the framework in which it is a function of organizing the speaker or writer's experience of the world [7]; the social function (the interpersonal function in Halliday's terms), is used to construct, nurture and signal human relationships; an expressive function, through which speakers signal information about opinions, prejudices, past experiences and so on; and textual functions, making written and spoken text.

The theoretical foundation in this study refers to SFL analysis [7] and multimodal SFL [6]. SFL theory is an approach that sees language as a source used for communication in a social context rather than as an abstract formal system. The word 'systemic' refers to the view of language as a network of interrelated systems (semantics, lexicogrammar, phonology) and functional terms, which indicate that the approach is related to the choice made by the speaker in the exchange of meaning through language. The exchange of meaning includes semantics (message content proposition), interpersonal semantics (including speech functions such as requests and phrases, as well as attitudes) and textual semantics (how text is structured as messages, for example, as given or new information). SFL has a lexicogrammatical concept, which is a concept that combines syntax, lexicon, and morphology as a system in analyzing speech in its functional roles such as agents, themes and mood. From the lexicogrammatical concept, SFL has a higher level of the concept called genre in its system concept.

The functional approach in language is often described as having the following main functions: 1) descriptive function (ideational function) that is organizing the speaker or writer's experience of the world and conveying information that can be expressed or rejected and testable; 2) social function (interpersonal function used to build, maintain and signal relationships between humans; 3) an expressive function, through which speakers signal information about opinions, prejudices, past experiences; 4) textual functions, making written text and coherent context [7]. In grammatical semantics, these functions are called semantic metaphors which are located in the text within the clause level. The thematic structures relate to the theme, and rheme, or structure of information or old and new topics and comments in which any component in clauses such as subject, predictive, complementary or adjudicative can be discussed and placed in a thematic position or the beginning of a more significant clause than any other location in a sentence.

Based on the explanation and exposure of the above theory, the modeling analysis is presented in Table 1.

2 RESULTS AND DISCUSSION

Social practices of colonial heritage: *Goa Belanda* is essentially a building object that has functions and structures. From the aspects of the building units and building components of *Goa Belanda*, we can interpret its structure and its function as a social practice of the object of the building. To interpret the object of *Goa Belanda*, aspects such as experience, interpersonal and textual, play a role as a means of meaning analysis.

The experiential meaning in multimodal SFL is the concept of user experience of architecture, the function of architecture and orientation. In a more detailed way, the experiential meaning of

Figure 1. Goa Belanda.

Goa Belanda can be explained in the way or layout of architecture in its environment, and the function of the architecture. The layout of the *Goa Belanda* is the position of the *Goa Belanda* between the building and the surrounding landscape. In position, *Goa Belanda* is in the hills. There are one main entrance, one exit and one door for logistics. There are five detention cells, a communications room, a guard room, eight multipurpose rooms, and one interrogation room. Then, the room layout of *Goa Belanda* is the entrance and exit stands, which are made separately and back to back. For *Goa Jepang*, there are four entrances that also serve as exits, and the layout of the four entrance are parallel. Besides the entrances, two ventilation ducts located to the right and left, and the layout of the ventilation duct themselves are similar both in the entrance and exit. The interrogation room is placed in the middle, adjacent to the multipurpose room. The layout of the multipurpose room and detention cell are side by side and adjacent to the hallway after the entrance. From the layout, there is currently no significant change. In conclusion, from the explanation of the *Goa Jepang* layout, this still describes the conditions and atmosphere that had occurred in the Dutch colonial period.

The function of the *Goa Belanda* architecture was original as a gateway for the sake of settlement in the area of Bandung. Over time, the initial function of the building was replaced with a military function, as the last bastion to defend the city of Bandung from enemy attack. The military function of *Goa Belanda*, among others, was as a command headquarters, the last line of defense, arms and ammunition storage, and the headquarters of allied communications. The same function also occurs in the *Goa Jepang* as a command post, last line of defense, the arsenal of weapons and ammunition, and communications headquarters. Viewed from the aspect of its function, currently, *Goa Belanda* functions as a tourist attraction with many additional functions such as education, economy, sport, and others.

The next meaning is the interpersonal meaning of *Goa Belanda*, which is the relationship between the building with the surrounding buildings, or building reference that is not around the architectural objects described in the relation/role of objects with other objects, and relation/role of the objects with humans. The relation/role of objects with objects is the meaning

Figure 2. Face of *Goa Belanda* currently.

of the relation of the object of *Goa Belanda* with the buildings and other objects and is the connection of the function of *Goa Belanda* to the function of other surrounding buildings. The interpersonal layout of *Goa Belanda* is nestled in a forest landscape with the majority of Ugandan Mahogany tree. In interpersonal functions, *Goa Belanda* is interpersonally positioned between the object itself and the objects around it. That is the function of military buildings to oversee the state of the region located in the lower area or downtown Bandung. The relation/role of the object with humans is the relationship or role of *Goa Belanda* with its users and is the object of having relationships as a means to defend territory, control territory and as a hideout. However, the meaning of *Goa Belanda* is as a means of colonialism defense of both the West and the East. This cave building also became a symbol of power or the power of colonialism, and a symbol of colonialism and violence during that period. The relationship of objects with the current human building is a socioeconomic relationship with the utilization of the building as the livelihood of some residents.

The final meaning is textual meaning, where the object of *Goa Belanda* is interpreted from the aspect of architectural coherence (construction detail of the architecture of the object) and its comparison with the construction of other architectures. From the aspect of textual meaning, the meaning represented by Goa Belanda is the relationship of the construction components from the object of Goa Belanda itself. Judging from the components of its architecture, the Gua Belanda has concrete, cement, and steel constructions as its main components. In interpreting textual meaning, the relationship between the architectural components of the *Gua Belanda* object is also related to the architectural component of other objects in other places. Before discussing the *Gua Jepang* in Bandung, the author wants to give an overview of the history of the *Gua Jepang* in the city of Lhokseumawe. The history of the Dai Nippon (Japan) army in the city of Lhokseumawe is very easy to find. One aspect is the existence of the *Gua Jepang* located in the hills of Cot Panggoi, in Gampong Blang Panyang. The location of the *Gua Jepang* is called 'Ku Rok Rok' by locals, which is a relic of the Japanese colonial period and which was used by the Japanese army as a hiding place and logistics at that time.

The relationship between the components of *Goa Belanda* with the surrounding buildings is the comparison of objects with other building components. The textual meaning of the *Goa Belanda* seen from the comparison between the objects of the *Goa Belanda* with similar buildings (other *Goa Belanda*) is very difficult to explain because the Netherlands only made caves in the city of Bandung alone. Therefore, the comparison with other objects is with the military object of *Gedung Sate*. Gedung Sate [16] is one of the colonial government heritage buildings that still stands majestically as a building that was once used as the *Department Peperangan* (Departement van Oorlog), located at Jalan Kalimantan no. 14 Bandung. The construction of the building began in 1908 and was completed in 1915. Bandung people called the building the House of Sabau. In Sundanese, *sabau* means smell and the unit of size is 7,096 m^2. *Gedung Sate* has a function similar to the *Goa Belanda* which has a function as the center of the last Dutch government if the first line of defense falls into the hands of the enemy. Another object of The Netherland heritage is Merdeka Building (Gedung Societeit Concordia), located on Asia Afrika Street, Bandung.

Images of the past, present, and future of the colonial heritage of the Dutch Cave are the meanings of cultural material objects. The representation of the meaning of the colonial heritage in the form of *Goa Belanda* is how the meaning of multimodal discourse is explained from the position and function aspects of the object itself. The position of *Goa Belanda* is in the hills of the highlands. The image of *Goa Belanda* has a function as a Dutch military installation during the colonial period which included functions as a fortress, hiding place, command and communication headquarters. In addition, the meaning of *Goa Belanda* conveyed that the building has difficult access and a defensive position against the opponent's attack The ideational meaning of *Goa Belanda* is reflected in how objects are constructed. At the time of its construction, *Goa Belanda* had diverse functions from socio-economic to military functions. *Goa Jepang*, on the other hand, has a function as an additional building for military activity, and the function of the *Gua Jepang*, in this case, is only used as a warehouse for ammunition, logistics, and communication.

Representation of *Goa Belanda* also interpreted the connection between the components of a solid object functioning for hundreds of years and which functioned to withstand heavy military attacks. The interpersonal functions and meanings of *Goa Belanda* are represented by the meaning of the relationship between *Gua Belanda* object with *Gedung Sate* and *Gedung Merdeka* (Societeit Concordia). When compared, the functions of the two objects are almost the same, as a means of military infrastructure to defend the colonial territory.

In the present, representation of *Goa Belanda* is interpreted as a legacy of colonial cultural history. *Goa Belanda* itself is currently one of the tourist attractions in the city of Bandung. On the other hand, the image is built as a marker of the history of robustness and greatness of Belanda colonial buildings, as well as a means of education, recreation and nature conservation. The colonial cultural heritage of *Goa Belanda* is essentially the reuse of the object for other purposes.

At the center of interpreting colonial heritage are the making of the meaning of the building itself and its historical context. The colonial legacy is not only tied to history, but it raises the present to create cultural value. The destruction of the material cultural values of *Goa Belanda* is related to the social values produced by humans in the context of the past. From the socio-cultural aspect, *Goa Belanda* reflects social and cultural values in the context of time. The cultural values of the colonial inheritance represented by Goa Belanda are interpreted from how these objects have functions and meanings that are related to the current, past, and future contexts. The building function of *Goa Belanda* emphasizes how building objects have meaningful values, explain structure, function, social relations and have a symbolic meaning of the human activity. In its meaning, the material culture of *Goa Belanda* also explains how people have used the object to interpret and overcome problems from various aspects. The social and cultural values that arise from material objects have changed over time. If the past, social values were to retain colonial power, colonialism, and values of struggle, while in the present, the values are historical and educational values of colonial occupation.

The historical heritage value of *Goa Belanda* is the value of the meaning of the object itself. The legitimacy of the historical heritage emphasizes the user's use of the object at the present moment. The ideological values and messages of the object of the building of the Dutch Cave at this time are the value and message of colonialism as a historical heritage. The message of material objects is how oppression, misery, fear of war and colonization are not shown entirely by the objects of buildings and objects surrounding them today, and what emerges is the romance of the colonial era.

3 CONCLUSION

As one of the three-dimensional objects that can be seen in everyday life, *Goa Belanda* is a form of a material object that has semantic and social meaning. In fact, material objects have dimensions of meaning that can be interpreted. As a multimodal discourse, each of these dimensions is an integral concept of analysis, in interpreting material objects comprehensively and critically. Material objects can be interpreted semantically by SFL-based methods, trying to explain the role and meaning of what is played in a three-dimensional visual communication in the form of material objects. In this way, at least, we can show how three-dimensional visual communication is slightly different from two-dimensional communication.

In representing material objects, the key meaning is in the narrative and the description of the landscape object itself. *Goa Belanda* is essentially a building object that has functions and structures. From the aspects of the building units and building components of *Goa Belanda*, we can interpret its structure and its function as a social practice of the object of the building. To interpret the object of *Goa Belanda*, aspects such as experience, interpersonal and textual, play a role as a means of meaning analysis. The social significance of material objects is explained by who the author (the maker) is and who the reader (user) is, and what forms and lines of communication of the material object as a whole unit of discourse. From the social semantic meaning, the cultural heritage of the object of *Goa Belanda* is the meaning of social practices aimed at building the meaning of common knowledge. In constructing cultural and ideological objects, material objects give meaning to how oppression, misery, fear of war and occupation are not fully represented by the objects of buildings and objects surrounding them today, and what emerges is the romance of the colonial era.

REFERENCES

[1] Antoš, Z. (2012). *Europski etnografski muzeji i globalizacija* (European ethnographic museums and globalization). *Muzeologija, 47*, 9–205.

[2] Gamble, C. (2004). *The basic archeology.* New York, NY: Routledge.

[3] Prown, J.D. (1982). Mind in the matter: An introduction to material culture theory and method. *Chicago University, 17*, 2.

[4] O'Toole, M. (2004). Opera Ludentes: The Sydney Opera House at work. In K.L. O'Halloran (Ed.), *Multimodal discourse analysis: Systemic-functional perspectives* (p. 13). London, UK: Continuum.

[5] Creswell, J.W. (2007). *Qualitative inquiry and research design "Choosing among five approaches"* (2nd ed.). Thousand Oaks, CA: Sage Publications.

[6] Kress, G. & Leeuwen, T. (2006). *Reading images.* London, UK: Routledge.

[7] Halliday, M. (2004). *Introduction to systemic functional linguistics* (3rd ed.). London, UK: Hodder Arnold.

[8] Fu, A.S. (2012). Materializing Spanish colonial revival architecture: History and cultural production in Southern California. *Home Cultures, 9*(2),149–172.

[9] Silverman, H. (2011). Contested cultural heritage: A selective historiography. In H. Silverman (Ed.), *Contested cultural heritage: Religion, nationalism, erasure, and exclusion in a global world.* New York, NY: Springer.

[10] UNESCO. (2017). What is meant by "cultural heritage"? Retrieved from www.unesco.org: http://www.unesco.org/new/en/culture/themes/illicit-trafficking-of-cultural-property/unesco-database-of-national-cultural-heritage-laws/frequently-asked-questions/definition-of-the-cultural-heritage/.

[11] Mujahidin, M. (2017, July 24). Benteng Gedong Dalapan, Sisa Penjajahan Belanda yang terlupakan di Cililin Kabupaten Bandung Barat [Gedong Dalapan fortress, forgotten Dutch colonial remnants in Cililin, West Bandung Regency]. *TribunJabar.* Retrieved from http://jabar.tribunnews.com/2017/07/24/benteng-gedong-dalapan-sisa-penjajahan-belanda-yang-terlupakan-di-cililin-kabupaten-bandung-barat.

[12] Hodder, I. (1991). The interpretation of documents and material culture. Retrieved from https://static1.squarespace.com/static/53568703e4b0feb619b78a93/t/5368dacae4b0a33222ab26f0/1399380682582/the-interpretation-of-documents-and-material-culture.pdf.

[13] Woodward, I. (2007). *Understanding material culture.* London, UK: Sage.

[14] Massey, A. (2000). *Hollywood beyond the screen: Design and material culture.* New York, NY: Berg.

[15] Kubler, G. (1962). *The shape of time: Remarks on the history of things.* Connecticut: Yale University Press.

[16] Pemerintah Provinsi Jawa Barat. (2017). Tourism potential: Historical building tourism 1. Bandung, Indonesia: West Java Provincial Government. Retrieved from http://jabarprov.go.id/index.php/potensi_daerah/detail/58.

English Linguistics, Literature, and Language Teaching in a Changing Era – Madya et al. (eds)
© 2020 Taylor & Francis Group, London, ISBN 978-1-03-224160-9

English and Javanese greeting expressions: A descriptive qualitative study on pragmatics

Ayu T. Andayani & Basikin
English Education Study Program, Graduate School, Yogyakarta State University, Yogyakarta, Indonesia

ABSTRACT: Due to the vast studies of cross-cultural pragmatics, a comparison of languages needs more investigation, especially in regard to the influence of culture. The current paper aims to describe various greeting expressions produced by English and Javanese users as well as to compare which language possesses more varied expressions. The main reason triggering the researchers to conduct the study is the emergence of English as a foreign language in Indonesia and the popularity of the Javanese language as the mostly used language in the country. Some factors, including culture, impact the diversity of greeting expressions. Therefore, the researchers conducted the current study to determine how culture influences the English and Javanese languages in expressing greetings. To achieve this goal, a descriptive qualitative study of pragmatics across culture analysis was carried out. The researchers utilized the expressions of greetings and their responses in English and Javanese as the object of the research. The data collection techniques were observations, in depth-interviews and questionnaires. The findings showed that English has a number of strategies to express greetings including formal greetings; informal greetings; the combination between formal and informal greetings; question greetings; statement greetings; the combination between informal greeting and statements; and the combination between informal greeting and questions. For Javanese, there are formal greetings; informal greetings; greeting by question; greeting by statement; greeting by invitation; greeting by complaint; greeting with particular utterances. The study also showed that the expressions produced in the Javanese language are more varied than those in the English language.

Keywords: pragmatics across cultures, greetings, language, English, Javanese

1 INTRODUCTION

A language must be considered as a very crucial matter in human life. It has a fairly significant role in the world. Language comes as the source of human life as well as power [1]. Thus, without language, human beings will be able to do nothing since they cannot communicate each other. Language is also regarded as a symbol for humans as social creatures. It exists to create a social life for humans. There is no real activity for humans without the presence of language [2]. However, language is admitted as being general, thus, it varies greatly depending on the place and community of people using it. Each place has its own specific language, which is only available and used in it and by its people who are living there. In addition, people from different places have different ways of speaking. The differences of language happen in most language devices. Greeting expressions come as one of the crucial and common language devices used to greet other people. Greetings are regarded as important and common in everyday social exchanges around the world. Appropriate greeting actions are critical for the establishment as well as maintenance of any interpersonal relationships. In addition, greeting expressions indicate permanence of personal relation signs and the recognition of another participant as a potential agent in an activity [3]. Greeting expressions are more suitably treated as a system of signals conveying other than just overt messages [4]. This language device exists in all languages in the world although it appears in different forms. Thus, greetings are varied in form and mode of expression depending on the language as well as culture. The emergence of cross-cultural pragmatic studies provides benefits for researchers to gain views on such differences of linguistic devices among different languages. Recently, a considerable number of studies have compared languages within the pragmatic field. The most obvious example is a project called the Cross-Cultural Study of Speech Act Realization Patterns (CCSARP) [5]. The project aimed to provide a database of speech acts in terms of requests and apologies, across eight different languages. Another purpose was to investigate dissimilar communicative strategies across languages and determine ranges of pragmatic mismatches [6].

Based on the afore-mentioned project, the researchers are eager to investigate more differences across different languages to widen the analysis and results of cross-cultural pragmatics in the world. Javanese and English are selected as the languages for comparison because of the major differences in context and settings. As is commonly known, the Javanese language is one of the most popular languages in Indonesia. It is now used by about 50% of Indonesians, who are distributed in most of the provinces in the country [7]. Meanwhile, English is also well known as an international language, which is regarded as a foreign language in Indonesia. It is also used by many people around the world as an international language. Hence, it can be concluded that both Javanese and English possess similarities in the majority of users. Even though English is not widely used in Indonesia, this language is still studied and used as a foreign language in the country.

Javanese and English undoubtedly differ in terms of expressing greetings. Javanese people obviously have their own strategies to convey greeting expressions, as well as people who speak English. In terms of expressions, English is one of the cultural products of Western culture or specified as British culture and has particular ways of greeting. Similarly, Javanese also has its own expressions to express greetings. As the most-used languages in different settings and users, both languages are worth studying, especially concerning greeting expressions. Due to the numbers of users as well as the culture influencing them, more differences in greetings might occur. Thus, an investigation of how the cultures of both languages influence the differences is beneficial to provide a description. Accordingly, it is beneficial to know and compare how these two languages differ in the way people implement greeting expressions as the result of their own culture. At this point, a pragmatic across culture study is suitable for comparing greeting expressions. To compare languages with such a pragmatic analysis, this study also applied a descriptive linguistics design in analyzing the data. A framework of descriptive linguistics is used to describe the strategies in conveying greeting expressions represented from each of the languages.

By knowing the differences, learners can benefit from proficiency in understanding linguistics in relation to culture and also about greeting expressions used by British and Javanese people under the theory of pragmatics. Besides, this study is expected to help provide a clear description about pragmatics across cultures and provide the expressions used by English and Javanese people in expressing greetings influenced by their own cultures.

As mentioned earlier, greetings are one of the linguistic devices categorized as adjacency pairs, because it has a response that is also called a greeting. According to Blum-Kulka [8], adjacency pairs occur when an utterance of a speaker makes a specific type of a response very likely. Dezhara et al. [6] also stated that adjacency pairs concern the relation between acts showing that a conversation contains frequently occurring patterns which are in pairs of utterance.

Therefore, as one of the adjacency patterns, greetings are considered as a speech event constituted by two parts, side by side, such as greeting–greeting [9,10]. A similar idea comes from Hornby, who states that a greeting is the first words or utterance used when one sees somebody or writes to somebody. It is an expression or act with which somebody is greeted [11]. For example:

- A: Hi
- B: Hi

A greeting consists of several interlinking behaviors including verbal, non-verbal, term of address and social context [10]. According to Hang [12], greetings are considered as 'ritualistic expressions' that are affected by any social factors, predominantly cross-cultural differences. Thus, a greeting is an expression that has a response by which the essence of culture and other social factors are greatly influenced. Irvine in Dezhara et al. [6] explains that greetings are an essential opening to all encounters and can be used as a description of when and where the encounter occurs. In a pragmatic view, greetings are more functional as illocutionary acts categorized as expressive meaning that could not be taken literally. This means, what is expressed to greet people might not be meant as it is, but more to show politeness. Therefore, the way people express greetings may vary considerably.

Greetings are utterances used by people when they first meet. The response to a greeting is called a greeting but its type varies depending on context and situation. In a pragmatic view, different greeting forms are greatly influenced by many factors related to culture. According to Cutting [10], there are some aspects that have an interlinking behavior with a greeting, namely: (1) verbal; (2) term of address; (3) non-verbal; (4) social context. Greeting forms are also classified into verbal and non-verbal [3,5]. In addition, Halliday (1973), in Kotorova [5], categorizes greetings into two aspects, time-bound and time-free. Time-bound greetings are those used in formal greetings, while time-free greetings are ritualized commonly in informal greetings.

Goffman stated that greetings provide the means of opening conversations appropriately, establishing and maintaining social relationship such as 'Hello' or 'Hi' [13]. In addition, the use of greetings in a conversation benefits the identification of the presence of communicators as well as to show their concern [10]. This means a greeting can recognize the speakers of the greeting itself and find out what kind of relationship exists between them.

A conversation usually has a beginning and an end. The starting part of a conversation sometimes can be called a greeting. According to Fieg and Mortlock [14], the beginning of a conversation will generally involve an exchange of greetings. Thus, a conversation is usually started by a greeting and then it is followed by a greeting. They also argue a lot about this introductory part of a conversation or this greeting phenomenon, which is highly influenced by the cultural setting [14]. It means the expression of a greeting will vary from group to group induced by its own culture. Greetings also involve the use of names or address terms that vary enormously, including who will speak first, what a suitable reply is and even what variety of language is used, which may also be tightly constrained by circumstances.

In common, English greeting expressions share some key formulaic expressions recurrently used in various informal contexts [13]. The expressions are 'Hi'+ (first name) followed by 'Hello'+ (first name). In addition, people tend to greet each other according to the time of the day.

Additionally, one major sense in English greeting expressions is about the topic. Hornby [13] found that in English culture, personal matters are regarded as one's privacy and people do not talk about them except with close friends. Thus, English speakers are habituated to greeting each other within linguistic routines like 'How've you been?' The other forms are like 'Nice day, isn't it?' or many other greetings that do not overstep one's private issues. These kinds of conversations are conventionally about food, health questions or the weather.

On the contrary, Javanese greetings are varied in expressions such as *sugeng enjing, sugeng, siang, sugeng sonten* and others which are formal expressions that are not only the common expressions used in daily communication [15]. Javanese people have other greeting types to greet other interlocutors that can be regarded as informal greetings. Besides, Javanese people also tend to use various intimate expressions to greet people to show how they respect each other.

Concerning the types of greeting, these vary greatly from one to the other. Given that English and Javanese are similarly regarded as major languages in different contexts, it is worthy to compare both in the aspect of greetings. It is absolutely certain that both languages have their own ways to greet people and of course many factors influence the variety. Therefore, this pragmatic across culture study was used to determine the way in which culture influences the expression of greetings. In addition, the variety of greeting expressions is also explored.

2 RESEARCH METHOD

A descriptive qualitative study under the grounds of pragmatic across culture analysis was used as the design of this research. This research design aimed to describe aspects of language depending on the cultural influence. The object of this research was greeting expressions of English and Javanese found in various data sources including movies, literary works and native speakers of Javanese. The data of this research were in the forms of dialogs containing greetings–greetings in the English and Javanese languages. There were two kinds of data sources applied in this study. The first data source was the data from English greetings which was found from English movies and literary works. The second source was about Javanese greetings gathered from interviews with five native Javanese speakers from different ages and social backgrounds. The data for the Javanese greetings were also gathered from question-naires and non-participant observations to get the real language use of Javanese.

This study was done in Yogyakarta province, in particular the districts of *Kulonprogo, Gunungkidul, Bantul* and *Yogyakarta* with 30 Javanese native speakers. To gather the data, the researchers implemented a triangulation method through interviews, observations and a questionnaire. In addition, a *metode catat* (noting technique) and recording method were also used to gather the data. Purposive sampling was used to find the most appropriate respondents for the interviews through selecting native speakers of different ages and social background. Besides, there were 30 open-ended questionnaires distributed to all the partici-pants. The instruments were focused on various types of greetings used by Javanese native speakers in different contexts and situations.

Overall, the researchers used an interactive model proposed by Miles et al. [16] to analyze the data. Data analysis was done by doing data condensation, data display, conclusion draw-ing and verification. Additionally, *metode padan ekstralingual* was also used to compare the data gathered from different sources. To address the issue of trustworthiness, the researchers combined methodological and data triangulation. This kind of triangulation is used to strengthen the credibility of the research result [17].

3 RESULTS AND DISCUSSION

Based on this investigation, the researchers found several strategies employed by native speakers of English and Javanese in expressing greetings. The differences and classifications are summarized in Table 1.

According to Table 1, it can be noted that both English and Javanese have formal and informal greeting expressions. However, the Javanese language seems to produce more varied utterances, including invitations, complaints and some specific utterances.

3.1 *English greeting expressions*

In English, various types of greetings were found including formal greetings, greeting by name, greeting with questions and greeting with statements. Each type is described and ana-lyzed in the following.

Table 1. Various greeting expressions both in English and Javanese language expressed by native speakers.

English greeting expressions	Javanese greeting expressions
Formal greeting	Formal greeting
Informal greeting	Informal greeting
Combination between formal and informal greeting	Greeting by question
Greeting by question	Greeting by statement
Greeting by statement	Greeting by invitation
Combination between informal greeting with statement	Greeting by complaint
Combination between informal greeting and question	Greeting with particular utterances

3.1.1 *Formal greeting*

As a time-bound greeting, formal greetings are initialed by a particular time, indicating when the greeting is expressed. Examples of English formal greetings are presented as follows:

- Miss Lidya: 'Good afternoon, Mr. James'.
- Mr. James: 'Good afternoon, Miss Lydia'.

Other examples are as follows:

- Mason: 'Morning'.
  Olivia: 'Morning'.
- Mase: 'Good morning'.
  Mason: 'Morning'.

3.1.2 *Informal greeting*

The other type of greeting is the informal greeting which does not indicate any particular time. Such greetings appear in the informal context such as between those having similar age and status. The informal greeting is sometimes expressed by using the words *hi* or *hello*. The other kinds of expressions used in an informal way are the use of names or just calling someone's name in greeting or the combination between those words and the names. Different from formal greetings, informal greetings do not consider the time when the greeting occurs. Examples are presented as follows:

- Samantha: 'Hello?'
  Mason: 'Hey'.
- Cliff: 'Hi!'
  Mason: 'Hi!'
- Charlotte: 'Lizzie'.
  Lizzie: 'Charlotte'.

3.1.3 *The combination between formal and informal greeting*

Another kind of greeting is the combination of formal and informal greeting. This is structured with both formal and informal expressions in a single conversation. Examples of this kind of greeting, found in the movie Boyhood, are presented as follows:

- Cooper: 'Afternoon, Sam'.
  Sam: 'Yeah'.
- A shopkeeper: 'Hi, good afternoon. What can I do for you today?'
  Mason: 'Hey!'

Greeting expressions with responses in the data show that English native speakers commonly use both formal and informal greetings to greet people. The context shows a situation which is very relaxed and informal, yet the speaker wants to treat another formally since the speakers have an age gap, so the combination of two kinds of greetings is used.

3.1.4 *Greeting by question*

Another variety of expression is made in different contexts. One of the types showing the variety of greeting other than formal and informal is greeting by question. The example below shows an expression containing a greeting using a question:

- Mr. Darcy: 'What are you doing here?'
  Miss Elizabeth: 'I'm a guest here'.

3.1.5 *Greeting by statement*
The following example, taken from the movie Boyhood, contains an expression of a greeting using a statement:

- Mase: 'Good to see you'.
 Catherine: 'Yeah'.

3.1.6 *The combination of informal greetings with statements*
Greetings in English also use a combination between an informal greeting and a statement. The expression containing the informal greeting is as an introduction and is then continued by a statement. An example is as follows:

- Dalton: 'Hey, you must be Mason'.
 Mason: 'Yeah. Dalton, right?'

3.1.7 *The combination between informal greeting and questions*
The next type of English greeting is the combination among greeting expressions. One combination that can be found in the English language is that between an informal greeting and a question, such as in the following example:

- Lily: 'Hey, Tammy, how you doing?'
 Tammy: 'Hey, nice to see you'.

3.2 *Javanese greeting expressions*

Javanese people are known as the friendliest human beings [15]. The way they express greetings is a reflection of the moral value of the Javanese culture. Literally, most Javanese people use greetings to maintain social life and social relations in society. The researchers found several greetings used by Javanese people, namely formal greetings, informal greetings, greeting by question, greeting by statement, greeting by invitation, greeting by complaint, greeting with particular utterances of *Mangga, Kulanuwun, Ndherek langkung* and *Nyuwun sewu.*

3.2.1 *Formal greeting*
This kind of greeting can emerge based on various situations surrounding it. The most crucial aspect influencing the variety of greeting is the time when a conversation between speakers occurs. Besides, different age, status and degree of intimacy also have an impact on the use of this greeting. Examples of Javanese formal greeting expressions are as follows:

- An adult woman: *'Sugeng enjing'.* 'Good morning'.
 An older woman: *'Sugeng enjing'.* 'Good morning'.
- A young girl: *'Sugeng sonten Bu'.* 'Good afternoon, Mrs.'
 An older woman: *'Sonten Mbak'.* 'Good afternoon, Ms.'

3.2.2 *Informal greeting*
This kind of greeting is sometimes expressed within medium to low stages of the Javanese language. Informal greetings are commonly used in any situations having a different time and place. Examples are as follows:

- A young man: 'Heh!' 'Hey'.
 A younger man: 'Ya!' 'Yes'.

- A 22 year old man: 'Hei!' 'Hey'.
  A man of similar age: 'Hei.' 'Hey'.

The conversations occur between two young Javanese men when they meet in a street in the morning. Both of the speakers use such expressions because they are of the same status and have a very close relationship. Hence, they use informal language to greet each other.

3.2.3 Greeting by question

There are some greeting expressions found in the Javanese language which are in the form of questions. The levels of language vary based on the contexts surrounding them, as in the conversation below.

- A girl: '*Saka ngendi?*' 'Where are you from?'
  A girl: '*Dholan Mbak*'. 'Just going somewhere, Miss'.

3.2.4 Greeting by statement

The other type of Javanese greeting is that conveyed by statements. Statements, as greeting expressions, sometimes have deeper purposes than just greeting someone. This type includes other various manners of greeting and it uses all three speech levels in the Javanese language. The forms differ from one another based on the context surrounding the conversation, as in the examples below:

- A young woman: '*Mlampah sekolah Dhik*'.
  'Just walking on school, Miss'.
  A younger woman: '*Nggih Mbak. Mangga Mbak*'.
  'Yes Miss. Excuse me'.

3.2.5 Greeting by invitation

Javanese people seem to invite other people. It is because their greetings are likely to be an expression of invitation to someone or asking someone to join them in doing something. However, it is only another way to greet people.

- A young girl: '*Ayo Dhik!*' 'Come on!'
  A younger girl: '*Nggih Mbak*'. 'Yes'.

3.2.6 Greeting by complaint

The researcher found another way of greeting in Javanese in the form of complaints. This kind of greeting contains a statement meaning to complain toward something or someone. Nevertheless, the speakers do not really complain to others. They just use it as another manner to greet people. The expressions are in the complaint form, but their meaning and sense express just another variety of greeting.

- A young woman: '*Dhik, sombong tenan*'.
  'You are so proud, Miss'.
  A younger woman: '*Hehe. Sori Mbak ora weruh*'.
  '(*laughing*) I am sorry I do not see you, Miss'.

3.2.7 Greeting with particular utterances

It was found that Javanese people use various forms of language to express greetings including *Mangga, Kulanuwun, Ndherek langkung* and *Nyuwun sewu*. Although the expressions are different, all of these forms are commonly used in similar contexts in which age and status gaps may possibly occur. Examples of each are described below. The data below contain a greeting expression using the form of *Mangga*:

• A man: 'Mangga'. 'Excuse me'.
  An older man: 'Nggih'. 'Yes, please'.

The next conversation contains a greeting expression using the form of *Kulanuwun*:

• An old man: 'Kulanuwun'. 'Excuse me'.
  An older woman: 'Mangga'. 'Yes, please'.

Similarly, the data below concern a conversation between two people of different ages. Furthermore, a greeting expression using the form of *Ndherek langkung* occurs.

• A man: 'Ndherek langkung'. 'Excuse me'.
  An older man: 'Nggih ati-ati'. 'Yes. Take care'.

The data below contain a greeting expression using the form of '*Nyuwun sewu*':

• An adult man: 'Lik, nyuwun sewu'. 'Excuse me, Uncle'.
  An older adult man: 'Mangga'. 'Yes, please'.

All the data presented in this section have similar contexts although different settings clearly occur. The typical context surrounding the speakers is the degree of intimacy as well as the age and social status. All of the factors obviously influence the use of those particular forms to express greetings in Javanese.

Based on the findings, it can be seen that various English greetings greatly depend on the situation, context and the speakers involved. More than that, it shows that the types, forms and formulas of greeting are taking into consideration various factors like age, status, sex and even culture [18]. Various contexts including time and place are the most aspects influencing the types of greeting [19]. As indicated above, it can be seen that English greetings are expressed mostly by using time-bound expressions such as 'Good morning' and 'Good evening'. In another sample, it can be noted that English greetings are also elaborated through time-free expressions such as 'Hello', 'Hi' and 'How are you?' [18].

In addition, different degrees of intimacy, connection and age also have an impact on how English greetings are expressed. The most common greetings are formal and informal greetings [18]. This shows a certain amount of informality being used by English speakers especially in greetings. Generally speaking, English speakers are not really concerned with social status [20].

Furthermore, the use of questions and statements are also used as greeting expressions. The combination of both formal and informal greetings along with the use of statements and questions may also emerge. This fact is giving a clue that English greetings are also used to portray any rules of social patterns as well as good manners [18].

In contrast, due to the influence of culture and other contexts surrounding greetings, the Javanese language is considered to have more productive greeting expressions than the English language. The considerable variations occurring in the expressions of greetings conveyed by Javanese people is because there are some aspects that may have an effect, especially the presence of the cultural influence on the language and the people who use it. Since Javanese people are well known as having a very respectful culture and being well- mannered [21], these behaviors reflect the people of Java in expressing greetings so they tend to create more varied ways of greeting.

Culturally, Javanese also creates a stereotype of being a friendly tribe and having great manners, so that they tend to express greetings in more ways [22]. Such stereotypes influence Javanese people to be able to greet others excessively, possibly in any conditions and to still maintain the harmony to other people as well as to the Javanese people [15]. For this reason, the expressions of Javanese greetings become varied depending on the speech levels.

The use of both time-free and time-bound greeting expressions also appears. For example, the use of '*Sugeng enjing*' and '*Sugeng ndhalu*' appear as examples of time-bound greeting expressions [23]. However, forms like 'Hi' and 'Hello' as time-free greeting expressions occur such as '*Heh*', '*Hei*' '*Ya*' and so on. These also indicate that both formal and informal greetings occur in Javanese culture. In addition, more expressions in the forms of questions, statements, invitations and complaints are also used by Javanese speakers. This indicates that the people are not only using greeting expressions as routine speech or any phatic communication [20], but more as a way to show hospitality, culture and tradition [23].

Javanese greetings are also varied in the forms of particular utterances. This can be denoted from the emergence of several technical terms in Javanese such as *Mangga, Kulanyuwun, Ndherek langkung* and *Nyuwun sewu* [15]. Those kinds of expressions might have similar meanings like 'Excuse Me' but they are regarded as more polite. As can be seen, such forms of greeting expressions are expressed to older speakers.

From the comparison, it can be concluded that the Javanese language is more productive since it produces more varied greeting expressions. From the analysis, it can be seen that more variations in the expressions of greeting are influenced by some aspects such as cultural and social background influencing the language and its users. Since Javanese people are well known as possessing a very respectful culture and being well-mannered [24], their behavior influences Javanese in expressing greetings. Therefore, they tend to create more varied ways of greeting.

4 CONCLUSIONS AND SUGGESTIONS

The results show that there are many factors influencing greeting expressions. Culture appears as the most one providing a contribution. Due to the culture covering age, sex, social status and so on, both English and Javanese greetings are varied. Hence, the function of greeting expressions is not only to greet someone but is expanded to a more essential role [25].

From the discussion, it can be concluded that Javanese people tend to produce more varied ways of greeting people than English. Therefore, it can be said that the Javanese language is regarded as having more varied greeting expressions than English. This is proven by the use of invitations, complaints and some particular utterances instead of just using time-free, time-bound, formal and informal greetings. This high variety of greetings in Javanese is a product of Javanese culture that respects friendliness. Furthermore, it has a major role in maintaining social harmony.

The English language, on the one hand, is regarded as varied in the use of formal and informal greetings. As can be seen in the findings, the use of formal and informal greetings is more varied than Javanese. Additionally, greeting expressions are also diverse in the forms of time-free and time-bound greetings. This strengthens the general and core function of greetings, which is to maintain social communication.

Lastly, it is truly recognized that the research is still far from complete. Due to the limitations of this research, future research and studies to expand the scope of the research in order to identify other varieties of greeting expressions of English and Javanese is required. In addition, the researcher hopes that further research will focus on other aspects of pragmatic across cultures study. More research subjects and objects from more varied data sources are needed to achieve a more comprehensive but detailed view concerning greeting expressions of both English and Javanese.

REFERENCES

[1] Victoria, F. (1995). *An introduction to language*. London, UK: Harcourt.

[2] Alwasilah, A.C. (1990). *Linguistik suatu pengantar. (Linguistic: an introduction)*. Bandung, Indonesia: Angkasa Bandung.

[3] Li, W. (2010). The functions and use of greetings. *Canadian Social Science, 6*.

[4] Firth, J.R. (1972). Verbal and bodily rituals of greeting and parting. *The Interaction of Ritual, 2*.

[5] Kotorova, E.G. (2014). Describing cross-cultural speech behavior: A communicative pragmatic field approach. *Procedia - Social and Behavioral Sciences, 154*.

[6] Dezhara, S., Rezaei, O., Davoudi, S. & Kafrani, R. (2012). A comparative study of greeting forms common among native male and female speakers of Persian. *Journal of Language Teaching and Research, 3*.

[7] Zuraya, N. (2017, August). Bahasa daerah di Indonesia. (Local languages in Indonesia). *Nasional Republika*.

[8] Blum-Kulka, S. & Olshtain, E. (1984). Requests and apologies: A cross-cultural study of speech act realization patterns (CCSARP). *Applied Linguistics, 5*(3), 196–213.

[9] Cook, G. (1989). *Discourse*. Oxford, UK: Oxford University Press.

[10] Cutting, J. (2002). *Pragmatics and discourse: A resource book for students*. New York, NY: Routledge.

[11] Schegloff, E.A. & Sacks, H. (1973). Opening up closings. *Semiotica, 8*(4), 289–327.

[12] Hang, X. (2009). A discourse and pragmatic analysis of hedges in academic papers. *Journal of Sichuan International Studies University, 4*, 154–160.

[13] Goffman, E. (1971). *Relations in Public. Microstudies of the Public Order*. London: The Penguin Press

[14] Fieg, J.P. & Mortlock, E. (1989). *A common core: Thais and Americans*. Yarmouth, ME: Intercultural Press.

[15] Purwadi, Mahmudi, & Nuning, Z. (2012). *Tata Bahasa Jawa. (Javanese Language structure)*. Yogyakarta, Indonesia: Putra Pustaka.

[16] Miles, M.B., Huberman, A.M. & Saldana, J. (2014). *Qualitative data analysis: A methods sourcebook*. Thousand Oaks, CA: SAGE Publications.

[17] McMillan, J.H. (2012). *Educational research: Fundamentals for the consumer* (6th ed.). Boston, MA: Pearson.

[18] Jibreen, M.K. (2010). The speech act of greeting: A theoretical reading. *Journal of Kerbala University, 8*(1), 1–25.

[19] Wardhaugh, R. (2006). *An introduction to sociolinguistics*. Oxford, UK: Blackwell Publishing.

[20] Nodoushan, M. (2006). The socio-pragmatics of greeting forms in English and Persia. *Journal of Language Society and Culture, 17*, 17–13.

[21] Li, W. (2009). Different communication rules between the English and Chinese greetings. *Asian Culture and History, 1*(2), 72.

[22] Trosborg, A. (2010). *Handbook of pragmatics: Pragmatics across language and cultures*. Berlin, Germany: De Gruyter Mouton.

[23] Moradi, R. (2017). Sociolinguistic aspects of the speech act of greeting in Persian and English. *Bulletin de la Société Royale des Sciences de Liège, 86*, 294–303.

[24] Wierzbicka, A. (2003). *Cross cultural pragmatics. The semantics of human interac*tion. New York, NY: Mouton De Gruyter.

[25] Innawati, I. (2016). The pragmatics of greetings reflected in the textbooks for teaching English as a foreign language in Indonesia. *Ahmad Dahlan Journal of English Studies (ADJES), 3*, 1–10.

Part II: Literature

English Linguistics, Literature, and Language Teaching in a Changing Era – Madya et al. (eds)
© 2020 Taylor & Francis Group, London, ISBN 978-1-03-224160-9

Ryunosuke Akutagawa's *Kappa:* Warning against the dangers and pitfalls of modernization

Orestis Soidi & Emzir
Language Education, Graduate School, Jakarta State University, Indonesia

J.H. Tamboto
Indonesia Language Education, Graduate School, Manado State University, Indonesia

ABSTRACT: The aim of this study is to determine the evil aspects of modernization which could jeopardize Japanese society at the end of the nineteenth century and the beginning of the twentieth century, as conceived in the novella *Kappa*. Structural semiotic analysis is used because the Kappa society can be regarded as an allegory of a modernized society. Such a society embodies dangers that can harm human nature and causes alienation of man from his human nature. In the case of Japanese society, it can also undermine the values of traditional Japanese society such as *ie* and *amae*. The novella also offers moral advice to avoid the pitfalls of medernization.

Keywords: modernization, danger, warning, society

1 INTRODUCTION

In the late nineteenth and early twentieth century Japan underwent a great change in all fields. This change was marked by the restoration of political power into the hands of the Emperor. It was known as the Meiji Restoration, which took place in 1868 [1]. Under the Meiji Administration, Japan underwent modernization in politics, government, military, education, economy and culture by learning from Western countries. As a result, there have been changes in Japanese people's social behavior, as well as social and economic relations. Social changes can cause turmoil in society which can potentially lead to community breakdown.

In times of change, any society needs people who have a keen view of the dangers hidden behind the changes. Among them are writers and poets, such as Ryunosuke Akutagawa. His novella *Kappa* warned the Japanese about the dangers and pitfalls that Japan may encounter in the process of modernization. *Kappa* highlights the changes in Japanese society and especially shows the dangers and pitfalls that lurk behind modernization, through an allegorical story of Kappaland. In Japanese traditional folk belief, a Kappa is a spirit infamous for being wicked and malicious. The novella *Kappa* uses Kappas as its characters to highlight the evil aspects of a modern society through the depiction of the modern society of the Kappas.

This study of Akutagawa's *Kappa* is aimed at providing an insight into the dangers that a society experiences related to a very fast modernization. It is the dangers that are brought by the features of modern society. Some of the features are anonymity, excessive exploitation of nature and indifference to local wisdom. Georg Simmel, as cited by Ferguson [2], stated the paradox of modern society which is characterized by the growth of anonymity and the increasing importance of personal identities. Mgbemene [3] points out that in the developing world, industrialization spells a higher level of pollution and uncontrolled exploitation. Widyastuti and Rosyada [4] show how more and more people become ignorant of local wisdom as a result of influence from the outside world.

57

Japanese society, in the era of modernization, resembles the current situation of this disruptive era. In the process of its modernization, Japan received a lot of influence from Western civilization. The values of modernization that came with it often collided with the traditional values of Japanese society. Today's society is also undergoing tremendously rapid changes because of the development of science and technology, especially information technology, which makes the influence from the outside world more intense. In this more globalized world, local values and wisdom are easily ignored. The findings of this study are not only relevant to the understanding of Japanese society in its modernization era, but also applicable in any society experiencing great changes. The warnings to the Japanese people against the dangers and pitfalls of modernization conveyed in *Kappa* can be applied to the world community today.

2   RESEARCH METHOD

This study uses a qualitative research approach with structural semiotic analysis. Structural semiotic analysis is used to examine the relationships between the components of the literary text as a sign framework. Structural semiotic analysis places a structural analysis into the socio-cultural context of a literary text [5]. Semiotic analysis is based on the theory of C.S. Peirce [6]. In Peirce's semiotics there are three elements namely the sign, its referent and the interpretant. Peirce also distinguished signs into three types: icon, index and symbol. Peirce's division of signs is based on the mode of representation and the relation of the sign to its referent. An icon works as a physical substitute for the referents. It represents the referents through resemblance. Photos, diagrams, images, metaphors are some examples of icons. An index represents the referent through indication. For example, 'asap' is an indication of fire. A symbol is a representation by convention. The sign and the referent are linked to each other by the force of historical and social convention. Words are examples of symbols, because the relation of words and the referents are defined through convention. Structural analysis is used to examine the relationship of novella structure such as theme, characters, plot and setting with the topic of modern society characteristics. Then, semiotic analysis is used to examine the meaning of those structural components as semiotic signs in a social context.

3   FINDINGS AND DISCUSSION

Akutagawa's *Kappa* tells about life in Kappaland, the land of the Kappas. In Japanese folklore, a Kappa is a water imp living in rivers. The Kappas in Akutagawa's *Kappa*, however, did not live in rivers. They lived in a society that resembled human society. Kappaland is a highly developed, highly advanced society in technology and industry. It is a modern society in which the novella's main character, Patient Number 23, lived for a while. By living in Kappaland, he was able to compare the modern society of the Kappas and Japanese society during its endeavors to modernize itself in the Meiji and Taisho eras. Through his sojourn in Kappaland he gained insight into the evil aspects of modern society. These aspects could jeopardize Japanese society as it became a modern nation.

The depiction of the Kappas and their community is used to show how Japanese people and society could become in the future and along with those changes, what dangers could arise. The Kappa community depicted in *Kappa* can be considered as a representation of developed and modernized Japanese society in the future. There are similarities between Kappa society and Japanese society. This means that the Kappa society in Akutagawa's *Kappa* is an icon of Japanese society, but not contemporary Japanese society. Rather it is an icon of a more modernized and more advanced Japanese society in the future. This is where traits in contemporary Japanese society resemble those of Akutagawa's Kappa society. In the future, Japanese society will become similar to Kappa society, if the tendency of contemporary Japanese society persists. Through the iconic relation between the Kappa society and the hypothetical Japanese society in the future, the novella delivers a warning against the dangers Japan will encounter as it becomes a modern society.

One of the characteristics of modern industrial society is anonymity. The main character of *Kappa* is a patient of a mental hospital outside Tokyo. He is not referred to by his name. Instead, he is referred to by his registration number, namely Patient Number 23. In a modern factory, workers are placed in a row at production lines and each worker works as a component of the production process. For the sake of efficiency, it makes sense for the management of such production lines to apply a number to each worker, which is more practical than remembering workers' individual names. Such managerial efficiency characterizes modern industry as an anonymous and impersonal system. A worker is equal to a screw or a gear in a large industrial machine. Such a modern industry erodes human personal relations and gives way to a mechanistic functional relationship. The main character of *Kappa* is a symbol of anonymity. He has no name but is referred to as a number because his individuality as a person is not important. The situation of the main character represents the situation of workers in a production line whose individuality is unimportant in the context of production. In modern industrial society, there is always a risk that a man is considered and treated only as part of a production system without any concern for his existence as a person.

Another characteristic is that modern society denies human nature as an intelligent worker and creator. In *Kappa*, this is illustrated in the depiction of a book factory. Patient Number 23 visited a book factory in Kappaland. The book factory amazed him because of its highly mechanized and simple process of book production. Books are produced just by inserting paper, ink and powder made of donkey's brain into a book machine. In five seconds, all kinds of books came out of the machine.

The depiction of the book factory in Kappaland shows how modern industry alienates man from his nature. The advance of technology contains risks that human nature as *homo faber* (man the creator) who creates things is denied. A book should be the product of a thoughtful human ratio. In the process of publishing a book, there must be a man who wrote the manuscript. The book production in Kappaland, however, abolished that necessity. It no longer needs a writer who processes his or her mind to write a book script. Everything is automated in the factory. In such a circumstance, the nature of a book-maker as a thinking creator or rational being is ignored. Unlike other products, the production of a book must first undergo a process of creation. Books cannot be modified in order to produce a different book. When it is revised, it remains the same book, not a new book. The publication of a book really presents human beings as creators. This process is unnecessary in the book factory in Kappaland. In such a factory, the nature of human as *homo faber* [7] is removed.

One of the materials used in the book production is a powder made from donkey brain. Donkeys are originally unfamiliar to the Japanese people. The Japanese later knew this animal primarily through the interactions with other cultures like China and Europe. Along with the introduction of the donkey, the connotative meaning of donkey and ass in English or *Esel* in German entered Japanese culture. Both donkey and ass in English, as well as *Esel* in German, have the additional meaning of dumb. With the use of donkey brain powder as the material for the production of books, it could be said that the production of such a book is a foolishness, and it produces only ignorance in varying degrees. The use of donkeys serves as a symbol of stupidity. It is a warning to Japan not to fall into the same stupidity (mistake) as other developed countries. The episode of the book factory is indeed a satire of industry or factory conditions of mass production in early Japanese modernization. Japan, at that time, produced cheap products that had no Japanese characteristics and did not bear any trace of the traditional high craftmanship that the Japanese are infamous for.

A society trying to become modern can also easily embrace a tendency to underrate or ignore local wisdom. In its struggle to become a modernized nation Japan was facing the risk of becoming a society whose economic system is contrary to the traditional Japanese economic system. In the traditional Japanese system, each working group or economy is based on the principle of family. Japanese managerial concepts consider a company as an *ie* (a family). In companies, the concept of *ie* is traditionally applied in terms of seniority and lifelong employment. The relationship in traditional Japanese companies is a familial one, and not a relationship of laborers and employers. The philosophy prevailing in traditional Japanese company is *amae*, a philosophy of interdependence based on personal relationships [8].

In traditional Japanese companies, both management and employees are interdependent on each other based on the understanding and recognition of shared common goals. Modern Japanese society could lose the philosophy of *amae* in its industrial relationships. However, modern Japanese industries did not apply the traditional Japanese system of *ie* and *amae*. On the contrary, they adopted the capitalistic system which separates the capital owner and workers. There are no interdependencies or any kind of familial relation in the capitalistic system. *Kappa* gives a warning against this danger through its depiction of Kappaland's economic system, which is purely capitalistic to its core. Workers are considered and are dealt with in terms of their advantageousness or profitableness. For workers who lost their jobs there is no government support or social welfare funds. Instead, when they lost their jobs and were no longer able to serve as workers, the Kappas found another way to take advantage of them. They slaughtered them and ate their meat, as Doctor Chack said:

「その職工をみんな殺してしまって、肉を食料に使うのです。ここにある新聞をごらんなさい。今月はちょうど六万四千七百六十九匹の職工が解雇されましたから、それだけ肉の値段も下がったわけですよ。」 [9] [We slaughtered the workers who lost their jobs and we ate their meat. Let's see what the newspaper said about it. The number of new unemployed people for this month reached 64,769; the price of meat goes down comparably].

This reveals another trait of a modern capitalist economy, which is usually expressed as *homo homini lupus* (men are wolves to each other). Consequently, in this kind of capitalist economic system, exploitation and oppression of the weak, namely the workers, easily occurs. With the introduction of the capitalistic system to Japanese society, Japanese entrepreneurs seemed to develop a capitalist mentality. In *Kappa*, Gael, the owner and director of a glass industry, is the symbolization of such an entrepreneur. For a capitalist, the main purpose of life is to make the biggest possible profit out of their capital. To achieve this, they exploit others. Such exploitation is depicted in *Kappa* in an episode about a war between the Kappas and the beavers. During the war, Gael made great profits by supplying bricks to feed Kappa soldiers. The danger of the capitalist mentality is that it ignores the principles of economics and employment of Japanese society based on a family philosophy (*ie*), and runs on economic principles learned from the West, which is deemed to be inhumane.

Nature is another object of exploitation in the capitalistic system. In the novella, there is an account of the Kappa religion called Viverism or Modernism. The god of Viverism or Modernism, namely The Tree of Life, bears two fruits. One is a golden fruit and the other is a green fruit. The golden fruit is the fruit of good, and the green fruit is the fruit of evil. The golden color in East Asian culture symbolizes strength, prestige and wealth [10]. This means that goodness, according to Viverism, is strength, prestige and wealth. On the other hand, the green color in traditional Japanese culture is a symbol of fertility and growth. Green also symbolizes immortality [11]. The Japanese word for green, *midori*, is used to refer to trees and plants, as when people say '*midori ga ooi*' meaning there are many trees and plants. So, green (*midori*) is an index of nature. The symbolization of golden and green shows the opposition between prestige and wealth pursued through modernization and nature, which serves only as a resource to be exploited. For modernization, nature is not an ideal to be protected but serves only as a means to be exploited for the sake of progress. It suggests that for the Kappas, idealizing nature is contrary to their concept of modernization. The modernization of Japan is driven by a desire to gain equal position with Western nations (prestige). For that, they build strength in the form of military and economic power (wealth).

In the final part of the novella, *Kappa* gives advice to not be easily plunged into the dangers of modernism by behaving like an old wise Kappa. Although his age was approximately 115 or 116 years, he has the body and appearance of a small child. He was born into the body of an old Kappa with white hair. As he grew up, his body grew into a young Kappa. The old Kappa symbolized a wise old man. He naturally has the characteristics of the wise. It was these qualities that saved him from the dragging stream of worldly life. According to his own explanation, being born as an old Kappa (60 years of age at birth), he was free from the passions of a young Kappa. Instead of getting older, he became younger, so he was free from the usual greedy impulses of an older Kappa to collect as much wealth as possible for an established life. These are the qualities that can save any human from being obsessed by anything else. Whenever he makes a program, a plan or an activity he can do it with more caution. This is a warning to the Japanese people to carry out modernization with the aim of providing a better life for the people and not because of an obsession to become a nation that is respected and equal with other developed countries. Thus, they would not be a nation as Ishihara described, a nation without morality whose actions are driven by a hungry mentality [12].

4 CONCLUSIONS

Akutagawa's *Kappa* is an account of a dystopian society, according to Ho [13]. In agreement with Ho's opinion, this research goes further by analyzing the purpose underlying the creation of the novella. Using a structural semiotic approach, it is clear that the depiction of a dystopian society is intended to demonstrate the evil aspects, the dangers and pitfalls hidden in any modernization process. Japan, which strived to modernize the nation to become as modern and strong as Western nations, undertakes many changes that can undermine the roots of its society and endanger the nation itself. Akutagawa's *Kappa* serves as a warning against such dangers and pitfalls, so that the process of modernization will not go in the wrong direction.

The reading of Akutagawa's *Kappa* in this way can give readers an understanding of the social condition in Japan as it undertook modernization. By understanding the problems that came with modernization and the way the Japanese people coped with it, we can learn how to manage our countries' development projects. With the knowledge we gained through Japan's experience of modernization, we learn how to reconcile our traditional values and the modern values adopted from Western countries to support a better life.

The characteristics of modern society, as shown in *Kappa*, which were originally meant as warnings to Japanese society in the era of its modernization against the dangers they could encounter, are still relevant as warnings to present society. Themes such as anonymity, indifference to local wisdom and excessive exploitation of nature, still require urgent attention.

REFERENCES

[1] Allinson, J.C. & Anievas, A. (2010). The uneven and combined development of the Meiji Restoration: A passive revolutionary road to capitalist modernity. *Capital & Class*, 34(3), 469–490.

[2] Ferguson, H. (2018). (Dis)appointment: Conspicuous absence in contemporary society. *Contemporary Social Science*, 11(1), 92–101.

[3] Mgbemene, C.A. (2011). The effects of industrialization on climate change. Fulbright Alumni Association of Nigeria 10th Anniversary Conference Development, Environment and Climate Change: Challenges for Nigeria, University of Ibadan, 12–15 September.

[4] Widyastuti, W.W. & Rosyada, A. (2017, April). Kearifan Lokal sebagai Bingkai Internalisasi Nilai-Nilai Nasionalisme dalam Era Globalisasi [Local wisdom as a frame for internalizing the values of nationalism in the era of globalization]. *Prosiding Seminar Nasional PKn-Unnes 2017, Penguatan Spirit Kebangsaan di Tengah Tarikan Primordialisme dan Globalisme* [Proceedings of 2017 PKn-Unnes national seminar, strengthening national spirit in the middle of primordialism and globalism].

[5] Nurgiyantoro, B. (1995). *Teori Pengkajian Fiksi* [Theory of fiction study]. Yogyakarta, Indonesia: Gajah Mada University Press.

[6] Danesi, M. & Perron, P. (1999). *Analyzing cultures: An introduction and handbook*. Bloomington, IN: Indiana University Press.

[7] Bergson, H. (1944). The creative evolution. New York, NY: Random House.

[8] Tanjung, A. (2012). Philosophie Amae dalam Perusahaan Jepang [The philosophy of amae in Japanese company]. *Ekasakti*, 22(1), 1–7.

[9] Akutagawa, R. (2014). *Kappa, aru aho no isshou* [Kappa, the life of an idiot]. Tokyo, Japan: Shinchousha.

[10] Bortoli, M.E., & Maroto, J.R. (2001). Colours across cultures: Translating colours in interactive marketing communications. In *Proceedings of the European Languages and the Implementation of Communication and Information Technologies (ELICIT) Conference. University of Paisley.*

[11] Mathers, C. (2018). What is the meaning of color in Japanese culture? Retrieved from http://www.ehow.com/about-6658499-meaningcolorjapaneseculture.html

[12] Ishihara, S. (1981). Satu Bangsa tanpa Moralitas [A nation without morality]. In Japan Center for International Studies (Ed.), *Kekuatan yang Membisu: Kepribadian dan Peranan Jepang* [*Silent strength: Japan's personality and role*]. Jakarta, Indonesia: Sinar Harapan.

[13] Ho, K.T. (1993). Kappa as a dystopia: A study of Akutagawa's anti-utopian thought. *Nachrichten der Gesellschaft für Natur- und Völkerkunde Ostasiens e.V. (NOAG)*, 153(1), 45–62.

English Linguistics, Literature, and Language Teaching in a Changing Era – Madya et al. (eds)
© 2020 Taylor & Francis Group, London, ISBN 978-1-03-224160-9

Disruptive creativity as represented by Jane Austen and Seth Grahame-Smith's *Pride and Prejudice and Zombies*

Ratna Asmarani
Faculty of Humanities, Universitas Diponegoro, Central Java, Indonesia

ABSTRACT: In the disruptive era of the twenty-first century, the emergence of disruptive technology is inevitable. This disruptive technology influences the literary world in the form of disruptive creativity. This paper aims to study the disruptive creativity adopted by Seth Grahame-Smith in his mash-up novel entitled *Pride and Prejudice and Zombies*, based on the canonical novel *Pride and Prejudice* by Jane Austen. The study focuses on the additional elements in the non-canonical novel; namely the horror and action in the form of zombies and martial arts. The concepts used to support the analysis concern this disruptive creativity. The method to collect data from the novel and from the supporting concepts is a close reading and the library research method. The qualitative method is used to analyze the data. Meanwhile, the contextual literary research is used to combine the analysis of intrinsic elements and extrinsic elements. The result shows that the disruptive creativity in the form of horror and action manifested in zombies and martial arts fights not only gives exciting violent action to the action-less canonical novel of Jane Austen but also gives a strong oriental touch to the British canonical novel in the hands of the American mash-up novel's originator, Seth Grahame-Smith.

Keywords: disruptive creativity, zombies, martial arts, mash-up novel

1 INTRODUCTION

As the literary world is not a vacuum, many events influence its development. The twenty-first century, also called the disruptive era, is characterized by the big change in the world of business and technology with the emergence of disruptive technology. Christensen describes the characteristics of the products of the disruptive technologies as follows: 'typically cheaper, simpler, smaller and, frequently, more convenient to use' [1]. The disruptive technology outsmarts the leading companies and gradually erodes its market because it offers things that are of interest for the low-purchasing-power class.

The same phenomenon appears in the literary world. The classical literary works that need seriousness and great interest to read often stay unread by the majority of common readers. According to Roh, the emergence of 'disruptive textuality' is driven by the 'impulse to emulate, improve upon, and recirculate' [2], which serves as a bridge between the exclusive classical works with the mass of common readers. Roh considers that the emergence of 'disruptive textuality' is a normal cycle in the development of literature to unsettle the exclusive center [2] in which it still mentions the original text but at the same time claims to make changes [2]. Thus, 'disruptive textuality' presents classical works in a new form for the consumption of a mass readership by 'appropriating canonical literature' [2]. In other words, 'literary disruption' is a creative process that takes time in its implementation.

One of the forms of 'disruptive creativity' is mash-up novels. A mash-up novel is 'a work of fiction that combines a pre-existing text, often a classic work of fiction, with a modern genre such as crime, fantasy or horror' [3]. *Pride and Prejudice and Zombies* is an excellent example of a mash-up novel. According to Diana Sheets, interviewed by Shaughnessy, the mixed title and

63

content interest both serious and pleasure-seeking readers with the deliberate bloody horror [4]. Thus, the mash-up novel as a form of disruptive creativity in the disruptive era tries to embrace two sides, the literary canon readers and the non-canon readers. LaPlaca states that mash-up is different from parody in that parody tends to combine sarcasm with humor, while mash-up tends to add new themes to the original work [5]. So, the main purpose of a mash-up novel is to reconstruct the original or canonical work by adding exciting elements.

The exciting action-packed addition to mash-up novels is often a combination of violence, horror, and inhuman characters such as vampires or zombies. *Pride and Prejudice and Zombies* (2009) by Seth Grahame-Smith, an American male writer (born 1976), while 'crediting Jane Austen as co-author' [3], combines the classic *Pride and Prejudice* (1813) by the British female author, Jane Austen (1775–1817), with the popularity of zombies in literature. Luckhurst defines zombies as the walking dead that are disgusting, fierce and contagious [6]. Referring to the presence of zombies, Browning et al. state that the existence of zombies in literary works indicates that humanity has decayed and needs rebirth [7]. Thus, the presence of zombies in literature has a hidden meaning, and is not just to evoke fear and horror in readers' minds. However, such a horrific atmosphere inflicted by a horde of zombies will attract lovers of horror and violence.

Even though belonging to the same group of inhuman characters, zombies have different characteristics from vampires. Hong, referring to the famous vampire story in the *Twilight* saga and the television series *The Walking Dead,* concludes that vampires are completely different from zombies in that vampires are classy and talented while zombies are lowly and repulsive [8]. This mash-up novel, although written by Seth Grahame-Smith, is based on an idea from Jason Rekulak [9]. When interviewed by Grossman, Seth Grahame-Smith states that the insignificant life of the characters in the original novel is like the life of the zombies ([10] in [11]).

Based on the account above, the purpose of this paper is to analyze the disruptive creativity in *Pride and Prejudice and Zombies* (*P&P&Z*). The focus of analysis is digging out the elements of disruptive creativity applied in the mash-up novel. This can be done through an implicit comparative perspective, bearing in mind the canonical novel *Pride and Prejudice* (*P&P*). Using this comparative perspective, the various elements of Seth Grahame-Smith's disruptive creativity are identified and discussed to establish their functions in making the mash-up novel interestingly different while still retaining similarities with the original novel. The result of this study helps encourage similar studies comparing a classical novel with its new, creative form, such as a canonical novel with its mash-up version, as is done in this paper.

2 RESEARCH METHOD

Close reading is used to collect data from the mash-up novel, and the supporting data to analyze the mash-up novel is collected through the library research method. For analyzing the data, a qualitative method is used. The literary analysis applied is a contextual one, which combines the analysis of the intrinsic elements and the extrinsic elements. The intrinsic elements focus on character, conflict and setting. These elements are useful to support the analysis of the extrinsic elements that focus on the elements of disruptive creativity; namely, the addition of horror and action in the forms of zombies and martial arts.

3 FINDINGS AND DISCUSSION

The influence of disruptive creativity is inevitable in literary works, in this case in the form of the mash-up novel *P&P&Z* [12], a non-canonical appropriation of the canonical novel entitled *P&P* [13]. The romantic novel of manners of the nineteenth century is developed into a romantic novel of violence and horror for the twenty-first century. The appropriation by introducing Eastern martial arts in the form of ninja and kung-fu skills mastered by the important male and female characters is essential to fight against the pullulating zombies threatening the human population of England. The mash-up novel *P&P&Z*'s success in combining Western tradition with Eastern martial arts enables it to attract the attention of common and/or young readers who feel that they do not have enough patience, time and literary ability to appreciate dense, high-brow, classical novels such as *P&P*.

Before discussing the disruptive creativity in the form of successful appropriation of the canonical novel, it is useful to appreciate the similarities still maintained in the non-canonical novel. Both *P&P&Z* and *P&P* have the same plot structure. The plot is about the Bennet family, which has five daughters whose mother's sole purpose in life is to marry them off to established gentlemen. The arrival of two single and wealthy gentlemen from London, Mr Bingley and Mr Darcy, into their neighborhood in Hertfordshire initiates the romance and conflicts triggered by pride and prejudice. Another maintained similarity is the characters. The family, relatives and neighbors of the Bennets, the families and relatives of the Bingleys and the Darcys, and the militia and officers in Meryton are all found in both novels. The setting of time, setting of place and the social setting are also the same in both novels.

Based on the maintained similarities, one of the forms of disruptive creativity that is applied to the canonical novel is accomplished by changing the famous opening of *P&P*: "It is a truth universally acknowledged, that a single man in possession of a good fortune must be in want of a wife" [13] turns into "It is a truth universally acknowledged that a zombie in possession of brains must be in want of more brains" [12] in *P&P&Z*. By changing this famous opening, the course of the story changes too, from implying domestic and peaceful married life to a horror story full of zombies. Another successful disruption involves the handling of the different views of life between Mr and Mrs Bennet. In *P&P*, their different views are implied by that of Mrs Bennet: 'The business of her life was to get her daughters married; its solace was visiting and news' [13]. However, in *P&P&Z*, their views are directly contrasted: "The business of Mr Bennett's life was to keep his daughters alive. The business of Mrs Bennett's was to get them married" [12]. By explicitly putting forward Mr Bennet's opinion, the mash-up novel immediately informs readers of the danger and conflict haunting the Bennet family in particular, and the population of England in general.

Disruptive creativity can also be seen in the leisure game played by the Bennet girls in the house of their aunt, Mrs Phillips. In *P&P*, it is called 'a nice comfortable noisy game of lottery tickets' [13], while in *P&P&Z* it is called 'a nice comfortable noisy game of Crypt and Coffin' [12]. Thus, it adds flavor to the haunting horror. Another form of appropriation in the disruptive creativity is the addition of the song lyrics:

When once the earth was still and dead were silent,
And London-town was for but living men,
Came the plague upon us swift and violent,
And so our dearest England we defend [12].

The lyrics of the song directly presented in *P&P&Z* emphasize the dangerous situation faced by England and its citizens. Thus, the song implies the impending actions involving violence, blood and zombies.

The combination of zombies, horror and Eastern martial arts creatively disrupts the classic novel *P&P*. The zombies are described in details as follows:

Unmentionables poured in; their movements clumsy yet swift; ... Their flesh was in varying degrees of putrefaction; the freshly stricken were slightly green and pliant, whereas the longer dead were grey and brittle—their eyes and tongues long since turned to dust and their lips pulled back into everlasting skeletal smiles [12].

The description of the dead people roaming the land of England is so vividly horrible that it arouses the sense of exciting horror loved by horror lovers. There are many other detailed descriptions of zombies in various types of age and gender throughout the story. These horrible creatures also appear everywhere and attack in various places, such as fields, roads, an orphanage, houses, and churches. This approach is successful in maintaining an atmosphere of teeming horror.

Another form of disruptive creativity applied in *P&P&Z* is the blending of Eastern martial arts within the tedious and domestic nature of Victorian manners in the canonical *P&P*. This is done in various ways. Specific words referring to Eastern martial arts can be found in *P&P&Z*, such as dojo, Shaolin Temple, Katana sword, master Liu, Kyoto masters, wet bamboo lashes, ninja, and kung fu. The constructed atmosphere of Eastern martial arts is further strengthened by the many fights against the zombies by the Bennet girls and Mr Darcy as, for example, when the zombies suddenly attack Netherfield Park while the mansion is full of guests having a party:

> As guests fled in every direction, Mr Bennett's voice cut through the commotion. "Girls! Pentagram of Death!" Elizabeth immediately joined her four sisters, Jane, Mary, Catherine and Lydia, in the center of the dance floor. Each girl produced a dagger from her ankle and stood at the tip of an imaginary five-pointed star [12].

The fighting skills and bravery of the Bennet sisters change the modest and domestic nature of the girls in *P&P* and thus brings the story alive with action and physical conflict.

Elizabeth (Lizzy) has an outstanding nature in *P&P*, whereas in *P&P&Z* she is described as having exceptional martial arts skills compared to her other siblings. She confidently claims to be "a student of Shaolin! Master of the seven-starred fist!" [12]. Her demonstration shows how capable she is of doing difficult physical exercise:

> She ... placed her hands upon the floor and lifted her feet heavenward—her dress kept in place by the modesty string. Holding herself thus, she then lifted one of her palms off the floor, so that all of her weight rested on but one hand ... she lifted her palm so that only one fingertip remained connected to the floor [12].

By adding martial arts skills to Lizzy's strong character, Lizzy retains her position as the leading female figure, which makes *P&P&Z* more exciting for common and/or young readers that love an action story.

To make Eastern martial arts as one of the new main themes in the disruptive creativity in *P&P&Z* more exciting, two Eastern martial arts are not only presented, but also contested.

This is creatively done through the haughty, upper-class figure of Lady Catherine, who is Mr Darcy's aunt, and Lizzy Bennet, who comes from a middle-class family living in the country. The rich Lady Catherine is very proud of studying ninja skills in Japan and looks down on Lizzy's kung-fu ability, obtained from studying in China. She arrogantly invites Lizzy to practice with one of her ninjas in her grand dojo, feeling confident that her ninja can easily embarrass Lizzy. Knowing the real motive of Lady Catherine, the brave Lizzy deliberately blindfolds herself while fighting the ninja:

> She delivered a vicious blow, penetrating his rib cage, and withdrew her hand—with the ninja's still-beating heart in it ...
> "Curious," said Elizabeth, still chewing. "I have tasted many a heart, but I dare say, I find the Japanese ones a bit tender" [12].

This kind of scene must be exciting for those readers who like bloody horror stories.

To create more excitement, the heated argument between Lady Catherine and Lizzy Bennet when Lady Catherine unexpectedly comes to the Bennets' house to forbid Lizzy from marrying Mr Darcy in *P&P* [13] is changed into a deadly duel full of martial arts skills between two female warriors in *P&P&Z*:

> After several minutes of flying about, attacking one another with force ... Lady Catherine's sword was dispatched with a well-aimed butterfly kick .... Elizabeth backed Lady Catherine against a wall, and held the tip of her sword to her wrinkled throat [12].

The tense duel surely excites the common and/or young readers that love a fully packed fight using sharp weapons.

Another creative disruption in *P&P&Z* concerns the grand Pemberley House owned by Mr Darcy. To maintain the oriental atmosphere, in *P&P&Z* the Pemberley estate is decorated with Eastern ornaments in strategic places:

Pemberley House ... a large, handsome stone building, made to resemble the grandest palaces of Kyoto ... the natural beauty of the Orient had been so little counteracted by English taste ... the stone dragons on either side of the bridge ... the solid jade door; ... The housekeeper came; a respectable-looking English woman, dressed in a kimono and shuffling about on bound feet [12].

The creative combination of East and West in Pemberley House successfully maintains the Eastern atmosphere of *P&P&Z* without ruining the beauty and grandeur of Pemberley House in the original novel.

The horrific atmosphere triggered by the unending appearance of zombies is carefully maintained in *P&P&Z* by introducing a new group of people called 'Reclaimers', who are basically zombie hunters who get money by trapping zombies and bringing them in cages to the 'Paymaster's shack' to be burned [12]. The emergence of the Reclaimers indicates that the existence of the zombies is uncontrollable. It also indicates the horror that will never stop haunting the life of the people of England, which causes horror lovers to enjoy reading *P&P&Z*.

Other changes also happen in *P&P&Z*, especially to the unpleasant characters. The first one is Charlotte Lucas, Lizzy's friend and neighbor who accepts the marriage proposal of Mr Collins, the cousin of the Bennet girls, after his marriage proposals to several Bennet girls are refused. Charlotte Lucas silently accepts the marriage proposal knowing that Mr Collins will inherit the property of the Bennets, because the Bennets do not have a son. In *P&P&Z*, Charlotte is described as being infected by the zombie plague due to being bitten by a zombie. Although she tries to hide this condition and only tells Lizzy [12], her condition worsens rapidly after the marriage. Mr Collins himself is an unpleasant character in *P&P*, thanks to his being a yes-man to Lady Catherine and his unembarrassed attitude to getting a wife. In *P&P&Z*, Mr Collins, a priest, commits suicide by hanging himself after performing his duty as a husband by beheading and burning his infected wife [12].

Another horrible change happens to Mr Wickham, the most controversial character. He is described as a handsome person who tries to get a girl with a fortune to be his wife. He also spreads a rumor portraying Mr Darcy as a cruel person. In *P&P*, after creating a scandal by running away with Lydia, Lizzy's youngest sister, he finally marries her after Mr Darcy finds their hiding place and pays off all his debts [13, p. 519]. In *P&P&Z*, his fate is worse. Mr Darcy, who is fed up with Mr Wickham's persistently bad attitudes and actions, finally loses his patience and, after settling Mr Wickham's big debts and securing his future, with Mr Wickham's consent, he imposes a severe physical punishment on Mr Wickham by paralyzing him forever [12].

4   CONCLUSION AND SUGGESTIONS

The creative disruption of blending Eastern martial arts and zombies gives the mash-up novel a new theme of horror, full of bloody fighting action and thus shifting the theme of romantic love haunted by pride and prejudice in a Victorian society that is full of modesty and domestic life in the original novel. The repeated appearances of zombies in various horrible states, the bloody fights against the crazed zombies and the appalling conditions of their victims are all used to satisfy the craving of lovers of bloody horror. However, the success of the mash-up novel in popularity and in financial terms may arouse questions concerning the original novel: is the original novel going to be remembered or forgotten? The original novel might be remembered in relation to its mash-up novel only. This means that the original novel is forgotten as an authentic work because common readers may feel it is enough to read only its mash-up version. Another possibility is that the original novel is remembered and read because of its mash-up version. This means that the original classic novel is revived by its mash-up version. It needs further research to understand the role of the mash-up novel in relation to its original novel and whether the mash-up version has a good or bad impact on its original novel.

REFERENCES

[1] Christensen, C.M. (1997). *Dilemma. When new technologies cause great firms to fail.* Boston, MA: Harvard Business School Press.

[2] Roh, D.S. (2015). *Illegal literature: Toward a disruptive creativity.* Minneapolis, MN: University of Minnesota Press.

[3] Balan, A. (2012, September 16). Monster mash(ups). *Ghost Cities.* Retrieved from https://anilbalan.com /tag/mashup-novels/

[4] Shaughnessy, M.F. (2013, April 28). An interview with Diana Sheets: Is the "mash-up" novel a monstrosity? *Education News.* Retrieved from http://www.educationviews.org/an-interview-with-diana-sheets-is-the-mash-up-novel-a-monstrosity/

[5] LaPlaca, C. (2012, July 10). The mash-up novel: A modern twist on old classics. *The Phi Beta Kappa Society.* Retrieved from http://www.keyreporter.org/PbkNews/PbkNews/Details/136.html

[6] Luckhurst, R. (2015). *Zombies: A cultural history.* London, UK: Reaction Books.

[7] Browning, J.E., Castillo, D., Schmid, D. & Reilly, D.A. (2016). *Zombie talk: Culture, history, politics.* New York, NY: Palgrave Macmillan.

[8] Hong, E. (2017, October 29). The age of the vampire has given way to the age of the zombie. *CNN.* Retrieved from https://edition.cnn.com/2017/10/29/opinions/vampire-zombie-popularity-opinion-hong/index.html

[9] Merritt, S. (2009, December 6). Pride and Prejudice and Zombies by Jane Austen and Seth Grahame-Smith. *The Observer.* Retrieved from https://www.theguardian.com/books/2009/dec/06/pride-prejudice-zombies-grahame-smith

[10] Grossman, L. (2009). Grahame-Smith, Seth. "Pride and Prejudice, Now with Zombies!" *Time.* Retrieved from Time.com.Web.

[11] Riter, A.V. (2017). *The evolution of mashup literature: Identifying the genre through Jane Austen's novels* (Master's thesis, De Montfort University, Leicester, UK). Retrieved from https://www.dora.dmu.ac.uk /bitstream/handle/2086/14209/Riter%20-%20MPhil%20Edited.pdf

[12] Austen, J. & Grahame-Smith, S. (2009). *Pride and Prejudice and Zombies.* Philadelphia, PA: Quirk Production.

[13] Austen, J. (2005). *Pride and Prejudice.* San Diego, CA: Icon Classics.

English Linguistics, Literature, and Language Teaching in a Changing Era – Madya et al. (eds)
© 2020 Taylor & Francis Group, London, ISBN 978-1-03-224160-9

Cultural term translation in the novel *Der Prozess* by FranzKafka: Analysis of translation methods and ideology

Sulfah Risna & Pratomo Widodo
Graduate School, Yogyakarta State University, Yogyakarta, Indonesia

ABSTRACT: This study aimsto describe the cultural terms found in the novel *Der Prozess* and its translation into *Bahasa* by reviewing the translation methods and translation ideology used. The study used a descriptive qualitative method. The data were a lingual unit with the cultural word. The data sources were taken from an authentic text of *Der Prozess* and its Indonesian translation. The results of the study were as follows. First, five types of cultural term categories were found: ecology, material (artifacts), social and political organization, social culture, and sign language and habits. The most common cultural terms were in the material category, while the ecological category had the least number of cultural terms. The study also identified seven translation methods: (a) Communicative (b) Free, (c) Literal, (d) Semantic, (e) Faithful, (f) Word-for-word, and (g) Adaptation. The method represents two different types of translation ideologies: foreignization, which is oriented to the culture of the source language, and domestication, which is oriented to the culture of the target language. Thestudy observed that translators are generally inclined to use the domestication ideology.

Keywords: cultural terms, translation methods, translation ideology

1 INTRODUCTION

Translation is an important activity in the process of understanding the culture of other nations. Translation activity concerns not only translators but also experts. Catford [1] argues that translation is an activity and that it is increasingly important. It's not only translators who are interested in translation activity, but also linguists, philosophers, writers, psycholinguists, language teachers, and even mathematicians. In the beginning, translation was perceived only on the paradigm of equivalence to assess whether a translation is "right or wrong". The terms of right and wrong are not just in the linguistic domain; in fact, they are more determined by factors outside the discipline of translation, such as the cultural factors by Schneider [2]. Schneider divides the definition of translation into two statements, but these statements actually confirm that translation must be seen as a process of reproducing equivalent terms between two languages, as well as the communication bridge between two cultures. Translation is considered as not only relating to the language aspect – as a cross-linguistic activity–but also as relating to culture as a form of cross-cultural communication because language is born from a particular cultural context.

There is a controversy over whether "language is part of a culture" or "culture is part of a language". "In fact, the translation might not separate from both aspects". Sutrisno [3] stated that language and culture are interrelated and influence one another. The cultural aspect needs to be considered in translation because language is part of a culture. Language is a cultural expression of the speaker, so it influences the way the speaker perceives the world. This statement becomes a dilemma for translators due to the translator's role as a mediator in intercultural communication, especially when translating the cultural terms of a literary work, such as a novel.

Newmark [4] classifies the cultural elements into five categories. These are: a) Ecology. The ecological culture includes geographical features, for example, flora, fauna, valleys, and hills. Each country has different terms for naming a geographic area. For example, the term "avocado" in English means *alpukat* in Indonesian. In this case, the Indonesian language has borrowed the meaning of avocado because there is no original concept of avocado fruit in Indonesia. b) Culture of material (artifacts).This includes food, clothing, houses, and vehicles. In the food category, it includes menus, food guides, and brochures containing foreign food terms, such as *kimchi* (Korean), *sushi* (Japanese), and *Soto* (Indonesian). c) Social culture. This includes work, games, entertainment, terms of kinship, sports, and art. The terms of social culture between two different cultures often become a problem in translation, for example, the word "sensee" in Japanese can mean a teacher, doctor or a person who has expertise in a particular field. d) Organizations, customs, activities, procedures, concepts, organization names, government positions, and the procedures of an organization. For example, the term *RT/RW* is only used in Indonesian culture. Another example is that the names of positions such as *treasury* are sometimes known as the finance ministry in other countries. e) Sign language and habits. In Indonesia and several other countries, the thumbs-up means agreement or a sign of approval. But Greece has a different meaning of this gesture: in this country, thumbs-up is considered impolite because the gesture is associated with an insult.

Basically, a mediator needs to be able to solve problems. There can be some practical problems when a translator does not understand the meaning of words, phrases, sentences, or paragraphs, and therefore does not understand the full message. Even when translators have understood the source language text, they may still have problems finding equivalent terms in the target language. In order to solve these problems, a translator can use an ideology. An ideology is the values, norms, and beliefs that became a motive for a translator in deciding the translation of a source text. Venuti (in Hoed, 2006 [5]) states that ideology has two opposite poles: a pole oriented to the source language and a pole oriented to the target language. Translators will always have to choose between these two positions. Venuti refers to the process of choosing the value of a foreign culture or making greater use of the source language as 'foreignization', and to the process of choosing to use the target value or make greater use of the target language culture as 'domestication'.

The translator ideology can be identified through the translation methods used by the translator when translating a specific work. Each method will represent a different ideology. There are several translation methods, and their use depends on the purpose of the translation. Translators often use one of the translation methods according to the type of text. Newmark [4] (pp. 45–47) proposed eight types of translation method, as illustrated in the V-diagram of Figure 1, where emphasis may be placed either on the Source Language (SL) or the Target Language (TL).

The eight types of translation method can be described as follows. First, word-for-word translation. This is considered to be the closest translation to the source language. It keeps the word order from the source language text and the translation of words is according to the meaning without conveying the context. Second, literal translation. According to Nababan [7], literal translation is in between word-for-word translation and free translation. It is usually applied when the structure of the source language is different from the target language

SL Emphasis	**TL Emphasis**
Word-for-word	Translation Adaptation
Literal Translation	Free Translation
Faithful Translation	Idiomatic Translation
Semantic Translation	Communicative Translation

Figure 1.   Types of translation method [4] (p. 45).

structure. Third, faithful translation. According to Machali [8], faithful translation tries to produce a contextual meaning of the source language text and is limited by its grammatical structure. Fourth, semantic translation. Semantic translation emphasizes looking for equivalence on the word level by keeping as close as possible to the culture of the source language. This method tries to convey the contextual meaning of the source language which is closest to the syntactic and semantic structure of the target language. Fifth, translation adaptation. According to Newmark [4], this is the freest of the translation types. It is usually used in the translation of drama and poems. Sixth, free translation. This method does not try to look for the equivalence of words or sentences, but it focuses on transferring messages at the level of paragraphs or discourses. Seventh, idiomatic translation. This translation method uses the impression of familiarity and idiomatic expressions that are not found in the source language text. Eighth, communicative translation. Communicative translation emphasizes the delivery of the message. It aims to produce translations in an acceptable and reasonable form in the target language. The different translation methods are described in a "V-diagram" which divides the translation methods into two groups: the translation method oriented to Bsu (the source text), also known as foreignization ideology, and the translation method oriented to Bsa (the target text), also known as domestication ideology. Each ideology consists of four translation methods which start from the closest relationship with Bsu to the furthest relationship with Bsu.

One kind of intercultural communication involving translation ideology is literary works, such as a translated novel. Typically, a novel has a distinctive interesting aspect, plus both intrinsic and cultural elements which are conveyed in the main text of the story. Translating novels is an attempt to bridge two different cultures and two different languages. An example of translating cultural terms in a novel is the word "Sessel" in the novel *Der Prozess*. In the German–Indonesian, Indonesian–German dictionary, Datje Rahajoekoesoemah (2009, p. 402) [10], the word "Sessel" means "Chair or Kursi" but in the translated Indonesian version, the translator has translated the word "Sessel" into "*kursimalas*", so thatthe cultural message is conveyed.

Based on this phenomenon, an analysis of the translation ideology of cultural terms in a novel needs to be conducted. The literary work for this particular study was a novel by one of the most influential German writers in the 20th century, *Der Prozess*by Franz Kafka and the novel translated by SigitSusanto. The study aimed to describe the method and ideology applied by the translator in translating the cultural terms of the novel *Der Prozess*into Indonesian.

2 RESEARCH METHOD

This research was a descriptive qualitative research which aimed to describe the research findings oriented to translation products. The units of analysis were lingual units such as words, phrases or sentences which had cultural terms. The objects of analysis were a German novel called *Der Prozess* and its translation into Indonesian for a book called "Process". The research steps are described in the following subsections.

2.1 *Observation*

Reading and analyzing the object, which is the texts of *Der Prozess* and the translated Indonesian version, was the first step. The lingual unit with cultural terms from both the source and target texts was then noted.

2.2 *Note-taking technique*

Identity method is a method of data analysis whereby the determiner tools are outside, detached, and do not become part of the language concerned or researched [9]. This particular study used translational and referential identity methods. The referential identity method was used to find out the cultural terms in the text of *Der Prozess* and their translation. Meanwhile, the translational identity method was used to find out the method and ideology of the translation. The technique was the technique of critical element segment which is a data analysis technique that sorts the linguistic units and analyzes them using determiner tools [9]. For this method, the sort segment was the referential sorting element where the determiner tools are another language.

2.3 *Data display of the results of data analysis*

The last step was the data display of the results of the data analysis. The data display or findings used two methods: formal and informal. Both methods are used to present the rules within the language. The informal method focuses on producing a verbal statement that is short, precise and clear, while the formal method focuses on symbols. .

3 DISCUSSION

3.1 *Findings*

3.1.1 *Cultural terms*
This study found 72 data items with cultural content. The data was obtained after analyzing the novel *Der Prozess* and its translation into Indonesian. The term culture is grouped into five cultural categories. From the results of the analysis, the most commonly found category of cultural terms is the material culture category, while the least commonly found is ecological culture. The number of terms can be seen in Table 1.

3.1.2 *Translation methods*
Based on the results of the analysis that found cultural terms, seven of the eight methods offered by Newmark [4] are used by the translators. More details are illustrated in Table 2.

Table 1. Cultural terms.

No.	Cultural term	Total	Percentage
1	Ecology	3	4.17
2	Culture of material	24	33.33
3	Social culture	17	23.62
4	Organizations, customs, activities, procedures, concepts	14	19.44
5	Sign language and habits	14	19.44
Total		72	100

Table 2. Translation methods.

No.	Method	Total	Percentage
1	Communicative	21	29.17
2	Free translation	19	26.39
3	Literal tranlation	14	19.44
4	Semantic translation	7	9.72
5	Faithful translation	6	8.33
6	Word-for-word	3	4.17
7	Adaptation	2	2.78
Total		72	100

Table 3. Translation ideology.

No.	Ideology	Total	Percentage
1	Foreignization	30	25.3
2	Domestication	42	74.7
Total		72	100

3.1.3 *Translation ideology*

Based on the findings of the translation method, the novel *Der Prozess* was translated into Indonesian predominantly using domestic ideology. The findings for the translation ideology used in the novel *Der Prozess* and its translation are shown in Table 3.

3.2 *Discussion*

3.2.1 *Cultural terms*

Based on the analysis of *Der Prozess*and its translation, 72 cultural terms were found, which covered the categories of ecology, material culture, social culture, social organizations, political organizations, sign language, and habits. The most common cultural term category was the material category, which had 24 data items;social culture had 17;organizations, customs, activities, procedures, and concepts had 14, while data, sign language and habits also had 14. The ecological category had the fewest terms. The following are examples of cultural terms of sign language and habit categories found in the *Der Prozess* novel and its translation:

> SL: **um Himmels willen**, *Josef*
> TL: **Demi Tuhan**, Josef

The term of *um Himmelswillen* refers to a person's expression when the interlocutor does not trust what is being stated. In Indonesian culture, people usually stated "Sumpah Demi Allah". The expression implies that the statement is true or a fact. This expression has become a habit for the target reader. Not only were the sign and habit language categories found, but also a number of ecological categories, such as:

> SL: *In diesem **Frühjahr** pflegte K. die Abende in der Weise zu verbringen...*
> TL: **Musim semi** itu K menghabiskan waktu malamnya dengan cara seperti berikut...

*Frühjahr*is one of four seasons in the subtropical region. Spring occurs at the transition from winter to summer, which takes place from March to May. It is very different from the season of the target reader area (Indonesia), which only knows two seasons: dry and rainy. Spring is a natural phenomenon which is part of the geographical state of a region.

3.2.2 *Translation methods*

Seven translation methods were found: (a) Communicative, (b) Free, (c) Literal, (d) Semantic, (e) Faithful, (f) Word-for-word, and (g) Adaptation. Based on frequency, the communicative method was the most common with 21 data items (29.17%). The free translation method had 19 (26.39%), the literal translation method14 (19.44%), the semantic translation method seven (9.72%), and the faithful translation method six(8.33%). The word-for-word translation method generated three data items (4.17%). Finally, the adaptation method produced two data items (2.78%). The following is one of the communicative translation methods found in the text.

SL:	*Sie haben sehr recht, denn es ist ja nur ein Verfahren, wenn ich es als solches anerkenne* (*Anda sangat benar, Karena itu hanya prosedur jika saya mengenalinya*)
TL:	Anda benar, sebab ini disebut persidangan hanya jika saya mengakuinya seperti itu

If the translator uses the word-for-word translation to translate the text in the above example, the translation will be difficult for the target reader to understand. The translator can try to transfer the meaning of the sentence communicatively so that the message can be conveyed naturally and acceptably in the target language. A literal translation method is also found in the analysis, as in the following example:

Example 1.

SL:	*Anna **soll** mir das Frühstück **bringen**.* (Anna harusnya saya sarapan membawa)
TL:	Anna **seharusnya mengantarkan** sarapan buat saya.

Example 2.

SL:	*Sagte K., sprang aus dem Bett und **zog** rasch seine Hosen **an***
TL:	Kata K, sembari melompat dari tempat tidur dan segera mengenakan celana panjangnya

The first example in Bsu is a *modal verben* sentence, where the verb is *bringen* at the end of the sentence. This case changes the language structure in the translation. Meanwhile, the second example is the sentence of *trennbare verben*. *Trennbare verben* is a verb that has two word parts, such as in the second example; there is a word *anziehen*. When conjugated, the verb prefix must be separated and placed at the end of the sentence into *Zog* and *an*.

3.2.3 *Translation ideology*

Based on 72 data on cultural terms, there were 30 data translated using methods that represented foreignization ideology and 42 data translated using methods that represented domestication ideology. These ideologies have an orientation that is the other's opposite, and shows a tendency for a translator to favor one of the two ideologies. Based on the percentage and frequency of the translation method used, we can conclude that domestication ideology was the predominant translation method used for the cultural terms of the novel *Der Prozess* and its translation into Indonesian, with a percentage of 58.34%. This clearly showed that the translator tried to transfer the culture of the source text into the culture of the target text by maintaining the culture of the target language. Examples of this translation ideology are:

SL:	*Sie haben sehr recht, denn es ist ja nur ein **Verfahren**, wenn ich es als solches anerkenne.*
TL:	Anda benar, sebab ini disebut **persidangan** hanya jika saya mengakuinya seperti itu

The text was translated using communicative translation methods so that the translation could be easily understand by the target reader. There will be a different result when the text is translated by a method oriented to the source language; for example, the word-for-word translation method will produce '*anda memiliki sangat benar, karena itu, jika saya mengenalinya seperti itu*'. The translation is free translation. Therefore, the readers must read the text repeatedly in order to understand the meaning.

4 CONCLUSIONS AND SUGGESTIONS

Based on our analysis of the method and translation ideology in the cultural term translation of *Der Prozess* into Indonesian, we can conclude the following points. First, translators tend to use translation methods oriented to the target language in translating lingual units with cultural meanings. Second, translators tend to adhere to the domestication ideology, which orients to the target language. The researcher hopes that the translator is able to choose the appropriate method in translating cultural terms and that they prioritize the information so that the readers understand the message, because not all readers have the same background, culture, and knowledge. Translators should have a good understanding of both cultures when acting as mediators in the translation process involving two different cultures.

REFERENCES

[1] Catford, J.C. (1978). *A linguistic theory of translation.* Oxford, UK: Oxford University Press.
[2] Schneider, H.W. (2007). *Allgemeine Übersetzungstheori: Verstehen und Wieder-geben (General translation theory: understanding and reproducing).* Bonn, Germany: Romanistischer Verlag.
[3] Sutrisno, M. (Ed.). (2005). *Teori-Teori Kebudayaan (Theories of culture).*Yogyakarta, Indonesia: Penerbit Kanisius.
[4] Newmark, P. (1988). *A textbook of translation.* London, UK: Prentice Hall.
[5] Hoed, B.H. (2006). *Penerjemahan dan Kebudayaan (Translation and culture).* Jakarta, Indonesia: Pustaka Jaya.
[6] Molina, L. & Albir, A.H. (2002). Translation techniques revisited: A dynamic and functionalist approach. *Meta: Journal des Traducteurs, XLVII*(4), 498–512.
[7] Nababan, M.R. (2003). *Teori Menerjemah Bahasa Inggris (Translating theory of English).* Yogyakarta, Indonesia: PustakaPelajar.
[8] Machali, R. (2000). *Pedoman Bagi Penerjemah (Guidelines for Translator).* Jakarta, Indonesia: GramediaWidiasarana Indonesia.
[9] Sudaryanto. (1993). *Metode dan Teknik Analisis Bahasa (Method and Language analysis Techniques).* Yogyakarta, Indonesia: Duta Wacana.
[10] Mahsun. (2012). *Metode penelitian bahasa: Tahapan Strategi, Metode, dan Tekniknya (Language research method; Steps of strategy, method and technique).* Jakarta, Indonesia: Rajawali Press.

English Linguistics, Literature, and Language Teaching in a Changing Era – Madya et al. (eds)
© 2020 Taylor & Francis Group, London, ISBN 978-1-03-224160-9

Digital literacy practices of English language learners: Indonesian context

W.H. Utami, D. Suherdi & P. Purnawarman
English Education, Indonesia University of Education, Bandung, Indonesia

ABSTRACT: The number of Indonesian Internet users around 13–18 years old in 2017 was 16.68% of an Internet-using population of 143.26 million people, and keeps increasing significantly. This age range represents the English language learners who spend most of their time daily connected to the Internet using digital devices. Besides using these devices for entertainment purposes, they also use them to learn English independently beyond the classroom. Accordingly, this study aims to identify types of digital practices employed by the learners in their attempts to learn English in the out-of-school setting in Indonesia. This study surveyed 25 high school students in Bandung by using closed and open-ended questionnaires. The quantitative and qualitative data were gathered and grouped into three categories of digital literacy practices as the findings. First, those digital natives who are learning English by locating and consuming digital content in their engagement online. Second, those who are also creating digital content as an enhancement of their language experience. Last, those communicating the digital content by interacting with others online. It can be inferred that there are three different types of digital practices that the learners are concerned with during their independent process of learning English. Further study of learners' perceptions and how each digital practice is contributing to the English language learning experience is recommended.

Keywords: beyond the classroom, digital literacy practices, English language learning

1 INTRODUCTION

The invention of the Internet has changed humanity and civilization, including the field of education. By connecting to the Internet, people can also access any information instantly and interact with anyone from their digital media, such as laptops, tablets and smartphones. Surveys conducted by the Indonesia Internet Service Provider Association (APJII) showed a significantly increased number of Internet users in Indonesia over the last ten years, from 20 million people in 2007 to 143.26 million people in 2017. More specifically, the educational activities they pursue are reading articles, watching video tutorials, sharing educational articles/videos, online courses and applying for schools/colleges. Furthermore, 16.68% of the Internet users in 2017 are around 13–18 years old, which represents the age of learners at high-school level. Thus, this phenomenon affects the educational field in terms of one's approach to learning in one way or another. Particularly for English language learning, learners can now get access to authentic language sources easily. In 2010, an estimated 27.3% of the global total Internet usage was in English, which indicates that besides being a global language, English is the most used language on the Internet [18]. It means that learners can get exposure digitally through their interaction with English sources and English speakers on the Internet. Moreover, they can learn both authentic and varied forms of English, as noted by "the English language learners now have the opportunity of experiencing different language registers and learning about formal and informal rules and conventions for participation [12]."

76

Particularly in Indonesia, where English is learned as a foreign language, most of the academic studies concerning Information and Communication Technology (ICT) or digital literacy practices related to English language learning are still in the formal education context or within the classroom only [7,14,17]. However, Lie [15] conducted a study of the combination of formal and informal learning and the use of a social media tool, Edmodo, to teach a course of pedagogy to a class of digital natives. The result shows that as an out-of-class communication forum to submit assignments, discuss relevant issues, exchange information and be used for housekeeping purposes, Edmodo can be useful in reaching out to the digital native students' learning process. It indicates that learning that is facilitated by digital media outside the classroom also has contributions to make to the learners' language experience. Another study of English language learning beyond the classroom was conducted by Setiasih [24] concerning the role of out-of-school activities that promote English literacy for young learners in Indonesia. One of its findings shows that technological tools used by the learners at home for learning English play an important role in promoting and developing their English literacy.

Thus, reflecting upon the fact that technology integration and utilization in Indonesia's English language classroom is still inadequate whereas Internet use is increasing, especially at the age of high school learners, the chance to learn English and get exposure to digital literacy practices outside the classroom is bigger. Moreover, it has been shown that exploration of language learning beyond the classroom is as important as formal education but is still limited, especially in the Indonesian context. Therefore, this study aims to investigate the digital practices that English language learners in Indonesia engage in outside the classroom that facilitate their learning experience of English by asking one research question: "What distinct types of digital literacy practices do learners engage in to facilitate their English language experience beyond the classroom?"

2 LITERATURE REVIEW

Scholars in this digital age, especially those who engage in the educational field and language learning, have studied the phenomena in the digital world: the people, and their practices happening online. Besides focusing on effective hardware, software and approaches that are useful for the learning experience, the people who spend time online are also being categorized into several groups according to certain considerations.

The discussion of labeling people started as early as the beginning of the twenty-first century, when the utilization of computers was becoming more significant. Prensky [23] came up with such terms as 'digital natives' and 'digital immigrants', where the distinction between those two labels is based on age, technical skills and learning preferences that differ between twenty-first-century learners and teachers. According to Prensky [23], digital natives are those who are fluent or 'native speakers' of the digital language of the Internet, computers and video games. They are the young adults or learners nowadays who were born and grew up with technology surrounding them. Meanwhile, those who were not born into the digital world, but who later adopted and become mesmerized by many or most aspects of the new technology, are called 'digital immigrants' and are the teachers of today.

There are several characteristics of digital natives and digital immigrants categorized by Prensky [23]. Digital natives are used to receiving information faster and prefer it in the form of graphics rather than text. They also like to multitask and parallel process. They function best when networked. They also prefer games to 'serious' work, which requires a fun way of learning. They are accustomed to the instantaneity of hypertext, phones in their pockets, a library on their laptops, online and downloaded music, instant messaging and beamed messages. On the other hand, the main characteristic of digital immigrants is that of turning to the Internet for information as the second option, unlike the digital natives. They do not believe that learning can be done while watching or listening to music.

Thus, misunderstanding and miscommunication between digital natives and digital immigrants is the single biggest problem facing education today [23]. The digital immigrants' ways of teaching are often different from the daily lives of digital natives, who are involved with digital devices for almost all activities in which their fingers are 'glued' to the gadgets [15]. As a consequence, the digital natives have little patience for the lectures of the digital immigrants who think that the 'old ways' of teaching can still be applied. The digital natives are no longer the generation who learn by step-by-step logic and 'tell-test' instruction. This miscommunication of the old ways of teaching is believed to be one of the reasons behind the autonomous or independent learning of the digital natives nowadays.

However, as the Internet has become the sole and first place for people to seek information at the moment, this kind of labeling turns out to be debatable. Bennet et al. [2] disagree with such terms that are rooted in age, technical skills and learning preferences, instead only to different types of people who engage online. They believe that socioeconomic and cultural factors also contribute to defining what kind of people are employing digital tools for learning. There are learners who do not have access or technology skills due to their economic and geographical background. It has been common knowledge that learners who live in rural and remote areas do not find it as easy as those who live in urban areas to get access to the newest technology and the Internet. Another difference in circumstance that also applies is between the learners whose parents can provide the digital tools such as laptops and smartphones and those who do not even have a television in their home. Furthermore, there are also learners who are simply uninterested in engaging actively online and using digital tools in most of their daily activities, even if they are capable of doing so. Moreover, if learners are actively engaged in the digital world, it does not always mean their engagement is for learning purposes. More specifically, concerning the age classification, White and Le Cornu [29] argue that no matter how old someone is, there are still those who acquire technological skills faster and those who struggle with them regardless of their age. Thus, it is not wise to generalize a generation into a quite narrow classification, as is proposed by Prensky [23].

Consequently, White and Le Cornu [29] propose an alternative to classifying people who engage online, based on their approaches or purposes in utilizing digital tools. They use the terms 'digital residents' and 'digital visitors', instead of using the metaphors 'tool' and 'place'. Digital visitors see anything digital like a website as a tool to attain their goal and task. Meanwhile, digital residents see it as a place in which they practically live. Digital visitors have certain reasons for not leaving any trace in digital space such as a digital identity, in the form of social media accounts or comments on blogs. They visit websites with a clear purpose to finish their task without interacting with others online. Just like using a tool, after they complete their task, the tool is returned to its place with no further additional activities that are unrelated to the task. Even though they are invisible online, it does not mean that they are handicapped in their use of technological skills. They just use the digital tools accordingly.

Meanwhile, digital residents are those who have a portion of their life that is in digital space. They have friends and colleagues with whom they share information and daily activities virtually. Just like a place, digital space is where they have a digital identity on social media accounts, belong and classify themselves into certain communities, and freely discuss ideas and opinions online.

Uniquely, these two terms are not two separate boxes but more like a flexible continuum where individuals can travel to either be more 'visitor' or more 'resident' in relation to a given aspect of digital space. As an example, a teacher might take a visitor approach while interacting with their students on the website where they are managing school-related tasks together. However, they might take a resident approach where sharing private life with their friends and colleagues. Thus, the continuum of visitor and resident can be illustrated as in Figure 1. Up to this point, it can be understood that the characteristics of digital natives quite resemble those of digital residents in one way or another. Yet, this research focuses on using the terms of digital residents and visitors instead of digital natives and immigrants, as they are more comprehensible.

Figure 1. The continuum of visitor and resident.

The concept of people who spend their time online can be extended further to what kind of engagement or activities they are involved in online. The skills they need to master their interactions are not limited to technical skills to operate the hardware and software alone, but also involve another set of required skills to engage accordingly in digital space, called 'digital literacy'. The notion of digital literacy was first proposed by Gilster [10] as "the ability to understand and use information in several formats from a wide range of sources that is presented via computers." As the Internet becomes the center of people's activities in information and communication technology, which is enriched by multiple media forms, the definition of digital literacy is widened as well. The word 'literacy' itself, which refers to one's ability to read and write in the first place, has added to a set of skills that includes the ability to manage the interpersonal and social process as well [12]. Thus, digital literacy can be defined as the ability to read and write in digital space with multimodal text, and at the same time establishing different kinds of relationship online accordingly.

The widely used term of digital literacy in research, especially in the educational field, results in a variety of its mapping of activities as well. Particularly for the engagement of language learners in the digital environment, Gee [9] identifies three digital literacy practices according to the digital literacy approach, namely accomplishing certain concrete actions using language, adapting in particular social groups, and creating an identity that belongs within a certain community. Furthermore, Spires and Bartlett [26] classify digital literacy practices into three categories: locating and consuming digital content, creating digital content, and communicating digital content, all of which involve simultaneously evaluating it critically. This is illustrated in Figure 2. Locating and consuming digital content includes the skills to search for information strategically and evaluate its accuracy and relevancy. This is followed by creating digital content, which involves the production of digital content in the form of multiple media. Moreover, understanding and manipulating the information and sharing digital content are what is meant by communicating digital content, which is facilitated by social networking sites.

Pegrum [21] and Dudeney et al. [6] also conceptualize digital literacy practices as a set of four overlapping skills corresponding to four main areas, namely language, information, connections and redesign. Language-based literacies include print literacy, texting literacy, hypertext literacy, visual and multimedia literacy, gaming literacy, technological literacy and code literacy. Information-based literacies cover search literacy, tagging literacy, information literacy, filtering literacy and attention literacy. Connection-based literacies are personal literacy, network literacy and participatory literacy. Redesign-based literacies are basically remix literacy.

As the most used language on the Internet nowadays and also the focus of this research, English is getting easier to access by learners. In 2010, an estimated 27.3% of global total Internet usage was in English [19]. Thus, learners can employ practices that benefit their English language learning experience. This implies that learning a language facilitated by digital media involves not only learning its grammar and lexis but also mastering its 'communicative function' and attaining 'pragmatic competence' in the language. Most learners are having interactions both with English language sources and also with speakers of the language. More specifically, according to Hafner et al. [13], being able to 'speak' a language in the digital age involves a whole host of new communicative

Figure 2. Digital literacies.

competencies including the ability to search for and critically evaluate large quantities of information in online databases, to construct meaningful reading paths through hypertext documents, to comment on the online writing of others in appropriate ways, to construct knowledge collaboratively through online platforms like blogs and wikis, to create multimodal texts that combine visual, aural and textual information, to remix online texts creatively, and to interact appropriately with others in a range of online spaces. Thus, learners are having many chances to learn in the digital environment.

The variety of digital practices that can facilitate the English language learning experience can be chosen consciously by the learners according to their preference and when to employ it. Furthermore, digital practices represent real language use where the language input is authentic and varied, unlike in the simulated and practice environment of the classroom [11,25]. As a consequence, learners can determine what kind of digital practices they want to engage in, to what extent they engage in digital practices for their language learning experience, and with whom they want to interact beyond the classroom.

Moreover, English language learning in this digital age then transforms learners into holders of several new roles. As Ware et al. [28] point out, "English learners are now seen as global communicators, sharers of local cultures, arbiters of misunderstandings and valued contributors to a growing global community." This happens as the result of many learners being likely to spend time socializing outside the classroom. Consequently, English learners use English more often to interact, communicate and participate in an online community, rather than using their first language. The exposure to English that they also get cannot be avoided during their online interaction. Thus, English language learning is now not only in the form of listening, reading, speaking and writing skills, but also requires students to have new 'digital' skills in the online environment. As noted by Godwin-Jones [18], language learners' participation online provides chances to experience a different language's registers, formal and informal rules, and conventions for participation. Therefore, in the process of learning English, at the same time learners also need to be acquiring skills to respond to anything that is going on digitally [27].

As it can take place anywhere, not only in the educational setting, language learning beyond the classroom actually contributes to the progress made by learners, especially in spoken and written communications. Palfreyman [20] shows that social networks can help learners to develop language skills beyond the classroom, in communities such as peer groups and the family. Specifically, in digital space, social networking sites offer many benefits toward greater and more successful informal learning, allowing learners to explore their own understanding within a supportive and non-threatening online environment [4]. Besides social networking sites, digital games also contribute to the language learning of learners, especially in English, because they are closely related to each other. As the meta-analysis conducted by Peterson [22] reveals, digital games offer different kinds of interaction that require the players to be using the language actively. Digital games provide real, meaningful and socially appropriate ways to accomplish a task in which language is the primary medium. In order to progress in the games, the players have to interact verbally with game objects or other players, and are exposed to cultural and linguistic knowledge that is different from that encountered in a textbook or in the classroom. According to Zheng et al. [30], the interaction that digital games offer is in the form of a request for help, the giving of an explanation, coordination of planned activities, reporting an action or asking for an alternative solution. This kind of interaction involves many players that have different backgrounds of language and linguistic knowledge. Consequently, they are required to be able to comprehend the language used in the game.

In contrast, a different finding is made in another study conducted by Lyrigkou [16], which focuses on learners' agency in terms of out-of-class language contact. It shows that without the conscious objective of language learning, learners actually lack agency in their own language learning experience. Their attitudes appear to hinder their active engagement with language sources outside the classroom, which interferes with further linguistic benefits. Moreover, regarding digital games for language learning, it should be noted also that there are negative social views of online gaming, which see it as an isolating, unproductive and dangerous activity [27]. Gaming is also not to everyone's interest nor the only way of learning a language outside the classroom, given the differences in gender preferences for game types [3]. Thus, there is a need for a critical evaluation and skill for every digital practice employed by learners as their preference for learning English in their leisure time beyond the classroom.

3 METHOD

3.1 Research design

This study was conducted under a mixed methods design which is in line with the purpose of the study, identifying digital practices of Indonesian digital natives in learning English beyond the classroom. In particular, it employed explanatory sequential mixed methods. Mixed methods research is a combination of quantitative and qualitative research methods in a single study, in which each approach is adding something to the understanding of a phenomenon [1]. Particularly in explanatory sequential mixed methods design, it involves both quantitative and qualitative data sequentially, which consists of two phases in conducting the research [5]. The first phase is where the researcher collects quantitative data, then followed by collecting the qualitative data. The priority of this design was the quantitative data, with the qualitative element used to follow up and refine the findings of the former [8].

3.2 Site and participants

The participants of this study were 25 students around 16–17 years old in a public high school in Bandung, Indonesia. All of the participants had been learning English as a foreign language at school for at least five years. At the time this study was conducted, they took English lessons twice a week, which is approximately for three hours. This school was chosen for several reasons. First, it was one of the model schools in Bandung into which many students had competed to be accepted, since they needed to have an average score of at least 85 as their final score in junior high school. This indicates that most of the students in this school are high achievers compared to students from other schools in the city. Second, the site of this study was Bandung, one of the big cities in Indonesia. This means that most of the advancement, especially in technology, is experienced first by people who live here. Thus, the reason for selecting the site and participants was due to the assumption that they were 'rich of information' in terms of owning digital devices (at least a smartphone and a laptop) and actively using the devices for their daily activities; they also understood common English terms, encountered both in the setting of the devices and those spread across the Internet. Therefore, they might provide varied and useful information regarding the types of digital practices they employ in learning English beyond the classroom. Details of the participants are shown in Tables 1 and 2.

Table 1. Possession of digital devices.

No.	Total of digital devices	Number of students	Percentage (%)
1	3 devices (smartphone, tablet, laptop)	13	52
2	2 devices (smartphone and laptop)	12	48

Table 2. Total time spent online.

No.	Time spent online per day	Number of students	Percentage (%)
1	3–4 hours	1	4
2	5–6 hours	3	12
3	7–8 hours	4	16
4	9–10 hours	8	32
5	11–12 hours	8	32
6	13–15 hours	1	4

3.3 Technique of data collection

The data in this study were taken from one source: a questionnaire. However, in the questionnaire, the types of question were both closed and open-ended. The questionnaire is divided into four sections. The first section is about the general information of the participants, which consists of their identities such as name, age and class. The second section is aimed at getting information about their possession of digital devices, the language in which they entered the setting, and general activities using those devices. The third section is about the frequency of digital practices they employ, specifically to learn English by using digital devices. The last section is follow-up questions from the third section, which specifically asks about the kind of digital practices, the sources and what language focus the participants engage in. By giving further open-ended kinds of questions in collecting the data, it is hoped to confirm the participants' feedback from closed questions.

3.4 Data analysis

As the first step in analyzing the data collected, the quantitative data were analyzed with descriptive statistics. After that, the qualitative data were also identified and coded. Then, all of the data gathered were grouped into several themes relevant to the types of digital practices. After this process was done, the data were then simplified and compared to the literature reviews, to be displayed in the results and discussion sections.

4 RESULTS AND DISCUSSION

As mentioned above, this study intends to address the question: "What distinct types of digital literacy practices do learners engage in to facilitate their English language experience beyond the classroom?" From the data gathered, the types of digital literacy practices can be classified into three categories, based on the framework proposed by Spires and Bartlett [25]: locating and consuming digital content, creating digital content, and communicating digital content.

4.1 Digital native, digital resident

Before elaborating on each type of digital literacy practices, the data show that all of the learners in this study have the characteristics of digital natives, just like those proposed by Prensky [23]. It can be seen from their age, technological skill, and learning preference. The learners are in the range are between 16 and 17 years old, which means that they were born and grew up with technology surrounding them. Their technological skill also reflects on the digital devices they possess; all of them have a smartphone to access digital space and even have either a laptop or tablet of their own. Moreover, it is supported by the fact that most of them (64%) spend their time connected to the Internet from 9 to 12 hours a day. Regarding the learning preference, all of the learners also admit that they use digital devices to support their learning experience, both in the classroom by doing assignments given by the teachers, and beyond the classroom by employing several digital practices in their leisure time. Thus, this result also indicates that all of the learners who participated in this study have a good economical background since their parents provide them with digital devices. Besides, the geographical background of the school also contributes to the 'nativeness' of these learners since they live in the urban area in which the Internet and digital devices can be accessed effortlessly.

However, when it comes to relating their activities in digital space according to the framework of White and Le Cornu [29], learners fall into both digital resident and digital visitor categories based on their preference of digital practices. There are three learners who feel uneasy to be active on social media and leave a digital identity. Thus, they enjoy other digital practices such as watching videos on YouTube and reading websites. It shows that even though there are those who are capable of being digital residents, they choose not to be for their own reasons. Besides these three, the rest of the learners are enjoying their label as digital residents who are involved actively on social networking sites. Since the digital resident and visitor are seen on a continuum, not two separate boxes, how resident they are has not yet been explored deeply.

4.2 *Digital literacy practices*

This present study is based on the framework of digital literacy practices proposed by Spires and Bartlett [26]. They categorize the digital literacy practices into three types: locating and consuming digital content, creating digital content, and consuming digital content. From these categories, there are various kinds of activities which take place as the learners spend time in the digital space. They will be elaborated below and with reference to other similar studies.

4.3 *Locating and consuming digital content*

The data gathered from the questionnaire found that the learners' digital practices are listening to songs from the online application (44%), followed by streaming TV series (24%), and playing online games (24%). Moreover, the activities that the learners do most often are also listening to songs (56%), translating by using online translation applications (52%), browsing English learning materials (48%), and streaming movies or TV series (44%). Thus, it shows that listening to songs and streaming movies or TV series are the digital practices that most of the learners regularly do. As the learners attempt to learn English using digital devices, all of these activities are using the English language by way of the songs, the TV series or the online games, even though it is not always spoken by native speakers of English. Most of the learners are listening to an online application that provides various kinds of music, just by connecting to the Internet without downloading it. Examples of online music applications used by the learners are Spotify, JOOX and SoundCloud. Furthermore, the most watched movies and TV series are *Harry Potter, Riverdale, The Ellen Show*, and *The Amazing World of Gumball*. These movies and TV series are in a variety of genre such as fantasy, crime, cartoons and talk shows. In addition, there is also a learner who admits that she likes to watch Korean drama but with English subtitles, so that she considers it as one of her ways to learn English.

Furthermore, besides watching English movies and TV series, most of the learners are also learning by watching videos provided on YouTube. The YouTube channels they regularly watch are rooted in their own interests, even though they are presented not only by native speakers of English but also by non-native speakers, as long as the content is in English. As an example, those who are interested in beauty tips regularly watch Liah Yoo's channel, a Korean beauty enthusiast who posts videos about skincare and make-up using the English language. Some of the learners also regularly watch Nessie Judge's channel on YouTube, an Indonesian public figure who often posts a video blog of her daily activity and her opinion on issues. Even though she is Indonesian, she often uses switch-code of Indonesian and English language on her videos. However, there are also some of learners who regularly watch a special channel for learning English that provides English materials, such as the LangFocus channel.

Regarding the online games the learners often play in their free time, they do not have to be games that are created for learning purposes, but most of the games are commercial ones using the English language. The digital devices they use are smartphones or tablets because they are convenient. The online game most played by the learners is a popular role-playing game named *Harry Potter: Hogwarts Mystery*. This game lets the players choose who they want to become and experience how it feels to be a student at Hogwarts, an imaginary wizardry school. The players can communicate with other in this game by using English and complete the challenges provided. Another example of an online game is *Plato*. This is a collection of many games that can be played by multiple players and provides a feature for chatting with friends. In addition, there is a game for learning language chosen by some of the learners named *Duolingo*. This provides many kinds of questions enriched with pictures and audio, rather than only using text forms. Its tagline is to learn language in a fun way.

On the other hand, the digital practices that the learners seldom follow are visiting website facilities for learning English (68%), browsing for any information by using English (64%), and reading websites that use English (48%). This means that the learners do these activities but not on a regular daily basis. Meanwhile, there are also activities that the learners never do, even though they are considered to be locating and consuming digital practices, such as reading online comics such as *WEBTOON* (44%).

4.4 Creating digital content

Among the four activities that involve creating or producing digital content, there is not a single digital practice that the learners regularly do. Only 28% of learners often write status posts or captions on their social media and 60% seldom do so. Most of the learners (76%) never write blogs, websites or fan fiction. Moreover, in terms of the creation of video with English content, 56% of learners never do it and 40% of them sometimes consider doing it as a digital practice for learning English. This result indicates that learners prefer lighter activities that do not take up much time. However, it does not mean that they avoid such things altogether but they consider them as activities that can be done when they have a lot of free time.

4.5 Communicating digital content

In terms of the digital practice related to communicating digital content, there is not a single person who always communicates in English through a chat application or social media, while 75% of learners report seldom doing this kind of activity as a digital practice for learning. Furthermore, learners have several choices of social media and chat application for learning, which include reading other people's status captions, reading English quotes, following accounts that provide English materials, and interacting with others in English. By employing these activities learners can acquire not only new vocabulary and sentence structure, but also information about their interests that they cannot get in the Indonesian language. Thus, the most used social media and chat applications they list that help them to learn English are Instagram, Line, Twitter, WhatsApp, and Tumblr.

From this variety of activities that learners employ, categorized as locating and consuming digital content, it can be inferred that learners choose activities that have entertainment purposes in preference to those that purposively teach English. It seems that learners get more enjoyment from those activities based on their interest which involve not just text and pictures, but also more in the form of audiovisual content, such as online gaming and watching videos. This kind of activity also gives a real context to language, not a simulated one as in the classroom. This is in line with the studies conducted by Godwin-Jones [11] and Sockett [25], where the digital environment provides authentic language input for learners. Especially for those who prefer playing online or digital games as an attempt to learn English, they have the chance to use English actively [22]. In addition, the interaction in digital games is also one of the reasons why learners choose them for learning English, which is in line with Zheng et al. [30]. However, learners who are interested in digital games are mostly boys and not all of the learners agree that digital games can help them learn English, which is in line with Boyle and Conolly [3].

On the other hand, learners seem less active when it comes to creating and communicating digital content as a digital practice for learning English. Most learners only produce digital content or use social media for learning English once in a while. Yet, the learners will hopefully be active in these kinds of activities since they are the representatives of their own community, such as their country, in the digital environment where everyone can meet and interact, as described by Ware et al. [28]. Furthermore, when the context of learning is compared to the classroom, the social networking site environment provides a more supportive and less intimidating space, especially for learning independently in leisure time [4]. In addition, creating digital content and interacting with others in online space is one of the digital practices that can help learners in their learning experience of English [13]. Thus, it can be concluded that most learners feel more relaxed learning English by employing a 'passive' kind of digital practice rather than a productive one.

5 CONCLUSIONS AND RECOMMENDATION

This study revealed that Indonesian learners, who are at high-school level and are active users in the digital environment, have employed several digital practices in their attempts to learn English outside the classroom. Their digital practices can be categorized into three types. First, locating and consuming digital content, which includes listening to songs from online applications, streaming TV series or movies, playing online games, translating through online translate applications, and browsing English learning materials. Second, creating digital content that involves writing status posts or captions on social media, writing blogs, websites or fan fiction, and creating videos with English content. Third, communicating digital content by interacting with others on social media or chat applications. Among these three types of digital practice, most of the learners are more eager to locate and consume digital content in preference to the other two types. Most of them prefer this first one when learning English beyond the classroom because most of the activities are based on their own interests or hobbies. Thus, it can be concluded that the learners employ three different types of digital practices for learning English for varying amounts of time, where the most frequent activities they engage in are those ones that have an entertainment purpose.

However, it should be noted that among these three different types of digital practice, critical evaluation by learners is needed to support their English learning experience. This study has not explored this issue, nor to what extent each digital practice employed contributes to the learning of English beyond the classroom. Moreover, the perceptions of learners regarding their activities of learning English in the digital environment also need to be revealed. Therefore, these shortfalls are strongly recommended for exploration by further studies.

REFERENCES

[1] Ary, D., Jacobs, L.C., Sorensen, C. & Razavieh, A. (2010). *Introduction to research in education* (8th ed.). San Francisco, CA: Cengage Learning.
[2] Bennett, S., Maton, K.A. & Kervin, L. (2008). The 'digital natives' debate: A critical review of the evidence. *British Journal of Educational Technology*, 39(5), 775–786.
[3] Boyle, E. & Conolly, T. (2008). Games for learning: Does gender make a difference? In T. Conolly & M. Stansfield (Eds.), *Proceedings of the 2nd European Conference on Games Based Learning* (pp. 69–76). Reading, UK: Academic Publishing.
[4] Buckley, C.N. & Williams, A.M. (2010). Web 2.0 technologies for problem-based and collaborative learning: A case study. In T.T. Kidd & J. Keengwe (Eds.), *Adult learning in the digital age: Perspective on online technologies and outcomes*. New York, NY: Yurchak.
[5] Creswell, J.W. (2014). *Research design: Qualitative, quantitative, and mixed methods approaches* (4th ed.). Thousand Oaks, CA: SAGE Publications.
[6] Dudeney, G., Hockly, N. & Pegrum, M. (2012). *Digital literacies*. New York, NY: Pearson.
[7] Floris, F.D. (2014). Using information and communication technology (ICT) to enhance language teaching & learning: An interview with Dr. A. Gumawang Jati. *TEFLIN Journal*, 25(2), 139–146.
[8] Fraenkel, J.R., Wallen, N.E. & Hyun, H.H. (2012). *How to design and evaluate research in education* (8th ed.). New York, NY: McGraw-Hill.
[9] Gee, J.P. (2012). *Social linguistics and literacies: Ideology in discourses* (4th ed.). New York, NY: Routledge.
[10] Gilster, P. (1997). *Digital literacy*. New York, NY: Wiley Computer Publications.
[11] Godwin-Jones, R. (2015). Contributing, creating, curating: Digital literacies for language learners. *Language Learning & Technology*, 19(3), 8–20.
[12] Hafner, C.A. & Jones, R.H. (2012). *Understanding digital literacies: A practical introduction*. New York, NY: Routledge.

[13] Hafner, C.A., Chik, A. & Jones, R.H. (2013). Engaging with digital literacies in TESOL. *TESOL Quarterly, 47*(4), 812–815.

[14] Hidayati, T. (2016). Integrating ICT in English language teaching and learning in Indonesia. *JEELS, 3*(1), 38–62.

[15] Lie, A. (2013). Social media in a content course for the digital natives. *TEFLIN Journal, 24*(1), 48–62.

[16] Lyrigkou, C. (2018). Not to be overlooked: Agency in informal language contact. *Innovation in Language Learning and Teaching.* doi:10.1080/17501229.2018.1433182

[17] Mali, Y.C.G. (2017). EFL students' experiences in learning CALL through project based instructions. *TEFLIN Journal, 28*(2), 170–192.

[18] Miniwatts Marketing Group. (2010). Internet world stats: Internet world users by language. Retrieved from http://www.internetworldstats.com/stats7.htm

[19] Palfreyman, D.M. (2011). Family, friends, and learning beyond the classroom: Social networks and social capital in language learning. In P. Benson & H. Reinders (Eds.), *Beyond the language classroom* (pp. 17–34). Basingstoke, UK: Palgrave Macmillan.

[20] Pegrum, M. (2011). Modified, multiplied, and (re-)mixed: Social media and digital literacies. In M. Thomas (Ed.), *Digital education.* New York, NY: Palgrave Macmillan.

[21] Peterson, M. (2010). Computerized games and simulations in computer-assisted language learning: A meta-analysis of research. *Simulation & Gaming, 41*(1), 72–93.

[22] Prensky, M. (2001). Digital natives, digital immigrants. *On The Horizon, 9*(5), 1–6.

[23] Setiasih, L. (2014). The role of out-of-school English literacy activities in promoting students' English literacy. *TEFLIN Journal, 25*(1), 62–79.

[24] Sockett, G. (2014). *The online informal learning of English.* London, UK: Palgrave Macmillan.

[25] Spires, H.A. & Bartlett, M.E. (2012). *Digital literacies and learning: Designing a path forward.* Raleigh, NC: Friday Institute, North Carolina State University. Retrieved from https://www.fi.ncsu.edu/wp-content/uploads/2013/05/digital-literacies-and-learning.pdf

[26] Tour, E. (2015). Digital mindsets: Teachers' technology use in personal life and teaching. *Language Learning & Technology, 19*(3), 124–139.

[27] Ware, P., Liaw, M. & Warschauer, M. (2012). The use of digital media in teaching English as an international language. In L. Alsagoff, S.L. McKay, G. Hu & W.A. Renandya (Eds.), *Principles and practices for teaching English as an international language* (pp. 28–46). New York, NY: Routledge.

[28] White, D. & Le Cornu, A. (2011). Visitors and residents: A new typology for online engagement. *First Monday, 16*(9). doi:10.5210/fm.v16i9.3171.

[29] Zheng, D., Newgarden, K. & Young, M. (2012). Multimodal analysis of language learning in World of Warcraft play: Languaging as values-realizing. *ReCALL, 24*(3), 339–360.

Part III:English Language Teaching in Changing Era

English Linguistics, Literature, and Language Teaching in a Changing Era – Madya et al. (eds)
© 2020 Taylor & Francis Group, London, ISBN 978-1-03-224160-9

Teaching critical thinking through reading to senior high school students

Adnan Zaid & Sri Sarjiyati
University of Technology Yogyakarta, Yogyakarta, Indonesia

ABSTRACT: It is a fact that critical thinking is one of the 21st century skills which is becoming paramount. It is a higher order of thinking which focuses on how facts are proven, arguments are built, and conclusions are drawn. In reading, it is more than just finding facts, or getting information from the reading material. It is assumed that critical thinking can be trained and developed via some ways. One of the ways may be conducted by means of teaching reading which promotes critical thinking. This involves students, while reading, to give comments, arguments, predict what is next, and draw conclusions based on the material they have read. However, this strategy will need a creative teacher who is able to make his/her reading class interesting, motivating, and challenging. This paper will explore on how reading activities can build critical thinking among senior high school students. It will deal with the procedures, materials, evaluation, feedback, problems, and students' comments on the application of the technique in learning critical reading through reading. A trial has been made for a reading class with this technique. Hopefully, this can inspire other teachers in teaching critical thinking in other settings.

Keywords: critical, reading, thinking, teaching

1 INTRODUCTION

The abundance of information in the society requires people to be critical in digesting the information. In reading, for instance, it is necessary to have a skill which enables one to think critically and synthesize what he/she reads. Otherwise, he/she will be easily influenced by what he/she reads. In this relation, it is is important to have a critical thinking skill in order not to be easily misled by written information. In line with this need, the government through Curriculum 2013recommends teachers to teach senior high students as to have the skill of critical thinking, creative and innovation, communication, and collaboration. It is hoped that teaching learning process should lead students to have High Order Thinking Skills [1]. The Ministry of Education, in the Implementation of 21 Century Skill Blueprint, 2017, highlights the importance of critical thinking ability in the nation's education agenda for the next decade.

The rapid advancement of technology has brought the new mandates and challenges so that critical thinking skills are necessary to be exercised and possessed by students. These changes have directly affected the teaching learning process and teacher's role. However, it is not easy to teach senior high students critical thinking when they are given printed material to read. It needs some great from the teacher to teach critical thinking. He/she has to apply a suitable technique that suits his/her class with its own unique environment. Both teachers and students should learn and practice how to think critically [2]. The teacher must create the classroom climate to be open, stimulating, and supportive so that the students may engage in critical thinking discussions or activities. Otherwise,students may not take the risk to engage with critical thinking processes [3].

89

2 THE TECHNIQUE TO BE APPLIED

Teaching Critical Reading may be conducted by using combination of SQ3R (Survey, Question, Read, Recite, Review) method and Socratic Questioning. It is assumed to be an effective way to train students to have critical thinking skill. SQ3R is reading study formula designed to have process and retention of written information.

The first step is Surveying which scans the piece of writing to establish its purpose and get the main ideas to look for (1) titles and headings to indicate the main topics and concepts being developed, (2) pictures, questions, bold or italicized print to emphasize important information, (3) introduction and conclusion to give the topics being covered as well as the purpose and first and last sentences in paragraphs, (4) Footnotes.

The second step is Questioning which students are asked to write questions to give purpose and improve concentration. This aids comprehension. The students are required to turn main headings and pictures into questions and jot down questions that they may have as they survey the material. In this questioning step, Socratic questioning can be adopted and adapted. It develops deep questions. Deep questions drive students' thought underneath the surface of things, and force them to deal with complexity. Questions of purpose force them to define their task. Questions of information require them to look at their sources of information as well as at the quality of their information. Questions of interpretation drive them to examine how they are organizing or giving meaning to information and to consider alternative ways of giving meaning. Questions of assumption trigger them to examine what they are taking for granted. Questions of implication demand them to follow out where their thinking is going. Questions of point of view push them to examine their point of view and to consider other relevant points of view. Questions of relevance require them to discriminate what does and what does not bear on a question. Questions of accuracy stimulate them to evaluate and test for truth and correctness. Questions of precision ask them to give details and be specific. Questions of consistency tell them to examine their thinking for contradictions. Questions of logic require them to consider how they are putting the whole of their thought together, to make sure that it all adds up and makes sense within a reasonable system of some kind [4].

Table 1. Types of Socratic questioning.

1. Questions for clarification:	1. Why do you say that?
	2. What do you mean by...?
	3. How does this relate to our discussion?
2. Questions that probe assumptions:	1. What could we assume instead?
	2. How can you verify or disapprove that assumption?
	3. On what basis do we think this way?
3. Questions that probe reasons and evidence:	1. What would be an example?
	2. What is.... analogous to?
	3. What do you think causes to happen...? Why?
4. Questions about Viewpoints and Perspectives:	1. What would be an alternative?
	2. What is another way to look at it?
	3. Why is the best?
	4. What are the strengths and weaknesses of...?
	5. How are...and ...similar?
	6. What is a counterargument for...?
5. Questions that probe implications and consequences:	1. What generalizations can you make?
	2. What are the consequences of that assumption?
	3. What are you implying?
	4. How does... affect...?
	5. How does... tie in with what we learned before?
6. Questions about the question:	1. What was the point of this question?
	2. Why do you ask this question?
	3. What does... mean?
	4. How does... apply to everyday life?

Another technique is Socratic questioning. It is at the heart of critical thinking and the following questions can be used by tutors to help draw information from their tutees. These are adapted from Paul's six types of Socratic questions

The third step is Reading. Students are asked to search for answers to the questions, to make notes and highlight main ideas that support the concept.

The fourth step is Reciting to help them to put the information into their long-term memory and put what they have learned into their own words.

The last step is reviewing the material to understand and remember it. Did they answer all of the questions and understand the information? Reviewing each time, one studies will eliminate the need to "cram" for a test.

3 PROCEDURE

Here are some steps of applying the technique of teaching critical thinking through critical reacding:

a. The teacher gives explanations about the purpose of the learning process that is to train the students to have critical reading.
b. The teacher gives some examples of Socratic questioning to ask deep questions.
c. The teacher gives examples about SQ3R.
d. Teacher tells the procedure of the learning process.
e. Teacher gives reading text about News item and gives students' worksheet.
f. Teacher guides students step by step to help students create deep questions in every type of questions.
g. Students do the task.
h. After 30 minutes teacher checks the students' work on questioning and how to raise deep questions.
i. Teacher and students discuss the students' work and give feedback on each step.
j. Teacher asks students to reread to find out the answers of the questions under the teacher's guidance.
k. Students continue to recite what they have read. They have to paraphrase the text by using their own sentences.
l. Students make a review on the text by making a summary of the text, give comments about the text using their own sentences.
m. To end the lesson, teacher gives evaluation and reflection on the teaching learning process and about the lesson. The teacher asks the difficulties and the obstacles that the students get when they do the tasks, and gives feedback on them.

4 THE STRENGTHS AND THE DRAWBACKS OF THE MODIFIED METHOD OF SQ3R AND SOCRATIC QUESTIONING

The modified method of SQ3R and Socratic has some strengths. It is a useful method to fully absorb written information. It helps students to create a good framework of a subject, into which the teacher can fit facts correctly. It helps students to set their own goal in getting bundles of information from any text. By using this method, students can break down reading texts into five easy-to-follow steps. Reading texts may be full with factual information that has been written in an essay form. Sometimes, it is hard to point out the main idea of the text.

By using this method, students can revise all the useful information in the text just in a few minutes when they want to do their revision. They can understand the text as fast as they can by using this method. They can break a long-boring text into an interesting note to read. Besides, they also can have a better understanding because it is easier to gain all the facts. SQ3R method encourages students to use their imagination and abstract reasoning abilities during developing question. One of the steps in this strategy is to create deep questions before reading. This is to ensure that their reading becomes an active search for answers instead of a passive activity. By asking questions, students will realize that short term goals will help them comprehend more difficult material. To create deep questions, they will have to imagine what kind of information that they want to know or what they are expecting from the text. This is called critical thinking. It will encourage students to think out of the box and to become more creative.

This method has also some weaknesses. It has five steps to be followed so that it will be time consuming. It needs a long period of time to complete just one topic. By following this method, muchtime is spenton just expecting the information that the students want to get. For example, to create many deep questions, the students have to survey the text and have to read the text more than once. To have better understanding, these steps have to be repeated twice or more. Students will not have enough time to focus on only one topic while they have a bundle of textbooks to read. This strategy is less effective for textbooks involving problem solving. This method needs a big effort to read frequently so that students can get the deep information [5].

5 METHOD

This study belongs to descriptive qualitative study. There is no statistical procedure in collecting and analyzing the data. The data were gathered by observing the process of teaching and learning in class and by giving questionnaires to the students involved in the application of the technique. The students involved were the second-year students of senior high school.

6 RESULTS

6.1 *Classroom atmosphere*

The classroom atmosphere was conducive. Students were active in doing the assignments although they were shy and doubtful to express their ideas at the beginning. Later, they were able to do their exercises as required. Some students found it hard to raise questions at the beginning. The teacher helped them build interrogative sentences at the start. As the classes moved on, the students seemed to enjoy their class and they felt free to express their ideas in their discussion. The teaching of critical thinking was quite successful in this case.

6.2 *Students response*

After the technique was applied, students were asked to give comments on the application of the technique. Most students responded in a positive way. Here are some comments made by the students.

One student said that the method was good but the material was too much and she got some difficulty in uderstanding long texts.

"In my opinion, this method is very good but for myself it is quite burdensome because class 12 has much material to learn and this material is quite difficult especially to interpret a long text, need more understanding to be able to understand the text.

Another student commentend that the learning method was interesting because it could train the students to think critically and it could make the students develop their vocabulary and grammar.

"In my opinion, this learning method is interesting because it trains students to think critically, develop vocabulary and grammar, but there are some troubles to understand the content of the text because a lot of vocabulary have not been understood and it is hard to make appropriate questions.

A student said that SQ3R method could make her more creative and thinking deeper.

"SQ3R learning makes me more creative and more thinking."

Another student commented that she was pleased with the introduction of SQ3R method despite her difficulties in raising questions.

"I am pleased with the SQ3R Method although I still have difficulties in making questions."

A student said that the method could train her to have a critical thinking skill with the reason that she could anlyze the given test further.

"Learning using this method can train critical thinking because I can analyze the text so I can think further."

7 CONCLUDING REMARKS

Teachers may teach critical thinking through critical reading although he/she may need to find out a suitable technique to deliver his/her teaching. One of the techniques that he/she can try is modified SQ3R method combined with Socratic questions.

This study shows that SQ3R method with Socratic questions could enhance the students to think critically. Yet, it took longer time to practice it. At least two meetings were needed to practice it. The first meeting was used for "survey, question, and read"; and the second meeting was used for "recite and review". The classroom was conducive. The students worked seriously and absorbedly. Yet, some students looked tensed.

The students responded positively to the use of the technique. They said that the technique was good and could make them think critically. At the same time, they could develop their grammar and vocabulary.

This technique needs a special effort from the teacher in terms of preparing suitable materials which enhance the students to think critically. The more challenging the material is, the more it can stimulate the students to think critically.

REFERENCES

[1] Permendikbud, No 21 Tahun 2016 tentang *Standar ISI.*
[2] Khojasteh, M., & Smith, J.W. (2010). Using Technology to Teach CriticalThinkingin HigherEducation: Look at an UndergraduateBusinessCourse. *Issues in Information System*, 11(2), 54–65.
[3] Black, S. (2005). Teaching students to think critically. *Education Digest*, 70(6), 42–47.
[4] Paul, R. and Elder, L. (1997). *Foundation for Critical Thinking*, Online at website: www.criticalthinking.org
[5] Ain Manaf. (2011). *The Strengths and the Weakness of SQ3R Method*. https://www.scribd.com/pres entation/58450438/Strength-and-Weaknesses-of-Sq3r

English Linguistics, Literature, and Language Teaching in a Changing Era – Madya et al. (eds)
© 2020 Taylor & Francis Group, London, ISBN 978-1-03-224160-9

Effects of a Think Pair Share strategy on Indonesian vocational higher institution students' English speaking skills

Alfi H. Miqawati & Fitri Wijayanti
English Study Program, Politeknik Negeri Jember, Jember, Indonesia

ABSTRACT: Several studies have shown that cooperative learning can improve students' understanding, academic achievement, social skills, self-esteem and ability to integrate and synthesize new material, while also helping to develop critical thinking, problem solving and decision-making skills. This study aims to examine the effect of cooperative learning with the Think Pair Share (TPS) strategy on students' ability to speak in the English Study Program, State Polytechnic of Jember. It employed a quasi-experimental design with a one-group pretest/post-test design. In this study, the subjects of research were first given a pretest (preliminary test) to understand the extent of their initial ability, before being given speech learning (speaking) using cooperative learning in the form of TPS. After this, the students were given a final test (post-test) to determine the extent of the influence of the treatment on learning outcomes (English speaking ability). A hypothesis test was aimed at understanding the difference in the learning results of the experimental and control groups. The results show that the implemented strategy (TPS) has a significant effect on improving students' English speaking skills.

Keywords: cooperative learning, think pair share, speaking skill

1 INTRODUCTION

English, as a foreign language in Indonesia, is taught and has become part of the national curriculum, starting from the level of basic education to that of higher education. In the context of higher education, mastery of English is not limited to functional mastery but also involves the academic realm and professional communication aspects. This requires innovation at every stage of learning so that the expected results can be achieved optimally.

Various methods are carried out by teachers so that students can master English in accordance with the objectives and learning outcomes that have been set. One of these is the implementation of cooperative learning, which replaces the closely controlled and teacher-centered system with a student-centered system in which the teacher and students share authority and control of learning (Bruffee [1]).

Bruffee mentioned that cooperative learning tends to assume knowledge as a social construct, thus, it can extend students' critical thinking, reasoning skills and understanding of social interactions, as they have more opportunities to be involved and take control of the learning process. In other words, cooperative learning is a type of active learning where students work or have a discussion in small groups (Zaitwan, 2013, in Hamdan [2]). Some studies indicate that cooperative learning increases students' understanding, the ability to integrate and synthesize new material, improve academic achievement, social skills, and self-esteem, and help develop critical thinking, problem solving and decision-making (Lujan & DiCarlo [3]; Goodwin [4]; Cortright et al. [5]). Thus, it can be concluded that cooperative learning is very useful for students, including those learning foreign languages that require complex oral and written competencies.

94

The teaching of Speaking II in the English Study Program, *Politeknik Negeri Jember* focuses on enhancing students' ability to speak in English by employing different communication strategies to be applied in professional/workplace use. The results of the preliminary study indicated that the lecturers teaching the subject, even though they have implemented student-centered learning, were still lacking variations in learning methods/strategies. For example, students were taught using conventional discussion methods (they were asked to work in groups, present their work or have group discussions). Effective learning strategies are needed because the strategies used so far have not made students highly motivated, nor actively participate in classroom activities or significantly improve their learning outcomes and speaking skills. In fact, speaking skills are very important because to interact socially, good communication skills are needed.

Implementing student-centered learning not only helps students to speak and discuss something in the classroom, but it should also create ways of being more innovative and creative. It is imperative that teachers design and apply interesting and challenging learning strategies and tasks that match students' styles so that they can be optimally facilitated and learning promoted (Aunurrahman [6]; Miqawati & Sulistyo [7]).

One effective cooperative learning variation of the in-class group exercise that can promote students' interest is Think Pair Share (TPS). In this case, a problem is given to the students and they need to solve it individually; then they are asked to compare their answer with their peers' answers. Finally, they synthesize a joint solution and may in turn share their solutions with the rest of the classroom members (Felder & Brent [8]). In other words, students have a time called wait time in which they think alone and then, with a group of friends, continue with the discussion. Through this strategy, they will find it easier to understand linguistic expressions relating to linguistic functions. Therefore, it is effective for the teachers to apply TPS in speaking activities.

Think Pair Share has empirically been proven to improve students' speaking skills. Some researchers have conducted research on the implementation of TPS in various learning contexts and showed significant results in improving students' language skills. Usman [9] conducted classroom action research to help improve the speaking skills of STAIN Ternate students with TPS strategies and the results showed that TPS could improve the students' speaking skills. The results of Brady and Tsay's [10] study also showed very positive results, such that this strategy succeeded in bringing about change and improving students' achievement in speaking skills. Desta's [11] study added additional proof that TPS is effective in improving junior high school students' speaking skills and increasing their motivation levels. However, most studies on the effectiveness of TPS have been conducted in primary school, secondary school and university settings. Few studies on how TPS is implemented in vocational higher education (polytechnic) settings have been conducted. Thus, there is only limited evidence to show the effectiveness of TPS in improving polytechnic students' English speaking skills. This study aimed to analyze the effect of cooperative learning with a TPS strategy on such students' ability to speak English.

2 RESEARCH METHOD

This study was a quasi-experimental study with a one-group pretest/post-test design. This type of research is often used to assess the value of a new learning method (Cohen et al. [12]). An initial speaking test (pretest) was carried out so that the effect of the implementation of the TPS strategy could be assessed. In other words, the research subjects were first given a pretest (initial test) to determine the extent of their ability before being given the 'treatment'. Thereafter, students were given the treatment, namely learning speaking using cooperative learning with a TPS strategy. After this treatment, the students who were the subjects of the study were given a final test (post-test) to determine the extent of the TPS influence on their learning outcomes (English speaking skills). Two different speaking prompts covering different topics were given to the students for the pretest and post-test (pretest: the environment; post-test: the Industrial Revolution 4.0). The students were asked to present their opinions related to the topics individually and respond to questions proposed by their peers. The criteria of success was the minimum standard score to pass the subject, which is 71 (B). Simply put, the research design used can be described as follows:

O1 ------ X ------ O2
Information:
O1 : initial test
O2 : final test
X : treatment (learning speaking using Think Pair Share)

The subjects of this study were second-semester students of the English Language Study Program at the Jember State Polytechnic in the 2017/2018 academic year. The total number of students was 69 and they were divided into three classes to maximize the implementation of TPS. Treatment was given seven times (including a pretest and post-test each time) based on the schedule of the Speaking for Group Activities course. Primary data, in the form of speaking test results, were obtained from the results of the pretest and post-test. Initial tests were given to determine students' ability in speaking for group activities before being given treatment in the form of learning with the TPS strategy. The final test was given to determine the level of progress or influence of learning speaking with the TPS strategy (i.e. after treatment). Aspects assessed included pronunciation, delivery and attitude, content, fluency and grammar.

Threats to internal validity were minimized because the treatments were conducted on the same day and taught by the same lecturer. The same materials and lesson plans for the three classes were utilized during the experiment.

For the sake of statistical assumption fulfillment, a normality test was conducted with the criteria for acceptance or rejection of the assumption at a level of significance of 0.05 (95 percent confidence). The data used for the testing were the results of the speaking post-tests. The result of the normality testing analysis was 0.065, showing that there was sufficient evidence to accept the hypothesis that the data obtained from the two groups' variances were homogeneous.

To find the effectiveness of the TPS strategy, a statistical hypothesis test was then conducted. Prior to it, a null hypothesis was formulated, which was that there was no difference in the students' speaking skills when taught by using the TPS strategy or through classroom discussion. Because the data was normally distributed, a t-test for dependent means was deployed for the statistical testing by comparing the result of the pretest and post-test. The level of significance was 0.05 to determine whether the implemented strategy contributed to the students' learning outcomes effectively or not.

3 FINDINGS AND DISCUSSION

The statistical results showed that the mean score of the initial test (pretest) was 65.31, while the mean score of the final test (post-test) was 71.97. Prior to the treatment, the students were asked to present their opinion on the environment and respond to their peers' questions. Meanwhile, the other topic, Industrial Revolution 4.0, was given for discussion. It could be inferred that the mean score of the post-test (the scores obtained after the treatment) was greater than that of the pretest. The mean difference between the two groups was 6.66. The detailed information of the means of the tests is presented in Table 1.

Table 1. Descriptive analysis summary.

Descriptive statistics			
	Mean	Standard deviation	N
Pretest	65.3188	9.6398	69
Post-test	71.971	10.6038	69

Table 2. *T*-test results.

Independent samples *t*-test	
T statistic	−3.8559
Degrees of freedom	136
Critical value	1.9771
95% Confidence interval	[−2.3075, 15.6119]

To answer the research problem related to the effectiveness of the TPS strategy in relation to the students' speaking skills, a *t*-test was carried out. The results showed that the observed significance level was lower than 0.05, meaning that there was a significant difference in the students' score before and after being taught using the TPS strategy. The result of hypothesis testing using the *t*-test can be seen in Table 2.

The result of the hypothesis testing showed that TPS has a significant effect on the students' English speaking skills compared to those taught using classroom discussion. The significant effect resulted from the implementation of the three phases (think, work in pairs, and share) carried out by the students during the experiment that triggered their active participation and cognitive processes. In the 'think' phase, students were given time to think about the questions or the problems proposed by the teacher. When they were given enough time to think, they could elicit their hesitancy and were able to organize their ideas. By organizing their ideas, they could identify the most important points, arrange them in a systematic way, and assure themselves that the ideas proposed were convincing enough and did not contain any misleading statements.

In the next 'pair' phase, students were asked to work with their peer, think out loud and conduct several 'negotiations' related to their ideas with their partner. In this phase, peer interaction was required and collaborative learning was promoted. In the last 'share' phase, the students presented the ideas refined with their friends to the wider class. To come up with their final ideas, each student, along with their partner, needed to synthesize their ideas, share their answers and reasons, and debate alternative solutions. This process stimulated the students' critical thinking.

Cooperation benefits students in many ways. As shown during the treatment process in this study, by working and sharing their ideas with their peers, the students are able to provide ample reasoning, are willing to listen to others' points of views and construct comprehensive understanding. From this experience, their critical thinking and reasoning skills can be valuable for adjusting themselves when they are dealing with professional and social environments. In other words, they can make reasonable and logical decisions in many different situations. Many studies have shown that cooperative learning helps students develop better high-level reasoning and critical thinking, increased willingness to listen, see, and consider the perspectives of others, construct new understanding, and make decisions in critical situations (McKeachie & Svinicki [13]; Gilles [14]; Kaddoura [15]).

The implementation of TPS in the classroom does not only result in an improvement in students' learning outcomes (speaking skills) but also heightens students' participation and motivation. During the teaching and learning process, the students paid very close attention every time the lecturer explained the materials, responding to their partner's opinion and willingly providing comprehensive ideas related to the topics given in each meeting. This would be unlikely to happen if the students were not motivated and interested in the teaching and learning process. It is in line with the results of studies conducted by Raba [16] and Zaim and Radjab [17], which show that TPS motivates and stimulates students to learn because it creates a fun learning atmosphere and allows them to have a good language learning experience. Thus, their oral communication skills can be improved. Zaim and Radjab also mentioned that variation of activities in the classroom can lead students to be more active in speaking.

All in all, the results of this study conformed to Robertson [18], in that the TPS strategy, as a part of collaborative learning, benefits students in the areas of peer acceptance, peer support, academic achievement, self-esteem and increased interest in learning. Gilles [14] also noted that by working cooperatively with their peers, students are more willing to listen to others' views, share ideas, clarify differences and construct new understandings. In other words, any kind of cooperative learning, including TPS, plays a pivotal role in the students' learning process. It can be concluded that cooperative learning is more effective than the traditional method of teaching, which is in line with the results of several other studies (Talebi & Sobani [19]; Thuy [20]).

The teacher also benefitted from TPS, in terms of the assessment process of the students' performance. While implementing TPS, the teacher can assess the students' understanding about certain topics using alternative assessment. The assessment is also called informal formative assessment, which occurs during student–teacher or student–student interactions (Ruiz-Primo [21]). The interactions taking place during TPS implementation allowed the teacher to observe the students' thinking and speaking. The students mentioned that they could enjoy their learning process without realizing that their performances were being assessed, unlike when they did tests based on pen and paper. As stated by Miqawati [22], such (alternative) assessment improves students' learning motivation and reduces their anxiety.

4 LIMITATION

The number of subjects in this study was only 69 vocational higher education students attending the same study program. This number is considered small in terms of sample size, and forms the major limitation of this study. Thus, it might not allow its findings to be generalized to all language teaching settings, especially higher educational settings in Indonesia.

5 CONCLUSION

Think Pair Share is a helpful teaching–learning strategy that can be applied in English language teaching settings to promote students' speaking skills. The findings of this study showed that collaborative learning, especially TPS, contributed significantly and positively to students' speaking skills. It can also be said that applying TPS as one of the alternative teaching–learning strategies appears to be helpful and suitable for developing students' speaking skills. The results showed that the students taught using TPS yielded higher speaking scores when compared to their scores before being exposed to TPS. This significant improvement was due to the three phases in TPS that arouse students' cognitive processes, critical thinking and cooperation, and which also lead to the promotion of students' soft skills, especially in making sound decisions and constructing valid arguments. The implementation of TPS also benefitted the teacher in terms of the assessment of the students' performance. The teacher was able to apply alternative asssessments during TPS activities and obtain reliable scores. The ample evidence provided by the present study can become a reference for teachers to implement TPS as one of the alternative strategies when teaching. Meanwhile, further studies of TPS in English language teaching with larger sample sizes and in different settings is highly recommended.

REFERENCES

[1] Bruffee, K.A. (1995). Sharing our toys: Cooperative learning versus collaborative learning. *Change: The Magazine of Higher Learning, 27*(1), 12–18.

[2] Hamdan, R.K.A. (2017). The effect of (Think – Pair – Share) strategy on the achievement of third grade student in sciences in the educational district of Irbid. *Journal of Education and Practice, 8*(9), 88–95.

[3] Lujan, H. &. DiCarlo, S.E. (2005). Too much teaching, not enough learning: What is the solution? *Advances in Physiology Education, 30*(1), 17–22.

[4] Goodwin, M.W. (1999). Cooperative learning and social skills: What skills to teach and how to teach them. *Intervention in School & Clinic, 35*(1), 29–33.

[5] Cortright, R.N., Collins, H.L. & DiCarlo, S.E. (2005). Peer instruction enhanced meaningful learning: Ability to solve novel problems. *Advances in Physiology Education, 29*(2), 107–111.

[6] Aunurrahman, A. (2010). *Belajar dan pembelajaran.* [Learning and Instruction] Bandung, Indonesia: Alfabeta.

[7] Miqawati, A.H. & Sulistyo, G.H. (2014). The PQRST strategy, reading comprehension, and learning styles. *Indonesian Journal of Applied Linguistics, 4*(1), 123–139.

[8] Felder, R.M. & Brent, R. (1994). *Cooperative learning in technical courses: Procedures, pitfalls, and payoffs.* Washington, DC: Division of Undergraduate Education, National Science Foundation.

[9] Usman, A. (2005). Using the Think-Pair-Share strategy to improve students' speaking ability at STAIN Ternate. *Journal of Education and Practice, 6*(10).

[10] Brady, M. & Tsay, M. (2010). A case study of cooperative learning and communication pedagogy: Does working in teams make a difference? *Journal of the Scholarship of Teaching and Learning, 10,* 78–89.

[11] Desta, R.A. (2017). Think Pair Share technique in teaching speaking skill. *Research in English and Education Journal, 2*(1), 37–46.

[12] Cohen, L., Manion, L. & Morrison, K. (2007). *Research methods in education.* New York, NY: Routledge.

[13] McKeachie, W. & Svinicki, M. (2014). *McKeachie's teaching tips: Strategies, research, and theory for college and university teachers.* Stamford, CT: Wadsworth Cengage Learning.

[14] Gilles, R.M. (2008). The effects of cooperative learning on junior high school students' behaviors, discourse and learning during a science-based learning activity. *School Psychology International, 29*(3), 328–347.

[15] Kaddoura, M. (2013). Think Pair Share: A teaching learning strategy to enhance students' critical thinking. *Educational Research Quarterly, 36*(4), 3–24.

[16] Raba, A.A.A. (2017). The influence of Think Pair Share (TPS) on improving students' oral communication skills in EFL classrooms. *Creative Education, 8*(1), 12–23.

[17] Zaim, M. & Radjab, D. (2014). Improving students' speaking skill by using Think-Pair-Share strategy at the second semester of Syariah Class A at language center of UIN SUSKA Riau. *English Language Teaching (ELT), 2*(1), 1–12.

[18] Robertson, K. (2006). Increase student interaction with "Think-Pair-Shares" and "Circle Chats". *Colorin Colorado.* Retrieved from http://www.colorincolorado.org/article/increase-student-interaction-think-pair-shares-and-circle-chats

[19] Talebi, F. & Sobhani, A. (2012). The impacts of cooperative learning on oral proficiency. *Mediterranean Journal of Social Sciences, 3*(3), 75–79.

[20] Thuy, L.T.B. (2015). An action research on the application of cooperative learning to teaching speaking. *TESOL Journal, 1*(2), 332–349.

[21] Ruiz-Primo, M.A. (2011). Informal formative assessment: The role of instructional dialogues in assessing students' learning. *Studies in Educational Evaluation, 37*(1), 15–24.

[22] Miqawati, A.H. (2019). Peer assessment practices in Indonesian higher education: The students' views. *Journal of English in Academic and Professional Communication, 5*(2), 57–64.

English Linguistics, Literature, and Language Teaching in a Changing Era – Madya et al. (eds)
© 2020 Taylor & Francis Group, London, ISBN 978-1-03-224160-9

Predict, Locate, Add, and Note (PLAN) strategy: An effective way to assist EFL students' reading comprehension in task-based learning

Annisa Rizqiana & Anita Triastuti
English Education Study Program, Graduate School, Yogyakarta State University, Yogyakarta, Indonesia

ABSTRACT: It is indisputable that one of the twenty-first century demands is to encourage students to be able to read effectively so that they can promote the language acquisition process and aid themselves to read various materials. Authentic reading tasks to teach reading may stimulate students to sense, to experience, to practice, and to understand the text more easily. Nevertheless, previous studies have revealed that the reading strategy implemented by teachers during the reading teaching and learning process does not always accommodate a communicative experience. Hence, the researcher attempts to describe a reading strategy to aid students' comprehension by implementing a Predict, Locate, Add, and Note (PLAN) strategy as an essential stage in students' reading comprehension. This paper concludes that the strategy can encourage students to think actively through strategic reading while carrying out effective and efficient reading in a task-based learning context.

Keywords: reading comprehension, task-based learning, PLAN strategy

1 INTRODUCTION

English as a Foreign Language (EFL) students consider reading as being a critical input within a complex matter, to obtain meaning from a text by actively thinking in order to understand the printed materials being read [15,17]. Thus, to be able to read comprehensively, students need a number of abilities to understand the words' meaning and their verbal interpretation, which makes such abilities a pivotal focus as a basis for English language learning [25]. Reading is an activity in which students are required to be involved during the process in order to comprehend what they read. Briefly, reading comprehension for students is not only about linking the words in a text, but also comprehending the ideas of the particular written text.

Due to the significance of reading comprehension, it functions to expand the students' knowledge of the language they read [32] and to improve their vocabulary [3,33] in relation to the learning and improvement of foreign language learning skills. When it comes to English learning, it is irrefutable that students often deal with and study various English written texts or printed materials, with which they will later be required to do several meaningful reading tasks to support their enhancement of language acquisition, particularly reading comprehension. The integration of authentic tasks into the learning process is designed to obtain an authentic reaction [8]. It will provoke students to appreciate the context required, to create understandable output, and to provide a more authentic classroom context. It proves that it is essential for them to gain access to English written texts, because they need to understand the written text and to develop their vocabulary through real-world tasks [20] via authentic texts such as a personal diary, newspapers, and labeling for their future needs.

Meanwhile, several studies related to reading comprehension in an EFL context have been carried out. Those studies recognize that EFL reading comprehension is a complicated and ongoing process that requires amelioration to solve. Students need to find specific and detailed information or grasp the main idea so that they are able to sense to experience, to practice, and to understand the text more easily. Such studies reveal that students find reading comprehension to be a difficult process, which has a clear relationship to success in effective reading, and this raises issues, namely the lack of awareness of appropriate strategies for reading comprehensively and proficiently in order to facilitate student learning [21]. Moreover, the preparation of teachers in demonstrating reading instruction to students becomes the fundamental issue [2]. This implies that it is mandatory for teachers to accommodate and to instruct students in a relevant reading strategy for comprehending texts in the future, and thus being able to attain reading comprehension.

The link between successful reading comprehension and a proper reading strategy has been studied broadly. Thus, the Predict, Locate, Add, and Note (PLAN) strategy is proposed for implementation to overcome such situations, as a research-based strategy that can develop students' higher-level thinking when reading English texts, making them more self-assured in reading and learning texts strategically [26,27]. Theoretically, this strategy presents a beneficial way to actualize students' ideas from the text, by stimulating background knowledge and generating a mind mapping that enables the students to monitor their comprehension and recognize the text more easily. In line with this study, students may improve their reading comprehension if they know about the PLAN strategy, and it is essential to understand the strategy in order to obtain good comprehension and fulfill the reading tasks. It leads us to discuss whether the strategy can aid students' reading comprehension, particularly in task-based learning; therefore, the researcher undertakes library research and uses a qualitative approach through a critical and in-depth study of relevant library materials to explore some main points in terms of reading comprehension, task-based learning, and the PLAN strategy with respect to the successful identification of a relevant reading strategy in a task-based learning context. The present study discusses the definition of reading comprehension, explains the definition of task-based learning, and elaborates the procedures of the PLAN strategy in task-based learning, in order to give an insight into how to implement the PLAN strategy in task-based learning as an assistance to teaching reading comprehension.

2 DISCUSSION

2.1 *Reading comprehension as an action to comprehend the written text*

Many scholars have specifically defined the terms of reading comprehension in an English Language Teaching (ELT) context. Reading comprehension involves the process of understanding what a student reads, which covers reminiscence, abstract thought, vision, and vocabulary knowledge in order to decode appropriately and to attain their needs and goals after reading [1,19,31]. This process includes their previous experiences and knowledge [28], because these are essential parts [14] in better knowledge of the discussed topic and in retaining the textual information through increased motivation [37] toward the text. It involves arranging what students have in their minds by applying prior knowledge as a basis to understanding the written texts, and to figuring out the vocabulary so that they are able to recognize the meaning of the text via various strategies [6]. It can be inferred that the process of text comprehension is how students extract the messages from printed materials and communicate with the text, which involves the students' thinking, previous knowledge and experience, and interaction with the assistance of reading instruction.

The reading comprehension process involves the students' struggle to read a written text that has certain messages, and to interact with it by understanding its meaning, underpinned by their prior knowledge [10]. They need intentional communication towards the author's message through interpretation of the text to understand the information in the language and the textual meaning. Nevertheless, students might have a variety of previous knowledge and experience that will influence their understanding of the text, which assuredly results in a different reading outcome. To anticipate this situation, it is suggested that teachers establish a contextual teaching process in which they may integrate information into the reading learning process [7]. It can be assumed that the existence of prior knowledge is critical in the comprehension process, to help students in relating to the topic they know and they learn. In addition, it is possible that students will have a different understanding and comprehension of the text due to their individual differences [13]. Regarding motivation, for instance, because students are working hard to establish the essence of the text [36], it can be ensured that they commit to reading comprehensively and determinedly; this is likely to leads to them becoming successful readers who are enabled to read a text effectively and efficiently. In brief, it indicates that they are required to digest and to transmit the information well to ensure their understanding of what and why they are reading; therefore, they can turn into successful readers.

Succinctly, reading comprehension is a process of reading a specific written piece with intent, to understand the information of the particular written text, benefitted by existing knowledge and the help of proper reading instructions.

2.2 Task-based learning as a method to develop students' reading comprehension

To attain EFL students' goal of reading comprehension, it seems probable that the existence of a task is considered as being a pivotal point [23] that focuses on the use of language meaningfully by emphasizing several tasks [30], namely learning the topic, finding the detailed information, or getting the main idea of the text. Some researchers have defined the task differently. The most popular definition of the task comes from Willis [38], as he defines the task as being an example of a classroom exercise that provokes students to comprehend, manipulate, produce or interact in relation to the target language in order to underline meaning. Task-based learning is to embody student-centered learning in the classroom and the context of language learning, since they have an opportunity to communicate and to interact in developing their ability to extend the target language [36]. It might be the most reasonable view of the correlation between the task's role and the students' activeness in acquiring the target language.

According to those definitions, the task in the reading classroom is seen as an activity that enables students, with the teachers' help, to comprehend the reading material, to manipulate the use of language, to produce their own language outcome based on the material used, and to interact with each other about their opinions in relation to the English material with a communicative goal. Therefore, the learning activity of reading comprehension should be purposeful in terms of language use. The activity should oblige students to actively participate in the process of reading. They can present their activity of making decisions such as designing a diagram with the information provided in a particular text or making an outline of the assigned text that might be referred to as a list of tasks to understand the text meaning; this is more crucial than reading form. It implies that having students engaged with meaningful reading tasks somehow makes the language learning more communicative to establish the outcome that indicates the students' understanding of language.

As identified by Willis [38], there are three fundamental stages of task-based learning: pre-task, task-cycle, and language focus. Briefly, the pre-task allows students to get meaningful exposure to extract their known words and expressions that relate to the topic. On the other hand, the task-cycle phase accentuates the understanding and phrasing of students to attain the outcomes of assigned tasks based on their results. The language focus phase, the last one, involves the student in analyzing and organizing the language to expand their concepts. Each phase has its own role that can contribute to student-centered learning. It can be deduced that task-based learning assists the students in acquiring language via a wide variety of reading tasks in keeping with the language used in the classroom.

2.3 The implementation of the PLAN strategy in task-based learning to enhance students' reading comprehension

The reading tasks mentioned previously, such as designing a mind map and summarizing a text function, are used to manifest students' understanding of the meaning of a text. To help them to understand a text, one of the reading strategies that can actively contribute to the development of students in comprehension is the PLAN strategy, by accessing prior knowledge, gathering extra information, and retelling the whole text. More prominently, it provides a modified mind map to stimulate their views and establish relationships between their conceptual understanding and the verification of the text, because it involves four steps: Predict, Locate, Add, and Note [26,27]. Because this strategy requires the students to implement reading instructions explicitly [18], it presumably leads to successful improvement of the students' text reading comprehension. The PLAN strategy attempts to benefit the students' metacognitive skills, in acquiring information from the printed materials to assist them in becoming strategic readers.

In connection with the use of the PLAN strategy in task-based learning in teaching reading comprehension, it is worth noting that it is important for teachers to make some preparations, for instance, in relation to the teaching scenario. The activity used is a type of task-based learning in which the goal is to manifest meaningful activities that fulfill the needs of the students' actual communication in reading comprehension. Students are required to read about what they need to interact and to communicate effectively. As suggested by Willis [38], the three stages of task-based learning are: (1) pre-task: to prepare for the implementation of a real task; (2) task-cycle: task – to assign the given task; plan – to prepare the result of the assignment; report – to report the task completion; (3) language focus: analysis – to evaluate the language rules; practice – to practice the grammatical form. The following are some examples of task-based activities to teach reading comprehension through the application of this PLAN strategy.

2.3.1 *Pre-task stage*

In this phase, the teacher explains the teaching and learning objectives. They present the discussion topic to be used in the classroom, for instance, recount text (personal diary). Then they divide the class into groups of four students, during which students are allowed to choose their own group. The first assignment for the groups is discussion of several questions related to the discussion topic [22], such as 'Have you ever told or written about your past experience? or 'Why do people tell of their past experience?'. The student groups are asked to discuss these questions to trigger their engagement in the learning activities, and to shape their interest in the particular topic as a warm-up step. This is supported by Ay and Bartan [5], that as the students' interest in the topic is sparked, it potentially contributes to their reading learning and achievement. Being responsive to a certain topic can cause students to show good performance. Furthermore, it would be harmful if their attention were distracted because it influences their self-confidence development. This indicates that the teacher should ensure that the students set their minds in order to be able to consolidate the specific topic. They may use Indonesian or English during the process of discussion according to the meaning in focus. At the end of the discussion, each group is asked with reporting their results in front of the class. To summarize, the role of the pre-task step is to assure the students' condition readiness to demonstrate their language ability communicatively.

2.3.2 *Task-cycle*

The next step of task-based learning is the task-cycle that consists of the task assignment, planning, and reporting, in which the implementation of the PLAN strategy is assimilated during the process because a specific strategy in task-oriented-reading assignments has previously been emphasized [24].

1. Task

This establishes the task to be carried out by the students and organizes them to work in small groups to fulfill the task goals; therefore, the teacher should be a facilitator in the classroom. It is categorized into two parts: listing (study of text information) and creating (summarizing). The following elaborates on these:

    1.1   Listing: Study of text information

            The teacher introduces the PLAN strategy and instructs the students to use it during the reading comprehension process. Here, the *Predict* step is applied by the groups.

After distributing a recount text entitled 'Holiday in Water Boom', for example, the teacher assigns the students to look at the title and to skim the text, guessing at the content and structure of the particular text. The aim is to get the gist in order to predict what may happen next, and to understand ideas as they are being experience, picturing the feasible content of the text through the creation of mental pictures in their minds or by designing a mind map, which is commonly made by circling to link lines inferring the relationships among the main topics, the general concept, and the specific one [34], using their own words based on what the passage says to visualize their prediction. They can be stimulated by questioning, for example, "Are you familiar with the Water Boom? What would you do if you were in the Water Boom?". This initiates a straightforward example of the relationship between prediction and idea visualization [9] that presents many opportunities to evolve their understanding of the text. When the students are able to guess what is likely to happen next, they will connect their prediction by reading continued to delineate a graphic organizer. This confirms the view of Radcliffe et al. [26,27], who state that the concept map usage can reveal the relationship between the textual information and the students' temporary understanding to illustrate their thinking and to visualize the connection of ideas effectively. As the students are drawing a mind map, they can incorporate new knowledge by organizing links to prior knowledge.

Nevertheless, this activity might be time-consuming [12] if the text is too long because the students should connect their previous knowledge in the process of text discussion. The teacher should make a careful selection of text appropriate to the students' level, which is critical in the reading comprehension process due to its contribution to successful text comprehension. In consequence, this leads to an increase in students' ability to manifest what they expect from the text. It can be deduced that connecting ideas is apparently advantageous in raising their engagement in determining a deeper meaning.

After that, the teacher guides the students to the next step in the strategy, namely *Locate*, in which they do not have to reread the passage as they have guessed at it in the previous activity. It is seemingly believed that they should have become sufficiently familiar with the text to discuss it. They need to place checkmarks next to known concepts and question marks next to unknown concepts. This is to transform the text strategically and efficiently through the application of their knowledge of text structure, and its manifestation is known as a schema [4], in which they are encouraged to put their knowledge of some parts in order, so as to be able to redeem the information in a more structured manner. As a result, it will remain in their long-term memory [16]. This helps them to connect the text in creating meaning. Next, in the *Add* stage of the strategy, the students include incorporate words, short phrases, or sentences into their map in order to acquire recent information that functions to record connections between their conceptual understanding and information, and in the text by marking links between their understanding of the concept and information in the text. They may discuss with their group members the difficult words identified in the text or, if they cannot find a word's meaning, they are allowed to ask the teacher to help them deliberate over such words; thus, the role of the teacher in this phase should be emphasized as a monitor. Then, they modify their mind mapping while reading, to stress those parts that should be addressed in order to ensure that they reveal the information needed to enlighten their confusion. From this, we can assume that this phase is used to annotate what students are reading during the process, in order to have a discussion and write corresponding text later.

1.2   Creating: Summarizing

This is to manifest an ultimate product that can be assessed by the class. It covers brainstorming and fact-finding. Now that the students have gained new understanding by considering the concepts and information in the text that they have identified and related to their own knowledge, summarizing is the final step of the PLAN strategy procedures. As a consequence, they complete a variety of tasks such as discussion and answering questions. This serves to confirm that they have been successful in their reading goals, from which eventually it can be inferred that they have become successful readers through the improvement of their skills in deriving meaning. They are able to gage their understanding through deep analysis of text, and at the end they can satisfy comprehension questions [11]. By utilizing new knowledge and associating what they have read with their own knowledge, they will be able to complete a task such as answering questions to ensure they fulfill their purposes in reading. In fewer words, the students advance their skills to solve the problems of comprehension as well as their abilities to conclude and to scrutinize.

2. Planning
   After accomplishing the tasks, the students should prepare to communicate the outcome, where they may take the chance to raise questions related to specific language items.
3. Reporting
   Throughout the task-cycle, emphasis is placed on the students' understanding and expression of the meanings of the text through presentation of their work findings, which is the summary of the text and the answers to the comprehension questions. As noted, other groups are allowed to make further comments and contrasts with their findings, because each group may have different answers from the others. It would be wise for the teacher to give comments and explanations to the class, yet this is not directly carried out during the reporting process. These activities appear to reinforce the claims of Burton [8], that the use of language in an authentic task underlines its communicative purpose and what students produce can be used to determine whether the learning objectives are successfully attained. Scrutinizing and making an outline based on the text they have read can lead to real-life language use as long as the teacher and students create a situation pedagogically, in which the final product of the students can be valued through their intensity of understanding and engagement with the text. Summarily, the participation of both teachers and students is involved in creating real-world activity.

2.3.3 *Language focus*

In task-based learning in reading comprehension, it is undeniable that language features and grammar cannot be disregarded; therefore, they should be taught in a contextual way. The teacher may start to give students assignments to analyze the rules of language, such as functional grammar, so that they can acquire basic ideas in relation to the utilization of language components. Because the students have been told that they will learn about recount text (personal diary), they are asked to highlight the language features of recount text that are simple past tenses, such as 'went', 'stayed', and 'decided'. The teacher, furthermore, may ask several questions related to the topic and allow the students to write any fruitful words, phrases, and patterns based on what the teacher has taught, while paying attention to other sentences in the text that have the same structure. Afterwards, for practice, the teacher provides several exercises for the students to accomplish; for instance, matching jumbled verbs in the simple past tense to the subject or object that they have found in the personal diary, or opening a dictionary to look up the meaning of particular words [29].

3 CONCLUSION

This paper is intended to discuss the use and the implementation steps of a PLAN strategy for EFL students in reading comprehension in task-based learning. The basic assumption of PLAN is that it is purposed as a tool to help students improve their reading comprehension by developing their prior knowledge, creating a mind map of a selected text, and proceeding through sequential phases to support active reading in order to accomplish reading tasks successfully. An opportunity is provided by the teacher to gain familiarity with the topic by reading the text, to guarantee the students' understanding through prediction and, by associating the textual content with that with which the students are already familiar, questioning in the reading process, and creating a summary. This approach can remove barriers to comprehension by preparing the students for reading, especially in organizing their reading and extending their comprehension. In spite of the favorable elements of the PLAN strategy, a specific issue might be detected in the strategy application in terms of the teachers' adequate preparation to try out the strategy in the classroom and to model it for the students. Yet, this study seeks to encourage researchers and teachers to create more conceptual papers with deeper exploration, particularly dealing with the implementation of the PLAN strategy to develop EFL students' reading comprehension.

REFERENCES

[1] Ahmadi, M.R. & Hairul, N.I. (2012). Reciprocal teaching as an important factor of improving reading comprehension. *Journal of Studies in Education, 2*(4), 153–173.

[2] Al Otaiba, S., Lake, V.E., Greulich, L., Folsom, J.S. & Guidry, L. (2012). Preparing beginning reading teachers: An experimental comparison of initial early literacy field experiences. *Reading and Writing, 25*(1), 109–219.

[3] Alessi, S. & Dwyer, A. (2008). Vocabulary assistance before and during reading. *Reading in a Foreign Language, 20*(2), 246–263.

[4] An, S. (2013). Schema theory in reading. *Theory and Practice in Language Studies, 3*(1), 130–134.

[5] Ay, S. & Bartan, O.S. (2012). The effect of topic interest and genre on reading test types in a second language. *The Reading Matrix, 12*(1), 62–79.

[6] Bolukbas, F. (2013). The effect of reading strategies on reading comprehension in teaching Turkish as a foreign language. *Educational Research and Reviews, 8*(21), 2147–2154.

[7] Brock, C.H. & Raphael, T.E. (2005). *Windows to language, literacy, and culture.* Newark, DE: International Reading Association.

[8] Burton, K. (2011). A framework for determining the authenticity of assessment tasks: Applied to an example in law. *Journal of Learning Design, 4*(2), 20–28.

[9] Campbell, E. & Cuba, M. (2015). Analyzing the role of visual cues in developing prediction-making skills of third- and ninth-grade English language learners. *The Catesol Journal, 27*(1), 53–93.

[10] Cassata, C. (2016). Strategies for struggling readers to increase reading comprehension in fourth graders. Education Masters. Paper 321. Retrieved from http://fisherpub.sjfc.edu/education_ETD_masters/321

[11] Chang, W. & Ku, Y. (2014). The effects of note-taking skills instruction on elementary students' reading. *The Journal of Educational Research, 108*(4), 278–291.

[12] Chiou, C. (2017). Analyzing the effects of various concept mapping techniques on learning achievement under different learning styles. *EURASIA Journal of Mathematics, Science and Technology Education, 13*(7), 3687–3708.

[13] Erdos, C., Genesee, F., Savage, R. & Haigh, C.A. (2010). Individual differences in second language reading outcomes. *International Journal of Bilingualism, 15*(1), 3–25.

[14] Falk-Ross, F. (2015). *Language-based approaches to support reading comprehension.* London, UK: Rowman & Littlefield.

[15] Gilakjani, A.P. & Ahmadi, M.R. (2011). A study of factors affecting EFL learners' English listening comprehension and the strategies for improvement. *Journal of Language Teaching and Research, 2*(5), 977–988.

[16] Gobet, F., Lane, P.C. & Lloyd-Kelly, M. (2015). Chunks, schemata, and retrieval structures: Past and current computational models. *Frontiers in Psychology, 6*,1–4.

[17] Grabe, W. & Stoller, F.L. (2001). Reading for academic purposes: Guidelines for the ESL/EFL teacher. In M. Celce-Murcia (Ed.), *Teaching English as a Second or Foreign Language* (pp. 187–203). Boston, MA: Heinle & Heinle.

[18] Jozwik, S.L. (2015). *Effects of explicit reading comprehension strategy instruction for English learners with specific learning disabilities* (Doctoral dissertation, Illinois State University, Normal, IL). ISU ReD: Research and eData, 415.

[19] Kintsch, W. (1998). *Comprehension: A paradigm for cognition.* New York, NY: Cambridge University Press.

[20] Klapper, J. (2003). Taking communication to task? A critical review of recent trends in language teaching. *Language Learning Journal, 27*(1), 33–42.

[21] Küçükoğlu, H. (2013). Improving reading skills through effective reading strategies. *Procedia - Social and Behavioral Sciences*, *70*, 709–714.

[22] Madya, S. (2013). Language teaching methodology: From the pre-method era to the post-method era. Yogyalarta, Indonesia: UNY Press.

[23] Nunan, D. (1989). *Designing tasks for the communicative classroom*. Cambridge, UK: Cambridge University Press.

[24] Ozuru, Y., Best, R., Bell, C., Witherspoon, A. & McNamara, D.S. (2007). Influence of question format and text availability on the assessment of expository text comprehension. *Cognition and Instruction*, *25*(4), 399–438.

[25] Phantharakphong, P. & Pothitha, S. (2014). Development of English reading comprehension by using concept maps. *Procedia - Social and Behavioral Sciences*, *116*, 497–501.

[26] Radcliffe, R., Caverly, D., Hand, J. & Franke, D. (2008). Improving reading in a middle school science classroom. *International Reading Association*, *51*(5), 398–408.

[27] Radcliffe, R., Caverly, D., Peterson, C. & Emmons, M. (2004). Improving textbook reading in a middle school science classroom. *Reading Improvement*, *41*(3), 145–156.

[28] Richards, J.C. (2006). *Communicative language teaching today*. Cambridge, UK: Cambridge University Press.

[29] Richards, J.C. & Schmidt, R.W. (2013). *Longman dictionary of language teaching and applied linguistics*. Abingdon, UK: Routledge.

[30] Samuda, V. &Bygate, M. (2008). *Tasks in second language learning*. Basingstoke, UK: Palgrave Macmillan.

[31] Snow, C.E. (2010). Reading comprehension: Reading for learning. *International Encyclopedia of Education*, *5*, 413–418.

[32] Stavonich, K. (2008). Matthew effects in reading: Some consequences of individual differences in the acquisition of literacy. *Journal of Education*, *189*(1–2), 23–55.

[33] Sternberg, R.J. (1987). Most vocabulary is learned from context. In M.G. McKeown & M.E. Curtis (Eds.), *Thenature of vocabulary acquisition* (pp. 89–106). Hillsdale, NJ: Erlbaum.

[34] Tajeddin, Z. & Tabatabaei, S. (2016). Concept mapping as a reading strategy: Does it scaffold comprehension and recall? *The Reading Matrix: An International Online Journal*, *16*(1), 194–208.

[35] Van den Branden, K. (2016). The role of teachers in task-based language education. *Annual Review of Applied Linguistics*, *36*, 164–181.

[36] Wigfield, A., Gladstone, J. & Turci, L. (2016). Beyond cognition: Reading motivation and reading comprehension. *Child Development Perspectives*, *10*(3), 190–195.

[37] Wigfield, A., Guthrie, J., Tonks, S. & Perencevich, K. (2004). Children's motivation for reading: Domain specificity and instructional influences. *The Journal of Educational Research*, *97*(6), 299–309.

[38] Willis, J. (1996). *A framework for task-based learning*. Harlow, UK: Longman.

English Linguistics, Literature, and Language Teaching in a Changing Era – Madya et al. (eds)
© 2020 Taylor & Francis Group, London, ISBN 978-1-03-224160-9

Professional development challenges for Indonesian English teachers

Astri O. Kuncahya & Basikin
English Education Study Program, Graduate School, Yogyakarta State University, Yogyakarta, Indonesia

ABSTRACT: Numerous studies on Teacher Professional Development (TPD) have indicated features of effective TPD programs. This attempt, however, has undermined the divergent contexts in which teachers are engaged and contributed to the drawbacks of existing TPD programs, especially in Indonesia. To this extent, there was a need for a study which identified the challenges of TPD programs faced by Indonesian English teachers. This library study was conducted by critically reviewing several related studies in the Indonesian context. Findings show that there are four main challenges, namely extrinsic motivation, lack of institutional supports, the gap between the teachers' needs and the program, as well as the lack of a sense of autonomy. These findings suggest that the challenges come from both internal and external aspects, and have an important implication for the policymaking in Indonesia.

Keywords: challenges, English teachers, teacher professional development

1 INTRODUCTION

In the last few decades, there has been a surge of interest in Teacher Professional Development (TPD) in the world of English Language Teaching (ELT). The topic started to gain its popularity as a result of an increasingly perceived importance in teachers and the teaching profession. Many studies have highlighted the contributions of TPD in terms of improving the teachers' competence, enhancing the students' learning processes and outcomes, reaching the schools' targets, and extending the current educational goals and changes.

Regarding the notion of TPD, many studies have offered vast and rigorous definitions. TPD is generally regarded as any learning opportunities for teachers to improve their practices and aid the students' development [4]. It can be either initiated by teachers themselves or requested by outside parties such as schools, local authorities, or even the national government. It can be in the form of formal activities such as attending a course, joining workshops and seminars, collaborating with colleagues, as well as informal ones such as surfing the net, reading journal articles, and watching documentaries related to teaching practices [15,16,20]. Therefore, it can be concluded that TPD is formal and informal activities done by teachers to enhance their teaching practices and facilitate their students' growth.

TPD benefits teachers in three distinct dimensions, namely personal, professional and moral dimensions. First, in terms of the personal dimension, TPD can improve the teachers' English proficiency, fulfill the teachers' personal interests and maintain their passions in ELT [20]. Looking at the professional dimension, it helps teachers to function successfully [1] by understanding the effective teaching of their subject matter [8], meeting the changes in the students' needs [1,14], catching up with the changes in ELT [1,20], and expanding their roles and careers [20]. In a similar vein, previous studies explained how TPD can improve professionalism by saying that it stipulates teachers with declarative knowledge (knowledge of English) and procedural knowledge (skills to perform teaching tasks) [12]. In regard to the moral dimension, teachers need TPD to be the best professionals that they can be, to nurture successful and thoughtful learners, and to shape future generations [1]. Finally, TPD benefits teachers in satisfying the teachers' personal thirsts, enhancing their professionalism and instilling moral value.

As for the students, the implementation of TPD may result in better learning achievements. As teachers' knowledge begins to improve, the teachers will be able to reflect on their classroom practices. Then, they transform their knowledge and reflection to improve their instruction and better meet the students' learning preferences. They will be able to differentiate instruction for all students [14], and as a result, can lead to an improvement in the students' learning achievements [16,21]. Thus, by improving the teachers' knowledge and practices, TPD can lead to the students' learning improvement.

Furthermore, research has shown that with TPD, not only teachers can strengthen their competence throughout their career [16], but also students can be competent and skilled [15]. At the same time, schools can reach and maintain a standard of high-quality teaching and excellent staff [15]. Thus, TPD enables schools to meet their expectations of the quality of the teaching, teachers and students. Finally, it can warrant the quality of education [21], and extend any educational changes to the grass-roots level. Finally, by implementing TPD, it will contribute to all educational stakeholders.

Being aware of its importance, many countries invest in TPD programs, one of which is Indonesia. The government of the Republic of Indonesia has regarded teacher professionalism as a prominent discussion. Therefore, it triggered the issuance of The Teachers and Lecturers Act Number 14 Year 2005 [18] that "explains the systems of teacher education, teacher recruitment and teacher career development which requires teachers to continuously develop their professionalism in relation to their teaching profession" [12]. As a result, the government has facilitated many TPD programs conducted locally and nationally, using face-to-face and online modes through the Subject Teacher Forum (MGMP) and other parties.

However, the result of the Teachers' Competence Test (UKG) in 2015 indicated that of all the teachers from 34 provinces, only those from ten provinces scored above the average score (53.05), namely teachers from Yogyakarta (62.58), Central Java (58.93), Jakarta (58.36), East Java (56.71), Bali (55.92), West Java (55.15), Bangka Belitung (55.10), West Sumatra (54.77), Riau Island (54.72), and South Kalimantan (53.14) [22]. Thus, teachers from 24 provinces score below average. The results of the test showed that: (1) most teachers in Indonesia have not met the demand of the government to possess sufficient pedagogic and professional competence, as tested in the teacher competence test; (2) the effectiveness of existing TPD programs in Indonesia is now in question.

Indeed, being English teachers in Indonesia is very challenging. As teaching has been regarded as a profession [20], it requires a special knowledge base of English and English language teaching, derived from specialized teacher education. In fact, the position of English as a foreign language in Indonesia drives teachers to always improve their proficiency after they graduate from teacher education [13]. Furthermore, they have to master four competences demanded by the government [18]. These four competences are pedagogic, professional, personal, and social competence [19].

Many publications on TPD only focus on the general features of the effective program, in isolation from the different contexts of the teachers and the teaching environment. For example, the literature-based study conducted previously has offered specific principles in designing effective professional development for teachers of English Language Learners (ELLs) [14]. Previous study revealed a number of steps in planning teacher professional development, one of which is by determining the needs of both the educational institutions and the teachers [20]. Most of them view TPD as "a process-product relation focusing more on recommending elements or components of effective programs, rather than on the mechanism of how such programs develop or improve the quality of teachers" [5]. Such publications disregard the teachers' personal perceptions, needs and challenges of certain types of TPD activities, so that the school and government stakeholders, and the policymakers, are unable to use them as the basis of evaluation to examine why certain types of TPD activities are not suitable for particular groups of teachers.

Therefore, it is crucial to investigate the challenges faced by English teachers when they undertake TPD programs. The ultimate aims are to identify the challenges, explain the causes, and finally to give a clear picture of TPD in Indonesia in general. It is expected that this study might enable program developers, school stakeholders, and policymakers to consider these challenges when designing and deciding future TPD programs.

This literature-based research was done in several steps. The first step was in reviewing the relevant studies about the challenges of TPD in Indonesia. There were at least five relevant studies that were chosen based on several categories, namely the topic, participants and setting. The topic and setting of relevant studies should be about the implementation of TPD in Indonesia and the participants of the studies should be English teachers or instructors at any Indonesian secondary school or university levels in which English is formally taught. The next step was in discussing the identified challenges with the existing literature and previous research done in other countries with similar contexts, followed by concluding and drawing up some implications of the study. The final steps were setting the limit and giving recommendations for the further research.

2 CHALLENGES OF TPD FACED BY INDONESIAN ENGLISH TEACHERS

From the review of the literature, it was found that there were at least four challenges faced by English teachers in Indonesia. The four main challenges include extrinsic motivation, a lack of institutional supports, the gap between the teachers' needs and the program, and a lack of a sense of autonomy. These are explained as follows.

2.1 *Motivation*

Although it is not the only determiner of the success of learning, researchers have acknowledged the importance of motivation in language learning [7]. It stipulates a drive or an effort to achieve a goal. There are at least two types of motivation, namely intrinsic and extrinsic motivation. Intrinsic motivation refers to the inner drive within individuals to engage in activities to gain "internally rewarding consequences, namely feelings of competence and self-determination". Meanwhile, extrinsic motivation can be defined as the effort of individuals to gain "reward from outside and beyond the self, for example money, grades, and positive feedback". A stockpile of research has indicated that intrinsic motivation is more powerful than extrinsic motivation. The reason is because the nature of intrinsic motivation reflects self-actualization and long-term retention, while the use of extrinsic motivation is likely to be addictive and dependent in nature.

In relation to the TPD program, one of the studies about the motivation to join the TPD program was conducted and it investigated the motivation to attend the training of genre-based English teaching by employing a survey study [6]. The participants were 202 English teachers at the level of junior secondary schools in Yogyakarta province. The data were collected using questionnaires and analyzed using descriptive statistics and MANOVA. The result showed that motivation in following the TPD program was mostly external. Participants confessed that the motivation to join the training included invitation from the local or national government and the assignment from the school or school principal. This motivation likely resulted from cultural orientation and the religion of the teachers. In relation to cultural orientation, participants had a high sense of interdependence with each other, so that they put aside their personal interests and gave priority to the group goals when joining TPD programs. Meanwhile, with regard to religion, it was claimed that participants happily received the assignment from their principal because they seemed to follow the rule of their religion, which mentioned that "obeying their leaders is almost a good deed, or *ibadah*".

The aforementioned study indicated that the English teachers' extrinsic motivation was stronger than their intrinsic motivation when attending TPD programs. This was not favorable for several reasons. First, extrinsic motivation was not a good predictor of successful TPD programs and it was intrinsic motivation which contributes to desirable learning outcomes [5]. In addition, as previously mentioned, the nature of extrinsic motivation was addictive and English teachers would depend much on it. Once they could not get these outside rewards, they would not be motivated to join the program. The result of the study also clearly explained the cause of low participations of English teachers in following TPD.

2.2 Institutional supports

There are two types of professionalism, namely individual and institutional professionalism [20]. Individual professionalism refers to the teachers' views and reflections related to their beliefs and practices. Meanwhile, institutional professionalism refers to "a managerial approach to professionalism" which intends to familiarize teachers with the required knowledge and standard of quality teaching practices, based on the regulation derived from ministries of education up to school principals. The goals of institutional professionalism are to improve the school performance, to facilitate the teachers' career development, and to achieve the students' desired learning outcomes. Therefore, institutions will always attempt to update the teachers' knowledge and skills that fit the schools' needs. One of the efforts is by conducting TPD in their environments or giving support for the teachers to follow TPD programs.

However, two previous studies [11,21] showed surprising results. Through a case study, the first study examined English teachers' attitudes toward Massive Open Online Courses (MOOCs), which provided TPD programs [21]. There were 24 informants and data were collected through questionnaire at the end of the program. The results revealed that the participants perceived the platform as a "well-organized and effective" means to improve their teaching skills. However, they lamented that their institutions did not provide follow-up activities for their previous TPD activities. Clearly, the absence of institutional and collegial supports had created a hindrance for English teachers in enhancing their teaching skills.

In a similar vein, the other case study [11] revealed the same results. It investigated the perceptions and experiences of Indonesian English-as-a-Foreign Language (EFL) university teachers in relation to TPD programs. There were six participants selected from purposive sampling and data were collected through interviews. One of the results of the study showed that there were at least five perceived barriers for TPD programs, namely lack of institutional supports, absence of PD programs, heavy teaching load, time management, and lack of information. In relation to the first barrier, participants stated that their institution's awareness of the TPD program was still low, so that it did not provide such TPD programs inside their environment. In addition, participants also addressed the issue of financial supports from the institution whenever they wanted to participate in TPD programs, which required some money.

Both aforementioned studies [11,21] mentioned that the absence of institutional supports leads to a hindrance for English teachers in joining or even following up TPD activities. Such absence of support could be in the form of program and financial support. It left teachers unable to upgrade their knowledge and skills, or to enhance their career development. If there was no improvement in such conditions, it might possibly result in the deterioration of the students' learning achievement and lead to a decline in the institutions' performance.

2.3 Teachers' needs

There has been a consensus that one of the features of a high-quality TPD program is that it should consider and meet the teachers' professional needs [2]. The term 'needs' represents the gap between what the participants of a program can do and should do to achieve the desired goals. Furthermore, 'needs' can be divided into learning needs and target needs [17]. Learning needs can be regarded as what individuals have to do in order to be able to learn. Target needs refer to what individuals need to do in a target situation, and they comprise of necessities (required knowledge), lacks (present knowledge), and wants (individual expectation).

However, 'needs' is regarded as multifaceted and changeable [10]. It means that before implementing a program, program developers should analyze the participants' needs using needs assessment instruments and use the result as the basis for developing the program. Also, needs assessment is useful to make participants of a program aware of their needs [10] and to warrant the content of the program to be relevant and useful for the participants. In relation to TPD programs, researchers have agreed that identifying the teachers' needs should be the first step in designing or planning professional development programs [20]. This is supported by relevant research [9], which states:

> *Effective programs can be achieved as long as the programs are based on teachers' needs. In other words, an effective professional development is possible when it responds to teachers personal needs. Therefore, before planning a professional development program, it is necessary to collect information about teachers' needs.*

However, in reality, a qualitative study [3] about the high-school teachers' voices in professional development revealed a contradictory result. The study intended to examine personal and collective voices of senior high-school English teachers in relation to TPD programs. Data were collected through interviews, observation and analysis of written statements and related documents. One of the results of collective voices in TPD programs was that there was a gap between the teachers' professional needs and the existing program. The study mentioned that the TPD programs contained repeated and irrelevant training and workshops, which resulted in teachers being bored. The reasons were because of the lack of communication with the party who conducted the TPD programs, and a reduction of the teachers' supervisions to merely administrative aspects

The decisions about what should be included and how it should be implemented should be based on the teachers' needs. The main reason was because the teachers become the central focus of the TPD programs and to improve their competence was the immediate goal of the TPD programs. If this requirement was not fulfilled, the program could be considered as being ineffective.

2.4 *Intention*

Another important discussion that entails TPD programs is whether teachers embrace the result of the TPD programs in which they were previously engaged. The word 'embrace' refers to the implementation of new knowledge and skills about curricula and teaching practices. One of the ways to predict such behavior is by investigating the teachers' intentions. There are two theories that can be used to predict behavioral intention, namely the Theory of Reasoned Action (TRA) and the Theory of Planned Behavior (TPB). TRA is useful to predict autonomous behavior and their predictors. Meanwhile, TPB can be applied if such restrictions on the teachers' sense of autonomy is detected. In the context of Indonesia, where TPD programs are mostly initiated by schools and government, TPB will be more suitable for use [5].

A relevant survey study has examined factors predicting the teachers' intention to embrace the result of TPD programs in relation to the introduction of genre-based teaching in Indonesia [5]. Participants of this study were 202 English teachers in the junior secondary school level in Yogyakarta province of Indonesia. Data were collected using a questionnaire called Intention to Implement the Genre-based English Teaching Scale (IIGETS), developed by the researcher, and were analyzed using structural equation modeling using SPSS Amos 20 software. The result showed that the teachers' intention of implementing genre-based teaching was influenced by facilitating factors and social pressures, rather than by attitudes.

From the aforementioned study, it could be concluded that English teachers did not consider their attitude toward certain teaching techniques when implementing the result of TPD. They had a lack of a sense of autonomy and tended to follow what was said to be important by the majority of people. This could cause a hindrance because the teaching context between one teacher and another might be different, in terms of such things as their goals, the students' needs, and the teaching environment. Therefore, it led to different treatments that teachers needed to implement into their practices. Teachers were the ones who knew what was best for themselves and their surroundings. Without a sense of autonomy, the decisions taken by teachers would eventually be misleading and fail to achieve the desired goals.

3 CONCLUSIONS AND IMPLICATIONS

There were at least four main challenges of the TPD programs for English teachers in Indonesia, namely extrinsic motivation, a lack of institutional supports, the gap between the teachers' needs and the program, and a lack of a sense of autonomy. It was implied that the future TPD programs should: (1) be initiated with the needs assessment in order to make sure that the programs were relevant and useful for teachers; (2) give opportunities for teachers to initiate and choose the TPD programs they needed, either at the institutional or personal level, so that it would increase the teachers' intrinsic motivation and sense of autonomy; (3) be supported by institutions where teachers worked in terms of financial supports or even follow-up activities, so that the teachers could have continuous TPD programs.

4 LIMITATIONS AND RECOMMENDATIONS

There were some limitations of this study. First, the nature of this research was a literature-based study in which the results had not been extensively and comprehensively proven with a longitudinal study. Also, the scope was limited to English teachers at the secondary school and university levels. Most importantly, the discussion was excluded from Continuous Professional Development (CPD) programs that were currently conducted by the government of the Republic of Indonesia.

Therefore, the researcher proposes three major recommendations. First, it is important to conduct a longitudinal study to prove the results. Also, it is suggested that the further research can expand the scope of discussions into all levels of education, if necessary. Last but not least, other researchers could investigate the same topic in relation to the implementation of CPD in Indonesia.

REFERENCES

[1] Alfaki, I.M. (2014). Professional development in English language teaching: A teachers' view. *British Journal of Education*, 2(7), 32–49.

[2] Al-Qahtani, H.M. (2015). Teachers' voice: A need analysis of teachers' needs for professional development with the emergence of the current English textbooks. *English Language Teaching*, 8(8), 128–141. doi:10.5539/elt.v6n8p128.

[3] Ashadi, A. (2010). School teachers' voice in professional development. In *Selected papers in ELT*. Jakarta, Indonesia: IIEF & RELO US Embassy.

[4] Avalos, B. (2011). Teacher professional development in teaching and teacher education over ten years. *Teaching and Teacher Education*, 27, 10–20. doi:10.1016/j.tate.2010.08.007.

[5] Basikin, B. (2015). I didn't like it… but I had no choice. In *International Conference of Education, Research and Innovation* (pp. 1–8). Retrieved from https://www.researchgate.net/publication/314299340_I_didn%27t_like_it_but_I_had_no_choice.

[6] Brown, H.D. (2001). *Teaching by principles: An interactive approach to language pedagogy* (2nd ed.). New York, NY: Longman.

[7] Basikin, B. (2016). *English teacher motivation and intention regarding their professional development program* (Dissertation). Retrieved from https://www.researchgate.net/publication/320761968_English_Teacher_Motivation_and_Intention_Regarding_Their_Professional_Development_Program.

[8] Carlisle, J.F. & Berebitsky, D. (2011). Literacy coaching as a component of professional development. *Read Write*, 24(7), 773–800. doi:10.1007/s11145-009-9224-4.

[9] Eksi, G. & Aydin, Y.C. (2012). English instructors' professional development need areas and predictors of professional development needs. *Procedia - Social and Behavioral Sciences*, 70, 675–685.

[10] Graves, K. (2000). *Designing language courses: A guide for teachers.* Canada: Heinle & Heinle.

[11] Hartono, R. (2016). *Indonesian EFL teachers' perceptions and experiences of professional development* (Master's thesis). Retrieved from http://knowledge.library.iup.edu/etd/1346

[12] Irmawati, D.K., Widiati, U. & Cahyono, B.Y. (2017). How do Indonesian professional English teachers develop their pedagogical competence in teaching implementation? *Arab World English Journal, 8*(2), 293–307. doi:10.24093/awej/vol8no2.21.

[13] König, J., Lammerding, S., Nold, G., Rohde, A., Strauß, S. & Tachtsoglou, S. (2016). Teachers' professional knowledge for teaching English as a foreign language: Assessing the outcomes of teacher education. *Journal of Teacher Education, 67*(4), 1–18. doi:10.1177/0022487116644956.

[14] Li, G. & Protacio, M.S. (2010). Best practices in professional development for teachers of ELLs. In G. Li & P.A. Edwards (Eds.), *Best practices in ELL instruction* (pp. 353–380). New York, NY: The Guilford Press.

[15] Mahmoudi, F. & Özkan, Y. (2015). Exploring experienced and novice teachers' perceptions about professional development activities. *Procedia - Social and Behavioral Sciences, 199*, 57–64. doi:10.1016/j.sbspro.2015.07.487.

[16] Mizell, H. (2010). *Why professional development matters.* Oxford, UK: Learning Forward.

[17] Nation, I.S.P. & Macalister, J. (2010). *Language curriculum design.* New York, NY: Routledge.

[18] The Republic of Indonesia. (2005). *Act Number 14 Year 2005 concerning Teachers and Lecturers.*

[19] The Republic of Indonesia. (2008). *Government Regulation Number 74 Year 2008 concerning Teachers.*

[20] Richards, J.C. (2015). *Key issues in language teaching.* Cambridge, UK: Cambridge University Press.

[21] Silvia, A. (2015). Coursera online course: A platform for English teachers' meaningful and vibrant professional development. *TEFLIN Journal, 26*(2), 228–246. doi:10.15639/teflinjournal.v26i2/228-246

[22] Ministry of National Education. (2015). *Hasil UKG tahun 2015.* Retrieved from www.kemdiknas.go.id/

English Linguistics, Literature, and Language Teaching in a Changing Era – Madya et al. (eds)
© 2020 Taylor & Francis Group, London, ISBN 978-1-03-224160-9

Automatic speech recognition to enhance EFL students' pronunciation through Google's Voice Search Application

Cherlie E. Rayshata & Dyah S. Ciptaningrum
English Education Study Program, Graduate School, Yogyakarta State University, Yogyakarta, Indonesia

ABSTRACT: Because the need for successful interaction in communication influences one's understanding, it urges speakers to at least have good pronunciation in order to avoid misunderstandings between speakers and listeners. Therefore, this research aims to discuss the utilization of automatic speech recognition to enhance Indonesian EFL students' pronunciation skill through Google's Voice Search Application (GVSA). The method for this research was Classroom Action Research (CAR). The participants of this research were five undergraduate female students who are studied from Non- English major. The data were collected using an observation checklist and test items. The data in this research is analyzed using percentages analysis. The result of this research showed that the students were able to enhance their pronunciation skills especially in the plosives consonant /t/, fricative consonant /s/, nasals consonant /m/, and approximant consonants /w/ and /l/, pure vowel /e/,/i/, and /æ/, and diphthong vowel/ej/ by using GVSA. Henceforth, it means that the importance of having a good pronunciation as show previously is one of the important aspects that must be pressed for Indonesian EFL students.

Keywords: Automatic Speech Recognition, Indonesian EFL students, teaching pronunciation, Google's Voice Search Application

1 INTRODUCTION

Successful communication is the aim of foreign language learning. In order to have successful communication, students should have good pronunciation skills. Without good pronunciation skills, communication in a foreign language will not run smoothly. In a conversation, incorrect use of vocabulary and grammar may not result in serious problems in communication. However, when students pronounce words or phrases incorrectly, they can create misunderstanding since the listener may not recognize the utterances very well making it difficult to get the meaning [1]. Therefore, students are expected to have good pronunciation since it is essential in communication.

In the English Foreign Language (EFL) context, pronunciation training requires more investment of time for EFL students to practice. However, EFL students have limited time to practice pronunciation in the classroom. Some foreign language teachers find that they do not have time to give proper attention to teaching pronunciation [2]. Some others teach English without considering pronunciation skills as well [3]. Indonesian language has different sounds and word stress patterns from English. For instance, for the word *laugh,* Indonesian students most probably pronounce it letter by letter, however, the correct pronunciation is /la:f/.

Thus, in addressing those problems, there should be some techniques and media that can be used to teach pronunciation to students. Some of the techniques to enhance students' pronunciation can be applied through singing, chanting, and pronouncing audio journals. Recently, some researchers have begun to use technology to teach pronunciation by using Automatic Speech Recognition (ASR). Some of these are PLASER (Pronunciation learning via automatic

115

speech recognition) and FluSpeak. PLASER and FluSpeak are not free, which make them unaffordable for Indonesian students. Hence, the researcher will discuss an application that can be downloaded freely to smartphones and computer, namely Google's Voice Search Application (GVSA). GVSA can be used by both EFL teachers and students in the classroom. In addition, by using this application, the user does not need to have native-like pronunciation since it tends to recognize sounds based on intelligibility. This paper then aims to discuss the utilization of automatic speech recognition to improve Indonesian EFL students' pronunciation through GVSA. Further, this research focused on finding a segmental feature or the sounds level in pronunciation teaching using GVSA since it cannot support other aspects like the supra-segmental level which focus on the intonation of sentence.

2 LITERATURE REVIEW

2.1 *Pronunciation*

Pronunciation is identified largely with the articulation of individual sounds and, to a lesser extent, with the stress and intonation patterns of the target language [4]. It means that pronunciation is a sound production which comes out together with articulation, intonation, and stress. According to the Oxford Advanced Learner's Dictionary, pronunciation is the way a language is spoken. This means that the knowledge of people in pronouncing some words represents the utilization of the language that they will use to communicate with others. Furthermore, another thing which has to be considered in pronunciation is that every single person has a different pronunciation style. However, as long as it is understood when it is received by the listener, it is called 'good conversation' [1].

On the whole, pronunciation is something that crucial to be learned especially by Indonesian EFL students. Although some experts believe that perfect native pronunciation in a second language is impossible for adults past puberty to attain [5], it does not mean that it is not important to teach. In the classroom, the teacher can still take students to higher level in teaching pronunciation since it becomes the most challenging skill to teach and it influences the way of how students speak in the classroom [6]. Therefore, the instruction while teaching pronunciation should be balanced with the instruction while teaching the other language skills (reading, writing, listening, and speaking) skills [7].

2.2 *Phonology*

There are many definitions of phonology in linguistic terms. Phonology is a study of how sounds can be distinctive in language, the pattern formed and the rules and regulations in terms of their use [8]. Furthermore, phonology can be defined as the range of sounds and their functions which are concerned with a particular language and the written principles to demonstrate the phonetic relation types which contrast and relate to the words and other linguistic units [9]. In short, phonology is the branch of linguistics that studies the way sounds occur in a particular language. In addition, phonology is concerned with existence of sounds, which is called the phonological environment. The phonological environment can determine the quality of phonemic of a sound in a given language.

2.3 *Segmental features*

A segmental features refers to a sound that can be analyzed without being connected to other features. It comprises of consonants and vowels [10].

2.3.1 *Consonants*
Consonants are related to the sounds and the place of articulation. According to Daniel et al. (as cited in Habibi, 2016), phonologically the consonant is the focus in terms of articulation [11]. Table 1 shows the list of consonants in English.

Table 1. Consonants [12].

	Bilabial	Labio-dental	Dental	Alveolar	Post-alveolar	Palatal	Velar	Glottal
Plosives	p b			t d			k g	
Fricatives		f v	θ ð	s z	ʃ ʒ			h
Affricates					ʧ ʤ			
Nasals	m			n			ŋ	
Lateral				l				
Approximants	w				R	j		

2.3.2 *Vowels*

Vowels are defined as the production of sounds without stricture in the vocal tract and they are called the original sounds by any friction noise unaccompanied [1]. Moreover, vowels consist of two components which are pure vowels and diphthongs. A diphthong is a special kind of vowel. Its sound begins by sounding the first letter then the movement is directed by the second letter. The list of vowels is presented in Table 2.

2.4 *Techniques for supporting pronunciation teaching*

At first, pronunciation teaching was neglected by many teachers, but in the 1950s and 1960s recognition in the importance of pronunciation began. In the 1960s, teachers used repetition and recitation to teach pronunciation. Unfortunately, in the 1970s and 1980s, pronunciation was considered an unnecessary element in language learning [3]. Additionally, it was considered that students would acquire pronunciation on their own through the input they received. Teachers taught grammar, vocabulary, culture, speaking, listening, reading, and writing but not pronunciation [3].

There are three important aspects of teaching pronunciation, namely perception, production, and prediction [14]. Perception of oral languages involves hearing, listening, seeing, and feeling. These aspects are related to the parts of speech which are necessary for pronunciation: lips, tongue, throat, vocal cords, sinuses, and facial muscles. Production of oral languages requires time to listen, process, form an answer, parts of language knowledge and activation of background knowledge. Prediction of oral communication needs to come through experiencing contexts differently. With the strategies of teaching prediction, EFL students swiftly progress to become autonomous students. Furthermore, there are some ways of teaching pronunciation such as elicited mechanical production, ear training for sound contrast, and sound for meaning contrast [15]. Thornbury [16] highlights that intelligibility is crucial in English pronunciation. He mentions some techniques of teaching pronunciation such as arranging cards of rhyming words, telling the story and lastly presenting speaking exercises.

Table 2. Vowels [13].

Original Vowels		Diphthongs
/i/ pin, English, business	/ɑ:/ car, art, heart, half	/ej/ take, pay, wait, ballet
/e/ bed, head, bury, exit	/ɔ:/ or, board, door, small	/aj/ five, sigh, height, buy
/æ/ cat, bag, apple, black	/i:/ sea, bee, people, receive	/ɔj/ noise, boy, lawyer
/ə/ the, a, woman, banana	/u:/ too, blue, fruit, fool	/aw/ no, road, sew, broken
/ʊ/ look, put, could, cushion		/a ʊ/ round, renown, doubt
/ɑ/ clock, what, because		/i ə/ here, deer, dear, fierce
/ʌ/ cut, come, mother		/eə/ care, air, mayor, prayer
/ɜ:/ girl, burn, word, heard		/ʊə/ poor, insure, tour, moor

Moreover, there are some ways to teach pronunciation, according to Moonasar [17], which focus on sounds, rhythm and stress, and the flow of speech.The sound are the technique which stresses on phonemes and phonics, it is comparing one sound to others. The activities include finding the different pronunciations of words, provide a pictures with the available words for students to read and presenting on it. Rhythm and stress focus more on the intonation of a sentence. It can be used in various ways. One technique to teach rhythm and stress is using song, the teacher will put the words randomly in the song to a new chant. Then, the students are asked to form a new chant to sing. Thus, it directly will help the students' learning pronunciation especially focus on the flow of speech stresses articulation.

Based on the explanation above, pronunciation should be given more attention, especially in Indonesian EFL classrooms. There must be methods, techniques, and teaching–learning aids to support students to learn and to teach pronunciation. Consistent repetition will enhance the student's pronunciation performance. However, those techniques make students rely on the teacher. They have to be taught and drilled accompanied by the teacher.

2.5 *Automatic Speech Recognition (ASR)*

In the learning process, ASR can be used as a supported technology that is able to recognize words which is spoken loudly by speakers [18]. Moreover, the system can provide feedback at sentence, word, or the text level which is spoken by speakers [3]. This feedback makes students aware of their mistakes which might also prevent them from producing further incorrect pronunciation. Furthermore, ASR enables students to practice pronunciation learning independently focused on words. It is very different from pronunciation teaching in the classroom. In the classroom context, some teachers teach English pronunciation regularly through printed pronunciation material using the phonetic alphabet and activities such as minimal pair drills, reading passages or dialogues, listening to a cassette, and imitating. Moreover, students would be very dependent on the teacher to learn each sound [19].

In addition, speech recognition provides an optimal solution to pronunciation learning [20]. Furthermore, it also helps students who are not confident at speaking in public. ASR lets students create possible "conversation" with the computer in a spoken dialogue system, which is useful, although the conversations can only be carried out within limited domains [21].

2.6 *Google Voice Search Application (GVSA)*

There are many available computer programs for supporting pronunciation learning in Computer-Aided Language Learning (CALL), such as the LISTEN project in 1994 by Mostow et al., Tell Me More Performance English [3], PLASER [22], FLUSpeak and the like. In this research, the researcher found that GVSA technology in which sounds can be recognized and simple feedback can be automatically given about the pronunciation. It can be used as a media to develop class activity.

Furthermore, GVSA tends to recognize sounds based on intelligibility, meaning that it does not require the speaker to have native-like pronunciation. In articulation, Google also recognizes the stress of the sounds. Thus, if the articulation and stress are intelligible for Google, Google will type the words correctly. If the pronunciation is not recognized, it types other words.

These are the steps for using Google's Voice Search:

1) Open the Google Search application in a smartphone;
2) Say "Ok Google" to it or touch the recorder symbol on the right side;
3) The app will direct users to the "listening" stage while they are speak;
4) Say the words users want to type;
5) Then, it will recognize the sound and type the words what users say;
6) Finally, after the words is typed, users are on the page

In addition, students can practice independently themselves outside and inside of the classroom. They only need to open the application on smartphones or computer and then speak to it. Moreover, the Google Voice Search application is usually installed in students' smartphones directly.

2.7 *Google Voice Search Application for Users*

While using GVSA, students not only get learning opportunities to learn pronunciation but also get corrective feedback. It can be used to support students to accomplish their learning goals. Moreover, the importance of feedback in language learning is discussed by Wang and Young [23]. There are two kind of GVSA feedback namely explicit feedback and implicit feedback. The explicit feedback affects the students' improvement of their error awareness. While, in implicit feedback, the feedback in Google's voice search is formed by the typed text appearing just after the users speak. In this way, the users will know their faults instantly after they speak.

3 RESEARCH METHOD

This research was designed using Classroom Action Research (CAR) in two cycles with four stages, namely plan, action, observation, and reflection. The participants of this research were five undergraduate female students with anon-English major, namely an economic major, a communication science major, and a mechanical engineering major. Their average age was 19 to 21 years old.

In collecting the data, the researcher used two instruments: an observation checklist and test items (pre-test and post-test). The observation checklist contained the list of vocabulary being tested which was used to check each student's intangibility in pronouncing words. The pre-test was used to gain information about the student's ability in pronouncing words through a reading test. Then, the post-test was used to collect information on the enhancement of the student's ability using GVSA. Additionally, the data were analyzed using percentage analysis.

4 RESULTS

The research was done in two cycles. Before the first cycle commenced, a pre-test was administrated. In the pre-test, the researcher used a reading test. She provided three themes of short texts on education, economic, and technology. Then, the students were asked to read the text one by one. After reading those three short texts, the researcher focused on vocabulary that were difficult or mispronounced by the students and listed them. The results showed that students made mistakes in pronouncing the words *lead, ask, sure, math, hidden, treat, weapon, trough, serve* and *fear*. In the next step, the researcher modeled the words' pronunciation one by one three times before allowing them to use GVSA.

Further, the researcher divided the students into two groups and gave them 20 words which had the same pronunciation as the previous ten words that the students mostly had difficultly pronouncing in the texts. The members of every group recorded their friends' pronunciation while they were using GSVA. Then they analyzed the data of their friends' pronunciation. If the word was intelligible, the members of the group would give a tick (✓) in the available column of vocabulary list, while if the word is unintelligible, the rater would give a cross (✗). While trying this application, some students complained about how the GVSA worked since it did not type words correctly even after trying many times. For instance, student 2 said *sure* but the GVSA typed *surf*. This may affect students' performance in pronouncing words if they practice independently. It also happened to the students with some cases of listed words. However, they enjoyed using it. After they tried for ten minutes, the researcher checked their pronunciation. The results of post-test 1 and post-test 2 are presented in Tables 3 and 4.

In Table 3, it can be seen that there were some words that were incorrectly typed by GVSA namely, *chaos* (40%), *ship* (40%), *height* (20%). Only student 4 could pronounce the word *bath (20%)* correctly using GVSA.

Table 3. Results of post-test 1.

No	Vocabulary	Student 1	Student 2	Student 3	Student 4	Student 5	Total	Percentage
1.	Letter	✓	✓	✗	✓	✓	4	80
2.	Late	✓	✓	✓	✓	✓	5	100
3.	Chaos	✓	✓	✗	✗	✗	2	40
4.	Axe	✓	✗	✓	✓	✗	3	60
5.	She	✓	✗	✓	✓	✓	4	80
6.	Ship	✗	✓	✗	✗	✓	2	40
7.	Mate	✓	✓	✓	✓	✗	4	80
8.	Bath	✗	✗	✗	✓	✗	1	20
9.	Issue	✓	✓	✓	✓	✓	5	100
10.	Height	✗	✗	✓	✗	✓	2	100
	Student's Score	7	6	6	7	6	32	64

Table 4. Results of post-test 2.

No	Vocabulary	Student 1	Student 2	Student 3	Student 4	Student 5	Total	Percentage
1.	Turn	✓	✓	✓	✓	✓	5	100
2.	Tree	✓	✓	✓	✓	✓	5	100
3.	Whip	✗	✓	✓	✓	✓	4	80
4.	Weather	✓	✓	✓	✓	✓	5	100
5.	Threw	✗	✓	✗	✗	✓	2	40
6.	Knew	✓	✓	✓	✓	✓	5	100
7.	Though	✗	✗	✓	✗	✗	1	20
8.	Sure	✓	✗	✗	✓	✗	2	60
9.	Feather	✓	✗	✓	✓	✗	3	40
10.	Clear	✓	✓	✗	✓	✓	4	80
	Student's Score	7	7	7	8	7	36	72

In Table 4, the researcher found that there were three words that were incorrectly typed by GVSA, namely *threw (40%)*, *though* (20%), and *sure* (40%). Only student 3 could pronounce the word *mate* correctly using GVSA. Additionally, four students improved their score by one point, while one student did not show improvement. In addition, no students gained a lower score than the first post-test.

Moreover, the researcher found that the word *sure* sounds as/s/and/ð/. It was proved by the result of the second post-test that only one student who was able to say the word containing the fricative consonant/ʃ/and the diphthong vowel/ʊə/, while the other four students needed extra time to practice since they were not able to produce the word *sure* (40%) using GVSA. It was also very difficult for them to be familiar with words especially for fricative consonant/θ/. In the pre-test, they learned how to pronounce *math*, but in two cycles they were not able to pronounce the words *bath* (20%) and *though* (20%) using GVSA. On the other hand, the results showed that the students were able to enhance pronunciation skills in plosives consonant/t/, fricative consonant/s/, nasals consonant/m/, and approximant consonants/w/and/l/, pure vowel/e/,/i/, and/æ/, and diphthong vowel/EJ/by using GVSA

Finally, the results in Tables 3 and 4 indicate that using GVSA can be used to enhance Indonesian EFL students' pronunciation. This can be seen from the enhancement of students' pronunciation in the result of post-tests in two cycles. However, the improvement was indicated by an increase in their score of only one point. This means that the improvement is not significant. This is probably because the time was not sufficient to explore students' pronunciation more.

5 DISCUSSION

Given the results of this study, the finding showed Indonesian EFL students' improvement when using ASR through GVSA while leaning pronunciation. This is similar result to previous studies [3,22,23] which indicated that using ASR was helpful for enhancing students' pronunciation especially for EFL students. These three previous studies showed a significant improvement when using ASR to teach students' pronunciation through experimental study. Nevertheless, the result of this study revealed that there was no significant improvement of students' scores while using GVSA to pronounce words.

Considering the time for practicing, it affected the students' performance. In this case, students found difficulties in saying words focused on words /s /, /ð /, /ʃ / or /θ/. They might be able to say words focused on /s/, /ð/, /ʃ/ or /θ/ and overcome other difficult words if they had the time to practice regularly especially while using GVSA. Stephen and Richards highlighted that it is very important to apply a drilling technique in teaching pronunciation skills. This technique represents a habitual approach for the students to be familiar with the target language that they have learned before. Thus, the students will have more time to practice [24]. Through repetition exercises, the students are also expected to be able to pronounce words well and the learning process in pronunciation terms will be more successful.

Furthermore, two of the students said that having correct pronunciation will help them to build self-confidence while speaking in public. GVSA can help them to decrease their speaking anxiety in the EFL classroom. Using GVSA, as one ASR technology, will be helpful for students since it tends to recognize sounds based on its intelligibility without have native-like pronunciation. These finding are supported by Mitra et al. [25], who highlighted that students will get certain feedback when using ASR to improve their pronunciation time after time. Therefore, using GVSA will reduce students' mistakes in pronouncing words.

Lastly, using the suitable technique in teaching pronunciation affected students' motivation. Motivation was one aspect that influenced students' pronunciation [26]. Based on the result of this study, GVSA can be used to build students' motivation since it will help the teacher to create various learning activities to teach students' pronunciation. And the researcher believes that students can improve their performance in pronunciation skills when they practice more in various activities created by teachers in the classroom.

6 CONCLUSIONS

Using GVSA as the teaching-learning aid can be used to enhance Indonesian EFL students' pronunciation. Moreover, the more treatment and given time for students to practice will be very effective for them to enhance their pronunciation skills while using GVSA. This application also has some advantages and drawbacks. It will be beneficial for teachers to create various learning activities in the classroom using GVSA. Additionally, the learning process will be more fun for the students while using GVSA, thus it can be used to directly increase students' confidence and motivation. It is also free to be install and it can be used anywhere and anytime as long as they have GVSA in their smartphone or computer. However, in some cases, GVSA cannot always capture the pronounced words correctly. It only focuses on recognizing sounds based on intelligibility, it is not focused on intonation.

In addition, for further researchers who are interested to analyze same topic, the researcher suggest to analyze *word stress* by using GVSA. For instance, student 1 pronounce word *environment* and he/she pronounce in stressing syllables EN *(ENvironment)*, while student 2 pronounce in stressing alphabet MENT *(environtMENT)*, GVSA may recognize those two kinds of stress or only one stress. Thereby, analyzing word stress that can be recognized using GVSA can be very useful for further researchers.

REFERENCES

[1] Jones, D. (1972). *The pronunciation of English*. Cambridge, UK: Cambridge University Press.

[2] Shooshtari, Z.G., Mehrabi, K. & Mousavinia, M.Z. (2013). A call for teaching pronunciation for Iranian school. *International Journal of Academic Research in Progressive Education and Development*, *2*(1), 455. Retrieved from http://www.hrmars.com/admin/pics/1684.pdf

[3] Elimat. A.K. (2014). Automatic speech recognition as an effective means for teaching pronunciation. *JALT CALL Journal, 10*(1), 21–47. Retrieved from http://eric.ed.gov/?id=EJ1107929

[4] Koasih, M.M. (2017). Native language interference in learning English pronunciation: A case study at a private university in West Java, Indonesia. *International Journal of Education and Research, 5*(2). Retrieved from http://www.ijern.com/journal/2017/february-2017/11/.pdf

[5] Leslie, M.B. (1980). Myths about interlanguage phonology. Paper presented at the National TESOL Convention in Colombia University, San Francisco. In G. Ioup & S.H. Weinberger (Eds.), *Inter-language phonology: The acquisition of a second language sound system* (pp. 168–175). Cambridge, UK: Newbury House.

[6] Fraser, H. (2000). *Coordinating improvements in pronunciation teaching for adult learners of English as a second language.* Canberra, Australia: DETYA.

[7] Miller, S.F. (2004). *Pronunciation and the adult ESL learner.* The University of Pennsylvania.

[8] Roach, P. (2009). *English phonetics and phonology: A practical course.* Cambridge, UK: Cambridge University Press.

[9] Crystal, D. (2018). *A dictionary of linguistics and phonetics* (6th ed.). Oxford, UK: Blackwell Publishing.

[10] Carr, P. (2008). *A glossary of phonology.* Edinburgh, UK: Edinburgh University Press.

[11] Habibi, M.W. (2016). *English pronunciation problem encountered by Indonesian advanced students.* Malang, Indonesia: UIN Malang.

[12] Lacy, P.D. (2007). *The Cambridge handbook of phonology.* Cambridge, UK: Cambridge University Press.

[13] Gebhardt, F. (2010). *English pronunciation.* Retrieved from https://www.slideshare.net/RUZANA HAMID/english-pronunciation-64579283

[14] Gottlieb, M. (2006). *Assessing English language learners: Bridges from language proficiency to academic achievement.* Thousand Oaks, CA: Corwin Press.

[15] Schmitt, N. (2002). *An introduction to applied linguistics.* London, UK: Arnold.

[16] Thornbury, S. (2016). CELTA. Cambridge, UK: Cambridge University Press. Retrieved from http://www.apps.emoe.gov.my/ipba/rdipba/cd1/article114.p

[17] Monasar, D. (2014). Teaching pronunciation [PowerPoint slides]. Retrieved from http://danielmoo nasar.wordpress.com

[18] Kim, I.-S. (2006). Automatic speech recognition: Reliability and pedagogical implications for teaching pronunciation. *Educational Technology & Society, 9*(1), 322–334.

[19] Murcia, C. Murcia, C.M., Brinton, D.M. & Goodwin, M.J. (1996). *Teaching pronunciation: A reference for teachers of English to speakers of other languages.* Cambridge, UK: Cambridge University Press.

[20] Neri, A., Cucchiarini, C. & Strik, H. (2001). Effective feedback on L2 pronunciation in ASR-based CALL. In *Proceedings of the Workshop on Computer Assisted Language Learning, Artificial Intelligence in Education Conference, San Antonio, Texas.*

[21] Zinovjeva, N. (2005). *The use of speech technology in learning to speak a foreign language.* Retrieved from http://www.speech.kth.se/~rolf/NGSLT/gslt.../Natalia2005.pdf

[22] Mak, B., Siun, M., Ng. M., Tam, Y., Chan, Y., Chan, Y.K., Leung, K., Ho, S., Chong, S., Wong, J. & Lo, J. (n.d.). PLASER: Pronunciation learning via automatic speech recognition. doi:10.3115/1118894.1118898.

[23] Wang, Y.H. & Young, S.S.C. (2014). A study of the design and implementation of the ASR-based iCASL System with corrective feedback to facilitate English learning. *Educational Technology & Society, 17*(2), 219–233.

[24] Stephen, T.R. & Richards, J.C. (2001). *Approaches and methods in language teaching.* New York, NY: Cambridge University Press.

[25] Mitra, S., Tooley, J., Inamdar, P. & Dixon, P. (2003). Improving English pronunciation: An automated instructional approach. *Information Technologies International Development, 1*(1), 75–84.

[26] Gilakjani, A.P. (2011). A study on the situation of pronunciation instruction in ESL/EFL classrooms. *Journal of Studies in Education, 1*(1). Retrieved from https:https://www.research gate.net/publication/315035214_A_Study_on_the_Situation_of_Pronunciation_Instruction_in_ESLEFL_Classrooms.

English Linguistics, Literature, and Language Teaching in a Changing Era – Madya et al. (eds)
© 2020 Taylor & Francis Group, London, ISBN 978-1-03-224160-9

Factors influencing anxiety of non-native English as Second Language (ESL) teachers in compulsory schooling

Cindyra Galuhwardani & Bambang W. Pratolo
English Education of Graduate Program, Universitas Ahmad Dahlan, Yogyakarta, Indonesia

ABSTRACT: Following a qualitative method approach, this study investigated the anxiety factors of non-native English as Second Language (ESL) teachers in compulsory schools (elementary school, junior high school and senior/vocational high school). This study involved four teachers as participants working at four different levels of school, and the data was collected through the qualitative method. The data collection instrument consisted of interviews, which were then transcribed. The findings derived from the qualitative data reveal that factors that make the teachers feel anxious are both teachers' and students' factors, including the students' language background, classroom management, teaching experience, student numbers and, most importantly, the teachers' physical condition. Teachers feel anxious in conditions such as when their physical condition is not good and when students are not competent enough to understand English material. All participants, especially the teacher at the elementary school, mostly used the Indonesian language instead of English as the medium of instruction.

Keywords: Factor, anxiety, ESL Teacher, compulsory schooling

1 INTRODUCTION

English as a foreign language has become one of the compulsory subjects taught in Indonesian schools, especially in secondary-level education such as junior and senior high schools. Having been taught the English language subject for at least six years, students are expected to master the four English skills, which are listening, speaking, reading and writing. However, various researches show that English mastery among students after they graduate from secondary schools is regarded as inadequate [1]. There are various reasons why Indonesian students' ability in the English language is low, and one of these is due to teachers' low competence in teaching English [1]. As teachers who are responsible for teaching English as Second Language (ESL), they are required to be professional [2] by having adequate knowledge and proficiency in English, including having sufficient speaking skills. However, many of these teachers feel anxious when they speak English for real communication such as in the classroom. This situation will affect students' learning in the classroom. In fact, Brown [3] stated that this self-anxiety will exacerbate many difficulties for learners in responding in speaking activities. In other words, if teachers experience anxiety in their teaching, they will not be able to teach English well.

A study conducted by Kim and Kim [4] about teachers' instruction in teaching a foreign language in the classroom showed that teachers' anxiety will affect their instruction. When students get incorrect information from their teacher, they will get confused and it will also affect their understanding of the lesson. Teachers can get nervous, anxious and even lose self-confidence if they are not well prepared for classroom activities and do not have the appropriate teaching material. Another study, conducted by Klanrit and Sroinam [5] in Thailand, about ESL teachers' anxiety in using English in their teaching reported that the source of teachers' anxiety was the students' attitude toward learning English. They noted that a language learner was always anxious about error correction in the classroom. As a teacher instructing in a non-native language, such as the English language, teaching causes anxiety. Stress will appear when they have difficulty using the English language.

Anxiety is a feeling of being tense, disturbed, and either feeling faintly threatened or feeling agitated [6]. The tendency of people with this feeling is that they mostly respond to such a situation with negative perceptions of themselves. They perceive that they do not have ideas to resolve the situation. Moreover, they worry about what they share, give, do and think because of the situation. According to Yoon [7], anxiety is a normal feeling that a person has when he or she suffers from either internal or external states, emotional feeling or uncertain conditions. When a person experiences something unexpected, he or she will usually feel nervous and tense. This kind of feeling is what psychologists consider as anxiety.

In this case, foreign-language anxiety affects non-native English teachers as well. Horwitz [8], as cited in Yoon [7], claimed that many non-native language teachers will feel anxious in their target-language classroom. Even though language teachers are supposed to be high-level speakers of their target language, their language mastery is a still ongoing work, and this is why most non-native language teachers are likely to have uncomfortable moments, particularly in speaking in the target language. In fact, before they began to teach the target language, they were language learners themselves. It showed that students were affected by language anxiety. Non-native language teachers might also be influenced by language anxiety because they have been language learners as well. Teachers used to be learners and their experience is the same as when they learned a foreign language. They learn how to perform standard English in front of their peers. This situation may cause a feeling of anxiety as they feel fear, apprehension, nervousness and lose self-confidence from a fear of making mistakes. Fear of negative evaluation is an apprehension that is based on the inability to make a proper social impression [9]. This is called a negative perception toward language evaluation, since they respond to themselves with negative feelings about the assessment.

Anxiety in teachers' language teaching can appear from various sources. It sometimes comes from the method, teachers' perspective toward the material, personality, lack of self-confidence or poorly prepared teaching procedures. There are a number of studies showing the factors or sources of teachers' anxiety in the classroom. Merç [10] reinvestigated the sources of Foreign-Language Teachers' Anxiety (FLTA) among ESL student teachers. The results showed that there were six sources of teaching anxiety: students and class profiles, classroom management, teaching procedures and being observed, mentors and miscellaneous. Merç [10] explained that anxieties related to student teachers are supposed to deal with lesson delivery. The number of students in a classroom was considered as a source of anxiety as well. Merç [10] also added that maintaining discipline has the second highest frequency among the anxieties of students and teachers when communication units are computed. Furthermore, some students and teachers indicated that they were stressful about how to reduce the noise in the classroom. Teaching procedures were an important source of foreign-language teachers' anxiety. It can be assumed that people may feel threatened when they encounter something that has never happened to them before.

2 RESEARCH METHOD

2.1 *Research design*

This study was intended to identify ESL teachers' anxiety in more depth in different levels of compulsory schooling. This is a descriptive qualitative research using individual interviews for data collection. Because this study aimed to investigate ESL teachers' experience regarding their anxiety in a naturalistic and situated concern as the basis of the inquiry [11], a descriptive qualitative design was chosen. In addition, a descriptive qualitative design was employed in order to study the phenomena through the ESL teachers' perspectives about their anxiety, paying attention to the context in which they emerge [11]. Thus, the descriptive qualitative study is found in direct (not disengaged or abstracted) experience, referring to experience as a direct value [12].

2.2 Research participants

Four ESL teachers, where one teacher represented each compulsory level of schooling (elementary school, junior high school, and senior or vocational high school) from various cities were chosen. In selecting the participants, purposive sampling was used and several criteria were applied. Purposive sampling is a sampling technique in which researchers apply their own judgment when choosing participants for the study [13]. The criteria employed to select the participants were, firstly, location of the author, secondly, the age of the participants, and thirdly, the level of schools in which they taught. The participants having these criteria were chosen in this study in order to answer the research questions appropriately.

2.3 Data collection technique

In this study, an individual interview was used as the data collection technique in order to collect information from the participants who discussed their interpretations in their particular environment in their lives through their own point of view [14]. In addition, this study used standardized open-ended interviews in which the participants were asked a similar number of questions in the same order using an open-ended format [14] in order to get maximum information about the detailed views and experiences of the participants. Besides, this kind of interview allowed the researcher to ask further questions. Following interviewing of the participants and transcription of the interview results, member checking, which is also known as informant feedback or respondent validation [15], was conducted as a way of ensuring the trustworthiness of the study. In the process of member checking, the participants were given the interview transcriptions to check the account of the interview. The four participants read the transcriptions, and agreed with the transcription accounts, meaning that the data transcribed was correct. This way, the credibility of the study was maintained.

2.4 Data collection instrument

In order to assist the interview sessions, semi-structured questions were developed as interview guidelines with the topics shown in Table 1, which gives information about the questions used in the interviews.

Table 1. Indicators and instruments of the interview.

No	Indicators
1	Class preparation a. Classroom management b. Teaching procedures c. Teaching and learning management d. Less knowledge of the material
2	Students and classroom profile a. The number of students b. Students' attitude toward learning English
3	Lack of self-confidence a. Worry about making mistakes b. Fear of English speech in the classroom c. Lack of teaching experience
4	Low level of language proficiency a. They use both FL & L1 b. Spend more time on structuring activities c. Focus on textbook
5	Physical condition a. Teacher in a poor health condition

Table 2. List of codes.

Factors contributing to anxiety	Code
AF: Classroom Management	AF-CM
AF: Teaching Procedures	AF-TP
AF: Teaching and Learning Management	AF-TLM
AF: Less Knowledge of Subject Matter	AF-LK
AF: Students' Attitude Towards Learning English	AF-SAE
AF: Lack of Self-Confidence	AF-SC
AF: Teaching Experience	AF-TE
AF: Number of Students	AF-NS
AF: Low Level Language Proficiency	AF-LLP
AF: Physical Condition	AF-PC

2.5 *Data analysis technique*

In this phase, data selection became a major issue and therefore only relevant data was selected and analyzed for categorization. In this coding process, the mass of the data was simplified, and the relevant data was selected, which was then categorized using big letters, small letters and numbers, and all irrelevant information was discarded [16].

3 FINDINGS AND DISCUSSIONS

The results in this study showed that the participants had many factors that made them feel anxious while teaching. The teachers felt anxious speaking in English because they were afraid that their students would not understand well what they said. The students did not have good English backgrounds from their families, so they became confused when the teachers gave them instructions in full English.

Based on Table 3, teachers' anxiety stemmed from many factors, but the dominant ones were the students' lack of discipline, inadequate preparation for teaching, teaching and learning management, students' minimum knowledge, the number of students in the classroom, and also the teachers' own factors such as teaching experience and physical condition.

3.1 *Anxiety factor: classroom management*

Three of the participants responded that they felt uneasy when they found their classrooms were not in order. It became stressful for them if they were not well prepared to enter the classroom. If the participants were not ready, the classroom activity would not be well-structured. The factor that played the greatest role in contributing to the participants' anxiety in class preparation was teaching procedures:

Table 3. Factors that contributed to anxiety.

Interview	Participants' answers/Anxiety Factors [AF]
1st	Students' discipline [AF-CM], teaching procedure [AF-TP], teaching and learning management [AF-TLM], teaching experience [AF-TE], difficulty in handling a big class [AF-NS], physical condition [AF-PC]
2nd	Students' discipline [AF-CM], preparing the procedure of teaching [AF-TP], worry of making mistakes [AF-SC], teaching experience [AF-TE], physical condition [AF-PC]
3rd	Teaching procedure [AF-TP], teaching and learning management [AF-TLM], small class is better [AF-NS], physical condition [AF-PC]
4th	Students' discipline [AF-CM], teaching procedure [AF-TP], teaching and learning management [AF-TLM], worry of making mistakes [AF-SC], not conducive class [AF-NS], physical condition [AF-PC]

Of course, students who have discipline can follow the class easily. [ES (Elementary School) Teacher]
I think yes, because the classroom becomes quiet and both of us, teacher and students, can be more focused. [JHS (Junior High School) Teacher]
Success in teaching procedure is absolutely important. [VHS (Vocational High School) Teacher]

Although some students were busy talking to each other, the teachers kept questioning them. Some students also ignored the teachers' explanation while the teacher wrote on the white board and explained the lessons. There were only a few students who responded to the teachers while the others just laid down their heads on the desk and slept. One of the teacher's problems in making his students focus on the lesson was also experienced by the participants of Merç's study (2011). Merç [10] reported that the teacher participants were stressed by getting students' attention. This demonstrates that poor classroom management can cause anxiety to teachers.

3.2 *Anxiety factor: class size*

Based on the interview, the large number of students caused teachers anxiety in using English in their teaching because the large classes had a tendency to produce uncontrollable noise. Three participants said that the number of students can affect their teaching performance:

I think yes, because in a large class you almost do not have time for real teaching, but have to handle the class. As I said before, my students are still young. [ES Teacher]
Yes, too many students, too much anxiety. [SHS Teacher]
Yes, because that is not conducive. When the teacher explains the material, other students make noise, so they can't hear well and can't understand well. I think the best number of students is about 20 students. [VHS Teacher]

The number of students in a class affects the psychological conditions, such as the anxiety of the learners [17,18,19,20]. Furthermore, Coates and Thoresen [17] suggested that, at some level, anxiety in classroom teachers may become detrimental both to the teachers themselves and to their pupils. They indicated that anxiety may be correlated with inappropriate student and teacher performance. Yoon [7] noted that foreign-language anxiety is a complex psychological factor for both teacher and learner.

3.3 *Anxiety factor: lack of self-confidence*

Based on the interviews, the students experienced difficulty in understanding the lessons when the teachers repeatedly made mistakes in using the target language. Students did not get what they expected from the materials they learned:

Some of my students sometimes correct me when I mispronounce words. [JHS Teacher]
My students who joined the English course always update their knowledge, and they sometimes protest to me when the material or the contents of the subject are not the same as what they learned at their English courses. [SHS Teacher]
Of course, they are still young so I always give them Indonesian instructions. [ES Teacher]
Yes. Because my students are not good in English. [SHS Teacher]

In contrast, some of the participants responded that they did not feel confident in using English as a medium of instruction in the classroom. Yoon's study [7] indicated that many teachers reported that they did not feel confident when teaching English through the English language. There was no practice among English teachers for using English in their daily conversations outside the classroom. Consequently, English was rarely used by them in a school environment.

3.4 Anxiety factor: physical condition

The factor of physical condition was the most important cause of anxiety for teachers, as they said that this factor could influence their performance and increase their anxiety.

Yes, because basically they are so noisy, if I got sick, I am afraid if I can't explain well to them. [ES Teacher]

Yes, absolutely yes. Because my students are unruly, so if I get sick I will be very anxious about them, my voice is very quiet because of course I cannot speak loudly, so they do not understand at all. [VHS Teacher]

Absolutely yes, because we become weak, so I feel anxious because the students do not understand what I said. [SHS Teacher]

Of course, because if we got sick, our voice is not loud, and we walk around in class less, and do not talk actively. [VHS Teacher]

The interviews revealed that physical condition played an important role in teaching activity. The respondents reported that the older their age, the more tired the teachers are. Furthermore, teachers had the responsibility to perform administrative tasks as well. Hence, they became exhausted when they had to teach their English classes. Coates and Thoresen [17] indicated that physical condition became the source of teachers' anxiety. As Pratolo [21] stated, the feeling of anxiety affects both physical and psychological conditions. Coates and Thoresen [17] also reported that many educators would agree that teachers' personality and mental health as they are reflected in classroom behavior are important. This showed that physical condition would influence both the teaching and learning processes.

4 CONCLUSIONS AND SUGGESTIONS

While much research into foreign-language teaching focuses on ability in the language itself, this present study focuses on the teachers' attitude in using English in the classroom. Our study reveals evidence of the source of anxiety among compulsory schooling teachers. Based on the data analysis, there are four primary factors causing teachers' anxiety: poor classroom management, large class size, lack of self-confidence and teachers' poor physical state. The findings show that teachers' anxiety comes from their personal states, their students and the classroom atmosphere. The findings of our study can provide important information about teachers' anxiety factors: having more awareness of teachers' anxiety means they can anticipate the problems in advance and resolve them accordingly.

REFERENCES

[1] Purwanti, E. (2016). *Building professional learning: Lesson study as a model of collaborative reflective in English as foreign language teaching in Indonesia* (Doctoral thesis, Faculty of Education, Monash University, Australia).

[2] Teacher and Lecturer Law. (2005). The constitution of the Republic of Indonesia. Retrieved from http://humas.unimed.ac.id/wp-content/uploads/2015/04/Undang-Undang-Nomor-14-Tahun-2005.pdf

[3] Brown, L. (2008). Language and anxiety: An ethnographic study of international postgraduate students. *Evaluation and Research in Education, 21*(2), 75–95.

[4] Kim, S. & Kim, J. (2004). When the learner becomes a teacher: Foreign language anxiety. *English Teaching, 59*(1), 165–185.

[5] Klanrit, P. & Sroinam, R. (2012). EFL teacher's anxiety in using English in teaching in the language classroom. *International Journal of Social Science and Humanity, 2*(6), 493–496.

[6] Rachman, S. (2004). *Clinical psychology: A modular course. Anxiety* (2nd ed.). Hove, UK: Psychology Press.

[7] Yoon, T. (2012). Teaching English through English: Exploring anxiety in non-native pre-service ESL teachers. *Theory and Practice in Language Studies, 2*(6), 1099–1107.

[8] Horwitz, E.K. (1996). Even teachers get the blues: Recognizing and alleviating non-native teachers' feeling of foreign language anxiety. *Foreign Language Annals, 29*, 365–375.

[9] Aydin, S. (2008). An investigation on the language anxiety and fear of negative evaluation among Turkish EFL learners. *Asian EFL Journal, 30*(1), 421–444.

[10] Merç, A. (2011). Sources of foreign language student teacher anxiety: A qualitative inquiry. *Turkish Online Journal of Qualitative Inquiry, 2*(4), 80–94.

[11] Denzin, N. & Lincoln, Y. (2005). Introduction: The discipline and practice of qualitative research. In N.K. Denzin & Y.S. Lincoln (Eds.), *The Sage handbook of qualitative research* (3rd ed., pp. 1–43). Thousand Oaks, CA: Sage Publications.

[12] Sherman, R.R. (1992). The idea of qualitative research. *CUHK Education Journal, 20*(2), 85–93.

[13] Black, K. (2010). *Business statistics for contemporary decision making* (6th ed.). Hoboken, NJ: John Wiley and Sons.

[14] Cohen, L., Manion, L. & Morrison, K. (2011). *Research methods in education* (7th ed.). London, UK: Routledge.

[15] Creswell, J.W. (2012). *Educational research: Planning, conducting and evaluating quantitative and qualitative research* (4th ed.). Boston, MA: Pearson Education.

[16] Miles, B., Huberman, M., Michael, A. & Saldana, J. (1994). *Qualitative data analysis: An expanded sourcebook* (2nd ed.). Thousand Oaks, CA: Sage Publications.

[17] Coates, T.J. & Thoresen, C.E. (1976). Teacher anxiety: A review with recommendations. *Review of Educational Research, 46*(2), 159–184.

[18] Soodak, L.C., Podell, D.M. & Lehman, L.R. (1998). Teacher, student, and school attributes as predictors of teachers' responses to inclusion. *The Journal of Special Education, 31*(4), 480–497.

[19] Blatchford, P., Edmonds, S. & Martin, C. (2003). Class size, pupil attentiveness and peer relations. *British Journal of Educational Psychology, 73*(1), 15–36.

[20] Bahanshal, D.A. (2013). The effect of large classes on English teaching and learning in Saudi secondary schools. *English Language Teaching, 6*(11), 49–59.

[21] Pratolo, B. (2015). *Exploring Indonesian learners' beliefs about language learning strategies through reflection* (Doctoral thesis, Monash University, Australia). Retrieved from https://core.ac.uk/download/pdf/82059045.pdf

English Linguistics, Literature, and Language Teaching in a Changing Era – Madya et al. (eds)
© 2020 Taylor & Francis Group, London, ISBN 978-1-03-224160-9

A descriptive case study on accommodating Turnitin to optimize the roles of portfolio-based assessment and self-assessment in students' writing process

Dewi Cahyaningrum, Hasan Zainnuri & Ngadiso
English Education Department, Sebelas Maret University, Central Java, Indonesia

ABSTRACT: Following the direction of the learner-centered approach, teachers need to provide assessment which is more learner-centered and authentic. In teaching writing in intermediate class, teachers found that students have a low inner motivation and joy to write meaningfully because they still have problems in writing; they are accustomed to receiving instruction from the teacher and then writing a text to fulfill the assignment or to write for the teacher, not for themselves. Portfolio-based assessment promotes students' participation and autonomy in assessing their own success. It is characterized by reflection that helps students to learn from experience and practice, and to bridge the theory–practice gap. In fact, facilitating students with a file documentation system is not easy for teachers. *Turnitin* provides a feature for documenting the students' work in the form of online portfolios. Turnitin also allows teachers to create and customize writing scoring rubrics to help students to work and assess their portfolio in terms of their own success in writing. This is a descriptive case study concerning the process of incorporating Turnitin to optimize the roles of portfolio-based assessment and self-assessment in students' writing process. The findings show that Turnitin optimizes: (1) the role of portfolio assessment; (2) the self-evaluation of the students' writing process.

Keywords: Turnitin, portfolio assessment, self-assessment, writing process

1 INTRODUCTION

In the twenty-first century, information literacy is needed for students in order to succeed academically and for their future job opportunities. There are many skills supporting this kind of literacy. One of the skills focused on in this article is writing. In general, it is increasingly important for students and others to have good writing skills. Through written text, people (students) can express both their ideas and feelings to inform, persuade and convince other people [15].

In practice, the results of observation and interview show that some difficulties are faced by intermediate students in developing ideas into a good paragraphs. Also found are mistakes made by some students in applying grammar rules, mechanics, punctuation and spelling. Moreover, the result of observation reveals some students as having low inner motivation and joy to write meaningfully. They are accustomed to receiving instruction from the teacher, and then writing a text to fulfill the assignment or to write for the teacher, not for themselves.

In this case, students are often blocked by the perception that the teacher is their only audience and reviewer. They have not clearly understood: (1) the aims of writing itself; (2) the importance of each single step in the writing process; (3) how to assess their own work through a self-assessment process. In this situation, teachers need to provide instruction, following the direction of a learner-centered approach, and assessment that is more learner-centered and authentic.

Effective writing follows the process covering pre-writing, organizing, drafting, revising, editing and documenting the final draft. Given this lengthy process, the teacher can use the strength of *Turnitin* (iParadigms LLC, Oakland, CA), which incorporates the collection and reviewing of artifacts. It provides a feature for documenting students' works in every single process of writing a text in the form of online portfolios. In addition, Turnitin allows teachers to create and customize writing scoring rubrics to help students to work through self-assessment on their portfolio in terms of their own success in writing. According to Seow, in Yugandhar [17], the teacher's guidance in students' writing is a significant technique in developing their writing process.

In general, this paper is reporting the result of a descriptive case study focused on Turnitin to optimize: (1) the role of portfolio assessment; (2) self-evaluation of the students' writing process. The findings explain how Turnitin achieves this.

2   LITERATURE REVIEW

2.1   *Instructional design for students' writing process*

Writing is considered a complex skill to be learned and mastered by students. It is the thinking process that generates, organizes, and exchanges with the reader's own ideas. Students have to be able to organize their ideas to construct sentences, use punctuation and spelling, and arrange their writing into cohesive and coherent paragraphs and text. Furthermore, students have to understand the steps in the writing process, which cover pre-writing, organizing, drafting, revising, editing and documenting the final draft. According to Kellogg and Whiteford [9], university undergraduates' writing skills are insufficient and need to be improved. In this case, teachers need to use learning instruction, helping students to accommodate several language components such as content, organization, vocabulary, language use and mechanics.

2.2   *Turnitin and portfolio assessment for students' writing process*

Turnitin is an electronic text-matching system. It is integrated into an assignments tool in all online classrooms. For the writing class, Turnitin provides a feature for documenting students' works in the form of online portfolios. Turnitin also offers a grade mark service covering rubric scorecards and grading forms that can be used to evaluate student work based on defined criteria and scales. It allows teachers to create and customize writing scoring rubrics to help students to work and assess their portfolio in terms of their own success in writing. Moreover, the use of Turnitin in the writing classroom can be categorized as instruction with the Internet and Web 2.0 social sites. Different from traditional language learning, accommodating the Internet and Web 2.0 social sites combines the benefits of classroom interactivity with personal and self-study [10].

A portfolio is an intentional collection of a student's performance, which contains the student's efforts, progress and achievement in one or more fields (Barrett's definition as cited in Wang and Liao [14]). Moreover, Hamp-Lyons and Condon [8] identified ten characteristics of a writing-portfolio as follows: (1) collection of more than one performance; (2) range of performances; (3) context-richness; (4) delayed evaluation; (5) promoting time for revision; (6) selection of writer's work; (7) student-centered control; (8) reflection and self-assessment; (9) growth along specific parameters; (10) measuring a learner's development over time. Furthermore, according to Burner [3], the main categories that constitute a portfolio are collection, selection and reflection.

In response to the need for alternative and more authentic assessment practices, portfolios have become a common alternative to traditional assessment methods [12]. The findings of a study conducted by Yurdabakan and Erdogan [18] indicate that portfolio assessment had a significant effect on writing skills. Another study, conducted by Fahed Al-Serhani [5], demonstrated that portfolio assessment had a significant positive impact on students' writing performance in general and sub-skills of purpose, content, organization, vocabulary, sentence structure and mechanics.

2.3 *Self-evaluation for students' writing process*

Andrade and Du [1] provide a helpful definition of self-assessment that focuses on the formative learning that it can promote. It is a process of formative assessment during which students reflect on and evaluate the quality of their work and their learning, judge the degree to which they reflect explicitly stated goals or criteria, identify strengths and weaknesses in their work, and revise accordingly. In the writing process, self-assessment is another factor that can support students' success. Fahimi and Rahimi [6] state that students need to be able to monitor the performance process, because not only the end-product is important but also the process by which it is attained.

3 RESEARCH METHOD

This research was conducted at the English Department of *FKIP* (Faculty of Teacher Training & Education), *Universitas Sebelas Maret*. The subjects of the research were the second-semester students of a writing class in the academic year 2017/2018. It uses descriptive case study as the research design, in which the researcher gained an in-depth understanding of the subject's perspective using a case study method. According to Yin [16], a case study is used when a 'how' or 'why' question is being asked about a contemporary case over which the investigator has little or no control, and when the focus is on a contemporary phenomenon within some real life context.

In this research, the researcher sought to gain an in-depth understanding of the case by collecting multiple forms of data [4]. In this research, the sources of the data needed by the researcher are events and documents. The research data were collected using qualitative methods. Data collection techniques were document analysis, interview and non-participant observation. The technique used for analyzing the data was qualitative data analysis. Miles and Huberman [13] describe the steps in qualitative data analysis as: (1) data reduction; (2) data display; (3) conclusion drawing and verification.

4 FINDINGS AND DISCUSSION

4.1 *Turnitin optimizes the role of portfolio assessment for students' writing process*

Turnitin provides a feature for documenting students' works in the form of online portfolios. On the students' page, students can access an assignment inbox that is home for any assignment that students might be working on. Students will find relevant dates for the assignment, and the time when they have to complete it. Assignments here refer to all the students' works in pre-writing, drafting, revising and finishing the text.

Turnitin also allows teachers to create and customize writing scoring rubrics to help students to work on and assess their portfolio for their own success in writing. Accommodating Turnitin in portfolio assessment supports the teacher in working collaboratively with students to help them become better writers. In the students' assignment inbox, they will find rubrics attached to the assignment. For students, these rubrics play a role as a guideline for writing and assessing their text.

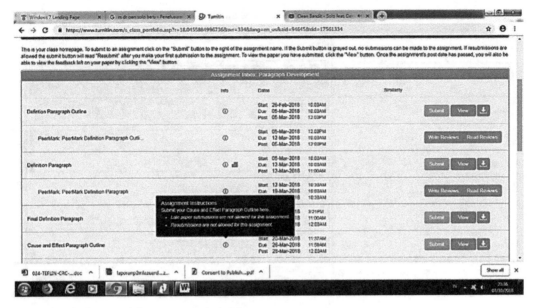

Figure 1. Assignment inbox: paragraph development.

In general, portfolio assessment is considered as an important tool to enhance students' better understanding of the writing process. It promotes participation by allowing students to select the work on which they will be evaluated, to reflect on their work, to take control of revision and to have the opportunity to produce substantive revision, in order to be granted the time to grow as writers. The findings indicated that portfolio assessment through Turnitin affects the students' writing performance in general and their sub-skills in content, organization, vocabulary, sentence structure and mechanics. In this case, accommodating the Internet and Web 2.0 social sites in the form of Turnitin in the writing classroom combines the benefits of classroom interactivity with personal and self-study [10].

This instructional practice is an example of the kinds of learning experiences to capture and gather insights so that lessons are more meaningful. Students are able to access their grades, work records, and teacher feedback on electronically submitted assignments. Access to this information increases communication between teachers and students and makes students accountable for their academic responsibilities [11].

4.2 *Turnitin optimizes the role of self- assessment for students' writing process*

Facilitating students with Turnitin provides the students with a file documentation system and assessment which is more learner-centered and authentic. Gallagher [7] maintains that reflection is a major component of portfolios as it helps students to learn from experience and practice. It helps students to bridge the theory–practice gap. Portfolio assessment promotes the students' participation and autonomy in assessing their own success.

According to Boud [2], all assessments, including self-assessment, comprise two main elements: *making decisions about the standards of performance* expected and then *making judgments about the quality of the performance in relation to these standards.* When self-assessment is introduced, it should ideally involve students in both of these aspects. Turnitin invites both teacher and student to work collaboratively to construct *standards of performance and assessment in the form of a scoring rubric.* In other words, Turnitin

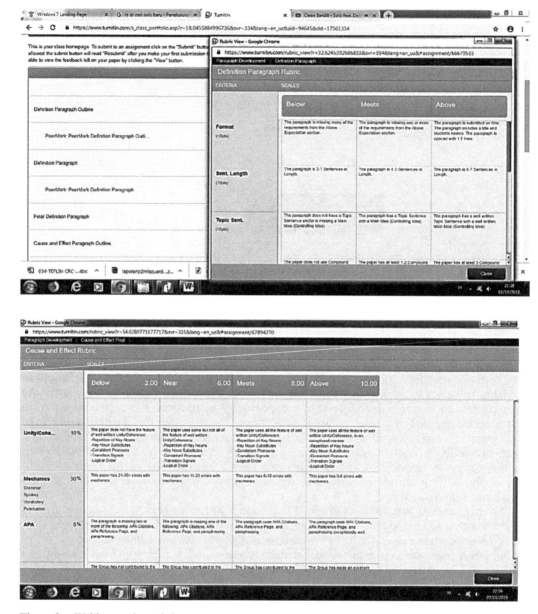

Figure 2. Writing scoring rubrics.

allows teachers to create and customize writing scoring rubrics to help students to work and assess their portfolio in terms of their own success in writing.

In general, the portfolio assessment is considered to be an important tool in enhancing students' understanding of the writing process and to encourage the students, giving them more confidence in analyzing their own writing (doing self-assessment) as writers. Students learn to reflect on their work, to take control of revision and have the opportunity to produce substantive revisions, thus being granted the time to grow as writers.

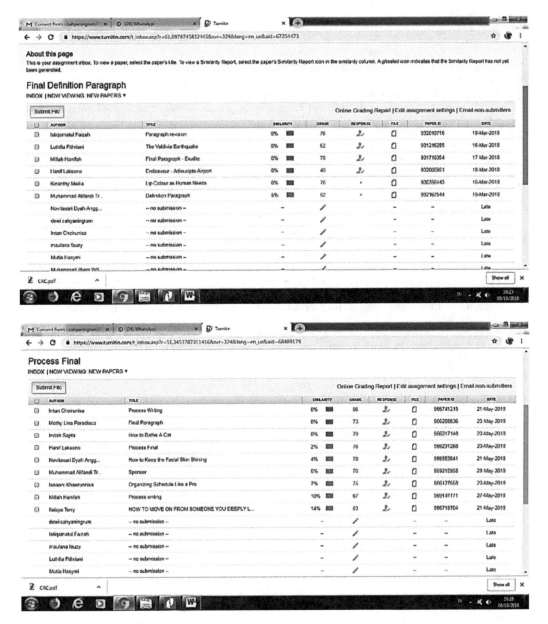

Figure 3. Students' writing scores.

5 CONCLUSIONS AND SUGGESTIONS

Turnitin can be categorized as instruction with the Internet and Web 2.0 social sites. For the writing class, Turnitin provides a feature for documenting students' works in the form of online portfolios. Turnitin also offers a grade mark service covering rubric scorecards and grading forms that can be used to evaluate students' works based on defined criteria and scales. It allows teachers to create and customize writing scoring rubrics to help students to work and assess their portfolio for their own success in writing. In general, this paper reports that Turnitin optimizes: (1) the role of portfolio assessment; (2) self-evaluation of students' writing process.

REFERENCES

[1] Andrade, H. & Du, Y. (2007). Student responses to criteria-referenced self-assessment. *Assessment and Evaluation in Higher Education, 32*(2), 159–181.

[2] Boud, D. (1995). *Enhancing learning through self-assessment.* London, UK: Kogan Page.

[3] Burner, T. (2014). The potential formative benefits of portfolio assessment in second and foreign language writing contexts: A review of the literature. *Studies in Educational Evaluation, 43,* 139–149.

[4] Creswell, J.W. (2012). *Research design: Qualitative, quantitative, and mixed method approaches.* Thousand Oaks, CA: SAGE Publications.

[5] Fahed Al-Serhani, W. (2007). *The effect of portfolio assessment on the writing performance of EFL secondary school students in Saudi Arabia* (Master's thesis, Taibah University, Saudi Arabia).

[6] Fahimi, Z. & Rahimi, A. (2015). On the impact of self-assessment practice on writing skill. *Procedia-Social and Behavioral Sciences, 192*(24), 730–736.

[7] Gallagher, P. (2001). An evaluation of a standards based portfolio. *Nurse Education Today, 21*(5), 409–416.

[8] Hamp-Lyons, L. & Condon, W. (2000). *Assessing the portfolio: Principles for practice, theory, and research.* Cresskill, NJ: Hampton Press.

[9] Kellogg, R.T. & Whiteford, A.P. (2009). Training advanced writing skills: The case for deliberate practice. *Educational Psychologist, 44*(4), 250–266.

[10] Köse, T. & Mede, E. (2016). Perceptions of EFL learners about using an online tool for vocabulary learning in EFL classrooms: A pilot project in Turkey. *Procedia-Social and Behavioral Sciences, 232,* 362–372.

[11] Manning, C., Brooks, W., Crotteau, V., Diedrich, A., Moser, J. & Zwiefelhofer, A. (2011). Tech tools for teachers, by teachers: Bridging teachers and students. *The Wisconsin English Journal, 53*(1), 24–28.

[12] Mayer, D.K. & Tusin, L.F. (1999). Pre-service teachers' perceptions of portfolios: Process versus product. *Journal of Teacher Education, 50*(2), 131–139.

[13] Miles, M.B. & Huberman, A.M. (1994). *Qualitative data analysis: An expanded source book.* Thousand Oaks, CA: SAGE Publications.

[14] Wang, Y.H. & Liao, H.C. (2008). The application of learning portfolio assessment for students in the technological and vocational education system. *Asian EFL Journal, 10*(2), 132–154.

[15] White, R. & Arndt, V. (1997). *Process writing.* Harlow, UK: Addison Wesley Longman.

[16] Yin, R.K. (1994). *Case study research: Design and methods* (2nd ed.). Thousand Oaks, CA: SAGE Publications.

[17] Yugandhar, K. (2015). Practicing teacher organized peer review to advance EFL students' writing skills. *International Journal on Studies in English Language and Literature (IJSELL), 3*(1), 25–29.

[18] Yurdabakan, I. & Erdogan, T. (2009). The effect of portfolio assessment on reading, listening and writing skill of secondary school prep class students. *The Journal of International Social Research, 2*(9), 526–538.

English Linguistics, Literature, and Language Teaching in a Changing Era – Madya et al. (eds)
© 2020 Taylor & Francis Group, London, ISBN 978-1-03-224160-9

Foreign language anxiety in relation to students' motivation: What's the matter?

Dyta Maykasari & Widyastuti Purbani
English Education Study Program, Graduate School, Yogyakarta State University, Yogyakarta, Indonesia

ABSTRACT: All foreign English learners have their own motivation. Sometimes many of them experience anxiety and fear toward second language (L2) learning. The aim of this study is to investigate the factors which contribute toward the Foreign Language (FL) anxiety and motivation and to seek the correlation among those variables. The participants of this study were the second year of graduate students in the English Education Department, Yogyakarta State University. There were 26 students who participated in this study. The data of the research were gathered through questionnaires of motivation [24] and Foreign Language Anxiety Classroom Scales (FLACS) [10]. The data were analyzed statistically using descriptive statistics, Pearson correlation and multiple regression. The result indicates that there is a significant and negative correlation between foreign language anxiety and motivation. The students' motivation factors are a significant predictor of foreign language anxiety.

Keywords: Foreign language anxiety, motivation, second language acquisition

1 INTRODUCTION

For foreign language learners, the terms of 'motivation' and 'anxiety' play the most important role in the learning process. Both of them participate as the basis of language achievement within language aptitude [7]. The researcher believes that motivation and foreign language anxiety refers to any individual differences which construct the language attainment. One's language achievement can be impeded when he/she is anxious and less motivated in language performance.

However, motivation takes a crucial role as a booster to achieve a high result in learning. The differences between those two aspects, which are anxiety and motivation, have a positive and negative impact on the learning process [5,12]. Therefore, this study will investigate the correlation between motivation and anxiety in a foreign language context. The correlation between motivation and anxiety on language learning will contribute to the positive impact for the teacher and researcher to increase the learning achievements.

1.1 *Students' anxiety in foreign language class*

The word 'anxiety' is common for human life, which refers to the human emotions of fear, worry, and unease [13]. Smith et al. [21] also mention that anxiety is the human body's response to a threat when someone feels endangered, worried, or under pressure in certain circumstances. From these perspectives, it can be said that anxiety is associated with the feeling of uneasiness, worry, nervousness, or even the fear that someone feels in a specific situation. Foreign language anxiety occurs in a foreign language context. Learners, who learn and use foreign language, experience nervousness, fear, worry, or even unease during language performance [10]. MacIntyre [17] explains that language anxiety is related to negative emotional reactions related to second or foreign language learning. Language anxiety is related to the dread of making mistakes, feeling worried, and perfectionism [20].

Horwitz et al. [10] introduce the traits of anxiety, which refer to people who permanently worry about everything. The traits are state and situational anxiety. The state anxiety involves situational anxiety, which is categorized as a specific anxiety reaction. The situational anxiety occurs in a specific situation, that is, the anxiety in a situation like public speaking or classroom participation. Language anxiety is included in the type of situational anxiety [16]. It means that language anxiety only occurs when learners feel apprehensive during a certain condition and situation in language learning. Anxiety has a negative influence on language production. Foreign Language Anxiety (FLA) occurs when the learners are exposed to some negative experiences in a foreign language context [10,17]. MacIntyre and Gardner in Gkonou [9] state that FLA constructs obstacles to the learners which make them lose their self-confidence, escape from classroom activities, or even deter them from making an effort during the learning process.

In addition, Horwitz et al. [10] classify the three factors of anxiety. These are (1) Communication apprehension, which relates to shyness on the interpersonal interaction. It involves the difficulties to communicate between individuals or in groups in speaking and also listening activities; (2) Test anxiety, which includes the performance anxiety, which is hindering due to a fear of failure; (3) Fear of negative evaluation, which represents the apprehension of someone's evaluation.

1.2 *Learning motivation*

Motivation is largely based on empirical studies that investigate how human psychology affects people's personalities and attitudes. Dörnyei [3] classifies the basic principles of motivation, which are called 'direction' and 'magnitude (intensity)'. These two dimensions reveal the word *choice*, where every person has the right to choose the tension of the particular action, and the word *effort* as the responsibility of their choice, which represents the activity in achieving the goal. It means that motivation reflects the human's responsibility and effort of their behavior to attain something.

By drawing the concept of motivation, Gardner [7] has his own views of second language (L2) motivation, which represents someone's desire to learn language by giving the efforts to achieve the language attainment. There are three components of L2 motivation: motivational intensity, desire to learn, and attitude toward the act of language learning. Another perspective of motivation is described by Noels et al. [18], who classify the L2 motivation into intrinsic and extrinsic motivation. The intrinsic motivation arises from the internal desire of someone to do an action. It occurs when the learners try to perform or achieve the learning intention wisely by themselves [12]. However, extrinsic motivation involves the external factors of the learners, which affect them to attain the goals in language learning.

On the other hand, Dörnyei [4] highlights the L2 motivational as being the self-system which integrates the language learning and psychology views (possible selves and future self-guides). The possible selves relate to "how the self regulates behavior by setting goals and expectations" [4]. The future self-guides concerns the ideal and ought selves, which describe the one's preferences and beliefs of what he/she would or must have. In addition, the terms of the L2 motivational system cannot be separated from imagery and vision [4].

According to Dörnyei [4], imagery involves the mental image of someone's desire. According to Markus and Ruvolo, as cited in Dörnyei [4], the imagery has a positive influence on the construction of someone in achieving goals. Drawing one's own images of actions can facilitate someone to attain his own intention. You et al. [25] believe that the image represents the subjective experiences of someone. In relation to motivation, imagery is the representation of vision. Everyone has a different vision, meaning that every single person has his/her own way to reach success or to determine the ideal L2. Creating the learners' vision gives a useful contribution to lead them to achieve the language attainment. There are nine categories of motivation which have been explained by You and Dörnyei [24]. They are ideal L2 self, instrumentally promotion, cultural interest, traveling, ought-to L2 self, instrumentality prevention, parental expectations, language learning experience, and intended effort.

1.3 The relation between motivation and anxiety in foreign language learning

Many researchers examine the correlation between motivation and anxiety in language learning. Liu and Chen [15] investigate whether motivation has a positive relation to the learners' language anxiety. The learners who are highly motivated to learn a foreign language, especially English, have lower anxiety levels during the teaching activities. This idea is also supported by the previous researcher [2,11,22]. Detailed examination between motivation and anxiety by Gardner [7], Horwitz et al. [10], Liu [14], and MacIntyre [17] reveal that those individual factors contribute to the significant effect on language proficiency. It can be derived that foreign language anxiety has a negative influence on the students' performance, which is affected by the other individual differences in language learning.

2 METHOD

2.1 The aim of the study

This study examined the correlation between the two variables of foreign language anxiety and motivation factors in the teaching-learning process. Then, it also explored which types of motivation predict the students' foreign language anxiety. Those factors of motivation and anxiety are extracted from the previous study [10,25]. The investigation of the correlation between foreign language anxiety and the motivational level will contribute to the significant influence for the teachers and students to improve the learning quality.

2.2 Participants

The data were gathered from the graduate students of the English Education Department, Yogyakarta State University. The populations of the participants are 34 students as the sample. They were randomly selected by the researchers. The survey was directly distributed by the researcher in the form of paper. Of those participants, there were only 26 participants who gave responses to the questionnaires. It means that there was a 76.47% response rate.

2.3 Instrument

The quantitative data were gained from the questionnaires. The instrument of this research is questionnaires adopted from the motivation questionnaires, which are developed and used in a Chinese survey by You et al. [25] and Foreign Language Anxiety Classroom Scales (FLACS), which is developed by Horwitz et al. [10]. There were 33 items of each variable. Those instruments used five Likert-like scales which are in the range between 1 and 5. The consistencies of those questionnaires are .70 for motivation questionnaires and .80 for FLACS, meaning that those instruments are reliable for use in this study.

2.4 Data analysis

To answer the research questions, the data were quantitatively analyzed using the application SPSS version 22. The researcher used descriptive statistics to answer the research question number 1, and correlation and regression analysis among those variables to answer the other research question.

3 RESULTS

The results of this study reveal the relation between foreign language classroom anxiety and learning motivation. The results are obtained from the exploratory factor analysis of the FLACS and Motivation scale. Table 1 presents the descriptive statistics of foreign language anxiety.

The table above shows the mean score and standard variation of the main variables. It was found that on the three types of anxiety, the means are approximately between 16.77 and 32.54. It is higher than the motivational factor variables. It indicates that when the students had a high level of anxiety, their motivation for learning English is low. Then, the Pearson product moment correlation coefficient analysis is carried out to investigate the correlation between those variables among the students in English-as-a-Foreign Language (EFL) learning. Table 2 shows the correlation between all main variables.

Table 2 shows the result of the correlation analysis of the Pearson product moment correlation. The table of correlation analysis indicates that there is a significant and negative correlation between anxiety subscales and motivation factors among graduate students in English language learning. Almost all motivation factors variables are negatively and significantly related to all foreign language anxiety factors. It means the increasing anxiety level has a negative impact on the students' motivation to learn English. The ought-to L2 self is the only motivating factor that is positively related to all three anxiety factors. It indicates that the students who relate to ought-to L2 self feel more anxious in communication, English test and for negative evaluation.

Table 1. Descriptive statistics of the main variables.

	Sample (N)	Mean	Std. deviation
Communication apprehension	11	25.46	5.093
Test anxiety	15	32.54	6.094
Fear of negative evaluation	7	16.77	3.922
Ideal L2 self	13	37.15	4.211
Instrumentality promotion	2	6.38	1.267
Cultural interest	1	3.73	.724
Traveling	1	3.50	.812
Ought-to L2 self	1	4.62	8.075
Instrumentality prevention	5	15.38	3.251
Parental expectation	2	5.23	2.065
Attitudes to L2 learning	4	16.54	20.196
Intended effort	4	12.23	2.103

Table 2. Pearson correlation matrix.

	1	2	3	4	5	6	7	8	9	10	11	12
Communication apprehension	1											
Test anxiety	.73*	1										
Fear of negative evaluation	.73**	.72**	1									
Ideal L2 self	−.39*	−.16	−.09	1								
Instrumentality promotion	−.19	−.19	−.16	.57**	1							
Cultural interest	−.28	−.21	−.46*	−.14	−.19	1						
Traveling	−.09	.15	−.14	.16	−.04	.44*	1					
Ought-to L2 self	.19	.08	.15	.05	.16	−.03	.35	1				
Instrumentality prevention	−.16	.040	.06	.58**	.63**	−.48*	.06	.11	1			
Parental expectation	−.06	.053	.04	−.19	−.48*	.50**	.26	.19	−.57**	1		
Attitudes to L2 learning	−.10	−.04	−.16	−.25	−.52**	.65**	.17	−.02	−.81	.79	1	
Intended effort	−.36	−.14	−.25	.16	−.01	.44*	.47*	.31	−.07	.44	.43	1

*Significant at .05 level; **significant at .01 level.

Table 3. Regression analysis for foreign language anxiety.

	Communication apprehension		Test anxiety		Fear of negative evaluation	
	β	T	β	t	β	T
Ideal L2 self	−.29	−.97	−.37	−1.09	−.02	−.06
Instrumentality promotion	.03	.10	−.06	−.17	−.15	−.47
Cultural interest	−.35	−1.20	−.50	−1.40	−.53	−1.60
Traveling	.22	.84	.42	1.43	.07	.25
Ought-to L2 self	.31	1.28	−.02	−.07	.17	.67
Instrumentality prevention	−.29	−.58	.54	.97	−.001	−.002
Parental expectation	−.02	−.07	.05	.12	.35	.98
Attitudes to L2 learning	−.01	−.016	.63	.95	−.08	−.13
Intended effort	−.41	−1.44	−.30	−.93	−.24	−.82
F(2,60)	1.38		.68		1.06	
AdjR^2	.11		-.13		.02	

The factors such as traveling, instrumentality prevention, and parental expectation are negatively and significantly related to communication apprehension. There is a significant and positive correlation between traveling and test anxiety but a negative and significant correlation is found in fear of negative evaluation. Moreover, instrumentality prevention and parental expectation are positively and significantly related to test anxiety and fear of negative evaluation.

The multiple regression is formed to answer the second research question. The nine motivation factors are regressed into each of three foreign language anxiety subscales. The regression analysis can be seen in Table 3.

Table 3 indicates that the students' motivation is 15%of the variance in communication apprehension toward English learning [F (2.60) = 1.38). Instrumentality prevention (β = .03, t = .10), traveling β = .22, t = 84) and ought-to L2 self (β = 31, t = 1.28) are the significant predictors of communication apprehension toward English in which ought-to L2 self is the most significant predictor.

In terms of text anxiety, the students' motivation accounted for 14% of the variance with F (2.60) = .68 and Adj R^2 = -.13. Traveling (β = .42, t = 1.43), instrumentality prevention (β = .54, t = .97), and attitudes to L2 learning (β = .63, t = .95) are the three significant predictors of anxiety during the test with attitude L2 learning being the most significant predictor.

For fear of negative evaluation, the motivation also accounted for 2% of the variance [F(2,60) = 1.06, Adj R^2 = 0.02]. Traveling (β = 0.7, t = .25), ought-to L2 self (β = .17, t = .67), and parental expectation (β = .35, t = .98) are the significant predictors of fear of negative evaluation with parental expectation being the most significant predictor.

4 DISCUSSION

The results reveal that the students possess anxiety toward the English class. The correlation between foreign language anxiety and motivation is significant and negatively related. It means that the higher the anxiety level of the students, the lower their motivation. The results also indicate that various types of foreign language anxiety are significantly correlated to motivation subscales. The students experienced foreign language anxiety, such as communication apprehension, test anxiety and fear of negative evaluation, influenced by their motivation.

Test anxiety is a great factor in students' anxiety. For statement number 21, statement *the more I study for a language test, the more confused I get* shows that the students feel worried to prepare the material before the test. They possess anxiety to be evaluated by their teacher and parents during language performance. The fear of testing is related to the academic system

[11]. Von Wörde [23] reveals that oral and listening tests are the most influential factors in test anxiety. The result of the oral test is also in line with speaking anxiety when the students are trying to produce the correct and accurate utterance without forgetting the choice and use of language [9].

In terms of foreign language motivation subscales, the ought-to L2 self possesses a high influence on the students' motivation. The students perceive duties, obligations, and duties to learn the language [3]. It means that the students' motivation to learn L2 is triggered by others. It is a matter of meeting expectations. For instance, their teacher has an expectation and forces their children to learn English.

The relation between foreign language anxiety and the ought-to self is interesting. There is a significant and positive correlation of the ought-to L2 self with all anxiety subscales. Therefore, the students who have high expectations in English learning have fear of communication, English test, and negative evaluation. However, the ideal L2 self, instrumentality promotion, cultural interest, attitudes to L2 learning and intended efforts are negatively correlated to the three foreign language anxiety factors. The students who have ideal English self and performance expectation are less anxious during English class. Then, the students who have cultural interests, attitudes toward English class and intended efforts do not have classroom anxiety. They are comfortable and at ease during the English class.

These findings are supported by previous studies that high anxiety in foreign language learning is associated with the students' motivation [1,3,16,19]. The students who have no motivation in language learning tend to be more anxious than the students who have encouragement to learn English.

Regression analysis was used to predict foreign language anxiety over foreign language motivation. It shows that traveling is a significant predictor of all anxiety subscales. It means that students who like traveling around the world experience higher anxiety during English language learning than the students who do not like traveling.

Therefore, the results of the study can make the English language learning practitioners aware of the individual differences in acquiring a foreign language. The negative correlation shows that the students who have high anxiety are less motivated during the class. To overcome this condition, the teachers should motivate the students in order to decrease their anxiety level.

5 CONCLUSION

This study has investigated the correlation between the factors of foreign language anxiety and motivation. These findings suggest that in general there is a significant and negative correlation between foreign language anxiety and motivation. The students of graduate school have high anxiety when they are not motivated enough to learn English. The empirical findings in this study involve three anxiety factors and nine motivation subscales in English language learning. The results of this research are limited to the number of participants who participated in this study. It affects the variance and confidence level of the data set. The teacher should be aware of the students' anxiety, motivation and any other individual differences in order to achieve the students' language attainments. For the future researcher, it would be interesting to explore the impact of foreign language anxiety and motivation toward the students' English proficiency. The relevant studies in different areas, such as students' aptitude, age, gender, and other individual differences, are also worth being discussed further.

REFERENCES

[1] Aida, Y. (1994). Examination of Horwitz, Horwitz, and Cope's construct of foreign language anxiety: The case of students of Japanese. *The Modern Language Journal, 78*(2), 155–168.

[2] Carreira, J.M. (2006). The relationship between motivation and foreign language anxiety: A pilot study. *JALT Hokkaido Journal, 10*, 16–28.

[3] Dörnyei, Z. (2001). *Teaching and researching motivation*. New York, NY: Longman.

[4] Dörnyei, Z. (2009). The L2 motivational self-system. In Z. Dörnyei & E. Ushioda (Eds.), Motivation, Language Identity and the L2 Self (pp. 9–42). Bristol, UK: Multilingual Matters.

[5] Dörnyei, Z. & Csizér, K. (2002). Some dynamics of language attitudes and motivation: Results of a longitudinal nationwide survey. *Applied Linguistics, 23*(4), 421–462.

[6] Ellis, R. (2012). Language teaching research and language pedagogy. Chichester, UK: John Wiley & Sons.

[7] Gardner, R.C. (1985). *Social psychology and second language learning: The role of attitudes and motivation*. London, UK: Edward Arnold Publishers. doi:10.1037/h0083787.

[8] Gardner, R.C., Lalonde, R.N. & Moorcroft, R. (1985). The role of attitudes and motivation in second language learning: Correlational and experimental considerations. *Journal on Language Learning, 35*(2), 207–227.

[9] Gkonou, C. (2011). *Anxiety over EFL speaking and writing: A view from language classrooms*. Studies in Second Language Learning and Teaching Department of English Studies, Faculty of Pedagogy and Fine Arts, Adam Mickiewicz University, Kalisz (pp. 267–281). Retrieved from https://pressto.amu.edu.pl/index.php/ssllt/article/view/5233

[10] Horwitz, E.K., Horwitz, M.B. & Cope, J. (1986). Foreign language classroom anxiety. *The Modern Language Journal, 70*(2), 125–132. Published by Blackwell Publishing on behalf of the National Federation of Modern Language Teachers Associations Stable. Retrieved from http://www.jstor.org/stable/327317

[11] Huang, H.W. (2005). *The relationship between learning motivation and speaking anxiety among EFL non-English major freshman in Taiwan* (Master's thesis). Taichung, Taiwan: Chaoyang University of Technology.

[12] Leaver, B.L., Ehrman, M. & Shekhtman, B. (2005). Achieving success in second language acquisition. New York, NY: Cambridge University Press.

[13] Lily, M. (2015). *Understanding anxiety and panic attacks*. London, UK: Mind (National Association for Mental Health).

[14] Liu, H.J. (2012). Understanding EFL undergraduate anxiety in relation to motivation, autonomy, and language proficiency. *Electronic Journal of Foreign Language Teaching, 9*(1), 123–139.

[15] Liu, H. & Chen, C. (2015). A comparative study of foreign language anxiety and motivation of academic- and vocational-track high school students. *English Language Teaching, 8*(3), 193–204. doi:10.5539/elt.v8n3p193.

[16] Lucas, R.I., Miraflores, E. & Go, D. (2011). English language learning anxiety among foreign language learners in the Philippines. *Philippine ESL Journal, 7*, 94–119.

[17] MacIntyre, P.D. (1995). How does anxiety affect second language learning? A reply to Sparks and Ganschow. *The Modern Language Journal, 79*(1), 90–99. Oxford, UK: Blackwell Publishing/ National Federation of Modern Language Teachers. Retrieved from http://www.jstor.org/stable/329395

[18] Noels, K.A., Pelletier, L.G., Clémen, R. & Vallerand, R.J. (2000). Why are you learning a second language? Motivational orientations and self-determination theory. *Language Learning, 50*(1), 57–85. doi:10.1111/0023-8333.00111.

[19] Papi, M. (2010). The L2 motivational self-system, L2 anxiety, and motivated behavior: A structural equation modeling approach. *System, 38*(3), 467–479. doi:10.1016/j.system.2010.06.011.

[20] Piechurska-Kuciel, E. (2008). *Language anxiety in secondary grammar students*. Opole, Poland: Uniwersytet Opolski.

[21] Smith, M., Lawrence, M.A. & Seagal, J. (2017). Anxiety disorder and anxiety attacks: Recognizing the signs and symptoms and getting help. Retrieved from http://www.helpguide.org/articles/anxiety/anxiety-attacks-and-anxiety-disorders.htm

[22] Tsai, C.C. & Chang, I. The study on motivation and anxiety of English learning of students at a Taiwan technical university. *International Journal of English Language Teaching, 1*(1), 24.

[23] Von Wörde, R. (2003). Students' perspectives on foreign language anxiety. Virginia Community College System. *Inquiry, 8*(1), n1.

[24] You, C. & Dörnyei, Z. (2014). Language learning motivation in China: Results of a large-scale stratified survey. *Journal of Applied Linguistics, 37*(4), 495–519. doi:10.1093/applin/amu046.

[25] You, C., Dörnyei, Z. & Csizér, K. (2016). Motivation, vision, and gender: A survey of learners of English in China. *Journal of Research in Language Learning, 66*(1), 94–123. doi:10.1111/lang.12140.

English Linguistics, Literature, and Language Teaching in a Changing Era – Madya et al. (eds)
© 2020 Taylor & Francis Group, London, ISBN 978-1-03-224160-9

The influence of Computer-Assisted Language Learning (CALL) to improve English speaking skills

D. Ratnaningsih, D. Purba, D. Wiratno & F. Nofandi
Politeknik Pelayaran Surabaya, Surabaya, Indonesia

ABSTRACT: The use of technology in learning English-speaking skills has grown rapidly. One such technology is the computer-aided learning media. The use of computer media in the field of education has many advantages as they are easier to access, disseminate and store. This study tries to determine how much influence the use of CALL media with lecture methods and discussion has on improving the cadets' English-speaking ability. This study uses a quantitative approach and descriptive-quantitative analysis that reveals the problems that occur during the English learning. Analysis of data used is statistical analysis by reviewing the learning process in learning activities using CALL with lecturing and discussion methods. The sample of this study are the cadets in classes A and B which consist of 50 cadets. The findings show a significant difference of use of CALL media in discussion method and lecturing for English-speaking skills.

Keywords: CALL, lecturing method, discussion method, speaking skills

1 INTRODUCTION

In the field of education, Politeknik Pelayaran Surabaya (the Surabaya Merchant Marine Polytechnic) is one of the vocational universities to continuously improve its graduates' abilities to meet the demands of industries such as shipping companies, port authorities, and all other employment relating to the maritime industry, both at home and abroad. One of the abilities that needs to be improved is the ability to communicate in English. This is in accordance with Sallis [13], who stated that all educational institutions should implement and standardize the management quality of their students; for example, educational institutions should promote sustainable quality programs to foster the ability expected from their graduates to communicate in English, to support the demand of the international maritime industry.

The world of education cannot be separated from technological developments, especially to support learning in higher education. The development of educational technology produces various concepts and educational practices that use computer media as a source of learning. This gives the perception that educational technology is the same as the media; this is actually contradictory because the media is only a tool to convey the content or material of the lesson. In the education system, technology has a role to support curriculum development, especially in design, development and implementation. Politeknik Pelayaran Surabaya itself also has a wide range of computer labs and simulators to support learning activities.

In connection with English learning, the use of technology in this course has grown rapidly. One of the examples of this is Computer Assisted Language Learning (CALL), which is a computer-aided language learning media. The use of computer media in the field of education has many advantages, as it is easier to evaluate the students' works such as grading, evaluating and creating tasks (Warschauer & Healey, 1998) while for students it is easier and faster to do the task and get feedback (Kessler, 2007).

Meanwhile, according to Levy (2005), "the definition of CALL is more succinct and broader as the search for study of applications of the computer in language teaching and learning", by which can be interpreted that CALL can be defined more concisely and widely as being a computer application for use in language learning.

However, based on observations, most of the learning activities in the classroom are still using the discussion and lecturing method. The report shows that the oral test scores and practice of cadets are still below average. Apart from the test scores, the time taken in speaking at the stage of questions and answers and explaining their ideas often highlights their difficulty in choosing vocabulary. Speech is also slow, and the cadets have less courage to start talking to lecturers or to classmates.

Therefore, with the availability of a language laboratory that has been equipped with a computer with the same number cadets in the class, it is planned to use CALL together with the method of discussion and lectures to improve speaking skills in the English language.

Thus, the aim of this study is to identify how much influence the use of CALL media has on the students' English-speaking skills when combined with the discussion and lecturing method.

2 THEORETICAL FRAMEWORK

2. 1 *English for specific purposes*

As Anthony [1] says, some people describe ESP as simply being the teaching of English for any purpose that could be specified. Others, however, are more precise, describing it as the teaching of English used in academic studies or the teaching of English for vocational or professional purposes [1] (pp. 9–10). Moreover, Ono and Morimura [11] explain that in ESP courses it is necessary for students to acquire an English proficiency which will allow them to communicate with English-speaking specialists all over the world, experience which will enable them to communicate with other nations on equal terms outside their own country, help their creative skills and self-motivation for exploring solutions to problems related to their professional domains, and give them an appreciation of diverse cultures in the world. Therefore, ESP in maritime English must be combined with such a comprehensive technology including CALL.

2.2 *Computer-Assisted Language Learning (CALL)*

Levy [8] states that "the definition of CALL is more succinct and broader as a search for study of applications of the computer in language teaching and learning", which could mean that CALL can be defined more concisely and extensively as being a study of computer applications in language learning.

Furthermore, CALL is not only considered as being simple desktop or laptop computer devices. It also includes the networks connecting them, peripheral devices associated with them, and a number of other technological innovations such as Personal Digital Assistants (PDAs), MP3 players, mobile phones, electronic whiteboards, and even DVD players which have a computer of sorts embedded in them [9].

CALL-based learning also has several advantages: 1) Fun: giving a sense of fun to learn for students; 2) Responsibility: giving students the opportunity to take responsibility for the mastery of the materials, that is, by doing the tasks required; 3) Active: students will play an active role in every activity during learning; and, 4) Communicative: many imaginative things that are difficult to visualize can be presented to students through computer simulations, so that such circumstances will facilitate and simplify the concepts in students' minds in understanding English (Iswanti & Lolita, 2010).

2.3 *Lecture method*

The lecture method can be called by the method of speech or lecture method. According to Djamarah [4], the lecture method is a way of teaching that is used to orally convey information or description of subject matter or a problem. This method of presentation is by direct narrative or explanation to the students. Thus, in this method the active role is played by the teacher/lecturer.

Furthermore, Djamarah [4] also mentions the advantages and disadvantages in the method of discussion. The advantages are that teachers/lecturers can master the class easily, easily organize seats in the classroom, can be followed by a large number of students, and can find it easier to prepare, implement and explain the lesson. The disadvantages are that the teachers/lecturers will become a verbalism, which makes the visual learning-style students lose attention; while the students can receive more information by listening, it will make them bored. The teacher/lecturer concludes that the student understands and is interested in his lecture (subjective interpretation), making students become passive, which is not suitable for shaping skills and attitudes and tends to place teaching positions as being the final authority.

2.4 *Discussion method*

Discussion in a broad sense is used to provide answers to serious questions or to talk about an objective problem. Whereas in a narrow sense, the discussion is the exchange of thoughts that occur in small groups or large groups to discuss topics of mutual interest, so that each participant expresses their opinions, both written and oral, about a problem or topic. Then the opinion is discussed with other members, so that the opinion can be obtained together [12].

Meanwhile, according to Mulyana[10], discussion can be defined as a responsive conversation that is woven by problematic questions that are directed to solve the problem. So, based on this understanding can be concluded that the method of discussion is one way to communicate actively by interacting and exchanging thoughts and opinions between one person and another. So the method of discussion in learning makes lecturers and students active in discussing the topic being studied.

2.5 *Speaking skills*

Speaking is an oral spoken process for expressing thoughts and feelings, reflecting on experiences, and sharing information. Ideas are the essence of what we are talking about and words are a means of expressing them. Speaking is a complex process because it involves the ability to have thought processes, discussion and social skills [5]. Meanwhile, according to Hornby [6], speaking is "to talk to somebody about something, to have conversation with somebody." So, speaking is an activity that someone does to someone else about a thing, or conversation activities that someone does with others.

According to Iskandar wassid and Sunendar [7], speech skills have a close relationship with listening skills. A speaker associates meaning and regulates interaction: who is to say what, whom, when, and about what. In the context of communication, the speaker acts as a sender, while the receiver is the recipient of the message that is the object of communication. Then, feedback (feedback) will appear after the news received and the reaction of the recipient of the message. Speech skills refer to the principle of stimulus-response, which is essentially the skill of producing a stream of articulation-sound systems to convey the will, the need for feelings, and the desires of others.

Furthermore, Penny [14] stated that speaking is one of the most important skills of all the four language skills because individuals who learn a language are referred to as the speakers of that language. Therefore, Davies and Pearse [3] explain that the main aim of English language teaching is to give learners the ability to use English language effectively and correctly in communication.

In this study, speaking skills are studied only in three categories: grammar, fluency and comprehension. The scoring rubric from Brown and Abeywickrama [2] is used.

Table 1. Speaking rubric [2].

Aspect	Explanation	Scale	Weight	Score
Grammar	Frequent grammatical errors even in simple structures; meaning is obscured.	1	4	
	Frequent grammatical errors even in simple structures that at times obscured meaning.	2		
	Frequent grammatical errors that do not obscure meaning; little variety in structures.	3		
	Some errors in grammatical structures possibly caused by attempt to include a variety.	4		
	Accuracy and variety of grammatical structures.	5		
Comprehension	The speech is incomprehensible; the speaker does not know anything about what he has said.	1	6	
	The speech is incomprehensible and the speaker knows little things about the speech.	2		
	The speech is difficult to understand; the speaker knows little things about the speech.	3		
	The speech is understood by listener; the speaker knows and understands about the speech.	4		
	The speech is easy to understand by both speaker and listener.	5		
Fluency	The speech is slow and exceedingly hesitant; difficult to perceive continuity in utterances.	1	10	
	The speech is frequently hesitant and jerky with some sentences left uncompleted.	2		
	The speech is relatively hesitation and unnatural pauses.	3		
	The speech is smooth with few hesitations.	4		
	The speech is smooth delivery.	5		
	Total Score			

3 METHOD

3.1 *Research design*

This study is quantitative research using an experimental design. This research involves two variables, which are independent variable or X variable (independent variable), and dependent variable or Y variable (dependent variable). The independent variable is English learning using CALL with lecturing and discussion methods. This X variable can be manipulated and controlled by the researcher, while the dependent variable is the English-speaking skills of the cadets. The instruments are the English Speaking Test which the validity and reliability already tested, while the main data is the speaking skill test scores.

The data analysis searched for the percentage of the cadets' speaking skill level in class A using CALL with discussion method, compared with class B using CALL with lecturing method, to know the effect of CALL media by using both methods in improving English-speaking skill.

To determine the value of each cadet, the researcher calculates from grammar component (G), fluency (F) and comprehension (C). The maximum value for G is 20, for C is 30 and the maximum value for F is 50 [2]. Then the pattern below is used:

$$X = G + C + F$$

While the descriptive analysis of mean scores using this formula is:

$$M = \frac{\sum X}{N}$$

where M = average level of speaking skills in English; ΣX = total sum of values; N = number of research subjects.

The mean scores will show improvement by cadets. If the average value is at least 75 then cadets are considered successful in reaching the Good category.

3. 2 *Participants*

Participants in the present study were 50 cadets of Politeknik Pelayaran Surabaya. They were studying ESP Maritime English in the academic year 2016–2017. These students were randomly chosen from the nautical department. The ESP syllabus used in the study is the syllabus mandated by the Ministry of Transportation Indonesia, which is a series of textbooks based on the International Maritime Organization (IMO) Model Course 3.17.

4 TECHNIQUE OF DATA ANALYSIS AND RESULT

The technique of data analysis in this research was the pretest and posttest in one group using CALL with lecturing method, and another group using CALL with discussion method. The oral test score was based on the scoring rubric from [2]. Those tests were analyzed using t-test to know the cadets' speaking skill, by comparing the scores in pretest and posttest.

The t-test in comparing the pretest in both groups showed that t count value has probability 0.501. Because the probability is less than 0.05, so it can be defined that there is a difference between the pretest results of the CALL group by the discussion method and the CALL group with the lecturing method. While in posttest, the t-count value has probability 1.301. Since the probability is > 0.05, then it can be said that there is a difference between the posttest results of the CALL group by the discussion method and the CALL group with the lecturing method. Finally, the score difference is shown below.

Based on Table 2, the significant improvement is acquired by the group which is using CALL with discussion method. In its post-test the mean score is 21.48, while another group which is using CALL with lecturing method achieved only 19 in mean score. So, the difference in value held by the CALL group with the discussion method, compared with the CALL group with lecturing method, is 21.48 > 19.

Moreover, the significant differences which are shown by the results of hypothesis testing proved that the value of t-count is greater than t-table at 5% significance level. It can be concluded that the use of CALL media using discussion method and lecture on English-speaking skill resulted in different outcomes in both groups, although higher results were achieved by groups using CALL by discussion method. This appears in the difference in value held by the CALL group with the discussion compared with the CALL group with lectures, which is 21.48 > 19.

Table 2. Score difference between CALL with discussion method and CALL with lecturing method.

Groups	Mean	Score difference
Pretest CALL with discussion method	19.0	+ 2.48
Post-test CALL with discussion method	21.48	
Pretest CALL with lecturing method	18.5	+ 0.5
Post-test CALL with lecturing method	19	

5 CONCLUSION

The conclusion that can be drawn from the research results and discussion of research data is that there is significant difference of use of CALL with discussion and lecturing method in improving the English-speaking skill. This can be seen from the results of hypothesis testing that shows that the value of t-count is greater than t-table at 5% significance level. Furthermore, it is also concluded that the group using CALL with discussion method achieve higher English-speaking skills than the group using CALL with lecturing method.

REFERENCES

[1] Anthony, L. (1997). Preaching to cannibals: A look at academic writing in engineering. In *The Japan Conference on English for Specific Purposes Proceedings, January 31, 1998.*

[2] Brown, H.D. & Abeywickrama, P.(2004). *Language assessment: Principles and classroom practices.* New York, NY: Pearson Education.

[3] Davies, P. & Pearse, E. (2000). *Success in English teaching.* Oxford, UK: Oxford University Press.

[4] Djamarah, S.B. (2002). *Prestasibelajar dan kompetensi guru.* Surabaya, Indonesia: Usaha Nasiona.

[5] Ellis, G. & Sinclair, B. (1989). *Learning to learn English: Learner's book.* Cambridge, UK: Cambridge University Press.

[6] Hornby, A.S. (2005). *Oxford Advanced Learner's Dictionary.* New York, NY: Oxford University Press.

[7] Iskandarwassid & Sunendar, D. (2009). *Strategipembelajaranbahasa.* Bandung, Indonesia: Rosda.

[8] Kessler. (2007). Formal and informal CALL preparation and teacher attitude toward technology. *Computer Assisted Language Learning, 20* (2), 173–188.

[9] Levy, M. (1997). *Computer assisted language learning: Context and conceptualization.* New York, NY: Oxford University Press.

[10] Levy, M. & Hubbard, P. (2005) Why call CALLCALL? (editorial). *Computer Assisted Language Learning, 18*(3), 143–149.

[11] Mulyana, E. (2006). *Menjadi guru profesional; Menciptakanpembelajaranaktif dan menyenangkan.* Bandung, Indonesia: RosdaKarya.

[12] Ono, Y.A. & Morimura, K. (2007). Effective methods for teaching technical English to Japanese engineering students: Case study at School of Engineering, The University of Tokyo. Professional Communication Conference, IPCC 2007, IEEE International, Oct 2007.

[13] Sahara, Fitiyah, Z.A. & Kusnadi. (2009). *KeterampilanBerbahasa Indonesia.* Jakarta, Indonesia: FITKUINSyarifHidayatullah.

[14] Warschauer & Healey. (1998). Computer and Language Learning; An Overvies. *Language Teaching, 31,* (57–71).

English Linguistics, Literature, and Language Teaching in a Changing Era – Madya et al. (eds)
© 2020 Taylor & Francis Group, London, ISBN 978-1-03-224160-9

Enhancing Indonesian elementary students' engagement in learning English through cooperative learning strategies

Emeral, Dyah S. Ciptaningrum, Elsa M. Marahati & Thuthut Kartikarini
English Education Study Program, Graduate School, Yogyakarta State University, Yogyakarta, Indonesia

ABSTRACT: Students' engagement is considered as being one of the influential factors in the teaching and learning process, particularly in language learning. When the students are engaged in the language learning process, they will focus and construct their own knowledge, and/or have a positive attitude toward the language, and/or get involved actively in interaction [13]. However, promoting student engagement seems to be challenging work for teachers as each student is naturally different in terms of background and knowledge. Therefore, the present study aimed at enhancing English-as-a-Foreign Language (EFL) students' engagement in the English learning process through the Cooperative Learning Strategy (CLS). To obtain the objective, the two cycles of Classroom Action Research (CAR) were applied. This study took place at one of the public elementary schools in Yogyakarta, particularly in grade five, which consisted of 28 students. Games, jigsaw, and project CLS techniques were utilized in the study. The data from on-going classroom observation were recorded with Narrative Observation Notes and then thematically analyzed. The overall result showed that there was a gradual improvement in the students' engagement in learning English and the class situation became more conducive during the teaching and learning process.

Keywords: engagement, Cooperative Learning Strategy (CLS)

1 INTRODUCTION

Students' engagement plays a pivotal role in the language teaching and learning process, particularly in language learning. When the students are engaged in the language learning process, they will focus and construct their own knowledge, and/or have a positive attitude toward the language, and/or get involved actively in interaction [13]. However, although it sounds worthwhile, promoting the students' engagement is challenging for teachers. This is because students are different in terms of their interests, needs, learning styles and purpose for learning English [10]. It is even more challenging if English is newly introduced to a class where most of the students have no previous knowledge about it. There will be a tendency that students might perceive English as being difficult, resulting in anxiety or poor motivation, which in turn inhibits the instructional process.

In an Indonesian context, English is taught as a compulsory subject at every level of education, with the exception of the elementary level. However, by referring to Law No. 62 of 2014 on Indonesian Ministry of Education and Culture, a great number of public elementary schools in Indonesia, especially in Yogyakarta, decided to equip their students with the English subject as an extracurricular program. Furthermore, in Chapter 4, Article 1 of this law, it is stated that the extracurricular program should promote the students' active participation and fun learning. Considering this principle, enhancing the elementary school students' engagement in learning English is crucial.

However, in class V A, where this study took place, it was found that students were totally less engaged in learning English. The result of 60 minutes on-going observation showed that most students did not pay attention to their teacher. They were talking to each other while the teacher was explaining the materials. Furthermore, only a few students were willing to respond to the teacher's questions. Similarly, when the teacher assigned them a task, the class became less productive and more chaotic. Surprisingly, the teacher confessed that the class was always this chaotic since English was first introduced and she believed that the students' poor engagement is mainly caused by the difficulties of English itself. Unfortunately, she took this situation for granted, as the only effort she made was to simply remind the students about the importance of English.

The observation and interview result indicated that the teaching strategies contributed to the students' having less engagement in the classroom. First, the materials were mainly delivered through lecturing, where the students were asked to sit and listen to the teacher's explanation during the class. This is in contrast to the characteristics of young learners who are energetic and physically active [11]. Furthermore, in assigning the task, the teacher always asked the students to do it independently. Nevertheless, it is important to highlight that in this school, English is first taught to fifth graders and in class V A, and only some students had experience in learning English in private courses. Thus, it can be inferred that the students' knowledge and ability in English varied. In line with this situation, most students confessed that the tasks were too difficult for them and that they needed help to accomplish them. Regarding this situation, the teaching strategy has been found to be a major determinant of students' reticence in the classrooms [7]. To sum up, an effective teaching strategy is necessary to enhance the students' engagement in learning English.

By reviewing the relevant literatures, the most suitable solution to the above problem seems to be by utilizing the Cooperative Learning Strategy (CLS). CLS is defined as *"instructional approaches in which students work in small mixed-ability groups"* [12]. Cooperative learning is different from ordinary group work since it functions to make students assist one another in order to achieve a certain goal [5]. The best number for a small group is no more than six people for the students to work effectively [2]. A great number of techniques of CLS can be applied, such as games, role-play, drama, project, interview, brainstorming, information gap and jigsaw [2].

During the implementation of CLS, the teacher is responsible for giving proper instructions and monitoring the group work [5]. A proper instruction is crucial to make students understand well what they are expected to do. If the instruction is not clear, the execution will not run as expected. In anticipation, the teacher can repeat the instruction or ask students to re-explain the instruction in their own way [2]. Additionally, if the task seems to be complicated to explain, simulation can be employed [2]. In the same way, the teacher needs to monitor the group work, and if necessary, he/she intervenes to help the students work effectively in their group [5]. It is undeniable that one of the important issues in relation to group work is that high-achievers are inclined to be dominating in it and avoid negotiation [6]. This situation is very harmful because when the high-achievers are dominating the group work, other students may become passive. Thus, to cope with this kind of situation, it is suggested that having students understand their own job description in a group is necessary [2].

There are studies which have proven the superiority of CLS in the language teaching and learning process [14,9,1]. In Vietnam, a study revealed that students who are instructed using CLS achieved higher scores than those who are taught using lecture-based teaching [14]. In another study, particularly in China, an intervention group who was taught using the CLS approach, performed better in speaking, listening and reading than those in a comparison group [9]. Similarly, a study in Iran indicates that CLS is successful in increasing Iran's junior high school learners' oral communicative competence, as well as their motivation in learning English [1]. Regarding these findings, CLS appears to be highly recommended to make students cognitively and affectively engaged in teaching and learning process.

Considering the problem in class V A and the superiority of CLS, this study attempts to enhance the students' engagement in learning English by applying the Cooperative Learning Strategy and address the two research questions below:

1. How does the Cooperative Learning Strategy help students become more engaged in learning English?

2. What is the class situation during the implementation of the Cooperative Learning Strategy?

2 RESEARCH METHOD

2.1 *Participant*

The participants of the study were 28 students of grade V A in one of the public elementary schools in Yogyakarta and their ages ranged between 9 and 11 years old.

2.2 *Research process*

Concerning the objective of this present study, to enhance the students' engagement in learning English through CLS, Classroom Action Research (CAR) is considered to be an appropriate design to apply. As its name suggests, CAR is expected to yield an improvement through actions in the educational setting [8]. This type of research comprises of planning, action, observation and reflection stages in each cycle [3].

2.2.1 *Cycle 1: Planning*

In this stage, the problems were carefully identified through 60 minutes of on-going classroom observation and interview with the classroom teacher and the students. As mentioned earlier, the result of the observation indicated that the inappropriate teaching strategies contributed to the students' having less engagement in the classroom since lecturing was dominating the teaching and learning process. Additionally, the interview result with the teacher confirmed that she always taught this way because she believed that having the students remember the rule is essential. However, the observation result showed that most students did not pay attention to her. The students were talking to each other when the teacher was explaining the materials. Furthermore, only a few students were willing to respond to the teacher's questions. The students were totally less participative and less enthusiastic during the class.

Another problem occurred when the teacher assigned the task. She asked the students to work independently in accomplishing the task. However, several students kept making some noises instead of starting to do the task and they ended up producing nothing. Besides, the teacher asked the students who had finished doing the task to write their answer on the whiteboard; meanwhile, others who had not finished still kept doing it themselves. Not long after, some of them decided to come to the teacher and/or their friends for help. This happened many times. Interestingly, there was a student who still did not understand what to do and he asked the teacher for further explanation. However, he still did not get proper explanation from the teacher. The teacher was inclined to ignore him, since she was more focused on other students who asked for feedback, and on checking the students' answers on the whiteboard. This situation made him ask his friends for help, but it still did not work since his friends were busy doing their own task. As a result, this student started making some noise. He played around and tried to go out of the classroom. He was then followed by other students who did not do the task. On the other hand, some students who finished doing the task earlier looked bored since they had to wait for their friends who were still doing the task. As a consequence, they started disturbing each other. This condition clearly made the class chaotic and out of control.

To obtain more precise information about the major source of the problem, we did an interview with three high-achievers, three medium-achievers and three low-achievers. Based on the interviews, it was revealed that both the low and medium-achievers found that the task was too difficult and that it took too much time to accomplish independently. Thus, they expected to work in a group or in pairs. On the other hand, one of high-achievers preferred to work by herself since she felt distracted by working together. She argued that her friends would rely too much on her. Meanwhile, the other two high-achievers were fine, whether or not they were assigned into a group. Interestingly, those three high-achievers found that the questions were too easy for them. Additionally, all of them agreed that listening to the lecturing for a long time was tedious.

In reference to the result of on-going classroom observation and interview, it is strongly believed that the inappropriate teaching strategy is the major cause of why students became less engaged and chaotic during the learning process. To overcome the problem, the teacher needs to facilitate students with a learning environment which enables them to assist one another during the learning process and which avoids too much lecturing.

In such a situation, CLS is considered relevant to apply. In implementing CLS, the researchers agreed that the first important thing is in making students enjoy the learning process. Thus, games were employed in the first meeting. Moreover, colorful nametags were prepared as a medium to assign students into groups. Based on the researchers' experience, assigning students into groups is not easy since they prefer to work with their close friends. By using colorful nametags, we simply distributed the tags to them and had them join the group with the same color of nametags. By doing so, the students would not realize that the group members had been determined by the researchers, as they were attracted to the colored nametag and perceived it as a part of the games. Additionally, in the next meeting of cycle one, we agreed to employ a more challenging task, that is, doing jigsaw. A challenging task is believed to contribute to the development of the students' cognitive level.

2.2.2 Cycle 1: Action

In the first meeting of cycle 1, puzzle games as one of CLS techniques was applied. The topic entitled "Profession" was taught by one of the researchers. Meanwhile, the classroom teacher participated as one of the observers. Firstly, the students were assigned into a group of four people. When assigning the students into groups, the teacher needs to consider at least one of the criteria such as native language, proficiency level, age, culture, gender, or interest [2]. However, in this study, the students were assigned into groups based on their proficiency level, since they are expected to assist one another in achieving the learning objective. The information of their proficiency level was obtained from Cambridge Assessment Test for Starter, which had been conducted for another project in this class. Each group consisted of a high-achiever, two medium-achievers and a low-achiever.

Next, the researcher made sure that the instruction was clear for the groups. Besides explaining it herself, she asked two students to re-explain the instruction in their own way. Furthermore, during the process, the researcher monitored the class, ensuring that the activities ran well. Additionally, whenever possible, the groups were free to ask the researcher for help. When they finished arranging the puzzle, each group stuck their group's puzzle on the whiteboard. After checking each group's puzzle, the researcher taught the students about the vocabulary of professions by writing down the name of professions under each puzzle, pronouncing each vocabulary word and asking the class to repeat. After that, the follow-up task was given to the groups to make them remember the meaning and spelling. In this task, each group was instructed to fill in the missing letters of several words and match them to the relevant pictures.

Then, in the second meeting of cycle 1, under the same topic and group member, the students were assigned to do a jigsaw. This activity required them to share information with their own group and other groups. Each group member was equipped with a card containing their own job description. Every high-achiever in the class was assigned to be "an expert" as those who gave information about what each profession does; meanwhile, the others were instructed to obtain information about what each profession does. However, to make sure that students were able to interact in the jigsaw activity, the researcher first drilled the previous materials in meeting 1 and explained about how to share information in English, and particularly on how to ask and answer question about what a certain profession does. Additionally, clear instruction was provided preceding the jigsaw activity. Moreover, to make it more precise to follow, the researcher invited one of the observers to perform the jigsaw simulation. Added to this, the researcher monitored the students during the activity.

2.2.3 Cycle 1: Observation

Since one's learning engagement is manifested in one's behavior, observation seems to be an appropriate way to collect the data. "Observation is best used to study actual behavior, and to study individuals who have difficulty verbalizing their ideas" [8]. The data from observations were then recorded into Narrative Observation Notes that are created as the researcher observes the events [3]. Putting it simply, Narrative Observation Notes can be regarded as the story of whatever events the researcher observes. Thus, the data obtained would be more systematic and comprehensive. In this study, we had three Narrative Observation Notes from the classroom teacher and two observers, which then were cross-checked among the observers before the data analysis.

The Narrative Observation Notes were analyzed thematically. To do so, there are several interrelated steps involved, as suggested by [4]. First of all, the researchers organized the notes to ensure the data were chronological and ready to analyze. This stage is known as data preparation. Second, the data were read thoroughly and interesting phenomena were coded - for example, CI for Contributes Ideas; H for Help; and, AQ for Asking Questions. After that, the codes were grouped into some themes which are related to the indicator of language learning engagement proposed by [1]; those are: constructing knowledge, having positive attitude toward language, and/or participating actively in interactions. Finally, the data were presented in a table, and to ensure accuracy, member checking was done.

2.2.4 Cycle 1: Reflection

After all actions in cycle 1 had been done, all researchers and the classroom teacher discussed the result. The following are the result of reflection on cycle 1:

i. The students' engagement in the learning process were improved in each meeting of cycle 1, and so this led to the next cycle being easier.
ii. Cycle 2 was carried out to validate the result of cycle 1;
iii. Assigning students into different groups is considered necessary that they would be able to deal with a number of different people;
iv. The researcher who teaches the class needs to talk louder since some students in the back row asked for repetition;
v. For the same reason as aforementioned, a more challenging task would be utilized.

2.2.5 Cycle 2: Planning

In this cycle, Word Wall Project as one of techniques in CLS was applied. This task was more complex than in cycle 1. The decision to apply this technique was aimed at improving the students' ability to cooperate with their friends, to empower creativity, and to recall their memory about previous materials in cycle 1. The tools for making the word walls, such as scissors, colorful markers, ropes, pictures and the example of a word wall were already provided by the researcher. Additionally, in assigning the students into groups, the researcher followed the same principles as the first cycle. The only difference was that the students did not work with the same members as in their previous groups. This was intended to make them able to cooperate with many different types of colleagues.

2.2.6 Cycle 2: Action

In this cycle, a new topic was introduced, which is about "Things at School". Each group was given a Logico board and a card consisting of many pictures related to the topic. The students should work in groups to match several things in that picture to the correct words by using colored buttons on a Logico board. During the process, the researcher walked around the class and checked the progress made by all groups. After all the groups had finished doing the task, the researcher instructed them to check the correct answers on the back of the cards and correct their answers.

For the main task, the researcher instructed all the groups to make a word wall based on the vocabulary they had learned from the Logico games. Before the students started doing the project, the researcher showed an example of a word wall, so that the students knew what a word wall looked like. Furthermore, while the researcher checked all the groups' progress, students were free to ask for help and suggestions from her. After all the students had finished their projects, they stuck their word wall on the whiteboard and the researcher taught them how to pronounce the words.

2.2.7 Cycle 2: Observation

In cycle 2, data collection techniques and instrument were the same as cycle 1, those being on-going classroom observation and Narrative Observation Notes, which were also thematically analyzed.

2.2.8 *Cycle 2: Reflection*

The result of cycle 2 supported the result of cycle 1; that is, the class engagement was improved which then made the class more conducive. Considering the satisfying result of CLS implementation on those two cycles, all observers agreed not to continue the cycle.

3 FINDINGS AND DISCUSSION

3.1 *Analysis of research question 1*

3.1.1 *The impact of CLS on class engagement during cycle 1*

This study is aimed at enhancing the students' engagement in learning English using CLS, and the result of the study indicated that CLS helps students to become more engaged in learning English. The engagement criteria in this context is when students focus and construct their own knowledge, and/or have a positive attitude toward the language, and/or get involved actively in interaction [13]. During the first meeting in cycle 1, students were willing to take part and work together with their group members to finish the assignment. When they were working on two sets of puzzles, almost all groups decided to share the tasks in which two members arranged a set of puzzles and the other two handled another set. Two members who had finished a set of puzzles quickly helped the other members who still worked on another set. Therefore, most of the groups could finish the puzzles on time. Interestingly, the low-achiever student, who found difficulty in understanding the task, engaged in this game. He even stood up from his chair to arrange the puzzles and acted as group leader who assigned the other members to work on another set, so that they could finish the puzzles on time. He also stayed calm in the classroom throughout the learning activity.

This kind of situation was also found during the follow-up task in which they were asked to fill in the missing letters and match the pictures. All the groups shared the task with their members, in which two members filled in the missing letters and the others looked for the correct picture. Interestingly, the high-achievers who at the first observation looked bored and disturbed their friends because they had nothing to do after finishing the task became focused on this task and helped their group members who had difficulties in choosing the correct pictures. As a result, they were not very noisy and did not disturb their friends.

In the second meeting of cycle 1, the students were given a jigsaw task. In this task, the students shared information with other groups related to what a person in a certain profession does. During the task, it was also revealed that the students, particularly the high-achievers, were not only willing to share information, but also to help their friends who had difficulty writing down the information in English. The high-achievers mentioned the words slowly several times and checked their friends' writing.

The above result indicated that heterogeneity of group membership benefited all group members since a small mixed-ability group is best to make students assist one another [12]. This arrangement made the low and medium-achievers accomplish the task or project easily as it enabled them to cooperate and learn from the members who are more knowledgeable. This situation was different from the previous situation or before the implementation of CLS, where many students were unable to accomplish the task as they were asked to do it by themselves or with no proper assistance. Similarly, this arrangement gave the high-achievers a more challenging task, that is, to help their friends in accomplishing the group work. As a result, they did not have the chance to loiter around the class or disturb their friends as they did before the implementation of CLS. Most students were focused on accomplishing their work. Besides the group arrangement, the technique of CLS encouraged students to be responsible in doing the task. The puzzle games and jigsaw piqued the students' curiosity and imagination, thus making the students enthusiastic in doing the task. Those activities are all relevant to the nature of young learners who are curious, energetic and physically active [11].

3.1.2 *The impact of CLS on class engagement during cycle 2*

The students' improved engagement was also observed in cycle 2, when they were instructed to work on Logico games and making a word wall project with their group members. When playing the Logico games, almost all the groups cooperated with their members in solving the game. They asked other members' opinions and discussed the solution. This indicated that students actively construct their own knowledge. However, among the seven groups, there was a group whose members were reluctant to participate in the Logico games and cooperate with other members. It is because the high-achiever in this group did not want to share the Logico with the other members and only solved it by himself. As a result, the other members found difficulty on doing Logico games since it was taken by the high-achiever. The researcher then tried to visit this group and directed the students but this situation was repeated several times. Therefore, the researcher made the decision to monitor them more intensively than other groups. Fortunately, in the end they could finish the Logico games together.

The situation when the high-achiever student did not want to share the Logico with the other members and only solved it by himself proved that high-achievers always have the potential to dominate the group work [6]. Nevertheless, this condition is also normal as another characteristic of young learners is to be egocentric and to relate new ideas to themselves [11]. Moreover, the present study also witnessed that such a situation is most likely to occur when the group members are not assigned specific work. Although having students understand their own job description in a group is necessary [2], in this kind of activity - playing Logico or other relevant games, it is actually impossible to assign what each member has to do. Therefore, when the high-achiever seems to be dominating, the teacher should be aware of this situation. She can interrupt the group by giving advice that they should be more cooperative. In short, it is essential to keep them under control so that every group member can benefit from the group work.

Furthermore, in the word wall project, all the groups were engaged since they discussed strategy to construct the word wall. For example, in group four, two members had tasks to stick a rope to papers with some glue while the other members wrote down the vocabulary of Things at School that matched with several pictures. This kind of participation was also observed in the other groups, in which they discussed some strategies about what to do first to make the word wall and helped other members who were still struggling with their tasks.

Added to this, in every pronunciation practice, the students enthusiastically repeated the researcher's pronunciation. Also, when the researcher asked the students to voluntarily pronounce the words themselves, most of them raised their hands as they wanted to be chosen. The same situation also happened when the researcher asked them questions to check their understanding of the materials. They were willing to respond to the teacher's question. These findings are relevant to the indication of learning engagement; that is, when the students are engaged in the language learning process, they will focus and construct their own knowledge, and/or have a positive attitude toward the language, and/or get involved actively in interaction [13]. Overall, the techniques above showed that students enjoyed the class, actively participated in responding to the researcher's questions and accomplished the task well.

3.2 *Analysis of research question 2*

3.2.1 *Class situation during cycles 1 and 2*

Besides the students' active participation, another thing noticed during CLS implementation was that the class had become less noisy and more conducive to learning. It is important to note that the term "less noisy" here means that the students did not spend their time discussing random things with other students which were not lesson-related. It was observed during the learning activity that the students mostly discussed about the tasks and projects given to them. There were also times when the students joked and played with other members, but they then went back to their discussion and projects quickly. In addition, during cycle 1 and cycle 2, all of the students stayed in the classroom. They did not get out of the class on purpose to play outside the classroom.

Furthermore, they also did not disturb their friends or do something that would make the class chaotic. This indicates that if the teacher is able to manage the class, it will be effective for English language learning [11].

In reference to this class situation, during the reflection, the classroom teacher confessed that she was impressed that CLS is successful in improving the students' engagement in learning English. She was motivated to use this strategy more often and interested in exploring other techniques of CLS.

4 CONCLUSIONS AND SUGGESTION

The above findings led to several conclusions: (1) CLS is proven to be an effective teaching strategy for the heterogeneous class as it encourages students to assist each other to obtain certain objectives and this benefits all students from all levels of proficiency; (2) CLS helps the teacher to manage the class properly; (3) CLS makes English learning become more enjoyable, resulting in students' active participation; (4) High-achievers always have the potential to be dominating in group work, and thus, the job description and the teacher's role as a monitor are necessary to control them; and, (5) however, the job description for each group member might not be suitable for every CLS technique, and thus, if the students tend to be dominating the group work, the teacher should pay more attention to the group.

However, since this study is limited to the subjects as mentioned above, there is a need to replicate this study in different contexts, so that the findings of the effects of cooperative learning can be compared. Additionally, other techniques of CLS can be explored in order to contribute to the CLS construct.

REFERENCES

[1] Azizinezhad, M., Hashemi, M. & Darvishi, S. (2013). Application of cooperative learning in EFL classes to enhance the students' language learning. *Procedia-Social and Behavioral Sciences, 93*, 138–141.

[2] Brown, H.D. (2007). *Teaching by principles: An interactive approach to language pedagogy* (3rd ed.). New York, NY: Pearson Education.

[3] Burns, A. (2010). *Doing action research in English language teaching: A guide for practitioners.* New York, NY: Routledge.

[4] Creswell, J.W. (2012). *Educational research: Planning, conducting and evaluating quantitative and qualitative research* (4th ed.). Boston, MA: Pearson Education.

[5] Johnson, D.W. & Johnson, R.T. (1999). Making cooperative learning work. *Theory into practice, 38*(2), 67–73.

[6] Lee, H.J., Kim, H. & Byun, H. (2015). Are high achievers successful in collaborative learning? An explorative study of college students' learning approaches in team project-based learning. *Innovations in Education and Teaching International, 54*, 1–10.

[7] Lee, W. & Ng, S. (2009). Reducing student reticence through teacher interaction strategy. *ELT Journal, 64*(3), 302–313.

[8] Lodico, M.G., Spaulding, D.T. & Voegtle, K.H. (2010). *Methods in educational research: From theory to practice* (2nd ed.). San Francisco, CA: John Wiley & Sons.

[9] Ning, H. & Hornby, G. (2010). The effectiveness of cooperative learning in teaching English to Chinese tertiary learners. *Effective Education, 2*(2), 99–116.

[10] Richards, J.C. (2015). *Key issues in language teaching.* Cambridge, UK: Cambridge University Press.

[11] Shin, J.K. & Crandall, J.A. (2013). *Teaching young learners English: From theory to practice.* Boston, MA: Heinle Cengage Learning.

[12] Slavin, R.E. (2006). *Educational psychology: Theory into practice.* New York, NY: Pearson Education.

[13] Marie, A., & Svalberg L. (2009). Engagement with language: interrogating a construct. *Taylor & Francis, 3*(4), 242–258.

[14] Tran, V.D. (2014). The effects of cooperative learning on the academic achievement and knowledge retention. *International Journal of Higher Education, 3*(2), 131–140.

English Linguistics, Literature, and Language Teaching in a Changing Era – Madya et al. (eds)
© 2020 Taylor & Francis Group, London, ISBN 978-1-03-224160-9

The implementation of intercultural language learning in teaching Indonesian as a foreign language to international students

Godlove Kiswaga
The Mwalimu Nyerere Memorial Academy, Tanzania

Anita Triastuti
English Language Education Study Program, Graduate School, Yogyakarta State University, Yogyakarta, Indonesia

ABSTRACT: In this global and digital era, we cannot avoid massive interaction of people from different cultural backgrounds. Although English has been used as an international lingua franca for many years, there is a vital reason to learn as many foreign languages as possible to couple with this multicultural phenomenon. These foreign languages have to be learnt in intercultural perspectives because intercultural language learning is essential to move learners from ethnocentrism to intercultural communicative competence (ethnorelativism). Learning, in this approach, also minimizes intercultural conflicts during interaction. Therefore, this study aims at exploring how intercultural language learning is implemented in teaching Indonesian language to international students. The study applied purposive sampling. The participants were seven international students studying at two universities in Yogyakarta, five from Africa and two from Asia. An Interview and open-ended questionnaires were used for data collection. The data were qualitatively analyzed. The results showed that intercultural language approach was implemented according to principles and processes [1 & 2]. However, most of the students recommended that the reflection in their cultures was not sufficient. These results imply that there is a need of adding more different sources to reflect the learner's culture. Moreover, deliberate consideration to compare the target culture and the learners' cultures should be highlighted.

Keywords: intercultural language learning, principles, processes, resources, intercultural transformation

1 INTRODUCTION

As the rapid and dynamic interaction of different people with different cultural background increases in this global era, intercultural communicative competence is highly demanded. Intercultural communicative competence is the ability to interact with people from different cultural background appropriately and effectively in all social contexts using foreign languages [3]. Hence, intercultural language learning approach becomes a right response to enhance learner's intercultural communicative competence in foreign language learning. Learning foreign language in this approach makes learners become the mediators between their own culture and the culture of the target language [2]. [3] describes the two stages in intercultural competence. The beginning stage is ethnocentrism, which is the tendency to view ones' own culture as the central to reality and followed by ethnorelativism, the conscious awareness that all behaviors exist within a cultural framework including one's own. Thus, intercultural language learning is very essential for the students to move from ethnocentrism towards ethnorelativism. Therefore, despite the use of English as a lingual franca by more than 7.5 billion speakers [5], it is very crucial to learn as many foreign languages as possible in intercultural perspective to be cultural mediators and communicate appropriately, effectively and to minimize intercultural conflicts in this 21st century multicultural global community.

Intercultural language learning in foreign language context does not mean foreign language learners who study foreign language and its culture as a body of knowledge solely, but rather it involves transformation of learners in the process of learning. The learners transform from linguistic and cultural positioning and develop intercultural identity, and as a result of engagement with another culture, the boundary between self and others are explored, resolved and redrawn [6]. [2] explains the term *"intercultural mediator"* to refer to the person who is intercultural competent as result of intercultural language learning orientation. Learners need to be mediators between their background culture and the culture of the target language. Further, he differentiated between intercultural mediator and bicultural person. The first involves the transformation of learners in attitude, knowledge, skills and cultural awareness, while the bicultural person only knows the comparison of more than one culture.

Intercultural language learning approach is the base of intercultural communicative competence in foreign language learning context. This perspective harmonizes linguistic competence, social linguistic competence, discourse competence and intercultural competence. If intercultural language learning is implemented effectively in foreign language context, learners will become intercultural competent and intercultural communicative competent. [3] distinguishes the two terms with the description that intercultural competence is the ability of people to interact in their own language with people from another country and from different cultural backgrounds and it comes as a result of knowledge, interaction, relating and discovery. While, intercultural communicative competence is the ability to use foreign language in interaction with different people from different cultural background including the ability to negotiate the meaning in different social context.

A number of research have been conducted on intercultural competence in relation to foreign language learning [7,8,9,10]. However, these studies differ in their focuses. While [10], and [9] investigated about the attitude and perceptions of intercultural competence in language teaching, [8] explored intercultural competence in language teaching and [7] conducted the study on factors that influence students' intercultural competence. In addition, those studies focused on English language, Thai language, Chinese language and Greek language.

Hence, little is known about the actual implementation of intercultural language learning in Indonesian context despite the existence of theories discussed by different scholars. Therefore, the focus of this paper is to describe how the intercultural language learning is implemented in learning Indonesian as a foreign language to international students from different countries in two universities in Yogyakarta. Particularly, the paper focuses on intercultural language principles, processes and resources. Therefore, the study is guided by the following questions;

1. How does the learning of Indonesian language apply the principles of intercultural approach?
2. How does the learning of Indonesian language apply the processes of intercultural language learning?
3. What are the resources used in learning Indonesian language in intercultural perspectives?

2   RESEARCH METHOD

This study was a qualitative research in which the data were collected from two universities in Yogyakarta Indonesia. Purposive sampling was applied in selecting the samples for the study. Seven international students were used as sample for the study.

The international students came from Asia and Africa. Two students were from Rwanda, two from Burundi (East Africa), one from Mali (West Africa), one from Nepal (Southern Asia) and one from Turkmenistan (Central Asia). All the students have different cultural backgrounds and languages. However, they are united by English as a lingua franca and they studied Indonesian language as a foreign language in intercultural perspectives.

The data were collected using open-ended questionnaires and semi-structured interviews. The questions for the questionnaire and the semi-structured interview were adapted from the principles and processes in intercultural language learning [1,2] and the Developmental Model of Intercultural Sensitivity [4].

3 FINDINGS AND DISCUSSION

3.1 *Principles in intercultural language learning*

Table 1. Principles of intercultural language learning.

	Active construction	Making connection	Social-interaction	Reflection	Responsibility
A	√	√	√	√	√
B	√	√	√	√	x
C	√	√	√	√	√
D	x	x	√	x	x
E	√	√	√	√	√
F	√	√	√	√	√
G	√	x	√	x	√

The table above shows that the principles of intercultural language learning are implemented as explained by most of the respondents in their questionnaires. However, respondents B, D and G showed doubt in some few principles. Respondent B said that responsibility was a problem in the implementation, respondent D claimed that only social interaction was implemented accordingly. Meanwhile, student G explained that making connection and reflection are still problems in the implementation of intercultural language learning. The principle which is mostly implemented effective is social interaction. This might be because the students live with the target language audience. Then, it is easy to interact with Indonesians and to exchange cultures through interview or different cultural workshops. From the findings, responsibility is still a problem. The students explained that they were not always motivated to consider their cultures in the learning process. However, mostly they study the culture of the target language. Furthermore, the students are lack of motivation to connect their cultural framework knowledge and the cultural framework knowledge of the target language. That is possibly the reason that connection as a principle does not seem to be implemented well as indicated by the findings.

The findings imply that although most of responses are positive regarding principles in intercultural language learning, there is a need to improve more the actual implementation to make students interculturally communicative. In supporting the effectiveness of the implementation of these principles, [11] suggests that the intercultural language learning materials of both cultures should be exposed to learners and encourage them to compare and contrast foreign culture and learners' own culture.

3.2 *Process in intercultural language learning*

Table 2. Students' responses regarding the process in the intercultural language learning.

Learners	Noticing	Comparing	Interaction	Reflection
A	√	√	√	√
B	√	√	√	√
C	√	√	√	√
D	√	x	√	x
E	√	√	√	√
F	√	√	√	√
G	√	√	√	x

The table above shows the responses of the students regarding the processes in intercultural language learning as stated by [1]. Most of the students responded positively, except student

D and G who confirmed that the comparison and reflection to their own culture and language were not sufficient in the process of studying Indonesian language. In learning language in intercultural perspectives, the comparison of the target culture and the learners' culture is very important and it enhances the reflection process. Hence, there is a need to pay attention to the international students' culture and the target culture in the learning process. Thus, learners will act as mediators between their cultures and the Indonesian culture. This is in support to [2] who highlighted the role of learners as mediators in intercultural language learning perspective so as to be interculturally communicative competent.

3.3 *Resources in intercultural language learning*

Table 3. The responses of seven international students on different resources in intercultural language learning.

Learners	Text books		Technology		Literary books		Tasks		Students presentation		community	
	TC	LC	TC	LC	TC	LC	T	C	TC	LC	TC	LC
A	1	0	1	1	1	1	1	1	1	1	1	0
B	1	0	1	1	1	0	1	0	1	1	1	0
C	1	0	1	0	1	0	1	0	1	1	1	0
D	1	1	1	0	1	0	1	0	1	1	1	0
E	1	0	1	0	1	0	1	1	1	1	1	0
F	1	1	1	0	1	1	1	1	1	1	1	1
G	0	0	1	0	1	0	1	0	1	0	0	0

The table above shows the responses of seven international students on different resources in intercultural language learning and how to apply them. TC represents the culture of the target language while LC represents the learners' culture. "1" represents the consideration of the culture, the presence of cultural elements, while "0" stands for absence of culture or no consideration of the particular culture. A-G stands for international students who learn Indonesian language and culture.

The findings show that most of the students responded that the seven resources were used in learning Indonesian language in intercultural perspective. All the resources mentioned by learners are relevant for the implementation of intercultural language learning as suggested by [2] [1],[12],[13],[14] and [15]. However, most of the students' responses show that most of the resources focused on Indonesian language and culture without including the language and culture of the learners, the cultures of the learners were included mostly in the students' presentation. In these presentations and projects, the students were able to notice, compare, interact and reflect in their own culture and Indonesian culture, while most of the resources such as textbooks, community, technology, literary books and different tasks focused on Indonesian language and culture only without deliberate inclusion of the learners' culture. In addition, there are other resources which can be used in learning language in intercultural perspectives. [2] suggests the authentic resources such as clothes, dances, cultural symbols (flags, coins, maps, games, images, cultural festivals and songs). This idea is supported also by [12,14] who add materials such as newspapers, role play and films. These materials were not mentioned by the respondents. However, it does not mean that they are not implemented in classroom context since classroom observation could prove this. In regard to this, [2] [12] and [15] explained gestures as very essential resources in intercultural language learning. They exemplified gestures such as kissing, bowing, kneeling down, weaving hands smiling and many others. These non-verbal clues vary in their meaning from one culture to another. Sometimes, they can be done in the same way, but the meaning is different, and the context is also different. Gestures are very important resources for international students who learn Indonesian language. By understanding gestures, they can become more interculturally communicative competent.

161

Therefore, concerning resources, there are several basic points which can be used as the criteria for evaluation of the materials to be used in intercultural point of view [1]. The materials should be interactive, involve the target culture and students' culture, make a student to do critical comparative analysis between the cultures, make the students change their attitude and understand better themselves and others. Hence, I suggest that all resources applied in learning Indonesian language may include the international students' culture and they may be used in the implementation along with the application of the principles and processes of intercultural language learning as suggested by [1] to make learners interculturally communicative competent.

3.4 *Responses from interview on intercultural language learning*

When the respondents were interviewed, most of their responses supported model suggested by [2]. Their responses revealed that intercultural communicative competence is implemented to the international students as they learn Indonesian language. For example, all the seven students were able to communicate with Indonesian people using Indonesian language and to interact with the community of Indonesia regardless of differences in cultural backgrounds, for example, different languages, different religions and different in levels of formalities, and different verbal and non-verbal expressions. This shows that the aspect of attitude (*savoir être*) is involved in intercultural language learning since students are open to interaction with people from different cultural backgrounds.

During learning Indonesian language, the students gained knowledge about different cultural practices and cultural products in Indonesian and from their friends from different countries. For example, all the students reported that they obtained knowledge on how to name different types of food in Indonesia with the corresponding time for eating in Indonesian culture. They also learnt non-verbal expressions such as not kissing with friends in public as they do in their countries, smiling more, bowing, touching chest when greeting, naming people by considering age and respect '*Pak*', '*Mbak*', '*Ibu*', '*Mas*', *etc*. These findings imply that the aspect of knowledge *(savour)* of the target language culture is gained as the international students learn Indonesian language. The respondents also reported that they were able to present their cultural products and practices in comparison to Indonesian culture. Each student presented types of food and their meanings, dances, clothes, and there was a special global cultural festival where each student showed food and cultural costumes to other people from different countries. This refers to skills of interpretation and relating *(savoir comprendre)*. For example, the students reported that they practice to play gamelan, *pencak silat*, and *wayang*, during learning process.. However, they were able to present their traditional dances to compare with Indonesian dances.

In learning Indonesian, the students have acquired knowledge and skills in Indonesian culture, and they were able to apply the knowledge and skills in actual context of communication. For example, one student from Rwanda reported that he became very social than before during studying Indonesian language and he would never stop *makan bersama in* his life as he learnt from *kenduri* a traditional from Indonesia. This means he learnt and acquired the spirit of togetherness by eating together as they were doing during studying Indonesian language. Another respondent from Turkmenistan reported that she has started using more polite language than before in speaking. She changed it after studying Indonesian language. She also reported that she has been more kind than before, and she no longer uses the left hand in giving things to people after learning Indonesian language *(savoir apprendre*/faire. This shows that she has been transformed interculturally to ethnorelativism stage in Developmental Model of Intercultural Sensitivity.

Moreover, the respondents involved in critical culture awareness in the process of learning Indonesian language. Most of the respondents reported how they evaluated the cultural products, practices and their perspectives in relation to their own culture. One of the respondents from Burundi reported that Indonesians use polite language, they are tolerant in their arguments, have so many names of food products, and normally they are not open when using their language if their meaning is not direct. Learning the context is very essential in interacting with the Indonesian culture. This is related to what is called critical cultural awareness (*savoirs'engager*) stated by [2], the student also promised that he will adapt and treat his family in friendly manner than he was doing before studying Indonesian language and culture for one year. This response also shows that the participant is in the adaption stage in ethnorelativism since he is capable of understanding the cultural differences, doing critical evaluation, and accepting other cultures and living within the two cultures.

Therefore, the responses from the interviews reveal that intercultural language learning is implemented by involving the change in the students' attitude, the ways they view their original cultures and their foreign culture, and how they interact with their friends from different cultural backgrounds. Furthermore, the students acquire knowledge of new cultures as they compare the target culture with their cultural backgrounds. They make actual practice of the knowledge they acquire. Finally, they are able to judge objectively and to adapt some of the cultural elements they prefer while preserving their identities. They are also able to interact peacefully and to live together in this globalized and digitalized era.

When the responses of the students were analyzed with Developmental Model of Intercultural Sensitivity, among seven students who participated in this research, six students were in the adaption stage in ethnorelativism. These were the students from Rwanda, Burundi, Mali and Turkmenistan. These students noticed the cultural differences, understood the differences accepted, and were ready to adopt some of the Indonesian culture. However, one student from Nepal was still in the denial stage in ethnocentrism because he could not accept the cultural differences. Therefore, he used his own culture as the center of reality to judge other cultures. The possible reason is that this student comes from monocultural background or he has not been exposed to the Indonesian culture to a great extent. On the other hand, it can imply that cultural transformation is a complex process, and normally learners change progressively from ethnocentrism to ethnorelativism with an unpredictable range of time.

4 CONCLUSION AND SUGGESTIONS

The findings and discussion on intercultural language learning principles, processes and resources have been presented. We found that the intercultural language learning principles, processes and reliable resources are implemented in teaching Indonesian as a foreign language to international students in the university in which this study was taken place. From the interview, we also found that some students have transformed their attitudes towards culture, knowledge, comparative skills in interpretation of intercultural values. Moreover, their cultural awareness is raised. In conclusion, the students are in the process of changing from ethnocentrism to ethnorelativism. However, more attention should be given on the inclusion of students' culture in the principles, processes and learning resources to make students more interculturally communicative competent. Additionally, we suggest more future research to be conducted by observing teachers and students as they learn in actual classroom context to achieve better results from multiple sources of data.

REFERENCES

[1] Liddicoat, A.J., &. Scarino, A. (2013). *Intercultural Language Teaching and Learning*. West Sussex: Wiley-Blackwell.

[2] M, Byram, (2008). *From foreign language education to education for intercultural citizenship*. Clevedon: Multilin gual Maters.

[3] Byram, M. (1997). *Teaching and assessing intercultural communicative competence*. Clevedon: Multilingual Matters.

[4] Bennett., M.J., & W. Allen, (1999). Developing intercultural competence in the language classroom. In Culture *as the core: Integrating culture into the language curriculum*, R.M. Paige, D. L. Lange & Y. A. Yershova (Eds.). Minneapolis: CARLA, University of Minnesota.

[5] British Council. (2013). *The English effect*. London: British Council Organization.

[6] Liddicoat, A. (2011). Language teaching and learning in intercultural perspective. In E. Hinkel (Ed.), Hand book of research in second language teaching and learning volume II (pp. 837–855). New York and London: Routledge Tylor & Francis group.

[7] Cui, Q. (2016). A study of factors influencing students' intercultural competence. *Journal of Language Teaching and Research, 7*(3), 433–439.

[8] Fungchomchoei, S., & Kardkarnklai, U. (2016). Exploring the intercultural competence of Thai secondary education teachers and its implications in English language teaching. *Journal: Procedia - Social and Behavioral Sciences, 236*, 240–247.

[9] Nteliou, E., & Kehagia, O. (2016). Intercultural perceptions among undergraduate students in English for Business. *International Journal of Language, Translation and Intercultural Communication, 4*, 98–109.

[10] Liu, S. (2013). Students' attitudes towards cultural learning in the English classroom: A case study of non-English major students in a Chinese university. *International Journal of English Language Education ISSN 2325-0887, 1*(3), 28–42.

[11] Fardini, S. (2014). Designing intercultural materials for EFL teaching/learning to young learners using Socio-pragmatic perspectives. *Proceedings of the 3rd UAD TEFL International Conference Yogyakarta*, pp. 351–363.

[12] Zhou, Z. (2017). Cross-cultural training and second language learning. *Asian Education studies, 2* (3), pp. 1–8, Sept. 2017, doi: 10.20849/aes.V2i3.176.

[13] Han, H. (2010). An investigation of teacher`s perceptions of culture teaching in secondary school in Xinjing, China. (Unpublished PhD Thesis), Durhan University, Retrieved from http://etheses.dur. ac.uk/109/

[14] Munir, A., Quareshi. A.H., Tahir, A., & Zubar, B.H. (2018). Shifting language paradigm: An integration of Five dimensions of culture in Teaching English as a foreign language in Pakistan. *International journal of English linguistics, 8*(5), 53–62.

[15] Sandorova, Z. (2016). The intercultural component in an EFL course- book package. *Journal of Language and Cultural Education, 4*(3),178–203. ISSN1339-4045 (print), ISSN 1339-4584 on line. doi: 10.1515/jolace-2016-0031.

English Linguistics, Literature, and Language Teaching in a Changing Era – Madya et al. (eds)
© 2020 Taylor & Francis Group, London, ISBN 978-1-03-224160-9

The implementation of MOOC using Schoology in second language acquisition towards students' learning outcomes

Hasan Zainnuri, Ngadiso & Dewi Cahyaningrum
English Education Department, Sebelas Maret University, Central Java, Indonesia

ABSTRACT: The advent of Massive Online Open Course (MOOC) is believed to offer an autonomous learning environment that minimizes the power structure between the teacher and students in English as Foreign Language (EFL) classes. Schoology, a learning management system, is one of potential platforms providing an undeniable possibility for educators looking for something between an academic social network and a learning management system. There has been little discussion and questions have been raised about whether theories of Second Language Acquisition (SLA) which are implemented using MOOCs or LMSs give impact on students' learning outcomes viewed from engagement framework. This paper aims to report how Schoology gives an impact on students' learning outcomes in second language learning in English classes at an Indonesian higher education. The qualitative case study employed semi-structured interviews and observations which involved 115 students enrolled in several English course subjects that adopted a blended learning method using Schoology. The findings explained how Schoology can link theory of SLA to classroom practice viewed from engagement framework towards students' learning outcomes in English language learning.

Keywords: MOOC, EFL, Schoology, engagement framework, learning outcomes

1 INTRODUCTION

Second Language Acquisition (SLA) is a conscious process where the learning of another language other than the First Language (L1) takes place. Similar with bilingualism and multilingualism, the process of SLA has to take place after the first language(s) has already been acquired. Therefore, SLA could also refer to the third, fourth, or fifth (so on and so forth) language the learner is currently learning. Strategies in language learning, or the steps that one take to learn a language, is very important in language performance. It is defined as "specific actions, behaviors, steps, or techniques — such as seeking out conversation partners or giving oneself encouragement to tackle a difficult language task — used by students to enhance their own learning" [1]. When learning a language, there are six strategies that learners use including memory, cognitive, comprehension, metacognitive, affective, and social.

Massive Open Online Courses (MOOCs) have become extremely popular in recent years. Among the more popular platforms for MOOCs are Coursera, Udacity, EdX, Udemy, Open Learning, and Schoology. MOOCs are a good example of the possible opportunities of higher education learning for both formal and informal courses. Educators may develop courses and offer them to the entire world using any of these platforms. Furthermore, English lecturers and teachers have the possibilities to design course materials in an e-learning environment combined with face-to-face teaching-learning process using one of the MOOCs platforms to find out the best practice of SLA theories in facilitating language learning.

Previous studies have reported that learning benefits in engaging with a MOOC and that it was advantageous to be able to study on the MOOC anywhere and at any time after enrolment [2]. Another research [3] found students' views about the educational values of MOOCs

165

as follows: expanding the knowledge provided in similar courses in their college (14%), acquiring new skills relevant to their daily life (14%), and interesting and a good way to acquire new knowledge (72%).

One type of MOOCs is a Learning Management System (LMS) which aids in offering a professional learning environment for students and teachers to support students in achieving mastery in content and developing skills and experiences with technology [4]. Moreover, several studies [5,6,7,8,9] suggested that Schoology is incorporated and integrated into English language learning and teaching. It is important, therefore, to find out the practical idea of SLA theories through the implementation of Schoology.

Engagement is an essential problem in the implementation of social networking LMS in English language teaching and learning. A number of researchers have reported many measures of student engagement were related positively with learning outcomes [10] and students who are actively engaged in learning learn more, learn better, and actually enjoy the classroom experience [11]. So far, however, there has been little discussion and questions have been raised about whether theories of SLA which are implemented using MOOCs or LMSs gives impact on students' learning outcomes viewed from engagement framework. In this study, the researcher reports an investigation on the implementation of Schoology to provide students with theory-to-practice of SLA viewed from engagement framework [2] consisting of teacher engagement, student engagement, cognitive engagement, and social engagement towards students' learning outcomes in English language learning. The major objective of this study was to investigate how Schoology LMS gives an impact on students' learning outcomes in English classes at an Indonesian higher education. This study aimed to address the following research questions: how the implementation of Schoology meets theories of SLA and gives an impact through the explanation of engagement framework.

The methodological approach taken in this study is a case study [12]. This study provides an exciting opportunity to advance our knowledge of the discussion of SLA theories on the implementation of MOOC by using Schoology towards students' learning outcome. The reader should bear in mind that the study is based on the application of integrating MOOC by using Schoology in three courses involving 115 college students. Therefore, the result of this study cannot be generalized.

The overall structure of the study takes form of five sections, including this introductory section. Section two begins by laying out the theoretical dimensions of the study. The third chapter is concerned with the methodology used for this study. The fourth section presents the findings of the research, focusing on the impact on the engagement framework towards students' learning achievement, namely: teacher engagement, student engagement, cognitive engagement, and social engagement. The fourth section also analyses the results of findings and data undertaken during the study. Finally, the conclusion gives a brief summary of the findings.

2   LITERATURE REVIEW

2.1   *MOOC, LMS, and Schoology*

Technology developments specifically by ICT have widely influenced learning processes. Among many computers based educational systems, MOOC and LMS will be discussed in this paper. MOOCs abbreviated from Massive Opening Online Course, which is created for unlimited participation and open access via the web worldwide. MOOCs have the special mission of expanding access to education worldwide, also pursuing the innovation of educating people online along with their partners [13].

Meanwhile, a Learning Management System (LMS) is a software application or Web-based technology used to plan, implement, and assess a specific learning process [14] as well as automate the administration of teaching-learning activities. LMS manages registers or users and course materials, gather data from learners, and provides analysis results to management. Typically, LMS offers an instructor with a way to create and deliver content, monitor student participation, and assess student performance [15]. In addition, LMS allows students to able to take benefit of interactive features, for example, online discussion, video conference, and online test.

One of the popular LMSs is Schoology which has some advantages in the learning process can improve learning through better communication, collaboration, and increased access to learning materials. Schoology has been chosen as the learning and teaching tools as well as a research material in educational studies.

2.2 *Schoology provides a meaningful learning experience*

Studies of blended learning aimed to reveal methodologically sound evidence of the impact of blended learning on the student experience. Learners gave a positive response in general when asked about their opinion of supplementary material being created online to support traditional teaching [16].

An English teacher or lecturer needs to create a great example of the kinds of learning experiences to grab students' attention, give them opportunities to learn with each other, and gather insights so that it makes lessons more meaningful. In general, Schoology provides two main aspects 1) interactive communication and 2) academic information exchange. Schoology offers teachers to make discussion questions, collaborative groups, or instruction for assignments that make dynamic interaction between students and their teachers become possible. For instance, students can participate in a reading workshop then they are able to ask questions and leave comments about classmates' book choices. Besides, teachers can participate in and monitor these student-led discussions. The other aspect that Schoology has capitalized on is the ability to deliver academic information to students. Within Schoology, students can access their marks, attendance data, and teacher advice on electronically-submitted assignments. As a result, communication between teachers and students can be increased through access to this information. Moreover, this benefit holds students accountable for their academic responsibilities [17].

2.3 *Schoology and its impact on English language learning*

Technology is an indispensable part of our lives in today's world, and thanks to the internet and the web 2.0 tools, the role of computers is increasingly becoming more and more significant in English language teaching and learning. Unlike traditional language learning techniques, with the internet and web 2.0 social sites, it is possible to combine the benefits of classroom interactivity with personal and self-study [18].

Research findings of the effectiveness of Schoology to improve the expertise of students' college in business writing is that the expertise result of subject in business writing can be increased through Schoology [7]. The suggestion of this study is Schoology as the supplement for traditional learning method is used to improve students' expertise college especially business writing.

A number of studies investigating the implementation of Schoology have found that: 1) blended learning using Schoology has a positive impact on students' learning motivation [19], 2) the implementation of Schoology e-learning platform helps students to improve their learning achievement [20], 3) Schoology m-learning platform installed in students' mobile device give them greater control over their EAP learning [5] and online peer review through discussion via Schoology can help facilitate in enhancing the college students' proficiency in Argumentative Writing [9], and 5) the online test using Schoology has been implemented in structure class of made the structure teaching-learning process more flexible and effective [9].

3 RESEARCH METHOD

This research was conducted to EFL learners enrolled in English language education department at a state university in Surakarta, Indonesia. Subject of this research was 115 undergraduate study who joined a MOOC in Schoology according to the available course and participated in eight weeks of study.

A case study research is adopted in this research offering the study of the phenomenon in its natural context [12]. The phenomenon in the research was the implementation of MOOC for English Language Learning using Schoology towards students' learning outcomes. Multiple methods of data collection were used including Likert-scale questionnaire and interviews. The analysis of questionnaire was assisted by Microsoft Excel and the interview data were coded through thematic data analysis [21].

This case study lasted for a whole teaching module consisting of 8 weeks. Within this process, the lecturer implemented the use of Schoology in the EFL classrooms. Meanwhile, the students answered quizzes, responded pre and post questionnaire, and communication with others through online discussion. At the end of this course, the lecturer provided a self-reflection response for students. As for the data collection process, questionnaires were administered to the participants before and after the application of Schoology and the result was compared. Classroom observations consist of students' point of view regarding the use and feature of Schoology in their learning. In addition, in-depth interviews including students record were also used.

4 FINDINGS AND DISCUSSION

4.1 *Schoology links the theory of Second Language Acquisition (SLA) to classroom practice*

In learning a language, one of the major concerns is applying theories and principles of SLA in ways to show their relevance to classroom practice. Several studies [5,6,7,8,9] have shown the integration of Schoology into English language learning and teaching in a blended learning classroom context. Blended learning refers to a combination of modes of web-based technologies (e.g. streaming video, audio, text and online discussions) or a combination of pedagogical approaches encompassing the main theories of learning (behaviorist, cognitivist, and constructivism) or a combination of the virtual and physical classroom [2]. In implementing blended learning, the lecturer needs to consider six strategies that learners use in learning a language including memory, cognitive, comprehension, metacognitive, affective, and social as well as engagement in teaching and learning process.

In this study, the researcher found that features of Schoology such as online quiz in the form of true or false, multiple choice, ordering, short answer, fill in the blank, or matching can encourage students in learning language through optimizing their memorizing ability. By creating a word-meaning map in their brain, students can find ways to remember better to aid in entering information into long-term memory, and then being able to retrieve that information. In addition, those features enable students to internalize the language in direct ways such as through reasoning, analysis, note-taking, summarizing, synthesizing, and outlining as a result of cognitive strategy that the learners use. The findings of this study also show that the learners adopt the comprehension strategy through guessing unknown words when listening and reading using above-mentioned Schoology features. Moreover, the implementation of learning English through Schoology enable learners to adopt the metacognitive strategy: plan, arrange, focus, evaluate on their own learning process. Features of Schoology also make students to be able to identify and monitor their own learning style preferences and needs such as organizing L2 materials. Lastly, the learners gather the benefits of learning language using Schoology by adopting the social/affective strategy. Students can control their feelings, motivations, and attitudes when in social situations or context in discussion feature of Schoology. For example, asking questions, communicating with others, facilitate conversation and interaction.

In addition to theory of SLA to classroom practice above, engagement is also necessary to be considered in language learning. It means the time, energy and resources students devote to activities designed to enhance learning at university [22]. Figure 1 presents the engagement framework [2] consisting of teacher engagement, student engagement, cognitive engagement, and social engagement (TSCS engagement). In Schoology, these engagement frameworks can be found in many features provided in this LMS to foster learning pedagogies such as updates, material resources, discussions, assignments, quizzes, homework, etc. The TSCS engagement framework can be seen in Figure 1 below.

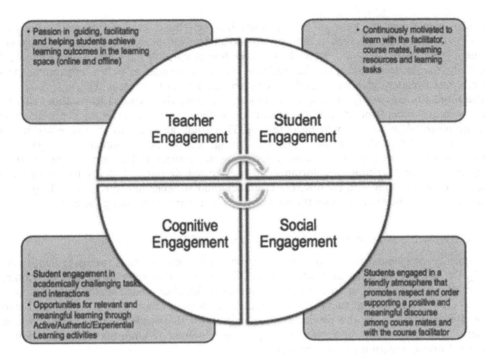

Figure 1. The TSCS engagement framework.

4.2 Teacher engagement in Schoology towards students' learning outcomes

Teacher or lecturer engagement framework focuses on the teacher's passion in guiding, facilitating, and helping students achieve learning outcome in the learning space (online and offline). In this study, the researcher not only provided oral presentations of the learning materials in the classroom, but also played the roles in MOOC using Schoology LMS as follow: answering questions, solving problems, sending messages to encourage students to participate in discussions/forums, leading the online discussion to improve students' engagement, and posting assignments and announcements related to the course.

Moreover, the researcher utilized Schoology to initiate online discussions over the content in this study. This would be beneficial to all students in improving their writing skills, and in learning the material. Schoology would allow the students who lack confidence to speak in the classroom to have a way to express their ideas and beliefs. These students may gain confidence through using Schoology and this may transfer over to the classroom [23].

In order to maximize the implementation of MOOC using Schoology, it is found that some considerations need to be applied. Based on the interview with the respondents, there are some aspects need to consider, namely, 1) visualization of abstract concepts by presenting multimedia features, pictures, animations and simulations as part of the learning materials and 2) clarity of explanations by using simple language and clear pronunciation of words by the teacher.

4.3 Student engagement in Schoology towards students' learning outcomes

Student engagement framework focuses on the perspective on students to continuously motivated to learn with the facilitator, course mates, learning resources and learning tasks. It means students need to achieve learning outcomes with the help of the teacher, classmates, and lesson materials and should learn diligently. In e-learning environment, student engagement is in the form of online discussion activity including asking and answering questions, providing feedback, and participation in submitting the assignments.

Student engagement has been well studied and it has been found that "engagement" is positively related to desired outcomes such as high grades and student satisfaction [24]. Student engagement is generally considered to be among the better predictors of learning and personal development. In this study, the researcher analyzed the students' learning outcomes as well as engagement from several courses namely essay writing, advanced grammar, and survival speaking.

The more students study or practice a subject, the more they tend to learn about it. Likewise, the more students practice and get feedback on their writing, analyzing, or problem solving, the more adept they should become [10]. This study also reveals that in essay writing class, it is found that students were engaged through the online peer-review feedback in the discussion activity provided in Schoology involving the lecturer and students to participate in reviewing students' writing. For instance, in peer-review activity, students try to guess the meaning of words they don't know, try to understand the meaning through looking at the word in context, and try to predict the meaning of some words by reading the essay.

4.4 *Cognitive engagement in Schoology towards students' learning outcomes*

In cognitive engagement framework, the researcher analyzed the student engagement in academically challenging tasks and interactions. Given tasks and tests in advanced grammar course, the students learning outcomes were increased. Another point analyzed was the opportunities for relevant and meaningful learning through active/authentic, and experiential learning activities. In this view, this finding of this study shows that students could cope with every activity given by the lecturer such as read Second Language reading materials. In addition, students learning outcomes were increased.

From the depth-interview with students, it is found that the variety of assignments which were applied by the lecturer could improve the cognitive engagement. It could be done by the lecturer through presenting diverse ways for grading to accommodate different learning styles.

4.5 *Social engagement in Schoology towards students' learning outcomes*

In this framework, the researcher viewed students' engagement in a friendly atmosphere that promotes respect and order supporting a positive and meaningful discourse among course mates and with the course facilitator. As a social network-based tool, Schoology allows teachers to interact with students. Schoology has the same design like Facebook in which messages are sent, conversations take place, statuses are updated, and information and other media are shared within a classroom network [17]. Therefore, Schoology provides supports and communication aspects by offering forums or discussions, sending social media messages, and operating chat components so that students receive assistance from the lecturer. Strong evidence of the effective communication was found when students were discussing online. For example, students encourage themselves to speak in English even though making a mistake, students reward themselves for good performance by leaving comment, and students try to speak in English using audio/video recording attachments to others.

5 CONCLUSIONS AND SUGGESTIONS

Implementing MOOC using Schoology has a great potential to change the learning strategies and environments in higher education. Practically, this implementation can link the theory of Second Language Acquisition (SLA) to classroom practice, concerning the strategies of language learning and engagement framework. Theories of SLA are successfully implemented using MOOC in Schoology which give impact on students' learning outcomes viewed from engagement framework. TSCS engagement frameworks, consisting of teacher engagement, student engagement, cognitive engagement, and social engagement, are necessary to be considered by the lecturer because it has an impact on students' learning outcomes in English classes at an Indonesian higher education.

The results of this study may enhance lecturers' and students' continuity in using Schoology. This study suggests the following aspects, namely clarity of explanations, visualization of abstract concepts, support and communication, and variety of assignments which should be considered by the lecturer in implementing Schoology in language learning.

REFERENCES

[1] Scarcella, R. & Oxford, R. (1992). *The tapestry of language learning: The individual in the communicative classroom*. Boston: Heinle & Heinle.

[2] Abas, Z. (2015). Fostering learning in the 21 st century through student engagement. *International Journal for Educational Media and Technology, 9*.

[3] Watted, A. & Barak, M. (2015). Students' preferences and views about learning in a MOOC. *Procedia - Social and Behavioral Sciences, 152*.

[4] Burgstrom, L. (2016). The impact of student completion requirements using an LMS (Learning Management System) on student achievement and fifferentiated instruction in the classroom.

[5] Ardi, Karyawati, & Lintang. (2017). Promoting learner autonomy through schoology M-learning platform in an EAP class at an Indonesian University. *Teaching English with Technology, 17*.

[6] Manning, C., Brooks, W., Crotteau, V., Diedrich, A., Moser, J. & Zwiefelhofer, A. (2011). Tech tools for teachers, by teachers: Bridging reachers and students. *Wisconsin English Journal, 53*.

[7] Sicat, A.S. (2015). Enhancing college students' proficiency in business writing via schoology. *International Journal of Education and Research, 3*.

[8] Strain-moritz, T.E. (2016). Perceptions of technology use and its effects on student writing. culminating projects in teacher development.

[9] Zainnuri, H. & Cahyaningrum, D. (2017). Using online peer review through siscussion via schoology to enhance college students' proficiency in argumentative writing: A case study. *Proceedings of the International Conference on Teacher Training and Education 2017* (ICTTE 2017). Atlantis Press.

[10] Carini, R.M., Kuh, G.D. & Klein, S.P. (2003). Student gngagement and student learning: Testing the linkages student engagement and student learning: How can we characterize the linkages.

[11] Park, C. (2003). Engaging students in the learning process: The learning journal. *Journal of Geography in Higher Education, 27*.

[12] Creswell, J.W. (2012). *Educational research: Planning, conducting, and evaluating quantitative and qualitative research*. Boston: Pearson Education.

[13] Li, P. (2007). Innovation in higher education: The effectiveness of disruptive technology in e-learning.

[14] Ismail, A.M. & Salih, A.A. (2018). The impact of blackboard LMS on teaching research method course for technology studies graduate students at the Arabian Gulf University. *International Journal of Information and Education Technology, 8*.

[15] Radwan, N.M., Senousy, M.B. & Riad, D.M. (2014). Current trends and challenges of developing and evaluating learning management systems. *International Journal of E-Education, e-Business, e-Management and e-Learning, 4*.

[16] Sharpe, R. Benfield, G. Roberts, G. & R. Francis. (October 2006). The undergraduate experience of blended e-learning: A review of UK literature and practice. The Higher Education Academy.

[17] Manning, C., Brooks, W., Crotteau, V., Diedrich, A., Moser, J. & Zwiefelhofer, A. (2011). Tech tools for teachers, by teachers: Bridging teachers and students. *Wisconsin English Journal, 53*.

[18] Kose, T., Yimen, E. & Mede. (2016). Perceptions of EFL learners about using an online tool for vocabulary learning in EFL classrooms: A pilot project in Turkey. *Procedia - Social and Behavioral Sciences, 232*.

[19] Wah, L.K. (2013). Understanding the blended learning experiences of English language teachers in a distance TESL degree programme in Malaysia. *Jurnal Teknologi (Social Sciences), 65*

[20] Low, P. (August 2017). E-learning implementation in foundation English class: Learners' Perspectives and learning achievement. *International Journal of Computer Theory and Engineering, 9*.

[21] Gall, M.D., Borg, W.R. & Gall, J.P. (1996). *Educational research*. White Plains, New York: Longman.

[22] Krause, L. (2005). Understanding and Promoting Student Engagement in University Learning Communities. Centre for the Study of Higher Education.

[23] Johnson, T. (2014). The Effects of Information and Communication Technology on Student Achievement.

[24] Chen, P.S. Gonyea, C.R. & Kuh. (2008). Learning at a distance: Engaged or not? *Innovate: Journal of Online Education, 4*.

English Linguistics, Literature, and Language Teaching in a Changing Era – Madya et al. (eds)
© 2020 Taylor & Francis Group, London, ISBN 978-1-03-224160-9

The effect of online extensive reading on building the reading fluency of EFL university students

Hendriwanto & Utut Kurniati
Department of English Education, Swadaya Gunung Jati University, Cirebon, Indonesia

ABSTRACT: Research on extensive reading (ER) has typically focused on the effect of reading programs on students' language proficiency rather than the topic of online extensive reading (ER) that relates to reading fluency. The present study examined how students build reading fluency, particularly their reading rate, automaticity, and comprehension. Several studies have suggested that extensive reading is required to build reading fluency [1,2,3]. Fifty EFL university students participated in an online extensive reading (ER) program comprising of eight meetings twice a week using ten graded readers. Three research questions were addressed: a) the effectiveness of online extensive reading, b) the amount of graded readers that should be read to develop reading fluency, c) if there is a difference in effect between learning simplified text and complicated text. The findings show that online extensive reading (ER) enhanced reading fluency. This implies that online extensive reading promotes the improvement of comprehension, automaticity as well as reading rates in a strategic way.

Keywords: Extensive Reading, Fluency, Graded Readers

1 INTRODUCTION

In the last decade, the demand for books to prepare for reading tests has increased rapidly. Extensive reading is believed to be an effective way of teaching a language, particularly the ability to read as well as language acquisition [4]. Extensive reading provides numerous benefits when utilized in the classroom. However, there is a lack of teachers who are able to carry out these activities during the learning process [5,6,7]. Extensive reading seems to be considered as lacking practical benefit in the classroom.

Extensive reading is derived from the paradigm that language learners have certain inputs and intake in facilitating language learning when acquiring a language. Extensive reading can be defined as a reading activity that is faster with the purpose of reading for pleasure and general information. Extensive reading was introduced for the first time by Killey in 1969. Studies on extensive reading have focused on the effect of reading speed [8] and listening skills [9] as well as teachers' and students' perceptions on extensive reading [10,11]. However, few studies have focused on fluency, particularly on EFL learners at the tertiary level.

A fluent reader is one who has the ability to read quantitatively. [12] illustrated that a fluent reader is like a good car driver who is able to drive and do other things at the same time, such as using their mobile phone or drinking, without paying attention to the road. This is the opposite to non-fluent reader who can only read the text they are given. It can be drawn that a fluent reader can read many more words in one minute; studies have shown that they are able to read 200 words per minute (WPM). Three research questions were posed to address the problem: a) Is online extensive reading effective for developing the reading fluency of students? b) Does the amount of reading material influence the improvement of the students' reading fluency? c) Do students who read simplified texts differ to students who read non-simplified text in relation to building students' reading fluency?

2 THE ROLE OF EXTENSIVE READING IN READING FLUENCY

The summary of the extensive reading study can be viewed on the table below to see how extensive reading develops reading fluency.

The studies above show that one who can read faster cannot automatically be defined as a fluent reader. Teachers must carry out appropriate steps in the classroom. The fluent reader will be able to read with ease and code toward reading materials. "The key to this definition of reading fluency is the combination of both reading rate and reading comprehension. Fluency is not one of these elements alone but the combination of both [17]. It is clear that reading fluency is a combination of speed reading and comprehension. Furthermore, "the ability to process text quickly not only at the alphabetic, word, sentence, and discourse levels but also the lexico-grammatical level, and in tandem with background knowledge" [2]. The fluent reader shows their ability to manage their time in reading. Based on international standards, a fluent reader is able to read 200 words per minute.

Meanwhile, texts that are easy to read will engage students to encode in lexis and morphosyntactics. The texts provided support to students to attain fluency in reading. Therefore, the fluent reader has two main characteristics: automaticity and speed reading. *Automaticity* is generally applied to the sub-lexical and lexical processing, whereas fluency also includes efficient processing beyond the lexical level [8]." With the background of automaticity, the reader employs multi-word units, morpho-syntax, and discourse organization as the basic one to build fluency in reading. *Speed Reading* is the main factor to build reading fluency, which is explained as "rapid access to semantic meaning, syntactic parsing, and knowledge of discourse structure, rapid semantic analyses of phrasal and intersentential relations [1]." Additionally, these terms were categorized into five types of readers: 1) remembering with 138 words, 2) process learning with 200 words, 3) reading process with 300 words, 4) skimming with 450 words, and 5) scanning with 600 words.

3 RESEARCH METHOD

The present study employed the pre-experimental research. Two groups of participants were involved in the study as volunteers and participated in a pretest and a posttest ($n = 25$ in the experimental group; $n = 20$ in the control group). Furthermore, the participants were divided into two categories, namely one group that read simplified text, while the other read non-simplified text.

Table 1. The summary of previous study.

No	Study	Participants	Reading Amount	Treatment Period	The average Reading Rate
1	Beglar & Hunt [13]	76 Students	57 texts	Two semesters	200,000 words
2	Beglar, et al [1]	97 Students	136,029 words from 9 books	One year	103.09/119.93 (16.84) words
3	Huffman [14]	66 students	Speed reading series	Two semesters	20.73 wpm .62 wpm
4	Karlin & Romanko [15]	110 students	85 pages 3000 words	Two Semesters	2000 words
5	Robb & Kano [16]	200 students	32 Texts	One year	No information
6	Sakurai [17]	70 Students	6–20 books	15 weeks	228 words and 262 words

4 FINDINGS AND DISCUSSION

Table 2 shows the descriptive statistics of the pretest and posttest. The alpha beta was measured to test the difference between both, where the resulting score was 0.025. Simplified text demonstrated the difference of significance with simplified text, $t(45) = -2.858$, $p < 0.001$. However, the scores of the pretest and posttest was not significant for simplified text, $t(45) = -1.64$.

4.1 The effectiveness of online extensive reading in developing reading fluency

The usage of a learning management systems platform for online extensive reading improves students' reading fluency, which in this case can be identified by viewing the reading rate. After meeting for 8 weeks, students who have read more than 20 graded readers can freely choose anything of their reading level in each folder, as shown on Picture 1. This relates to the principle of extensive reading where students read what they want to read [18].

There were six-grader reader level material in the folder of LMS Schoology that could be accessed by all participants. They read for a certain time then have to report on the log of the reading report. They have to write down the title, how many words or pages they read, and what their responses to the story were.

Table 2. Descriptive statistic of simplified text and non-simplified text.

		Min	Max	Mean	SD
Simplified Text	Pretest	16	43	33.55	4.64
	Posttest	22	50	36.60	6.11
Non- simplified Text	Pretest	15	57	36.50	9.15
	Posttest	21	57	42.02	9.15

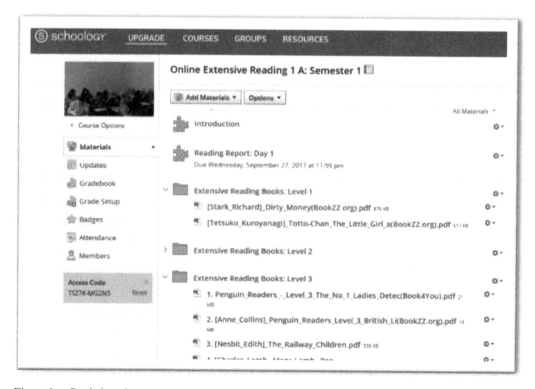

Figure 1. Graded reader.

To measure reading fluency in numerical form, the participants were given a test to read one text in one minute, as seen on the table below. The three components measured were accuracy, prosody, and reading rate where each separate component was measured according to the number of words the students managed to read. The indicators of fluency are presented on the table below.

The reading rates of the experimental group in the pretest approximately measured 120 and 124 words per minutes (wpm). After the treatment, the experimental group read at an approximately an equal rate at 130 words per minutes (wpm); however, the reading rate of the control group where the students read printed storybooks was lower compared to the online extensive reading group, measuring 127 wpm. ANOVA was measured to compare the reading rates between both groups and showed the result was statistically significant in F(2, 130) 1/4 91.70, p < .001 as well as for the effect size (eta squared 1/3 .65). These results indicate that the reading speed of the online group was faster than the control group which had changed slightly after the treatment.

4.2 *Simplified text and non-simplified text in reading fluency*

Anderson (2014) proposed that students are exposed to two types of texts: narrative and expository texts. Students may be exposed to these two types of texts during reading activities. Narrative texts can assist in developing students' imagination and creativity.

Table 3. The indicators of fluency.

Number of students	Number of Words	Words per minute
10	100–150	40 words
22	150–250	65 words
23	250–300	80 words

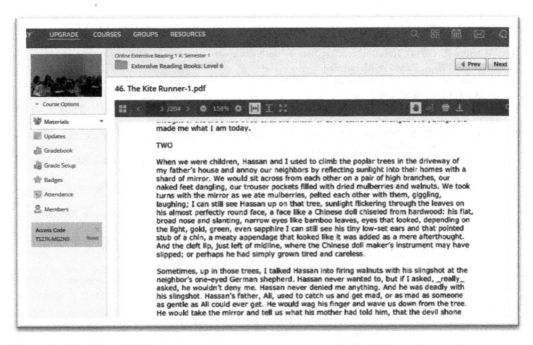

Figure 2. Reading materials.

The reading materials were available to access in LMS so that students can read them online. The higher the level of reading, the more difficult the reading materials. In the picture above, it can be seen that the difficulty of reading material seem to entice the students to further engage in reading activities. One page is approximately 200 words in length. This way the students can read in a few minutes while they catch the meaning of the text.

5 CONCLUSION AND SUGGESTIONS

To conclude, empirical findings have shown that reading fluency can be developed through online extensive reading. The result of the study implies that online extensive reading is recommended to improve the reading fluency of students. Therefore, both simplified and non-simplified texts will encourage students to think critically. Online extensive reading improves students' reading fluency.

The effectiveness of online extensive reading can statistically be found with the use of graded readers to build reading fluency. However, there were different results between learners using simplified and complicated texts. The findings indicated the role of online extensive reading (ER) in enhancing reading fluency. This implies that online extensive reading promotes building comprehension, automaticity as well as reading rate in a strategic way.

ACKNOWLEDGEMENTS

The writer would like to thank the directory of research of RISTEK DIKTI. Special thanks also to my colleagues and all participants in this study.

This work was supported by the Directory of Research and RISTEK DIKTI Indonesia. (Grant NumberSK: 0045/E3/LL/2018. No: 0790/K4/KM/2018.

REFERENCES

[1] Beglar, D., & Hunt, A. (2011). The effect of pleasure reading on Japanese university EFL learners' reading rates. *Language Learning, 62*(3), 1–39.

[2] Waring, R. (2014). Building reading fluency with extensive reading," in Muller et al. *Exploring EFL fluency in Asia*. Palgrave Macmillan.

[3] Y. Iwahori, Y. (2008). Developing reading fluency: A study of extensive reading in EFL. *Reading in a Foreign Language, 20*(1), 70–91.

[4] Maley, A. (2015). Extensive reading: maid in waiting in Tomlinson, B. *English language learning materials*. Continuum.

[5] Huang, Y. (2015). Why don't they do it? A study on the implementation of extensive reading in Taiwan. *Cogent Education, 2*(1), 1–13.

[6] Jacobs, G. M., & Renandya, W. A. (2005). Making extensive reading even more student centered. *Indonesian Journal of Applied Linguistics, 4*(2), 102–112.

[7] Nakanishi, T. (2014). A meta-analysis of extensive reading research," *TESOL Quarterly., 49*(1), 6–37.

[8] Beglar, D., & Hunt, A. (2014). Pleasure reading and reading rate gains. *Reading a Foreign Language, 26*(1), 29–48.

[9] Stephens, M. (2015). Why extensive reading and listening to audio books may not be enough. *Reading Matrix, 15*(2), 252–255.

[10] Byun, J. H. (2014). Korean EFL teachers' perspectives about their participation in an extensive reading program (Unpublished doctoral dissertation). The University of Texas at Austin.

[11] Chou, I. (2014). Reading for the purpose of responding to literature: EFL students' perceptions of e-books," *Computer Assisted Language Learning, 29*(1), 1–19.

[12] Rasinski, T. (2014). Fluency matters. *International Electronic Journal of Elementary Education, 7*, 3–12.

[13] Huffman, J. (2014). Reading rate gains during a one-semester extensive reading course. *Reading in a Foreign Language, 26*(2), 17–33.

[14] Karlin, O., & Romanko, R. (2010). Examining multiple variables within a single ER setting. *The Reading Matrix*, *10*(2), 181–204.

[15] Robb, T., & Kano, M. (2013). Effective extensive reading outside the classroom: A large-scale experiment. *Reading in a Foreign Language*, *25*(2), 234–247.

[16] Sakurai, N. (2015). The influence of translation on reading amount, proficiency, and speed in extensive reading. *Reading in a Foreign Language*, *27*(1), 96–112.

[17] Anderson, N. J. (2014). A curricular model for reading: The inclusion of extensive reading. *TESL Reporter*, *46* (1&2), 1–9.

[18] Day, R. R. (2015). Extending extensive reading. *Reading in a Foreign Language*, *27*(2), 294–301.

English Linguistics, Literature, and Language Teaching in a Changing Era – Madya et al. (eds)
© 2020 Taylor & Francis Group, London, ISBN 978-1-03-224160-9

English teachers' perceptions of the implementation of character education in Curriculum 2013

Heni Puji Lestari & Bambang Widi Pratolo
English Education, Universitas Ahmad Dahlan, Yogyakarta, Indonesia

ABSTRACT: The implementation of character education in Curriculum 2013 plays an important role in the development of education in Indonesia. However, the change of this new curriculum requires teachers to have more knowledge and experience to integrate character education into their teaching. The main purpose of this study is to describe how teachers implement character education in the English class. Besides, this study aimed at identifying the advantages and challenges of implementing character education in Curriculum 2013. A descriptive qualitative method that was grounded in ethnographic design was utilized. Data were collected through in-depth interviews with six English teachers working at different junior and senior high schools in Yogyakarta, Indonesia. The interviewees had experience in teaching ranging from one to eight years. The data were analyzed by qualitative techniques based on pre-determined categories standing for each of the interview questions. After that, the researchers summarized the findings from the data and drew a conclusion. The results of the study indicated firstly, that most of the teachers accepted and knew the existence of character education in Curriculum 2013. Second, teachers inserted character values in their teaching by integrating them into the learning activities, learning materials, learning culture and assessments. Third, implementing character education can provide some positive impacts on students' lives. Fourth, there were some challenges in implementing character education in Curriculum 2013, as teachers also found several problems and difficulties. Therefore, most of them hope that assessing character in Curriculum 2013 should be evaluated, improved and designed more simply.

Keywords: character education, Curriculum 2013, English teachers' perceptions

1 INTRODUCTION

A curriculum is a guideline for the planning, contents, methods, materials of learning to facilitate students' learning and teaching implementation in the educational process, to achieve the goals that have been set. Ekawati [1] argued that a curriculum is the arranged association of students with instructional substance, material, assets and procedures for assessing the achievement of instructive destinations. A curriculum is one of the main components of education in all countries including Indonesia. Therefore, the curriculum has a very important role in providing a fundamental reference concerning what students should learn and achieve.

Curriculum change in Indonesia has occurred periodically since the birth of the country [2]. Before the School Based Curriculum (SBC) was executed, some curricula, for example, the 1968 curriculum, the 1975 curriculum, the 1984 curriculum, the 1994 curriculum and the 2004 curriculum were implemented in Indonesia. The reasons put forward by the Ministry of Education and Culture of the Republic of Indonesia to replace the SBC with Curriculum 2013 were the current global challenges, required competencies, current negative phenomena particularly among young people and discouraging perceptions among Indonesians regarding education [3].

There are differences between the SBC and Curriculum 2013. Among others included in Curriculum 2013, teachers must consolidate character education in the learning activities in the classroom. In SBC, character education was incorporated into one or two subjects such as civic education and religion but in Curriculum 2013 all subjects have to include character education in the learning process. In this case, the teacher has a role to integrate good values that are suitable with their subject of teaching. In fact, Curriculum 2013 is an extension of the SBC in several components. The main purpose of this curriculum is to improve the potential of learners to be someone who has faith, good character, confidence, learning success, who is responsible, democratic and contributes to society [4].

Character education is needed to solve the problem of students' morality and character that always decreases over time. Character education in Curriculum 2013 is emphasized for the purpose of balancing hard skills (cognitive and psychomotor) and soft skills (affective) of students. The inclusion of character building in Curriculum 2013 is important due to some negative phenomena emerging recently, such as fights among students, use of drugs, corruption, plagiarism, cheating and social unrest [4]. Because of these problems, the government puts character education as a core competence of Curriculum 2013. The government named character education in core competence two (KI 2) in all subjects because it is important aspects for moral education. Therefore, Curriculum 2013 has a big role in implementing character education to improve the good character of students in Indonesia.

Lickona says that character is 'a reliable inner disposition to respond to situations in a morally good way', adding that 'so conceived character has three interrelated parts: moral knowing, moral feeling, and moral behavior' [5]. According to Lickona, good character includes knowledge of goodness, and cause intention of goodness, and lastly actually doing good. In other words, character refers to a set of knowledge, attitudes, motivations, habits and competences.

Ki Hajar Dewantara (the Indonesian education father) defines education as 'an effort to advance the character, mind, and body of children, in order to advance the perfection of life that is alive and bring the child in harmony with nature and society' (as cited in Yulia and Helena, 2015, p.3) [6]. Therefore, education is very important in building and developing students' knowledge, skill and character.

English is the most-learned foreign language in Indonesia. It is a compulsory subject that is taught from the lower education level to the higher education level. Language is beneficial to teach good character by using good words and expressing the words in a good way. Therefore, character values can be developed through the English subject. Character value development through the English subject is expected to have a positive impact on the children and the nation's development [1]. However, in terms of the implementation of Curriculum 2013 in the English subject, not all English teachers can integrate it in a learning process. There are differences between the ideal of the implementation of Curriculum 20013 with what really happens on site. Therefore, the study to investigate English teachers' perceptions of the implementation of character education in Curriculum 2013 is worth undertaking.

2 RESEARCH METHOD

A descriptive qualitative approach is used in this research. According to Creswell [7], qualitative research is:

> an approach for exploring and understanding the meaning individual groups ascribe to a social or human problem. The process of research involves emerging questions and procedures, data typically collected in the participant's setting, data analysis inductively building from particular to general categories and the researcher making interpretation of the meaning of the data. (p. 295)

It is grounded ethnographic design since it aims to improve knowledge about the implementation of character education in English Curriculum 2013. Ethnography is 'a strategy of inquiry in which the researcher studies an intact cultural group in a natural setting over a prolonged period of time by collecting, primarily, observational and interview data' [8].

In this study, the researcher interviewed six teachers who had one to five years' experience in teaching English at different levels of school in Yogyakarta. All the participants have similar educational and economic backgrounds. Six teachers volunteered to participate in this study based on their experience as English teachers. For ethical reasons, the teacher participants were given pseudonyms; teacher A (female and had more than five years' experience), teacher B (female and five years' experience), teacher C (female and four years' experience), teacher D (male and three years' experience), teacher E (female and two years' experience) and teacher F (female and six months' experience).

The purpose of this study was to explore the language teachers' perceptions of implementing character education in English Curriculum 2013. A semi-structured interview technique was employed to gather information from all the participants. A semi-structured interview was chosen because the researchers had the opportunity to further elaborate the information from the participants based on their responses on the previous questions. While conducting the interviews, the researchers took note of the participants' opinions and recorded the sessions using a tape recorder and also the voice note facility in the WhatsApp application.

The data collection through interviews was conducted in 2017/2018 academic years. Face to face interviews occurred in the places that teachers suggested. The interviews ranged from 30–60 minutes. The researchers conducted the interviews and asked for more information in detail to determine how they implemented character education in Curriculum 2013, which was developed by the Ministry of Education (Kemendikbud) of The Republic of Indonesia for the English subject in secondary schools.

In analyzing the data, the researchers employed a descriptive analysis method. In other words, the data were collected from the participant teachers through in-depth interviews. First, the data were coded, then these codes were classified and evaluated according to several categories. Considering the research questions, these categories were pre-determined by the researchers, using 20 questions in the interviews with some further questions to unearth more detailed information based on the answers. The interpretations of the data of teachers' opinions on the implementation of character education in Curriculum 2013 are explored in the following findings.

3   FINDINGS AND DISCUSSION

In this part, the results of the study are presented for each research question. The perceptions of the interviewed teachers on the implementation of character education in Curriculum 2013 are presented according to the categories based on their responses to the questions given in the interviews. This part is divided into four main sub-sections based on the research questions, namely: English teachers' thoughts about character education in Curriculum 2013, the implementation of character education in Curriculum 2013, advantages and challenges of character education in Curriculum 2013.

3.1   *English teachers' thoughts about character education in Curriculum 2013*

The results of the data analysis reveal some English teachers' perspectives on character education in Curriculum 2013. They shared their experiences and understanding about the issue. Table 1 summarizes the teachers' perceptions regarding character education in Curriculum 2013. Within the categories, teachers' experience of teaching English can support the data to know their knowledge about character education.

Most of the teachers know that Curriculum 2013 is different, as it provides character building and moral values for the student. Below are some teachers' perceptions about character education in Curriculum 2013:

A curriculum emphasizes student character. In order that learners are not only experts in subject material, but also that their character is well developed (Teacher C)

Another noted that character education can build the attitude and skills of the student:

The 2013 curriculum focuses on life skill and character education, where students are required to understand the material, be active in the process of discussion or presentation, have good manners and discipline (Teacher E)

One teacher also wrote that character education can provide some good attitudes for students, such as:

Character education is inserted during the learning process in the classroom. Such as being courageous, responsible, polite, courteous, showing respect, appreciation etc. (Teacher B)

Another teacher expressed about social and environment can build the student's character:

Character education begins when the process of learning further extends in their daily life at school/even at home (Teacher C)

Table 1 explains what the teachers think about character education. They pointed out that character education focuses on character building, moral values, attitudes and skills of the students. Character education is aimed to make students not only smart in their cognitive domain (thinking) but also affective one (emotion/feeling) such as their attitude. They believe that character education is the teaching of core values for students to develop good characters. Several teachers also said that character education should improve students' individual leadership and communicative competence. They also said that character education needs to be contextual and consider social and environmental aspects. It is also found that the implementation of Curriculum 2013 has as its purpose to build students' good character in the aspects of knowledge, skills and attitude. This is in line with the findings of a similar study by Darsih [9], who states that 'the previous curriculum only focuses on improvement of knowledge and skill or cognitive aspect and did not pay attention to attitude and students' creative thinking' (p. 195). Therefore, teachers not only teach knowledge but also life skills, what students need to know to live in the world. Implementing character education for students can also build students' life skills and good character, such as being independent, brave, responsible, polite, confident, respectful and appreciative of others. However, it is not sufficient that implementing character education in Curriculum 2013 is just conducted in classrooms, it should be supported by social and environmental aspects to build and practice their good habits and behaviors. Because students spend much time in school, school should offer the opportunity to support and help them to reach the full potential of their good character. It is also developing a positive school climate or culture and bringing out the best attitude for students at the school. Character education in this curriculum is important and beneficial for everyone, so it has to involve school staff, parents, students and community members to support this curriculum for making an effective academic process.

Table 1. English teachers' thoughts about character education in Curriculum 2013.

Teachers' perceptions	Participants (N = 6)
Character building	6
Moral values	4
Attitudes and skills	2
Contextual and communicative	1
Independent learner	1
Social and environmental aspects	1

3.2 The implementation of character education in Curriculum 2013

This part describes the implementation of character education in Curriculum 2013 by English teachers in the classroom. From the categories, the teachers implemented character education in materials and activities.

First, most of the teachers used some activities for implementing character education in their teaching English:

Presenting the results of the discussion in front of the class. It builds the student's confidence and they are not shy (Teacher B)

Then, other teachers integrate learning materials with character values in the English class:

Using appropriate techniques suggested by the Ministry of Education, that is through learning materials that contain moral values, through texts used, e.g. discussion of inspiring characters (Teacher F)

Several teachers use a scientific approach to generate student-centered learning in the class for supporting character education implementation:

The emphasis of character building in each learning and also the transformation from EEK (Ekploration, Collaboration and Confirmation) to a scientific approach here by observing, questioning, processing, presenting, concluding, creating (Teacher D)

Other teachers said that the school environment also supports building character education for students:

A conducive learning environment plays an important role in the process of character building students (Teacher E)

The last teacher also wrote that using our own culture can implement character education in the English language:

By integrating their own cultural values with the cultures and foreign languages they learn (Teacher E)

Table 2 confirms that teachers have implemented the character education of Curriculum 2013 in their teaching and learning processes. First, some of the teachers use some activities to implement character education such as brainstorming, warming up, discussion and presentation to build character value for students. For example, the students have to discuss in their group and also present their ideas. This activity can build their confidence to speak in front of others. Since learning English is a matter of habit, students must practice it in their daily activities. Second, some teachers say that they integrate their learning material with character education, for example studying English through narrative texts. From the narrative text a student can get moral value from the story of the text. Integrating materials with character education was similar to a previous study by Ratih [10], who argued that 'in the materials, the teacher inserted the character values directly and indirectly. It means the character values can be seen from the words used and the content of the materials' (p. 101). Next, the teachers suggest that students also have to know the differences between their local culture and a foreign culture. Teachers can

Table 2. The implementation of character education in Curriculum 2013.

Teachers' perceptions	Participants (N = 6)
Using some activities to support character education	6
Integrate learning material with character value	4
Scientific approach	4
School environment supports character education	2
Integrate original culture with foreign culture	1

share good values of both cultures with the students. Because Curriculum 2013 uses the scientific approach, students can observe, question, process, present, conclude and create to improve their knowledge and skills. One of the teachers said that language and art are appropriate lessons to build character education for the students because English language has text, dialog, an expression that supports the students to implement their speaking and communication. For example, students study a narrative text to know the moral value of the text. Teachers also said that the environment can influence students' character. It comes not only from the school environment but also from their family and neighborhood lives. The last finding is to integrate local culture with a foreign culture. This is very important to improve cultural awareness among students. Teachers can take the same positive values which exist in both cultures and integrate them into the teaching and learning process.

3.3 *Advantages of character education in Curriculum 2013*

As shown in Table 3, it was found that character education provides positive effects for students from internal and external factors. Table 3 presents the advantages of implementing character education in Curriculum 2013 according to English teacher participants.

Here are the advantages of implementing character education in Curriculum 2013 according to English teachers' perceptions.

First, character education can encourage students to be more independent and communicative:

> *By practicing speaking English, students' confidence will grow so that they are more independent and confident to convey their ideas.* (Teacher B)

Second, character education can help students to be more active, creative and innovative:

> *Students are required to be more active, creative and innovative in every problem that they have to solve in the school* (Teacher E)

Third, character education can improve good knowledge and moral attitude for a student:

> *Assessment of all aspects; attitudes, skills and knowledge will better represent the students themselves* (Teacher D)

Fourth, character education can increase the level of confidence and religion of the students:

> *In Curriculum 2013, there is a spiritual assessment that makes students have faith and caution to their respective God* (Teacher D)

The last, teachers can motivate the student that the assessment is not only from their knowledge but also from their attitudes and morals:

> *By telling them that their score are not only from their lessons but also their daily behavior. It will make students more trying to form a better person and character* (Teacher C)

In this study, the researchers found some advantages identified the six English teacher participants including: first, encouraging students to be more independent and

Table 3. Advantages of implementing character education in Curriculum 2013 (n = 6).

Teachers' perceptions	Participants (N = 6)
Improve students to be more independent and communicative	4
Help students to be more active, creative and innovative	3
Improve knowledge and moral behaviors of students	2
Increase students' spiritual and religious life	2
Assessment can be from exam score and moral aspects	1

communicative in that they can do their activity in the classroom through discussion and presentation with their group confidently. Another example is that students can work together in groups to complete their assignments, which helps them learn and practice the skills to work together so every student can contribute their ability to participate in this activity. As they work together in their groups, students have a chance to improve their skills to speak with other people confidently. Second, implementing character education can help students to be more active, creative and innovative. These skills improve their study skills in all subjects, making them responsible for their learning activities. Third, teachers confess that implementing character education at school could improve students' knowledge and moral behaviors. Character education also explores feelings and the ability of students to improve their behavior inside and outside the school environment. Fourth, character education in the school can support students to increase their spirit of religious life. It is very important to build and improve their faith. Assessment in Curriculum 2013 is not only from subject exams but also from their moral life such as behavior, including how they interact with other students and their teachers. Therefore, implementing character education in the English language classroom can have positive impacts for the students. The students are not only smart in their cognitive domain but also in their affective domain, which is proven by having good character or in the Indonesian language 'cerdas berkarakter' (smart and acquiring prominent characters).

3.4 Challenges of implementing character education in Curriculum 2013

On the other hand, some challenges were also recorded This section provides data on the aspects the teachers perceived as being challenging in implementing character education in Curriculum 2013.

The following is an example of what the teachers said regarding the assessment of character education as being very complicated:

> The teachers' assessment system is too complex, there are so many teachers who are not mentally ready for the 2013 curriculum (Teacher D)

Other aspects that impact the implementation of this curriculum are a lack of teacher experience and creativity and also a lack of appropriate materials:

> This curriculum demands teachers to be more creative, lack of understanding of teachers with the concept of scientific approach, lack of teachers skills in designing lesson plans, mastering authentic judgment (Teacher D)

Several teachers also argue that this curriculum is not well developed, government hope can student-learning center, but in the reality, it is still teacher-learning center:

> Curriculum 2013 is expected already centered students, but teacher-centered learning is still much going on many subjects especially English Subject (Teacher D)

Table 4 provides information on aspects of the teaching and learning process that the English teachers consider as challenging in implementing character education. All teacher participants said that implementing character education in the classroom is not easy. The teachers complain about the assessment of character values, which is very detailed and complex, making them find it difficult to do it. The scoring criteria not only focuses on competence aspects but also on character aspects. In Curriculum 2013, teachers assess students not only from knowledge but also their competence and attitudes inside and outside of the classroom. This kind of assessment is very complicated as the teachers must know every individual student very well. The next is the lack of teacher experience and creativity, which causes difficulties implementing character education. In addition, lack of appropriate extra resources and materials are possibly negatively affected by the curriculum. This is in line with the result of previous research by Iyitoğlu and Alci [11], which described that 'teachers listed the weaknesses of the curriculum as

Table 4. Challenges of implementing character education in Curriculum 2013.

Teachers' perceptions	Participants (N = 6)
More detailed and complex assessment	6
Lack of teacher experience	2
Lack of teacher creativity	2
Lack of training from government	1
Lack of guidance	1
Time consuming	
Dominant teacher-centered	1
Poor student confidence	1
Lack of appropriate materials	1

a lack of motivation for the students to speak, lack of materials to help them learn English effectively, lack of communicative activities' (p. 10). The teachers did not have enough information on how to implement the curriculum. All of the problems came from many aspects such as lack of teacher experience, lack of teacher creativity, lack of training from government, lack of appropriate materials and lack of guidance. Therefore, these problems become the weakness of implementing Curriculum 2013. Since the assessment of this curriculum is more complicated and difficult, it needs a lot of time to implement it. Another challenge is that many students do not feel confident and are passive in the learning activities so the class becomes dominated with teacher-centered learning even though the purpose of Curriculum 2013 is student-centered learning.

Furthermore, to solve these problems, some of the teachers hope that the government would give training about character education in Curriculum 2013 and also how to implement it. It is also appropriate if the government provides a guidance book for teachers to help them implement this curriculum. The teachers also have to be active in searching for information about the implementation of moral education in Curriculum 2013 through books or the Internet, asking other teachers or attending workshops or seminars about the issue.

4 CONCLUSION AND SUGGESTIONS

Based on the findings and discussion presented, some conclusions can be drawn. First, teachers were aware and positively received the change of curriculum, from the SBC to Curriculum 2013. Second, teachers have included character values in the lesson plans, teaching materials, learning activities and assessments. Third, implementing character education can provide some positive impacts on students' lives. Fourth, several challenges were still encountered while implementing character education in Curriculum 2013. As a result, teachers, as the main actors in education, have a significant role in implementing character education in their teaching and learning processes. Therefore, teachers have to be open-minded, creative and innovative to provide and improve their teaching performance. It would be beneficial for teachers and students if the government would listen and consider their opinions. The governments need to involve teachers from urban and rural schools in the improvement process of Curriculum 2013 to make sure that the implementation would be smooth and not find any significant barriers in the field. The assessment process in Curriculum 2013 needs to made simple and easy so that teachers do not spend too much time on administrative tasks. The government should improve the training and guidance for teachers, for example, though more workshops or teacher training about Curriculum 2013. The government should also supply more resources and guidance for implementing character education in Curriculum 2013.

REFERENCES

[1] Ekawati, Y.N. (2016). The implementation of Curriculum 2013: A case study of English teachers' experience at SMA Lab School in Indonesia. *ELLD Journal, 7*(1), 84–90.

[2] Pratolo, B. (2015). *Exploring Indonesian leaners' beliefs about language learning strategies through reflection* (Unpublished thesis, Monash University, Australia). Retrieved from http://core.ac.uk/dow load/pdf/82059045.pdf

[3] Muth'im, A. (2014). Understanding and responding to the change of curriculum in the context of Indonesian education. *American Journal of Educational Research, 2*(11), 1094–1099.

[4] Kemendikbud. (2013). *Curriculum 2013: SMP/ MTs basic competencies. Jakarta, Indonesia: Research and Development Agency.*

[5] Lickona, T. (1992). *Educating for character, how our schools can teach respect and responsibility.* New York, NY: Bantam Books.

[6] Anugrahwati, Y. & Helena, I.R.A. (2015). The integration of second core competence (KI 2) of Curriculum 2013 in English classes. *Journal of English Language Teaching, 4*(1), 1–8.

[7] Creswell, J.W. (2014). *Research design qualitative, quantitative, and mixed methods approaches* (4th ed). New York, NY: SAGE Publications.

[8] Creswell, J.W. (2009). *Research design qualitative, quantitative, and mixed methods approaches* (3rd ed). New York, NY: SAGE Publications.

[9] Darsih, E. (2014). Indonesia EFL teachers' perception on the implementation of 2013 English curriculum. *Journal of English Education, 2*(2), 192–199.

[10] Ratih, I.A.M. (2017). The analysis of classroom character education in English lessons based on the Curriculum 2013. *Journal of Psychology and Instruction, 1*(2), 97–105.

[11] Iyitoğlu, O. & Alci, B. (2015). A qualitative research on 2nd grade teachers' opinions about 2nd grade English language teaching curriculum. *Journal of Elementary Education Online, 14*(2), 682–696.

English Linguistics, Literature, and Language Teaching in a Changing Era – Madya et al. (eds)
© 2020 Taylor & Francis Group, London, ISBN 978-1-03-224160-9

Raising English students' intercultural awareness through cultural texts

Indah Permatasari & Erna Andriyanti
English Education Program, Yogyakarta State University, Yogyakarta, Indonesia

ABSTRACT: Along with globalization and the advancement of technology in foreign language teaching, intercultural awareness (IA) has become one of important aspects to be addressed in English teaching and learning activities. IA promotes knowledge, understanding and tolerance, which later shapes how people think and behave in relation with the language they learn. Nevertheless, very limited efforts have been done by Indonesian lecturers to raise students' intercultural awareness during their teaching practices. They tend to focus more on grammar, vocabulary, and phonology with less attention to the cultural aspects of English spoken by European and American communities. Thus, this research aims to explain the role of cultural texts in raising students' intercultural awareness in English classroom. Based on interviews with two English lecturers and seven students majoring in petroleum engineering program, cultural texts are considered useful in raising students' intercultural awareness as students can learn English best through printed materials. Moreover, the knowledge reflected in these texts is critical parts of the sociocultural-dimension of literacy. Yet, lecturers are suggested to conduct further classroom-based study in order to investigate its effectiveness in English classroom.

Keywords: intercultural awareness, English language teaching, cultural texts

1 INTRODUCTION

The function of English as lingua franca has resulted in the recognition of English as the global language for communication. This global use of English involves its variation in space, that is, the notion of the range of "Englishes". These variations further have been generally divided into three concentric circles, with English as a native language in the inner circle, English as a second language (ESL) in the outer circle, and English as a foreign language (EFL) in the expanding circle [1]. With its wide use as the foreign language in many sectors, English in Indonesia belongs to the expanding circle. This situation resulting a challenging demand that ask Indonesian lecturers to include culture as parts of language learning in their English classroom [2]. This demand arises due to the fact that language and culture cannot be separated from each other [3,4]. Language and culture are closely related as language is the presentation of a culture [5]. This means that if someone wants to understand a language, it is very important for him/her to study the culture of that language [6].

Further, many experts have already researched the importance of intercultural awareness in EFL teaching [5,2,7,8,9]. According to them, it is imperative for lecturers to stress the importance of intercultural awareness to the students in their EFL classroom as it helps students to acquire new values and morals. It fosters the existing ones as well as establishing positive attitudes among students which in turn motivate them to learn foreign languages. Additionally, it is the cognitive aspect of intercultural communication and refers to the understanding of cultural conventions that affect how people think and behave [10]. That is to say, intercultural awareness is a crucial part in an intercultural approach to foreign language teaching and it is an essential prerequisite for developing students' intercultural communicative competence (ICC) [8].

Nevertheless, the fact speaks different. Indonesian EFL teaching has been less satisfactory in the last few decades [11]. This condition happens as very limited efforts have been done by language lecturers to raise students' intercultural awareness during their EFL teaching practices. At both level of school and university, the Indonesian English-teaching focuses more on the rules of English such as grammar and phonology, rather than on the culture of English communication [12]. Also, lecturers often fail to put their awareness of the importance of incorporating culture in teaching into action [13]. As a result, many students have difficulties in intercultural communication in spite of their positive attitude toward intercultural awareness.

In relation to that, several studies [14,15,16,17] have researched the role of literature in EFL teaching as it is the best ground for the genuine exploration of English culture especially in the context of European and American culture [18]. Moreover, studying literature in EFL classroom is also advantageous for a number of reasons [19], such as:

a. providing meaningful contexts,
b. involving a profound range of vocabulary,
c. enhancing imagination and creativity,
d. developing cultural awareness: it encourages critical thinking, and it is in line with CLT in which students become the active and autonomous participants while lecturers become the facilitators, guides, and active planner of the teaching and learning processes.

In addition, as the knowledge reflected in cultural texts are critical parts of the sociocultural dimension of literacy [20], cultural texts are suggested to be used as one of the learning materials in EFL classroom. The term cultural texts refer to objects, actions, and behaviours that reveal meanings [21]. These texts can be used to help students interpret what people from different communities do, not simply what they do not do when compared to the dominant group in the society [22]. However, limited studies had been conducted to investigate their roles in raising Indonesian students' intercultural awareness. This study was intended to raise students' intercultural awareness through the teaching and learning of English. The relevant cultures are those related to English as spoken by European and American communities because the standard English usually taught in Indonesia is from the inner circle and Indonesian culture since the participants are Indonesian students. Therefore, the main question of this study is: what is the role of cultural texts in helping English lecturers to raise students' intercultural awareness? Specifically, this main question was investigated using the following questions.

1. What are the students' opinions of intercultural awareness?
2. What are the lecturers' conceptions of their students' attitude towards intercultural awareness?
3. In what way do the lecturers teach English to the students in EFL classroom?

2 RESEARCH METHOD

This research was a qualitative study based on less guided-interviews conducted with two English lecturers and seven first semester students majoring in petroleum engineering study program in the faculty of mineral technology, in one of the state universities in Yogyakarta. The lecturers and the students were chosen to represent the real condition of EFL teaching administered in the previous semester. Particularly, these less guided interviews were designed so as to give meaningful voice to both group participants. Moreover, qualitative study was used as it can explore general views on and everyday practices relating to EFL teaching and intercultural awareness conducted by the lecturers, and the views of students about such practices.

In conducting the interview, I explained the purpose of the study to the participants and asked them to participate by answering the questions based on their experiences in their one-semester English classroom. Most of the participants indeed agreed and shared their stories related to the questions being asked. Then, to gain rich information from each interview, I allowed each informant to answer the questions in the way he/she chose, according to individual understanding and emphases. Finally, I analysed all of the data collected from the interviews using qualitative data analysis that consists of reducing the data, displaying the data, drawing conclusion and verification [23].

3 FINDINGS AND DISCUSSIONS

Here, the findings and discussions of the interviews are described under the three questions below.

3.1 *What are the students' opinions about intercultural awareness?*

All of the seven students said that intercultural awareness is very important in EFL learning. When the researcher asked them about some advantages that they might get in learning the target language's culture, most of the students answered that it cold foster their confidence in speaking English and enrich their knowledge about the people they were speaking to. Further, they said that by knowing the interlocutors' culture, they could maintain the conversation and avoid misunderstanding well. In other words, the students believed that it is hard for them to survive in a particular community or country unless they understand its language and culture. Examples of their statements are following.

As long as it is positive, why not? We need other people; we need to have interaction with them to develop ourselves. That is why language is present. Culture was born because of interaction, and interaction is a result of a language. (Student A)

In my opinion, having a positive attitude towards a foreign language and its culture is important. (Student B)

When asked about their thoughts related to several aspects which appear to be different from Indonesian culture, most of the students tended to become open-minded. In their point of view, it is common different nations to have differences. For them, differences are treasures that make this life beautiful. As Indonesians who are used to cultural complexity, they did not consider those differences a problem as long as they are able to filter them. However, one student said that there is no difference between Indonesian and foreign cultures. For her, sticking on Indonesian culture is the most important thing to do when communicating with foreigner. These two different opinions are summarized as follows.

I see differences as an asset of knowledge that can be learned. Being a nationalist is important but it does not mean that we close our eyes to see and learn other cultures. (Student E)

I think we must stick on our culture. We must stick on Indonesian culture if we are Indonesian because sharing the same interest will build up the conversation. (Student C)

The students' responses in the interviews show that six out of seven students have positive attitude towards foreign language and its culture. They tended to be open-minded and viewed differences as an asset to appreciate their own culture. However, they were rarely had opportunities and learning materials which discuss the cultural aspects of the target language they are learning. This might bring the students in difficulties in maintaining good conversation in an intercultural communication.

Intercultural communication is the symbolic exchange process where individual from two different cultural backgrounds or communities communicate in an interactive situation [24]. It is closely related to ICC as it is the ability to interact with people from another country and culture in a foreign language [25,26]. ICC involves not only a set of knowledge, skills and attitudes about knowing the self and the other, but it also includes the skills to deal with them in a non-judgmental way [8]. Thus, students of a foreign language who want to have effective intercultural interaction must be equipped with this set of abilities as it can train them to become intercultural speakers in an intercultural communication.

3.2 *What are the lecturers' conceptions of their students' attitude towards intercultural awareness?*

After interviewing the students, I interviewed the two English lecturers. They explained that most of the students are willing to learn the English and its culture happily. According to them, most of the students are categorized as *jaman-now* 'present generation' students who do not view differences as something dangerous. This happens because the advancement of technology helps them to easily access whatever information on the Internet in any time and in any situation. However, some students were reported to be less motivated in learning English. This condition happened as they got bored with the teaching materials used inside the classroom. Following are comments in the lecturers' interview.

So far, all of my students are having positive attitude towards the foreign language and the culture being learned inside the classroom. (Lecturer A)

There are some students who still see learning English and its culture as something boring. Maybe this is because the materials are less challenging for them. This was reflected on their behaviour inside the classroom in which tended to be demotivated and underestimate the learning activities. However, most of the students are having positive attitude toward learning the culture of English speakers in US and Europe. (Lecturer B)

In relation to the situation above, both lecturers A and B explained that they always tried to motivate the students inside the classroom. According to their statements, one of the ways that they use to foster the students' motivation is by stressing the advantages of learning the culture of English speakers in US and Europe. However, simply giving motivation is not enough to change someone's belief or attitude. According to lecturer B, students need to experience it themselves until they truly understand about what is really happening. That is, it is very important for lecturers to provide activities that allow students to interact with the cultural aspects of the target language being learned.

I cannot simply change my students' belief or opinion about this issue. For me, students need to experience it themselves so that they can fully understand about the importance of intercultural awareness. (Lecturer B)

The lecturers' explanation implies that these two lecturers are not aware of the importance of incorporating culture in teaching into action (see also 13]. The lecturers seemed to be aware that introducing US and European cultures is important in EFL classroom. However, their action stopped at the level of oral motivation only. There were no examples or opportunities that allow students to experience the cultures during the learning practices. As a result, many students lack of ICC, which is crucial to help them compare and mediate between different cultural norms present in intercultural communication [4].

Yet, teaching culture in EFL classroom is believed as indispensable necessity for many students to learn and improve their knowledge and communication skill of the target language being learned [27]. This is because the ultimate goal of foreign language teaching is to help students grow out of the shell of their mother tongue and their own culture [28]. In other words, the more the students understand the target language's culture, the more they will be able to become speakers who respect others' value as well as their way of acting and thinking without prejudice and discrimination [8].

3.3 *In what way do the lecturers teach English to the students in EFL classroom?*

Related to the EFL teaching practices, findings show that the two lecturers mostly used materials related to grammar, vocabulary, and phonology inside the classroom. Even when they talked about cultural aspects of US and Europe, the discussion was just in the beginning of the lesson and not so deep that it could raise their students' intercultural awareness. When I interviewed the students, most of them also stated that they usually learned about writing a CV, writing a postcard, doing interview simulation, et cetera. Following are some of their statements.

We learned how to write a CV, how to write a postcard, how to infer paragraph, and do interview simulation related to jobs. (Student A)

My lecturer told me about how to make a good CV. She also explained me about the differences between Indonesian CV and American CV. (Student G)

Conversely, when I interviewed the lecturers, one of them mentioned that she indeed reminded the students about the interconnection between language and culture. She also mentioned that she used various kinds of media to help her teaching. Nonetheless, all of those actions were done in the other major (English education study program). This can be seen on the following fragment of interview.

I always reminded my students about the need of learning the target language culture, especially in my sociolinguistics class. For media, of course I used various media to deliver the materials to students. (Lecturer B)

It can be concluded that the teaching and learning of culture is lacking. If the lecturers want to achieve the ultimate goal of foreign language teaching, it is important for them to use materials or activities which allow students to notice, compare, reflect, and interact with the culture of the foreign language they are learning [29]. Moreover, the interviewed lecturers did not seem to have a desired attitude of language lecturers who integrate culture in language teaching although incorporating culture in their EFL classroom might improve their teaching practices (see also 30].

Additionally, when the researcher asked the students about types of materials that they like most; six students said that they can learn English best when it is in print. Further, they explained that they can easily understand the meaning as they read the texts in pictures, stories or video. This statement was also proven by their lecturers. In this regards, cultural texts might be helpful for raising the students' intercultural awareness as they allow readers or writers become text user and text critic, and help students to understand how texts are used in various context for various purposes and functions, and how texts reflect particular viewpoints and ignore others [20]. By using cultural texts that are suitable with their major, students will be able to notice, compare, reflect, and interact with various people coming from various cultural backgrounds better.

4 CONCLUSIONS AND SUGGESTIONS

Based on the discussions above, the data collected through interviews showed that six out of seven students had positive attitude toward the culture of the target language being learned. Moreover, the lecturers also said that they had done some efforts to motivate and train students' intercultural awareness inside the classroom. Nonetheless, findings from observation showed a contradictory result—the lecturers did not put their awareness of the importance of incorporating culture in teaching into action [see also 13]. Thus, most of the students were saying that they have difficulties in interacting with people in an intercultural communication. In this regard, cultural texts might be opted as one of the effective media to raise students' intercultural awareness inside the classroom. However, due to the limitation of this research, further classroom-based studies are needed to investigate its effectiveness in raising students' intercultural awareness in English classroom.

REFERENCES

[1] Kachru, B.B. (1985). Standards, codification and sociolinguistic realism: The English Language in The Outer Circle. In R. Quirk, & H.G.W. (Eds.), *English in The World: Teaching and Learning The Language and Literatures* (pp. 11–30). Cambridge: Cambridge University Press.

[2] Kourova, A. & Madianos, D. (2013). Intercultural awareness and its role in enriching students' communicative competence. *The International HETL Review*, Special issue.

[3] Liddicoat, A.J., Scarino, A., Papademetre, L. & Kohler, M. (2003). Report on intercultural language learning. *Science and Training*. Canberra: Commonwealth Department of Education.

[4] Baker, W. (2011). Intercultural awareness: Modelling an understanding of cultures in intercultural communication through English as a lingua franca, *Language and Intercultural Communication*, 197–214.

[5] Mahadi, T.S.P & Jafari, S.M. (2012). Language and Culture. *International Journal of Humanities and Social Science, 12*.

[6] Brogger, F. (1992). *Culture, language, text*. Oslo: Scandinavian University Press.

[7] Liu, C. (2016). Cultivation of intercultural awareness in EFL teaching. *Journal of Language Teaching and Research, 7*, 226–232.

[8] Barany, L. K. (2016). Language awareness, intercultural awareness and communicative language teaching: Towards language education. *International Journal of Humanities and Cultural Studies, 2*(4).

[9] Kusumaningputri, R. & Widodo, H.P. (2014). Promoting Indonesian university students' critical intercultural awareness in Tertiary EAL classrooms: The use of digital photograph-mediated intercultural tasks. *System*, 49–61.

[10] Rong Zhang & Steele, D. (2012). Improving intercultural awareness: A challenging task for Japan. *Procedia of Social and Behavioral Sciences*, 52–63,

[11] Kirkpatrick, A. (2007). Teaching English Across Cultures: What do English language lecturers need to know how to teach English. *English Australia Journal, 23*(3).

[12] Sulistiyo, U. (2016). English language teaching and EFL lecturer competence in Indonesia, *Proceedings of the Fourth International Seminar on English Language Teaching (ISELT-4)*, 396–406,

[13] Yeganeh, M.T. & Raeesi, H. (2016). Developing cultural awareness in EFL classrooms at secondary school level in an Iranian educational context. *Procedia Of Social And Behavioral Sciences*, 534–542.

[14] Tasneen, W. (2010). Literary texts in the language classroom: A study of lecturers and students views at International School in Bangkok, *Asian EFL Journal, 12*(4).

[15] Segal, N. (2015). From literature to cultural literacy. *Humanities*, 68–79.

[16] Rodrigues, R. (2016). Using literary texts for teaching English: Benefits, limitations and application.

[17] A. Chouhan. Teaching English language through literature: A critical study. *International Journal of English Language Literature and Humanities*, 266–271.

[18] Bagherkazemi, M. & Alemi, M. (2010). Literature in the EFL/ESL classroom: Consensus and controversy. *Linguistic and Literature Broad Research and Innovation, 1*(1).

[19] Van, T.T.M. (2009). The relevance of literacy analysis to teaching literature in EFL classroom. *English Teaching Forum, 3*, 2–9.

[20] Kucer, S. & Silva, C. (2005). *Teaching the dimensions of literacy*. New York: Routledge.

[21] Malley, S. & Hawkins, A. Examining culture as text, (Online), Retrieved from www.engagingcommunities.org/proposing-the-ethnographic-research-project/3a-examining-culture-as-text/, July 2018.

[22] Larson, J. & Marsh, J. (2005). *Making literacy real: Theories and practices for learning and teaching*. London: SAGE Publications

[23] Miles, M.B. & Huberman, A.M. (1994). *Qualitative data analysis (2nd ed)*. California: SAGE Publications.

[24] Ting-Toomey, S. (1999). *Communicating across cultures*. London: The Guilford Press.

[25] Byram, M. (1997). Teaching and assessing intercultural communicative competence. Multilingual Matters, Clevedon.

[26] Byram, M., Gribkova, B. & Starkey, H. (2002). Developing the intercultural dimension in language teaching: A practical introduction for lecturers. Strasbourg: Council of Europe.

[27] Gorjian, B. & Aghvami, F. (2017). The comparative study of EFL lecturers and learners' perceptions on the importance of teaching culture, *Journal of Applied Linguistics and Language Learning*, 71–78.

[28] Kaikkonen, P. (2001). Intercultural learning through foreign language education, in Kohonen, V., Jaatinen, R., Kaikkonen, P. & Lehtovaara, J. (Eds), *Experiential Learning in Foreign Language Education*, 61–105, Essex: Longman.

[29] Liddicoat, A.J. & Scarino, A. (2013). *Intercultural language teaching and learning*. West Sussex: Blackwell Publishing.

[30] Karabinar, S. & Guler, C.Y. (2012). The attitudes of EFL lecturers towards teaching culture and their classroom practices, *Journal of Education and Social Research, 2*, 113–123.

English Linguistics, Literature, and Language Teaching in a Changing Era – Madya et al. (eds)
© 2020 Taylor & Francis Group, London, ISBN 978-1-03-224160-9

Tertiary students' anxiety in speaking English

Muamaroh, Nur Hidayat & Sri Lestari
Universitas Muhammadiyah Surakarta, Central Java, Indonesia

ABSTRACT: The objective of the study was to investigate tertiary students' level of language anxiety. There were 531 respondents from four universities who participated in this study. The study used close questionnaire as an instrument for data gathering. The data were analyzed quantitatively using descriptive statistics, T-test, and ANOVA. Based on descriptive statistics results, all participants had moderating of anxiety levels (mean = 73.94). It was found that 92 participants (17.3%) had high language anxiety, 354 students (66.7%) had moderate rating of anxiety levels and 85 students (16.0%) had low language anxiety. There was no significant (sig = 0.127) difference between state and private universities students based on T-test (t = -1.528), and both had moderate level of language anxiety. This study also found that female students had higher language anxiety (mean = 74.86) than male students (mean = 70.97), and its difference was considered as significant (sig = 0.010) based on T-test (t = 2.596).

Keywords: students' anxiety, English as a foreign language, tertiary level

1   INTRODUCTION

Anxiety plays an important role in language learning [1]. Consequently, many students experienced with language anxiety. There were more than half of foreign language learners ever have experiences related to language anxiety in their language classroom [2]. Anxiety is a complex affective concept associated with feelings of uneasiness, frustration, self-doubt, apprehension, or worry [3]. Zhang [4] stated that anxiety is psychological tension that the learner experiences in performing a learning task. Anxiety is considered as one of affective variables that can negatively influence students in learning a foreign language to have language learning experience in class [5, 6]. The concept of anxiety refers to emotional state of apprehension, tension, nervousness, and worry mediated by the arousal of the automatic nervous system Kumaravadivelu [7]. Anxiety refers to feeling of fear, worry, and unease caused by external or internal potential threats [8]. Thus, anxiety is related to psychological aspects such as feeling of worry, difficulty, and tension.

Furthermore, Horwitz et al, [9] stated that the concept of foreign language anxiety (FLA) refers to an individual self-perception, feelings and behaviors related to classroom language learning, arising from the uniqueness of the language-learning process. Moreover, MacIntyre [10] elaborated that Foreign Language Anxiety (FLA) is feeling of tension and apprehension specifically associated with second or foreign language contexts, and negative emotional reaction arousal when learning or using a second or foreign language. As a result, students' anxiety might reduce their language acquisition and their motivation to study the language. Therefore, they grow to be more fearful in using English to communicate in English in class. Spielberger [11] considered any form of stimulation that could trigger state anxiety will reduce students' self-confidence and, therefore, their willingness to communicate.

Pappamihiel [12] divided anxiety into state and trait anxiety. State anxiety occurs when learners are exposed to particular conditions or situations, while trait anxiety is a person's tendency to feel anxious regardless of the situations they are exposed to. Similarly, Mesri [13] classified anxiety into three types: trait, state and situation-specific anxiety. Trait anxiety is considered as an aspect of personality; that it is more permanent disposition to be anxious. State anxiety is an apprehension that is experienced at a particular moment as a respond towards a definite situation. Situation-specific anxiety is an apprehension that is aroused at a specific situation and event. Different individual has his/her own level of anxiety [14].

There were some studies on the correlation between anxieties and foreign language performance that obtained different findings [1, 15, 16, 9, 17, 6, 18, 19].

A study by Kord and Abdolmanafi-Rokni [1] found that there was a negative correlation between language anxiety and speaking performance. On the other hand, Rastegar and Karami's study [15] discovered that there was a significant negative relationship between foreign language classroom anxiety (FLCA) and willingness to communicate (WTC). Sanaei et al [20] found that low average of anxiety among students can be positively correlated to the main speech fluency indicators. As the participants are more fluent in a language, they will produce more accurate sentences. Foreign language anxiety has negative impact on performance in foreign language classroom [16, 9, 17]. A study by Park and Lee [6] found that learners' anxiety level was negatively related to their oral performance. Cameron [18] discovered that minimizing students' anxiety will enhance their "state of readiness" to communicate in English. Fang and Dong [19] argued that students who have higher anxiety also have lower English speaking ability.

Since English speaking ability is important for Indonesian students, the government made some efforts to improve EFL learners' communicative competence by producing a new curriculum called Curriculum 2013. The curriculum emphasizes language learners to use English actively, which includes scientific approaches to give students many opportunities to use English orally. However, feeling of language anxiety might become a great obstacle for them to use their English and it is relevant in Indonesian context and also in other countries that consider English as a foreign language. Therefore, as this study explored learners' anxiety to speak English, we believe it is an important research since there has been not many research focusing on this issue within Indonesian context and in particular at the tertiary educational level.

2   RESEARCH METHOD

The participants of this study were undergraduate English department students from two public universities and two private universities located in Central Java. Five hundred and thirty one students who took English speaking subject became the participants of this study. They were taken randomly from these four universities. There were 405 female and 126 male students. They have been studying English as a foreign language. At the beginning of the study, the researchers gave brief explanation of the study objectives, and if they agreed to join this study voluntarily, then they had to sign a consent form that we already provided. The instrument used to gather data was close questionnaire adapted from the Foreign Language Classroom Anxiety Scale (FLCAS), which was developed by Horwitz et al [9]. The close questionnaire had been tried out to students who were not included in this research. The result of the pilot experiment showed that the content of all items in the questionnaire could be understood by participants. The reliability of the questionnaire was 0.891, which means all items were reliable and proper to use.

Based on the pilot experiment result, 24 items of close questionnaire matched to the study purpose were used. The close questionnaire was translated into Indonesian to avoid misunderstanding from students A Likert-type scale with five possible responses (1 to 5) to each item of the questionnaire was used. The scale ranged from (1) for "None at all" to (5) for "a great deal." Descriptive statistics was employed to analyze the acquired data based on two variables: type of university and the students' gender. T-test was also used to observe whether there were some significant differences between two variables, while ANOVA was used to observe whether there were some significant differences among the variables.

3 FINDINGS AND DISCUSSION

Based on the results of close questionnaire, important findings related to the students' language anxiety based on their university background and gender were found. The findings are explained in the following tables:

3.1 The students' language anxiety at tertiary level

The study showed that from 531 participants, it was found that 85 students (16.0%) had low language anxiety level, 92 students (17.3%) had high language anxiety, and 354 students (66.7%) had moderate language anxiety level.

3.2 The students' language anxiety based on students' type of university

In view of descriptive statistics analysis, it was revealed that students from private universities had slightly higher language anxiety level (mean = 74.51) than those enrolled at public university students (mean=72.28). Even though the difference was not significant (sig = 0.127), as measured using T-test (t = -1.528), both students from public and private universities had moderate language anxiety level.

To understand the difference of language anxiety level from all participants taken from four universities, ANOVA analysis was used to analyze the data.

Table 3 revealed that students from four universities had no different language anxiety based on the result of ANOVA analysis (F = 1.544). This means that the different among them was not significant (sig = .202).Therefore, it can be concluded that all students from four universities whether they were from public and private universities had moderate language anxiety level.

Table 1. The students' language anxiety at tertiary level.

Score	Category	Frequency/N	Percent
X < 59.168	Low	85	16.0
59.169 < X < 88.710	Moderate	354	66.7
X > 88.711	High	92	17.3
		531	100.0

Table 2. The result of language anxiety between public and private universities.

Type of university	N	Mean	Standard Deviation	Std Error Mean	t	Sig (2-tailed)
Public university	137	72.28	13.800	1.179	−1.528	.127
Private university	394	74.51	15.068	.759		

Table 3. Students' anxiety based on ANOVA analysis.

	Sum of Squares	Df	Mean square	F	Sig
Between groups	1007.313	3	335.771	1.544	.202
Within groups	114636.510	527	217.527		
Total	115643.823	530			

3.3 The students' language anxiety based on gender

Based on descriptive statistics analysis in Table 4, there was different significance (sig = 0.010) between female and male students based on T-test (t = 2.596). It was because mean for females students was higher (mean = 74.86) than those of male students (mean = 70.97). This means that there was significant effect of gender on the level of language anxiety.

The following is the result of close questionnaire related to factors which caused students' anxiety in using their English.

According to the results of descriptive statistics, this current study found that there were six highest factors which influenced participants' language anxiety based on the questionnaire results. The findings were illustrated in Table 5. Among six factors, the feeling that other students or classmates have better English speaking ability was the strongest factor which caused anxiety on students with the mean score of 3.58 and standard deviation (SD) of 0.975. The next highest factor was concern about the consequences of failing in their foreign language class with the mean score of 3.55 and SD of 1.0.90. Speaking in English without preparation was the next highest factor which made students anxious (mean = 3.38 and SD=1.097). Their language teacher (mean = 3.33 and SD

Table 4.   The result of language anxiety based on gender.

Gender	N	Mean	T test	Sig (2-tailed)
Female	405	74.86	2.596	.010
Male	126	70.97		

Table 5.   The foreign language anxiety scale.

No	Statement	Mean	SD
1	I never feel quite sure of myself when I am speaking in my foreign language class	3.02	0.961
2	I tremble when I know that I'm going to be called on in language class	2.98	1.042
3	I get nervous when I don't understand every word the language teacher says	2.86	1.020
4	I keep thinking that the other students are better at languages than I am	3.48	0.985
5	I am usually at ease during tests in my language class	2.83	0.797
6	I start to panic when I have to speak without preparation in language class	3.38	1.097
7	I worry about the consequences of failing my foreign language class	3.55	1.090
8	In language class, I can get so nervous I forget things I know	3.22	1.128
9	It embarrasses me to volunteer answers in my language class	3.01	1.003
10	I would not be nervous speaking the foreign language with native speakers	2.96	0.887
11	Even if I am well prepared for language class, I feel anxious about it	3.18	1.012
12	I feel confident when I speak in foreign language class	2.95	0.912
13	I am afraid that my language teacher is ready to correct every mistake I make	2.89	1.079
14	I can feel my heart pounding when I'm going to be called on in language class	3.09	1.052
15	I always feel that the other students speak the foreign language better than I do	3.58	0.975
16	I feel very self-conscious about speaking the foreign language in front of other students	3.34	0.933
17	Language class moves so quickly I worry about getting left behind	3.04	0.998
18	I feel more tense and nervous in my language class than in my other classes	2.91	1.109
19	I get nervous and confused when I am speaking in my language class	2.91	1.028
20	It frightens me when I don't understand what the teacher is saying in the foreign language	3.09	1.018
21	I feel overwhelmed by the number of rules you have to learn to speak a foreign language	2.77	0.980
22	I am afraid that the other students will laugh at me when I speak the foreign language	2.88	1.131
23	I would probably feel comfortable around native speakers of the foreign language	2.71	0.912
24	I get nervous when the language teacher asks questions which I haven't prepared in advance	3.33	1.051
	Total participants	531	100

= 1.051) and the speaking class itself made students anxious (mean = 3.22 and SD = 1.128). Finally, inability to understand the learning materials (mean = 3.09 and SD = 1.018) was also highest factor which made students anxious.

The finding of this research was consistent with the study conducted by Gopang, et al [21] who found that students had moderate level of language anxiety within the context of Pakistan. The results of this study is also in line with Yang's study (2017) who explained that the language anxiety level of female students (M = 2.962) was higher than male students (M = 2.838) based on descriptive statistics analysis, although its difference was not statistically significant (t = 1.810).

Nevertheless, the finding of this study conflicted to Tsai's study [22] who investigated university students within the context of Taiwan. It was found that there was no significant difference between male and female students in language anxiety of speaking English. In contrast, this current study found that there was significant difference (sig = 0.010) based on T-test (t = 2.596) between male and female university students. Female students had higher language anxiety (mean = 74.86) than male students (mean = 70.97). This corresponded to the study conducted by Çubukcu [23] who found that there was no significant difference between female and male students regarding their anxiety.

On the other hand, this current study found that there was significant difference between female and male students (sig = 0.010) based on T-test (t = 2.596). This supported the study conducted by Mahmoodzadeh [24] who discovered that the female students were found to have more experience in foreign language speaking anxiety.

4 CONCLUSION

The study found that all participants from four universities had moderate level of language anxiety (66.7%). This study also found that female students had higher language anxiety level (mean = 74.86) than those of male students (mean = 70.97). Its difference was considered as significant (sig = 0.010) based on T-test (t = 2.596). This study showed that six strongest factors which caused anxiety towards students to use their English speaking ability were related to their perception of classmates who have better English skills, concern that they will fail in their foreign language class, speaking English without preparation, the language teacher, the speaking class itself, and the inability to understand the learning materials.

The limitation of this current study relates to the factors which caused anxiety towards language learners in using their English and the efforts to minimize and reduce their anxiety in using English. Therefore, it will need further research on this topic. Due to students and cultural situation, government policy, teachers' competence and their qualification, learning facilities and learning context of this study, the findings of this current study may not be generalized in all situations due to limited number of participants, which was limited to four universities consisting of two public universities and two private universities in Central Java, Indonesia.

REFERENCES

[1] Kord, S. & Abdolmanafi-Rokni, S. (2016). The relationship between self-efficacy and anxiety and speaking ability of Iranian intermediate EFL learners. *Modern Journal of Language Teaching Methods, 6*(9), 2251–6204.

[2] Wörde, V.R. (1998). *An investigation of students' foreign language anxiety*. Retrieved on March 7, 2011, from http://www.Eric.ed.gov/ERIC web portal

[3] Scovel, T. (1978). *The Effect of affect on foreign language learning: A review of the anxiety research.* https://doi.org/10.1111/j.1467-1770.1978.tb00309.x. Retrieved from https://onlinelibrary.wiley.com/doi/abs/10.1111/j.1467-1770.1978.tb00309.

[4] Zhang, L.J. (2001). ESL students' classroom anxiety. *Teaching and Learning, 21*(2), 51–62.

[5] Wörde, V.R. (2003). Students' perspectives on foreign language anxiety. *Inquiry, 8*(1), 21–40.

[6] Park, H., & Lee, A.R. (2005). *L2 learners' anxiety, self-confidence and oral performance*. Retrieved from pdfs>hyesook",1,0,0>www.paaljapan.org>pdfs>hyesook

[7] Kumaravadivelu. B. (2006). *Understanding language teaching: From method to postmethod*. Available from: https://www.researchgate.net/publication/242086730_Understanding_Language_Teaching_From_Method_to_Postmethod [accessed at Dec 03 2018].

[8] Grupe, D.W., & Nitschke, J.B. (2013). Uncertainty and anticipation in anxiety: An integrated neurobiological and psychological perspective. *Nature Reviews Neuroscience, 14*, 488–501.

[9] Horwitz, E.K. (1986). Preliminary evidence for the reliability and validity of a foreign language anxiety scale. *TESOL Quarterly, 20*, 559–562.

[10] Macintyre, P.D. (1999). Language anxiety: A review of literature for language teachers. In D. J. Young (Eds.), *Affect in foreign language and second language learning* (pp. 24–43). New York: McGraw Hill Companies.

[11] MacIntyre, P.D., Dörnyei, Z., Clément, R., & Noels, K.A. (1998). Conceptualizing willingness to communicate in a L2: A situational model of L2 confidence and affiliation. *The Modern Language Journal, 82*(4), 545–562. doi: 10.1111/j.1540-4781.1998.tb05543.x.

[13] Pappamihiel, N.E. (2002). English as a second language students and English language anxiety: Issues in the mainstream classroom. *ProQuest Education Journal, 36*(3), 327–355.

[14] Mesri, F. (2012). The relationship between gender and Iranian EFL learners' foreign language classroom anxiety (FLCA). *International Journal of Academic Research in Business and Social Sciences, 2*(6), 147–156.

[15] McDonald, A.S. (2001). The prevalence and effects and test anxiety in school children. *Educational Psychology, 21*(1), 89–98.

[16] Rastegar, M., & Karami, M. (2015). On the relationship between foreign language classroom anxiety, willingness to communicate and scholastic success among Iranian EFL learners. *Theory and Practice in Language Studies, 15*(11), 2387–2394.

[17] Aida, Y. (1994). Examination of Horwitz, Horwitz, and Cope's construct of foreign language anxiety: The case of students of Japanese. *The Modern Language Journal, 78*, 155–168.

[18] MacIntyre, P.D., & Gardner, R.C. (1991). Methods and results in the study of anxiety and language learning: A review of the literature. *Language Learning, 41*(1), 85–117.

[19] Cameron, D. (2015). 'In New Zealand I feel more confidence': The role of context in the willingness to communicate (WTC) of migrant Iranian English language learners. *International Journal of English Studies IJES*. http://revistas.um.es/ijes

[20] Fang, P.G., & Dong. Y. (2010). A study on college students' anxiety to spoken English. *Canadian Social Science, 6*(2), 95–101.

[21] Sanaei, O., Zafarghandi, A.M., & Sabet, M.K. (2015). The effect of classroom anxiety on EFL learner's oral narratives fluency: The case of intermediate level students. *Theory and Practice in Language Studies, 5*(7),1390–1400. Doi:http://dx.doi.org/10.17507/tpls.0507.11

[22] Gopang, I.B., Bughio, F.A., Memon, S.A., & Faiz, J. (2016). Foreign language anxiety and learner beliefs in second language learning: A research timeline. *Theory and Practice in Language Studies, 6* (8), 1591-1595. doi: http://dx.doi.org/10.17507/tpls.0608.10

[22] Tsai, C. (2014). English as a foreign language speaking anxiety among university of technology students in Taiwan. *Modern Journal of Language TeachingMethod, 4*(4), 44–48.

[23] Çubukcu, F. (2008). A study on the correlation between self-efficacy and foreign language learning anxiety. *Journal of Theory and Practice in Education, 4*(1):148–158.

[24] Mahmoodzadeh, M. (2012). Investigating foreign language speaking anxiety within the EFL learner's interlanguageSystem: The case of Iranian learners. *Journal of Language Teaching and Research, 3*(3), 466–476. Doi:10.4304/jltr.3.3.466-476.

English Linguistics, Literature, and Language Teaching in a Changing Era – Madya et al. (eds)
© 2020 Taylor & Francis Group, London, ISBN 978-1-03-224160-9

Developing integrated English learning materials of Islamic content based on instructional analysis: Design-based research

Muhammad Saifuddin & Dwi Nurcahyani
Universitas Pesantren Tinggi Darul Ulum Jombang, East Java, Indonesia

ABSTRACT: English learning material should be well developed based on formulated learning goal. It should also be able to assist students to learn English well. For achieving learning goal, instructional analysis helps teachers identify students' learning level and specific learning skill. To do so, it is essential to design learning materials which meet students' way of learning. Besides, in relation to educational purposes, well integrated language skills are often suggested. This research aimed at developing English material based on instructional analysis. A design-based research was applied. The data were gained from the result of a syllabus analysis and a questionnaire. The data were in terms of learning objectives identification. In addition, since this research focused on Islamic content, some Islamic resources were selected accordingly. This Islamic content was adapted based on the students' level of difficulties. As a result, English learning material was developed to promote students' integrated skills to achieve their cognitive, affective, and psychomotor objectives while learning English.

Keywords: material design, instructional analysis

1 INTRODUCTION

Learning English requires learners to practice a lot and have the performance ability that they need to equip themselves with the four language skills. Being able to perform their language enables them to easily use the language properly [1]. However, learners sometimes have difficulties learning English. In that case, students are essentially guided in how to learn. On the other hand, good learning materials should also facilitate their way of learning and assist learners to attain the learning goal. These learning outcomes should be clear and specific describing learners' competences. Therefore, teachers should be careful in determining and formulating learning objectives.

When learning objectives have been arranged systematically, they will determine the learning content. Both learning objective and content of the material should be formulated at the beginning as a planning. The formulation refers to the principles of how instructional design is applied and by the purpose of maintaining good learning quality. The benefit of appropriate material design is to maintain learning quality [2]. Consequently, the purpose of learning material design avoids some misleading objectives which do not measure students' exact competence. Providing developed learning materials helps students how to learn and how to perform its presentation [3].

In an English learning context and to maintain the educational learning standard, providing sustainable English learning materials which meet students' expectations will affect their English development. In fact, it is not only about the material but also how teachers and students act their role [4]. Regarding teachers' efforts, they should focus on what the students need and what they are able to do. However, learners experienced differently. Teachers often neglected the outcome. This could lead to problems with unsuccessful learning. Then, teaching material design is proposed to encounter unsuccessful learning.

Designing teaching materials provides a good analysis of students' needs. Sustainable design should be developed based on the formulated goals. Therefore, it can be done through instructional analysis. Farid and Saifuddin note that the use of common books for learning International English Language Testing System (IELTS) does not seem to meet test takers' needs, especially in terms of writing tests [5]. They provided purposefully designed IELTS writing materials for those who wanted to take the IELTS test. Some designs may also emphasize certain language skills for which they provide the syllabus of English for Academic Purpose (EAP) [6]. In addition, these designs are accountably suggested for certain material.

Dick and Carey explain that it begins by analyzing the instructional goals followed by analyzing performance objectives. The analysis includes instructional goals analysis, and sub-learning outcomes analysis [7]. Doing the instructional analysis helps to identify and measure psychomotor skill, cognition, verbal information skill, and affective domain. Meanwhile, sub-learning outcomes analysis evaluates the arrangement; whether they are well - developed systematically and procedurally or not. Dick and Carey proposed models of instructional analysis:

1. Hierarchical Approach

   It indicates learners' competence which should be maintained systematically. The previous skills will determine their learning to the next level. It means that one sub-learning outcome should be mastered first and becomes the prerequisite to the next learning outcome mastery. This model is specialized by a vertical line. Additionally, this competence is also recognized as cognitive competence.

2. Procedural Approach

   The procedural approach is classified as the psychomotor domain. This approach illustrates that some abilities have the same position in a series of learning but are not prerequisites for other competences. This approach is usually depicted with horizontal straight lines which are not required but the level of difficulty increases from easy to difficult.

3. Cluster Approach

   In this approach, students' abilities are grouped according to one specific goal. This grouping is not based on the dependence of ability on another and is not hierarchical, but students must master all of them.

4. Combination Approach

   In applying this approach, a hierarchical, procedural and grouping model is combined. This has meaning, to be able to have psychomotor skills, intellectual abilities, verbal information and attitudes must be systematically combined in accordance with the rules used in instructional design.

Taking account into the provided models of instructional analysis, they emphasize on systematic arrangement of learning outcomes and to figure out typical competence depicted in the formulated outcomes. This analysis is used since it focused on developing learning materials which met cognitive, psychomotor, and affective abilities. Thus, integrative learning could be maintained. On the other hand, to get unity of a good learning process, there are several sources that need attention. This refers to the success rate of learning that is not only determined by one factor. These factors are as follows [8]:

1. Learning context; formal, non-formal.
2. Learning requirements; learning objectives, syllabus, methods, evaluation.
3. Students; level of ability, character, previous experience.
4. Teacher; teaching style, teaching vision.
5. Material; learning activities, learning methods, exercises, texts.

Foremost, the benefits of the teaching material design is that it requires learners to make their own decisions and builds up decision-making and enables them to elaborate the reasons for them [9]. As it proposes more advantages and significances, this study aimed at figuring out the needs of learning materials suited to learners' level based on instructional analysis, and presents a teaching material design under Islamic content, since this study emphasizes Islamic values integrated into learning contents.

2 RESEARCH METHOD

This study aimed at developing integrated learning material of Islamic content based on instructional analysis. This learning material covered the integration of language skills to build students' language proficiency. Thus, the research design used was design-based research. This research design focused on the research and development which involved certain processes of development to validate a particular product [10]. Seels and Ritchey [11] further indicate that this design based research is applied to analyze design, development, and evaluation systematically, practically and effectively.

This study used instructional analysis to figure out the formulation of the syllabus used. By this, it identified the formulation of learning outcomes, learning materials, learning activities, and evaluation. The results of the conducted instructional analysis, supported by some supporting data gained from observation and questionnaire, were the basis of developing the learning material. The procedure of the study is described in Figure 1.

This study involved the students of Unipdu University who were in their first semester and took English Consortium. The participants were students from Math Education, Islamic Studies, Information Systems, Health and Science, and the Administration Department. The focus of this material development was that the material was developed specifically for those who were non-English students.

To collect the data, this study used more than one research instrument concerning the needs of the data. Observations and a questionnaire were applied. Observing the teaching and learning process led to the identification of the learning activities used. Besides, its purpose was to see the appropriateness between the activities used by the teacher and the basic competences formulated based on the syllabus used. Meanwhile, a questionnaire attempted to gain more information about the students regarding their competences in terms of cognitive, psychomotor, and affective learning domains.

3 FINDINGS

3.1 *Instructional analysis on current syllabus*

In a syllabus, the description of achieving the learning outcomes should be clearly formulated. This is because the syllabus also describes how students learn through learning stages; from easy to difficult or from understanding to application. These stages clearly refer to learning activities which were particularly formulated to basic competence or sub-learning outcomes. Obviously, to measure how learning outcomes were achieved, systematically formulated sub-learning outcomes or basic competences were needed to determine what the level of learning was. Thus, instructional analysis was carried out. This instructional analysis measured how well the sub-learning outcomes were arranged to attain the learning outcomes designed by the teachers of the English Consortium.

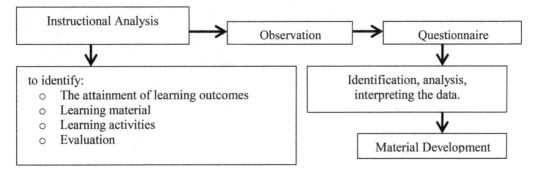

Figure 1. Research design.

The analysis covered the formulation of the learning outcomes into some sub-learning outcomes and the procedure of how they were developed in order to have a clear analysis on the approaches of the instructional analysis used. As was previously described, the approaches used to analyze the syllabus were hierarchical, procedural, cluster, and a combination approach. Every approach used in this analysis described how students gained their knowledge through learning activities.

Looking at its learning outcomes, the syllabus stated the description of the final competence students should master at the end of the learning process. It further described that students were expected to be able to explain Test of English as Foreign Language (TOEFL) learning material, including listening, structure, and reading as well as apply their understanding to do simple tasks. The previous syllabus stated that learners were able to explain TOEFL material including listening part A, B, and C; structure and written expressions; reading comprehension; and able to use their understanding to do simple task appropriately.

In relation to the formulation of the learning outcomes, they should clearly cover the pedagogical, psychomotor, and affective learning domains. How the three domains remained as the stated learning objectives was based on the operational action verbs used. The action verbs stated in previous syllabus were 'explain' and 'apply. In terms of the analysis based on Bloom's taxonomy [12], the cognitive domain expressed in the formulated learning outcome reflects the stage of 'analysis'. In the analysis stage, students master the ability to break down, determine and relate one part to another. Meanwhile, the psychomotor domain is reflected in the stage of 'manipulation', the second stage of the taxonomy. However, the affective domain was not expressed well in this learning outcome.

Based on the instructional analysis in this study, it was identified that there were 14 sub-competences developed to achieve the learning outcomes. These 14 sub-competences varied in terms of the approach used. The classification of the approach used was based on the operational implications of the learning stages and their learning materials. Figure 2 shows the result of instructional analysis on the current syllabus used:

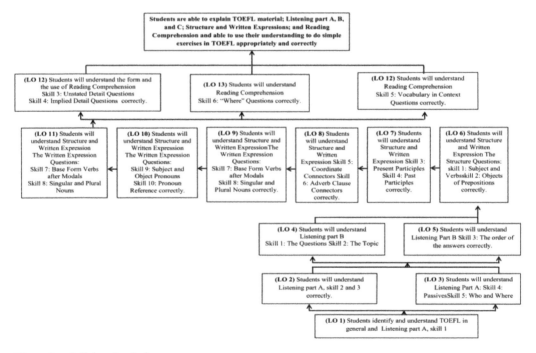

Figure 2. Syllabus Analysis.

The instructional analysis shows that there were three approaches used, hierarchical, procedural, and cluster. Every approach used implied the meaning of the description of the sub-competences. In fact, there were two different things described in this analysis. The content of the materials were systematically arranged. However, the written action verbs each sub-learning competence did not describe the level of students learning stages. It was revealed that the action verb used in all sub-learning outcomes was 'understand'. Although the organization of the learning materials were properly arranged, they could not achieve the learning outcome because of the improper action verbs used for different stages of formulated sub-learning outcomes.

3.1.1 *Hierarchical approach*
In the hierarchical approach, the attention is on the orientation of the sub-learning outcomes in that they must relate to one another. In other words, the learning stages remain either the same or higher level. Thus, the beginning formulated sub-learning outcome at least showed the same level of learning mastery or the next sub-learning outcome must be formulated in higher level and of course the subject mastery must relate one another, one is as prerequisite to the another next step. The following is an example of the hierarchical approach:

Based on Figure 3, the organization of this approach shows that in order to attain LO 4 and 5, students should master LO 2 and 3. Moreover, if Figure 3 was analyzed in a line from LO 1 to LO 2 and 3 to LO 4 and 5, the approach was there. What referred to this figure is that students' were brought gradually from mastering listening part A to part B. Learners should master the LO 2 and it should come first before going to the LO 4 and 5.

The weaknesses in this analysis relate to the systematic procedure of formulating the sub-learning outcomes. Most of the sub-learning outcomes used the same action verb which only referred to the same level of 'Understanding' based on Bloom's taxonomy. It was always impossible to achieve the 'Analysis' taxonomy as stated in the learning outcome if the formulation of the sub-learning outcomes using appropriate action verbs was not set properly.

3.1.2 *Cluster approach*
This approach did not obligate the close relationship in which one competence relied on another but rather they refer to complete competences needed to attain a higher level. However, the main point of this approach is that the competences should not be stages but should be equal so that students get the whole required competence to gain the next level.

Figure 4 explains the cluster approach. It is indicated by one arrow creating two different paths of arrow competences, which were competences that had an equal level of competence and should be mastered. In addition, there were two pairs of cluster approach noted in LO 2, LO 3 and LO 4, LO 5. In this case, between LO 2 and LO 3, they indicated no relation in which to gain LO 3, it was not needed to gain LO 2 first or vice versa. In LO 2, students were expected to be able to understand the listening material in part A, while in LO 3 students were still expected to be able to understand the listening material in part A as well but they had

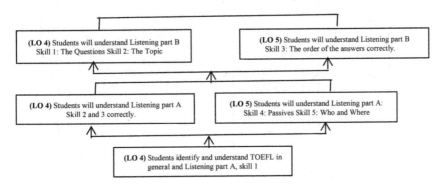

Figure 3. Hierarchical approach analysis.

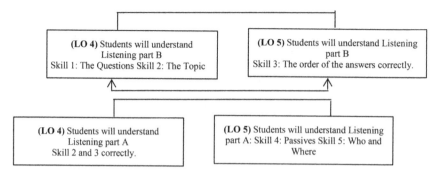

Figure 4. Cluster approach analysis.

different learning contents. When those competences in LO 2 and LO 3 had not been mastered then it was hard for the students to achieve LO 4 and LO 5 because to achieve those competences, they must gain those in LO 2 and LO 3.

3.1.3 Procedural approach

This approach analyzed competences at equal level and as a series of learning activities. One competence should not be a prerequisite to the others but the competences should show that the level of difficulty should be systematic; from the easiest to the most difficult. This is because the procedural approach describes students' psychomotor skills.

The horizontal flow of the arrows draws series action done by the students. Those series of action describe the level of difficulties from the materials. The beginning competence, LO 6, stated that students should master how to identify subject and verb of the sentence which was categorized as easiest. Then, it went to the next competence still about understanding the pattern of the sentence as in LO 7, but it was more difficult than the previous one.

3.2 Identification of learning domains

In the case of the results from the instructional analysis, there were some points identified relating to the description of learning outcomes reflecting the three learning domains; cognitive, psychomotor, and affective. The affective domain was neglected in the syllabus. None of the formulated learning outcome refers to affective domain.

Referring to the result of the instructional analysis, the formulation of the sub-learning outcomes seemed unattainable. The action verbs used from one sub-learning outcome to the other showed no indication of the accomplishment of the learning stages. Besides, almost all sub-

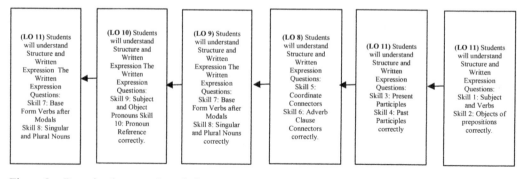

Figure 5. Procedural approach analysis.

Table 1. Analysis of cognitive domain.

Cognitive domain (Anderson & Kathrwohl, 2001)	Action verbs
Creating	-
Evaluating	-
Analyzing	-
Applying	-
Understanding	Understand (LO 1 – LO 14)
Remembering	Identify (LO 1)

learning outcomes used 'understand' as the action verb showing cognitive domain. Table 1 describes the analysis of suitability between learning domain and action verbs used in the syllabus.

In detail, there must be some more action verbs used to achieve the learning outcome. The syllabus stated 'Analyzing' was the learning outcome. Therefore, the sub-learning outcomes should gradually apply learning stages based on the taxonomy. In other words, formulated sub-learning outcomes should also be set in a stage of 'Analyzing' in order to achieve the competence. It can be said that the analysis figured out that there were missing learning taxonomy stages, which were 'Applying and Analyzing'. This was also supported by the data from the questionnaire, as shown in Table 2:

Seventy percent of the participants in this study claimed that their learning experience was at the remembering stage. There were also different responses that the learning activities also varied in cognitive taxonomy, for example; evaluating involved 13% and creating 10% of the participants. It was also still questionable that their learning competence should be at analyzing. Some students experienced analyzing some tasks and creating some work. However, these two types of activities were not the stage of 'evaluating' and 'creating' since the learners' activities focused on the handbook.

4 DISCUSSION

4.1 *Implications for developing integrated learning material*

The results of the instructional analysis and identification of the learning taxonomy became the basis and guidance to develop the material. There were two fundamentals requiring consideration; firstly, in order to build learners' English performance and proficiency, there must be systematic and procedural formulation of learning outcomes related to the learning taxonomy. This was also to create quality of learning which fosters students' involvement. This high involvement is said to have a profound effect on the outcomes of learning [13]. The learning taxonomy represented what students do. Moreover, it is like a 'stair', one needs to be accomplished before going through to the next stage. However, what was missing in the

Table 2. Learners' level of cognitive attainment.

Levels based cognitive taxonomy	Participants (%)
Remembering	70
Understanding	23
Applying	24
Analyzing	15
Evaluating	13
Creating	10

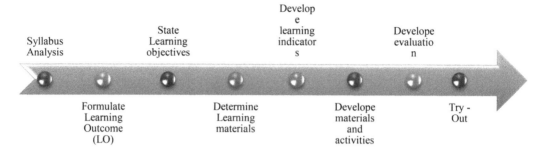

Figure 6. Phases in material design.

previous syllabus, based on the findings, was that there were no indications of the 'applying' and 'analyzing' learning taxonomy, especially the cognitive domain. Figure 6 illustrates the research stages to develop the materials.

The content of the learning material used was Islamic since the students were in an Islamic university. Certain topics would trigger their enthusiasm to learn as they felt engaged and they found no difficulties to understand them. As mentioned, a product-based design using religious aspects increasingly motivated the students and improved their enthusiasm [14]. The Islamic content was chosen based on the result of a questionnaire and expert judgment related to university-based-character building. The intended material development still focused on the students' English language skills.

This material design put more emphasis on utilizing the four language skills. It aimed at challenging students to use their English alive. Applying integrated skills generates learners' English to authentic use of language and attracts them to communicate with others naturally [15]. The developed materials were broken down into some topics and meetings. Every topic led to formulated sub-learning outcomes under the consideration of cognitive, psychomotor, and affective domains. Additionally, the competences represented an integration of language skills. Students were expected to be able to use their language competence to perform their language skills.

As the integrated materials concerned Islamic content, the first step was to formulate the learning competence – what the students were expected master or to be able to do. The formulation of the competence was based on the learning taxonomy.

The intention of the learning outcome was to allow the students to master the basic principles of English usage to be able to perform their language skills to communicate either in oral or written form. To have meaningful and effective learning outcomes, the learning taxonomy; cognitive, psychomotor, and affective domains, should be explicitly presented in order to measure its achievement easily. It can be stated that the next sub-learning outcomes must developed based upon this learning outcome and that the competence should cover the three learning domains. Furthermore, to develop this learning material, ADDIE Analysis, Design,

Table 3. Formulating learning outcomes.

Competences	Competence description	Scope of learning material
Cognitive	Analyze (C4)	Basic principles of English usage; reading comprehension, listening, speaking, writing, sentence structure within Islamic content
Psychomotor	Demonstrate (P3)	Language performance
Affective	Integrate (A4)	Ethics and cultural background

Learning Outcome:
Students will be able to analyze the basic principles of English usage; reading comprehension, listening, speaking, writing, sentence structure within Islamic contents by demonstrating their language performance integrated to the ethics and cultural background

Development, Implementation, Evaluation) design was used. The stages of the design are analysis, design, development, implementation, and evaluation.

4.2 Islamic content as learning material and sources

Learning sources was very essential in this material development. As the learning content of this material concerns Islamic content, there are hundreds of sources available. However, there were some considerations in the selection. These are:

4.2.1 Accessibility

Students prefer using learning sources which are accessible. They find no difficulties to get the source. The purpose is that it enables students to always have reviews. Especially, some available references on the book allow them to search. Taking the benefits of authentic materials motivates them and exposes them to real use of language. There are some resources used including websites, books, and magazines. The scope of the material taken from different resources is based on common Islamic studies given to the students to understand culture, norms, and ethics.

4.2.2 Culture based

The Islamic contents used in this material development were based on the main Islamic studies; five pillars of *Islam*, six pillars of *iman*, and *rosul ulul azmi*; and were based on local Islamic studies; visiting family, Islamic figures, and Eid in Indonesia.

4.2.3 Language proficiency

Not all authentic sources can be taken as learning sources and learning material. There must be some considerable selection. Language proficiency means considering the level of difficulty representing how the language is used in those sources, whether it is understandable for the students, whether the vocabularies are commonly understood, and whether the sentence structures are easily understood or not.

4.2.4 Adaptable

More sources are not usually addressed for learning. They are sometimes reading articles. When the learning sources found are limited, then adaptation techniques are helpful.

5 CONCLUSION

To liven students' language skills, it is needed to design learning material which motivates students to learn through stages and integrated. Instructional analysis was essentially conducted since it aimed at measuring the attainability of the learning outcomes and the support of the sub-learning outcomes. Moreover, instructional analysis used to determine that the learning taxonomy was explicitly stated in the learning outcomes. The development of the learning material of Islamic content tends to ease their language performance and is also useful for their Islamic content understanding. Finally, developing integrated learning material must reflect on the learning taxonomy, including cognitive, psychomotor and affective domains, in order to lead learning activities successfully.

ACKNOWLEDGMENT

Appreciation and gratitude to Direktorat Riset dan Pengabdian Masyarakat, Dirjen Pengusulan Riset dan Pengembangan, Kementerian Riset, Teknologi dan Pendidikan Tinggi, who financed *Penelitian Dosen Pemula* 2018 under the title Pengembangan Bahan Ajar Bahasa Inggris Konsorsium untuk Mahasiswa Non-Bahasa Inggris di Lingkungan Pesantren Berdasarkan Analisis Instruksional.

REFERENCES

[1] Gao, Y. & Barlett, B. (2014). Opportunities and challenges for negotiating appropriate EAP practice in China. In T. Liyagne & T. Walker (Eds.), *English for academic purposes (EAP) in Asia: Negotiating appropriate practices in a global context.* Rotterdam, The Netherlands: Sense Publishers.

[2] Richards, J.C. (2001). *Curriculum development in language teaching.* Cambridge, UK: Cambridge University Press.

[3] Nation, I.S.P., & Macalister, J. (2010). *Language curriculum design.* New York, NY: Routledge.

[4] Amerian, M. & Poramid, S. (2018). Language teachers' beliefs on materials use and their locus of control: Case studies from Iran and Japan. *Indonesian Journal of Applied Linguistics.* 7(3), 583–593.

[5] Farid, A. & Saifuddin, M. (2018). Designing IELTS writing material for learners with low level of English proficiency based on needs analysis. *Journal of Research in Foreign Language Teaching.* 1(1), 49–61.

[6] Junining, E. (2015). Designing a syllabus of collaborative English teaching for physics study program. *Journal of English Education and Linguistic Studies.*, 2 (2), 1–12.

[7] Dick, W. & Carey, L. (1990). *The systematic design of instruction* (3rd ed.). New York, NY: Harper Collins.

[8] McDonough, J., Shaw, C. & Masuhara, H. (2013). *Material and method in ELT: A teacher's guide* (3rd ed.). Oxford, UK: John Wiley & Sons.

[9] Navarro, E.H.A. (2015). The design of teaching materials as a tool in EFL teacher education: Experiences of a Brazilian teacher education program. *Ilha do Desterro.*, 68, 121–137.

[10] Borg, W.R & Gall, M.D. (1983). *Educational research: An introduction.* New York, NY: Longman.

[11] Seels, B.B. & Ritchey, R.C. (1994). *Teknologi pembelajaran: Definisi dan kawasannya* (Trans. D.S. Prawiradilaga). Jakarta, Indonesia: IPTPI LPTK UNJ.

[12] Anderson, L.W. & Krathwohl, D.R. (2001) *A taxonomy for learning, teaching, and assessing: A revision of Bloom's taxonomy of educational objectives* (Abridged ed.). Boston, MA: Allyn & Bacon.

[13] Helme, S. & Clarke, D. (2001). Identifying cognitive engagement in the mathematics classroom. *Mathematics Education Research Journal,.* 13(2), 133–153.

[14] Syafi'i, M.L. & Gestanti, R.A. (2017). Developing English materials for EFL learners at Islamic junior high school. *Journal of English Education and Linguistic Studies.*, 4(2), 199–220.

[15] Oxford, R. (2001). Integrated skills in the ESL/EFL classroom. *ERIC Digest.* Rertrieved from http://www.cal.org/ericcll/digest.

English Linguistics, Literature, and Language Teaching in a Changing Era – Madya et al. (eds)
© 2020 Taylor & Francis Group, London, ISBN 978-1-03-224160-9

An investigation into the English language writing strategies used by Indonesian EFL graduate students

Nanik Rahmawati
Indonesia Endowment Fund for Education, Indonesia
English Education Department, Sebelas Maret University, Surakarta, Jawa Tengah, Indonesia

Endang Fauziati & Sri Marmanto
English Education Department, Sebelas Maret University, Surakarta, Jawa Tengah, Indonesia

ABSTRACT: This study is aimed at investigating the English language writing strategies used by Indonesian EFL graduate students at an academic writing class. The concern was to determine the types of writing strategies which are employed by the learners and to identify the factors contributing to the use of the writing strategies employed. The students were taught the strategic knowledge of how to write texts in a foreign language. The study applied a qualitative method approach. Since this is a case study structured interviews, observations and documentation are employed in collecting data. The implications of the study could include improvements in learning and teaching of academic writing and the design of new teaching syllabi that concern the strategic teaching of English writing in the future.

Keywords: writing strategies, foreign language learner, qualitative, case study

1 INTRODUCTION

English has become one of subjects examined in national exams in Indonesian schools. Moreover, it is included in the national examination from junior until senior high school level. This means that every student should master this language. Thus, English learners should master every language skill such as writing.

In addition, mastering English writing skill is not an easy task. Many students still find difficulties in producing words in their writing. Thus, writing strategies play an important role to increase learner's writing ability. Every learner has preferred writing strategies before, during and after writing. And there must be a reason why they use writing strategies employed. Those become the concern of the writer.

Furthermore, this study focuses on writing strategies based on the three writing stages proposed by Petric and Czarl (2003, p. 210–211). These stages are before, during and after writing. Before writing includes time planning, mental planning, no plan, experts' model reference and outlining. During writing includes introduction first, sentence verification, pharagraph verification, outline revision, language transfer, sentence simplification, positive grammar and vocabulary, synonym, dictionary, and peer cooperation. Finally, after writing includes introduction first, sentence verification, paragraph verification, outline revision, language transfer, sentence simplification, positive grammar and vocabulary, synonym, dictionary, and peer cooperation.

The findings of current study will be analyzed in the light of this theory in order to gain an insight into the Indonesian graduate students who take academic writing class for their postgraduate preparation context.

Oxford (1990, p.201), states that:

'Learners need to learn how to learn, and teachers need to learn how to facilitate the process. Although learning is certainly part of the human condition, conscious skill in self-directed learning and in strategy use must be sharpened through training.'

In conclusion, both collaborative and independent learning in the language classroom are important aspects of the language teaching pedagogy. Consequently, this research has the following aims: to determine the types of writing strategies employed by the learners and to discover what factors contributing to the learners' English writing strategies.

Little researches on English writing strategies of Indonesian English-asa-Foreign-Language (EFL) graduate students has been conducted. Thus, the authors initiated research in this area especially on Indonesian graduate students who take academic writing classes for their postgraduate school preparation.

In defining the term 'writing', there are various ideas proposed. According to Rivers (1981, p. 294), writing is conveying information or expression of original ideas in a consecutive way in the new language. Furthermore, in scoring students' writing, the authors apply Brown's scoring rubric. Brown in 2001 (p. 357) states that content, organization, discourse, syntax, vocabulary, and mechanics are the required categories to evaluate writing. Writing strategy is defined as the sequence in which a writer engages in planning, composing, revising and other writing related activities (Penuelaz, 2012, p. 83). In their opinion, writing strategies are a sequence of activities instead of a single one.

2   METHOD RESEARCH

2.1   *Research setting*

This research was conducted at the Universitas Gadjah Mada Language Training Center. The subjects of this researchs were six students of an academic writing class at the Universitas Gadjah Mada Language Training Center. All were in a group of graduate students who intended to pursue their studies at at higher level like postgraduate degree and were taking this short course as part of their academic preparation. The six students belonged to a class called the Test-of-English-as-a-Foreign-Language (TOEFL) preparation and academic writing class, in which case the writer only focuses on their academic writing activity.

This research is categorized as a qualitative research. Qualitative research is a research which focuses on understanding social phenomena from the perspective of the human participants in natural settings and it does not begin with formal hypotheses, but it may result in hypotheses as the study unfolds (Ary et al., 2010, p. 22). The type of this research is a case study research.

2.2   *Data collection*

In collecting the data, the authors conducted observations, interviews and a test. The interview used in this research was developed based on Petric and Czarl's (2003) writing strategies inventories.

To gather data of the students' writing mastery, the researchers used a test. According to Brown (2004, p. 3), a test is a method of measuring a person's ability, knowledge, or performance in a given area (domain). A test can be defined as a systematic procedure for observing one's behavior and describing it with the aid of numerical devices or a category system (Syakur, 1999, p. 5).

2.3   *Trustworthiness*

All studies need valid data to prove the credibility of the data so the data collected needs trustworthiness. Creswell (2012, p. 259) defines triangulation as the process of corroborating evidence from different individuals (e.g. a principal and a student), types of data (e.g.

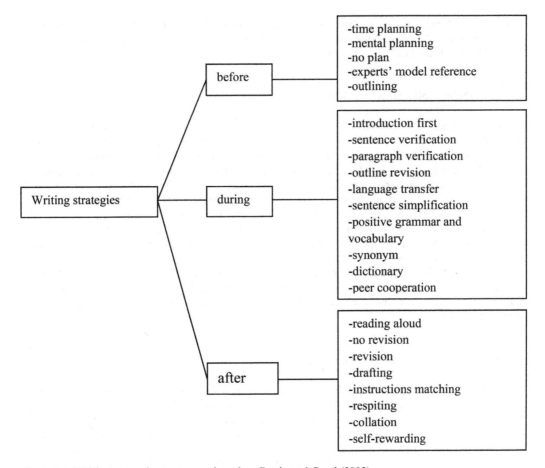

Figure 1. Writing strategies taxonomy based on Petric and Czarl (2003)

questionnaire and interviews) or methods of data collection (e.g. documents and interviews) in descriptions and themes in qualitative research. Triangulation often includes: (1) direct observation by the researcher within the environments of the case (2) probing by asking case participants for explanations and interpretations of 'operational data' and (3) analyses of written documents and natural sites occurring in case environments (Woodside, 2010, p. 6). In this research, the researchers used observational field notes and interviews as the triangulation method to maintain the validity of the collected data.

2.4 *Data analysis technique*

In analyzing the data, the researchers used the flow model proposed by Miles and Huberman (1994). Miles and Huberman (1994, p. 10) demonstrated that there are three stages that should be undertaken in using the flow model, those are data reduction, data display and conclusion drawing/verification. Those three stages should be done in order.

Data reduction refers to the process of selecting, focusing, simplifying, abstracting, and transforming the data that appear in written up field notes or transcriptions (Miles & Huberman, 1994, p. 10) . A display is defined as an organized, compressed assembly of information that permits conclusion drawing and action (Miles & Huberman, 1994, p. 11).

The third stream of the analysis activity is conclusion drawing or verification. From the very beginning of the data collection, the qualitative analyst is beginning with what the things mean (Miles & Huberman, 1994, p. 11).

3 FINDINGS AND DISCUSSION

The research finding involve two parts, which are: (1) types of writing strategies employed by the subjects; and (2) the reason why they employ such writing strategies. In this research the writing strategies are categorized into three major types. These are before writing, during writing, and after writing categories. Afterwards, each type consists of several more specific activities. Before the start of writing there are some activities that are identified as being employed by the respondents. Those activities are time planning, experts' model preference, and outlining strategy.

During writing, there are some activities that are identified as being employed by the respondents, these are introduction first, sentence verification, paragraph verification, outline revision, language transfer, positive grammar and vocabulary, sentence simplification, synonym, dictionary and peer cooperation activity.

After writing, the strategy deals with the activities employed by the students after the writing activity. In this part, there are some activities that are identified as being carried out by the respondents, these are reading aloud, revision, drafting, instruction matching and self-rewarding activity.

4 CONCLUSION AND SUGGESTION

In regard to the findings of the two research objectives, there are two conclusions arising which can be drawn from the preliminary studies. First, there are major strategies employed by the subjects. Before writing, they carried out time planning, experts' model reference, and outlining activities. Moreover, in the middle of the writing activity, they carried out introduction first, sentence and paragraph verification, outline revision, language transfer, positive grammar and vocabulary, sentence simplification, synonym, dictionary, and peer cooperation activities. Then, after writing, they carried out reading aloud, revision, drafting, instruction matching and self-rewarding activities.

Secondly, the factors identified as contributing to the use of writing strategies can be students' beliefs, students' awareness, students' language proficiency, writing time, writing type, and writing activity environment.

The implications of the study could be improvements in learning and teaching of academic writing and the design of new teaching syllabi concerning the strategic teaching of English writing in the future.

As noted, this research involved a relatively few number of subjects and small area of research coverage. In addition, this research deals with writing mastery as a research variable, yet there are still many other potential variables in existence. Additionally, this research did not utilize a questionnaire to identify the types of writing strategy and factors behind their use. So the suggestion for future researchers is to conduct a research related to writing strategy in a wider or different area of research coverage.

REFERENCES

[1] Abdul-Rahman, S. (2011). *An investigation into the English academic writing strategies employed by students of HE in the NE of England with particular reference to their nationalities and gender.* (Doctoral thesis, University of Sunderland, UK)

[2] Berg, B.L. & Lune, H. (2014). *Qualitative research methods for the social sciences.* 8th ed. Harlow, UK: Pearson Education.

[3] Bryman, A. (2012). *Social research method* (4th ed.) New York, SNY: Oxford University Press.

[4] Cohen, A.D., 1998. *Strategies in Learning and Using a Second Language*. New York: Addison Wesley Longman Limited.

[5] Fowler, Jr., F.A. (2009). *Survey research methods* (4th ed., ch 6). Los Angeles, CA: SAGE Publications.

[6] Griffiths, C. (2008). *Lessons from good language learners*. Cambridge, UK: Cambridge University Press.

[7] Hyland, K. (2003). *Second language writing*. Cambridge, UK: Cambridge University Press.

[8] Kasper, L.F. (1997). 'Assessing the metacognitive awareness of ESL student writers'. *Teaching English as a Second or Foreign Language*, 3(1). Retrieved from www.tesl-ej.org/wordpress/issues/volume3/ej09/ej09a1/

[9] Miles, M.B. & Huberman, A.M. (1994). Qualitative data analysis. California: Sage publications inc.

[10] Oxford, R.L. (1997). Cooperative learning, collaborative learning, and interaction: Three communicative strands in the language classroom. *The Modern Language Journal*, 81(4), 443–456.

[11] Oxford, R.L. (2011). Teaching and researching language learning strategies. Harlow, UK: Longman.

[12] Penuelaz, A.B.C. (2012). The writing strategies of american university students: focusing on memory, compensation, social and affective strategies. Estudios de lingüística inglesa aplicada. 77–113.

[13] Petric, B., & Czarl, B. (2003). Validating a writing strategy questionnaire. System, 31, 187–215.

[14] Rivers, Wilga M. (1981). Teaching foreign language skill. USA: The University of Chicago.

[15] Syakur. (1999). Language Testing and Evaluation. Surakarta: Departmen Pendidikan dan Kebudayaan Republik Indonesia, Universitas Sebelas Maret.

[16] Wolfersberger, M. (2003). 'L1 to l2 writing process and strategy transfer: a look at lower proficiency writers'. *Teaching English as a Second or Foreign Language*, [e-journal] 7 (2). Retrieved from http://tesl-ej.org/ej26/a6.html

[17] Woodside, A.G. (2010). Case study research: theory, methods, practice. Boston college: Emerald Group Publishing Limited.

English Linguistics, Literature, and Language Teaching in a Changing Era – Madya et al. (eds)
© 2020 Taylor & Francis Group, London, ISBN 978-1-03-224160-9

Let's speak: Encouraging students to speak up in the classroom through project-based learning

Nur I. Muslim, Yulia N. Hidayah, Iffah Mayasari & Ashadi
English Education Study Program, Graduate School, Yogyakarta State University, Yogyakarta, Indonesia

ABSTRACT: This study was to investigate the implementation of project-based learning to improve the speaking skills of 23 grade-seven students in learning descriptive texts. These participants studied in a public junior high school in regency in the southeast part of a Special Region in Indonesia. This research applied a classroom action research that implemented a wall magazine as the project in the first cycle, while the second cycle was a lapbook, a simple file folder that contains a variety of pictures, and other materials that covers detailed information about a certain topic. In addition, speaking rubrics, interview guidelines, and questionnaire items were used to collect the data. The results of the study indicate that this type of project-based learning can improve students' speaking skills especially in learning descriptive text as well as their creativity and collaborative learning.

Keywords: Project-based learning, speaking skill

1 INTRODUCTION

Speaking is an important skill in language learning that needs to be taught. Speaking may involve presenting reports or presenting a viewpoint on a particular topic as part of a work or academic study [1]. Speaking allows students to express their ideas, receive information, and respond to an interlocutor. Furthermore, based on the 2013 curriculum, one of the objectives in English language teaching is that students are able to communicate in written and spoken forms. Therefore, it is highly required that students master speaking skills in order to communicate and to achieve the goal of learning English at school.

However, based on the observation in a public junior high school located in the southeast part of the province of Yogyakarta Special Region, Indonesia, it was found that students have several problems in speaking related to pronunciation, fluency, grammar, vocabulary, knowledge, and anxiety. Thus, to improve students' speaking skills, researchers considered using project-based learning as an appropriate strategy. Project-based learning has the potential to create powerful and memorable learning experiences for students [2]. In project-based learning, it is possible to create meaningful learning because students are more engaged in their learning process. Project-based learning allows students to learn by doing in applying their ideas [3]. It also develops and improves students' creativity and taking responsibility for working individually, in pairs, or in groups. Pair-work requires rather little organization on the part of the teacher and, at least in principle, can be activated in most classrooms by simply having students work in pairs, but group-work will probably require greater role differentiation between individuals as well as a certain amount of physical reorganization of the classroom [4]. Moreover, when students work collaboratively in a group, it will create an independent team because every member has to finish their part to complete a successful final product [5].

In implementing a project, there are five key features as guidance [3] such as driving questions, situated inquiry, collaborations, using technology as tools to support learning, and the creation of artifacts which also includes feedback. Those features will help teachers in implementing project-based learning to support the teaching and learning process. Moreover, teachers can also use four steps as practical guidance for sequencing project activities in the classroom such as speculation, designing the project's activities, conducting the project, and evaluation [6]. Thus, classroom activities are designed to make students actively engage in learning activities and make them free to share their ideas and opinions. Additionally, by implementing this learning approach, teacher can make the learning activity enjoyable and improve students' micro and macro skills of English of which one is speaking skills.

Some researchers proved that project-based learning can improve speaking skills and students' productive skills in an EFL context [7][8]. Project-based learning is suitable for students' autonomous learning consciousness and effectively improves students' listening comprehension and speaking ability [7]. Besides, project-based learning also encourages students' participation in the learning process, which makes them engage and learn more [8]. Therefore, through project-based learning, teachers can design meaningful activities which help students improve their language skills.

Considering the successful implementation of project-based learning and the problems faced by students in the classroom, this present study aims to seek the answers to the following questions, 'How does the implementation of project-based learning improve the speaking skills of grade-seven students of a junior high school?'

2 METHOD

2.1 Methodology, participants, and research setting

This research used classroom action research design adopted from Burns model [9], which involved a substantive act with a research procedure to find the improvement. The research was conducted in grade seven in a public junior high school in a regency in the southeast part of the province of Yogyakarta Special Region, Indonesia. The participants of the study were 23 students. They were first grade studying in their second semester. They attended the class twice a week and each session lasted 80 minutes.

2.2 Research instruments

To achieve the research objectives, quantitative and qualitative data were utilized. For quantitative data, a speaking test was used to gather data in order to find out if the students improved their speaking skills. This study implemented a speaking rubric adapted from a speaking assessment proposed by Brown (2004) and included five aspects; grammar, fluency, pronunciation, vocabulary, and their creativity during the project [10]. Those aspects covered the micro skill of speaking. The score was analyzed using a t-test. On the other hand, for qualitative data, questionnaire items and interview guidelines were applied to gather data about students' perceptions during the implementation of the project-based learning. The questionnaire consisted of four multiple-choice items based on the students' views about the project, their participation during the project, their belief of improvement from the project, and their confidence in presenting the project through an oral presentation.

Moreover, there were two items which asked about the strengths and weaknesses of the project implementation. In addition, the interview protocol comprised semi-structured questions to confirm the data from the questionnaire and elicit students' perceptions of the project. There were three general questions included in the interview protocol intended to address the research objectives.

2.3 Research procedures

This study was carried out in the third and fourth months of the second semester in the academic year 2017/2018. Since it was a classroom action research, in order to achieve research objective, researchers did two cycles. Both the first and second cycles were conducted in three meetings.

In the first cycle, the teacher used a wall magazine as the project and the topic was about describing animals. The project was done in groups consisting of four or five students with different speaking proficiencies. Before starting the project, the students were given some inputs related to how to produce descriptive texts in written forms which would help them when speaking. The teacher implemented drilling and repetition in order to encourage the students' speaking skills. Because of the time limitation, the zoo wall magazine project was assigned as homework. Therefore, in the last meeting of cycle 1, the students gave oral presentations about their wall magazines in order to allow the teacher to assess their speaking performance.

In the second cycle, the teacher proposed a lapbook as a project to improve students' speaking skills in descriptive texts. The topic was about things around the house. The students completed the project in groups, and the members were similar to the previous project. In addition, the students were given inputs related to the theme and the topic which helped them in producing spoken texts. Furthermore, the teacher also gave some worksheets as inputs and exercises before presenting the project. The teacher also taught the students how to present their work in front of the classroom. Moreover, the project was done in the classroom in the second meeting. In the first meeting, the students were given stimulation and schemata about the topic and project, then, in the third meeting, the students presented their lapbook projects, and the teacher assisted their speaking and creativity through their oral presentation.

3 FINDINGS AND DISCUSSION

3.1 *Preliminary study*

Before this study, the teacher had implemented project-based learning that integrated with Information and Communication Technology (ICT) based learning. ICT was applied to support students in conducting the project because they were interested in making videos as a medium for practicing their speaking. However, the teacher found that the students still faced some difficulties in pronouncing words, creating phrases and sentences, producing vocabulary and fluent speech, and were anxious about talking in front of the camera and their friends. Furthermore, the students also had difficulties in using the technology to record and edit their videos. Therefore, the teacher decided to implement project-based learning, but not using the technology, thus the students were only focused on their speaking skills and the content that they presented. In addition, project-based learning is applicable to different types of learners and learning situations and requires the active engagement of students and their efforts over an extended period of time [11]. Project-based learning also contributes positive learning outcomes, and helps students improve their cognition, work ethic, and interpersonal skills in the EFL classroom [12]. In relation to teaching speaking, the use of project-based learning enables students to have a positive learning attitude while learning speaking skills in the classroom.

3.2 *Cycle 1*

In this cycle, the teacher implemented a wall magazine as a project for teaching how to describe animals. In the first meeting, the teacher divided the students into groups consisting of four or five students and explained that they had to make a wall magazine and present it in front of the classroom to practice their speaking skills at the end of the topic. Then, the teacher showed music videos about animals in the zoo. Through the video, students got input about how pronounce and describe the animals. The teacher asked the students to mention the animals seen in the video and gave them worksheets that asked them to name and identify the characteristics of the animals. Furthermore, in the second meeting, teacher asked the students to describe some animals in a few short sentences. In this activity, the students prepared content for their wall magazines. They were free to ask the teacher about the content and the teacher gave them feedback. Then, in the third meeting, students presented their project in groups.

As result, the students' speaking score decreased compared with the one in the preliminary study. In the preliminary study, the students' speaking score was an average of 69.34; meanwhile, the students' speaking score of their wall magazine presentations in Cycle 1 was an average of 62.82. However, based on the interview results, the students conveyed that they liked to engage in learning activities such as making a wall magazine as a project in the classroom. In line with the questionnaire result, 95% of the students liked to learn through the wall magazine project, and 81% of them could participate in the learning process through these projects. Moreover, 71% of the students believed that through project-based learning, they could improve their participation during the learning process, while the rest were not sure. In addition, 67% of the students were confident in presenting their project, although the rest did not really feel confident presenting in front of the class.

Based on the observations while students presenting their projects, most of them were shy and felt uncomfortable standing and speaking in front of their classmates which indicated as anxiety. Students' anxiety in communication in English can be enervating and can affect students' adaptation to the target environment and the achievement of their educational goals [13]. Additionally, anxiety reactions can be classified as reflecting worry such as self-deprecating and task-irrelevant thoughts, or emotionality such as blushing or a racing heart, stammering and fidgeting [13].

Moreover, based on reflection stage result, the students' anxiety arises because the teacher was focused on giving input and asked them to prepare their draft instead of improve their linguistic knowledge related to speaking. In order to be able to speak, students need to emphasize points such as speech production, conceptualization (in terms of its discourse type, topic, and purpose) and formulation of the idea, articulation, self-monitoring and repair, automaticity, fluency, and managing talk (interaction, turn-taking, and paralinguistic) [14]. On the other hand, because students were asked to speak in front of the classroom in the form of an oral presentation, providing examples or model speeches was suggested [15]. However, we did not give enough examples as input and models for the students to present their projects in front of the classroom. Those components influenced students' performance which needed to be improved in the next cycle.

3.3 Cycle 2

In this cycle, the teacher implemented the lapbook as the project in order to help students improve their speaking performance. A lapbook project is applicable for implementing in teaching English to young learners since it is very interactive. Teaching English can be practiced using a lapbook as it initiates students to learn by doing. In line with that, a characteristic of our students is that they like to create something and actively move around [16]. So, students could grasp the teaching process easier through the lapbook project and the teaching process would be student-centered.

In the first meeting, the teacher gave input using song and shared the lyrics with the students, thus they had the chance to practice pronunciation through the song lyrics. The teacher also asked the students randomly to pronounce some words, phrases, sentences, and sing the song. Through this activity, teacher could learn the students' problem and what they lacked. After that, the teacher divided the students into groups but the members of the groups were different to the previous cycle. Then, the teacher explained the topic and the learning objective that the students were to make and present a lapbook as a project with the topic of describing things around the house. The teacher showed them an example of a lapbook. The teacher also gave an example of text about things around the house, and asked the students to read together with the teacher. After that, the teacher asked the students randomly to read sentences from the text and gave feedback. In the second meeting, the teacher gave the students a worksheet with guidelines for making their descriptive text and a model of a lapbook. After that, the teacher asked each group to read their passage. Moreover, the teacher also gave a model of how to present a lapbook in the front of class and asked the students to practice

217

presenting their project. The project was done as homework. Then, in the last meeting, the students presented their project and the teacher gave them feedback.

As the result, the students' speaking score was increased to an average of 87.82. This average score indicated that their speaking ability was above the government standard which is 75.00. In line with the speaking score, based on interviews, the students enjoyed the project and presenting in front of their friends, because they had practiced before the presentation and could show their work to their classmates. Moreover, based on the questionnaire result, 81% of the students liked to learn and participate in the lapbook making project. In addition, only 61% believed that this project could improve their speaking ability, and 65% of them were confident about presenting their project but this was because this project was new to them compared with the previous one.

Furthermore, based on the result, project-based learning improved the students' speaking skills as well as their confidence in speaking in front of the class because, through the project, students had opportunities to develop their confidence as well as their self-esteem and positive attitudes about the learning process [17]. Additionally, based on observations, the students were eager to learn through pictures, as the process of creating the wall magazine as well as the lapbook project contained many pictures which provide in lapbook as teaching media for visual thinking [16]. Through this project, the students were helped to think through pictures since the lapbook project was rich with printed pictures and encouraged students' creativity.

4 CONCLUSIONS AND SUGGESTIONS

Teachers can implement project-based learning to improve students' speaking skills in the EFL classroom. This strategy is applicable to high school students with different types of learners in various learning situations that can activate student engagement. However, this study focused only on two projects proposed by the teacher and researchers that were applied in a classroom in order to improve the speaking skills of the students. In the first project, the teacher was focused on giving input without providing adequate knowledge on presenting the project, so that in the second project, the teacher gave more activities to make students practice their speaking skills. Thus, further research is needed to investigate the implementation of project-based learning to integrate more language skills for different levels of students.

REFERENCES

[1] Nation, I.S.P. & Newton, J. (2009). *Teaching ESl/EFL listening and speaking.* New York, NY: Routledge.

[2] Krauss, J. & Boss, S. (2013). *Thinking through project-based learning: guiding deep inquiry.* Thousand Oaks, CA: Corwin Publishers.

[3] Krajcik, J.S. & Blumenfeld, P.C. (2006). Project-based learning. In Sawyer, R.K. (Ed.), *The Cambridge handbook of the learning sciences* (pp. 317–333). New York, NY: Cambridge University Press.

[4] McDonough, J., Shaw, C. & Masuhara, H. (2013). *Materials and methods in ELT: A teacher's guide* (3rd ed.). Oxford, UK: Wiley-Blackwell.

[5] Bell, S. (2010). Project-based learning for the 21st century: Skills for the future. *The Clearing House, 83,* 39–43.

[6] Kriwas, S. (1999). *Environmental education: A handbook for educators.* Athens, Greece: Ministry of Education.

[7] Yiying, Z. (2015). Project-based learning in Chinese college English listening and speaking course: From theory to practice. *Canadian Social Science, 2*(9), 40–44.

[8] Lasauskiene, J. & Rauduvaite, A. (2015). Project-based learning at university: Teaching experiences of lecturers. *Procedia - Social and Behavioral Sciences, 197,* 788–792.

[9] Burns, A. (2010). *Doing action research in English language teaching.* New York, NY: Routledge.

[10] Brown, H.D. (2004). *Language assessment: Principles and classroom practices.* New York, NY: Pearson Education.

[11] Blumenfeld, P.C., Soloway, E., Marx, R.W., Krajcik, J.S., Guzdial, M. & Palincsar, A. (1991). Motivating project-based learning: Sustaining the doing, supporting the learning. *Educational Psychologist, 26*(3), 369–398.

[12] Kettanun, C. (2015). Project-based learning and its validity in a Thai EFL classroom. *Procedia – Social and Behavioral Sciences, 192*, 567–573.

[13] Woodrow, L. (2006). Anxiety and speaking English as a second language. *RELC, 37*(3), 308–328.

[14] Thornbury, S. (2005). *How to teach speaking*. Harlow, UK: Pearson Education.

[15] Richards, J.C. (2008). *Teaching listening and speaking: From theory to practice*. New York, NY: Cambridge University Press.

[16] Mastellotto, L. (2016). *Using lapbook in teaching English to young learners*. TESOL Val d'Adige – TEYL Symposium. Bolzano, Italy: University of Bolzano.

[17] Fragoulis, I. (2009). Project-based learning in the teaching of English as a foreign language in Greek primary schools: From theory to practice. *EnglishLanguage Teaching, 2*(3), 113–119.

English Linguistics, Literature, and Language Teaching in a Changing Era – Madya et al. (eds)
© 2020 Taylor & Francis Group, London, ISBN 978-1-03-224160-9

Investigating self-correction strategies for oral grammatical errors and their merit in language acquisition among EFL learners

Nurul Marlisa & Ashadi
English Education, Yogyakarta State University, Indonesia

ABSTRACT: Self-correction strategies for grammatical errors in language production are one of the pivotal issues that receive ample attention during the past decades within the discussion of second language acquisition. Although abundant research has been carried out to discover the empirical support of self-correction strategies performed to grammatical errors, ones with concern on oral grammatical errors have yet to be fully substantiated. In order to move this line of research further, this survey study was addressed to fill the gap by identifying the variations of frequent self-correction strategies to treat the grammatical errors frequently made by adult learners of English. The data were collected by means of questionnaire towards 20 participants who have been learning English for more than 10 years. This present study found four self-correction strategies namely avoidance, output modification/recast, form negotiation, and speaking pauses that are commonly employed by the respondents to treat their frequent errors such as word choice, verb tense error, and sentence structure errors. The mentioned self-correction strategies are somehow overly seen as negative transfers (crosslinguistic influence) in second language acquisition, yet this research showed that they possibly turn out to be positive opportunities for helping language learners develop and strengthen their self-correction sense. This contrast and other evidences found suggest that there is a need of further studies to be undertaken as abundant room of gap on this issue is widely open for further progress.

Keywords: oral grammatical errors, self-correction strategy

1 INTRODUCTION

Grammaticalization is an essential process in language acquisition whereby language learners build their grammatical proficiency in terms of morphological and syntactical constrains [1]. The continual process along with the increase of grammar registry allows language learners to gradually produce language, as a means to communicate, in more complex and structured way. Well-structured language production undeniably enhances its comprehensibility in transferring the intended message in communication processes [2]. Consequently, for becoming competent language users, language learners are expected to possess sufficient grammatical knowledge to accurately construct utterances and add meaning to them. In other words, they need to know the grammatical system of the language so that they can communicate with others properly.

However, it is indisputable that speakers of other languages will get through trial and error in the areas of grammar since performing other languages accurately is somehow considerably difficult for non-native speakers [3]. In other words, language production often evolves a process of hypothesis and trial whereby error occurrences are inevitable [4]. The errors may occur on the level of words, phrases, as well as sentences. More specifically, language learners are assumed to mostly commit errors in terms of part of speech, temporal expressions, determiners, pluralized nouns, as well as word orders within phrases or sentences [2,5].

The above-mentioned errors apparently emerge as the result of crosslinguistic influences [2]. The rationale underlining this notion is that the first language (L1) may influence the second language (L2) acquisition and so forth. Languages can share similarities and even big differences assumed to contribute in language learners' confusion while learning and using L2. The existing knowledge of L1 may influence L2 development by delaying the progress in which language learners naturally manage the information they are about to utter. It reflects that crosslinguistic influences can be concluded as negative transfers from L1 to L2 [2]. The negative transfers can be manifested in errors such as omission, avoidance, underuse, and overuse [2]. The transfers, somehow, hinder language learners to use language competently.

In contrast, the occurrence of grammatical errors is not always seen as a negative transfer [6]. Errors are assumed to play a vital role during the language learning process to widen the learners' knowledge scope and become a learning opportunity, which may help them reach automaticity in language production [7]. It is thought to be a good evidence of the learners obtaining new construction rules of the language.

However, continuous errors can gradually result in error fossilization, a process in which incorrect linguistic features become a permanent part of the way a person speaks or writes a language, when they are not treated correctly [8]. The errors made may be stored into long term memory after done incessantly. Consequently, the outcome of this gradual process is automaticity that leads language learners to automatically keep producing language with grammatical errors [2]. Therefore, once language learners have a fossilized form, it is difficult to remedy it with further instruction.

Having said that, monitoring errors is an important attempt to carry out for avoiding language learners from fossilization. Error correction is considered pivotal for language learners to help them improve their accuracy. A study by Nan, Surasin, and Brudhiprabha [9] found out that the mostly used error correction is corrective feedback from others, for instance, teachers and friends. However, for language learners especially adult learners, corrective feedback is not effective for use [10]. It is because they usually prefer self-correcting their own errors than being corrected by someone else [10,11]. For adults who are no longer learning English in formal institutions may find it difficult to frequently ask for corrective feedback from capable teachers or friends. They are considered to have high self-esteem that makes them difficult to receive correction or feedback from others [12]. Meanwhile, they may work best on their errors if they are aware of and accustomed to self-correction. The most commonly practiced self-correction strategies are devices for delaying the production of the next lexical item [13]. The delay provides speakers time to search more appropriate words or tense for repairing their previous utterances or do other actions to carry out the conversation [14]. Accordingly, a study conducted by Rieger [15] found out that adult learners of English in German often employ repetition as a self-correction strategy whose function is to gain linguistic and/or cognitive planning time for the speaker in producing accurate language. Furthermore, if error correction is intended to be meaningful, a combination of different types of error correction strategy should be employed so that they can build awareness, confidence, and responsibility for their own learning.

Self-correction strategy for errors can be applied in both written and oral language production. Accordingly, some researches [16,17,18] have been conducted to discuss the strategies to self-correct the written language production, yet only small amounts concern with the strategy for self-correcting oral grammatical errors [2]. Having mentioned the fact, the use of self-correction strategies for adult learners in terms of oral grammatical errors is worth to be elaborated more since the ways by which adults self-correct their errors may be different from one another. This leads to the variation of self-correction strategies among individual. An interesting new question to fill the gap is therefore to reveal the variety of self-correction strategies used by adult learners of English to treat their frequently made errors and the possible significances of the strategies towards learner's language acquisition. This present study is expected to add to the growing of studies on self-correction strategies for oral grammatical errors. The results of this study are also expected to be beneficial for independent adult learners of English to train themselves to self-correct their oral grammatical errors and improve their grammatical accuracy specifically in speaking.

2 RESEARCH METHOD

2.1 Research design

This present study is classified as a group-administered survey intended to gain information on the issues of oral grammatical errors frequently made by the non-native adult speakers of English; further actions they do to deal with them; and types of self-correction strategy used by them. This study was done through these following steps adapted from Denscombe [19].

2.2 Research setting

This present study was conducted in Yogyakarta on 2nd until 7th of January 2018. The participants of this research were chosen through cluster sampling with a set of demographic variables including age and length of English learning experience. Twenty participants, with age ranging from 23 to 27 years old classified as adults, were taking part in this study. They were non-native adult speakers of English who basically speak the same first language which is Indonesian yet different mother tongue as they come from different regions in Indonesia. They have been learning English for more than 10 years. All of them are currently studying English education in a university in Yogyakarta. As English learners who have been practicing English for years, they are assumed to be more aware of their frequent errors and strategies they usually employ to encounter the errors.

2.3 Data collection technique and instruments

This study used survey as the main data collection technique. For the survey, a questionnaire was used to gain quantitative and qualitative data. The questionnaires contained 5 questions in the form of both close and open-ended questions. The first part of the questionnaire is the identification form on which the respondents were required to write their name, age, and time length of learning English. Three of its questions are close-ended ones intended to gather respondents' data on (1) their frequency of making oral errors – whether it is always, often, sometimes, rarely, or never, (2) their reaction towards oral grammatical errors – whether they ignore the errors or immediately correct them, and (3) their frequent oral errors (taken from the list proposed by Norrish in 1983 [2]). Furthermore, the last two questions are open-ended

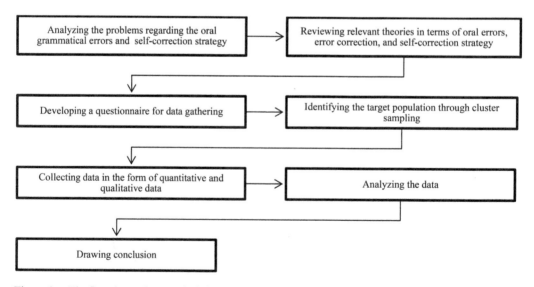

Figure 1. The flowchart of research design.

ones for which the respondents should answer what self-correction strategies are frequently used by them and how effective those strategies are.

2.4 *Data analysis*

The data analysis of this study was descriptive statistics intended for examining the quantitative data in terms of their frequency of occurrences. Descriptive statistics, considered as the heart of quantitative data analysis, were chosen since they offer an effective way to provide a brief summary of quantitative data such as the number of types of errors and self-correction strategies. As this analysis is only limited to present summations, qualitative data analysis was employed to provide comprehensive analysis that can support the statistical findings. Within the qualitative analysis, the qualitative data were being mapped based on the similarities, scrutinized by contrasting and comparing them, and interpreted to draw conclusions.

3 FINDINGS AND DISCUSSION

The data in the field yielded that most of the respondents, about 55% of them, reported to often make grammatical errors while speaking although they have been learning English for a quite long time. Only 10% of them admitted that they always make that kind of errors. Meanwhile, the rest of them, about 35%, said they do not frequently make such errors. The findings indicate that all of the respondents, regardless their length of English learning experience, are unable to perfectly perform grammatical accuracy while speaking. It confirms the belief that performing L2 competently for most L2 learners is difficult and probably taking a long-time process. It also affirms that grammatical errors are inevitable in the process of L2 learning [3,4].

However, they did some efforts to correct the errors they made. Eighteen of them stated that they immediately corrected the errors they made and only two of them who chose to ignore the errors. This fact shows that the participants, somewhat, possess awareness in language production. The awareness encourages them to control and monitor their own speech production as well as make their errors as sources of learning [7]. It is a good sign that the participants have a high opportunity to successfully self-correct oral errors they make.

Meanwhile, regarding the oral grammatical errors frequently made by the participants, the results of the questionnaire are shown in the following table.

According to Table 1, it is found out that most of the participants encountered six types of oral errors. The types of errors are similar with some of those proposed by Ortega [2] and Norrish [5]. They mention that the frequent errors usually committed by language learners are incorrect part of speech (word choice), temporal expressions (verb tense), determiners (omission of article), pluralized nouns (verb form), as well as word order (sentence structure). Among the errors, only three types of errors are mostly committed by the participants and they occur on words and sentences level.

Table 1.   Types of oral grammatical errors.

Types of errors found in the field	Frequency
1. Subject and verb agreement	4 (20%)
2. Verb tense	13 (65%)
3. Verb form	8 (40%)
4. Sentence structure	14 (70%)
5. Word choice	11 (55%)
6. Omission of articles	5 (25%)

Furthermore, in terms of self-correction strategy, the data in the field revealed five common self-correction strategies employed by the participants. First, two of the participants mentioned that they simply waited for other speakers to correct their errors since, in some occasions, they were not aware of their errors or preferred to leave their errors when no one corrected them. It implies that among the participants, only small numbers of them rarely perform self-correction strategy yet they depend on other to appoint their errors. The fact confirms that adults mostly prefer self-correcting their own errors [11].

Second, twelve of the participants tended to negotiate for grammar forms when they encountered grammatical errors. They often mentioned the same words in many forms while recalling which word form should be used in the statement they want to utter. They said that they mostly do the form negotiation when they dealt with verb tense and word choice. The action of negotiating form occurs as it is supported by learners' initiation [2]. It reflects that learners' autonomy plays role in promoting their willingness to correct their own errors [7].

Third, twelve of them often avoided certain grammar forms when they were not so sure how to use them. They preferred to use another grammar form by replacing or simplifying the grammar form. This action represents the phenomena of avoidance in second language acquisition. As mentioned previously, avoidance is one of the types of negative transfer in learning L2 [2]. It is believed to contribute in learners' low L2 proficiency, yet in the field, it considered helpful for the participants to produce more appropriate language that is grammatically correct [6].

Fourth, fourteen of them often modified the grammar within utterances they said wrongly. They modified the utterances by reformulating the previous utterances into new ones they perceived as correct. This action refers to the concept of recast where speakers tend to change the whole wrong utterances into other correct utterances. This strategy is quite similar with negotiating form, yet it is performed to the whole utterance while negotiating form commonly focuses on word level.

Lastly, eleven of them said that they frequently spent the time to think first before they spoke. They often made pauses while speaking to give them time formulating utterances in their mind before uttering them. Sometimes they think first of what they want to say in their mother tongue and turn it into the L2 after they figure out the whole information they want to convey. It indicates that L1 can delay the process of language learners to produce the language in L2 [2]. However, somehow it is perceived beneficial by the participants as they can strengthen their memory on the vocabulary and grammatical forms.

Regarding the self-correction strategies mentioned previously, the participants mentioned that their self-correction strategy was quite effective to help them minimize their oral grammatical errors. By using the self-correction strategy frequently, they felt that their grammar was improved. They mentioned that, so far, it helped them strengthen their awareness to speak properly using correct grammar, avoid them making the same errors although it took times, sharpen their grammatical knowledge, and develop their creativity in formulating utterances.

4 CONCLUSIONS AND SUGGESTIONS

4.1 *Conclusions*

Based on the discussion in the previous section, several conclusions can be drawn to answer the research questions. First, there are three most frequent oral grammatical errors made by adult learners namely word-choice, verb-tense, and sentence-structure errors. The errors reflect that most adults have grammar difficulties at the word and sentence level. Second, adult speakers of English mostly have a high awareness and willingness to correct their errors. It indicates that the use of self-correction strategy may work best for them to deal with their oral grammatical errors. Third, there are five self-correction strategies used by adult learners yet only four promoting autonomous self-correction. They are avoidance, output modification/recast, form negotiation, and speaking pauses. The mentioned self-correction strategies actually represent the effect of crosslinguistic in second language acquisition known as negative transfers. Those phenomena are perceived as having negative influence towards L2 learning, yet, in this respect, they may turn as positive opportunities for helping language learners develop their self-correction sense. Fourth, the self-correction strategies are perceived beneficial by adult speakers of English. It indicates that other speakers of English may apply the same self-correction strategies to be more accurate speakers and gain the same benefits as the participants. Lastly, the fact that every participant has their own self-correction strategy and frequently makes oral grammatical errors even though they have been learning it for years leads to the belief that every speaker of English consciously or unconsciously has their own self-correction strategy for oral errors and also possibly commit other types of language errors in both oral or written production.

4.2 *Suggestions*

This present study is still far from perfection. It focused on identifying the variation of both oral grammatical errors and self-correction strategies to deal with them, yet it had not gone deeper on elaborating the other possible types of oral errors, the process of which each strategy is used by a large number of speakers, and the effectiveness of each strategy in helping speakers produce accurate utterances. Therefore, it is suggested for other researchers who are interested in second language acquisition to conduct similar research with some modifications such as adding the number of participants to collect more accurate and representative data and selecting participants with different range of age and other demographic variables. This present study also opens a new perspective on negative transfer which is worth to be elaborated more comprehensively, probably within the different research genres. Lastly, other researchers are suggested to enrich the literature regarding the self-correction strategy for oral grammatical errors as well as for other types of errors in language production.

REFERENCES

[1] Bassano, D., & Hickmann, M. (Eds.). (2013). *Grammaticalization and first language acquisition: crosslinguistic perspectives, 50*. Amsterdam: John Benjamins Publishing.

[2] Ortega, L. (2014). *Understanding second language acquisition*. London: Routledge.

[3] Brown, H.D. (2001). *Teaching by principles (2nd Edition)*. New York: Pearson Education.

[4] Sabboor, M., Raja, H., Albasher, K. B., & Farid, A. (2016). Error treatment in teaching English to EFL adult learners: A study in current English Language Teaching Practices in Native/Non-Native Divide Context in Saudi Arabia. *Journal of Applied Linguistics and Language Research*, 3(5), 1–16.

[5] Norrish, J. (1983). *Language learners and their errors*. Basingstoke: Macmillan.

[6] Tomkova, G. (2013). *Error correction in spoken practice* (Doctoral dissertation, Masarykova univerzita, Filozofická fakulta).

[7] Krashen, S. (2009). The comprehension hypothesis extended. *Input Matters in SLA*. Clevedon: Multilingual Matters, 81–94.

[8] Richards, J.C., & Schmidt, R. (2002). *Longman dictionary of applied linguistics and language teaching (3rd ed)*. Harlow, UK: Longman.

[9] Nan, Z., Surasin, J., & Brudhiprabha, P. (2015). Self-correction Strategies Employed in Spoken English by Chinese First-year College EFL. *HRD Journal*, 6(1), 149–161.

[10] Rezaei, S. (2011). *Corrective feedback in task-based grammar instruction*. Saarbrücken, Germany: LAP LAMBERT Academic Publishing.

[11] Edge, J. (1993). *Essentials of English language teaching*. London: Longman.

[12] Knowles, M. (1980). What is andragogy, *The modern practice of adult education, from pedagogy to andragogy*, 40–62.

[13] Fox, B.A., Hayashi, M., Jasperson, R. (1996). Resources and repair: a cross-linguistic study of syntax and repair. In: Ochs, E., Schegloff, E.A., Thompson, S.A. (Eds.), *Interaction and Grammar*. Cambridge: Cambridge University Press, pp. 185–237.

[14] Schegloff, E.A., Jefferson, G., Sachs, H. (1977). The preference for self-correction in the organization of repair in conversation. *Language*, 53, 361–382.

[15] Rieger, C.L. (2000). Self-repair strategies of English–German bilinguals in informal conversations: The Role of Language, Gender and Proficiency. *Doctoral dissertation*, University of Alberta.

[16] Forbes, K. (2018). The role of individual differences in the development and transfer of writing strategies between foreign and first language classrooms. *Research Papers in Education*, 1–20.

[17] Thao, N.T.T., & Anh, N.D. (2017). Error correction in teaching writing skill. *Journal of Development Research*, *1*(1), 24–28.

[18] Anindyawati, F., & Fauziati, E. (2017). The instructional delivery of writing course at English department of ums: A naturalistic study. *Kajian Linguistik dan Sastra*, *27*(1), 28–39.

[19] Denscombe, M. (2010). *The good research guide: for small-scale social research (5th Edition)*. McGraw Hill.

English Linguistics, Literature, and Language Teaching in a Changing Era – Madya et al. (eds)
© 2020 Taylor & Francis Group, London, ISBN 978-1-03-224160-9

Proposing literature circle strategy to enhance students' reading comprehension in EFL classroom

Nurus Sa'adah & Erna Andriyanti
Yogyakarta State University, Yogyakarta, Indonesia

ABSTRACT: Traditionally, many teachers give rigid question-answer exercises which include some texts to be answered by students in reading classroom. This strategy is commonly used by most of EFL teachers in the classroom but this conventional reading comprehension activity does not provide students opportunity to share what they have read. This mixed-method research is aimed to find out students' needs and wants as well as their interests and difficulties in reading classroom in second grade of a senior high school in Yogyakarta. A questionnaire was developed to collect the main data and 25 students participated in responding this questionnaire. To support the result of the questionnaire, the writers also conducted observation in the classroom and interviewing the teacher. The preliminary data analyses showed that the students in EFL classroom need a strategy which can help them improve their reading skill, increase their vocabulary, and enhance their social skill, which all can lead to better learning in reading class. This paper proposes a strategy that can be used by the teachers in EFL reading classroom through the use of Literature Circle Strategy to develop the students' reading comprehension skill while also increase their social skill needed during successful reading process.

Keywords: literature circle strategy, reading classroom, reading comprehension, EFL classroom

1 INTRODUCTION

Many scholars addressed that comprehension is certainly the most important reading skill [1]. Reading comprehension is important in all levels of education because it enables learners who are struggling with their academic and literary tasks to overcome their problems [2]. Reading comprehension occurs during "the process of extracting and also constructing meaning trough interaction and involvement with the written language [3], through which readers are able to understand the content of the texts" [4].

In some countries, reading comprehension becomes one of problems in the classroom [5], including EFL classroom [1]. The students are given rigid question-answer exercises in the classroom to ensure that they have comprehended the content of various texts given by the teacher from the textbook. In this common style of teaching reading, the students are asked to answer the following text questions without any discussion with the other students. In some classes, teachers adopt multiple choice exercises in which the students are asked to respond the question related to reading comprehension while the teacher plays a role in giving right answer to the questions [6].

Many students in EFL context, including Indonesia, do not like to read English texts because they have limited vocabulary [7] and this will affect their ability in comprehending the texts. When they do not know the meaning of some words of the first paragraph in reading a passage they read, they will feel demotivated to continue reading the next paragraph. Thus, when they are asked to respond some questions related to the text, they will fail to answer correctly because they do not comprehend the content of the text. This becomes another problem of teaching reading comprehension in EFL classroom. Teachers should emphasize vocabulary learning and create a vocabulary-rich environment, and incorporate extensive or independent reading [8].

The conventional reading activity does not provide a good opportunity for EFL students to share what they have read [6]. It cannot help students engage in interactive reading task and communicative reading activity [7]. When teachers defend to use their current method for teaching reading comprehension in the class, it might be difficult for them to help their students successful in their reading class. An inappropriate strategy used to teach reading in the classroom will make students have less motivation and interest in reading the text. To motivate students to learn English, teachers should be able to build students' awareness toward the importance of reading English texts. This way can support their students' successful learning.

Those facts indicate that teachers in EFL context should find teaching reading strategy that is suitable for their classroom context because the learning strategy will determine success in language learning [9]. Furthermore, by using appropriate reading strategy, it will help students to understand and obtain meaningful information from the text they have read [10]. There are some components in achieving successful reading program in EFL context [11]. They are extensive amount of reading time in the classroom, direct strategy instruction on reading comprehension, opportunities for collaboration, and opportunities for discussion on respond to reading.

In line with the previously mentioned reasons, this article suggests the strategy that can be used by EFL teachers for their reading classroom. Literature Circle Strategy, developed by Daniels [7] is the strategy that draws on some principle that can support students in activating their motivation and engagement in reading comprehension. By most account, Literature Circle Strategy had been a valuable addition to many kids' school experience, helping to grow more self-sustaining, lifelong readers [12]. This paper aims at proposing Literature Circle Strategy to develop students' reading comprehension and social skills needed in reading classroom.

2 RESEARCH METHOD

This study applied a mixed-method approach, with questionnaire, observation, and interview as methods of data collection in an Islamic senior high school in Yogyakarta. This Islamic school was located on a street in Mantrijeron, Yogyakarta. This study was conducted at a reading class of second grade, with 25 students and the teacher as the research participants.

Based on a preliminary study conducted in July, 2018, the researcher conducted a need analyses on reading classroom by distributing questionnaires to the participating students. Students should respond to 19 questions related to their reading interest and reading comprehension using Likert-scale with 5 options (Strongly Agree-5, Agree-4, Neutral-3, Disagree-2, and Strongly Disagree-1). This questionnaire was aimed to know the students' needs, lacks, and wants in reading class. Besides the questionnaires, the researcher also conducted class observation and had an interview with the teacher.

3 FINDINGS AND DISCUSSIONS

This study was aimed to find out students' needs and wants as well as their interests and difficulties in reading classroom in second grade of a senior high school in Yogyakarta. The questionnaire consisted of 19 question items and was distributed to 25 students. The researchers also conducted an unstructured interview with the teacher of the class to find out the students' difficulties as well as the needs of the students for successful reading comprehension. Descriptive statistics was performed to analyze the questionnaire data.

Referring to the result of the questionnaires, the data showed that 15 of 25 students liked to learn English. Most of the students agreed that they liked to learn English. Figure 1 shows the result of the first question (Q1) of the questionnaire. In the second question (Q2), the result shows that the students did not have definite answers whether they liked reading or not because more than half of students in the class were neutral regarding their preference of reading. The result of this question is shown in the Figure 2.

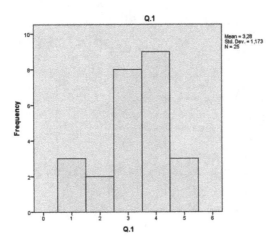

Figure 1. Q1: I like English subject.

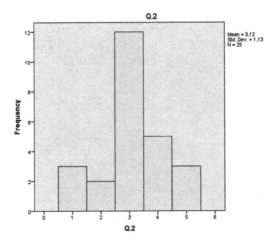

Figure 2. Q2: I like reading in English subject.

The result of the questionnaire also revealed that the students needed various types of techniques or strategies in their reading classroom. This was reflected from the answer of Q11 and Q12. Most of the students responded that they were interested in the lesson when the teacher gave them various ways of teaching, like showing pictures or playing the movie/video for their reading class. Figure 3 and 4 show the students' responses of Q11 and Q12. Most of the students agreed that they were not interested in the strategy used by the teacher because only one strategy was implemented in several meetings, thus it made them bored and less motivated in the reading class.

Related to students' lack of reading comprehension skill, the result reported that they got difficulties in comprehending the texts and gaining information of the texts (Q7 and Q8). These difficulties affected their ability in doing the exercise after reading the text (Q9). Figure 5 shows the students' responses for the seventh question of the questionnaire. Most of the students agreed that they had problems in comprehending the content of the text. Another factor that could affect students' reading comprehension was their vocabulary mastery. The third question of the questionnaire asked if the students were able to understand the text when they knew the meaning of the words (Q3). Most of the students agreed that vocabulary mastery could help them in improving their reading comprehension skill. Figure 6 shows the students' responses related to question number 3.

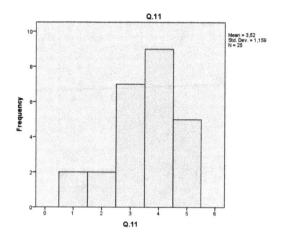

Figure 3. Q11: I am not interested in the teacher.

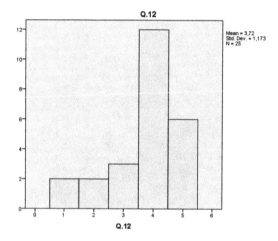

Figure 4. Q12: The teacher uses monotonous strategy in teaching reading.

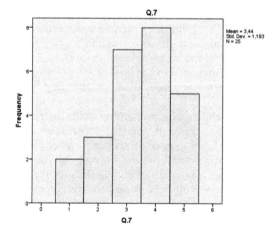

Figure 5. Q7: I get difficulties in comprehending a reading text.

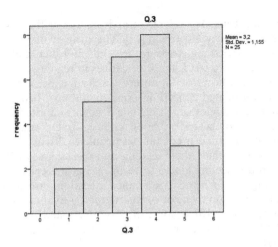

Figure 6. Q3: I understand a text when I know the meaning of the words.

To support the result of the questionnaire, the researchers also conducted classroom observations. The researchers found some problems during the teaching and learning process. For instance, students were not enthusiastic in following the class activities. They did not respond to the teacher's talk and just kept silent in the class. When the teacher asked them the meaning of a word, most of them were not responsive to the teacher because they did not bring a dictionary in the class. After they read, the teacher asked them to share what they got from their reading in front of the class. Most of the students were not willing to do it in front of the class because they said that they were not ready.

Another type of supporting data is interview results from the teacher. The teacher stated that the students had low vocabulary mastery. It affected their motivation in reading the texts. As a result, they could not answer most of the questions. Besides that, the teacher admitted that she had tried to practice some handbooks but she still could not find an appropriate handbook compatible with her students' characteristics. Another result regarding to media used, the teacher said that she did not have sufficient time to prepare teaching media because of work load. She taught the students through lecturing and providing games, if needed. Further, she said that she taught the students text genres separately with the lesson discussed on that day. The reason was because she explained all kinds of texts at the same meeting to give more understanding of the differences among them. The strategy used by the teacher could make students lose their motivation in the reading class. Based on the result of the questionnaire, the students preferred to have reading class with materials having more pictures. Using short video could also be an alternative to help the students comprehend a text better.

Based on the findings above, the researchers propose one strategy that can be used by the teachers in EFL classroom, especially Indonesian teachers to solve several problems faced by students as well as the teachers. The strategy is called Literature Circle Strategy. The important points and the implementation of this strategy are discussed in the following section.

3.1 *Important points in literature circle strategy*

"Literature Circle is a small, peer-led discussion group, that has chosen to read the same story, poem, article or book" [12]. It can be used to discuss any types or genres of texts, including fictions, nonfictions, chapter books, picture books, textbooks, articles or poems. Through the activities of literature circles, students are expected to have an interaction with peers and their chosen text through ongoing discussion. They are also expected to guide their own instruction by making connection and focusing on issues that are meaningful to them

[13]. Literature Circle is a forum for students to articulate their thoughts, opinions and questions about common material they have read [14]. The strategy of Literature Circle traditionally has been used to teach fictional texts rather than non-fictional ones. However, some researchers motivate educators to use Literature Circles in reading textbooks [15]. As the success with fictional texts, the concept of Literature Circles has been extended to enhance content area of vocabulary and related concept in nonfictional text. It believes that there are "11 key ingredients" for literature circles which include Students choose their own book, 2) Small temporary groups are formed, based on book choice, 3) Different groups read different books, 4) Groups meet on e regular, predictable schedule to discuss their reading, 5) Students use written or drawn notes to guide their reading and discussion, 6) Discussions topic come from the students, 7) Group meeting aimed to be open, natural conversation about books, so personal connections, digressions, and open-ended questions are allowed, 8) The teacher serves as a facilitator, not a group member or instructor, 9) Evaluation is by teacher observation and student self-evaluation, 10) A spirit of playfulness and fun pervades the room, 11) When books are finished, readers share with the classmates and then new groups form around new reading selection [16].

As an instructional practice, the implementation of Literature Circles is grounded in the social learning perspective and reflects the Socio-Cultural Theory [17]. It falls under the category of a social learning perspective. The theory explains that activities take place in cultural context; therefore, literacy development is understood by exploring the culture, social, and historical context in which children have grown [18]. Literature Circles are consistent with the Socio-Cultural Theory [19]. As students participate, they learn from other group members by talking about books and making different connection.

3.2 Implementing literature circle strategy in EFL classroom

There are several steps in implementing Literature circles strategy in ESL, EFL, or in classroom of English speaking country. Procedures in implementing this strategy that suit EFL classroom includes:

3.2.1 Reading material selection

Reading materials used in literature circles are important to stimulate meaningful discussion among the students [20]. In selecting texts to use in Literature Circle, some authors have suggested some criteria which include: comprehensible to students with different abilities and interests, reflect students' language needs and skills, address issues/topics relevant to students' lives, and provoke thinking and discussion by the students [21].

As the result of class observation and interview during the reading class, the text given by the teacher did not support students' different abilities and interests because the material was just taken from the textbook given by the government. The material still needed some modifications to adjust with the issue or topic related to students' lives. The teacher also should find an appropriate text used in Literature Circle which can support thinking and discussion among the students.

3.2.2 Community building

A primary function of Literature Circle strategy is to create classroom community in which students and teacher can learn from each other [22]. Teachers should discuss the following topics with the students: how to handle difficult words, how to respond and provide feedback for another participant, how to select topic for discussion, and how to get along as a group [20].

The observation result showed that during the teaching and learning process students did not have a good cooperation with the teacher. They just kept silent when they did not understand the material or the task given by the teacher. As a result of preliminary study, the teacher and students did not have a good communication in the classroom. Through the implementation of Literature Circle Strategy, the community building between teacher and students is expected to be better.

3.2.3 *Number of participants in each circle*

In Literature Circle, four to eight participants are the ideal number for implementing this strategy because students need time and opportunities to share their idea and to respond to other members in thoughtful and probing ways [23]. Based on the classroom student participants, the class consisted of 25 students and it could be divided into five groups. Each group would include five students. In implementing this strategy, the teacher participant can modify the role of Literature Circle so that it will be appropriate with the number of the students in a group.

3.2.4 *Preparation for discussion*

One of the aims of preparation for discussion is not only making students familiar with the text being read but also being prepared to fulfill various different roles in the discussion. Not as the way the research participant teacher did before, she just made a group and gave students material to be discussed. However, the teacher here should explain that in the Literature Circle Strategy there are several roles that should be understood by every student in each group. The teacher can give example activity of each role before starting the discussion. From that, the students are expected to have good understanding of what role that will be played by them during the discussion session.

3.2.5 *Sharing and discussion*

After finishing the discussion preparation, students should start their discussion. They should bring the discussion sheets as the guidance for the discussion, but some researchers believe that the discussion should not be limited by these [30]. When the teacher participant will implement this strategy later and students does not fully understand on Literature Circle Strategy, teacher participant must give an appropriate model discussion behavior, such as how to response the readings, give respectful feedback to the interpretation of others, how to be a good listener and should have a good questioning skills. There are six roles which are implemented in Literature Circles Strategy [19], and those roles of Literature Circle can be implemented by the interviewed teacher in this study are as follows: 1) *Group Discussion Leader (GDL)*, 2) *Summarizer*, 3) *Connector*, 4) *Word Master*, 5) *Passage Person*, and 6) *Culture Collector*

There are many instructional advantages in implementing Literature Circle Strategy in EFL context around a reading comprehension strategy. Literature Circle Strategy allows students to enjoy and interpret the book/text [25]. They can gain control over independence through authentic questions around text. Implementing Literature Circle Strategy in EFL classroom does not only develop students' reading abilities but also contributes to improve students' communication skills and to foster social and interpersonal skills. The benefits of Literature Circle Strategy which some studies have identified include [26]: a) Stronger reader-text relationship, b) Improved classroom climates, c) Enhanced degrees of understanding, and d) A learning environment more conductive to the need and abilities of English language learners.

4 CONCLUSION

There are a lot of problems faced by teachers in implementing strategy for their classroom. In EFL classroom, English teachers sometimes use strategies inappropriate with the students' needs and wants. This kind of situation will affect students' performance and their ability in comprehending knowledge. Students in EFL classroom need a strategy which can help them improve their reading skill, increase their vocabulary, and enhance their social skill, which all can lead to better learning in reading class. This paper proposes a strategy that can be used by the teachers in EFL reading classroom through the use of Literature Circle Strategy to develop the students' reading comprehension skill while also increase their social skill needed during successful reading process. Teachers in EFL classroom can use and modify this strategy based on the situation and context of their classroom.

REFERENCES

[1] Widodo, H.P. (2015). Engaging students in Literature Circles: Vocational English reading programs. *Asia-Pacific Edu Res*, *25*(2), 347–359. doi:10.1007/s40299-015-0269-7.

[2] Irawati, D. (2016). Effectiveness of Literature Circles on students' reading comprehension. *IJOLTL*, *1*(3). Retrieved from http://ijoltl.pusatbahasa.or.id.

[3] Hedgcock & Ferris. (2009). *Teaching readers of English: Students, texts, and contexts.* New York: Routledge.

[4] O'Malley, J.M., & Pierce, L.V. (1996). *Authentic assessment for English language learners: Practical approaches for teachers.* White Plains: Addison Wesley Publishing Company, Inc.

[5] Li, F. (2010). A study of English reading strategies used by senior middle school students. *Asian Social Science*, *6*(10), 184–192. Retrieved from http://ccsenet.org/ass.

[6] Harvey, M. (2012). *Reading comprehension strategies for elementary and secondary school students.* Virginia, VA: Lynchburg College.

[7] Daniels, H. (2006). What's the next big thing with literature circles?. *The National Council of Teachers of English*, *13*(4), 10–15.

[8] Carrison, C., Ernst-Slavit, G., & Spiesman-Laughlin, J. (2009). Creating opportunities for "grand conversations" among ELLs with Literature Circles. In J. Coppola & E. Primas (Eds.), One classroom, many learners: best literacy practices for today's multilingual classrooms. *International Reading Association*, 91–117.

[9] Rogers, W., & Leochko, D. (2006). *Literature circles: Tools and techniques to inspire reading groups.* Manitoba, Canada: Portage & Main Press.

[10] Wilfong, L.G. (2009). Textmasters: Bringing literature circles to textbook reading across the curriculum. *Journal of Adolescent & Adult Literacy*, *53*(2), 164–171.

[11] Daniels, H. (2002). *Literature circles: Voice and choice in book clubs and reading groups.* Markham, ONT: Stenhouse Publishers.

[12] Davidson, K. (2010). The integration of cognitive and sociocultural theories of literacy development: Why? How?. *The Alberta Journal of Educational Research*, *56*(3), 246–256.

[13] Tracey, D.H., & Morrow, L.M. (2012). *Lenses on reading: An introduction to theories and models.* New York: The Guilford Press.

[14] Fountas, I.C., & Pinnell. G.S. (1996). *Guided reading: Good first teaching for all children.* Portsmouth, NH: Heinemann.

[15] Varita, D. (2017). Improving reading comprehension through Literature Circle. *English Education Journal (EEJ)*, *8*(2), 234–244.

[16] Maher, K. (2013). Literature circles: Acquiring language through collaboration. *Proceedings of 2013: 2nd World Congress on Extensive Reading.* Seoul, Korea.

[17] Nation, I.S.P. (2009). *Teaching ESL/EFL reading and writing.* New York: Routledge.

[18] Furr, M. (2004). *Why and how to use EFL literature circles.* Retrieved from http://www.eflliterature circles.com/howandwhy2.html.

[19] Stein, D., & Bede, P.L. (2004). Bridging the gap between fiction and nonfiction in the literature circle setting. *The Reading Teacher*, *57*(6), 510–518.

[20] Farinacci, M. (1998). "We have so much to talk about": Implementing literature circles as an action-research project. *The Ohio Reading Teacher*, *32*(2), 4–11.

[21] Peralta-Nash, C., & Dutch, J.A. (2000). Literature circles: Creating an environment for choice. *Primary Voices K-6*, *8*(4), 29–37.

[22] King, C. (2001). I like group reading because we can share ideas: The role of talk within the literature circle. *Reading*, *35*(1), 32–36.

[23] Brabham, E.G., & Villaume, S.K. (2000). Questions and answers: Continuing conversations about literature circles. *The Reading Teacher*, *54*(3), 278–280.

[24] Gilbert, L. (2000). Getting started: Using literature circles in the classroom. *Primary Voices K-6*, *9*(1), 9–16.

[25] Clower, S.M. (2006). Using Literature Circles to improve literacy skills of English language learners.. *All Regis University Theses.* Retrieved from http://epublications.regis.edu/theses.

[26] Lin, C. (2004). Literature circles. *Teacher Librarian*, *31*, 23–26.

English Linguistics, Literature, and Language Teaching in a Changing Era – Madya et al. (eds)
© 2020 Taylor & Francis Group, London, ISBN 978-1-03-224160-9

The representation of cultural elements in the promotion of intercultural communicative competence in senior high school EFL textbooks in Indonesia

Oktavia Herawati
Graduate School of Education, College of Social Sciences and International Studies, University of Exeter, UK

ABSTRACT: This study aims to examine the promotion and development of Intercultural Communicative Competence (ICC) within the English Language Teaching (ELT) textbooks used in public senior high schools for grade X (the lowest grade) and XII (the highest grade) in Indonesia. Relevant literature by Byram [4], Holliday [3], Cortazzi and Jin [16], and Baker [17,9], is used as the research framework for the examination. The *content analysis* method is used to answer the research aim. The results were arrived at by analysing the frequency of three aspects of ICC representations: 1) the three key components of Intercultural Communication Awareness (ICA); 2) the cultural elements which cover large culture (large C) (that is, *products* and *persons*) and small culture (small c) (that is, *practices* and *perspectives*); and 3) cultural sources (that is, *home (H), target (T)* and *international (I)* cultures). Regarding the findings, the analysis found that the ICC promotion and development decreased from the grade X textbook to the grade XII one. Recommendations are tentatively suggested in terms of the development of teaching and learning, pedagogy, and material development. The limitations of this study include the absence of teachers' and students' perspectives.

Keywords: Intercultural Communicative Competence (ICC), English Language Teaching (ELT), Intercultural Communication Awareness (ICA), cultural elements, large culture, small culture, cultural sources

1   INTRODUCTION

The modern era, i.e. the technology development, e.g. the internet development, which leads people to live with no border, creates a bubble of post-modernism. The existence of diverse culture becomes inevitable. This situation eventually increases the amount of intercultural communicator. Interestingly, Romanowski [1] stresses that the intercultural communicators experience a communication failure which is caused not by their linguistic competence but by their Intercultural Communicative Competence (henceforth ICC). Therefore, he emphasises that "linguistic competence is no longer a sufficient prerequisite of communicative success because communication has to be understood as more than a mere exchange of information and sending of messages" [1]. It implies that foreign language teaching, including English Language Teaching (henceforth ELT), should be more focused on preparing the learners to become successful communicators through not only considering linguistic competence (for example, grammar and vocabulary) but also the ICC (that is, learners' sociolinguistic competence and knowledge of other cultures, their intercultural communication skills, and their attitudes and behaviour).

In a context in which I have been into it, in 2013, the Indonesian government arranged a *2013 ELT Curriculum* which the main goal is to meet of global demands in which the intercultural communication is inevitably needed. Consequently, the curriculum objectives embody the ICC elements - the knowledge, skills, attitudes, and behaviour - that are needed to develop learners' ICC. It is expected to see the ICC implementation within the relevant material. Hence, this study intends to examine the ICC development promoted throughout the ELT core textbooks, entitled *"Bahasa Inggris"* (English Language) used in the lowest grade (grade X) and the highest grade (grade XII) in public senior high schools, in Indonesia.

2 THE NOTION OF CULTURE

The notion of culture is elusive, and its definitions tend to be quite abstract [2]. Holliday [3] uses his idea to divide culture into two main groups: 1) large culture (large C); and 2) small culture (small c). The large C which is non-essentialist, concerns ethnic, national and international entities that are easily recognised, such as traditional cloth, food, language, public figures, names. Meanwhile, the small c (essentialist) is quite difficult to distinguish because it is significantly concerned with an understanding of the emergence of behaviour, for example, the way people think of things - why people decide to celebrate the Thanksgiving Day.

3 THE PEDAGOGY OF INTERCULTURAL COMMUNICATIVE COMPETENCE (ICC)

Byram [4] believes that ICC of which Critical Cultural Awareness (henceforth CCA) is a part, is needed in terms of achieving successful intercultural communication. According to Byram [4], CCA is "an ability to evaluate critically on the basis of explicit criteria perspectives, practices, and products in one's own and other cultures and countries." (p. 53). According to Kim and Paek [5], *products* refer to "a system or code" which may include four aspects, namely "artefacts, places, institutions, and art forms" (p. 91). *Practices* refer to instances of communication, such as communication that occurs in daily life [6]. Finally, *perspectives* involves "particular perceptions, values, and beliefs, and that guide people's behaviours in cultural practices" [5]. Thus, according to Moran (2001, as cited in [6]), Celik and Erbay [7], and Kim and Paek [5], an awareness of culture is not complete without including a *"person"* as the representation of a particular culture or community. Therefore, the concept of CCA involves understanding the areas of *perspectives, practices, products* and *persons* (henceforth *4Ps*) in one's own and others' cultures and countries.

In terms of CCA within foreign language learning, Baker [9] stresses that CCA entails "knowledge, skills, and attitudes" that should be "developed by the language learner, which can then be utilised in understanding specific cultures and in communicating across diverse cultures" (p. 65). The way to develop the CCA is by developing an awareness of intercultural communication (henceforth ICA), that is, viewing culture as "fluid, fragmented, hybrid, and emergent" [9], p. 65–66). This ICA might enable learners to see culture as a non-essentialist, that is, a dynamic behaviour. This awareness might be beneficial for the learners in terms of achieving the ICC. For example, when the representation of foreign culture appears during

Table 1. ICC dimensions *(Byram ([4] emphasis in original)).*

	Skills interpret and relate *(savoir comprendre)*	
Knowledge of self and others; of interaction: individual and societal *(savoirs)*	Education political education critical cultural awareness *(savoir s'engager)*	Attitudes relativising self valuing others *(Savoir etre)*
	Skills discover and/or interact *(savoir apprendre/ faire)*	

the English learning, the students could break cultural stereotypes which place limits of the understanding of "human behaviour" and "intercultural discourse" because stereotypes reduce "human activity to just one or two salient dimensions and consider those to be the whole picture" [10] p. 169). Byram [4] proposes five ICC dimensions which can be used to equip intercultural communicators to succeed in intercultural communication, including:

In terms of the practical implementation of the ICC, it can be implemented within the curriculum, explicitly through the curriculum objectives [4,2], which, in turn, should be evident in the material produced to achieve them [11,12,13,14]. In other words, the ICC can be implemented in foreign language learning through the content of the material. However, a textbook should not only cover the cultural elements common to English-speaking cultures, such as the UK and USA, but also other foreign cultures worldwide and the local cultures which the learners belong to [15]. Cortazzi and Jin [16] classify cultural sources into three main groups, namely: 1) *Home Culture (H)*; 2) *Target Culture (T)*; and 3) *International Culture (I)*. The *H* refers to the culture of the learners' home countries, so, in this study, is Indonesian. The *T* refers to the culture of countries where English is a first language, including the UK, USA, Ireland, New Zealand, Canada, or Australia. Finally, the *I* refers to cultures where English is not spoken as the first language, such as Malaysia, Singapore, Japan, China, Korea, the Netherlands, Italy and Turkey. They should then be covered in a balanced way.

4 THE DEVELOPMENT OF INTERCULTURAL COMMUNICATIVE COMPETENCE (ICC)

Based on the mentioned concepts, Baker [9,17] reflects that ICC development could be assessed using the three key components of ICA. Baker proposes three components that could be used to indicate ICC development. The first component concerns the "basic cultural awareness", which focuses on "an ability, or the development of an ability, to articulate one's own culture and 'others'; [...] at the level of broad generalisations or stereotypes." In other words, the understanding of culture is still on the essentialist level [17]. The second component is named "advanced cultural awareness" and involves an ability to understand other cultures and compare and mediate between them. The perspective of culture hence moves away from the essentialist. The third component is the key component of ICA, namely, "Intercultural Awareness", which focuses on an awareness of culture as fluid and dynamic, requiring an ability to mediate and negotiate between cultural frames by, for example, taking the role of a mediator in a cross-cultural interaction.

5 METHODOLOGY

This study used a qualitative methodology with a *content analysis* as the method to analyse the data. It was included textual and visual (e.g. images) features within the samples, which were the textbooks for grades X and XII used in public senior high schools in Indonesia. Regarding research reliability and validity, I use: *1) stability* (with myself being the one coder that analyses the data consistently); and *2) accuracy*, ensuring that the research framework is designed on the basis of relevant categories. Meanwhile, the validity of this study is achieved through *semantic validity*. Regarding the data analysis procedure, the development of ICC is judged by analysing the beginning (grade X) and the end of the learning process (grade XII).

In terms of content analysis, to carry out the analysis in this study, firstly, the data are collected. The research framework which was designed by referring to the literature reviewed was then outlined (it is by indicating the frequency of ICA components, cultural elements (large C and small c (i.e. *products, persons, practices*, and *perspectives*), and cultural sources (*H, T* and *I*) throughout the textbooks). A numeric conclusion was made, based on counting the number of times an item appeared and translating this into percentages. Finally, the numeric results were interpreted, and the findings were discussed descriptively (in words) in relation to the aim of this study.

6 FINDING AND DISCUSSION

I examined the development of Intercultural Communicative Competence (henceforth ICC) throughout the textbooks by looking at the three main aspects of: 1) the three components of Intercultural Communication Awareness (henceforth ICA); 2) cultural elements; and 3) cultural sources, respectively. I present the findings in relevant tables respectively below. This is followed by the relevant discussion.

Tables 2–4 show the findings of ICA components found throughout the textbooks. This followed–by Table 5 which shows the frequency of ICA representations throughout the textbooks.

To summarize, it can be seen the second and third ICA components in both textbooks are mainly promoted through reading comprehension activities, particularly through sharing and discussion of the texts with peers (see Table 3 and 4). In terms of the frequency, Table 5 shows that the grade X textbook has more ICA components than the grade XII one: 62% compared with 38% respectively with the highest domination of ICA component number 1 in both textbooks.

Table 2. Example of ICA component number 1.

Grade X	Grade XII
Chapter 1: Reading task 2: Comparing an American's (Hannah's) letter and a Malaysian's (Saidah's) letter. By comparing the two letters, Alia (an Indonesian) could see the different ways of communicating (i.e. the way to communicate, e.g. Hannah starts her letter by using "Hello", meanwhile, Saidah uses "Assalamualaikum").	Chapter 9: Observing and Questioning: Through the reading passage, the students may have a chance to learn about international cultural *products*; that is, the history of pottery brought by Persians.

Table 3. Example of ICA component number 2.

Grade X	Grade XII
Chapter 10: Speaking Task 2 and 3: Asking the students to choose and share information of a public figure (using references). This task may give students the chance to develop their awareness level 1 and 2 through familiarising themselves with cultural *products, persons,* and even *practices* (if the students could go beyond the products and persons) of home, target and international cultures.	Chapter 10: Reading: Sharing/discussing a report text of a particular ethnicity. This task might give the students chance to develop their understanding of their own/target/international cultural products and cultural practices.

Table 4. Example of ICA component number 3.

Grade X	Grade XII
Chapter 13: Reading Comprehension: The task may *familiarise* students with the cultural *products, persons*, and *practices* of international culture (Japanese culture). The *practices* could be the practice of praying in a temple. In addition, this part gives students the chance to familiarise themselves with the *perspectives* in the reading text, such as the reason why the couple prays to God (this relates to beliefs and perspectives).	Chapter 10: Reading: Sharing/discussing a report text of a particular ethnicity. This task might give the students the chance to develop their understanding of their own/the target/international cultural *products* - cultural *perspectives*.

Table 5. The frequency of ICA components throughout the textbooks.

Components	Grade X (%)	Grade XII (%)
1	38	23
2	5	3
3	4	3
TOTAL	47 (62%)	29 (38%)
FINAL TOTAL	76 (100%)	

Regarding the samples of cultural elements, they are presented in Table 6 below:

Table 6. Samples of large C (*products* and *persons*) and small c (*practices* and *perspectives*) – Grade X and XII.

GRADE X

Cultural Sources	Large C		Small c	
	Products	Persons	Practices	Perspectives
Home	Indonesia (a country)	Andrea Hirata (an Indonesian novelist)	Practices of Heroes Day Celebration in Indonesia on 10 November.	Chapter 13: Pic. 12.2. represents the famous symbol of Malin Kundang (People believe that the stone represents the Malin Kundang incarnation).
Target	Minnesota (a city in the USA)	JK. Rowling (a British novelist)	No data (-)	No data (-)
International	Picture 4.2. in chapter 4 represents Taj Mahal in India	Siti Nurhaliza (a Malaysian singer)	Practices to ask permission for marriage from the King (Issumboshi legend)	Issumboshi legend passage (p.157): *"Please give us a child, "they asked God every day".* – showing their belief in God

GRADE XII

Cultural Sources	Large C		Small c	
	Products	Persons	Practices	Perspectives
Home	Orang Utan (a protected local animal)	Basuki "Ahok" Tjahaja Purnama (former of Jakarta governor	P.149: Chapter 10 – Observing and Questioning (Reading): *"Baduy Dalam wears white and black cloth as clothing, meanwhile .... Some people say ...into their daily lives."*	Chapter 4 (a belief in God – dialogue 3 by Nina)
Target	Microsoft Corporation	Harold Pinter (English playwright, screenwriter, director and actor)	Mr. Peterson ["Mr." which is followed by the last name]	No data (-)
International	Latin language	Maher Zain (a Lebanese-Swedish singer)	No data (-)	No data (-)

Following Table 6, the Table 7 below presents the frequency of cultural elements:

Table 7. The frequency of large C and small c references throughout the textbooks.

4Ps	Grade X (%)	Grade XII (%)	TOTAL
Products	475	327	
Persons	93	17	
Large C	568 (62%)	344 (38%)	912 (100%)
Practices	15	8	
Perspectives	20	5	
Small c	35 (72%)	13 (28%)	48 (100%)

To summarise, the percentage of representations of large C elements in the grade X textbook was higher (62%) than in the grade XII textbook (38%) (see Table 7). Nevertheless, most of the references in both textbooks were to *products* (802 times appearance). A similar result was found for representations of the small c elements; the textbook grade X represents small c elements more frequently than the grade XII one does: 72% as opposed to 28%. Overall, the grade X textbook captures cultural elements more frequently than the grade XII one does.

Finally, Table 8 below displays the findings of cultural sources found throughout the textbooks, followed by Table 9 which presents the frequency of cultural sources. The frequency of references to the cultural sources decreased from textbook grade X to grade XII: from 63% to 37% with *H* as the domination.

In a way to discuss the findings, I discuss them respectively. Analysis of the first aspect, which is components of ICA, focused on the opportunities provided by the activities or tasks in the textbooks. Whether both teachers and students use these opportunities, is unfortunately beyond the scope of this study. According to Baker [9,17], to achieve ICC, the last (third) component should be achieved because this involves an awareness of culture beyond the large C elements. In other words, if a student is conversant with the last component, this helps them

Table 8. Samples of cultural sources representation.

Cultural Sources	Grade X	Grade XII
Home	Indonesian flag, Cut Nyak Dien, a practice of calling an elder by using "Mr." followed by first name (Mr. Mosleh), etc.	Baduy tribe in Indonesia, Basuki "Ahok" Tjahaja Purnama (former of Jakarta governor).
Target	The United States of America (USA) Oprah Winfrey, JK. Rowling, etc.	Seattle in the USA, Harold Pinter, Mr. Peterson ("Mr" followed by the last name)
International	South Korea football team, Mother Theresa, Issumboshi, etc.	African continent, Persian pottery, Ottoman empire.

Table 9. The frequency of cultural sources throughout the textbooks.

Cultural Sources	Grade X (%)	Grade XII (%)
Home	341	220
Target	131	91
International	131	46
TOTAL	603 (63%)	357 (37%)
FINAL TOTAL	960 (100%)	

to mediate between different cultures and to see culture as fluid, dynamic, and non-essentialist [9,17]. It would appear to be essential to increase exposure to the three components from the grade X textbook to the grade XII one, although, the findings show that the frequency of representations of the three components decreases from 62% to 38%. Moreover, ICA component number 1 dominates in both textbooks. Therefore, these findings - 1) the decrease in representations of the ICA components, and 2) the domination of the first component - serve to strengthen the finding that ICC does not seem to bet well-developed in the textbooks.

In terms of the cultural element, Baker [9,17] suggests that, in terms of developing the ICC, an understanding of culture should be developed by seeing it as flexible and non-essentialist, not the opposite. Byram's [4] five *savoirs* can be used to develop ICC and are concerned not only with large C but also with small c elements, especially the *Savoir S'engager (perspectives and practices)*. The findings show that both large C and small c representations decrease from textbook grade X to grade XII. Other than that, in the two textbooks studied, the greatest number of references was to *products* (475 & 327). This finding is in line with the study undertaken by Celik and Erbay in 2013 in the English as a Foreign Language (EFL) context, in which they conclude that ICC is not well-promoted in the textbooks since the element of *products* dominates throughout them. To be able to achieve ICC, knowledge of small c elements is needed because this might influence the attitude, behaviour, and skills of people engaging in intercultural communication [17]. In addition, the five *savoirs* proposed by Byram [4] implicitly need such knowledge for example, the Critical Cultural Awareness (CCA), which needs an understanding not only of cultural *products* but also of *practices* and *perspectives* [4,17,5]. The facts of the decrease representation of cultural element from textbook grade X to XII and *products* domination strengthen the findings that the textbooks do not thoroughly develop ICC in the students.

Regarding references to cultural sources (*Home (H), Target (T)*, and *International (I)* cultures), the findings show that, even though the representation of cultural sources decreased from textbook grade X (63%) to grade XII (37%), interestingly, most references were to the *H* culture (341 & 220). Byram's (1997) concept of ICC, particularly the CCA as a part of the five *savoirs* tenet, suggests that to embed the ICC, understanding of one's own culture is needed. This is supported by Baker [17,9], who argues that understanding one's own culture might help reflection on other cultures, which leads to an ease in mediating between one culture and another. In other words, they might develop Byram's five *savoirs* (1997), which include relevant ICC knowledge, attitudes, and behaviour.

Nevertheless, *T* and *I* are no less important than *H*. Gray [15] and Yuen [6] suggest that textbooks should represent elements of *H, T* and *I* cultures equally in light of the rapid growth of intercultural communication, and English being the main Lingua Franca (ELF). This implies that equally covering elements of *H, T, I* cultures in ELT textbooks might contribute more to the development of ICC. Unfortunately, elements of *H, T*, and *I* cultures are generally not only represented in an imbalanced way in each textbook but are also decreasingly portrayed throughout the books. This finding further strengthens the conclusion that ICC is not well-developed in the textbooks. Interestingly, the grade X textbook seems to be more committed than the grade XII textbook to promoting ICC, despite the grade XII one being designed for more senior students. However, even though the grade X textbook seems more concerned with ICC, both textbooks are presumably could not highly promote the ICC.

To conclude, the findings of this study did not meet my expectations and the three indicators of development of ICC (the ICA components, cultural elements, and cultural sources) decreased in the frequency of representations. The reduction in the frequency of references to the relevant elements may be a result of the time when the textbooks were revised; the latest revision of the grade X textbook is 2017, whereas the latest textbook for grade XII was revised two years previously, in 2015. This shows that the set of textbooks is not revised simultaneously.

7 CONCLUSIONS AND SUGGESTIONS

This study has provided an insight into the field of Intercultural Communicative Competence (ICC) development and promotion within two EFL textbooks. It has concluded that the textbooks do not promote and develop ICC well. This can be seen from the frequency of representations of three aspects of ICC, which decreased from the grade X textbook to the grade XII one. This finding might indicate the lack of ICC awareness of the stakeholders (the curriculum policy makers) and the textbook authors. Hence, I propose three points of suggestions. The first point is the need for consistency in ICC development. Thus, paying attention to the neglected content of ICC is needed. In terms of the second suggestion, it is the need to develop ICC awareness for the stakeholders (the curriculum policy maker) and authors, teachers, and students. Finally, making a long-term commitment to ICC is also recommended. However, this study is limited to the absent of teachers' and students' perspective. Hence, a further longitudinal study which includes their perspectives, the use of additional material, and the relevant assessment might be suggested.

REFERENCES

[1] Romanowski, P. (2017). Intercultural communicative competence in English language teaching in Polish state colleges. Cambridge: Cambridge Scholars Publishing.
[2] Hall, J.K. (2002). *Teaching and researching language and culture.* Great Britain: Pearson Education.
[3] Holliday, A. (1999). Small cultures. *Applied Linguistics, 20*(2). 237–264.
[4] Byram, M. (1997). *Teaching and assessing intercultural communicative competence.* Clevedon: Multilingual Matters.
[5] Kim and Paek (2015). An analysis of culture-related content in English textbooks. *Linguistic Research, 32.* 83–104.
[6] Yuen, K. (2011). The representation of foreign cultures in English textbooks. *ELT Journal, 65*(4), 458–466.
[7] Çelik, S. & Erbay, S. (2013). Cultural perspectives of Turkish ELT coursebooks: Do standardized teaching texts incorporate intercultural features? *Education and Science, 38*(167), 336–352.
[8] Byram, M., et. al. (1997). Teaching-and-learning language-and-Culture. Clevedon: Multilingual Matters No. 100.
[9] Baker, W. (2012). From cultural awareness to intercultural awareness: culture in ELT. *ELT Journal, 66*(1), 62–70.
[10] Scollon, R. & Scollon, S.W. (2001). *Intercultural communication* (2nd ed.). Oxford: Blackwell Publishing Ltd.
[11] Nunan, D. (1988). *Syllabus design.* Oxford: Oxford University Press.
[12] Brown, J.D. (1995). *The element of language curriculum.* Boston: Heinle & Heinle Publisher.
[13] Richards, J.C. (2001). *Curriculum development in language teaching.* Cambridge: Cambridge University Press.
[14] Nation, I.S.P. & Macalister, J. (2010). *Language curriculum design.* New York: Routledge.
[15] Gray
[16] Cortazzi, M., & Jin, L. (1999). Cultural mirrors. *Culture in second language teaching and learning,* 196–219. Cambridge, England: Cambridge University Press.
[17] Baker, W. (2011). Intercultural awareness: modelling an understanding of cultures in intercultural communication through English as a lingua franca. *Language and Intercultural Communication, 11*(3), 197–214.
[18] Textbook grade X: Kementrian Pendidikan dan Kebudayaan Republik Indonesia (*Indonesian Ministry of Education and Culture*). (2017). Bahasa Inggris. Jakarta: Jakarta: Pusat Kurikulum dan Perbukuan, Balitbang, Kemdikbud.
[19] Textbook grade XII: Kementrian Pendidikan dan Kebudayaan Republik Indonesia (*Indonesian Ministry of Education and Culture*). (2015). Bahasa Inggris. Jakarta: Jakarta: Pusat Kurikulum dan Perbukuan, Balitbang, Kemdikbud.

English Linguistics, Literature, and Language Teaching in a Changing Era – Madya et al. (eds)
© 2020 Taylor & Francis Group, London, ISBN 978-1-03-224160-9

The significance of teacher's talent in improving students' engagement in EFL classroom

Puspita Wijayati & E. Andriyanti
English Languange Education, State Univeristy of Yogyakarta, Yogyakarta, Indonesia

ABSTRACT: This study aims at describing and explaining teacher's talent as a significant factor to improve students' engagement in ELT Classroom. The data were taken through observation and interview at a Vocational High School (VHS) in Yogyakarta. The participants were 32 students at the eleventh grade of culinary study program and I as the English teacher. Data were analyzed by using the social-cognitive theoretical framework by Jones (2009) and the theory of student engagement by Fredricks, Blumenfeld & Paris (2004). The result of this study showed that the teacher's talent is significant to improve the students' engagement at this particular VHS. The students showed positive engagement after the teacher improved the teaching strategy and applied the teacher' talent. There were three characteristics of students' engagement that appeared during classroom observation: (1) good attendance and involvement, (2) interest, enjoyment, or sense of belonging to the instructional process, and (3) seeking more challenges.

Keywords: teacher's talent, students' engagement, instructional process

1 INTRODUCTION

Students' engagement has been among issues always researched in order to improve an instructional process. This is done to overcome the problem of poor engagement in the classroom that can end up with poor student achievement and behavior such as interest, time on task, and learning enjoyment if it is less [1]. Engagement is presumed to be malleable, responsive to contextual features, and amenable to environmental change [2] that can be seen by students who have passion, excitement, desire to learning, a sense of belonging and achievement, and also a connection with those who support learning [3].

Improving students' engagement can be challenging for some teachers as a classroom is always dynamic. Therefore, the role of teacher is very important because a teacher will shape and reshape the outcome of the students [4] and this is a big responsibility. The way a teacher teaches in the classroom will determine the successful of the students in the learning process and even after the process. In order to reach the specific goal in teaching, a teacher should not only facilitate the students but also make them understand the importance of a single subject, in this case, English as foreign language (EFL) for their future life. The characteristics of a good teacher are represented by the principles of an interactive teacher. The principles include roles as a controller, a director, a manager, a facilitator, and a resource [5]. Using a different perspective, [3] argues that teachers need to consider five aspects such as: (1) empowerment, (2) usefulness, (3) success, (4) interest, and (5) caring if she wants to succeed in conducting the instructional process. However, to be a good teacher is not easy and I experienced it. I often found many of my students looked bored, unmotivated, talked among themselves, laid their heads down on their table, and neglected me as a teacher. Those conditions showed students' low engagement in class, which could lead to low achievement and behavior. Those might happen due to my teaching performance. I realized that I taught the students with conventional methods such as explaining the theory for so long and asked the students to do the task afterwards. There were no fun and engaging activities. Applying new strategies in the classroom could be done in solving these problems. In this case, something should be done and one of the ways is by applying fun learning activities. The activities can be fun if the teacher has ability in delivering the materials. Previous study has shown that teachers' non-verbal behaviors can play a highly important and essential role on learners' motivation in language classroom [14]. In order to have that behavior, teacher should be aware in their own talent. Talent generally refers to developing domain-specific abilities [6]. In addition, one of talent approaches, the talent construct, is seen as being related to will, perseverance, motivation, interest, and passion [7] if teachers do not have the talent, applying those theories of teaching will only be wishful thinking.

This research is done to solve the problem, especially to improve students' engagement by improving the teacher's role and performance. Relevant to this case, talent is used in teaching to grab students' attention and focus. The use of the term teacher's talent is because it really represented the way teaching and learning happened in the classroom. Talent in applying the teaching technique, strategy, and or media is used for example, I told my students about how English could be beneficial for their future by showing them my experiences in reaching some success through English. In front of the classroom, I performed my skill (my talent) in becoming a Master Ceremony at international events that I think can bring me to a better life. Sometimes, I sang a song to attract their focus if they seemed lost. Most of the times, icebreaking was used as well. Students were amazed and their attention was totally grabbed. Learning English became fun and interesting. Moreover, they realized that English is very important that even can change their life. As a result, their performance in the classroom was improved because they made efforts and they became more engaged as they showed (1) good attendance and involvement, (2) interest, enjoyment, or sense of belonging to the instructional process, and (3) seeking more challenges after the class was finished.

2 RESEARCH METHOD

2.1 *Type of the research*

The design of this action research was based on the spiral model suggested by Kemmis and Mc Taggart (1988). A class action research was chosen because it gives more great value of extending teaching skill and obtain more understanding of teacher's self, classroom, and as well as the students [9]. I planned, acted, observed and reflected on the implementation of teacher's talent combined with some strategies, technique, and media to improve students' engagement. Before the action, a preliminary study was conducted by doing observation and interview with the help of two collaborators, who were another English teacher and a student-teacher from a state university practicing the same field. Those were done in order to prevent the bias of this research. That process was done in order to know the crucial problems needed to be solved soon.

2.2 *Setting of the research*

The research was carried out in a state vocational high school in Yogyakarta. The school has five programs, namely culinary, tourism agent, skin and hair beauty, fashion, and hospitality. Categorized as a good school, this school has an A accreditation and some facilities such as computer laboratory, free internet connection, practice room, library, and hall. The school applies a block system for English teaching. It means that the English lesson is conducted in the first two weeks of each month. There are two meetings of English lesson in one week. The students' origins vary. They come from various regions in Yogyakarta and from outside Yogyakarta.

2.3 Participants and subjects of the research

The research was conducted at class X-2. The study involved me as the English teacher and 32 students, consisting of 2 male students and 30 female students.

2.4 Instrument

This research included qualitative and quantitative data. In collecting qualitative data, observation and interview were used [9][10][11]. Three instruments of observation were designed: field notes, observation checklist, and students' engagement rubric. The purpose of using field note was to capture in brief description of what happened during the instructional process in the form of notes. The observation checklist was used to observe the teacher and students in the classroom using designed criteria. Next technique is interview, which was done by collaborators to get students' opinions, feelings, or perceptions towards the teaching and learning process that occurred. Meanwhile, quantitative data were gained through the students' engagement rubric adopted from [12] to score students' engagement. There were five aspects to observe students engagement such as posture, focus, responsibility, participation, and time completion. The students were observed and scored from 1 until 4. At the end of the cycle, the students' engagement would be categorized as disengaged (0–5), slightly engaged (6–10), fairly engaged (11–15), and fully engaged (16–20).

2.5 Data analysis

This research used five stages in analyzing the data, as suggested by [9]. First, assembling the data was done by rereading and reviewing the data from observation and interview in order to get the important points. Second, coding the data was doneto classify qualitative data and quantitative data. The qualitative data were obtained from observation and interview. The quantitative data were obtained from students' engagement score. The third stage was comparing the data, which was done to see any similarities or differences between observation and interview results. In addition, the data of students' engagement were also presented in the form of pie charts. The fourth stage is the description of the data after doing the third stage. Lastly, reporting the outcome was done to show the results of the study.

There are validity criteria by Anderson [9], and the triangulation by [9]in making sure that this research is valid. The validity criteria consist of (1) democratic validity, by including the collaborators in this study; (2) outcome validity, that was used to identify the outcome from the action as consideration for the next cycle in determining whether it was successful or not; (3) process validity, which was done by conducting this research from February to May 2018; (4) the catalytic validity, which was obtained by my knowing the participants' understanding at the end of the meetings; and lastly (5) dialogic validity, which was done through discussion and review. Collaborators give their suggestions and advices.

The triangulation was also conducted in the study, namely time triangulation and researcher triangulation. In the time triangulation, the data were gained during February to June 2018. Meanwhile, researcher triangulation was used by involving collaborators as observers in the research to avoid bias and give reliability in the observation.

3 RESULTS AND DISCUSSION

3.1 The problems in pre-observation

According to the observation checklist and interview transcript, the researcher found out two big problems related to the instructional process in this school. Those problems were: (1) students' low engagement in English learning; and (2) the teachers' monotonous and inappropriate teaching techniques. The description of the problems obtained through preliminary study could be seen below:

Table 1. Problems in pre-observation.

NO	Problems	Indicators
1.	The students' low engagement in English learning	- The students often did not answer or respond to the teacher's questions. - Most of the students did not do the homework and seemed bored. - The students did not pay attention to the teacher and were not engaged when dealing with activities in the classroom.
2.	The teachers' monotonous and inappropriate teaching techniques	- The teacher did not use various teaching techniques and interesting activities. - The teacher did not use various media. - The materials were not varied. - The teacher just explained about the language and gave written tasks.

3.2 *Teacher's talent in improving students' engagement*

Jones argues that if a teacher wants to be successful in teaching, s/he should consider five aspects. The first one is the design of empowerment [3]. Teachers should design the instructional process to empower students. Empowerment refers to the amount of perceived control that students have over their learning [3]. In the first cycle I conducted the teaching and learning process using media such as power point and puzzled-words game as the strategies to empower my students in learning. I also asked my students to do a short dance that turned out into fun and exciting part of my teaching.

In this case I used my talent in showing the students how to do the dance that can be the media as well to learn English vocabularies, for example, about parts of body. I used proper pronunciation and gestures in order to catch their attention. After that, I divided the students into some groups and they played a game in which they arranged words into a good sentence. I gave them a chance to feel that they had a control of their own learning process. Unfortunately, after applying this strategy, another problem occurred. Some shy students were not confident to express their ideas and show their efforts in front of their friends. Therefore, in cycle II, I made up my teaching strategies by facilitating those students who were not confident in the classroom by motivating them and choosing activities that included topics they could choose by themselves. [13] mentions that good teachers are those who support learners to be more confident and thoughtful. I also set up my class by asking my students to make their own rules when doing game-based instructions [13]. These strategies have been promoted by [9] who say, in order to empower students a teacher can provide rationales for rules and directions. As a result, these efforts were successful in increasing their activeness as they were excited to talk about something they loved and competed in something they had made up by themselves.

The second aspect is the design of usefulness. As a teacher, I had to ensure that students understood why a material was useful. In every topic, I tried so hard to make them understand and realize that a particular material would be very beneficial for them in the future. I did it either at the beginning of the class or at the end of the class. This strategy surprisingly had a strong impact because previously I neglected this part as a way to improve the students' engagement. After doing this, most of my students became more motivated in learning English. Those who were not, had in their mind that English is something related to their future career. It is proven by their statement in the interview session after the cycles.

The third aspect is the design of success. I considered this part as the most challenging because I had to make sure that my students would achieve success by doing the task or after learning. In cycle I, my students were bored with some situations, for example, when they faced materials they had understood or given before. In this case, I realized that I needed to make efforts to overcome this problem by providing my students with more challenging activities. Therefore, in cycle II I conducted a small project they should finish with their group.

This strategy was successful in gaining students' attention in learning autonomously. They would be proud if they could finish the challenge.

The next aspect is the design of interest. Jones says "instructors should think beyond creating interesting classroom activities to thinking about how they might incorporate aspects of instruction that foster in students a more enduring interest in the course content" [3]. In this aspect, I tried to look for some topics my students might like but never know before. I tried to brows on the Internet about something unique and most of the time I brought other cultures to the class so that the students learnt something new from my subject that might be memorized by them in the next time because the cultures might be new for them. This strategy was done in every meeting of my first and second cycle. This was one of the best ways to engage my students in learning English.

The last aspect is the design of caring. This part needs teacher's talent because it is almost impossible to love and care about something, in this case, the students, if people do not have passion and talent. Previously, I had done this way but I did it explicitly that my students were being quite spoiled. After knowing what I should have done, I improved the way I taught my students by being caring but firm and discipline. I never believed before that this simple strategy could have a big change to the way my students saw me as their teacher. They became more respectful.

Using my talent in applying some theories of teaching in my class was successful because students showed improvements in some aspects. They mention three types of engagement and their indicators [2].

First, students had shown their behavioral engagement. During my teaching, there were only two students who were absent to my class because of joining a competition. Some of my students obeyed the rules and showed good attitude in accordance with social norms. They respected me as their teacher.

The next indicator was related to the emotional engagement. In this case, I admit that not all my students were happy of my teaching style, but fortunately most of them were interested in the learning process especially when they had to do the task because it was so fun. The rest of my students who were not as happy as the others should have more serious attention and treatment because it was so hard to motivate them.

The last indicator was related to the cognitive engagement. This part mostly related to the concept of design of success in my previous point. Some of my students became more curious of some materials because it was much challenging for them. By this process, their cognitive engagement could be improved.

The number of students who were engaged was presented in the following pie chart using a rubric adapted from [12] that indicated fully engaged in the range of 16–20, fairly engaged in the range of 11–15, slightly engage in the range of 6–10, and disengaged in the range of 0–5.

The data were collected from the observation during meetings 1 and 2 in the first cycle. All collaborators scored the students' engagement in the rubrics during the process of teaching and learning. Based on the findings from the observation, this chart shows that 76% of students in the classroom were categorized as fairly engaged. They paid attention to the teacher's explanation and seemed interested in the materials during the class. However, they kept silent when the teacher asked questions. Some of them were shy and confused of what to say and what to do. Meanwhile, 21% of students were fully engaged to the teaching and learning process.

Their gesture and body language indicated that they gave their 100% attention to the teacher's explanation and the activities. Not only their body language but also their responsibility in doing the task was also great. They did the task on time, enthusiastically, and actively. Only 3% of the students were slightly engaged during the teaching and learning process. All of them did not give a good attention to the class and were sleepy most of the time. They put their body on the table and sometimes, they just talked among themselves. Even though this cycle showed a quite good result, it was needed to confirm and improve some aspects that did not work in cycle 1 that could cause students fairly and slightly engagement. It was hoped to have increased number of the fully students' engagement.

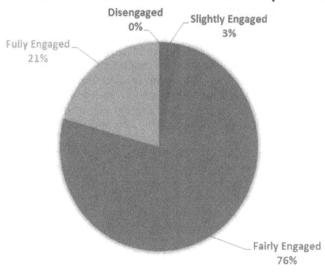

Figure 1. Students' engagement result cycle 1.

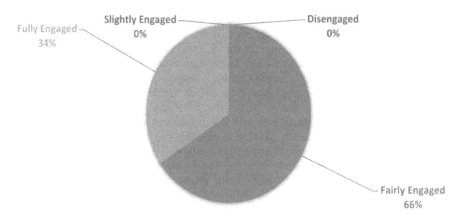

Figure 2. Students' engagement result cycle 2.

The chart showed the more number of students who were fully engaged. There were 34% of the students engaged in cycle 2. Compared to cycle 1, this number increases. It can be seen from students who paid more attention to the teacher's explanation and activities in the production phase. More students focused on the learning process compared to the previous cycle, which was only 21%. Not only paid attention to the teacher, they also actively involved in the teaching and learning process. However, there were still some students who did not fully focus on the teachers and the teaching and learning process. There were 66% students who were fairly engaged. This number was fewer compared to the previous cycle, which was a good indication as some of them had changed into the fully engaged ones. From the chart, it can be concluded that there were improvements on students' engagement in cycle 2 as there were no students who were slightly engaged and disengaged.

This study has found that the teacher's talent really could improve some aspects. The first was related to me as the teacher. I knew that everyone should have a talent in order to distribute the theory in the book to the practice. In my view this is one of the great ways to be a good teacher. The second was the way of teaching. Talent will definitely influence how the students will accept everything that comes from the teacher. If the teacher can explain the materials interestingly, no matter how hard and boring the material is, the students will be engaged of the subject. The third, the teacher's talent has an impact to my student's understanding on how English can be useful to their future life. This will turn out to the improvement of their engagement in the classroom. They become more enthusiastic and active in the classroom. It can be said that teacher's talent is a significant factor in improving students' engagement in EFL classroom. The talents applied in my case, I believe can also be applied to the other students other than culinary students. This is because based on what I experienced, students tend to choose learn English in the fun ways. In bringing the fun activities, teachers' talent is extremely needed. Without talent, teacher will only deliver the material but not in the fun ways.

4 CONCLUSION AND SUGGESTIONS

This study aims at describing and explaining teacher's talent as a significant factor to improve students' engagement in ELT Classroom. The result of this study showed that the teacher's talent in applying the theory of teaching is a significant factor in improving students' engagement. It is proven by students' behavior, emotions and cognitive aspects that show their enthusiast in learning English. The theory of Jones was used in teaching English to my class [3]. The talent I used for teaching were related to the way I spoke, the way I taught, the way I explained, and the way I motivated my students. All aspects were wrapped into a good performance with a good voice so that all objectives of materials could be given to the students efficiently. This study also provides some suggestions for further study in the same field. Further researchers may choose the same topic as this study with modified strategies that are especially dedicated to the students who were demotivated even though efforts had been made. The challenges for the next researchers are to approach those kinds of students with the same or other methods so that the students can all be facilitated.

REFERENCES

[1] L. Taylor and J. Parsons. (2011). Improving Student Engagement. *Current Issues in Education*, 14.
[2] J.A. Fredricks, P.C. Blumenfeld, P.C., and A.H. Paris. (2004). School engagement: potential of the concept, state of the evidence. *Review of Educational Research*, *74*, 59–109.
[3] B.D. Jones. (2009). Motivating Students to Engage in Learning: The MUSIC Model of Academic Motivation. *International Journal of Teaching and Learning in Higher Education*.
[4] Madya, S. (2013). *Metodologi Pengajaranbahasa: Dari Era Prametode Sampai Era Pascametode*. Yogyakarta: UNY Press.
[5] Brown, H.D. (2001). *Teaching by Principles: An Interactive Approach to Language Pedagogy (2nd Edition)*. New York: Pearson EducationInc.
[6] D.W. Chan. (2010). Talent Development from a Positive Psychology Perspective, *Educational Research Journal* 《教育研究學報, 25*.
[7] E. Gallardo-Gallardo, N. Dries, and T. Gonzalez-Cruz. (2013). What is the meaning of 'talent'in the-world of work?. *Human Resource Management Review, 23(4)*, 290–300.
[8] S. Kemmis and R. McTaggart. (1998). *The Action Research Planner (3rd Edition)*. Geelong: Deakin University.
[9] A. Burns. (2010). Doing action research in English language teaching: a guide for *practitioners*. New York: Routledge
[10] J.W. Creswell (2012). *Educational* research: planning, conducting, and evaluating quantitative and qualitative research (4th ed.) Boston: Pearson

[11] M.G. Lodico, D.T. Spaulding, and K.H. Voegtle. (2010). *Methods in Eduational Research: from Theory to Practice (2nd ed.)* San Fransisco: Jossey-Bass

[12] L. Parn. (2006). An in-depth study of student engagement. (Master's Thesis). Retrieved from https://digitalcommons.unl.edu/cgi/viewcontent.cgi?referer=https://www.goo-gle.com/&httpsredir=1&article=1023&context=mathmidsummative.

[13] Sotto, E. (2016). When teaching becomes learning: A theory and practice of teaching (2nd ed.). London: England Continuum Education.

[14] J.S. Negi. (2009). The Role of Teachers' non-verbal Communication in ELT Classroom. *Journal of NELTA, Vol. 1 4*, No. 1–2.

English Linguistics, Literature, and Language Teaching in a Changing Era – Madya et al. (eds)
© 2020 Taylor & Francis Group, London, ISBN 978-1-03-224160-9

English language learning needs of culinary students in vocational school

Richa A. Shara & Erna Andriyanti
Yogyakarta State University, Indonesia

ABSTRACT: The aim of this study is to identify the English language learning needs of students of culinary major at vocational high school. Learning English at vocational school is certainly different from high school with regard to the graduate competencies expected by their major. One popular major at vocational school is culinary, that provides many opportunities for graduates to work together with foreigners or is sent to work abroad. However, preliminary studies showed that the English language materials and activities obtained by culinary students were not much different from those learnt by public high school students. Therefore, knowing what students' needs is important. Questionnaires were distributed to 62 students of tenth grade (first year) culinary major to disclose the students' preferences in learning English. The result of the needs analysis showed that writing was the hardest skill for the culinary major students. They preferred to learn writing on topics suitable to their major. They also reported the activities that they prefer in learning writing. Finally, the results of this study are expected to open opportunities for materials developers to design learning materials in accordance with what is needed and desired by students, especially for culinary major.

Keywords: Culinary major, need analysis, vocational school

1 INTRODUCTION

Needs analysis is a crucial part of the process of making and developing syllabi and learning materials. Needs analysis is a procedure performed to gather information about what students need. It is usually done to find out what language skills the students need in a particular course and to identify what they have and have not known yet [1]. It emphasized the analysis of the awareness of the needs in the target situation [2]. However, needs analysis stage is often forgotten in the syllabus and material planning. Previous studies showed that needs analysis was often not formally carried out whether in a school program or university [3,4,5] so that the learning process did not really facilitate the students to achieve the graduate competence. Considering its usefulness, many researchers began to conduct needs analysis as a first step in designing programs, syllabi, or materials.

Needs analysis can be conducted for a variety of specific purposes, such as in vocational school majors as it can help the success of the implementation of a program [6]. The ESP program is prepared for learners with specific needs, such as students in vocational school. There are differences in English learning for students who have specific purposes to those who do not [7]. In fact, learning English in vocational school is certainly different from those in public senior high school regarding the graduate competencies expected by their major. The differences between majors and courses show that students' needs in learning are also different. Related to this, Owolabi [8] mentioned several objectives of ESP: i) to identify learners' specific needs; ii) to make learners learn the specific English required for their use in specific professions without compromising standard; iii) to learn the vocabulary peculiar to a specific profession and iv) to assist learners attain the needed level of confidence in the use of English that will enable them perform optimally in their respective professions.

Teachers have a role in organizing an effective learning process, in which they must be aware of what students need and want, as well as the ability and potential of students [9]. Students' need and what they will do after completing learning should be the basis for teaching [7]. The syllabus and course should be made specifically in relation to the needs of students on the courses so that learning becomes more ideal [4]. An observation in a vocational school in Yogyakarta, Indonesia, reveals important information about the culinary major, one of the popular departments. It has the vision to prepare graduates who have sufficient knowledge and skills in the areas of restaurant servicing, kitchen production, pastry and bakery, and entrepreneurs. In vocational school, the students get training, internships, and industrial practices that cannot be found in public schools. The culinary major intends to prepare intermediate skillful workers in serving food and beverages in restaurants and hotels, making food and beverage products, pastry and bakery products, as well as to produce graduates who are ready to work independently in the catering sector. Graduates of this department can continue their studies in universities according to their major. They can also explore many professions such as food stylists, caterers, personal chefs, nutrition experts, cruise ship staff, teachers or mentors in cooking classes, bakers, also pastry chefs. Culinary major provides many opportunities for the students to work together with foreigners or be sent to work abroad after graduating. They will likely be engaged in English texts related to food and cooking. Their professions have particular standards so that they need to learn more specific materials related to culinary to be able to perform optimally in the future.

Brief interviews with the English teachers disclosed that the curriculum used in learning English was no different from that of public high schools. The English language materials and activities obtained by the students were not much different from those in public high schools. This is very unfortunate especially because the culinary major has the possibility to apply more English. The materials the students deal with should have been connected to culinary. There were limited topics of culinary contained in the English books, which were most often used in the learning process. Teachers looked for additional materials on the Internet, but due to time constraints, the results were less optimal. To overcome this problem, research to develop the English curriculum and learning materials for culinary major is imperative to help teachers and students to get better and more appropriate learning support.

This paper deals with research and development and reports the first step of a need analysis in English learning. It was done to find out the extent to which students know what is best for them, and adjust the learning process with the graduates' expected competencies. Since a need analysis supports student-centred learning, it is important to include students' opinions in making decisions [10]. Therefore, knowing what students' needs, lacks, and wants is also important. For this reason, the aim of this study was to find the English language learning needs of the students of culinary major in vocational high school. The results of the needs analysis reported are a small part of a research and development project, which follows the procedure proposed by Masuhara in Tomlinson [11]: (1) needs analysis; (2) goals and objectives; (3) syllabus design; (4) methodology/materials; and (5) testing and evaluation.

2 RESEARCH METHOD

The participants were 62 tenth-grade students of culinary major in a vocational high school in Yogyakarta, Indonesia. The students were between the ages of 15 and 16. The data were gathered during the academic year of 2017-2018 when participants had studied for approximately one semester. A questionnaire was distributed to collect data concerning with the English learning needs of vocational students. The questionnaire was developed with reference to the culinary graduate competence.

There were 42 statements listed in the questionnaire. Statements number 1 to 5 related to students' lack of learning English. Statements number 6 to 9 were learning difficulties of culinary major students. Statements number 10 to 25 were preferred input materials of culinary major students in studying listening, reading, writing, and speaking. Statements number 26 to 42 were preferred learning activity of culinary major students in studying listening, reading, writing, and speaking. Before the questionnaire items were used, peer review was done by a number of English Education graduate students, and expert judgments were also carried out by two qualified lecturers in the English curriculum development fields.

The research data were obtained by asking the participants to choose the statements in the questionnaire that best represent their situation. They might choose more than one statement and since the questionnaire was open-ended so students could also write their own answers in the empty column available for each topic. The data derived from the questionnaire were summarized into percentages and analysed using a descriptive statistical method.

3 FINDINGS AND DISCUSSION

There were four major points that became the focus of the questionnaire distributed to students. First, the learning lacks of the culinary students. Second, the difficulties they encountered related to English learning. Third, the input materials that the students want to support the English learning process. The fourth was the activity that they prefer to be done in English learning. Broadly speaking, the points in the questionnaire were related to four main skills, namely listening, reading, writing, and speaking, as these are the main skills that the students learn in vocational school.

The main point of Table 1 is the lacks of culinary major students in learning English. Each statement relates to learning activities that are generally carried out in class. The results of the questionnaire showed that 72.58% of students still cannot arrange sentences in English correctly. The results of the questionnaire showed that the majority of students were still lacking in writing and speaking compared to other skills.

There are not many differences with the results in the previous table; students apparently still choose writing as the hardest skill. The activity such as writing ideas was the main problems often experienced by students. Relatively fewer students considered speaking and reading as the skill with problems that are often encountered. Meanwhile, students did not seem to find many difficulties in listening such as understanding a daily conversation. These results indicated that students found more difficulty in mastering productive skills rather than receptive skills, especially in writing.

In the next section, students mentioned the input materials which they wanted most. For listening skill, almost all students reported their preference to listen to a cooking tutorial in comparison with listening to news and information about culinary. For reading skills, 44 students wanted

Table 1. The learning lacks of culinary major students.

Statements	Frequency	Percentage
Arranging sentence in English correctly	45	72.58%
Pronouncing the English words correctly	32	51.62%
Using the English words in the sentence	27	43.55%
Confidently stating an opinion in English	24	38.71%
Understanding short conversation in English	3	4.84%
Other...	3	4.84%

Table 2. The learning difficulties of culinary major students.

Statements	Frequency	Percentage
Writing down ideas in English	36	58.06%
Understanding text in English	34	54.84%
Doing English daily conversation	17	27.42%
Understanding daily conversation in English	9	14.52%
Other...	4	6.45%

Table 3. The preferred input materials of culinary major students.

Statements		Frequency	Percentage
Listening	Cooking tutorial	46	74.19%
	Television cooking show, for example, cooking contest show	28	45.16%
	Conversation talking about culinary	18	29.03%
	Latest news about culinary	11	17.74%
	Other...	8	12.90%
Reading	Short functional texts such as ads, memos, menus, etc.	44	70.97%
	Review on culinary	31	50%
	Newspapers, recipes, and magazines	21	38.87%
	Descriptive text, recount text, procedure text, etc.	18	29.03%
	Other...	3	4.84%
Writing	Recipes, food, and beverage menu	40	64.52%
	General information about people, things, places, or events	32	51.62%
	Reviews about restaurants and food	24	38.71%
	Memo of customer' orders	16	25.81%
	Other...	1	1.61%
Speaking	Cooking tutorial	35	56.45%
	A conversation about culinary	23	37.10%
	Television cooking show, for example, cooking contest show	20	32.26%
	Latest news about culinary	17	27.42%
	Other...	7	11.29%

Table 4. The preferred learning activity of culinary major students.

Statements		Frequency	Percentage
Listening	Recognizing certain information in a monologue/dialogue	31	50%
	Recognizing the phrase	22	35.48%
	Answering questions verbally	18	29.03%
	Determining true or false statements	14	22.58%
	Answering questions in written form	12	19.35%
	Other...	3	4.84%
Reading	Understanding texts and translating them into Bahasa Indonesia	46	74.19%
	Answering questions based on the information in the texts	25	40.32%
	Reading aloud	13	20.97%
	Indicating true and false statements	12	19.35%
	Other...	3	4.84%
Writing	Completing a missing text	31	50%
	Writing a simple and short text	24	38.71%
	Recognizing errors in a sentence and correct them	18	29.03%
	Arranging jumbled sentences into a complete paragraph	15	24.19%
	Other...	7	11.29%
Speaking	Exchanging information	38	61.29%
	Role-play	26	41.93%
	Memorizing dialogue or monologue and practicing it in front of the class	17	27.42%
	Having a discussion about particular topic	16	25.81%
	Other...	2	3.22%

shorter texts such as memos, menus, and food review articles and 18 students still choose general input such as descriptive text, recount, or procedure. Not much different from the results of listening and reading skills, the input that the students wanted in writing is also related to recipes and food. Lastly, just like listening skill, students stated they liked materials about a cooking tutorial for speaking skill. To conclude, the input materials chosen by students are in accordance with the major they were taking. The students seemed to believe that the best input for learning English is something related to culinary. This is certainly very reasonable and shows that students were able to recognize what they really needed in learning. Providing the right input hopefully will be able to increase students' willingness to learn, especially with topics that suit their interests.

The following table shows the preferred English learning activities which were considered to help the learning process to become more effective and produce satisfactory outputs and outcomes. These results can be linked to the previous table which describes the preferred input materials in learning English. The learning activities were grouped based on their respective skills.

In listening activities, 31 students choose activities that involve recognizing certain information in a monologue or dialogue in the audio listening played. Whereas activities such as answering questions from audio apparently did not really attract the students. Furthermore, for reading activities, 46 students like something related to translating text into their first language. Apparently, there were still 74.19% of the students who considered this kind of activity very useful in understanding English. Other interesting activities were answering questions based on the information in the texts. Meanwhile, for the writing activity, students like semi-guided activities such as completing the jumbled text, followed by writing a short text. The last, 38 students like speaking activities with the aim to exchange information. 26 students also showed their interest in role-play activities. Overall, the results of the questionnaire showed the activities that were preferred by culinary students which might support the process of their English learning to be more interesting. Broadly speaking, students like a variety of activities and are not stuck in one type of activity. From the activities mentioned, the teacher can design how these activities will be carried out in class and relate them to input material that students like.

4 CONCLUSIONS AND SUGGESTIONS

Students are able to mention the difficulties experienced while learning English and recognize what is best for them whether it is related to topics or learning activities through needs analysis. Findings from the research showed that students prefer to learn English on topics according to their major which is culinary. The results also exposed the students' difficulty in mastering productive skills, especially in writing. The students were also able to identify their preferences in learning the four English major skills including the topics and activities that attract their interest. The information and data obtained might have an impact on curriculum development and English language learning in the future, especially for culinary majors in vocational high school.

Finally, the results of this study were expected to give opportunities for materials developers to design learning materials in accordance with what is needed and desired by students, especially for culinary major. This result is also beneficial to those who can help in improving and developing the English learning process of culinary major at vocational school. For the improvement in future research, the instruments in preliminary observation can be added in order to produce more complete data. The number of participants can also be added and classified according to gender or class level. Lastly, the extension of the topic on the questionnaire can also be supplemented by adding other factors besides the four main skills which would have an effect on the learning process.

REFERENCES

[1] Richards, J.C. (2001). *Curriculum Development in Language Teaching*. Cambridge University Press.
[2] Hutchinson, T., & Waters, A. (1987). *English for Specific Purposes*. Cambridge University Press.
[3] Chostelidou, D. (2010). A needs analysis approach to ESP syllabus design in Greek tertiary education: A descriptive account of students' needs. *Procedia Social and Behavioral Sciences, 2*, 4507–4512.
[4] Karimi, P., and Sanavi, R.V. (2014). Analyzing English language learning needs among students in aviation training program. *Procedia Social and Behavioral Sciences, 98*, 852–858.
[5] Aliakbari, M., & Boghayeri, M. (2014). A needs analysis approach to ESP design in Iranian context. *Procedia Social and Behavioral Sciences, 98*, 175–181.

[6] Rashidi, N., and Kehtarfard, R. (2014). A needs analysis approach to the evaluation of Iranian third-grade high school English textbook. *SAGE Open*, 1–9.

[7] Cunningsworth, A. (1983). Needs analysis – a review of the state of art. *System, 11*(2), 149–154.

[8] Owolabi, D. (2012). Attaining linguistic proficiency in the EFL/ESL adult classroom through English for specific purposes: The Nigeria example. *TESOL Journal, 6*, 109–122.

[9] Bada, E., and Okan, Z. (2000). Students' language learning preferences. *TESL Journal, 4* (3). Available at: http://www.writing.berkeley.edu/TESL-EJ/ej15/a1.html.

[10] Gozuyesil, E. (2013). An analysis of engineering students' English language needs. *Procedia Social and Behavioral Sciences, 116*, 4182–4186.

[11] Tomlinson, B. (1998). *Materials development in language teaching*. Cambridge University Press.

English Linguistics, Literature, and Language Teaching in a Changing Era – Madya et al. (eds)
© 2020 Taylor & Francis Group, London, ISBN 978-1-03-224160-9

Narrative story cards for ELT: A report on their development and effectiveness

Richard J. Stockton
English Department, Binus School Serpong, South Tangerang, Banten, Indonesia

ABSTRACT: This is a report on research and development of story cards for ELT based on Jungian archetypes, and testing demonstrating improvement in narrative writing versus text-book and PowerPoint taught groups. Improvement may be due to seven ways English language teaching metaphorical associative cards (ELTMAC) games can benefit English language learning: Jungian researchers finding improved language memory in tests with archetypal metaphorical associative cards is corroborated. The cards are scalable to learner level; the 59 cards can be named with the most frequent English words. Recent magnetic resonance imaging (MRI) studies support Jung's claim that archetypes are universal neural structures; ELTMAC therefore transcends intercultural boundaries and accesses language parts of the brain. The cards are based on fairytale, i.e. European folklore; as both English and fairytales originating in the Bronze Age Indo-European dispersal, the game imparts cultural competence via Whorfian synergy. Story helps us understand ourselves; hence ELTMAC develops L2 identity. Fairytale confronts the realities of life, allowing meaningfulness to reemerge in ELT classrooms where commercial or social-political forces are censoring it. And, narrative card games are adaptable to broad uses.

1 INTRODUCTION

Teaching English language, I became familiar with a number of narrative card games for ELT, but felt there was something wrong with many of them. These games tended to form streams of random events without any plot or meaning. So I began to develop my own set of story cards, based on fairytale. During these trials, I sometimes had an eerie sense that the game cards were bringing up thoughts and feelings from deep in the psyche. This led to a research and development question: would it be possible to design a narrative story card game for ELT based on the archetypes and journey? And an action research question: could an archetype and journey-based ELT card game significantly benefit English language learning?

1.1 *Archetypes*

Carl Jung is one of the most influential psychologists. Jung coined the terms "archetypes" and "collective unconscious" and laid down the founding work. Jung's archetypes resemble Plato's forms. Jung was also aware that Augustine used the term archetypes, and that alchem-ist and astrologer Paracelsus advanced the idea. His most important influence however, was Kant's categories of understand in which our ideas are "pre-configured" and "structured by modes of perception and thinking that are universal and collective" [1, p.68]. Of these archetypes, "like the instincts, the collective thought patterns of the human mind are innate and inherited" [2, p.75]; they are universal, "regardless of history, gender, race, geography, or time" [3, p.21]. Commonly discussed archetypes are: the self, persona, the shadow, anima and animus, the great mother, the wise old man, the trickster, fog, twins, the ouroboros, and the journey. Science has given some support to Jung's idea of inborn archetypal neural structures, locating them within the Default Mode Network (DMN). The DMN is involved in

257

daydreaming, nighttime dreaming, "autobiographical thinking" [4], and significantly here, in representing global meaning of passages. Using MRI with English, Mandarin, and Farsi speakers, Dehghani *et al.* "demonstrate that neuro-semantic encoding of narratives ... is systematic across both individuals and languages" [5, p.6098].

1.2 *Narrative*

Bruner distinguishes between facts on one hand, and "narrative" on the other, though some insist narrative thought informs even scientific paradigms [6]. Narrative is hence the sequenced telling of "motivations, goals, actions, events, and outcomes", and, narratives "structure our understanding of the world and of ourselves" [7, p.21].

That there is some sort of structure and sequence to narrative has been understood since ancient times. For Aristotle, a plot follows a rule of three, it has a beginning, middle and end [8, 1450b]. Georges Polti found 36 possible dramatic situations [9]. W.H. Auden's was convinced all genres contain the same six stages [10]. More recently, Booker has analyzed stories into seven basic plots [11].

In the early 20th Century folklorist Antti Aarne designed a catalogue of tale types, from myths and creation stories, to fables and fairytales, and even bawdy stories and jokes. His system was organized around motif. Motifs are specific actions of agents in a story, they are the smallest narrative units. The current final format, the Aarne-Thompson-Uther classification system (ATU), indexes over 40,000 motifs [12, p.20].

A very different approach however was taken by Soviet era folklorist Vladimir Propp. His *Morphology of the folktale* revolutionized his field [13]. Propp discovered functions, 31 of them. "All fairytales are of one type in regard to their structure" [14, p.23]. He was able to describe fairytales by the syntagmatic sequence of functions underlying the motifs. While Propp's work was suppressed by the Communists, many continue to develop the insight. Joseph Campbell's work shows all myth worldwide underlied by the same tri-part "monomyth" consisting of departure from the familiar world, trial and initiation, and finally return [15].

"The development ... of the postmodern critical approaches, particularly poststructuralism and cultural materialism, has brought about a marked devaluation of the theories of Eliade, Jung and Campbell" [16, p.12]. Claude Lévi-Strauss was impressed by Propp, Propp on the other hand took considerable slight as Lévi-Strauss reduced his functions into an atemporal table of binaries. What Lévi-Strauss's though shares with Propp is that the words of a story create another level of "supermeaning" or "metalanguage" [17, p.188]. Lévi-Strauss saw this level's meaning changing depending on cultural context, though for Propp, all stories have only one eternally fixed meaning. Paradigmatic post-structuralist like Barthes followed [18], and the school of narratology founded by Todorov [19]; interest in AI narrative intelligence in computing descends significantly from Propp.

1.3 *Fairytale*

"The term "fairy tale" resists a universally accepted ... definition" [20, p.322]. It sits closely associated with world folklore, myth, epic, saga, and legend. For J.R.R. Tolkien, fairytales are defined by their setting and stock characters [21]. Fascist and Traditionalist, Mircea Eliade, sees fairytales as the remnants of ancient religions [22]; this was roughly also Propp's view [23]. What differentiates fairytale from folklore is that fairytale is specifically European folklore. da Silva and Tehrani trace many fairytales to Proto-Indo-European Bronze Age origin; Jack and the beanstalk being among the oldest [24]. Etymologically, "fairytale" comes from the French *contes de fees*; coined by *Ancien Régime* countess Marie-Catherine d'Aulnoy. Salon fairytales drawing on "the supernatural powers of fairies, sorcerers, and other "pagan" figures obviously run counter to a Christian world view" [25, p.8]. This was "literary fairytale", a kind of disruptive social criticism; indeed, d'Aulnoy ended up in the Bastille, then exiled. From the early 19th Century, fairytales began to be collected by the likes of Charles Perrault and the brothers Grimm, produced for children, and progressives like Oscar Wilde took to the medium [26]. Another group also began to take an interest in fairytale too ... For the Nazis, European folktales were "considered to be holy or sacred Aryan relics" [27, p.141]. Spurning literary fairytale, to the Nazis, "the classical fairy tale ... offered compensation to ... people who felt bypassed by swift socioeconomic and techno-logical changes" [28, p.153].

1.4 *MAC*

Metaphorical associative cards (MAC) have been used in psychology for at least a century, Rorschach's ink blot test being the most well-known. Popova and Miloradova explain that, "the psychological mechanisms of the cards' action is connected with ... identification, meta-phor, association, ... archetypes, ... and some others" [29, p.208]. Another MAC deck, OH cards, was developed by artist Ely Raman; "OH cards grew out of his involvement with ... pop art, his study of psychology, and ... Tarot" [30]. Raman also created a fairytale based OH deck, *Saga*. The Asian Storytelling Network hosts a series of OH teacher training in ser-vices; and Richard Martin has written specifically on using OH cards in ELT [31].

1.5 *Storytelling in ELT*

Lucarevschi reviews the literature on the effectiveness of storytelling for ELT, finding it more effective across receptive and productive skills, grammar, vocabulary and pronunciation than traditional methods like textbook based lessons; the success is attributed to storytelling lessons being "fun, engaging, and highly memorable" [32, p.23], and "comprehensible input" [33, p.33]. Hsu's [34] and Atta-Alla [35] add improvement may stem from students writing their own fairytales and telling them, not only listening.

2   RESEARCH METHOD

2.1 *Research and development*

The game first inspiring me to start developing ELTMAC was a medieval fantasy set of 36 cards from an ELT workshop. One of the great things about that game is its curious and ambiguous drawings, one could see one card as a storehouse, or a secret code, or maybe a town map. Its failure however, is too many, mostly male, bad-guy characters, the result being insufficient literary devices to guide plot development. My ELTMAC style is based on analytical psychologist Lance Storm's suggestion that the cards could have, as in the ASI set, "artistic simplicity and accuracy, and students should find them pleasing to look at" (Personal Communication, 2018). As well as ambiguous cards, I include two which are purely abstract; and I aimed for gender balance in characters. While an ELTMAC deck ought to be arche-typal, it oughtn't to be sexist. Women have been an important part of fairytale since at least French salon, but fantasy genre games have tended to be male biased [36]. Hence, I considered Erich Neumann's iconic analysis of female archetypes in my choice of female characters for the deck [37].

Another narrative card game with some flaws is snakes and ladders with "place", "actions", and "character" distributed along the route, and ending with "they lived happily ever after" [38: p.71]. The game limits mood to happy endings; but the biggest problem is no plot structure. To support plot development, the ELTMAC deck has cards suggestive of sequence such as a key and a door, and suggesting elements of fiction, for instance dialogue bubbles or reversal.

A narrative game with a winning formula has learners throw dice to choose settings and characters from lists, and finally a plot from "looking for treasure", "having a toothache", or "cooking some soup"; the students then write the narrative in stages, "At the beginning", "after that", and "finally" [39, p.60]. I made a tiled game board for ELTMAC that scaffolds beginning, climax and resolution to aid the emergence of plot. Rules and game variations I adapted from *OH Cards quick start guide* [40].

ELTMAC cards need to represent the mythic archetypes. I used *Ring of the Nibelungs* (2004), *Snow White and the huntsman* (2012), and *Game of thrones* (2011-2017) to guide what cards to include. And, the needs of language learning have to be taken into account. I used basic level names for the cards, and then thesauruses to compile synonyms and superordinate and subordinate names. I profiled the list against a corpus linguistics database to ensure all cards would be namable with the most frequent English words [41]. In class, students in fact used a surprisingly rich pallet of vocabulary. "Knowing these topic-related words is a phenomenon" likely due to familiarity with the fairytale genre (Personal communication, Paul Nation, 2018).

While personally, Propp, Campbell, or Eliade's spiritual approach was the greater inspiration, the post-structuralist perspective, i.e., binaries, figures large too; ELTMAC contains opposites like day/night, male/female, fruit/flower, fire/water, dog/cat and the levels tree/forest, one/many, and commoner/noble.

2.2 *Testing*

My research design follows that suggested by psychoanalyst Milena Sotirova-Kohli, "Create two groups of English learners ... Then proceed with English teaching in both groups, use the cards only in one of the groups and after the course is over compare the results" (Personal communication, 2018).

The research was carried out at one of the largest private English institutes in Indonesia. All subjects were 8 to 11 years old young learners, with upper intermediate English, CEFR A2 by the institute's level placement test. I collected control group data from 16 classes totaling 117 students. These groups were taught a fairytale vocabulary and elements of fiction lesson with a textbook and supporting PowerPoint. The test group consisted of five classes totaling 28 learners and were taught to the same aims, but using ELTMAC decks to play a story creation game with oral retelling. These classes followed a lesson plan I developed that opened with discussion of what fairytales are and examples. The students were then introduced to basic elements of fiction and asked to divide a fairytale they were familiar with into beginning, middle and end. Next the learners formed small groups and the ELTMAC decks were distributed, the learners looked through the cards and asked vocabulary questions about them; frequently students intuitively grouped the cards into type, setting, characters, props and so on. The groups then used the cards and tiled game board to plan out their own fairytales. Lastly, I prompted the groups to retell their fairytale to me, and I questioned them about elements of fiction in their story. All classes were finally assessed with a fairytale writing task that starts with the prompt, "Once upon a time there was a young, brave princess ..." [42].

3 FINDINGS AND DISCUSSION

The writing was graded against a general writing rubric that includes "lexical command" and "communicative competence" [43]. The average writing task score for the 117 fairytales of the control group came to 84.42%. The average score for the 28 learners of the test group who played ELTMAC games instead was 89.57%, a difference of 5.15%. The p value for a two-tailed t test is 0.037. If the level of statistical significance is assumed to be 0.05, as commonly set in social science, the null hypothesis would be rejected and the results are statistically significant. Classes who played narrative story card games based on Jungian archetypes wrote significantly better fairytales as assessed against the writing rubric.

One simple explanation for the improved narrative writing of the group who had ELTMAC lessons is that young learners prefer playing games over textbooks and PowerPoint and hence the lesson content made a much greater impression. Deeper considerations suggest however the better fairytale writing may emerge from the seven following ways ELTMAC can benefit English language teaching.

Memory—Memory has long been a concern in language instruction [44, p.45].

Rosen, Smith, Huston & Gonzalez have demonstrated, with native speakers of English, improved memory recall using 40 flashcards based on the Archetypal Symbol Inventory (ASI) [45]. The ASI was designed against dictionaries of symbols, and the Archive for Research in Archetypal Symbolism. Bradshaw and Storm get similar results using a multicultural Australian group [46]. Brown and Hannigan replicate the test with bilingual English-Spanish speakers [47]. Sotirova-Kohli *et al.* find the results with a Swiss German group [48]. And Sotirova-Kohli, Rosen, Smith, Henderson, and Taki-Reece find an "8%" memory advantage using *Tensho* style Chinese characters [49, p.125], which evolved from ancient pictographs, therefore retaining archetypal imagery. The implication seems to be that archetype inspired flashcards have an affect on memory in inter-cultural, interlingual learning.

L2 identity—Some philosophers, Owen Flanagan for instance, go as far as seeing the emergence of self-consciousness in narrative capacity [50]. Storytelling helps language learners create their L2 identity. Fairytales in particular, Mitchell tells us, "are marvelous vehicles for gaining insights and learning about ourselves" [51, p.264].

Alexander Pushkov, who uses OH cards in his counseling practice, says that the games facilitate changes in character for his clients [52]. ELTMAC games and narrative production engage learners in developing their identities as English speakers.

Trans-cultural—The archetypes of the collective unconscious are the same "in any part of the world" [53, p.69]. The cards and stories speak to learners regardless of their socio-cultural situation.

Cultural competence—Language learners "need to recognize the language of codes and signs and to view their ... experience beyond the literal level" [54, p.3]. Using fairytale with language learners is "preparing them to read cultural codes and interpret mythical language from a context that is simple and easy to understand" [55, p.3]. While all cultures have folklore, the fairytale is specifically European. Fairytales promote English discourse via Whorfian synergy with the culture and values embedded in European fairytale language. Every culture/ civilization has a defining narrative; for the West, according to Oswald Spengler, that is Faust [56]. In ELT, Goh explains, "introducing ... fairy tales in the classroom will help introduce learners to Western society's style of thinking" [57, p.62].

Category and corpus linguistics—Aristotle's conception of categorization, with its 10 categories, dominated for more than two millennia [58]. Rosch problematized Aristotle's view of how cognition organizes, proposing categories don't have clear-cut criteria and boundaries [59]. Hence, in MAC decks, "there are no "correct" interpretations of the pictures", narratives develop out of "our own perceptions and interpretations" [60, p.1]. As well she says, categories have a "basic level", the most frequent English word, but also meaning on "superordinate" and "subordinate" word levels [61, p.7], making thoughtfully designed ELTMAC decks scalable to learner level.

Meaningfulness—In TESOL, where commercial interests, social-political forces, and political correctness have been altering content, censoring what might offend [62], fairytale, which often deals in the realities of life, can resupply the authenticity that has slipped away.

Broad use—Wright has published no less than 94 tasks for narrative story card games [63]; so English language teachers who would like to try developing their own ELTMAC decks, will hopefully have some guidance from the discoveries and suggestions laid out in this report, and many ideas for use in their classrooms.

4 CONCLUSIONS AND SUGGESTIONS

To the research and development question, the answer is that it is possible to develop a narrative story card game for ELT based on Jungian archetypes and journey. The ELTMAC deck is the result. To the action research question, the result is that ELTMAC games significantly improved learner's English narrative writing, while the games were no doubt fun to play, gains may be due to deeper ways archetypal story cards can benefit English language learning. Going into the future, Semetsky and Delpech-Ramey (2012) implore educators to further "explore the role of the unconscious in learning" [64, p.69]. Unfortunately, very few publications on analytical psychology are appearing in the field of TESOL, hopefully this research might inspire others to bring Jung and archetypes into ELT.

REFERENCES

[1] Gill, G.R. (2003). Northrop Frye and the phenomenology of myth [Doctoral thesis]. McMaster University, Hamilton, Canada,
[2] Jung, C.G. (1964/1988). (Ed.) *Man and his symbols.* New York, Doubleday,
[3] Mills, J. (2013). Jung's metaphysics. *International Journal of Jungian Studies*, 5(1), 19–43.
[4] Buckner, R.L., Andrews-Hanna, J.R. & Schacter, D.L. (2008). The brain's default network: Anatomy, function, and relevance to disease. *Annals of the New York Academy of Sciences*, 1124, 1–38,
[5] Dehghani, M., Boghrati, R., Man, K., Hoover, J., Gimbel, S. I., Vaswani, A. & Kaplan, J.T. (2017). Decoding the neural representation of story meanings across languages. *Human Brain Mapping*, 38(12), 6096–6106.
[6] Bruner, J. (1986/2009). *Actual minds, possible worlds.* USA: Harvard University Press,
[7] Lakoff, G. & Narayanan, S. (2010). Toward a computational model of narrative. In AAAI Fall Symposium: Computational Models of Narrative. USA: AAAI Press, pp. 21–28, 2010.
[8] Aristotle. (2000). Poetics (S.H. Butcher, Trans.). USA: A Penn State Electronic Classics Series Publication, 4th Century.
[9] Polti, G. (1895/1924). The thirty-six dramatic situations (L. Ray, Trans.). Franklin, Ohio: James Knapp Reeve.
[10] Auden, W.H. (1968). The quest hero. In N.D. Isaacs & R.A. Zimbardo (Eds.), Tolkien and the critics: J.R.R. Tolkien's The lord of the rings. London: University of Notre Dame Press, pp. 40–61.
[11] Booker, C. 2004. *The seven basic plots: Why we tell stories.* London: A&C Black,
[12] Uther, H.J. (2009). Classifying tales: Remarks to indexes and systems of ordering. Folks Art-Croatian *Journal of Ethnology and Folklore Research*, 46(1), 15–32.
[13] Propp, V. (1928/1968). Morphology of the folktale (L. Scott, Trans.). New York: University of Texas Press.
[14] Propp, V. (1946/2000). Историческиекорниволшебнойсказки [Historical roots of the wonder tale]. Moscow: Хгбиринт.
[15] J. Campbell. (1949/2004). The hero with a thousand faces. USA: Princeton University Press.
[16] Gill, G.R. (2003). Northrop Frye and the phenomenology of myth [Doctoral thesis]. Canada: McMaster University.
[17] Lévi-Strauss, C. (1984). Structure and form: Reflections on a work by Vladimir Propp. *Structural Anthropology, 2*, 115–145,
[18] Barthes, R. (1975). An introduction to the structural analysis of narrative (L. Duisit, Trans.). *New Literary History*, 6(2), 237–272.
[19] Todorov, T. (1971). The 2 principles of narrative. *Diacritics 1*(1), 37–44,
[20] Haase, D. 2008 (Ed.). The Greenwood encyclopedia of folktales and fairy tales (Vol. 1). Westport, CT: Greenwood Press,
[21] Tolkien, J.R.R. (1947). On fairy-stories. Oxford: Oxford University Press.
[22] Eliade, M. (1963). Myth and reality (W.R. Trask, Trans). New York: Harper & Row Publishers.
[23] Propp, V. (1946/2000). Историческиекорниволшебнойсказки [Historical roots of the wonder tale]. Moscow: Хгбиринт.
[24] da Silva, S.G. & Tehrani, J.J. (2016). Comparative phylogenetic analyses uncover the ancient roots of Indo-European folktales. *Royal Society Open Science*, 3(1), 1–11.
[25] Seifert, L.C. & Stanton, D.C. (2010). Enchanted eloquence: Fairy tales by Seventeenth-Century French women writers. Toronto: Iter Inc. Centre for Reformation and Renaissance Studies.
[26] Zipes, J. (1995). Breaking the Disney spell. In E. Bell, L. Haas & L. Sells (Eds.) From mouse to mermaid: The politics of film, gender, and culture. USA: Indiana University Press, 21–42.
[27] Zipes, J. (2012). Fairy tales and the art of subversion: The classical genre for children and the process of civilization, 2nd Ed. New York: Routledge.
[28] Zipes, J. (2012). Fairy tales and the art of subversion: The classical genre for children and the process of civilization, 2nd Ed. New York: Routledge.
[29] Popova, G. & Miloradova, N. (2014). Psychological mechanisms of the use of metaphoric associative cards in individual counseling. *Psychology and Pedagogics*, 42(5), 207–217
[30] Moore, J. 1999. OH cards: The game of inner vision. Positive Health, 45.
[31] Martin, R. Tell a tale, n.d. Retrieved from http://www.tellatale.eu
[32] Lucarevschi, C.R. (2016). The role of storytelling in language learning: A literature review. Working Papers of the Linguistics Circle of the University of Victoria, 26(1), pp. 23–44.

[33] Lucarevschi, C.R. (2016). The role of storytelling in language learning: A literature review. *Working Papers of the Linguistics Circle of the University of Victoria, 26*(1), 23–44.

[34] Hsu, Y. (2010). The influence of English storytelling on the oral language complexity of EFL primary students [Master's thesis]. National Yunlin University of Science & Technology, Yunlin, Taiwan.

[35] Atta-Alla, M.N. (2012). Integrating language skills through storytelling. *English Language Teaching, 5*(12), 1–13.

[36] Miller, S.R. (2013). Gender bias in American video gaming. Em-Journal. Retrieved from http://em-journal.com/2013/10/gender-bias-in-american-video-gaming.html.

[37] Neumann, E. (1955/1972). The great mother: An analysis of the archetype (R. Manheim, Trans). USA: Princeton University Press.

[38] High Flyers, Book J. (2016). English First. Switzerland: Sigmund International S.à.r.l Luxembourg.

[39] Trailblazers, Book 7. (2016). English First. Switzerland: Sigmund International S.à.r.l Luxembourg.

[40] OH cards quick start guide. Germany: OH Verlag, 2003.

[41] T. Cobb. Compleat Web VPv.2 [Computer program]. (2018). Retrieved from https://www.lextutor.ca /vp/comp/.

[42] Writing task. High Flyers, Book J. (2016). English First. Switzerland: Sigmund International S.à.r.l Luxembourg.

[43] Writing rubric. High Flyers, Book J. (2016). English First. Switzerland: Sigmund International S.à.r.l Luxembourg.

[44] Kelly, L.G. (1969). 25 centuries of language teaching: An inquiry into the science, art, and development of language teaching methodology 500 BC – 1969. USA: Newbury House Publishers.

[45] D.H. Rosen, S.M. Smith, H.L. Huston and G. Gonzalez. (1991). Empirical study of associations between symbols and their meanings: Evidence of collective unconscious (archetypal) memory. *Journal of analytical psychology, 36*(2), pp. 211–228.

[46] S. Bradshaw and L. Storm. (2013). Archetypes, symbols and the apprehension of meaning. *International Journal of Jungian Studies, 5*(2), 154–176.

[47] Brown, J.M. & Hannigan, T.P. (2006). An empirical test of Carl Jung's collective unconscious (archetypal) memory. *Journal of Border Educational Research, 5*, 114–120.

[48] Sotirova-Kohli, M., Opwis, K., Roesler, C., Smith, S.M., Rosen, D.H., Vaid, J. & Djonov, V. (2013). Symbol/meaning paired-associate recall: An "archetypal memory" advantage? *Behavioral Sciences, 3*(4), 541–561.

[49] Sotirova-Kohli, M., Rosen, D.H., Smith, S.M., Henderson, P. & Taki-Reece, S. (2011). Empirical study of Kanji as archetypal images: Understanding the collective unconscious as part of the Japanese language. *Journal of Analytical Psychology, 56*(1), 109–132.

[50] Flanagan, O.J. (1992). Consciousness reconsidered. USA: MIT Press.

[51] Mitchell, M.B. (2010). Learning about ourselves through fairy tales: Their psychological value. *Psychological Perspectives, 53*(3), 264–279.

[52] Pushkov. 2011. Presentation of associative-metaphorical cards (OH cards).Morning Cocktail (live broadcast) [Video file], Retrieved from https://www.youtube.com/watch?v=gav5zC2tOMU.

[53] Jung, C.G. (1964/1988). (Ed.) *Man and his symbols.* New York: Doubleday.

[54] Goh, L. (1986). Using myth, folktales and fairy tales in the adult ESL classroom [Master's thesis]. Vancouver, Canada: Simon Fraser University,

[55] Goh, L. (1986). Using myth, folktales and fairy tales in the adult ESL classroom [Master's thesis]. Vancouver, Canada: Simon Fraser University,

[56] Spengler, O. (1937). Decline of the West, (C.F. Atkinson, Trans.). New York: Alfred A. Knopf.

[57] Goh, L. (1986). Using myth, folktales and fairy tales in the adult ESL classroom [Master's thesis]. Vancouver, Canada: Simon Fraser University,

[58] Aristotle. (2002). *Categories* (E.M. Edghill, Trans.). Blackmask Online.

[59] Rosch, E. (1978/1998). Principles of categorization. Cognition and categorization. In G. Mather, F. Verstraten & F. Anstis (Eds), The motion after effect. USA: The MIT Press, 251–270.

[60] OH cards quick start guide. Germany: OH Verlag, 2003.

[61] Rosch, E. (1978/1998). Principles of categorization. Cognition and categorization. In G. Mather, F. Verstraten & F. Anstis (Eds), The motion after effect. USA: The MIT Press, 251–270.

[62] Smith, D. (2003). Uncovering the spiritual dimension of language teaching [Conference presentation]. TESOL, Baltimore, USA.

[63] Wright, A. (1995). Story telling with children. UK: Oxford University Press.

[64] Semetsky, I. & Delpech-Ramey, J.A. (2012). Jung's psychology and Deleuze's philosophy: The unconscious in learning. *Educational Philosophy and Theory, 44*(1), 69–81.

English Linguistics, Literature, and Language Teaching in a Changing Era – Madya et al. (eds)
© 2020 Taylor & Francis Group, London, ISBN 978-1-03-224160-9

EFL adult learners' perceptions of language anxiety toward speaking performance

Rini Ardiani & Bambang W. Pratolo
English Education, Universitas Ahmad Dahlan, Yogyakarta, Indonesia

ABSTRACT: A considerable number of foreign as well as second language learners suffer from language anxiety when they step into the language classroom. This research drew on a small study which was carried out at a private university in Yogyakarta to understand the factors that affect English as a Foreign Language (EFL) adult learners' language anxiety toward speaking performances. The purpose of this study is to report findings from the qualitative interview data on the factors of EFL adult learners' language anxiety toward speaking performance. The participants were six postgraduate students who were chosen randomly. The data were collected through semi-structured interviews guided by an interview protocol. The demographic data were analyzed descriptively while the interview data were transcribed and analyzed line by line to generate and develop codes and themes. An analysis of the interview data revealed five major themes, including (1) linguistic difficulties, (2) cognitive challenges, and (3) lack of practice in speaking English. Some ways to deal with language anxiety are also explained and suggestions for future study are provided.

Keywords: Perceptions, language anxiety, speaking performance

1 INTRODUCTION

English as a Foreign Language (EFL) has been challenging for Indonesian students. The positive thing is that learners are motivated to learn English because it is the official language of many international and professional organizations. But, unfortunately, it is not easy for Indonesian students to learn English because they have some challenges in learning it, including anxiety. Horwitz, Horwitz and Cope [1] defined anxiety as 'the subjective feeling of tension, apprehension, nervousness, and worry associated with an arousal of the autonomic nervous system' (p. 125). They discussed foreign language anxiety as 'a distinct complex of self-perception, beliefs, feelings, and behaviors related to classroom language learning arising from the uniqueness of the language learning process' (p. 128). This means that language anxiety is an awkward feeling and psychological pressure that learners experience when learning a language or accomplishing a task [2]. Even students at a higher level of education may have anxiety around foreign language learning.

Factors that could contribute to speaking anxiety are linguistic difficulties, cognitive challenges, a lack of information in the first language, competitiveness, and the role of teachers. The study conducted by Kayaoğlu and Sağlamel [3] among Turkish students stated that students' language anxiety is caused by linguistic difficulties including: vocabulary, pronunciation, grammar and sentence structure; cognitive challenges including fear of failure (failing to communicate, failing in exams, making mistakes, and failing in front of others); lack of information in the first language; competitiveness; the teacher's role, which leads students to have a high level of anxiety and low confidence in their language performance. Motivation can be another reason for being anxious. Tanveer's study showed that anxiety can be caused by intrinsic motivation. Accordingly, students' beliefs, opinions and lack of language instruction can lead to a higher level of anxiety. Other factors such as the social and cultural environments can also be reasons for anxiety-provoking situations [3]. Students' anxiety might also be related to gender: a survey of previous studies showed that gender influences the level of foreign language anxiety among learners [4,5,6,7,8,9].

With regard to the effects of anxiety, students might face some challenges or difficulties in expressing themselves in the language with effects that may be academic, cognitive, social or personal [9]. These kinds of effects may produce negative feelings in learners when they come to communicate in the target language and can affect their performance, especially when speaking. In one study, Aydin [10] stated that there are some negative correlations between achievement and anxiety. Firstly, EFL students may suffer from language anxiety provoked by factors including: not being prepared for classroom activity; being apprehensive about communicating with teachers, peers, and native speakers; teachers' questions and corrections in the classroom environment; assessments and negative attitudes towards English courses. Secondly, language anxiety is caused by the feeling of being afraid of being evaluated by others. This consists of fear of negative judgments by others, of making an unfavorable impression on others, of making verbal or spelling mistakes, and of displeasing others. Being afraid of negative evaluation is a general factor of foreign language anxiety. This negative evaluation leads to the fear of being called on in class; assessment anxiety; communication apprehension with peers, native speakers, and teachers; fear of making mistakes while speaking; negative attitudes towards language learning, and feeling anxious when teachers ask questions and make corrections of their performance.

Language anxiety can affect students' speaking performance in many ways. A study conducted by Kayaoğlu and Sağlamel [3] among Turkish students stated that students are visibly different when they are anxious. They believe that some differences occur when they feel anxious, and these effects can be physical, psychological, cognitive, linguistic, and behavioral.

A number of previous studies have investigated language anxiety for EFL students at university level [3,10,11,12,13,14,15,16]. This study is an attempt to explore how language anxiety affects EFL adult learners' speaking performance. It aims to answer the research question on the perceptions of EFL adult learners about language anxiety regarding speaking performance. This research question then leads to two supplementary questions: How does language anxiety affect EFL adult learners' speaking performance? How do EFL adult learners deal with language anxiety?

2 RESEARCH METHOD

Our investigation used a qualitative approach because it involved a small-scale study and looked at EFL adult learners' perceptions and interpretations of the factors in language anxiety regarding speaking performance. This was useful and practical because it allowed the researcher to conduct an in-depth analysis of the data [15]. The study was conducted at an Indonesian private university in Yogyakarta with six EFL students who were in the first year of a postgraduate program in English education. A purposeful sampling with a convenient case strategy was used, following what Creswell [17] described as 'the concept of purposeful sampling used in qualitative research. This means that the inquirer selects individuals and sites for the study because they can purposefully inform an understanding of the research problems...' (p. 125) and 'convenience cases, which represent sites or individuals from which researchers can access and easily collect data' (p. 126).

A semi-structured interview was used to collect the data and was carried out in April 2018. The process of collecting the data involved recruiting the participants first, then conducting the research by doing an interview which lasted between 10 and 15 minutes. The interview was recorded with the researcher's mobile phone. The demographic data were then analyzed descriptively in the form of data transcription of the information given by the participants. The interview data were transcribed and analyzed line by line to identify the categories among the data. In order to guarantee the trustworthiness (Lincoln & Guba, 1985, cited in [18]) of this study and to verify the accuracy of the data, findings, and interpretations [19], the

Table 1. Participants' background information.

No.	Name	Gender	Age	Major	Current Status
1	Lisa	Female	24	English Education	First-year study
2	Feby	Female	24	English Education	First-year study
3	Tania	Female	25	English Education	First-year study
4	Akbar	Male	24	English Education	First-year study
5	Fendi	Male	25	English Education	First-year study
6	Indra	Male	26	English Education	First-year study

researcher then returned the interview data transcriptions to each participant to ensure that the data remained valid and had not been manipulated.

3 FINDINGS AND DISCUSSION

This study was intended to report on some of the factors of English language anxiety regarding speaking performance as experienced by EFL adult learners at a private university in Yogyakarta, Indonesia. The analysis and discussions were organized according to the participants' accounts, feelings, and thoughts regarding the factors of English language anxiety that they experienced. An analysis of the interview data revealed three main categories that related to EFL adult learners' perceptions: (1) linguistic difficulties, (2) cognitive challenges, (3) lack of practice in speaking English.

It cannot be denied that many EFL students experienced difficulties using the English language, especially when speaking. The finding has also shown, in terms of the first supplementary research question, that there are some obstacles faced by EFL adult learners, especially when speaking English in public. At the start of language learning, a learner will face some difficulties with the language learning process, understanding grammar and other language aspects. If that student becomes anxious about this, then they become uncomfortable in making errors, resulting in anxiety. Thus, the first factor, and possibly the most significant aspect for EFL adult learners, is linguistic difficulties due to speaking anxiety. Although the learners are in higher level education, the study shows that they still face difficulties in speaking English, especially anxiety. Of the linguistic difficulties, vocabulary and pronunciation were reported to have the strongest effect on students' speaking performance. Most of the participants stated that it was vocabulary and mispronunciation of words (P1, P2, P3, P4 and P6) that made it challenging for them to speak in front of others because they didn't have enough vocabulary to speak fluently. Grammar (P1, P2, P3 and P4) was also reported as a linguistic difficulty due to language anxiety around speaking performance [3].

From the interviews carried out during the study, linguistic difficulties appeared to be one of the factors in the language anxiety which influenced students' speaking performance. Participants stated that they felt anxious about English due to a variety of problems. Five of the participants admitted that difficulties in pronunciation, lack of vocabulary and grammatical knowledge were the main factors that led them to feel anxious or hesitant in speaking English. Comments they made included:

'In English, I felt difficulty in translating because I do not know the vocabulary and the grammar for speaking; I think it is hard for me' [P1/Lisa]

Table 2. Themes of factors in EFL adult learners' speaking anxiety.

No.	Theme	Participants (N = 6)
1	Linguistic difficulties	5
2	Cognitive challenges	5
3	Lack of practice in speaking English	3

'Yeah, of course, it is about pronunciation, grammar and also vocabularies' [P2/Feby]

'... First, less of vocabulary, then lack of pronunciation, yeah, I think those are the basis of factors that make me feel anxious, lack of vocabulary and afraid of mispronouncing and nervous to confront the audience' [P3/Tania]

'Of course, it is about the misspelling, grammatical errors, and lack of vocabulary' [P4/Akbar]

'Lack of vocabulary mastery and mispronounce, and also lack of practicing speaking English' [P6/Indra]

The data above indicates that the participants were challenged in speaking English due to a lack of vocabulary and grammar. Some of them stated that they could not speak English because they did not know how to spell the words and use the vocabulary appropriately. They said they required more time to think about the vocabulary and grammar, which made it hard for them to speak freely in front of others. This finding supports Pratolo's [20] study which identified that lack of vocabulary could cause a language learner to feel anxious. One of his student participants confessed that she would get stuck, and that if she forgot an English word while speaking in English with an English native speaker then she wouldn't be able to think of anything. Pratolo's research participant, who was also an EFL adult learner, believed that to be able to communicate well with people, she had to know every single word that she spoke and heard. Failure in this endeavor would inevitably lead to language anxiety.

Participants also reported that cognitive challenges such as being scared of negative responses from others and a lack of confidence would disturb their speaking performance. They cited fear of negative responses from others, including being disparaged by friends (P1) and being interrupted by the lecturer (P3), as crucial factors that make students feel anxious when speaking or presenting in front of the class [3]. Cognitive challenges were reported as the next factor that influences students' speaking performance and were split into four categories: speaking unsuccessfully in front of the audience; failure in delivering a message; worry about making mistakes; lack of confidence. Three of these – speaking unsuccessfully in front of the audience, failure in delivering a message, and worry about making mistakes in front of the audience – can be grouped as 'being frightened of negative responses from others'. The participants in this study reported fear of negative responses from others as making them feel anxious when speaking in front of others. Five of the participants reported that they had felt anxious or afraid when they tried to communicate or perform in front of the class, especially in front of their friends and the lecturer. Two students shared their perspectives about being frightened of negative responses from others, commenting:

'I think because my English is not good, they became more attentive to me, and sometimes I feel that my friends underestimated me, and I also worry that my lecturer will interrupt me when I am speaking. This will make me nervous' [P1/Lisa]

'Yeah, of course, especially when I talk or speak to a person who is smarter than me. And I love it more to speak English directly to native speakers because they appreciate us more than Indonesian people' [P1/Lisa]

'Sometimes I am afraid to speak in front of the class, I am afraid for making mistakes in my words or mispronounce some pronunciation, and it might be interrupted by the lecturer or friends' [P3/Tania]

'... Because I am so nervous. And I am afraid that the audience (friends and lecturer) will not understand what I am presenting about' [P6/Indra]

Consequently, fearing negative responses from others was one of the things that made students worried or hesitant to speak English. Being disparaged was a crucial reason why they were nervous about speaking English. In addition, they sometimes thought that their friends were smarter than them. This kind of feeling makes participants afraid of being disparaged by their friends or the lecturer when they make mistakes in speaking in front of the class. It also showed that the students were scared to use their English because they were afraid of making mistakes and that they would be interrupted by the lecturer.

Lack of confidence due to the informal or formal situation can be another factor leading to cognitive challenges. Three *students shared their perspectives:*

'I am still afraid to speak to my friends and lecturers, feel doubt, and lack of confidence ...' [P1/Lisa]

'For the informal situation such as speaking English with my friend for just making some jokes I do not feel anxious at all but for the formal situation such as for doing a presentation in front of lecturer I feel a little bit anxious, even sometimes I feel nervous' [P4/Akbar]

'So, I felt anxious when I want to speak English because I am not confident with my vocabulary use' [P6/Indra]

The data above showed that participants are willing to speak according to the situation. However, most of the participants are not confident about speaking in front of others, especially in formal situations and for academic purposes, such as presenting something. They even felt anxious about speaking in front of an audience. Some of the students also believed that language is for communication (P6). Failing to communicate can lead to a substantial decrease in motivation [13]. The findings revealed that even students at a higher level could be less motivated when they felt anxious. Several factors are predicted as sources of foreign language anxiety, such as age, academic accomplishment, a previous high school experience with foreign languages, and students' current language course [16]. It was found that older students had higher language anxiety than younger ones. Some changes become obvious when learners get anxious. As the result of cognitive challenges, students were afraid to speak, nervous, and they felt anxious. Language anxiety can affect students in many ways and have various effects, such as physical and psychological, cognitive, linguistic, and behavioral [3].

Another factor influencing English language anxiety within the EFL adult learners' speaking performance as reported by the participants in this study was 'lack of practice in speaking English', especially for practicing English speaking performance [16]. The findings revealed that some students have a reduced speaking performance not only because of linguistic difficulties and cognitive challenges but also because of the lack of practice in speaking English. Not having a partner to speak with or being in a particular learning environment may also lead to this problem [3]. Within this categorization, some students reported that they felt anxious to speak due to less practice in speaking English. Three students shared their perspectives:

'It was rare because at that time the class was so boring, make me feel bored, and the learning process was monotonous' [P1/Lisa]

'It was rare because I have limited partners to speak English' [P5/Fendi]

'Less practicing and lack of support from my friends' [P5/Fendi]

'It is rare. I think the teachers were boring and my friends, they are passive in English and only one or two students are active in class' [P6/Indra]

'Lack of vocabulary mastery and mispronounce, and also lack of practicing speaking English' [P6/Indra]

Based on the experiences shared by the participants above, a number of facts are revealed. It was found that the participants felt anxious due to lack of practice in speaking English because they don't have much experience in speaking English. They shared that they rarely speak English because they have no chance to speak it. They stated that the learning environment made it hard for them to practice English. They felt that the learning environment was boring and the teachers and students (and/or friends) were not especially active in speaking English.

We have already mentioned that language anxiety could be affected by gender [4,5,6,7,8]. In fact, this concept is confusing. While there are many studies that still consider the effect of gender on language anxiety within speaking performance debatable, this present study has revealed one fact: based on the interview and the information gained from the participants, we conclude that there were no significant differences of language anxiety between male and female students. Both sexes have the same feeling of language anxiety toward speaking performance.

All of the students noted that they felt anxious when they speak publicly. They stated that there are many factors that impact their performance. To answer the second supplementary research question, many ways have been offered to deal with language anxiety. The participants also have their own ways to cope with it. Some of them mentioned that it's important to keep practicing and to make friends to learn English or just to have a partner for speaking with (P1, P3 and P6). According to Jones [21], language anxiety can be considered as part of a culture-based syndrome. It is the condition in which students feel humiliated or embarrassed when they are interacting with others. Making friends or being with friends who have the same culture or study background as them somehow helps students to deal with language anxiety. Some other participants mentioned doing some physical exercise (P1, P2 and P4), while one mentioned listening to English music and watching motivational videos to improve their motivation for learning English (P5). Physical exercise, in particular, is seen to help students refresh their minds and reduce anxiety.

4 CONCLUSION AND SUGGESTIONS

A number of reasons, effects, and ways to cope with language anxiety were examined from the students' perceptions obtained in the interviews. The study revealed that linguistic difficulties (vocabulary, grammar, and pronunciation), cognitive challenges (fear of negative responses from others and lack of confidence), and a lack of practice in English were considered as factors that could affect language anxiety, leading to a failure in speaking performance. The students did find some ways to deal with language anxiety, but this issue still needs more attention, especially in terms of the cognitive challenges of language anxiety. Thus, teachers should pay more attention to these students. They should be aware that students are sensitive to being judged by other students. They should arrange the learning environment in such a way that students can feel more comfortable and relaxed. The most important thing is that teachers give students more time for speaking exercises, for example, by drilling the students to practice speaking in every lesson. In short, they should be given more opportunities for speaking practice. For students to be successful in the future, they should also increase their confidence in speaking. They should practice public speaking because it will help them improve their speaking skills. Students can learn from native speakers or through videos on YouTube. Overall, students need to be more proactive.

REFERENCES

[1] Horwitz, E., Horwitz, M. & Cope, J. (1986). Foreign language classroom anxiety. The Modern Language Journal, 70, 125–132.

[2] Xiao, Y. & Wong, K.F. (2014). Exploring heritage language anxiety: A study of Chinese heritage language learners. The Modern Language Journal, 98(2), 589–611.

[3] Kayaoğlu, M.C. & Sağlamel, H. (2013). Students' perceptions of language anxiety in speaking classes. Journal of History Culture and Art Research, 2(2), 142–160. doi:10.7596/taksad.v2i2.245.

[4] Tanveer, Muhammad. 2007. Investigation of the Factors that Cause Language Anxiety for ESL/EFL Learners in Learning Speaking Skills and the influence it Casts on Communication in the Target Language. Glasgow: University of Glasgow.

[5] Naghadeh, S., Naghadeh, M., Kasraey, S., Maghdour, H., Kasraie, S. & Naghadeh, N. (2014). The relationship between anxiety and Iranian EFL learners' narrative writing performance. International Journal of Psychology and Behavioral Research, 3(6), 602–609.

[6] Chanprasert, C. & Wichadee, S. (2015). Exploring language learning anxiety and anxiety reducing strategies of the first-year students taking a foreign language course. Journal of Social Sciences, Humanities, and Arts, 15(1), 131–156.

[7] Lian, L. & Budin, M. (2014). Investigating the relationship between English language anxiety and the achievement of school-based oral English test among Malaysian form four language learners. International Journal of Learning, Teaching and Educational Research, 2(1), 67–79.

[8] Alsowat, H. (2016). Foreign language anxiety in higher education: A practical framework for reducing FLA. European Scientific Journal, 12(7), 193–220. doi:10.19044/esj.

[9] Bell, S.M. & McCallum, R.S. (2012). Do foreign language learning, cognitive, and affective variables differ as a function of exceptionality status and gender? International Education, 42(1), 85–105.

[10] MacIntyre, P.D. (1998). Language anxiety: A review of the research for language teachers. In D.J. Young (Ed.), Affect in foreign language and second language learning (pp. 24–25). Boston, MA: McGraw-Hill.

[11] Aydin, S. (2008). An investigation on the language anxiety and fear of negative evaluation among Turkish EFL learners. Asian EFL Journal, 30(1) 421–444.

[12] Zhiping, D. & Paramasivam, S. (2013). Anxiety of speaking English in class among international students in a Malaysian university. International Journal of Education and Research, 1(11), 1–16.

[13] Tüm, D.Ö. & Kunt, N. (2013). Speaking anxiety among EFL student teachers. H.U. Journal of Education, 28(3), 385–399.

[14] Waseem, F. & Jibeen, T. (2013). Anxiety amongst learners of English as a second language: An examination of motivational patterns in the Pakistani context. International Journal of Humanities and Social Science, 3(16), 174–184.

[15] Gopang, I.B., Bughio, F.A. & Pathan, H. (2015). Investigating foreign language learning anxiety among students learning English in a public-sector university, Pakistan. The Malaysian Online Journal of Educational Science, 3(4), 27–37.

[16] Ahmed, N.F. (2016). An exploration of speaking anxiety with Kurdish university EFL learners. Journal of Education and Practice, 7(27), 99–106.

[17] Creswell, J.W. (2007). Qualitative inquiry & research design. Thousand Oaks, CA: Sage Publications.

[18] Mukminin, A., Noprival, Masbirorotni, Sutarno, Arif, N. & Maimunah. (2015). EFL speaking anxiety among senior high school students and policy recommendations. Journal of Education and Learning, 9(3), 217–225.

[19] Creswell, J.W. (1998). Qualitative inquiry and research design: Choosing among five traditions. Thousand Oaks, CA: Sage Publications.

[20] Pratolo, B. (2015). Exploring Indonesian learners' beliefs about language learning strategies through reflection (Doctoral thesis, Monash University, Australia). Retrieved from https://core.ac.uk/download/pdf/82059045.pdf.

[21] Jones, J. (2001). A cultural context for language anxiety. EA Journal, 21(2), 30–39.

English Linguistics, Literature, and Language Teaching in a Changing Era – Madya et al. (eds)
© 2020 Taylor & Francis Group, London, ISBN 978-1-03-224160-9

The differentiated types of role play for enhancing speaking in contextual learning

Sarah M. Azizah & Dyah S. Ciptaningrum
English Education Study Program, Graduate School, Yogyakarta State University, Yogyakarta, Indonesia

ABSTRACT: Contextual learning is defined as learning that occurs in the most effective and natural manner, which is associated with classroom theory alongside real-world applications. It is believed that the purpose of contextual learning is to reconnect work and education so that learning can occur effectively in the context of its natural use. In addition to this, the students need to be fluent enough speakers to be able to build communications with their, possibly foreign, future coworkers. One classroom activity that meets these requirements is role play. Among the many advantages of role play, it is said to be able to recreate real-life situations by giving students the space to practice with their peers. This has also been proved by some previous studies, which used different types and techniques of role play. Hence, this literature-based paper aims to develop the idea of using role-play activities to enhance students' speaking skills in a contextual instructional process. However, certain types of role play might or might not work in a particular context. Thus, knowledge of the different types of role play is essential for teachers so that they are able to select the proper technique for their own students.

Keywords: Role play, contextual teaching, speaking

1 INTRODUCTION

Learning by context has been highly favored in the teaching of language, because it emphasizes relationships with the real world. Contextual learning is defined as learning that occurs in the most effective and natural manner, which is associated with classroom theory alongside real-world applications [1]. It is believed that the purpose of contextual learning is to reconnect work and education so that learning can occur effectively in the context of its natural use. However, the teaching of English in vocational high schools is still lacking in context, even though the students will need it in real-life working situations for their future occupation.

The goal of language teaching today is to be able to use language for meaningful communication [2]. In order to have meaningful communication, Johnson and Morrow [3] proposed that students should know the purpose of speaking, what to speak, with whom, and where to speak, and how to use appropriate language. Once they understand these, the students need to be fluent enough in speaking to build communications with their peers and, possibly foreign, future coworkers. As emphasized by Harmer [4], fluency can be achieved by involving students in real-life situations that require communication. The classroom activity needs to be centered on the students and to have more meaningful speaking activities. Unfortunately, the teaching of English is oriented too much on text and the national final exam, with not enough consideration given to speaking.

One classroom activity that can meet the requirements of meaningful communication is role play. There are two researches from Indonesia regarding students' speaking skills and role play. Both researches found out that the use of role play can improve students' speaking skills [5,6]. There has also been research on this in Thailand. Oradee [7] combined role play with discussion and problem solving to develop the students' speaking skills. From all of this research, it can be said that role play is able to recreate real-life situations by giving students the space to practice with their peers. It can also increase students' engagement and inter-action, because role-play activities can be fun in the classroom.

Hence, this literature-based paper aims to develop the idea of using role-play activities to enhance students' speaking skills in a contextual instructional process. However, certain types of role play might or might not work in a particular context. Thus, knowledge of the different types of role play is essential for teachers so that they are able to select the proper technique for their own students. The proper use of role play in the classroom can give more context and meaning to students' learning.

2 ROLE PLAY IN ENGLISH LANGUAGE TEACHING

The use of role play in English language teaching is not new. There are a lot of studies about role play that have been done by researchers. Dent-Young [8] explained that role play is basic-ally a way of taking a broad range of experiences into a narrow classroom learning situation, which can stimulate the students' imaginations and their communication with other students. In addition, Nurbaya et al. [6] thought that role play could be used as a method for teaching speaking by setting up the students in situations in pairs or groups. Similarly, Andresen [9] defined role play as pretend play with people taking on roles. In other words, role play is a communicative activity that can help students to practice their speaking with each other by imagining they are undertaking a role in real life, based on the given context and also on their social life.

The teacher has an important role in the process of role play, as they need to give instructions and guide the students to explore the possible situations that could occur in the given context. After that, it will depend on the students' imagination to develop the dialog and the situation. The context given by the teacher is usually a real-life situation that has been brought into the classroom. The main purpose is to give students a glimpse of how to converse in different situations in the real world. As for vocational students, it can also prepare them to enter their future workplace, especially if they are going to work with foreigners.

There are some characteristics that should be fulfilled before implementing role play, according to Jones in [4]. The first is the reality of function, which requires students to think of themselves as real participants in the given context. Also, a simulated environment is important to create the right mood. The teacher needs to set up the classroom for different situations. The third is about structure. Students must know how the activity will be con-structed. They must be given the essential information in order to carry out the implementa-tion effectively.

Meanwhile, Ladousse [10] gave some classroom management hints of things to be avoided before implementing role play. The teacher must be able to distinguish between noise and chaos. Noise might be a problem if the class next door complains. Role play needs to begin with pair work, rather than group work, and with only short activities at first until students get used to it. The teacher needs to give clear instructions and make sure that the students have understood the situation and what is on the cue cards before starting. To avoid noise, the teacher should always have a follow-up activity ready for those groups that finish the role play before the others. Finally, it is necessary to set a strict time limit and make every attempt to stick to it. This way, the students will learn to be disciplined and the teachers will be able to control the next activity.

Liu and Ding [11] stated that role play is an applicable method for animating the teaching and learning process, arousing the students' interests, and building language acquisition in an exciting way. Further, Nurbaya et al. [6] said that role play is useful for teaching speaking because it provides students with the chance to practice communication in different social per-spectives and roles, and also allows the students to be more active and to place themselves in another person's position for a whi le. In short, role play helps the students to have more interaction with each other and increases their motivation. Moreover, Harmer [4] explained that role play will be most effective when it is open-ended, so that different students have different views of what the outcome should be, and a consensus has to be reached.

Rao and Stupans, in Hidayati and Pardjono [12], argued that role play is effective in three major learning domains: affective, cognitive, and behavioral. By placing the students in another person's position for a while, they also practice empathy and the ability to put things in perspective [12]. Also, Streep [13] assumed that role playing encourages and deepens authentic learning by allowing the students to understand another person's life and experiences, while also growing their own self-awareness. Streep also said that the verbal, physical and intellectual demands of role playing improve communication abilities and foster improvement of the psychomotor, cognitive and emotional learning domains.

Despite all of these advantages, students could react negatively to the implementation of role play. Some of them may have low motivation, be less enthusiastic, have poor self-confidence, be shy, or have a fear of making mistakes [14]. The duration of the implementation of role play may also influence its success or failure. We cannot predict the emotional reactions of the students, either to the idea of the role play itself or to the content of the role play [15]. Moreover, the teacher may come up with a variety of objections to role play. Ladousse [10] thought that the aspects of classroom management need to be carefully and highly considered. Teachers with limited resources may also find it hard to create situations and choose the proper role play to be used in their classroom. For these reasons, the teacher needs to consider many things before actually implementing role play in the classroom. It needs to be implemented step by step so that the teacher can evaluate the classroom reaction and resolve any problems.

3 DIFFERENTIATED TYPES OF ROLE PLAY

In this section, some types of role play that are discussed in the literature and research will be explained.

3.1 *Role play for young students*

The activity of role play can be done with students of all ages and with different levels of knowledge. The difference will be in the complexity of the instructions and the tasks. Chesler and Fox [16] argue that role play could have tremendous advantages for elementary and secondary schools. They proposed some advantages of role play for young students. The main point is that role play is an active instructional technique, which allows students to participate socially and behave freely while, at the same time, observing the new behavior of others.

In line with this, Andresen [9] also practices role play with young students. He believes in the Vygotsky notion of a zone of proximal development because students are in this zone when they are playing a role. Vygotsky's notion asserts that, until the age of about three, linguistic meaning is dominated by the activities the children are actually involved in and by the concrete objects they are dealing with [9]. Hence, role playing for young students focuses more on daily life activities, where the students' vision is limited to their surroundings and becoming adult just like their parents. A simple example of the topic could be how they usually chat with their friends.

3.2 *Oral instruction role play*

The role-play instructions need to be understood by the students before they are able to take part, especially if it is in a foreign- or second-language classroom. Students who are still learning the new language may be confused about what to do during role play. In this regard, Dent-Young [8] also investigates what the particular relevance of role play may be for the foreign- or second-language teacher. Dent-Young [8] suggests that oral instruction might be best if it is the first time that students have tried role play in that class. The teacher will give oral instructions for each role assigned to a group of students. This is considered to be the best method because the teacher can immediately tell if everyone has understood. Students have more chances to express themselves spontaneously. Students are not allowed to write down the conversation they are going to have before performing it, in order to avoid a scripted performance. The points highlighted in this activity are the separate instruction, the teacher's response and the motivation. The teacher should give an exaggerated response in order to make it clear that he is not judging but reacting to each character. The motivation is given in the instructions to provide conflict and to help to develop the conversation naturally. Another major consideration is whether the role-play situation should relate to the students' own culture or the culture of the target language. It is, of course, clear to us that role play is contextual so that it needs culture to give it context.

3.3 Real-play

Al-Arishi [17] proposed real-play as one type of role play, which gives students a taste of how the real-life situation would be. This type of role play accommodates the desire for realism, which is described by McArthur [7]. The realism view points out that the things done in the classroom have to relate to real life 'out there' beyond the classroom walls. The textual material should be authentic, and the oral practices should be meaning-based rather than structure-based. Furthermore, Widdowson [17] demands the use of activities that are able to engage students in a real-world situation without requiring rehearsals, so that they can be as natural and authentic as possible. Real-play role play fits the desire for realism because it brings the possible daily conversations that might happen in real life into the classroom. This type of role play will be suitable for the students in specialized high schools, because they can imagine what their future occupation will be. The teacher's role is to give examples and depictions of what future occupation is suited to them. For example, greetings, asking for directions, ordering something in the public space, and so on.

3.4 Surreal-play

Another type of role play is surreal-play, which is also called imaginative role playing. As its name suggests, it is the opposite of real-play. Surreal-play focuses more on contemporary language learning in order to stress the promotion of self-expression or the inner world of each student's mind [17]. This type of role play may fulfill humanistic desires because, according to Rivers [17], it has resulted in the inclusion in language learning materials of sharing and developing understanding of others' feelings and needs. In surreal-play, fantasy becomes more important, and reality is less so (Shadow in [17]). Students are asked to solve a problem that they would not normally have to face in daily life. They are asked to come up with a plan that they would never have thought about before. This will allow for a free flow of imagination and self-expression. In a similar way to drama, surreal-play needs imaginary characters and problems that can either be about the student's world or, maybe, another or imaginary world. While children and teenagers like to imagine themselves in different situations, such as when playing games, surreal-play may not be a daily classroom activity because it will be hard for beginner students to build a conversation without background knowledge.

4 CONCLUSION

To conclude, each type of role play has its own benefits, according to the students' needs and the teacher's ability to adapt. If English teachers in foreign- or second-language classrooms want to use role play in the classroom, they must consider the students' level of cognitive ability in order to be able to match the type of role play to their students' needs. There are both advantages and drawbacks to role play when it is applied in the classroom. However, some experts have also given consideration to how to prepare for role play and to anticipate any associated chaos. Context is one of the factors to consider, which is closely related to culture and social life. Through role play, students are trained to be able to communicate using English in a real-life situation. This paper suggests some types of role play that can be used inside the classroom. As a result, it is hoped that more students will be able to utilize language to create meaningful communication.

REFERENCES

[1] Bolt, L. & Swartz, N. (1997). Contextual curriculum: Getting more meaning from education. *New Directions for Community Colleges, 1997*(97), 81–88. doi:10.1002/cc.9709.

[2] Richards, J.C. (2006). *Communicative language teaching today*. New York, NY: Cambridge University Press.

[3] Johnson, K. & Morrow, K. (1981). *Communication in the classroom*. Harlow, UK: Longman Group.

[4] Harmer, J. (2001). *The practice of English language teaching*. London, UK: Longman.

[5] Sumpana, S. (2010). *Improving the students' speaking skill by role play* (Thesis, Universitas Muhammadiyah, Surakarta, Indonesia).

[6] Nurbaya, S., Salam, U. & Arifin Z. (2016) Improving students' speaking ability through role play. *Jurnal Pendidikan dan Pembelajaran, 5 (10)*. http://jurnal.untan.ac.id/index.php/jpdpb/article/view/17115/14610.

[7] Oradee, T. (2012). Developing speaking skills using three communicative activities (Discussion, problem-solving, and role-playing). *International Journal of Social Science and Humanity, 2*(6), 533–535. doi:10.7763/IJSSH.2012.V2.164.

[8] Dent-Young, J. (1977). Role-play in language teaching. *RELC Journal, 8*(1), 61–68.

[9] Andresen, H. (2015). Role play and language development in the preschool years. *Culture & Psychology, 11*(4), 387–414. doi:10.1177/1354067X05058577.

[10] Ladousse, G.P. (1987). *Role-play*. Oxford, UK: Oxford University Press.

[11] Liu, F. & Ding, Y. (2009). Role-play in English language teaching. *Asian Social Science, 5*(10), 140–143. doi:10.5539/ass.v5n10p140.

[12] Hidayati, L. & Pardjono, P. (2018). The implementation of role play in education of pre-service vocational teacher. *IOP Conference Series: Materials Science and Engineering, 296*, 012016. doi:10.1088/1757-899X/296/1/012016.

[13] Streep, M. (2015). *Role-playing enlivens the classroom*. Retrieved from www.tolerance.org/sites/default/files/general/edcafe.pdf.

[14] Nguyen, T.K.T. (2017). How can role-plays increase speaking participation for the working adult students? *IOSR Journal of Research & Method in Education, 7*(1), 57–67. doi:10.9790/7388-0701015767.

[15] Woodhouse, J. (2014). Role play: A stage of learning. In J. Woodhouse & D. Marris (Eds.), *Strategies for healthcare education* (pp. 71–80). Oxford, UK: Radcliffe.

[16] Chesler, M. & Fox, R. (1996). *Role-playing methods in the classroom*. Chicago, IL: Science Research Associates.

[17] Al-Arishi, A.Y. (1994). Role-play, real-play, and surreal-play in the ESOL classroom. *ELT Journal, 48*(4), 337–346. doi:10.1093/elt/48.4.337.

English Linguistics, Literature, and Language Teaching in a Changing Era – Madya et al. (eds)
© 2020 Taylor & Francis Group, London, ISBN 978-1-03-224160-9

Looking at learner engagement in a digital multimodal-based instruction

Siti Kustini
English for Specific Purposes at Electrical Engineering Department, Banjarmasin State Polytechnic, Banjarmasin, Indonesia

ABSTRACT: Student engagement is regarded as a crucial aspect in today's education and has been called "the holy grail of learning" [1] because of its correlations to academic achievement, persistence, and satisfaction. This paper reports an investigation of learner engagement in English for Specific Purposes (ESP) classroom practice in which multimodal pedagogy is used as the overarching framework in the overall instructional procedures. Digital multimodal texts were utilized as learning tools for this study to provide opportunities for learners to learn different multimodal text types; to promote alternative ways of reading, interpreting, and text composing; and to facilitate learners to develop their multimodal communicative competence. This study employed both quantitative and qualitative approaches. The quantitative data were gained from questionnaires, and the qualitative data were obtained from classroom observation and students' personal narratives. The participants of this study were fifty-three semester two students of ESP classes in a state polytechnic in Banjarmasin. The findings of this study revealed that the integration of digital multimodal texts in ESP classrooms could lead to the improvement of learners' engagement in learning. The results confirm the need to reconceptualize ESP instruction in that multimodal approach is integrated in the teaching and learning process as it promotes positive learning outcomes.

Keywords: digital, engagement, ESP, multimodal

1 INTRODUCTION

This study attempts to explore learner engagement in a digital multimodal-based instruction in ESP classes. A digital multimodal-based instruction is primarily designed to accelerate learning in the 21st century in which students are encouraged to actively and naturally engage in the constructions of digital texts using a range of multimodal resources. Digital multimodal texts combine linguistic, visual, audio, and other non-verbal forms of expression to represent meaning potential in digital environment. These texts are utilized in this study as learning tools to provide opportunities for learners to learn different multimodal text types; to promote alternative ways of reading, interpreting, and text composing; and to facilitate learners to develop their multimodal communicative competence. The theoretical framework for this pedagogical instruction is derived from the concept of multiliteracies and multimodality. Multiliteracies is a term introduced by a group of literacy scholars known as the New London Group (NLG) in 1996. These literacy experts believed that literacy in the twenty-first century should extend beyond reading and writing printed texts to involve all various ways of communication to make meanings (i.e. through combinations of linguistic, gestural, audio, visual, tactile and spatial semiotic modes) as well as an "appreciation of diversity of textual, contextual, social and cultural conventions that influence the use of these modes for different people in different situation" [2,3]. The New London Group's agenda of introducing multiliteracies learning for students was two-fold: students were expected to have access to the diverse forms of communication necessary to apply in multiple contexts, and students were encouraged to be active citizens in an increasingly complex globalized world. Thus, to accomplish this challenge, the NLG suggested a new approach to literacy teaching called multiliteracies pedagogy. This pedagogy was developed and organized into two sections: the "what" of literacy pedagogy and the "how" of literacy pedagogy. The "what" of multiliteracies pedagogy draws from multiple modes of meaning making to support a design process of literacy learning. The "how" of multiliteracies pedagogy draws from a range of relationships between four components: situated practice, overt instruction, critical framing, and transformed practice.

This pedagogy also takes into account of the concept of multimodality which views that "language is but one of the communicative resources through which meaning is (re)made, distributed, and interpreted" [4]. Thus, a key principle of the theory of multimodality is that all communication is multimodal, and any communicative event entails simultaneous use of multiple modes which may realize meanings that complement, extend, and/or contradict each other [5].It is contended that multimodal learning environments allow learners to construct and interact with specific contexts of language use in that learners gain awareness of the linguistic elements they need in order to create appropriate contexts of language use and to complement these with their specialized content [6]. By engaging learners to design multimodal artifacts, it provides them greater flexibility and creativity in their language learning. Multimodality, thus, engages learners in a "complex process of sense making" [7] which is based on the social interactions between language and the other semiotic systems represented.

Recently, there has been an exponentially increased interest on the study of student engagement as this variable of learning is regarded to be the driving force for positive educational outcomes [8]. However, the study on the exploration of learner engagement in a digital multimodal in ESP classroom remains limited. Therefore, this study is considered important that it can be beneficial in the contribution of adding insights to research in engagement area. It is assumed that students' active engagement leads to students' success in the learning process. The more students engage with the ideas, the environment, and other learners in the learning process, the better the ability and the knowledge they will gain. This is supported by [9]'s idea stating that active engagement will likely result in an improvement in student learning. Disengagement will disrupt learning and threat their future success. Accordingly, it is essential to create and construct learning instruction that captivates student to have a high degree of engagement in the knowledge acquisition. Thus, this study has significant contribution both theoretically and practically to inform the degree of learner engagement in the instructional program.

A plethora of learning engagement definitions has been proposed, yet many educational experts have not reached any agreement in defining this term precisely because of its broad and complex meanings [10,11]. Researchers used various terms to define engagement in learning, including student engagement, academic engagement, school engagement, and learner engagement [12]. Some scholars refer to learner engagement as "an educational bottom line" [13] and "the holy grail of learning" [1] for its correlation to academic achievement, persistence, and satisfaction. Learner engagement is concerned with the investment of cognitive and emotional energy to accomplish a learning task [14,15]. Some others view engagement as a multidimensional construct that includes different types of engagement such as behavioral, emotional, and cognitive engagement [8]. In the context of this study, the two meta-constructs (i.e. cognitive and emotional) of engagement will be highlighted as they are considered as the primary factors of students' success in learning. Cognitive engagement (CE) is defined as the focused effort learners give to effectively understand what is being taught, including self-regulation and metacognitive behaviors [8]. [15]argues that CE is composed of attention, effort and persistence, time on task, cognitive strategy use, absorption, and curiosity. Emotional engagement (EE) is related to the students' emotional reactions to their learning experiences such as interest, frustration, and boredom. EE, [15] proposed, consists of positive energy indicators, including interest and enjoyment, happiness, and confidence, along with negative energy indicators such as boredom, frustration, and anxiety. The model of learner engagement from [15] will be used as framework for data analysis for this study.

2 RESEARCH METHOD

2.1 *Research design*

The purpose of this study is to explore the extent to which students are engaged in the learning process using a digital-multimodal based instruction. To achieve this particular aim quantitative and qualitative inquiry embracing a case study design was conducted. This case study design was selected for two reasons. First, this study was carried out in a "small case, a single case" [16] and it "focused on one particular instance of educational experience or practice" [17]. The second aspect was that this study utilized multiple sources of evidence [18] including observations, questionnaires, and students' personal narratives.

2.2 *Research site and participants*

This study was conducted in Informatics Engineering Study Program under the Electrical Engineering Department of a state polytechnic located in Banjarmasin, South Kalimantan, Indonesia. This site was chosen primarily due to its feasibility. The researcher has been a teaching member in the research site for almost 12 years that it is easy to get access to it. In addition, the researcher's familiarity with the situation in the research site was expected to lead to more natural conduct of the study.

The participants of this study were fifty-three semester two students taking an English course in the academic year 2017/2018. The English course offered in this semester was English for Specific Purpose (ESP) program in which the content-specific English language related to students' field of study was introduced. The participants were heterogeneous based on their age, sexes, and areas of origin. The age-range of the participant was from 18-19. Given the natural setting and heterogeneity enabled this study to study things as they are without manipulating the environment where ordinary events and behaviors are studied in their everyday context.

2.3 *Data collections and analysis*

Multiple data resources were utilized for this study including observations, questionnaire, and students' personal narratives. The observations were conducted during the implementation of teaching program. The documentation of the observation known as field notes was carried out right after each session ends. The aim of observation was to capture unique behaviors related to student engagement. The second data was from questionnaire responses. The questionnaire focused on measuring student engagement which was adopted and modified from [15] model of engagement. The original items were in English. To ensure the participants' complete comprehension of the instrument, the items were translated into Bahasa Indonesia. Bahasa Indonesia is the participants' national language. The questionnaire consisted of 33 items in which all dimensions of CE and EE were covered. Response format conducted categorical data using a five-point Likert type scale ranging from 1 (never) to 5 (all the time) or other five-response variations such as 1 (not at all interested) to 5 (extremely interested). Although the questionnaire was not validated prior to distribution, this instrument was carefully constructed based on the principle Usefulness, Satisfaction, and Ease of Use (USE) suggested by [19]. The last data resource was students' personal narratives. These data were used to support the results from observation and questionnaire. In analyzing the data, thematic coding was utilized for observation and students' personal narratives. The students' responses from the questionnaire were processed using SPPS version 22 to get descriptive statistics informing frequencies percentage of each response.

3 FINDINGS AND DISCUSSION

The data analysis in this study was thematically presented based on the construct of engagement model proposed by [15]. She argues that engagement is manifest via cognitive and emotional indicators and contributes to desired learning. Cognitive Engagement (CE) is comprised of several factors indicating the quantity (i.e. attention, effort and persistence, time on task) and the quality (i.e. cognitive and metacognitive, deep concentration or absorption, and individual interest or curiosity). Emotional Engagement (EE) consists of positive engagement (i.e. enjoyment, happiness, and confidence) and negative engagement (i.e. boredom, frustration, and anxiety).

As it was mentioned earlier, the whole instructional process in this study strictly followed the pedagogical framework of multiliteracies proposed by the New London Group (1996). The framework comprises of four components: situated practice, overt instruction, critical framing, and transformed practice. Fourteen meetings of multiliteracies ESP program were set up. In regards teaching materials, authentic multimodal texts were used. The authentic texts are not only in the form of printed-based materials but also non-printed materials. During the instructional process, students were required to construct digital multimodal texts in the form of mini magazine and video presentation. Several applications to design and compose these texts were introduced. The students managed to accomplish the tasks to their potential. The sample of the students' works can be accessed at this web address: https://www.youtube.com/watch?v=wFwHRPaiDPw. To get students more engaged, Learning Management System (LMS) of *Schoology* was used during the teaching program. This LMS allows teacher and students to have online conversation, to upload and download learning materials, post assignments, and other instructional activities.

3.1 *Students' Cognitive Engagement (CE)*

In terms of CE, the data from the observation reveals that students showed high degree of attention, effort, and persistence during the teaching program. Students were also cognitively engaged and immersed as they got through activities in the classroom. This can be seen from the task completion, class participation, and strategies used in comprehending the learning materials. Students were also active in asking questions, exchanging ideas with friends, enthusiastically answering teacher's questions, making evaluative comments, etc.

These observation findings were supported by the data gained from the students' personal narratives. Below is a sample of students' journal excerpts produced:

We started basic materials by learning multimodal texts. It's true that learning multimodal text is more efficient than English-printed text. She also explained that each picture was not made freely. Each picture had some meanings. They gave us some information. Furthermore, colors in a picture are exactly had their own meaning. The class is very interesting today. It makes me curious to learn more about it. I feel motivated to learn English more and I can't wait for the next meeting (Aksa, Journal March 8th, 2018).

It can be seen from this excerpt that cognitive engagement was indicated by student's curiosity in learning and accordingly this had led student's high degree of motivation to learn. This evidence confirms the statement that high level of cognitive engagement can lead to increased motivation, and subsequently promote positive learning outcomes.

The questionnaire data also produced similar results to those in observation and students' personal narratives. The overall students' responses related to cognitive engagement in learning can be seen in Table 1.

It can be seen from Table 1 that the quality and quantity of engagement were demonstrated by the students during the learning process. The level of learning attention was quite high that only 3.8% and 2% of students showed little attention during the learning process. Interestingly, the efforts that students put into the class activities were at the average level of 62.3%. These data inform teachers to design activities that encourage learners to be actively engaged in the activities. In terms of efforts to learning, the students showed high efforts in learning the materials or the activities (39.6%) during the program implementation. The data concerning the level of concentration indicated that students had good concentration (64.2%) in the learning process.

3.2 *Emotional Engagement (EE)*

In regards with EE, which is related to students' emotional reactions to their learning activities in the classroom, the data reveal that students showed high degree of positive emotional

Table 1. Responses to students' CE ($N = 53$).

Question	Response				
My mind wandered during the class activities.	Never 7.5%	Rarely 67.9%	Sometimes 20.8%	Often 3.8%	All the time 0%
Describe your level of attentiveness during the class activities.	Not attentive at all 0%	Not very attentive 2%	Moderately Attentive 19%	Quite attentive 47%	Extremely attentive 13.2%
Compared to other courses, the effort I put into class activities has been:	Extremely low 0%	Low 5.7%	About average 62.3%	High 28.3%	Extremely high 3.8%
Even when the class was uninteresting, I made an effort to learn.	Never 1.9%	Rarely 9.4%	Sometimes 34.0%	Often 39.6%	All the time 15.1%
To what degree did you thoughtfully analyze and evaluate the information presented?	Not at all thoughtfully 0%	Not very thoughtfully 1.9%	Moderately thoughtfully 28.3%	Quite thoughtfully 37.7%	Extremely thoughtfully 32.1%
Describe your level of absorption/deep concentration during the class activities.	Not at all absorbed 1.9%	Not very absorbed 5.7%	Moderately absorbed 26.4%	Quite absorbed 64.2%	Extremely absorbed 1.9%

Table 2. Responses to students' EE (N = 53).

Question	Response				
I felt happy during the class activities.	Never 0%	Rarely 5.7%	Sometimes 45.3%	Often 43.4%	All the time 5.7%
After attending the class, I felt confident about my ability to succeed in course.	Never 3.8%	Rarely 7.5%	Sometimes 28.3%	Often 50,9%	All the time 9.4%
Describe your level of happiness during the class.	Not at all happy 0%	Not very happy 9.4%	Moderately happy 39.6%	Quite happy 39.6%	Extremely happy 11.3%
Describe your general anxiety during the class.	Not at all anxious 24.5%	Not very anxious 47.2%	Moderately anxious 17.0%	Quite anxious 7.5%	Extremely anxious 3.8%
Describe your level of interest during the class.	Not at all interested 1.9%	Not very interested 3.8%	Moderately interested 37.7%	Quite interested 43.4%	Extremely interested 13.2%

engagement. Students felt happy doing things in the classroom (43.4%); they were confident enough to succeed in course (50.9%], and they were interested in the learning design implemented (43.4%). The illustration of students. EE can be seen in Table 2 below.

The analysis of students' reflective journals also showed the similar results. This can be seen from the journals written by the students below:

I think the way the teacher teaches made us interested and we did not get bored during the lesson because in every slide of presentation, the teacher explained the material clearly with a little bit jokes. I hope in the next week's meeting I can better understand the lessons given by the teacher (Arga, March 1st, 2018).

My opinion, the teacher is a good lecturer because she can turn the class atmosphere that the class is not boring. And her explanation is very understandable. Besides the learning system is very good (Doni, April 12th, 2018).

From the results of data analysis, it seems that the findings of this study are in line and support previous studies in this area. It is reported in several studies on digital multimodal compositional practices that students were indicated to have high level of engagement. For instance, the study conducted by [20] reporting that the multimodal projects assigned for the students in their study had led to student higher level of engagement and longer attentive period in the task completion. The project was the production of Claymation tests which aimed to develop their English language skill along with synesthetic abilities. At the initial stage of the classroom activities the students showed very little engagement in learning due to their low levels of English proficiency and sociopolitical condition. Gradually, students' level of involvement increased. In [21] study also showed students' increased level of engagement in their findings. Exploring writing and text construction practices using in technology-mediated environment, this study suggests the use of digital media to enhance students' creative possibilities in the construction of new dynamic texts and build learning about the elements of design into the instruction. Other studies with similar results including [22], [23], and [24].

4 CONCLUSION AND SUGGESTIONS

Helping students engage in learning is an important issue in classroom practices for it leads to an excellent educational outcome. To this end, teachers are required to provide motivating learning experiences and to create a classroom environment that gives all students the best opportunity to learn. This article explores how learners are engage in the class environment in which digital multimodal texts are extensively exposed. The results indicate that the digital multimodal-based instruction has positive impacts on student cognitive and emotional engagement. It is therefore suggested that teachers shift their teaching practices to incorporate more multimodal texts in the classroom.

REFERENCES

[1] Sinatra, G.M., Heddy, B. C., & Lombardi, D. (2015). The challenges of defining and measuring student engagement. *Educational Psychologist, 50*(1), 1–13. doi:10.1080/00461520.2014.1002924.

[2] New London Group. (1996). A pedagogy of multiliteracies : Designing social futures. *Harvard Educational Review, 66*(1), 60–92.

[3] Cope, B., & Kalantzis, M. (2015). *A pedagogy of multiliteracies: Learning by design.* United Kingdom: Palgrave Macmillan.

[4] Jewitt, C. (2008). Multimodality and literacy in school classrooms. *Review of Research in Education,* 32, 241–267. doi: 10.3102/0091732X07310586.

[5] Kress, G. (2010). *Multimodality: A social semiotic approach to contemporary communication.* New York, NY: Routledge.

[6] Plastina, A.F. (2013). Multimodality in English for specific purposes: Reconceptualizing meaning-making practices. *Revista de Lenguas Para Fines Específicos, 19,* 385–410.

[7] Jewitt, C. (2006). *Technology, literacy, learning: A multimodal approach.* London and New York: Routledge.

[8] Fredricks, J.A., Blumenfeld, P.C., & Paris, A.H. School engagement: Potential of the concept, state of the evidence. *Review of Educational Research, 74*(1), 59–109.

[9] C. Bryson, & L.H. (2007). The role engagement in inspiring language teaching and learning. *Innovations in Education and Teaching International, 44*(4), 4–14.

[10] Dörnyei, Z. (2001) Motivational strategies in the language classroom. Cambridge: Cambridge University Press.

[11] Russell, V.J., Ainley, M., & Frydenberg, E. (2005). Student motivation and engagement. *Schooling Issues Digest.* Australian Government, Department of Education, Science and Training.

[12] Reschly, A.L., & Christenson, S.L. (2015). Jingle, jangle, and conceptual haziness: Evolution and future directions of the engagement construct. In Christenson, S.L., Reschly, A.L., & Wylie, C. (Eds.), *Handbook of research on student engagement,* pp. 3–19. New York, NY: Springer.

[13] Coates, H. (2006). *Student engagement in campus-based and online education: University connections.* New York, NY: Routledge.

[14] Astin, A.W. (1984). Student involvement: A developmental theory for higher education. *Journal of College Student Personnel, 40*(5), 518–529. Retrieved from https://www.middlesex.mass.edu/tutoring services/downloads/astininv.pdf.

[15] Henrie, C.R., Halverson, L.R., & Graham, C.R. (2016). Measuring student engagement in technology-mediated learning: A review. *Computers & Education*, *90*, 36–53. doi:10.1016/j.compedu.2015.09.005.

[16] Stake, E. (1985). Case study, In Nisbet, J., Mergary, J., & Nisbet, S. (Eds.), *World yearbook of education 1985, Research, policy and politics*. London: Nicholas Publishing Company.

[17] Freebody, P. (2003). *Qualitative research in education. Interaction and practice*. London: SAGE Publications.

[18] Yin, R.K. (1993). *Applications of case study research*. Newbury Park, California: SAGE Publications.

[19] Lund, A.M. (2001). Measuring usability with the USE questionnaire. *STC Usability SIG Newsletter*, *8*(2), 3–6, Retrieved from http://garyperlman.com/quest/quest.cgi?form=USE.

[20] Hepple, E., Sockhill, E.M., Tan, A., & Alford, J. (2004). Multiliteracies pedagogy: Creating claymations with adolescent, post-beginner English language learners, *Journal of Adolescent and Adult Literacy*, *58*(3), 219–229. doi: 10.1002/jaal.339.

[21] Edwards-Groves, C. (2011). The multimodal writing process: Changing practices in contemporary classrooms. *Language and Education*, *25*(1), 49–64, doi:10.1080/09500782.2010.523468.

[22] Munns, G., Zammit, K., & Woodward, H. (2008). Reflections from the riot zone: The fair go project and student engagement in a besieged community. *Journal of Children & Poverty*, *14*(2), 157–171, doi:10.1080/10796120802335888.

[23] Zammit, K. (2011). Connecting multiliteracies and engagement of students from low socio-economic backgrounds: Using Bernstein's pedagogic dis- course as a bridge. *Language and Education*, *25*(3), 203–220, doi:10.1080/09500782.2011.560945.

[24] Ntelioglou, M.B.Y. (2012). *Drama pedagogies, multiliteracies and embodied learning: Urban teachers and linguistically diverse students make meaning* (Doctoral dissertation). Ontario Institute for Studies in Education/University of Toronto, Toronto.

English Linguistics, Literature, and Language Teaching in a Changing Era – Madya et al. (eds)
© 2020 Taylor & Francis Group, London, ISBN 978-1-03-224160-9

Developing the model of teaching materials for ESP (English for Specific Purposes)

Stefhani R. Rahmawati, Emzir & Aceng
Language Education, State University of Jakarta, Jakarta, Indonesia

ABSTRACT: The need to communicate in the foreign language, especially English, is currently prevalent throughout the globe to the extent it is usually one of the major requirements in several job advertisements. This calls for the development of English learning materials to match the specific area of need. Therefore, the goals of learning English for Specific Purposes, in this case, Professional Nurses, is to help the students broaden their vocabularies in relation with nursing to have the ability to explain and communicate with their patients in the language. This study made use of qualitative research to determine suitable teaching materials and data were collected through the use of field notes and questionnaires. The subjects included student nurses of Gatot Soebroto Nursing Academy. The data were analyzed through the use of a descriptive approach. The results showed that four skills including interesting book layout needed in developing English learning materials for Student Nurses.

Keywords: Development, model of teaching materials, ESP

1 INTRODUCTION

According to Tomlinson, materials development is both a field of study and a practical undertaking. As a field of study, it underlines the importance of the principles and procedures of the design, implementation and evaluation of the materials; while as a practical undertaking, it focuses on the production, evaluation and adaptation of the materials. Ideally, both of them are interactive in that the theoretical studies inform and are informed by the development and use of classroom materials. It refers to anything which is done by writers, teachers or learners to provide sources of language input, to exploit those sources in ways which maximize the likelihood of intake and to stimulate purposeful output. The materials developers must be able to provide materials as input, so that the languages can be effectively learned [1].

Materials include anything which can be used to facilitate the learning of a language. They can be linguistic, visual, auditory or kinesthetic, and can be in the form of printed materials, live performance or display, or on cassette, CD-ROM, DVD or the internet.

Tomlinson focuses on six principles for materials development. They are (1) Exposing the learners to language in authentic use, (2) Helping the learners to pay attention to features of authentic input, (3) Providing the learners with opportunities to use the target language to achieve communicative purposes, (4) Providing opportunities for outcome feedback, (5) Achieving impact in the sense that they arouse and sustain the learners' curiosity and attention, and (6) Stimulating Intellectual, aesthetic and emotional involvement [2].

Specialized languages usually refer to the specific discourse used by professionals and specialists to communicate and transfer information and knowledge. There are as many specialized languages as there are professions. This is what has usually been known as Languages for Specific Purposes or, when applied to English, English for Specific Purposes (ESP), i.e., the special discourse used in specific settings by people sharing common purposes [3].

According to Dudley & Evan and St John, ESP focuses on characteristics distinguishing it from other areas of English Language Teaching: specific language skill needs; specific genres and language relate to them; and methodology reflecting the discipline(s) or professions to which the language needs relate. They also stated that there are two characteristics to outline the major features of ESP: Absolute and Variable Characteristics. There are three points discussed in Absolute Characteristic. They are: (1) ESP is defined to meet specific needs of the learners; (2) ESP makes use of underlying methodology and activities of the discipline it serves; (3) ESP is centered on the language (grammar, lexis, register), skills, discourse and genre appropriate to these activities. While Variable Characteristic pays attention to four points: (1) ESP may be related to or designed for specific disciplines; (2) ESP may use, in specific teaching situations, a different methodology from that of General English; (3) ESP is likely to be designed for adult learners, either at a tertiary level institution or in a professional work situation. It could, however, be for learners at secondary school level; (4) ESP is generally designed for intermediate or advanced students. Most ESP courses assume some basic knowledge of the language systems, but it can be used with beginners [4].

English for Nurse focuses on the specific ways in which nurses use English both in the clinical setting as well as in nursing education. Bosher found out that both academic skills and clinical skills are necessary for success in nursing program. He had conducted a number of need analyses to determine the objective, subjective, and learning needs of the student nurse that led to the development of the materials in English for nursing [5].

The aim of this research was to produce a text book which gave high priority to the language forms students would meet in their science studies and in turn would give low priority to forms they would not meet.

2   METHODS

2.1   *The participants*

The participants of this study were 59 student nurses of Gatot Soebroto Nursing Academy who were on their third semester.

The total of 59 questionnaires were distributed. Participants were given a time limit of 30 minutes to return the completed questionnaires due to time constraint. All students returned the questionnaires within the given time.

2.2   *The instrument and procedure*

This Research is designed as a Research and Development study with qualitative approach (Jolly and Bolitho in Tomlinson [1]). Researcher used questionnaires as the main instrument for the data collection to obtain information from the student nurses especially on their opinions about the book being used that need to be developed and the topics that meet their need based on the syllabus. Besides questionnaires, I also did some observations and took notes when the developed book was being used in the classroom.

There are some steps in this design. First is the Identification of Need Material. On the first step, the Researcher analyzed whether the book used by student nurses needs to be developed or not. Next is Exploration of need. The Researcher distributed the questionnaires to the participants and lecturers to know what need to be developed. There was also a list of topics in the questionnaires and they gave check marks to the topics which met their needs, and left it blank if the topic was not suitable with the syllabus. The third step is the Contextual realization of the materials. The Researcher collected the data received from exploration of need (need analysis) and tried to find suitable materials based on it. After that, Pedagogical realization of the materials. The Researcher developed the first draft of the materials. Then she asked help from the expert to give their suggestions. The fifth step is the Production of the materials. This was the step of producing the second draft. The draft was ready to be used as a field test. Next is the Students use of materials. As the developed material was used as a field test, the Researcher observed in the classroom and took notes. The notes were used as the basis of evaluating the second draft to be the final draft. . The last but not least is the Evaluation of materials against agreed objectives Based on the observation and field notes, the Researcher evaluated the materials and prepared to produce the final draft

The steps above answered the problems about the condition of the book being used, what materials needed by the student nurses, and the model of ESP materials.

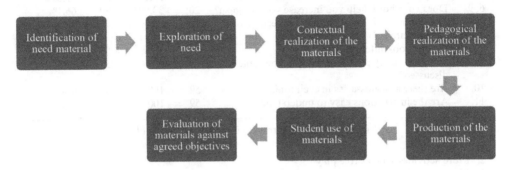

Figure 1. The simple chart of the design created by Jolly and Bolitho.

3 FINDINGS

The results are sorted into three sections; each section addresses one of the research questions. The first section answers the first research question: What is the condition of the book being used? The second section covers the second research question which investigated the materials needed by the students nurse. As for the third and final section, it answers the third research question: What have been developed as the model of ESP materials?

1. The Condition of the Book being Used
   Based on the students' Identification of Need Materials and the Exploration of Need, there are some findings about the condition of the book.
   (1) There was no Listening Comprehension Materials
      Most of the time, the lecturers read a conversation, helped by one of the students to give an example of the correct pronunciation and tones. Sometimes, they brought a video downloaded from *you tube* and created their own questions that later must be answered by the students.
   (2) Conversation examples were provided but less practices
      There were examples of conversations in every chapter and the students worked in pair and practice them. But, there was no instruction for the students to create the similar activities.
   (3) Need more pictures
      More pictures needed to show different kinds of activities related to nurses' duties in wards. These pictures could also be used as a source of conversation activities during the teaching-learning process.
   (4) The book was not colorful; not interesting
      The students gave suggestions to provide colorful pictures, especially related to medical instruments; if it is possible, to give the real pictures of the instruments.
   (5) No guidance for the lecturers to use the book.
      There were two lecturers who taught English there. From the interview, the lecturer said that they needed a *teacher's book* as guidance in every chapter, so they could easily notice whether they had reached the goals or not.

Table 1. Identification of need materials.

No.	Questions	Yes		No	
	For Student Nurse				
1.	Does your book have Reading section?	59	100%	0	0%
2.	Does your book have Listening section?	2	3.38%	57	96.6%
3.	Does your book have Speaking section?	59	100%	0	0%
4.	Does your book have Writing section?	59	100%	0	0%
5.	Do you have many activities for each section?	5	8.47%	54	91.5%
6.	Does your book help you increase your English?	20	33.89%	39	66.1%
7.	Does your book answer what you need in your working area?	12	20.33%	47	79.66%
8.	Is your book interesting?	2	3.38%	57	96.6%
9.	Are there many pictures related to the topic discussed?	0	0%	59	100%
10.	Are there any glossaries in each topic?	59	100%	0	0%
11.	Are the instructions easy to understand?	59	100%	0	0%

Write any suggestions to help improve the text book

1. More pictures
2. More activities such as role play
3. More activities for listening comprehension
4. Should be colorful
5. Need teacher's manual

Table 2. The list of topics given in the questionnaires.

Number	Topic	Important	Not Important
1.	Establishing A Relationship	59	0
2.	Handling phone call	2	57
3.	Asking and showing rooms in the Hospital	59	0
4.	Nurse's Duty in Wards	59	0
5.	Medical Equipment	59	0
6.	Telling Time, date and Doctor's Schedule	50	9
7.	Parts of The body and Health Problems	59	0
8.	Presentation	10	49
9.	Reporting Health Problem and Diagnosing	59	0
10.	Questions to fill in pain assessment form	43	16
11.	Positioning A Patient	59	0
12.	Asking and Telling about measurements	59	0
13.	Taking blood sample, sputum sample, and stool sample	59	0
14.	Reinforcing Dietary Program	59	0
15.	Walking Aid	59	0
16.	Psychological help	0	59
17.	Explaining Medication	59	0
18.	Checking the Vital Signs	59	0
19.	Explaining Medication	59	0
20.	Admission to Hospital	1	58

Based on the Identification of the need materials, the book being used at the moment did not provide listening section, and there were not many various activities in each session. Some of the materials provided in the book did not answer what they need to support their jobs and there are not many pictures to support the materials. Therefore, the participants considered it as boring materials.

2. The materials needed by the students nurse
From the list of topics given to the participants, only 16 were chosen. Those 16 topics were then developed in the new materials.
3. The Developed materials
Based on the condition of the book being used and the students' need of the materials, the first and the second draft were made. Those two drafts became the base of creating the final materials. The new materials provided four skills, with various activities, and the topics were based on what matched the students need. On the process of creating the drafts, the researcher also got some suggestions from some experts. The following were the suggestions given by the experts.
a. First Expert
Generally, the developed model has been in line with the theory. You need to pay attention on some points to make it better. The details can be seen in the questionnaires.
b. Second Expert
Overall, the final draft has fulfilled the good criteria. Even though it is taught as a whole language, you need to clarify which aspects become the focuses of each meeting.
c. Third expert
According to me, the materials are very good. It's simple but easy to understand. It has four language skills and the exercises are comprehensive. Do not forget to add more exposure, so that they can still learn about English even when they are not in the classroom.

4 DISCUSSIONS

The developed materials were equipped with pictures, four skills of English with exercises. With respect to its importance, Dudley-Evans and St John [6] mentioned that key graphic representations such as lists, columns, tables, matrices, tree diagrams, charts and mind maps can be very helpful in extracting and reorganizing the information in ESP textbooks. Alemi and Ebadi [7] said that illustrations can be an integral part of ESP courses and its justification is that they make ESP courses more tangible and understandable. Erfani [8] claimed that pictorial context can be an innovative alternative for most of the current ESP textbooks lacking this feature. It is emphasized that such pictures must be educationally valid. Those pictures must be relevant with the learners' need and purposefully into the text.

Therefore, the researcher needed to develop the teaching materials based on what the students need to support the use of English in the working area.

5 CONCLUSIONS

The data from the students' questionnaires and the field notes have illustrated a number of issues which need to be considered as they offer significant implications for developing this ESP textbook. First of all, the finding of the study revealed the need of listening comprehension audio and exercises. The students needed a lot of exposure of the pronunciation, tones and example to imitate when they created their own conversation. The second finding was exercises on conversation practices. This finding could be combined with the third one, which was the need of pictures, since pictures could help the students get the idea in what situation they were going to get involved in conversation. Colorful pictures in this textbook were only limited to the pictures of the implementation done by the nurse to the patients, while the pictures of the medical instruments would be the real pictures with smaller scales. The last finding was the need of teacher's manual for lecturers. The teacher's manual provided some activities that can be used by the lecturers to support the teaching and learning process.

REFFERENCES

[1] Tomlinson, B. (2007). *Developing Materials for Language Teaching*. London: Continuum.
[2] Tomlinson, B. (n.d.). *Materials Development in language Teaching* (2nd ed.). Cambridge: Cambridge University Press.
[3] Hutchinson, T., & Water, A. (2006). *English for Specific Purposes*. Retrieved from https://assets.cam bridge.org/97805213/18372/excerpt/9780521318372_excerpt.pdf
[4] Dudley-Evans, T. (1998). *An Overview of ESP in the 1990s*. Presented at the The Japan Conference on English for Specific Purposes, Fukushima.
[5] Bosher, S., & Smalkoski, K. (2002). From needs analysis to curriculum development: Designing a course in health-care communication for immigrant students in the USA. *English for Specific Purposes*, *21*(1), 59–79.
[6] Dudley - Evans, T., & St. John, M. J. (1998). *Developments in English for Specific Purposes. A Multi-Disciplinary Approach*. Cambridge: Cambridge University Press.
[7] Alemi, M., & Ebadi, S. (2010). The Effects of Pre-reading Activities on ESP Reading Comprehension. *Language Teaching and Research*, (September 2010). https://doi.org/10.4304/jltr.1.5.569-577.
[8] Erfani, S.M. (2012). Pictures Speak Louder Than Words in ESP, Too! *English Language Teaching*, *5*(9 July 2012). https://doi.org/10.5539/elt.v5n8p164

English Linguistics, Literature, and Language Teaching in a Changing Era – Madya et al. (eds)
© 2020 Taylor & Francis Group, London, ISBN 978-1-03-224160-9

The integration of character education in reading classes at the English education department

Sugirin, Siti Sudartini & Ani Setyaningsih
English Education Department, Universitas Negeri Yogyakarta, Indonesia

ABSTRACT: At the school level, the Indonesian Ministry of National Education/ IMONE [1] has published a guide for developing education in the nation's culture and character. However, at the university level, it is the responsibility of each through its instructors to make efforts in developing the students' character. As instructional materials are one strategic means of nurturing values [2], this study aims to describe (1) how instructors in Reading classes select the reading materials for the teaching purposes; (2) the extent to which moral values are included in their selection criteria; (3) the strategies used in highlighting the values and activities devised to nurture the intended values. This qualitative study documented the reading materials used in Reading classes from Semesters I to IV. A qualitative data analysis technique [3] was employed. The research team examined the materials and categorized them based on the semester and the cultural and character values integrated, and the criteria for the moral value inclusion. The findings show (1) the criteria for including character values are based on Lickona's [4] 10 moral values and the IMONE's 18 character values; (2) all the four instructors selected the materials for teaching purposes, however, only two intentionally selected the moral values to be included, one lecture made use of any moral values found in the selection, and one lecturer focused on the language and skills development only; (3) highlighting the values is done through relating the similarity and contrast between foreign and local values; (4) comprehension, discussion, and reflection sessions are activities devised to nurture the intended moral values.

Keywords: character education, instructional materials, explicit and implicit modes

1 INTRODUCTION

When reference is made to the goal of the Indonesian national education, i.e. to develop the learners' potentials to be pious and obedient humans of noble character, healthy, knowledgeable, intelligent, creative, autonomous, democratic and responsible as citizens [5], it is clear that all the elements of the national education must work hard to realize the goal. However, character education, which is mandated to uplift the nation's character, has not shown significant impacts after fifteen years of its implementation.

The death of a soccer group (Persija) supporter at the hands of the opposing group (Persib) supporters even before the soccer match was started on Sunday 23 September 2018 [6] is an example of the failure of character education in this country. A clash between student groups at a university also happened earlier, Saturday, 15 September 2018 at Jalan Raya Lenteng Agung Timur, Jagakarsa, South Jakarta. A physical combat was also demonstrated by two members of the People's Representatives at the Parliament Building complex, Senayan, Jakarta, Wednesday 8 April, 2015 [7]. What makes greater concern is that a clash also took place between groups of junior high school gangs (29/09/2018) which made Yogyakarta police detain 25 students found carrying weapons [8].

289

Why do all of these clashes happen? The Indonesians are friendly and well known for the culture of "gotong-royong" (sharing the burden and working together). This cooperative spirit has a long history and has been inherited from generation to generation. That a clash between groups has happened in a peaceful city such as Yogyakarta is beyond the public expectation (Jalaluddin, 2016).

As stated by a social observer, Ramadhan [9], the factors causing clashes by school children are: first, the failure of the school to nurture ethical values in real life. The school pays more attention to academic achievement than attending to ethical values. Second, with the presence of the latest technology, such as smartphones, there is a wider gap in children-parent relationship. Phubbing has hit smartphone users, young or old. Third, the gap in children-parent relationship hampers the transformation of family values from parents to children.

In addition, a psychologist, Riani (as reported by Solichin [10]) states that clashes start from a disharmonious family which is unable to bring up the children with love. As a result, when the children grow into adolescents, they tend to become provocateurs and seek attention from the world outside the family. These adolescents tend to play truant and violate school regulations. The boys tend to play the role of heroes, seeking supports from classmates by protecting whoever is being harassed by the classmates, the teacher, or students from other schools. Some schools are notorious for having an enemy. Without a proper solution by the school management, this enmity will be maintained and passed on to next generations.

In efforts to solve the problems, Riani (Solichin [10]) suggests the following: (1) parents should be the good role models of the good family values and communicate well with their children, (2) the school must have clear and firm rules so that students will make every effort to adapt themselves to the rules, (3) teachers should treat all the students fairly, (4) the school should provide space and activities so that they can develop their talents and interests, and (5) the school should involve them in social activities to nurture their empathy.

Whether efforts have been made to respond to the suggested solutions above is still a question but these examples of violence and clashes mentioned earlier prove that there is something wrong with the implementation of character education in this country. Family, school, and community are all responsible for the failure, and educators, including teachers of English should feel that school has substantial contribution to the success or failure of nurturing the students' character and the character of the nation. Character education should not be interpreted as a separate discipline taught by special teachers such as teachers of religion and civics, but it must be incorporated into many or all the disciplines, including that of the teaching of English as a foreign language.

The problem is that the English language teaching conducted so far runs as if it has nothing to do with the domain of character education, whereas the nature of the English language teaching may accommodate ample opportunities and potentials for the integration of cultural values and moral values upheld by the community, which make up the core of character education. It must also be noted that language and culture are intertwined [11,12] so that teaching English also has the potential of foreign cultural infusion which may not be in line with the character values adhered by our community. Hence, English as an international language which dominates the language of the internet (Lotten [13]) has great potentials of contributing to problems related to cultural differences. As a matter of fact, the study conducted by Sugirin, Sudartini & Nurhayati [14] shows that there are examples of the insertion of foreign cultures in the SMA English textbooks through the media of pictures and the texts used. However, there can also be values which may reinforce the appreciation of the Indonesian cultural values, moral values and character of the nation.

It should, therefore, be the concern of all the individuals involved in the teaching of foreign languages, including English, in the school level or in the higher education level, that there is always space for the infusion of values, regardless of whether they are in contrast or in harmony with our own. Hence, a critical study on the practice of teaching English focusing on the materials content is required. This study, therefore, focuses on the critical analysis on the textbooks and resources used in Reading classes in the English Education Department of a university educating prospective teachers of English.

The choice of reading classes is based on the importance of reading in the students' academic development, while materials content plays a strategic role in transferring values in education. The importance of reading in life can be seen from Koda & Zehler [15] who assert that without sufficient *reading proficiency students will have problems for further learning. Similarly,* Lyon [16] claims that anyone having no reading proficiency *in our literacy-driven society will most probably miss the opportunity to achieve productive life. Although reading skills do not guarantee success for the people (*Grabe [17]) without these skills it will be difficult to be successful in life. In addition, as reading is conventionally always related to the manipulation of texts, a reading class has the greatest opportunity to expose the students to various types and a considerable number of texts.

As mentioned earlier, materials content plays a strategic role in transferring values in education. Asrom [2] notes that there are some published textbooks which are educationally misleading. He proposed that the government should take more care in evaluating and determining textbooks acceptable for publication. Therefore, selecting and developing materials or modules need considering aspects that would accommodate the maximum benefits obtained through the use of the materials selected and developed. In this regard, Richards and Schmidt [18] suggest that the use of appropriate modules will allow for flexible course organization and learners will have a sense of achievement because modules provide clear, specific, and measurable objectives.

It is also worth noting that while intending to evaluate the course materials already used by the reading instructors of a higher education institution educating student-teachers of English, the results of the study will also be used to design a course book to complement the existing course materials. When a teacher selects course book for use with her particular class, it has to be context-dependent [19].

The context dependency is related to the choice of prospective teachers or student-teachers as the target of character education. While currently learning to develop themselves as students, who must be armed with values they need in order to be able to function properly as persons and members of the community, they also need to learn how to make their prospective students develop themselves as persons who will be good members of their community.

As the evaluation of the existing course materials will be used as a basis for revision or adaptation of the materials, post-course report on the learners by subject instructors is needed [19]. The report should include how the instructors select materials for teaching purposes and highlight the extent to which moral values are included in their selection criteria.In addition, the extent to which these values are 'taught' during the reading lessons, what instruction strategies are used to highlight these values during the lesson, and what activities are used should also be included in the report.

As the textbooks and materials resources have been chosen to be the focus of the study, the questions to be answered in this study are (1) how do the instructors select materials for teaching purposes and the extent to which moral values are included in their selection criteria? (2) what character values were present in the existing Reading course materials and how these values were represented? (3) what strategies do the instructors use to highlight these values in the lesson? and (4) what activities are used to transfer these values? Hence, the study aimed (1) to describe how the instructors select materials for teaching purposes and the extent to which moral values are included in their selection criteria; (2) to identify the character values present and how they are represented; (3) to describe the strategies used by the instructors to highlight these values in the lesson; and (4) to describe the activities used to transfer the intended values.

Theoretically, this study was expected to enrich understanding about the selection of course materials for teaching purposes which considers the integration of character education values, the strategies used to highlight character education values, and the activities used to transfer the values. Practically, the results of the study will be valuable input for reading instructors in developing the expertise in selecting and using reading course materials which meet the teaching purposes and at the same time nurture the character values of the students.

For the student teachers, the experience of joining the reading class directly expose them to ways of building awareness about the importance of character education and to provide a model of how to integrate it in the teaching learning process as reflected in the materials used. For the English Education Department this study was expected to provide some basis for the policy in regard to the practice of course materials selection, teaching and learning strategy development and activities devised to nurture character values. Hence, course materials play an important role in skills building and character building.

In regard to the role of course materials in the teaching and learning process, Fasso, Knight, & Knight [20] note that they are used to integrate discipline knowledge and help teachers in developing students' learning outcomes. A textbook constitutes a learning package related to a course unit. It can be in the form of printed materials for the learners to read which may also be completed with related tasks. Basically, a textbook is a book used as a guide for teaching and learning process in the classroom [18]. In the context of the English language teaching, a textbook is part of a collection of books containing materials for teaching various language skills or only focusing on the discussion of one language skill (e.g., reading). This study focuses on the reading course materials (a textbook, sections of a textbook, journal articles, magazine sections, news items, brochures, and other items used as a source of learning). To contextualize the learning focus to the real life experience some authors suggest the use of authentic texts.

Heitler [21] defines authentic materials as any texts written by native English speakers for native English speakers. As authentic materials bring learners into direct contact with a reality drawn from up-to-date source, such as newspaper, they can be directly relevant to learners' needs. As such, they are the best means that could encourage them to attempt to communicate in English without much hesitation.

As stated earlier, this study is concerned with the condition of the nation which has shown signs of the ineffectiveness or even the failure in implementing character education. The failure applies not only to the young such as school-aged children but also to respectable members of people representatives who supposed to be models who should set examples for the implementation of character education.

The basic concept of character education can be traced from two main terms, education and character. Education is a consciously planned effort to create a learning atmosphere conducive for learning processes to happen so that the learners are able to actively develop their potentials in order to possess the power of religious spirit, self-control, personality, knowledgeableness, noble character, and the skills required for themselves, the community, the nation and the country [3].

Nucci & Narvaéz [22] propose that education can be interpreted as all the endeavors teachers make to encourage the development of the students' learning, despite the awareness that moral development and character building are not merely the result of the teaching and learning process at school. However, the school, one of the three pillars of education, has a paramount role in building the students' character and personality. Meanwhile The Board of Research and Development of Curriculum Center of the Ministry of National Education [1] defines character as the trait, attitude, morality, or personality of someone built as a result of the internalization of various virtues believed and utilized as the foundation for perceiving, thinking, behaving, and acting.

The term *virtues* in this context should be understood as a set of values, morals, and norms, such as honesty, courage to take actions, reliability, and respecting others. One's interaction with others grows and nurtures the character of the community and that of the nation. Hence, the nation's character can only be built through the character development of the individuals. However, as human beings live in a specific social and cultural environment, one's individual character development can only happen in his/her own social and cultural environment. This means that the development of the nation's culture and character can only be conducted in an educational process which does not separate the learners from their social environment, community's culture, and the culture of the nation [1].

Therefore, in this regard, Berkowitz & Bier [23] assert the important role of the two of the three pillars of education – the family and the community – in character education when they claim that:

1. *character education is the deliberate effort to develop good character based on core virtues that are good for the individual and good for society.*

2. *character education is any deliberate approach by which school personnel, often in conjunction with parents and community members help children and youth become caring, principled, and responsible.*

However, it must be kept in mind that making children and youth become caring, principled, and responsible, character education needs role models. Our young generations need examples of the noble value application, not merely programs or slogan highly packaged but away from practical applications of the targeted values [24].

Related to the implementation of character education at school Lickona [5] mentions ten main values - *wisdom, justice, fortitude, self-control, love, positive attitude, hard work, integrity, gratitude* and *humility*. Meanwhile, the Indonesian Ministry of National Education (2010) suggests eighteen values – religiousness, honesty, tolerance, discipline, hard work, creativity, autonomy, democracy, curiosity, nationalism, patriotism, achievement-praising, communicativeness, peace-loving, love of reading, environmental care, social care, responsibility.

Fundamentally, therefore, the concept of character education is closely related to local culture or local wisdom. The term *local culture* is associated with local tradition which textually means traditions inherited from generation to generation (from the ancestors) continually performed in the community, based on the judgment and belief that the existing practice is considered the best and the truest (Pusat Bahasa, 2008: 1483). From the term *tradition* (noun) comes the word *traditional* (adjective) representing an attitude or way of thinking and acting-which always firmly adheres to the norms and traditions inherited. The concept of tradition is closely related to the concept and the domain of locality. Hence, local wisdom refers to inherited attitude and way of thinking adhered to by members of the community as they are considered the best and the truest.

This study, which is the continuation of the previous studies, concerns the big theme – cultural insertion and character value integration in the teaching of English as a foreign language in Indonesia. The first multi-year study (Sugirin, Sudartini, Nurhayati, and Suciati, 2011-2013) was on the development of a multicultural-based English textbook as a means of the local culture maintenance. The initial survey on the books used at the junior high school level indicated the presence of the foreign culture insertion in the forms of pictures, illustrations, and texts. The absence of adequate explanation about the introduced phenomena may lead to possible cross-cultural misunderstanding. The second study (Sugirin, Widyantoro, and Sudartini, 2012-2014) was on the development of a model of integrating cultural values in the teaching of English in vocational and senior high schools.

The initial step of this present study found data related to the integration of Western and Indonesian cultures in the contents of the teaching and learning materials used. The authors included a number of character values in the course materials mostly used by the instructors participating in the study. As the purpose of evaluating the existing materials is for the basis of developing a textbook which caters for teaching purposes as well as integrating character education values, questions related to materials selection which includes character education values, strategies and activities devised to nurture these values will be addressed.

2   METHOD

In line with the aims of the study, a qualitative approach is employed in this study. The data were texts in English as found in the textbooks, journal articles, news items or other learning materials used in developing the students' reading skills in a higher education, particularly in the English Education Study Program, the instructors' criteria in selecting the course materials, strategies in highlighting the character values, and activities devised to nurture the intended character education values. Data were collected through (1) documenting the English textbooks and other learning materials commonly used in teaching and learning process in the English Education Study Program in the last academic year, i.e. September 2017 to August 2018; (2) reading the documents/textbooks and other materials used that included character education values; (3) categorizing the contents based on the values integrated; (4) interviewing the instructors in selecting the materials, strategies used to highlight character education values, and activities devised to nurture the intended values. The key instruments of the research were the researchers themselves as *'human instruments'*, complemented by the documentation guide. The data were then analyzed using the qualitative data analysis technique suggested by [4], involving three steps - data condensation, data display, and inference drawing.

The values were first grouped based on the units found in the related semesters. The same value appearing in different units was counted once. Values having similar or related meaning were grouped as one family. The value families were then classified based on the categories of the values proposed by [5,1]. The values which did not belong to the two categories were assigned a new category. In order to find out the utilization of the selected materials, interviewing the instructors were focused on what strategies they used to highlight the values in the teaching and learning process and what activities they used to nurture the intended character education values.

3 FINDINGS

The findings of the study consist of two parts: (1) the general description of the study and discussion on content of the character education values in the textbooks and other materials used and the utilization of the course materials to nurture the character education values, and (2) discussion on the findings in details.

3.1 *General description of the findings*

The teaching of reading which is basically intended to develop the students' reading skills runs for four hierarchical classes in four semesters, each earning two credit units. The classes are *Reading for General Communication* (semester 1), *Reading for Information and Enjoyment* (semester 2), *Reading for Literary Appreciation* (semester 3), and *Reading for Academic Purposes* (semester 4).

Based on the result of tracing the course descriptions and the course outlines of the reading classes, other than books there are also complementary materials such as handouts used by the instructors in the academic years 2016-2017 and 2017-2018.The following is a list of books and materials used in the reading classes identified.

Reading for General Communication - ENG6209/2 credits/Semester 1
1. Mikulecky, B. & Jeffries, L. (1996). *More reading power.* New York: Wesley Addison
2. Longman, Shepherd, J. F. (1987). *College vocabulary skills.* Boston: Houghton Mifflin.
3. Thornbury, S. (2002). *How to teach vocabulary.* Essex: Longman.
4. Shepherd, J. F. (1987). *College vocabulary skills.* Boston: Houghton Mifflin.
5. Flemming, L. (2006). Reading resources. Retrieved January 29, 2009 from http://dhp.com /~laflemm/reso/mainIdea.htm
6. Herszenhorn, D.M. (2009, January 28). Components of Stimulus Vary in Speed and Effi ciency.The New York Times. Retrieved from http://www.nytimes.com/2009/01/29/us/polit ics/29assess.html?_r=1&scp=5&sq=how%20effective%20the%20huge%20program%20of %20tax%20cuts%20&st=cse
7. Stolberg, S. G. (2009, January 29). White house unbutton formal dress code. The New York Times. Retrieved from http://www.nytimes.com/2009/01/29/us/politics/29white house.html?hp
8. Maker, Janet. Lenier, Minnette, (1991). *College Reading Book. Third Edition.* California: Wadsworth.
9. Glenn, C. Miller, R. K., Webb, S. S., Gray, L. & Hodges, J. C. (2004). Hodges' Harbrace Handbook. New York: Thomson Wadsworth.
10. http://esl.about.com/od/readinglessonplan1/a/Reading-Comprehension-Skills-Scanning.htm

11. http://www.ereadingworksheets.com/free-reading-worksheets/reading-comprehension-worksheets/context-clues-worksheets/

Reading for Information and Enjoyment - ENG6210/2 credits/Semester 2
12. Martin, Montgomery, et al. 2006. *Ways of Reading*. Routledge
13. Grenall, Simon & Swan, Michael. 1986. *Effective Reading*. Cambridge University Press
14. Pasternak, Mindy & Wrangell, Elisaveta. 2007. *Well Read 3*. Oxford
15. Lee, Linda &Gundersen, Erik. 2001. *Select Reading (Intermediate)*. Oxford University Press
16. Gairns, Ruth & Redman, Stuart. 2005. *Natural English (Pre-Intermediate) – Reading and Writing Skills*. Oxford

Reading for Literary Appreciation – 2 credits/Semester 3
17. Mikulecky, Beatrice S. & Jeffries, Linda. 2007. *Advanced Reading Power*. Pearson Education. New York
18. Wiener, H. S. &Bazerman, C. (1988). Reading skills handbook.(4th ed.). Boston: Houghton Mifflin.
19. Montgomery, Martin et.al. 2007. *Ways of Reading*. Routledge. New York

Reading for Academic Purposes/2 credits/Semester 4
20. Brown, H. D. 2007. *Principles of Language Learning and Teaching, Fifth Edition, pp. 5–8:* White Plains, NY: Pearson Education. *Language, learning, and teaching*
21. Lindeman, G. & Sanchez, M. F. 2009. The Role of Language Education in Sustainable Development. *IberoAmerica Global*. Vol 2 No 1, Feb. 2009. Pp.142–150.
22. Kilgour, David. 1999. *The Importance of Language*. Calgary: Southern Alberta Heritage Language Association. Pp. 1–3.
23. Saleh M. Al-Salman. 2007. Global English and the Role of Translation. *SWE Journal*. Volume 9. Issue 4 Article 9.
24. Firman, H. & Tola, B. 2008. The Future of Schooling in Indonesia. *Journal of International Cooperation in Education*, CICE Hiroshima University, Vol.11 No.1, pp.71-84.
25. Lin Shen & Jitpanat Suwanthep. 2011. E-learning Constructive Role Plays for EFL Learners in China's Tertiary Education. *Asian EFL Journal*. Professional Teaching Articles. Vol. 49 January 2011. Pp 3–27.
26. Tovani, Cris. 2000. *I Read It, but I Don't Get It*. Portland, Maine: Stenhouse Publishers. Pp. 13–21.
27. Ford, E. H. & Emery, E.1954. *Highlights in the History of the American Press*. London: OUP. Pp. 362–370.
28. American Heart Association. 2003. Risk Factors for Heart Disease. In *Heart and Stroke Facts*. Pp. 36–45.
29. Greene, I. 2003. *How to Improve Self-Esteem in the African American Child*. Second edition. San Diego: P. S. I. Publishers. (Forewod, 102–143)

3.2   *Units of the books containing character values*

From the close and critical reading of the texts in the book sections and the complementary materials used in teaching the reading skills, the integration of character values were identified. Nine of 10 Lickona's [5] main values and twelve of the 18 IMONE's [1] values were found in the course materials used.However, only two of the four instructors intentionally selected the materials by considering the inclusion of Lickona's main character education values and IMONE's mandated character education values. The following outliners the character education values found in the reading course materials from semesters 1 to 4.

   Reading for General Communication (Semester 1) has 9 units containing character education values in 1 out of 11 books used.**Reading for Information and Enjoyment (Semester 2)** has 13 units containing character education values in 4 out of 5 books used, while **Reading for Literary Appreciation (Semester 3)** provides 3 units in 1 out of 3 books, and **Reading for Academic Purposes (Semester 4)**accommodates 9 units in 9 out of 10 books used.

3.3 Character education values found in the units

The following is a list of character education values found in the 34 units used in the teaching of reading. The values are presented in three groups: the Lickona's group, the Indonesian Ministry of National Education's (IMONE's) group and the new group.

3.4 Modes of presenting the character values

The close reading of the books shows that there are two modes of presenting the character education values. Some of the units present the values by explicitly mentioning the intended values in the topic of the unit. Some others present them implicitly. It is the task of the lecturer to manipulate the texts in the exercises and discussion sections in order that the students can see and learn the intended values.

As only two instructors intentionally selected the character education values to be included in the course materials, these two instructors were also the ones who intentionally identified the values and discussed the values in the teaching and learning process. Where relevant, they related the foreign values to similar ones in the Indonesian context. For example, one instructor related Thanksgiving Day to currently revived traditions of post rice harvest or pre-sugar cane harvest celebrations in some areas in Java. The third instructor made use of any moral values found in the selection without deep consideration in selecting and nurturing the values, and the fourth instructor focused on the language and skills development. Meanwhile,

Table 1. Nine of 10 Lickona's (2004) main values.

fortitude, self-confidence, commitment	*justice*, respect, responsibility, respect for human rights
gratitude, gratefulness	*love*, patriotism, loyalty, empathy
hard work, diligence, seriousness	*positive attitude*, optimism, vigor, zest
humility, decency, simplicity, modesty	*wisdom*, decision making
integrity, consistency, faithfulness	

Table 2. Twelve of the 18 IMONE's (2010) values.

achievement-praising, social prestige	*nationalism*,
autonomy, independence, freedom,	*peace loving*, peace
creativity, innovation	*religiousness*
democracy, equality	*responsibility*
discipline	*social care*, care
honesty	*tolerance*, compatibility, harmony
love of reading, love of learning	

Table 3. The non-suggested values.

cooperative spirit, collaboration competition	professionalism
dependability, reliable, trustworthiness	power, supremacy, dominance
intelligence, sensibility, common sense,	role model, leadership
open-mindedness	self-appreciation, self-acceptance, self-esteem
	self-direction, self-reliance
	thrift, prudence

Note: *the values written in italics are those suggested in the related documents.*

the values are integrated in explicit and implicit modes. In the explicit mode, the author explicitly uses the word representing the value such as "responsibility" while in the implicit mode the author presents a text in which the instructor and the students have to make an inference of what character value is intended though the given text.

In regard to the activities to nurture some intended character education values, three instructors have reported that text comprehension, discussion, and reflection sessions have been considered fruitful in encouraging the students to internalize the values intended. In the reflection session some students expressed silent agreement that cheating in the exam was a common practice in their past. Even the instructor focusing on the language and reading skills development found the three activities effective in achieving the goals of the instruction.

4 DISCUSSION

Regardless of the reasons behind the choice of the books or complementary materials used in the teaching of Reading, it can be seen from Table 1 that the values included in the books already represent 9 of the 10 main values suggested by Lickona [5] in character education. Table 2 shows that 12 of the 18 IMONE's values are found in the books and the complementary materials used in the teaching of Reading. Beyond the two groups there are still a number of non-suggested values identified.

It is worth noting that some of values in Table 3, which are not included in the IMONE's value group, are in fact characteristic values of the Indonesian people. Collaboration or cooperative spirit, for instance, is a prominent character value highly upheld by the Indonesians and should be inherited by the young generations. Cooperative spirit known as "gotong royong" (Jalaluddin, 2016) is the spirit of working hand-in-hand that has brought Indonesia into its independence. This spirit is up to now highly valued, especially in the countryside and suburban areas. This spirit is the capital of the nation that has enlightened the burden of the government in facing disasters such earthquakes, tsunamis, volcano eruptions, landslides, and the others. Without undermining the role of the international aids, it can be said that disasters in Aceh (2005), Yogyakarta (2006), Lombok (2018), and Palu and Gorontalo (2018) have all been made manageable because of the collaborative spirit of all the walks of life of the Indonesian people. This value should be one of the main values listed in the Indonesian character education values.

Another important value is "leadership" or "role model" that should characterize all the government officials, heads of institutions, and public figures including members of the Indonesian People's Representatives. These people should set examples for the public, particularly for the youth if character education in this country is to be successful. If these people can play the role of role models for the public, particularly the young, formal character education programs will be no longer necessary [24]. It can be seen from the tables above that not all the character education values appear in the units of the books used. This may be due to the purpose of the selected texts. The instructors may have based the selection more on the authenticity of the texts rather than on the theme. As the focus is on the reading skill development, they seek texts considered authentic for the purpose. As Heitler [21] and Kilickaya [25] claim, authentic materials bring learners into direct contact with a reality drawn from up-to-date source, such as newspaper, they can be directly relevant to learners' needs.

Contextualizing the course materials as suggested by Tomlinson [19] has been one of the strategies an instructor used to attract the students' interest. For example, Thanksgiving Day has been related to currently revived traditions of post rice harvest or pre-sugar cane harvest celebrations in some areas in Java, Indonesia. Other than making the text interesting, the unit has also made the students search for new words or phrases to express themselves in the discussion session and task completion.The instructor focusing on the language and reading skills development has found contextualizing course materials effective in achieving the goals of the instruction. Despite lacking the mandated character education value, focusing on the language and skills development is, in fact, an important goal of language teaching and learning [26].

5 CONCLUSION

Despite the focus on reading skills development as the main purpose of the Reading classes, some instructors have selected course materials containing character education values as suggested by Lickona as well as those mandated by IMONE. However, some have not based the selection on such criteria. From the point of view of the main purpose of the Reading classes, the materials may have met the requirement; however, from the perspective of the implementation of character education as mandated by the MONE, much still needs to be done by the instructors of the Reading classes. Hence, the integration of character education in reading classes at the English education department is still an effort worthy of making.

REFERENCES

[1] Ministry of National Education. (2010). *The development of the nation's culture and character education: A school guide.* Jakarta: the Ministry of National Education, the Board of Research and Development of the Curriculum Center.

[2] Asrom, H. (2015). Beredar, Buku Ajar Menyesatkan (Circulation of Misleading Textbooks). *Kedaulatan Rakyat*, 5 April, page 12 columns 4–7.

[3] Ministry of National Education. (2003). Act of the Republic of Indonesia Number 20, Year 2003 on National Education System. Jakarta: Ministry of National Education.

[4] Miles, M.B., Huberman, A.M., & Saldaña, J. 2014. *Qualitative Data Analysis. A Methods Sourcebook.* 3rd Edition. Los Angeles: Sage.

[5] Lickona, Thomas. (2004). *Character Matters: How to Help Our Children Develop Good Judgement, Integrity and Other Essential Virtues.* New York: Touchstone. Simon & Schuster, Inc.

[6] Tehusijarana, K.M. & Dipa, A. (2018). Death of Persija fan at hands of Persib hooligans sparks outrage. *The Jakarta Post*, September 24.

[7] Ihsanuddin. (2015). Breaking News: Dua Anggota DPR Adu Jotos di Gedung DPR. Accessed on 15/ 06/2018 from *http://www.tribunnews.com/nasional/2015/04/08/breaking-news-dua-anggota-dpr-berkelahi-di-gedung-dpr.*

[8] Edi, P. 2018. Polisi amankan 25 pelajar SMP akan tawuran di Yogyakarta. Accessed on 2 October 2018 from https://www.google.co.id/Merdeka.com.

[9] Arjawinangun, K.B. (2018). Tiga Faktor Penyebab Tawuran di Kalangan Pelajar. Accessed on 13/ 02/2018 from *https://metro.sindonews.com/read/1281615/170/ini-tiga-faktor-peyebab-tawuran-di-kalangan-pelajar-1518449935.*

[10] Solichinc, (2018). Faktor Penyebab Pelajar Suka Tawuran dari Psikolog. Accessed on 22/10/2018 from *http://lampung.tribunnews.com/2018/07/04/faktor-penyebab-pelajar-suka-tawuran-dari-psikolog.*

[11] Williams, G. 2010. ESL Teaching: How language and culture are interdependent. *Language Study.* November.

[12] Foley, W.A. (2001). *Anthropological Linguistics: An Introduction.* Oxford: Blackwell Publishers Inc.

[13] Lotten, M. (Ed.). (2013). *Languages for the Future.* London: British Council.

[14] Sugirin, S., Sudartini, S. & Nurhayati, L. (2012). *Developing a model for character education integration in the English language teaching at senior high school.* Seminar proceeding, Universitas Negeri Yogyakarta.

[15] Koda, K. & Zehler, A.M. (2008). Conceptualizing reading universals, cross-linguistic variations, and second languageliteracy development. In K. Koda & A.M. Zehler (Eds.). *Learning to Read Across Languages: Cross-Linguistic Relationships inFirst- and Second-Language Literacy Development.* New York and London: Routledge Taylor & Francis Group (pp. 1–9).

[16] Lyon, G.R. (2005). *Why Reading Is Not A Natural Process.* Bethesda, Maryland: Center for Development and Learning, National Institutes of Health (NIH).

[17] Grabe, W. (2009). *Reading in a Second Language: Moving from Theory to Practice.* Cambridge: Cambridge University Press.

[18] Richard, J.C. & Schmidt, R. (2002). *Longman Dictionary of Language Teaching and Applied Linguistics* 3rd*Edition.* Edinburgh: Pearson Education Limited.

[19] Tomlinson, B. 2009. *Principles and procedures of materials development for language learning.* New York: Continuum.

[20] Fasso, W., Knight, B.A., & Knight, C. (2014). Development of individual agency within a collaborative, creative learning community. In M. Khosrow-Pour (Ed.), *Encyclopedia of information science and technology* (3rd ed., pp. 7519–7528). Hershey, PA: IGI Global Press.

[21] Heitler, D. 2005. Teaching with Authentic Materials. Pearson Education. Accessed from http://www.pearsonlongman.com/intelligent_business/images/teachers_resourse/Pdf4.pdf.

[22] Nucci, Larry P. and Darcia Narvaés. (2008). *Handbook of Moral and Character Education*. New York: Routledge.

[23] Berkowitz, Marvin W. & Melinda C. Bier. (2005). *What Works in Character Education: A Research-Driven Guide For Educators*. St. Louis: University of Missouri Press.

[24] Sugirin. (2018). Role models in language acquisition and character education. *Character Education for 21st Century Global Citizens* (ISBN 978-1-138-09922-7). London: Taylor & Francis.

[25] Kilickaya, F. (2004). Authentic materials and cultural content in EFL classrooms. *The Internet TESL Journal, X(7)*.

[26] Uso-Juan, E. & Martinez-Flor, A. (2006). Approaches to language teaching and learning: Towards acquiring communicative competence through the four language skills. *Current Trends in the Development and Teaching of the Four Language Skills*. Berlin: Walter de Gruyter G. Williams, G. 2010. ESL Teaching: How language and culture are interdependent. *Language Study*. November 2010.

English Linguistics, Literature, and Language Teaching in a Changing Era – Madya et al. (eds)
© 2020 Taylor & Francis Group, London, ISBN 978-1-03-224160-9

The implementation of the Moodle platform to help teachers develop blended learning in the field of Teaching English as a Foreign Language (TEFL)

Tchello Kasse & Anita Triastuti
English Education Study Program, Graduate School, Yogyakarta State University, Yogyakarta, Indonesia

ABSTRACT: This paper presents a narrative review of the literature in relation to the implementation of Moodle to help teachers develop blended learning in the field of Teaching English as a Foreign Language (TEFL). Although much research has been done regarding the use of Moodle in teaching and learning processes, some shortcomings still exist in this discipline. The Moodle implementation does not cover all of the universities of the world. Further studies are needed to help teachers to understand more about it and to master its use in order to foster the blended learning approach. This paper intends to examine the extent to which Moodle has been given attention by the previous studies, and from which aspects it has mainly been studied, so that teachers can benefit from it to find better teaching methods. This paper also offers useful information that will provide additional insights in relation to Moodle and the ways that teachers can use it efficiently during their teaching. Moodle and blended learning will be successfully applied by colleges and universities around the world. The information provided in this paper will empower teachers, students and school administrators to acknowledge the crucial value of Moodle in English language teaching and enable them to obtain excellent results and improve their teaching and learning strategies.

Keywords: ICT, Moodle, blended learning, teacher, student, EFL

1 INTRODUCTION

In this era of global digitalization, it is hard to talk about education without mentioning the use of Information and Communication Technology (ICT). ICT intervenes in every single part of human life, including Humanities, Social Science, Law, Natural Science, Technology and Medicine. In education, ICT plays a key role in terms of conducting research, collecting data, teaching and learning. While using ICT, with just a click of a mouse we can access mountains of information from around the world [1]. Additionally, in reference to the field of education, the use of ICT has made it easier than ever for teachers to be able to exchange their experiences, points of view, ideas, and feelings with learners. Also, many of them can see their teacher training programs get improved on site or remotely at a very low cost [2]. It has been claimed [2] that ICT can be used in many places, where it can enable both teachers and students to study their respective courses. As education is one of the foundations of economic and social development factors, ICT facilitates a growing number of people to get access to schools and enables them to have a better education that matches their interests.

There are lots of ICT tools available for teachers: computers, internet, projectors, smartphones, e-mailing facilities, online classes, video conferencing, and so on. These tools make both teaching and learning English more attractive and convenient. Also, ICT enables teachers to save a great deal of time, prevents them from having to travel home, gives them energy for working and helps them save money when working at school. For students, they can learn whatever they want by using ICT tools at any time and in any place [3]. Therefore, ICT plays an incredible role in Teaching English as a Foreign Language (TEFL) [1].

ICT has emerged gradually in the educational sector, dealing with the pedagogical philosophy based on constructivism that is supported by a Learning Management System (LMS) such as Moodle. Henceforth, the Moodle platform will be known as one of the most used open source e-learning platforms, as it gives teachers the possibility to create online courses with access given to registered students only. This platform allows teachers and students living in different geographical areas to exchange information through synchronous and asynchronous communications [4]. The benefits of Moodle are multiple. Moodle facilitates educational communities to share information, it develops a student-centered approach, and finally it strengthens social interaction [5]. However, the Moodle platform is difficult to use for some teachers. In this regard, teachers first need to learn how to manipulate electronic devices. Nevertheless, the flexibility of the Moodle platform allows teachers' uploaded materials to be accessed by the learners at any time and from any place they might be. It also permits a series of interactions between teachers and students. Students have enough time to thoroughly discuss and share ideas about the topics presented by their respective teachers before the class starts. But in order to obtain the advantages that come from using Moodle, one important element must be highlighted: the need for an internet connection, without which there is no way to use Moodle. Furthermore, teachers using Moodle will have full control of their students' track records. The activities are checked throughout by the use of the internet. Teachers can see what students did during a certain timeframe for assignments, quizzes, forums, chats, and so on. [6]. For example, [6] argued that one teacher claimed: 'I use Moodle for uploading and sharing documents. I use Moodle for uploading listening activities because it's easy for students to be online and then they can attend to the listening text. Mostly, I use it for listening exercises, not for reading.' This shows how important the teachers found the use of Moodle in teaching listening skills. Regarding these statements, teachers have to be well equipped in both material and resources, otherwise they cannot use Moodle in the teaching process. Therefore, using Moodle requires the potentiality of having both money and technology.

In the field of education, when supported by ICT, the concept of Blended Learning (BL) has become one of the hottest teaching approaches, as it empowers a large number of students to actively gain access to the materials provided by teachers. BL offers a flexible and customizable time frame for each student to learn at their own pace [7]. Many students are happy when the courses are taught face-to-face and in live using via Internet. Therefore, BL also decreases the stress and anxiety of learners, since students perform much better when they interact by using ICT tools [8]. BL permits teachers to be more productive because it helps students to work comfortably when learning languages and technology. Also, it gives them a positive attitude and increases their learning motivation [9]. Nevertheless, the concept of BL must first be understood by the teachers who are engaged in the teaching profession. In addition, [10] explained that studies showed that, by 2019, 50% of high school courses will be made available and taught online. Moreover, today's younger generation is more focused on this digital era and they are exposed to and use technology from the age of one [10]. In this case, it is crucial to make sure that teachers will have the opportunity to learn how to use computers, become proficient in English, and work very hard on technological knowledge. Otherwise, making the internet available to everyone will not help teachers who are not familiar with ICT tools to teach effectively using Moodle. Therefore, pre-training sessions regarding the use of ICT would be very helpful for teachers who are not computer literate.

BL facilitates easy access to global resources and material appropriate to learners so that they can use them to improve their learning achievements. Moreover, BL increases students' vocabulary knowledge, as they are given opportunities to navigate through the internet and check the meaning of terms [11]. It has been said [12] that teachers who use BL by mixing the online system with the traditional way of teaching do best of all. Likewise, a study conducted at the University of Wisconsin – Milwaukee suggested that students learn much more in BL courses compared to traditional classroom courses. Even though that statement is true, we should focus on the availability of the internet. Without that, there is no BL at all. Therefore, BL and Moodle strongly require an internet connection so that they can be operational.

Although Moodle has been combined with other ICT devices, such as computers, smartphones, and tablets, in order to teach English effectively, there are still English-as-a-Foreign Language (EFL) teachers with a very low level of awareness of the importance of using Moodle to develop BL. Barriers to ICT integration in education did exist in many institutions due to its high level of costs, the lack of mastery of its functionality, and its level of acceptance. This has been argued by [13], who said that BL received little attention in its implementation. Difficulties ranged from a lack of communication, lack of institutional support, problems in adopting new technologies, and a lack of electronics means. Moreover, old methods of instruction are still applied in some universities and teachers carelessly do not pay attention to the fact that using Moodle can help to improve the teaching process [13]. Therefore, in this era of digitalization, the use of Moodle and BL must be supported by the developed countries so that the necessary equipment and internet connection can be available for all teachers.

Based on what has been mentioned above, the current study began with a narrative review of literature that explains largely how Moodle can help teachers to understand more about BL so that they can take advantage to use it in schools. If they were not aware of this, teachers would miss out on the advantages that ICT brings us, and they would find themselves in a disadvantageous situation when it came to teaching. A combination of previous studies allowed the researcher to collect a series of data about the use of Moodle and BL for teaching EFL students. Data in this research are sourced from documentation (documents-based data). Therefore, this paper will definitely discuss the use and importance of the Moodle platform to increase teachers' awareness of preparing and delivering teaching material in the field of TEFL, which will finally develop BL.

2 INFORMATION AND TECHNOLOGY COMMUNICATION

ICT is a useful instrument for developing education [14]. It permits people to have access to education so that they can develop educational materials, especially in teaching and learning. Today, ICT makes information and social media available to all people, even those living in remote areas. ICT is considered as a top source of information for our daily activities. However, a lack of ICT in education means that learners only have access to a poor amount of knowledge and experiences in various domains: teaching, business, tourism, and so on [14]. Therefore, we can assume that ICT is extremely important for teachers, but they need an internet connection in order to deliver the lessons to the students. Also, the government should help us to have ICT materials at the lowest price, because the underdeveloped countries have sufficient problems if they want to buy them, due to a lack of money and infrastructure. Therefore, governmental help is greatly needed in schools.

In contrast, it is clear that ICT is not used only for teaching, but can also be used for gaming, communicating, and for science and technology. A study at the University of Zagreb showed that, while using ICT, students are very much more competent when they play games in learning English [15]. In the same study, it is shown that ICT offers great possibilities for students to learn English. They can use various ICT tools that help them to access the learning materials that they need to boost their education. Despite large publications promoting the use of ICT in education, ICT is sporadically and insufficiently used in education. Therefore, results showed that 67.7% of the students being surveyed asserted that the frequency of ICT use is very satisfactory, and 27.1% claimed that ICT is used sometimes. However, every 20th student thought that ICT was never used in their faculty to help with learning EFL. This is why the importance of ICT use in schools should be highlighted, so that it can cover many educational institutions [15]. In order to facilitate the use of ICT in learning for all students, the governments need to make sure that the cost of ICT is low enough for everyone to access.

3   ICT AS AN EFFECTIVE TOOL IN TEACHING EFL

Using ICT tools helps both teachers and learners to acquire knowledge. As the technology is advancing at a high speed, teachers have to just as quickly update their competences when using it. This means that teachers should not wait to see the end of ICT development, but they need to develop themselves alongside ICT [16]. Moreover, ICT assists teachers and students to have creative ideas in a learner-friendly environment. When ICT is applied in a classroom setting, the following advantages are gained. Firstly, students are highly motivated to undertake classroom activities given by their teachers. Secondly, they get access to a wide range of information that they need to help them attain their goals [16]. To do this kind of work, students also have to be techno savvy. That is to say that they need to be competent in using computers, cell phones, tablets, and so on.

Students who learn from PowerPoint get new ideas and concepts to enhance their four English language skills. In addition, LCD projectors are today being used on a daily basis in our classrooms. They help in creating bulleted PPT notes for the learners [16]. Furthermore, the World Wide Web (WWW) cannot be ignored in this era of technology. The WWW offers a variety of possibilities to collect data for learning English by navigating the internet. It aids the improvement of the four language skills, which are listening, speaking, reading, and writing, by using authentic material, such as audio songs, online videos, and web pages downloaded from the internet [16]. Although ICT has become extremely important in teaching EFL, not all teachers can afford it due to its cost, which might be very high for some users. Therefore, people should not forget its affordability, mastery of manipulation, and knowledge of using it.

Another study conducted by [17] revealed that ICT should be used to change from a teacher-centered approach to a student-centered approach. That means that ICT can develop a teaching approach that can be combined with the traditional method of instruction to build BL. It is not only computers or LCD projectors that are considered to be ICT tools; radio, television, and telephones are also part of ICT. He showed that over 80% of information on the internet is written in English. This shows how interesting English language is today. What is unbelievable is that non-native English speakers outnumbered the native speakers [17]. Therefore, ICT helps the development of English to be well spread around the world and teaching English at school has impacted the advancement of ICT.

4   E-LEARNING

ICT creates distance learning approaches, new opportunities to develop education and training by using software and applications (e-learning), and a BL format by combining traditional classroom activities and those of ICT tools, such as computers [14]. For tens of thousands of years, it was difficult to meet and share knowledge. However, technologies have considerably changed this constraint. Now, through the newly developed approach called e-learning, people can finally learn everything they want from each other at any time and in any place, in any of the four corners of the world. E-learning is therefore defined as the use of information and computer material to make knowledge happen [18]. In addition, e-learning marshals computers and online networks to execute some pedagogical instructions. The combination of computers and internet connection gives the user the possibility to design teaching materials and deliver them virtually, for example, to students of EFL.

In the same year, another definition was given by [19], stating that e-learning is commonly understood as the use of information and communication technology devices to serve in a teaching and learning environment. Similarly, there are other technical terms referring to e-learning, such as online learning, virtual learning, distributed learning, network and web-based learning. These terms are used when talking about e-learning in general. They are terms that are used when referring to educational processes that require the combination of the internet and ICT tools to perform asynchronous and synchronous activities in teaching and learning [19]. According to [20], e-learning is any use of the web and internet connections to create learning activities. Finally, [21] argued that e-learning can be defined as learning by using electronic devices. In short, e-learning has become the use of the internet and computers to learn language.

5 BENEFITS OF E-LEARNING

E-learning facilitates learners to access the knowledge, multimedia resources, and teaching software that are available on the internet [21]. Learners become more and more flexible in terms of time and place. They can learn freely, based on their needs. Moreover, it enables multinational enterprises to adopt quick training strategies, and implement them for targeted training. Briefly, e-learning is helpful in education, so schools need to have a good technology infrastructure for education.

A survey study conducted by [22] classified four forms of e-learning. Firstly, the traditional form, in which there is no use of technology at all. Secondly, the web-based course, which works with computer and internet. All the communications and activities are done online. These courses use web-based technologies. They use the system to manage the content or just use web pages to help communicate the course plans to the students. Thirdly, the hybrid or BL form, which replaces the traditional courses to online activities. In these classes, the teacher combines the present course with e-learning. A large part of the course uses the internet, through discussion forums, with limited face-to-face meetings. Fourth, the online form, which happens when the learner takes the course at distance. The entire course is delivered online without any face-to-face contact with students. All these types of e-learning forms make learning easier for students provided they have the required elements for implementing the e-learning types, such as the material from which the course delivery happens.

6 MOODLE PLATFORM

It has been stated by [23] that Moodle is a free learning management system that allows the user to develop useful teaching material for online courses. In addition, Moodle is a course management system that many universities, colleges, K–12 schools, businesses users, or any other user can use to add web technology to their courses for teaching [24]. In addition, [25] argued that Moodle was created by Martin Dougiamas in 1999 as an open source course management system, so it is free. Moreover, [26] defined Moodle as a course management system used to develop courses via the internet. Furthermore, [27] stated that Moodle can be considered to be one of the fastest growing free and open source virtual learning environments around the world.

It was suggested by [28] that the number of contact hours in traditional face-to-face teaching are not enough for students to understand what they need to learn. As a result, Moodle can be implemented to activate and increase their English language skills, and also to make them independent learners. To support the use of Moodle, [28] recommends that teachers should implement it within BL, because this allows learners to support each other. Therefore, the implementation of Moodle is of paramount importance in teaching EFL since it is strongly connected to BL, so that students can learn effectively and efficiently. On the other hand, the Moodle platform has been researched by [29], who confirms that the Moodle platform has the main tools that teachers like when developing their teaching material. Moreover, the Moodle platform is used for BL, distance education, flipped classroom and other e-learning projects.

7 MOODLE ACTIVITIES

These activities can be used to enable students to develop their language proficiencies and also make them independent learners [28]. The first activity is chatting. This is a module that helps learners to have a real-time discussion by using the internet. After that comes the choice activity. This one enables teachers to ask a question and offer a multitude of answers that students can choose from. Additionally, the database activity helps learners to create, maintain, and find a collection of records. Their vocabulary and grammar are developed by reading text files, and also their English pronunciation development is helped through listening to authentic audio materials, such as those from native speakers, BBC news, VOA, and so on. External tool activity helps students to interact by using learning resources and activities from different websites. All these happen when the conditions of use are available: materials and an internet connection.

8 MOODLE RESOURCES

The following Moodle resources are designed to help students to develop their language proficiency through accessing information in various formats. Books are an important resource for learning any language. A file resource is also available for teachers to use for sharing presentations, mini websites, or drafts of files for some software programs, such as Photoshop for example. In addition, we have label resource, which is used for inserting text and multimedia into a course page. Moreover, page resource is a page that enables the teacher to develop a website resource by using a text editor. Finally, a URL resource helps teachers to make a web link as a course resource. Documents, images, or any other content that is available on the internet can be offered to the students. Moodle has indeed become important as it allows teachers to use the teaching resources on the website.

9 USEFUL FEATURES OF MOODLE

Instead of creating a Hyper Text Markup Language (HTML) page editor and sending the documents that are being created in a server, the teacher can directly use a web form to store the syllabus on the server. Online forums and chats serve as a communication tool between instructors and students, and also between the students themselves during their studies both inside and outside of the classroom. In addition, chats help the learners to quickly and easily interact with other students who are in a remote area. Online quizzes are very practical. The teachers can do these in a simultaneous way, which is to say that, at the same time as the quiz is made, the students can work on it and submit it to the teacher, who can give feedback immediately. The online grade book gives students the opportunity to see their work performance in real time. It is important to mention that only students who are well equipped can do this in comfort. The others have to visit cyber cafes or get connected via a relative's laptop in order to see one of these features.

In addition, this system helps to keep students' grades secure and prevents their identities from being posted in public places. Moreover, the online grade book only gives students permission to see their own grades, not those of others. Furthermore, research revealed that using the internet to score students work helps a lot with motivating them in their learning process. Therefore, it is really secure for students in terms of keeping their identity private.

The implementation of the Moodle platform is an easy process for teachers of EFL [29]. Firstly, they give assignments, such as projects, presentations, essays or reports, which allow them to push students to prepare digital content in any format, which can then be submitted by uploading it to the server. Secondly, it enables teachers to elaborate on forums or discussion boards. Forum refers to the posts that can be placed on the Moodle website allowing participants to discuss things freely, and they can receive all posts in their inboxes. Thirdly, live chat enables attendees to have a real-time exchange using the internet. Fourth is the content, in which teachers can develop lessons that end with a question, plus a number of possible answers. The last factor deals with the students whose teachers ask them to think about a particular topic. Students can edit and refine their answers in a given time.

10 THE CONCEPT OF BLENDED LEARNING (BL)

It was argued by [30] that BL is the combination of face-to-face meetings and online learning methods using computers and the internet. In addition to that, [31] defined BL as a combination of different tools, teaching methods and learning styles using an online network for delivering courses to learners. Further, [31] said that BL is a way of teaching at distance by using technological devices, such as high tech, television, internet, voice mailing, or conference calling, combined with a traditional way of teaching. Without mentioning the material, BL works only when one of the required materials, such as a computer and the internet, is available.

11 ADVANTAGES OF BLENDED LEARNING

There are numerous advantages of using BL, according to [32]. Learning can be more targeted, focused, delivered bite-size, and just-in time. Also, learners can interact with the tutor without moving from one place to another. In addition, learners can interact with their peers both inside and outside of school. Learning materials are readily accessible for all of the students who are registered to the class. Finally, a variety of techniques can be utilized by maximizing different technologies. All of these are feasible if the teachers are trained well how to use it and if they are given the necessary teaching materials for this purpose.

12 CONCLUSION

The combination of Moodle with traditional face-to-face instruction makes teaching successful using the BL approach. Teachers are invited to experiment using Moodle because of its unlimited effectiveness. Students always gain more knowledge and understanding than they would have done using the traditional teaching model. Therefore, it is highly recommended for English teachers to implement Moodle in the educational institutions where they work, providing that they are good at manipulating electronic devices.

REFERENCES

[1] Akhtar, S. (2016). Role of ICT in the enhancement of English language skills among the learners. *Journal of Technology for ELT*, 6(2).

[2] Ghayifekr, S. & Rosdy, W.A.W. (2015). Teaching and learning with technology: Effectiveness of ICT integration in schools. *International Journal of Research in Education and Science (IJRES)*, 1(2), 175–191.

[3] Ammanni, S. & Aparanjani, U. (2016). The role of ICT in English language teaching and learning. *International Journal of Scientific & Engineering Research*, 7(7), 2.

[4] Teixeira, L., Alvelos, H. & Costa, C. (2012). The use of Moodle e-learning platform. *Conference on Enterprise Information Systems*. Procedia Technology 5.

[5] Jeong, K.O. (2017). The use of Moodle to enrich flipped learning for English as a foreign language education. *Journal of Theoretical and Applied Information Technology*, 95(18).

[6] Suppasetseree, S. (2010). The use of Moodle for teaching and learning English at tertiary level in Thailand. *International Journal of the Humanities*. doi:10.18848/1447-9508/CGP/v08i06/42964

[7] Teach Thought Staff. (2017, August 29). *Re. The benefits of blended learning*. [Web log comment]. Retrieved from https://www.teachthought.com/technology/the-benefits-of-blended-learning/.

[8] Yuen, A.H.K. (2011). Exploring teaching approaches in blended learning. *Research and Practice in Technology Enhanced Learning, 6*(1), 3–23.

[9] Karkour, I. (2011). A blended learning model for teaching reading in English as a foreign language. *Teaching English with Technology, 14*(4), 17–31.

[10] Buono, J. (2017, August 21). *Re. Blended learning: Why it's taking the lead in education.* [Web log comment]. Retrieved from https://blog.cognifit.com/blended-learning/.

[11] Tosun, S. (2015). The effects of blended learning on EFL students' vocabulary enhancement. *Procedia - Social and Behavioral Sciences, 199*, 641–647.

[12] Khan, I.A. (2014). Effectiveness of blended learning for teaching of English. *Research Journal of Recent Sciences, 3*(3), 78–85.

[13] Ghazizadeh, T. & Fatemipur, H. (2017). The effect of blended learning on EFL learners' reading comprehension. *Journal of Language Teaching and Research, 8*(3), 606–614. doi:10.17507/jltr.0803.21.

[14] BMZ Strategy Paper. (2013). *Information and communication technology.* Federal Ministry for Economic Cooperation and Development: Berlin.

[15] Oreski, P., Mikulan, K. & Legac, V. (2017). The use of information and communication technology in foreign language teaching/learning in school and at home. *Yearbook of the Faculty of Education.* XIV.

[16] Samuel, S. & Pulizala, R. (2014). Role of ICT in English language teaching. *International Journal of Innovative Research and Development.* ISSN 2278–0211 (online).

[17] Ibrahim, A.M.I. (2010). Information & communication technology in ELT. *Journal of Language Teaching and Research, 1*(3), 211–214.

[18] Horton, W. (2006). *E-learning by design.* San Francisco, CA: John Wiley & Sons.

[19] Naidu, S. (2006). *E-learning. A guidebook of principles, procedures and practices.* New Delhi, India: Sanjaya Mishara.

[20] Horton, W. & Horton, K. (2003). *E-learning tools and technologies.* Indianapolis: Wiley Publishing.

[21] Benraouane, S.A. (2011). *Guide pratique du e-learning.* Paris, France: Dunod.

[22] Allen, E. & Seaman, J. (2016). *Tracking online education in the United States.* Babson Survey Research Group and Quahog Research Group: Oakland, CA 94611.

[23] Rice, W.H. (2008). *E-learning course development.* Birmingham, UK: Packt Publishing.

[24] Cole, J. & Foster, H. (2008). *Using Moodle* (2nd ed.). USA: O'Reilly Media.

[25] Berg, D.R. (2014). *Student attitudes towards using Moodle as a course management system.* International Conference on Recreation and Leisure Industry & Language Application.

[26] Nash, S.S. & Rice, W. (2010). *Moodle 1.9 teaching techniques.* Birmingham, UK: Packt Publishing.

[27] Stanford, J. (2008). In the mood for Moodle. *English Teaching Professional, 54*, 58–60.

[28] Soliman, N.A. (2014). Using e-learning to develop EFL students' language skills and activate their independent learning. *Creative Education, 5*, 752–757. doi:10.4236/ce.2014.510088

[29] Elhawwa, T. (2017). The implementation of Moodle platform through lecturer's perspectives at English department. *Journal on English as a Foreign Language, 7*(2), 227–240.

[30] Garrison, D.R. & Vaughan, N.D. (2008). *Blended learning in higher education.* San Francisco, CA: John Wiley & Sons.

[31] Procter, C. (2003). *Blended learning in practice.* Education in a Changing Environment, Conference Proceedings. ISBN 0902896660

[32] Thorne, K. (2003). *Blended learning. How to integrate online and traditional learning.* London, UK: Kogan Page.

English Linguistics, Literature, and Language Teaching in a Changing Era – Madya et al. (eds)
© 2020 Taylor & Francis Group, London, ISBN 978-1-03-224160-9

Administering a need analysis survey to young EFL learners in Yogyakarta

Thuthut Kartikarini, Dyah S. Ciptaningrum, Emeral, Elsa M. Marahati & Septiana W. Setyaningrum
English Education Master Program, Graduate School of Yogyakarta State University, Yogyakarta, Indonesia

ABSTRACT: A growth of interest in teaching English at a younger age has triggered an emergence of Teaching English for Young Learners (TEYL) in Indonesia. Though English is not a compulsory subject taught in elementary schools, some public elementary schools in Yogyakarta run it as an extracurricular program. Either as a compulsory subject or an extra-curricular program, an appropriate EYL curriculum should be designed in order to achieve the best learning outcomes. In designing a curriculum, a need analysis plays an important role in investigating learners' needs of learning English. However, there has been a lack of atten-tion in conducting a need analysis of EYL from viewpoints of young learners themselves. Fill-ing this gap, a cross-sectional survey design using a questionnaire was conducted in order to assess students' wants and needs of English learning through twenty-seven of the fifth graders of SDN(Public Elementary School) XYZ 1 Yogyakarta in Academic Year 2017/2018. The questionnaire was distributed to know the students' wants in learning topics, ways of learning, modes of work, and a place of learning. Findings revealed that dream jobs and hobbies were the students' most favorite topics. In terms of learning preference, they enjoyed learning Eng-lish through games and picture stories. Learning in the classroom through group work was the students' favourite place of learning and mode of work. These findings serve as a basis for the teachers and stakeholders in the school to design an appropriate curriculum for the EYL program addressing the learners' needs, wants and necessities.

Keywords: English for young learners, need analysis

1 INTRODUCTION

Teaching English for Young Learners (TEYL) in Indonesia has begun since Curriculum 1994 with the issue of *SK Mendikbud* (Minister of Culture and Education Decree) No 060/U/1993. This regulation justified the teaching of English as a local content starting from the fourth grade of elementary school [1]. This policy has been shifted in Curricu-lum 2013 allowing the teaching of English as an elective extracurricular program for elementary school students. As stated in the Regulation of the Minister of Education and Culture of Republic of Indonesia Number 62, the Year 2014 on extracurricular activity in primary and secondary education, the implementation of elective extracurricular pro-gram must follow two principles. They are active participation and fun learning. Thus, TEYL in Indonesia is supposed to be conducted in fun ways and invite the young learn-ers to participate actively in the classroom.

However, reality does not meet expectation. TEYL in Indonesia has been facing some obs-tacles and its practices are still far from the aforementioned principles. There are two major problems of TEYL in Indonesia which might become sensible reasons for the government to shift the English subject from an intra curricular activity to extracurricular one in the current curriculum. They are a low quality of English teachers in public elementary schools and insufficient facilities, teaching aids and media [1]. It is revealed that 724 out of 1415 elementary school English teachers in ten regencies in South Sulawesi have never attended to English Teacher Training College. Added to this, most of them neither have received a proper English training for young learners nor had adequate experience in TEYL [2]. Moreover, pre-service and in-service education have not been sufficient to train student teachers and teachers to teach English at primary level. Lack of expertise and quality teacher educators contribute to the situation [3]. These findings imply that most elementary school English teachers do not have competent knowledge and skill in teaching English to young learners. They are not well equipped with the skill and ability to create enjoyable learning experiences for young learners. Limited facilities and resources were also major problems faced by EFL primary school teachers in Kuala Tungkal, Indonesia [4]. Hence, with a higher demand of teaching English at younger and younger ages, TEYL practices in Indonesia need to straighten up to grasp success.

The success of TEYL can be achieved if the teaching and learning activities meet the nature of children, how children learn, and how children learn a language. Children should be given activities and task which cater their characteristics as individuals who are(a) energetic; (b) spontaneous; (c) curious; (d) imaginative; (e) easily distracted; (f) egocentric; (g) social; (h) active learners – they learn by doing and interacting with their surroundings; (i) dependent on the teacher's support and scaffolding; (j) in need of a learning environment resembling their L1 acquisition; (k) in need of meaningful exposure and practice when learning a language; (l) not keen on explicit grammar explanations [5]. In terms of their proficiency level, the five to seven years old children belong to level one, the beginner stage while the eight to ten years old ones can be both in level one or level two since they might have been learning English for some time [6].

Additionally, TEYL can be implemented successfully under following conditions; (a) appropriate EYL curriculum; (b) appropriately trained EYL teachers, and (c) sufficient facilities [7]. The curriculum and learning materials are emphasized to be essential points in the teaching and learning process. Moreover, a continuity of English curriculum between primary schools and secondary schools should be maintained for the sake of students' smooth transition of learning English and teachers' source of help in fulfilling their students' needs of English [5]. However, it has not been implemented in Indonesia. An absence of a standard-based EYL curriculum in Indonesia has made TEYL practices out of focus. As a result, the teachers find difficulties in determining learning goals and materials for their students. Thus, the standard-based and appropriate EYL curriculum is necessary to be developed for the success of TEYL in Indonesia. EYL curriculum planners are required to be realistic about the children's ability to do and achieve within the limited amount of instruction that they get on a weekly basis [8].

Consequently, in designing a curriculum, it is essential to conduct need analysis. Need analysis is mainly used to identify learners' needs [9; 10]. It is closely related to English for Specific Purposes (ESP) that makes it different from General English [11]. Need analysis ensures that the curriculum will be relevant and meet the learners' satisfaction [9]. It can be a source of information about learners' perceived and present needs, and their potential and unrecognized needs [10]. In the other word, it identifies the learners' lacks – their present knowledge, necessities – required knowledge, and wants – subjective needs [11]. Although need analysis has some limitations such as a possibility for missing or inaccurate information about what learners' needs in the future, it acts as a foremost reminder for teachers and curriculum planners that the final aim of language teaching is to make the learner able to communicate [12].

Related to TEYL in Indonesia, previous studies have been conducted to investigate the needs of learning English for the elementary students. A need analysis of fourth and fifth graders of three public schools in Jakarta through a questionnaire, interviews and documents revealed the young learners' preferences of learning materials and ways of learning [1]. Findings revealed that in terms of learning material the students wanted to study music and songs, animals, arts & literatures, jobs, and family. In terms of ways of learning, the learners' needs were writing diaries/stories/teacher's explanation/summaries/sentences/names of fruits/names of animals, studying textbooks & exercise books, reading books/comics/magazines/English conversation, listening to music/teachers/conversation, making presentation, looking meaning up in a dictionary, working in groups, playing games, using English words in real conversation, and making dialogues. Another study revealed the target needs and learning ones for the third and fourth graders in an integrated Islamic primary school in Depok, West Java [13]. The findings showed that the target needs were tackling English language in the classroom and the daily lives, focusing on vocabulary building and its development, using familiar topics for the sake of vocabulary mastery, and utilizing various stimulating instruments to encourage the students to use English in their daily lives. Furthermore, the learning needs revealed that children learned English easier from concrete objects found in their daily lives and a presence of visual aids.

Though the aforesaid previous studies explored the young learners' wants and needs of their English language learning, a need analysis of EYL should be administered by every school which conducts TEYL as an extracurricular program since each school must have different vision and mission, learning objectives, and learners' needs. In light of the above, this study focused on investigating the needs of a specific group of fifth graders in *SDN* (Public Elementary School) *XYZ 1 Yogyakarta*. This school had been running EYL program as an extracurricular activity for its fifth graders for almost a year. However, this school had neither developed its own curriculum nor administered the need analysis to investigate its students' needs. As a result, it also faced the common problem in TEYL, which was the out of focus TEYL practice. Therefore, a need analysis for this school was urgently needed. This study is then aimed to investigate the students' needs of learning English in this school and assess their current knowledge in order to find out their learning gap. Hopefully, the data can serve as a basis to design the EYL curriculum for this school.

2 RESEARCH METHOD

The study employed a cross-sectional survey design [14]or one-shot survey design [15] since it wanted to measure current needs of the fifth graders in learning English at one point of time. *SDN* (Public Elementary School) *XYZ 1 Yogyakarta* was selected as the subject of the research since (a) it was one of Yogyakarta State University (YSU)'s lab schools – the schools which were being developed by YSU and the local government to be far better quality ones [16]. Therefore, as a student of YSU, the researcher also shared a responsibility to improve the academic quality of this school by helping it to design an appropriate EYL curriculum; and, (b) it had run TEYL for the fifth graders as the extracurricular program for one year, yet it had neither developed its own curriculum nor administered the need analysis to investigate its students' English learning needs.

This school conducted the EYL program once a week for the fifth graders. There were two classes in the fifth grade with twenty-eight students in each class. Each meeting began after the school hours. It lasted for sixty minutes. Using the convenience sampling, the researchers selected class 5 A as respondents because they were convenient to the researchers' schedule. There were twenty-eight students in total, yet there was one student absent during the need analysis administration.

A questionnaire was developed as the research instrument since this study addressed only a few variables i.e. learning topics, ways of learning, modes of work, and a place of learning [14]. The questionnaire containing four questions in total allowed the students to indicate their existing knowledge and expected knowledge by checking the appropriate column. Since the students were still in the beginner level, pictures describing different literacy contexts were shown to help them mark the contexts that were related to them [17]. Moreover, the questionnaire could collect information from a group of students in short period of time and it was easy to summarize the responses [7,14]. Another reason for administering a questionnaire for the fifth graders was due to the children's cognitive development. Children at the age of eleven years old were between Piaget's concrete and formal operational stage [5] in which they were considered as mature enough to reflect their English learning experience and convey their wants in learning English [10].

To check the questionnaire validity, expert judgment as evidence based on test content [14] was utilized. Moreover, a pilot study involving five students from Class 5 B helped the researchers to determine the survey's validity and reliability. Those five students voluntary answered the questionnaire and joined the interview related to the clarity of the questionnaire. Based on the pilot study, the alteration was mainly made on question number one. This question was then equipped with pictures to help learners grasp an idea about what the theme is about. Moreover, the researchers found that the questionnaire could be answered in approximately 15 minutes, thus no change about time allocation. After being validated, the questionnaire was distributed directly at a research site in order to obtain a high response rate. The gathered data from the questionnaire were then analyzed using the descriptive statistical analysis.

3 FINDING AND DISCUSSIONS

This study aimed to investigate the fifth graders' English learning needs of *SDN* (Public Elementary School) *XYZ 1 Yogyakarta in* Academic Year 2017/2018.There were four questions in the questionnaire. The first question was related to the students' preferred topic. The second one was about the students' learning ways of learning. The third one was related to modes of work, either they preferred working individually, in pair, or in group. The last one was about the students' favourite place of learning. The students were allowed to pick more than one answer.

Findings from the questionnaire were presented as followings:

Figure 1 above gives information that the top three favorite themes are *cita-cita, hobi,* and *sekolah*. There was 20% of students who picked *cita-cita* as their most favourite topic, meanwhile 19% of students wanted to learn about *hobi*. Those who wanted to learn about *sekolah* were 13%. This result reveals that the learning materials should be developed with more emphasis on *cita-cita, hobi,* and *sekolah*. However, it does not mean that the rest of themes will be excluded from the learning materials. They are given in smaller portions since they are also closely related to the children's daily lives that will be beneficial for the young learners' vocabulary mastery [13]. Furthermore, by personalizing what the children learn, it will help them strengthen their language learning and fulfil their egocentric nature [5].

Figure 2 shows that 46% of students enjoyed learning English through games. 25% of students also loved to learn English through picture stories. This finding confirms previous finding [10] revealing that most young learners loved playing games while studying English. Moreover, songs, stories, games, videos, role plays are some activities suggested to engage children and keep them interested in learning English. The language used in those activities should also be authentic and contextualized similar to their first language acquisition since

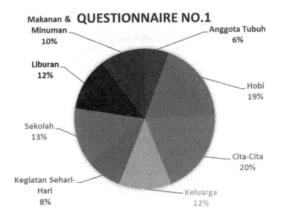

Figure 1. Result from question no 1.

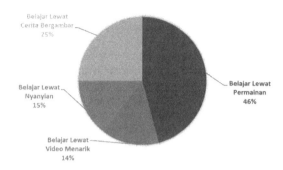

Figure 2. Result from question no 2.

the children will be motivated to learn and use English if they know a real purpose for using English [5].

Children are social [5]. They love playing with their peers and cooperating with them. This statement confirms with the finding which shows that 58% of students preferred working in groups and 24% in pairs. Meanwhile there was only 18% of students who liked to work individually. Furthermore, a previous study [18] showed that techniques of working in teams and especially in pairs promoted learners' speaking fluency. An interaction in pair work could facilitate an increase in the level of interactions among learners. Having a learner-learner interaction, the learners in pair work could create a relaxing or fear free environment. Thus, it could reduce an affective filter inside the classroom. On the other hand, although individual work could work better for other language learning elements like reading, writing, listening, and even pronunciation, it could not promote the learners' speaking fluency because the interaction was between learner-teacher which could prevent the learners from talking freely. The young learners should speak out to build their oral English proficiency. Thus, putting them in pairs or groups can help them achieve that goal.

Although children mostly love doing outdoor activities, the finding from the question number 4 shows an unexpected result that 63% of students preferred studying in the class, while 11 out of 27 students want to study out of the class. Both learning in the classroom and outside the classroom should be established in TEYL. However, it should be emphasized that the EYL teacher is supposed to provide some opportunities for the students to interact with real life objects connected to English language they are learning [5]. It is because the children learn best by practicing and interacting with their environment.

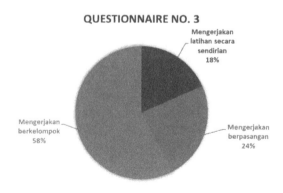

Figure 3. Result from question no 3.

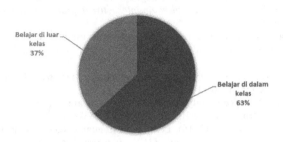

Figure 4. Result from question no 4.

4 CONCLUSIONS AND SUGGESTIONS

Findings revealed that dream jobs and hobbies were the students' most favorite topics. In terms of ways of learning, they enjoyed learning English through games and picture stories. Learning in the classroom through group work was the students' preferred mode of work and place of learning. The findings from this study is expected to make the English teachers in *SDN XYZ 1 Yogyakarta* aware of their learners' needs of learning English and provide an opportunity for them to revise their current teaching methods and materials that can address the learners' actual needs. Therefore, this school can achieve the best learning outcomes. However, since this cross-sectional survey design studied a small sample, there is an urgency to conduct a similar survey design with larger sample. Thus, the sample will show characteristics closest to the target population. As a result, it will be beneficial for further R&D research conducted by EYL teachers and curriculum developers in designing an appropriate curriculum for young EFL learners in Indonesia.

REFERENCES

[1] Sihmirmo, P. (2015). The needs analysis of English learning for the fourth and fifth graders. *Eduscience, 1* (1). Retrieved from http://ejurnal.esaunggul.ac.id/index.php/EDU/article/view/1183/1078.
[2] Sikki, E.A.A., Rahman, A., Hamra, A., Noni, N. (2013). The competence of primary school English teachers in Indonesia. *Journal of Education and Practice, 4* (11). Retrieved from https://www.iiste.org/Journals/index.php/JEP/article/view/6461/6462g.
[3] Zein, M.S. (2012). *Language teacher education for primary school English teachers in Indonesia: Policy recommendations* (Doctoral dissertation, The Australian National University, Canberra, Australia). Retrieved from https://www.researchgate.net/publication/300909051_Language_Teacher_Education_for_Primary_School_English_Teachers_in_Indonesia_Policy_Recommendations.
[4] Abrar, M. (2016). *Teaching English problems: An analysis of EFL primary school teachers in Kuala Tungkal.* Conference proceedings of ISIC 2016 Academic Conference. Retrieved from https://www.researchgate.net/publication/314280291_kTEACHING_ENGLISH_PROBLEMS_AN_ANALYSIS_OF_EFL_PRIMARY_SCHOOL_TEACHERS_IN_KUALA_TUNGKAL.
[5] Shin, J.K., & Crandall, J.A. (2013). Teaching young learners English: From theory to practice. Boston: Heinle Cengage Learning. Retrieved from https://books.google.am/books?id=50b_ygAACAAJ.
[6] Scott, W.A., and Yterberg, L.H. (1990). *Teaching English to children.* London, UK: Longman.
[7] Sutarsyah, C. (2017). Pembelajaran bahasa Inggris sebagai muatan lokal pada sekolah dasar di propinsi Lampung. *AKSARA Jurnal Bahasa Dan Sastra, 18* (1). Retrieved from http://jurnal.fkip.unila.ac.id/index.php/aksara/article/view/12633/9811.
[8] Zein, M.S. (2017). Elementary English education in Indonesia: Policy developments, current practices, and future prospects. *English Today, 33* (1). Retrieved from https://www.researchgate.net/publication/306107932_Elementary_English_education_in_Indonesia_Policy_developments_current_practices_and_future_prospects.

[9] Nation, I.S.P., & Macalister, J. (2010). Language curriculum design. New York: Routledge[2] Brown, H.D. (2001). *Teaching by principles: An interactive approach to language pedagogy (2nd ed.)*. New York, NY: Longman.

[10] Tzotzou, M.. (2014). Designing and administering a needs analysis survey to primary school learners about EFL learning : A case study. Preschool & Primary Education, 2(1),59–82. https://doi.org/10.12681/ppej.62.

[11] Hutchinson, T., & Waters, A. (1987). *English for specific purposes: A learning-centred approach.* Cambridge: Cambridge University Press.

[12] Cunningworth, A. (1983). Need analysis: A review of the state of the art. *System, 11* (2). Retrieved from http://sci-hub.tw/https://doi.org/10.1016/0346-251X(83)90025-8.

[13] Sunengsih, N., & Fahrurrozi, A. (2016). Learners' Language Needs Analysis of English Subject in Azkia Integrated Islamic Primary School. *IJEE (Indonesian Journal of English Education), 2*(1), 86–100. https://doi.org/10.15408/ijee.v2i1.1483.

[14] Creswell, J.W. (2012). *Educational research: Planning, conducting and evaluating quantitative and qualitative research* (4th ed.). Pearson Education, Inc.

[15] Lodico, M.G., Spaulding, D.T., Voegtle, K.H. (2010). *Methods in educational research: From theory to practice (2nd ed.)*. San Fransisco, CA: Jossey-Bass.

[16] Nurhadi. (2014, January 8). Pencanangan Lab School UNY. *UNY*. Retrieved from https://www.uny.ac.id/?q=berita/pencanangan-lab-school-uny.html.

[17] The CAELA Guide for Adult ESL Learners. (n.d.). Retrieved from http://www.cal.org/caela/scb/III_A_AssessingLearnerNeeds.pdf.

[18] Hosseini, S.H., Bakhtiarvand, M., Tabatabaei, S.A comparative study on the effect of individual, pair, and team work on speaking fluency of Iranian elementary EFL learners. *International Journal of Sciences, Basic, and Applied Research, 4* (8). Retrieved from https://www.researchgate.net/publication/246044421_A_Comparative_Study_on_the_Effect_of_Individual_Pair_and_Team_work_on_Speaking_Fluency_Of_Iranian_Elementary_EFL_Learners.

English Linguistics, Literature, and Language Teaching in a Changing Era – Madya et al. (eds)
© 2020 Taylor & Francis Group, London, ISBN 978-1-03-224160-9

Improving speaking skills through role plays for nursing students in Indonesia context

Tri W. Floriasti & Indah Permatasari
English Education Program, Yogyakarta State University, Yogyakarta, Indonesia

ABSTRACT: This research was aimed to explain the teaching and learning activities that improve the speaking skill of Nursing students through the use of role plays. Based on the classroom observation and interview that had been conducted, it was revealed that there were problems regarding to students' speaking skills, teaching techniques, and teaching materials used inside the classroom. In this regard, some teaching activities using role plays was created to be used in a classroom action research for improving students' speaking skills. This research was conducted in two cycles. The participants were 22 students in Nursing programme and the English teacher. The data obtained during the research were qualitative data and quantitative data. The qualitative data were obtained from observations and interviews, while the quantitative data were gained from tests. Based on the post-test administered in each cycle, the teaching activities using role plays were proven to give significant improvements on students' speaking skills. Findings from classroom observation and interviews with both students and English teacheralso showed that videos, worksheets, role play cards and feedbacks were effective in improving students' motivation to study English inside the classroom.

Keywords: Speaking skills, role plays, teaching activities and materials

1 INTRODUCTION

Speaking is a-must-have skill for many EFL students in Indonesia. It is a process to convey and to share ideas and feeling orally. A good speaker is someone who can carry on a conversation reasonably competently [1]. The ability to speak fluently presupposes not only knowledge of language features, but also the ability to process information and language on the spot [2]. Thus, knowing the socio-cultural rule and turn-taking rule in speaking is much needed [2] as the better students can use English for communication with the society, the higher level of their English language mastery. Here, sociocultural rules deal with the sociocultural background of the interlocutors (their culture, their behaviour, their preferences, et cetera) while turn-taking rules deal with the timing when to speak.

Nevertheless, many people often find speaking as a difficult skill to master. From a classroom observation conducted in one of the private vocational high schools in Klaten, many students were considered to have low English speaking ability. According to the English teacher's statements during interview, this situation happened as most of the students were having low English vocabularies and were facing difficulties in pronouncing and combining English words into good English utterances. These conditions showed that there are indeed several aspects which make speaking difficult—clustering, word redundant, reduce form, performance variables, colloquial language, rate of delivery, stress, rhythm and intonation, and interaction [1]. In this regards, English teachers need to equip students with strategies that make speaking less difficult—improvising, discarding, foreignising, and paraphrasing [2].

However, finding from students' interview showed that the monotonous materials and techniques used by the teacher were the reasons for their low skills in speaking and low motivation in studying English. Further, the fact that the teacher never used any interesting media during the teaching and learning also made them bored to study English inside the classroom. Therefore, teachers are suggested to use role plays as one of the techniques to be used in English classroom. Role plays are fun and help many shy students to speak out by providing them with a mask [3]. They give students opportunities to be creative and permit them to have a rehearsal time which has effect of lowering their anxieties [4]. Thus, the purposes of this research are to know:

1. whether the English teaching activities using role plays do interest students in their learning practices, and
2. whether they improve students' speaking skills.

2 RESEARCH METHOD

This research used two-cycle classroom action research model [5]. The participants were 22 first year female students majoring in nursing program in one of the private vocational high school in Klaten. They were chosen as they need to use English frequently but have limited chances and learning materials that can help them improve their speaking skills. To collect data, I used both quantitative and qualitative data collection techniques. Quantitative data were gained from spoken tests and qualitative data were obtained from observations and interviews. Particularly, I used speaking rubric to assess students' speaking performance, observation guideline to observe everything happened during the teaching and learning processes, interview guideline to find out about both students' and English teacher's opinion towards the action, and I used camera and recorder to create documentation.

To analyse the data, then, I employed Microsoft excel and qualitative data analysis that consists of reducing the data, displaying the data, drawing conclusion and verification [6]. Microsoft excel was used for finding the mean scores of students' speaking performance before and after each treatments. Meanwhile, the qualitative data analysis was used to analyse the results from students' and teacher's interviews.

3 FINDINGS AND DISCUSSIONS

Since this was a two-cycle action research that collecting data through both quantitative and qualitative method, the findings and discussions will be described under two sub-sections below.

3.1 The teaching activities in cycle I

This cycle was conducted after classroom observation, interview, and pre-test to gain data about the students' preliminary speaking skills were administered. From the classroom observation and interview, it was found out that the students have low motivation to learn English. This happened as the used materials were focusing too much on reading and writing rather than listening and speaking. Moreover, the teacher also never used any media in her teaching practices. All this time, the students were only asked to complete exercises inside the textbook. If only there was a speaking activity, it is only listen and repeat activity. Similarly, finding from pre-test also showed the low achievement on students' speaking skills. Therefore, improvements on the English speaking teaching activities were needed to be conducted by the teacher to improve students' speaking skills inside the classroom.

To do this, planning on the implementation of cycle I was created—this cycle lasted for 2 meetings. First, describing people based on their professions, nationalities, and physical appearances was chosen as the topic of discussion during this cycle. Here, to make the teaching and learning activities less boring, innovation on the teaching materials, media, and activities was conducted.

In relation to the materials, contextual materials were provided by the teacher. Contextual materials in this matter were dialogues and videos that are related to the students' need and subject area. In relation to the media, pictures, Microsoft Power Point and LCD projector as well as black board were used to deliver the materials. Meanwhile, role play was administered at the end of this cycle in order to give innovation on the speaking activities inside the classroom. All of them were delivered to the students through PPP method [see 2].

Based on the data collected through interview with English teacher, finding showed that the implementation of cycle I was quite successful in helping students to improve their speaking skills. According to her, the materials and media used were helping students to practice their speaking skills during role play.

So far, the used of handout and video are good in helping students to gain interest in the teaching and learning activities. Role play was also helpful in facilitating students to practice their speaking skills. (English teacher)

Moreover, based on students' interview, it was also found out that students could get a good input for role play by watching the video. This proved that video could give students realistic models to imitate for role play [7]. Further, it could help students see how people behave in the culture whose language they are learning by bringing into the classroom a wide range of communicative situations [7]. Following are several comments on the students' interview.

"I like role play because it is fun. It allows me to become anyone I want." (Student A)

"This activity is very fun. Besides, the handout and situation provided by the teacher can help me creates the dialogue that I need to perform later." (Student B)

Yet, even though the use of role play could attract students' interests in learning English, finding from post-test showed that there still little improvement on students' speaking skills in terms of pronunciation, vocabulary, grammar, fluency, and comprehension. According to the discussion with the English teacher, this condition happened as there were still many students who felt shy and afraid of making mistakes in doing the role play. Besides, the chaotic situation also made them hard to concentrate.

The use media and worksheet for role play indeed improved the students' interest in the teaching and learning activities. However, there were still many students who are shy and reluctant to perform they role play. Some of them also still had wrong pronunciation and grammar, and the class was also too chaotic. (English teacher)

This situation proved that time is needed to develop and set up a role playing situation and some learners may be shy or anxious when asked to do role play in front of the class [8]. Therefore, better preparation and time management are needed for the implementation of cycle II.

3.2 *The teaching activities in cycle II*

As what has been explained in cycle I, the use of role play does interest students in learning English inside the classroom. However, there is no significant improvement on the students' speaking skills. This situation happened due to the limitation of role play in which making students shy and making the situation inside the classroom chaotic [9]. In this regards, further intervention was done by implementing points to remember when setting up a role play [3, 10].

Similar to the previous cycle, this cycle was run for 2 meetings. It used pictures, video, LCD projector, black board, and role play as the media and activities. However, additional time and better preparation were done by the researcher. This time, the topic of discussion was about expressions used for command and request. This was done in order to teach students with how to deal with patients later in their future career. In relation to the materials, several expressions for command and request, dialogue, video, role play cards, and more vocabulary lists related to the topic were provided for the students. Here, more vocabulary lists were used to train students' pronunciation and vocabulary.

In relation to the media, similar treatment was applied. That is, researcher used Microsoft Power Point, LCD projector and black board to deliver the materials to students. Then, role play was also used at the end of this cycle. What made this cycle different compared to the previous one was the focus of learning—researcher focusing more in enriching students' vocabulary and motivating them to bravely practice their pronunciation. Moreover, researcher gave more time for students to practice their dialogue before performing the role plays. Better classroom management was also conducted by the researcher with the help of the English teacher.

Finally, from the classroom observation and interview with students, findings showed that the re-implementation of role play was successful in improving the students' speaking skill and familiarizing them with English words. The motivation that was given was also successful in making the students more confident in performing the role plays without looking back at their texts. In addition, the actions of giving feedback and additional time were very useful for the students to create and practice their dialogue. Following are some of their statements.

"I start to like role plays more. This is because it helps me to improve my confidence. Now, I am also able to perform dialogues without looking back at my notes again." (Student C)

"I like role plays because it can enrich my vocabulary. The handout provided by the teacher also helps me create my dialogue better. Moreover, the additional time also gives me more time for practice." (Student D).

Furthermore, similar findings were also found in a discussion with the English teacher on the reflection phase. During the discussion, the English teacher said that there was a great improvement on the students' enthusiasm of the English learning activity. According to her observation, the videos and handouts provided for the students were very helpful in enriching their vocabulary [see also 11, 12]. Also, the additional time given to the students motivated them to create better and better dialogues. This can be seen from the following fragment of interview.

Many students seem to gain more confidence in performing their role plays. They are also enthusiastic in completing the worksheet for role plays. The media and additional time given by the teacher also boost their motivation in learning to speak English. (English teacher)

In addition to that, the scores on post-test 2 also showed that there is an improvement on students' speaking skills compared to those in pre-test and post-test 1. So, it is clear that there are significant improvements on the students' speaking skills through the use of role plays [see also 13, 14]. This was in line with the theory which stated that a role play is a very useful dress rehearsal for real life and helps many shy students to speak out by providing them with

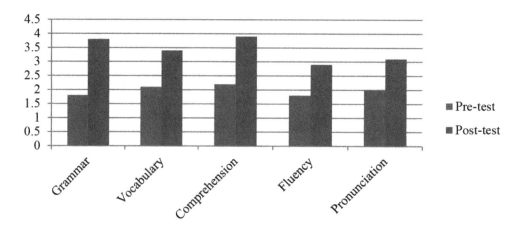

Figure 1. Students' mean scores of five speaking aspects in the pre-test and post-test.

a mask [3]. What need to be noted here is that it is very important for teachers to have enough information about their students' preferred learning style and roles in teaching [15, 16]. In sum, the comparison between the mean scores of students' pre-test and post-test scores is summarized on Figure 1 below.

4 CONCLUSION AND SUGGESTION

Based on the students' speaking mean scores on both cycles, it is proved that role plays help shy students to improve their speaking skills during their English classroom. From the interviews conducted with students, the use of video and handout as input were very effective in helping them to create the role plays [see 15]. Video and handouts helped students enrich their vocabulary of the topic being discussed and role play cards facilitated them with certain contexts that made their performance easier. Similarly, finding from the English teacher's observations also showed positive improvements on students' speaking performance. It is because many students started to be active and do not afraid of making mistakes during the role plays. Giving motivation and additional time for practice were claimed as the reason for this condition to happen. Nevertheless, as this research was carried out in a particular area using specific research subjects, findings might be different depending on the subjects and additional interventions used. Therefore, further classroom-based studies are needed to investigate its effectiveness in other subject areas.

REFERENCES

[1] Brown, H.D. (2001). *Teaching by principles: An interactive approach to language pedagogy* (2nd ed). New York: Pearson Education.
[2] Harmer, J. (2001). *The practice of English language teaching*. Essex: Longman.
[3] Ladousse, G.P. (1987). *Role play*. Oxford: Oxford University Press.
[4] Brown, H.D. (2004). *Language assessment: Principles and classroom practices*. New York: Pearson Education.
[5] Burns, A. (2010). *Doing action research in English language teaching: A guide for practitioners*. New York: Routledge.
[6] Miles, M.B. & Huberman, A.M. (1994). *Qualitative data analysis* (2nd ed). California: SAGE Publications.
[7] Cakir, I. (2006). The use Of video as an audio-visual material in foreign language teaching classroom. *The Turkish Online Journal of Educational Technology–TOJET*, ISSN: 1303-6521, 5(4), 9.
[8] Jones & Bartlett. Classroom Skills for Nurse Educators: Specific Classroom Skills, (Online), Retrieved from www.jblearning.com/samples/0763749753/49753_CHO3_FINAL.pdf, February 2016.
[9] Woodhouse, J. (2007). *A stage of learning strategies for healthcare education: How to teach in the 21th century*, 71–80, Oxford: Oxford University Press.
[10] Anderson, J. (2006). *Role plays for Today: Photocopiable Activities to Get Students Speaking*. Guildford: Delta Publising.
[11] Wright, A. (1976). *Visual Materials for the Language Teacher*. Essex: Longman.
[12] Rivers, W.M. (1981). *Teaching Foreign Language Skills*. Chicago: The University of Chicago Press.
[13] Rayhan, J.M. The Impact of Using Role Play Techniques on Improving Pupils Speaking Skill for Primary School, (Online). Retrieved from http://www.iasj.net/iasj?func=fulltext&aId=91556, August 2015.
[14] Sinurat, N.M. & Saragih, W. (2012). Improving Vocational Students' Speaking Skill through Role Play Technique, (Online). Retrieved from http://jurnal.unimed.ac.id/2012/index.php/eltu/article/download/1126/896, February 2016.
[15] Brown, H.D. (2007). *Principles of Language Learning and Teaching*. New York: Pearson Education.
[16] Ortega, L. (2009). *Understanding Second Language Acquisition*. New York: Hodder Education.

English Linguistics, Literature, and Language Teaching in a Changing Era – Madya et al. (eds)
© 2020 Taylor & Francis Group, London, ISBN 978-1-03-224160-9

Developing students' reflective skills in the teaching and learning of reading in the disruptive era

Umi Rachmawati
English Education Study Program, Graduate School, State University of Yogyakarta, Yogyakarta, Indonesia

ABSTRACT: In the disruptive era, the teaching and learning of reading is required to apply meaningful activities that make a positive impact on the students' outcomes. The four Cs (Collaborative, Communicative, Critical Thinking, and Creative) are proposed due to the rapid development of ICT. One of the four Cs is the ability for critical thinking, which requires the students to have reflection skills. The ability to criticize texts will be beneficial in reflecting on the students' learning. In fact, the understanding of reflecting learning is still low, so that the students do not clearly understand why they are learning something and what the benefits of learning it are. Thus, reflecting on the students' learning is viewed as an influential aspect in the success of teaching and learning. This study is a classroom action research that has been done in a senior high school and is aimed at developing the students' reflective skills in their reading classes. The classroom action research was done in two cycles in order to examine the changes that took place during the process of the teaching of reading through the use of computer-assisted language learning. The findings of the study show that the students had different learning behavior after they had undertaken the reflection process. Their individual reflection alters their ability to develop their own learning goals so that their learning is more meaningful. Positive changes in the students' attitude during the learning were also found during the learning. Moreover, the improvement in their learning output was also proven. The process and principles of conducting reflective teaching during reading classes are now discussed further.

Keywords: reflective learning, teaching reading, digital learning

1 INTRODUCTION

The teaching of reading has changed from using paper-based texts to the digital teaching of reading, with all of its challenges and opportunities. The use of digital learning forces the teachers to not only have the ability to teach, but also to know how to organize the class based on their learning needs. A basic mastery of the pedagogical content and technological knowledge [1] can improve teaching and learning in the disruptive era. The students, as digital natives, should be accommodated by the use of various authentic learning materials [2] from the internet. The skill of criticizing texts and navigation skills are hugely necessary for the teachers. The skill of navigating the digital media [3] to access more positive inputs needs to be accompanied by the mastery of critical thinking skills. The students, as digital natives, should already be familiar with the massive unfiltered websites that harm their self-development through critical thinking. Critical thinking is also needed to support the students' reflection on their learning in order to improve their self-organization.

Reflective learning plays an important role in the teaching of reading [4,5], as it enables students to sort and develop the value of their own learning experiences. Reflective learning is the ability to criticize the learning content in order to make a positive improvement to their learning. This involves deep thinking about their experiences and reflecting on the students' seriousness and consciousness in learning. Senior high school students are in the period of finding their best figure. They need the skill of thinking independently to make their transformation from their reflection.

To support students' self-reflection, teachers need to apply reflective teaching. It is one of the teachers' jobs to accommodate the students' reflection on their learning. Based on the preliminary study conducted by the researcher in several senior high schools in Indonesia, many teachers did not consider the reflection stage during their teaching. Most of the teachers still focus on the achievement in the final examinations. This means that the teaching focuses more on reading comprehension, in order to enable the students to deal with the English reading tests. As a result, the output is concentrated merely on the final scores, which might be meaningless for the students' self-development. It is crucial, then, to motivate the teachers to provide more reflective teaching and learning.

Regarding the importance of reflective skills, teachers and students need to be ready to face the challenges of reflective teaching. The practice of undertaking reflective activities during teaching is problematic for the teachers, since it becomes a conceptual portmanteau [6]. Practicing reflective learning requires qualitative process sensitivity. Taylor [7] states that there is a need for a more critical approach to qualitative data in order to reveal the truth of 'what really happened' and suggests that narration related less to facts and more to the pressure to show a competent professional individual

As mentioned earlier, the focus of the teaching and learning of reading in senior high schools in Indonesia is mostly on the achievement of the final results, which means the students' final examination. The whole process of teaching and learning is mostly aimed at making sure that the students are ready for the final examination. This influences the preparation, process, and evaluation of the learning. The main purpose of learning, transformation, has not been achieved. The transformative process comes after the process of reflection. In other words, reflective teaching plays an important role in teaching and learning. To enable both the students and the teacher to make their reflections, there should be a practical way of teaching that highlights the process of learning instead of the final achievement. The characteristics of classroom action research mean that the teaching and learning process can be more focused.

2 REFLECTIVE TEACHING

Reflective teaching is a willingness to participate in constant self-appraisal and development. It is concerned with aims, consequences, and technical efficiency [8]. The learners propose their learning aims or goals and need to be ready to deal with the consequences they will discover during their learning. The details of the activities are varied and should train the students' higher order thinking skills that will be the students' challenges. In order to deal with the challenges, the students must be ready to make use of the technical aspects. The students can undertake efficient learning through technical efficiency. Reflective learning is evidence-based learning, which is aimed at supporting the development of higher standards of teaching.

The development of the students' reflective skills was done dealing with the perspectives on the professions, including knowledge, skills, attitudes, and awareness [9]. Reflective practice is viewed as the ability to examine their own professional attitude and practices in order to improve their performances and relevant skills [10]. The reflection can be undertaken using different methods in different pedagogical contexts [11]. Becoming a reflective teacher refers to moving beyond the knowledge of discrete skills to the knowledge of integrated and modified skills to actualize new strategies [12]. Reflective teaching is aimed at developing the students' life skills beyond the goals of teaching.

The success of language teaching is also influenced by the teacher's role, particularly in constructive teaching. Reflective teaching obliges the teacher to stimulate the students' reflective skills through using their critical thinking skills. To achieve this, the teacher should know the position and roles in the class. Neuman and Blundo, in Gray and Gibbons [13], share the idea that the teacher should act as a provider to the students instead of being an expert. Maintaining the students' current changes are another problem for the teacher, since they have to deal with the students' portfolios, which might be presented in the students' journals. Paper-based journals can also be problematic in other ways [14]. They require the students to write quickly, which is sometimes difficult to read. The use of online media for reflection supports the students' reflective activities, and this can be an alternative for the less motivated students or the less confident ones. Online journals enable the students and the teacher to experience the real conditions of teaching and learning. Journals are a means of developing habits that can be used to assess the practical value of reflection [15]. Teachers are required to be able to provide changes for the students in order to accommodate their learning shift. In this role, the teacher should be knowledgeable and constructive.

Actually, reflective teaching is cyclical in nature. Dewey [17] elaborated seven basic stages of the reflective process. These are reflect, plan, make provisions, act, collect evidence, analyze evidence, and evaluate evidence. The teacher starts the reflective teaching by organizing a plan of teaching and learning. This plan is made in order to make provisions for the students' learning. Following it, the teacher acts out the plan and provisions that have been developed. During the act stage, the teacher collects evidence. The evidence is analyzed and then evaluated in order to accommodate the students' reflections. After the evaluation, the teacher goes back to the reflection stage, and this is followed by the whole process of reflective teaching. The process of reflective teaching is depicted in Figure 1.

In relation to the learning principles in reflective teaching, it is crucial to consider the teacher's roles. Teachers are informed decision makers and they thoughtfully analyze previous experiences in preparation and teaching, while also promoting thinking about teaching and learning [17]. The teacher is expected to be able to solve problems in the classroom. She or he also needs to be aware of the assumptions regarding the teaching. Understanding the institutional and cultural context of the teaching is another of the teacher's roles in reflective teaching. The teacher needs to participate in the development of the curriculum and in changes in the school. Their last role is to seek professional development opportunities. These roles are all required in order to achieve success in the teaching and learning process.

There are some components of reflective teaching that can be used to measure its effectiveness: understanding, teaching methods, interdisciplinary subjects, and the strengths and weaknesses of the lesson. Cruickshank [18] states that reflective teaching shares several components and characteristics. A learner satisfaction form should be completed in order to evaluate the reflective teaching.. The class reflects upon and discusses the different teaching acts that took place after the reflective teaching sessions. The upcoming teacher is chosen (designated) and the cycle repeats. Richards [19] states that critical reflection can trigger a deeper understanding of the teaching. This means that successful teaching results in more students understanding

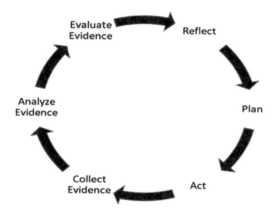

Figure 1.   The basic stages of reflective teaching [16].

the learning materials. Reflective learning is also developed from careful reflection on the teacher's past experiences and this can lead to more effective planning and teaching [17]. Lastly, a reflective teacher formulates rules, principles, and philosophies in order to be a better decision maker, planner, and more successful teacher. Conducting these steps in every cycle of teaching shows that the teaching is a success.

3   THE TEACHING OF READING

Reading is part of communication. It is an interaction between the writer and the readers through texts, which enables the readers' to expand their knowledge and to make sense of the print [20]. Today's teaching does not only focus on the reading comprehension. As extracted from Munzenmaier and Rubin [21], Bloom's Taxonomy has been changed or revised based on the current conditions and trends of today's teaching, including reading. The students should not only deal with the evaluative tasks of reading, but also the creative task of reading. The demands of the current condition forces students to think deeply about what they need to support their self-development.

With regard to the development of ICT, Richards [19] also presents reading skills for the digital age. The readers should be able to search quickly through and evaluate great amounts of information. They also have to create coherent reading pathways through complex collections of linked texts. The ability to make fast connections between widely disparate ideas and domains of experience is another reading skill in the digital era. Finally, the readers should be able to read multimodal documents that combine words, graphics, videos, and audios. Extensive reading involves reading through longer texts, which might help the students to acquire a good vocabulary, content knowledge, familiarity with the syntactic structure, knowledge about genres, and reading rate [22]. To deal with the longer passages, the readers may conduct some strategies to improve their reading speed. Galla, in Stone [23], presents the strategies needed for proficient reading, namely: asking questions, making predictions, making connections, visualizing, determining important information, synthesizing, and making inferences.

4   RESEARCH METHOD

This study was a classroom action research following Burns [24] design, which facilitates the gathering of qualitative data to solve the problems addressed in this study. The main purpose of classroom action research was to develop the students' reflective skills during the teaching of reading. It was done in cycles and implemented using the computer-assisted reflective transformative reading instructional model. As mentioned earlier, reflective teaching deals with qualitative data. Thus, the implementation of classroom action research was undertaken in order to support the collection of qualitative data, as discussed. The qualitative data were gathered from observations, interviews with the students and the teacher, and the students' feedback on the classroom action research. These data were in the form of field notes, interview transcripts, and discussion reports. These three sources of data were used to consider the data triangulation. The data were analyzed qualitatively to reveal the emic of the findings.

The subjects of the classroom action research were the students of class XI IA 3 in a public senior high school. This class was selected based on the preliminary study. This class needed to have more reflective teaching to support their self-organization. The learning characteristics supported the students to have more reflective learning. The learning activities were presented through the use of a website developed by the researcher. The main role of the researcher was as the classroom action research planner, and the English teacher was the research collaborator. The researcher taught the students during the class and the teacher observed the activities undertaken during the learning session. Both the teacher and the researcher made a report from each meeting and discussed all of the meetings in order to improve the learning.

5 DISCUSSION

The classroom action research was run following the plan prepared in the planning phase. There were two cycles, with four meetings per cycle. The first cycle was much more difficult than the second cycle, since the students were not familiar with the reflection phase. The teacher taught the class by approaching the students by giving easier learning activities before the teaching went into more varied and complicated learning or prospective to action [24]. The teacher also provided opportunities for the students to communicate, both face to face and through social media such as What'sApp and email. Communication through digital media enables the students to keep on communicating while they are pursuing other interests [25]. The students' reflection was reported in the field and the criteria of successful reflective learning was achieved, although it did not reach 100%.

Based on the classroom action research conducted, this study offers several findings on the students' reflection. The first is that the students had not previously experienced detailed reflective activities. From the observation of the teaching, the teacher did not provide any reflection for the students. This was confirmed by the students' feedback on the reflection stage, saying that the teacher never did that kind of activity.

S: 'We never have this kind of reflection activity.'
R: 'At the end of the lesson, did the teacher review what you have learned?'
S: 'She did not. She only gave additional task as homework.'

During the teaching and learning, the students also showed their confusion regarding the reflection stage. The students did not know how to respond to the questions addressed in the reflection stage, since they had never done this activity. Theoretically, reflection can be an evaluation process for the teacher regarding the success of the teaching [24].

Secondly, reflection is a learning habit that can enable both the students and the teacher should be able to facilitate the process of reflection. The students reflected on their learning while the teacher reflected on the teaching. This would help the students develop better learning. The main role of the teacher in reflective teaching is to be a facilitator [26]. The teacher reflects on what they have done and this improves the teaching and makes it more successful. The teacher should make this a habit of administering the main purpose of education. Patience and hard work are needed to support reflective teaching and learning. The more the students reflect, the more familiar they will be with the subject.

Thirdly, reflective learning and teaching requires the teacher's sensitivity. This means that the teacher is expected to be very sensitive and understanding of the students' current learning position. Responsive teachers help the students to improve their academic motivation [27]. The teacher should be able to check the students' learning and correct any possible misunderstandings that they might make. In responding to the students' questions and comments, the teacher is expected to make inferences and provide suitable learning activities to support the students. Being close to the students is a successful method of reflection, since there are many students who are so introverted that the teacher could not really get a good idea of students' understanding of the subject .

The whole process of reflective teaching successfully achieves the goals of learning by considering some of the components of reflection. In this study, the components of successful reflective teaching and learning are goal achievement, teaching methods, interdisciplinary subjects, and the strengths and weaknesses of the lesson. The main purpose of the teaching was to train the students' critical thinking during the teaching of reading. The students' achievements regarding their critical thinking skills were measured. The results show that there was a significant difference between the pre- and post-tests of the students' critical thinking. Taken from the mean of each test result, the pre-test mean is 5.51 and the post-test mean is 7.02. This shows that a great improvement had been made in the students' critical reading.

The second indicator of successful teaching through reflective learning is teaching methods. Based on the field notes of the classroom action research, the teacher combined some teaching methods in order to not only achieve the learning goals but also to meet the students' current learning needs during the teaching. The teacher made some revisions in terms of the methods applied. For example, self-regulated learning was the first consideration. After the teaching began, the self-regulated learning during the class was changed into collaborative learning. Student learning and motivation are considered to be interdependent processes that cannot be completely understood separately [28]. The self-regulated learning emphasized the students' autonomous learning. This means that the teaching methods had been changed due to the needs of the class. Another indicator of successful teaching is the interdisciplinary subjects involved in the class. Based on the learning materials developed by the researcher, the explanation texts were administered to provide more critical activities for the students. The content of the texts not only included knowledge of the language but also knowledge of the world. In this case, biology and history were two of the subjects that supported the teaching of reading. The selection of the learning materials in the second cycle was also undertaken based on the students' reflection.

The next indicator is the strengths and weaknesses of the lesson. Reflecting is the ability to sort out the positive and negative impacts of the learning. At the end of the teaching and learning session, the students were asked to complete a reflection form. The reflection form was used to show the students' own feelings and understanding of the learning. The reflection form was used as the first consideration when preparing for the next meeting's activities. The students wrote about the strengths and weaknesses of the lesson they experienced in their own journal. Journaling is a learning tool in reflective practice, in which the online ones will provide more benefits and there are no marked drawbacks [7]. Mostly, the reflection stage was the hardest part of learning, since the students rarely practiced reflection during their learning. The students stated that their teacher never asked them to think of what they had done during the lesson. Another fact about reflection is the students' absence of understanding the purpose of their learning. The students' information was the researcher's source of making betterment of their instruction.

6   IMPLEMENTATION OF THE PRINCIPLES OF REFLECTIVE TEACHING IN THE READING CLASS

This study implemented a number of the principles of reflective teaching in the reading class. It is proven that the teaching of reflective reading requires more than just ordinary teaching. Several aspects of language teaching and reflective learning should be accommodated and married in harmony in order to achieve the main purpose of teaching. (1) The teacher should consider the need for individual learning. Reflection is an independent process of thinking. Different students will face different learning experiences. Considering individual learning needs will alter the students' self- organization through the teacher's consideration and attention. (2) The teacher is supposed to employ both content knowledge and knowledge of the language, but also life skills. In the 21st century, the students not only need to master the learning content but also the real life skills, for example navigation and critical thinking skills. The teacher should consider these aspects in the process of reflection. (3) The teacher believes that no argument is wrong. The teacher should realize that each student will have a different point of view and opinion on a certain topic. The teacher should be able to accommodate the differences by motivating the students to share their critical thinking during their reflection. (4) The teacher's elaboration should be clear and vivid. When conducting the process of reflection, many teachers and students have not previously experienced reflective learning. The teacher needs to give clear instructions in order for the process of reflection to succeed. (5) The teacher should emphasize that learning focuses on the process of learning and not on the final results. Many students only focus on the final results without considering the process they have gone through. Neglecting the process of learning will mean that the students are unable to make their own reflection, something that is beneficial for the students' self-organization. (6) The students create goal setting for further learning. Although the focus of learning is not on the final result, the students should make their own learning goal. This will be varied and depend on their current learning position. Organizing the students' learning condition and goals will enable the teacher to maintain the teaching and learning process. (7) The teacher is the students' friend. Communication between the teacher and the students is very rigid, and the student can feel reluctant to communicate with the teacher personally. Considering this, the teacher is expected to be able to act as a partner in learning. This will open up close communication for the students with the teacher. (8) The teacher and the students refer back to the students' portfolio. It was quite difficult for the teacher to maintain the reflections of the whole class without any notes. Thus, the teacher should make a portfolio for the students during the teaching and learning process. Checking the students' progress is one of the most important jobs undertaken by the teacher. A portfolio will help the teacher to control the students' learning achievements and lead the teacher to make better plans for the students' learning. (9) The teacher's sensitivity is important for the students' success in reflection. As shown previously, the reflection stage is a new activity for the students and this will force the students to be able to state their learning achievement, reflect on their current understanding and solve problems related to their learning achievement. Lastly, (10) the teaching should balance both the hard and soft skills in reflection. Sometimes, the teacher only focuses on the hard skills with less attention given to the students' soft skills. If the students have developed their soft skills and embedded them in their behavior, this will influence their reflection. These principles of reflective teaching are highlighted both before, during, and post teaching.

7 CONCLUSION

The teaching of reading does not only refer to the teaching of comprehension skills but also to the preparation of real life skills. Facilitating the students to have more reflective reading requires both time and energy from all parties in teaching and learning. Accommodating the reflective learning motivates the teacher to facilitate the students' self-organization. Principles of reflective learning during the teaching of reading should be considered in order to achieve the main purpose of the reading class in the disruptive era.

REFERENCES

[1] Jang, S.J. & Chen, K.C. (2010). From PCK to TPACK: Developing a transformative model for pre-service science teachers. *Journal of Science Education and Technology, 19*(6), 553–564.
[2] Tomlinson, B. (2012). Materials development for language learning and teaching. *Language Teaching, 45*(2), 143–179.
[3] Alkali, Y.E. & Amichai-Hamburger, Y. (2004). Experiments in digital literacy. *Cyber Psychology & Behavior, 7*(4), 421–429.
[4] Wilhelm, J.D. (2016). *"You gotta be the book": Teaching engaged and reflective reading with adolescents.* New York: Teachers College Press.
[5] Brookfield, S.D. (2017). *Becoming a critically reflective teacher.* New Jersey: John Wiley & Sons.
[6] Morrison, K. (1996). Developing reflective practice in higher degree students through a learning journal. *Studies in Higher Education, 21*(3).
[7] Taylor, C. (2006). Narrating significant experience: Reflective accounts and the production of (self) knowledge. *British Journal of Social Work, 36*, 189–206.
[8] Pollard, A., et al. (2005). *Reflective teaching.* London, UK: A & C Black Publishing.
[9] Narvaéz, C.Q. (2010). *How can the practice of reflective teaching promote professional development in each of the constituents of teacher education- knowledge, skills, attitudes and awareness?* Retrieved from http://www.eumed.net/rev/tlatemoani/02/cqn.pd.
[10] Clarke, R. & Croft, P. (1998). *Critical reading for the reflective practitioner.* Oxford, UK: Elsevier Butterworth- Heinemann.
[11] Rodman, G.J. (2010). Facilitating the teaching-learning process through the reflective engagement of pre-service teachers. *Australian Journal of Teacher Education, 35*(2), 20–35.
[12] Larrivee, B. (2000). Transforming teaching practice: Becoming the critically reflective teacher. *Reflective Practice, 1*(3), 293–307.
[13] Gray, M. & Gibbons, J. (2002). Experience-based learning and its relevance to social work practice. *Australian Social Work, 55*(4), 279–291.

[14] Phipps, J.J. (2005). E-journaling: Achieving interactive education online. *Educause Quarterly*, *28*(1). Retrieved from http://www.educause.edu/apps/eq/eqm05/eqm0519.asp?bhep¼1.

[15] Quinn, D. (2010). Authenticity in reflection: Building reflective skills for social work. *Social Work in Education*, 29(7),778–791.

[16] Moore, K.D. (2015). *Effective instructional strategies: From theory to practice* (4th ed.). London, UK: Sage Publications.

[17] Dewey, J. (1933). *How we think: A restatement of the relation of reflective thinking to the educative process*. Chicago: Henry Regnery.

[18] Cruickshank, D.R. (1987). *Reflection teaching*. Reston, VA: Association of Teacher Educators.

[19] Richards, J.C. (2015). *Key issues in language teaching*. Cambridge, UK: Cambridge University Press.

[20] Ruddle, M.R. (2005). *Teaching content reading and writing*. Hoboken, NJ: John Wiley & Sons.

[21] Munzenmaier, C. & Rubin, N. (2013). *Perspective Bloom's Taxonomy: What's old is new again*. California: The eLearning Guild.

[22] Lembs, K., Miller, L.D. & Soro, T.M. (2010). *Teaching reading to English language learners*. New York, NY: The Guilford Press.

[23] Clarke, R. & Croft, P. (1998). *Critical reading for the reflective practitioner*. Oxford, UK: Elsevier Butterworth-Heinemann.

[24] Burns, A. (2005). Action research: An evolving paradigm?. *Language Teaching*, *38*(02), 57–74.

[25] Waycott, J., Bennett, S., Kennedy, G., Dalgarno, B. & Gray, K. (2010). Digital divides? Student and staff perceptions of information and communication technologies. *Computers & Education*, *54*(4), 1202–1211.

[26] Smith, S.V. & Karban, K. (2006). Developing critical reflection within an interprofessional learning programme. In 36th Annual SCUTREA Conference, 04 July 2006-06 April 2006, Leeds.

[27] Kiefer, S.M., Ellerbrock, C. & Alley, K. (2014). The role of responsive teacher practices in supporting academic motivation at the middle level. *RMLE Online*, *38*(1), 1–16.

[28] Zimmerman, B.J. (1990). Self-regulated learning and academic achievement: An overview. *Educational Psychologist*, *25*(1), 3–17.

English Linguistics, Literature, and Language Teaching in a Changing Era – Madya et al. (eds)
© 2020 Taylor & Francis Group, London, ISBN 978-1-03-224160-9

Out-of-class language learning activities: A case study of good language learners

Wawan Cahyadin
English Language Education, Universitas Halu Oleo, Kendari, Indonesia

Halijah Koso
English Literature, Universitas Halu Oleo, Kendari, Indonesia

ABSTRACT: This study examined the out-of-class language learning activities (OCLLAs) undertaken by good language learners in the Indonesian EFL context and their specific local context. It employed a descriptive qualitative case study. Eight students from English department of UNIDAYAN chosen as good language learners participated in this study. This study firstly identified and described the out-of-class English learning activities conducted by the participants through a four-week diary/journal and questionnaire. Afterwards, the tendency of the students to particular skills-based OCLLAs was explored further through interview. It found that the participants involved in a variety of language learning activities outside the classroom. Furthermore, it found that the participants tended to engage more frequently in productive skills-related OCLLAs particularly in speaking with considerable time allocation. The tendency was caused by internal and external factor. Internally, their belief in the importance of speaking and their low-inhibition of using English in public encouraged them to practice more spoken English. While externally, positive experience from OCLLAs, neutral/positive perception of community and the availability of native speaker enhanced their motivation and extended their opportunities to practice oral English directly with native speakers.

Keywords: out-of-class language learning activities, Indonesia EFL context, specific local context, good language learner

1 INTRODUCTION

Out-of-class language learning refers to students' activities to enhance their skills and knowledge of language outside the classroom [1]. The term 'autonomous learning' is also used to refer to the same definition as the decision to do the activities is in principle made by students themselves without teacher's control. Benson [2] prefers to use 'language learning beyond the classroom' and divides it into three main categories: self-instruction which involves the use of resources that replaces the role of teachers; naturalistic learning, by which learners interact with native speakers; and self-directed naturalistic learning, in which language learners establish a naturalistic situation to learn the target language with further focus on pleasure or communication.

For quite some time now a number of studies have found that while engaging with foreign language out-of-class time, learners tend to develop receptive skills of reading and listening rather than productive skills of speaking and writing [3,4,5]. Studies have also discovered the positive causal relationship between students' engagement in learning activities outside the classroom with their language proficiency and classroom achievement. Inozu et al [6] for instance, revealed that students' out-of-class language learning experiences contribute to their learning outcomes of four language skills development (listening, reading, speaking and writing) and language aspects (grammar and vocabulary). Reading and listening improved most compared to speaking and writing. Similarly, Sunqvist [7] found that English learning beyond the classroom correlated positively and significantly with both students' oral proficiency level and the size of their vocabulary.

Although those research works have quite extensively described out-of-class language learning activities as well as their important contribution to learners' language proficiency and achievement in the target language, they still look at language learners in general. It is poorly understood how 'good language learners' in EFL context deal with their language learning outside the classroom. In addition, it is noticeable that very little effort if not to say none, has been made to examine how learners' specific local context structured their out-of-class language learning activities particularly good language learners. Norton and Toohey [8] suggest that "learner of English participate in particular, local context in which specific practices create possibilities for them to learn English" and thus it could not be negligible.

The aim of this study is to further extend our knowledge of out-of-class language learning activities by particularly focus on good language learners. It seeks to address questions what out-of-class language learning activities (OCLLAs) these particular learners engage with in Indonesia EFL context and their specific local context and why they tend to engage most in particular skills-based OCLLAs rather than in the rest of the skills. By answering these questions, the current study is expected to firstly give insight into how the good language learners in the Indonesian EFL context engage in language learning activities outside the classroom and more importantly, how these activities shape the good language learners.

2 RESEARCH METHODOLOGY

2.1 *Research design*

The study used a descriptive case study that was analyzed through qualitative method. Case study refers to a "detailed examination of an event which the analyst believes exhibits the operation of identified general theoretical principles" [9] and it is conducted for a certain period of time. This study was to detail the out-of-class English learning conducted by the good language learners for the duration of four weeks and therefore, case study method matched the purpose of the study.

2.2 *Research subject*

The subjects of this research were undergraduate students at the fourth year of study at English study program of **UNIDAYAN** University Baubau. They were selected through purposive sampling. In purposive sampling the researcher selects participants who satisfy certain qualities or criteria [10] and three criteria of good language learners were set. First, the participants share majority or all of the characteristics of good language learners which were identified through assessment of personal learning style and strategy use. These characteristics were adapted from Brown's [11] maxim for good language learning. Second, the participants are high-achievers, marked not only by his/her strong GPA ranging from 3.5 - 4.0 of four-scale but also by their successful participation in regional/national English events and non academic involvement in professional activities where English proficiency is highly required. Third, the participants engage actively in various out-of-class language learning activities, which is one of the traits of good language learners as most research suggested and substantiated [12,5]. As a result, 8 students were identified as good language learners and taken as the participants.

2.3 Data collection

The data for this study were collected through diaries and journal, questionnaire and semi-structure interview. Self-reported diaries and journal detailed the students' exposure and contact with English as well as their reflection on their experience on daily basis for the duration of four weeks. The questionnaire was adapted from Hyland [4] and Pearson [3] which requested students' demographic information, their attitude towards using English in different situations, the part English played in their daily life and the OCLLAs they engaged in. Meanwhile, the semi-structure interview was to gain in-depth information obtained from the two previous instruments concerning the students' attitude and belief toward English and their out-of-class language learning activities. Special attention was paid to why the students tend to engage most in particular language skills-based activities.

2.4 Data analysis

For the data analysis, the researcher used Miles and Huberman's steps for qualitative data analysis [13]. Firstly data reduction, by which data on OCLLAs were categorized based on language skills categories. Secondly data display, by which data were presented in the form of matrices presenting the OCLLAs, the frequency as well as the time allocation. Lastly, the researcher drew and verified conclusion.

3 FINDINGS AND DISCUSSION

3.1 Finding

3.1.1 Out-of-class English learning Activities (OCLLAs) carried out by the students

This study shows that the participants engaged more in speaking skills-based OCLLAs (168 mentions) and dedicated a large portion of their time (247 hours) to carry them out (see Table 1). The OCLLAs such as *speaking with Indonesian colleagues in pair, speaking at the meeting, speaking with one self and speaking with foreigner* contribute most to the dominance of speaking skills. Listening skills-based OCLLAs are the second highest (146 mentions; 216.25 hours), followed by writing (84 mentions; 119.52 hours) and reading (38 mentions; 30.20 hours). There are only few participants (4 mentions; 2.77 hours) who studied grammar independently out-of-class time. This study has therefore been inconsistent with the previous studies in which receptive skills were the most often carried out OCLLAs.

3.1.2 Reasons of the students to engage most in speaking skills-based OCLLAs

The study finds that there are a number of reasons that influence the tendency of the participants in speaking skills-based OCLLA both internally and externally. Internally, their belief in speaking ability as an indicator of English mastery motivated the students to perform speaking more frequently and at the same time dedicated their time a great deal. Their low-inhibited act about using English in public arena was in favor of such belief. While externally, positive experience from speaking skills-based OCLLAs led them involved more in speaking. Moreover, neutral/positive community's attitude towards people using English and local affordance particularly the availability of native speakers in the community provided them with good environment and extended their opportunities to use and practice spoken English.

3.2 Discussion

The study shows that the participants engaged in a variety of different language learning activities outside the classroom. Self-directed naturalistic learning is the most dominant carried out. In self-directed naturalistic learning, the learner arranges a naturalistic learning situation purposively to learn the language, but in the middle the focus is more on something other than language such as pleasure and communication [2]. This means that outside the classroom

Table 1. Students'exposure/contact with English by language skills.

No	OCLLA	Freq (x)	Time (hour)
1	Receptive skills-related activities		
1.1	Watch TV program/movies	71	161.75
1.2	Watch video file	4	1.67
1.3	Listen to songs	63	47.45
1.4	Listen to English audio (speech, recording)	8	5.38
1.6	Read novel	8	6.7
1.7	Read article	11	5
1.8	Read book	12	12
1.9	Read e-book	5	3
1.10	Read narative text	2	3.5
	Total	184	246.45
2	Productive skills-related activities		
2.1	Speak with indonesian colleagues face 2 face	51	64.55
2.2	Speak with colleagues on the phone	9	9.50
2.3	Speak with foreigner/native speakers	13	53
2.4	Speak with foreigner on the phone	1	0.12
2.5	Speak with one self	28	8.23
2.6	Speak at the meeting	40	63.5
2.7	Speak at English radio program (guest)	13	17
2.8	Speak at English radio program (host)	7	14
2.9	Speak when teaching	12	15
2.10	Speak with native speakers via skype	1	2
2.11	Writing article for blog	4	7
2.22	Write email to foreigner	3	3
2.23	Chat with Indonesian friend	1	1
2.24	Chat with foreigner	32	69.5
2.25	Write English text	10	15.5
2.26	Text mobile message	28	14.02
2.27	Write status in facebook	6	9.5
	Total	252	366.42

the students tend to engage in activities which not merely entail the language use and linguistic material but also are enjoyable and communicative at the same time. Menezes [14] states that the OCLLAs primarily the ones to do with cultural product such as movies, songs and interaction with expatriates have become the source of contact of good language learners with English in EFL context. It means that the good language learners in this study engaged in OCLLAs that are commonly performed by good language learners in EFL context. This finding conforms to Lamb [5] who discovered the similar OCLLAs when investigating sixteen students in Jambi, five of whom were high achieving students. Ibadurrahman [15] who investigated the OCLLAs carried out by senior high school students in Bandung West Java also found the similar activities except *playing video games*.

Furthermore, this study finds that *speaking with native speakers/foreigners* and *reading English newspapers/magazine* were structured by the students' specific local context. While the former was frequently performed (mean = 3.75), the latter was rarely performed (mean = 1.40). Lamb [5] and Ibadurrahman [14] by contrast found the former to be very scarcely performed, revealed by the number of mention (2 mentions only) and the low mean figure (mean = 0.53). While the finding of the two previous studies was apparently common in Indonesian EFL context where the opportunity to have contact directly with native speakers very little exists, the finding of this study was locally specific. The specific local context appeared to adequately offer the students with good range of opportunities to speak with foreigners. It was expressed by the participants during the interview as one student put it: *"there are many foreign students coming to*

Lambusango to do research and I meet them each year". Another student commented that: *"I teach also Mr. Stephen Bahasa Indonesia, they live in front of KPU office in Palatiga."*

On the contrary to former, the latter was rarely rated by the participants (mean = 1.40), approaching 'never'. In fact, English materials such as newspaper and magazine were hardly ever available in Baubau and neighboring areas. Similarly, the high achiever group in Ibadur-rahman [15] read magazine (mean = 0.64) very scarcely. It seems that local affordance both in this study and in Ibadurahman [15] constrained the participants to learn English from printed mass-media material. The study of Lamb [5] also indicated the similar finding. Local affor-dance is among other things that shapes the students' specific local context [16], leading to being context-specific of the two OCLLAs in the current study. While the former is made pos-sible, the latter is constrained.

The participants tended to engage more in productive skills in general and speaking skills-based OCLLAs in particular and this study has therefore conflicted with a number of previous studies (i.e. [17,4,6,15]). Such tendency is unexpected since the availability of speaking oppor-tunities in EFL countries is commonly known to be very limited [5,14,18]. Besides, it is unex-pected because Indonesian EFL learners are believed to be largely passive [5] as it has been previously found by Ibadurrahman [15]. Therefore, it reveals that Indonesian EFL learners are not necessarily passive as it is commonly believed (i.e. [5,15]). Instead, the participants were highly active as it is shown by the frequency and the time allocation. There are several factors that influenced the tendency. Internally, the students' high belief on the importance of speaking skill is a main reason. One participant for example put it:*"speaking skill is the first skill I want to master, it makes me comfortable and confident in English, I want to be guide, accompany for-eign guest, speak to investor maybe".* Such belief is confirmed by Walls [19] by saying that that students' perception or personal belief highly affect their out-of-class learning. If we refer to Ushioda [20], the participants are intrinsically motivated to develop speaking skills and at the same time, extrinsically motivated to pursue certain kinds of job. Their low inhibition also affected their tendency to speak the language more often. One participant for example, put it: *"I don't care about people judgment it is about me and my English, when I speak English in public, because if I consider what people say about me I will get stuck on my English, I would not lose my chance just because of what people think about me".* Ellis [21] holds that low inhibition encourages learners to take risk and it is required for rapid progress in language learning.

Externally, positive experience from carrying out speaking skills-based OCLLAs seem also to influence the tendency. One participant for instance put it: *"I like learning in English meeting because there are friends, we are stimulated to speak when seeing friend speaking English".* It is probable that after having such positive experience, they became more motivated to engage more frequently in the OCLLAs. According to Ellis [22] with such positive experience the learners acquired resultative motivation. Another reason is neutral and positive community's perception towards people using English in public arena that enabled the participants to create more opportunities to use and practice English publicly. One participant for example put it: *"when I speak English in public I ever attended meeting in Pantai Kamali and many children came to look at us but the adult I think they don't have any judgment, no judgment, they just masa bodoh".* Moreover, the participants made contact and interacted with native speakers quite intensively which in turn extended their opportunities to practice more spoken English. One participant for example put it: *"there are many foreign students coming to Lambusango to do research and I meet them each year".* Another participant put it: *"actually Baubau very sup-port us, because every tourism event in Baubau they [the local government] always invite me like last month, the cruise ship Liver Odesy came to Baubau, I was a guide and the Sail Komodo 2013 a couple of days ago".* A few of participants also made contact with expatriates from English-speaking countries living in their community. One participant for example put it: *"I teach also Mr. Stephen Bahasa Indonesia [and his friends], they live in front of KPU office in Palatiga".* The availability of the native speakers in those cases is affordance [23,14] which the environ-ment offers to which the language learners act or with which the students interact. This envir-onment enabled the participants to speak English with the native speakers more often as well as allotted their time considerably and this caused their tendency to productive skills OCLLAs primarily speaking. Norton et al., [8] term this environment as 'specific practice' which creates English learning opportunities and that's why this study corroborates their study.

4 CONCLUSIONS AND SUGGESSTIONS

Despite the limitation of research participants due to the case study, the findings may lead to several conclusions. Firstly, in the Indonesian EFL context the learners who are good language learners tend to involve more frequently and more intensively in productive skills-based OCLLAs rather than they do for the receptive skills related ones. Secondly, the OCLLAs that the learners carry out are commonly similar to those in other EFL contexts. However, the learners' specific local context along with the typical affordance it provides could distinguish the tendency, frequency and time spent on particular skill-based OCLLAs. It is noteworthy that speaking with foreigners/native speakers and reading newspaper/magazines are two context-specific OCLLAs. Finally, it is evident that individual, social factors and local affordance account for the students' tendency over speaking skills. This study has in several ways opened pathways to future studies in the field of out-of-class English learning activities and autonomous learning. It could be replicated in different context involving a larger number of participants.

REFERENCES

[1] Shen, L., Tseng, C., Kuo, S., Su, Y., & Chen, M. (2005). A preliminary study of college students' out-of-class English learning activities. *Annual Bulletin, 31*, 464–475.

[2] Benson, P. (2011). *Language learning and teaching beyond classroom: An introduction to the field*. In P. Benson, & H. Reinders (Ed.), Beyond the language Classroom, 7–16. New York: Palgrave Macmillan,

[3] Pearson, N. (2004). The idiosyncracies of out-of-class language learning: A study of mainland Chinese students studying English at tertiary level in New Zealand. *Proceedings of the Independent Learning Conference 2003*. Downloaded on 24 April 2012. Available from http: independentlearn ing.org/ILA/ila03_pearson.pdf.

[4] Hyland, F. (2004). Learning autonomously: contextualizing out-of-class English language learning. *Language Awareness, 13*(3), 180–202.

[5] Lamb, M. (2002). Explaining successful language learning in difficult circumstances. *Prospect*, 17/2, 35–52.

[6] Inozu, J., Sahinkarakas, S., Yumru, H. (2010). The nature of language learning experiences beyond the classroom and its learning outcomes. *US-China foreign language, 8*(1),14–19.

[7] Sunqvist, P. (2011). *A possible path to progress: out-of-school English language learners in Sweden*. In P. Benson, P & H. Reinders (Eds.), Beyond the Language Classroom, 106–118. New York: Palgrave Macmillan.

[8] Norton, B., & Toohey, K. (2001). Changing perspective on good language learners. TESOL Quarterly, 35/2, 307–322.

[9] Mitchell, J. C. (1983). Case and situation analysis. *The Sociological Review*, 31, 187–211.

[10] Koerber, A., McMichael, L. (2008). Qualitative sampling method. *Journal of Business and Technical Communication*. Downloaded on 11 May 2013. Available from http://jbt.sagepub.com.

[11] Davies, M., J. (2011). *Are the characteristics of a 'good' language learner identifiable?: An examination of the 'good' language learner assumption in a young learner EFL classroom*. Downloaded on 7 May 2013. Available from http://www.birmingham.ac.uk/Documents/collegeartslaw/cels/essays/ younglearner s/Daviesessay2GLLessaybank.pdf.

[12] Brown, H. Douglas. (2007). *Teaching by principles: an interactive approach to language pedagogy*. Third Edition. New Jersey: Prentice Hall Inc.

[13] Miles, M.B., Huberman, A.M. (1994). *Qualitative data analysis*. (2nd ed). California: Sage Publication.

[14] Menezes, V. (2011). *Affordance for language learning beyond the classroom*. In P. Benson, P & H. Reinders (Ed.), Beyond the Language Classroom, 59–71. New York: Palgrave Macmillan.

[15] Ibadurrahman. (2011). *Out-of-class language learning activities and students L2 achievement: A case study of Indonesian students in senior high school*. Unpublished Thesis: International Islamic University Malaysia.

[16] Palfreyman, D. M. (2011). *Family, friends and learning beyond the classroom: social capital in language learning*. In P. Benson, & H. Reinders (Ed.), Beyond the Language Classroom, 106–118, New York: Palgrave Macmillan.

[17] Intaraprasert, C. (2007). Out-of-class language learning strategies and Thai university students and learning English for science and technology. *Journal of science technology and humanities*, *1*(1), 1–18.

[18] Guo, S. (2011). Impact of an out-of-class activity on students' English awareness, vocabulary and autonomy. *Language education in Asia*. Downloaded on 12 April 2013. Available from doi: 10.5746/LEiA/11/V2/12/A07/Guo.

[19] Dang, T.. (2012). Leaner Autonomy: a synthesis of theory and practice. *The Internet Journal of Language, Culture and Society*, *35*, 52–67.

[20] Ushioda, Ema. (2008). *Motivation and Good Language Learner*. In C. Griffith (Ed.), Lessons from good language learners, 19–34. Cambridge UK: Cambridge University Press.

[21] Mohseni, A. & Ameri, A. (2010). Inhibition revisited in EFL learning/teaching. *Journal of Language and Translation*, 1/1, 39–50.

[22] Ellis, Rod. (1997). *Second language acquisition*. Oxford: Oxford University Press.

[23] Van Lier, L. (2004). *The ecology and semiotics of language learning: A sociocultural perspective*. Dirdrecht: Kluwer Academic Publisher.

English Linguistics, Literature, and Language Teaching in a Changing Era – Madya et al. (eds)
© 2020 Taylor & Francis Group, London, ISBN 978-1-03-224160-9

Investigating an individual's clarity of enunciation with the Orai application: Implications for L2 assessment

Widya R. Kusumaningrum & Rangga Asmara
Universitas Tidar, Magelang, Indonesia

ABSTRACT: The disruptive era in English-as-a-Foreign Language (EFL) teaching allows the perception of world Englishes to proliferate. It allows people to talk English with their L1 accent, but it also raises a new problem in enunciation. This study attempts to explore the effect of the Orai application on the individual's clarity of enunciation in final devoicing minimal pairs. Investigated under quasi-experimental research with Non-Equivalent Group Design (NEGD), this study ran the dependent Analysis of Variance (ANOVA). The study compared two groups of university students within the age range of 20–21 years old, with each group having the same L1 background (Indonesians) (N = 40): (1) an Orai experimental group, measured with the Orai application (artificial intelligence), and (2) a non-Orai control group, rated by two EFL teachers (human intelligence). The current study presented the quantitative data in the form of the participants' responses to the pretest and posttest. The findings showed that the implementation of the Orai application was more objective and accurate in investigating the participants' clarity of enunciation than rating by EFL teachers, while the non-Orai control group tended to receive a changeable and subjective rating, which might be impacted by having different background knowledge, tiredness, fatigue, concentration, and the halo effect. It is concluded that the results have implications for L2 assessment, particularly for nurturing assessment for learning.

Keywords: Clarity of Enunciation, L2 Assessment, Orai Application, Gamification, Artificial Intelligence

1 INTRODUCTION

Living in the 21st century, with technology development and its rapid changes, has affected the status of English. English has accelerated its position from an international language into a global lingua franca. It has become the central means of communication, which is widely spoken in all aspects all over the world. It has spread extensively and rapidly as a dominant language. However, at the same time, this significant spreading has resulted in the ramification of English into greater varieties as the result of localization and nativization [1]. In this regard, English has expanded its domain into larger areas, such as the outer and expanding circles of English users [2]. It has led to the notion of world Englishes.

Coined by Kachru, a Kashmiri-American linguist, in 1986, the term world Englishes refers to the institutionalized varieties of English [2]. World Englishes centers on the notion of inner, outer, and expanding circles. The inner circle symbolizes the countries that have the traditional bases of English and give English the status of being their first language, such as in the United Kingdom and the United States. The outer circle includes some countries where English plays an essential part in the nation. These outer circle countries have an historical connection to the language (for example, British Commonwealth countries). Meanwhile, the expanding circle countries include the rest of the world, where the status of English is only as a foreign or international language without any historical relationship with the language [3]. This last circle raises new problems as it lets Non-Native English Speakers (NNESs) use English with their L1 interference, such as Indonesian English or Javanese English. Supporters of world Englishes legitimize the use of these world varieties of English.

Conversely, this world Englishes paradigm raises a new problem regarding the clarity and accuracy of enunciation. The following studies discuss the criticism regarding how NNESs articulate, enunciate or shape the sounds [4,3,5,6,7]. Jenkins [4] underlined that although some NNESs try to maintain intelligible and comprehensible pronunciation for international use, some others may still be substituting /t/ and /d/ for /θ/ and /ð/. A similar concern is also pointed out by Wenfang [3]. She highlighted the implication of the world Englishes paradigm and for the language teaching in China. and raised the notion of Chinese English model for attaining international acknowledgment. Another study was done in Japan by Saito [5] He identified some enunciation features that might cause problems for Native Japanese Speakers (NJSs), such as the eight English-specific segmental /æ/, /f/, /v/, /θ/, /ð/, /w/, /l/, /ɹ/. Another study was conducted in one of the Southeast Asian countries, i.e. Thailand. Khamkien [6] emphasized that many Thai students had difficulties with the consonant sounds, vowel sounds, and clusters, particularly with the final cluster consonants such as /l/ and /ch/. Dlaska and Krekeler [7], who did a study in East and Southeast Asia, including Indonesia, rated the participants as having difficulty in discriminating the voiced labiodental fricative and labiodental voiced semivowel due to the Bahasa Indonesia interference. However, there have been minimal studies done in this area.

Related to 21st century learning, which emphasizes technology, this study tries to integrate the use of technology, i.e. the Orai application, in order to understand and assess the Indonesian learners' clarity of enunciation. As has been claimed by the developer of the application, Orai is used for measuring some speaking microskills, such as speech rate, pauses, stresses, pitch ranges, and clarity. Later, this study emphasizes the use of the Orai application for assessing individual clarity and limits the object to the final devoicing minimal pairs, both voiced consonants (/b/, /d/, /g/) and voiceless consonants (/p/, /t/, /k/), since students of English have difficulty in enunciating some of the voiced and voiceless words of the above consonant phonemes. Thus, this study proposes the research question:

'How effective is the Orai application for assessing individual clarity of enunciation on final devoicing minimal pairs, both voiced consonants (/b/, /d/, /g/) and voiceless consonants (/p/, /t/, /k/), in comparison with the traditional and standardized test?'

2 RESEARCH METHOD

2.1 *Research design*

To answer the research question above, we used quasi-experimental research with Non-Equivalent Group Design (NEGD). In this NEGD, we involved two groups of the intact/experimental group with Orai intervention (later called EGOI) and the control group without any intervention (CGNO).

2.2 *Participants*

The study compared two groups of university students within the age range of 20–21 years old, with each group having the same L1 background (Indonesians) (N = 40): (1) an Orai experimental group, measured with the Orai application (artificial intelligence) (N = 20), and (2) a non-Orai control group, rated by two EFL teachers (human intelligence) (N = 20). The participants were purposively selected from the 120 students. The rationale for selecting them was that they were considered to have the same speaking level.This study was carried out from late August to mid-September 2018.

2.3 *Instrument*

Using the non-equivalent group design (NEGD) with pretest-posttest design, this study measures the individual clarity of enunciation on final devoicing minimal pairs, both voiced consonants (/b/, /d/, /g/) and voiceless consonants (/p/, /t/, /k/). To support the data, other instruments were used, such as audio recordings, transcriptions, and observations.

2.4 Procedure

In order to investigate the effect of the Orai application on the individual clarity of enunciation when focusing on final devoicing minimal pairs, both voiced consonants (/b/, /d/, /g/) and voiceless consonants (/p/, /t/, /k/), both groups were given the same pretest. They were asked to work with partners and take turns to record their partner's recitation of some minimal pairs and then send the audio recording by email. Meanwhile, for the posttest, the CGNO was asked to do the same as for the pretest procedure while the EGOI, as the experimental group, received the Orai intervention. The overall posttest scores for both groups were compared to see the statistically significant difference shown in their performance. To examine the efficacy from the pretest to the posttest, the study was done in six meetings of 100-minute lessons.

To estimate and investigate the individual clarity of enunciation, the study developed a rubric using the Likert scale, as follows.

2.5 Data analysis

The data analysis techniques used were descriptive statistics and parametric inferential statistics. Descriptive statistics were used to ensure the equality level of both the intact and control groups and to see the normality of the data. The average scores of the pretest and posttest from both groups were compared and analyzed by considering the skewness and kurtosis values in the tables. After the normality was statistically identified, this study ran the parametric inferential statistics to see the effect of the Orai intervention on the participants' clarity of enunciation, particularly on final devoicing minimal pairs, both voiced consonants (/b/, /d/, /g/) and voiceless consonants (/p/, /t/, /k/), by using the dependent Analysis of Variance (ANOVA).

3 FINDINGS AND DISCUSSION

3.1 Descriptive statistics

The average pretest and post-test scores from the two groups were investigated under descriptive statistics. The pretest and post-test scores were compared using the speech enunciation rubric.

Table 1. Enunciation clarity rubric.

Enunciation category (final devoicing minimal pairs)	Excellent (4pts)	Good (3pts)	Fair (2pts)	Poor (1pt)
Voiced consonants (/b/, /d/, /g/)	Correct, articulate, and distinct in pronunciation	Occasional in-articulation or inaccuracy in pronunciation.	Multiple inaccuracies in pronunciation; poor word separation. Sentences trail off toward the end.	Slurred and indistinct.
Voiceless consonants (/p/, /t/, /k/)	Correct, articulate, and distinct in pronunciation	Occasional in-articulation or inaccuracy in pronunciation.	Multiple inaccuracies in pronunciation; poor word separation. Sentences trail off toward the end.	Slurred and indistinct.

Table 2 shows the descriptive statistics used for examining the normal distribution of the data. Both EGOI and CGNO were equal, with the mean scores for the pretest 68.65 and 68.60, respectively. The normal distribution was investigated by using skewness and kurtosis values. The data from all of the phases or steps from the pretest and post-test were statistically analyzed. From the skewness range of 0.58–0.93, the skewness value (Zskew) of the pretest and post-test for the EGOI could be drawn into 1.04, 1.01, and 0.77, 0.53 for the CGNO respectively. The Zskew indicated the normal distribution. Kurtosis analysis was done in order to understand the density of the score distribution. From the table above, it can be seen that the kurtosis values were in the range of 0.54–1.18, with the kurtosis value (Zkur) of the pretest and post-test for the EGOI could be drawn into 0.49, 0.74, and 2.31, 0.96 for the CGNO respectively. It can be assumed that the data either had a histogram shape that was rather flat on top or had a platykurtic shape. However, the raw data were still considered normal, so they could be used.

3.2 Inferential statistics

In order to understand the effect of the Orai intervention as a tool for seeing the participants' clarity of enunciation, focusing on final devoicing minimal pairs, both voiced consonants (/b/, /d/, /g/) and voiceless consonants (/p/, /t/, /k/), this study used the dependent analysis of variance (ANOVA).

Table 3 displays that the F-value was 24.94, which was higher than the F-crit 4.10 ($\alpha = 0.05$), with the P-value less than the α (0.05). This confirmed that the Orai intervention has a significant influence on the overall participants' clarity of enunciation.

Table 4 indicates the ANOVA results of the traditional enunciation test for the CGNO. As shown in the table, the F-value was 0.98, which was less than the F-crit 4.10 with ($\alpha = 0.05$), and the P-value was higher than the α (0.05). This affirmed that the traditional test was not significant to elicit the participants' clarity on pronunciation.

3.3 The final devoicing minimal pairs

To investigate the use of the Orai application as the intervention in eliciting the participants' enunciation on the final devoicing minimal pairs, both voiced consonants (/b/, /d/, /g/) and voiceless consonants (/p/, /t/, /k/), we used the minimal pairs in isolation rather than in a non-isolated condition. This procedure allows the participants' conscious level and awareness to be actively involved. The Orai application has some features that record the participants' voices and transcribe them in alphabetic letters, rather than in international phonetic alphabets. Once the application recognizes and understands the participants' articulation or enunciation from the way they shape their sounds, the application starts to transcribe it in phonetics.

Table 2. Descriptive statistics for the participants' pretest and post-test.

Group	Test	N	Lower	Upper	Mean	SD	Skewness	ZSkew	Kurtosis	ZKur
EGOI	Pretest	20	64	77	68.65	3.45	0.93	1.04	0.54	0.49
	Posttest	20	69	80	73.60	2.78	0.90	1.01	0.82	0.74
CGNO	Pretest	20	65	75	68.50	2.85	0.84	0.77	2.53	2.31
	Posttest	20	66	75	69.25	2.70	0.58	0.53	1.05	0.96

Table 3. Summary of analysis of variance (ANOVA) for EGOI.

Sources	SS	df	MS	F	P value	F crit
Between groups	245.03	1	245.03	24.94	0.00	4.10
Within groups	373.35	38	9.83			
Total	618.38	39	15.86			

Table 4. Summary of analysis of variance (ANOVA) for CGNO.

Sources	SS	df	MS	F	P value	F crit
Between groups	4.90	1	4.90	0.98	0.32	4.10
Within groups	190.70	38	5.02			
Total	195.60	39	5.02			

Based on the principles, the issue regarding the final devoicing minimal pairs, both voiced consonants (/b/, /d/, /g/) and voiceless consonants (/p/, /t/, /k/), was investigated as follows.

Table 5 verified that the pretest – posttest changes of the EGOI outperformed the CGNO in the three types of final devoicing minimal pairs. This might have been affected by one of the features, which is called 'transcript'. The 'transcript' feature documented the sound produced by the participants. Once the sound was loud enough to catch, this feature rated the participants with grades A-D and then transcribed it.

It became clear and visible that the application might recognize the participants' voices and transcribe them consistently, in comparison to the two teachers who might have significantly different background knowledge Other aspects, such as tiredness, fatigue, concentration, and the halo effect, might cause subjectivity and therefore impact on the assessment and evaluation process.

Table 5. Summary of the final devoicing minimal pairs.

Final devoicing minimal pairs	Task	The pretest – posttest changes	
		EGOI	CGNO
Voiced/b/- voiceless/p/	Tab – Tap	0.48	0.063
	Cub – Cup	0.43	0.069
	Robe – Rope	0.49	0.064
	Cab – Cap	0.56	0.072
	Rib – Rip	0.48	0.068
Voiced/d/- voiceless/t/	Mad – Mat	0.53	0.071
	Bad – Bat	0.65	0.081
	Bed – Bet	0.45	0.063
	Kid – Kit	0.49	0.077
	Sad – Sat	0.64	0.086
Voiced/g/- voiceless/k/	Pig – Pick	0.41	0.067
	Bag – Back	0.42	0.054
	Dog – Dock	0.45	0.063
	Dug – Duck	0.42	0.064
	Clog – Clock	0.31	0.059

Table 6. Comparison of the final devoicing minimal pairs in the 'transcript' feature.

Final devoicing minimal pairs	Task	Participant 4	Participant 11	Participant 18
Voiced/b/- voiceless/p/	Tab – Tap	Tap – Tap	Tap – Tap	Tap – Tap
	Cub – Cup	Cub – Cup	Cub – Cup	Cub – Cup
	Robe – Rope	Rope – Rope	Rope – Rope	Rope – Rope
	Cab – Cap	Cap – Cap	Cap – Cap	Cap – Cap
	Rib – Rip	Rib – Rip	Rip – Rip	Rip – Rip
Voiced/d/- voiceless/t/	Mad – Mat	Mad – Mat	Mat – Mat	Mat – Mat
	Bad – Bat	Bet – Bet	Bet – Bet	Bet – Bet
	Bed – Bet	Bet – Bet	Bed – Bet	Bet – Bet
	Kid – Kit	Kid – Kit	Kit – Kit	Kit – Kit
	Sad – Sad	Sad – Sad	Sad – Sad	Sad – Sad
Voiced/g/- voiceless/k/	Pig – Pick	Pig – Pick	Pick – Pick	Pig – Pick
	Bag – Back	Bag – Back	Back – Back	Bag – Back
	Dog – Dock	Dock – Dock	Dog – Dock	Dog – Dock
	Dug – Duck	Duck – Duck	Duck – Duck	Duck – Duck
	Clog – Clock	Clock – Clock	Clock – Clock	Clock – Clock

4 CONCLUSIONS AND SUGGESTIONS

Focusing on the investigation of the effect of the Orai application on the individual's clarity of enunciation on final devoicing minimal pairs, this study implemented quasi-experimental research with non-equivalent group design (NEGD) and dependent analysis of variance (ANOVA). The findings concluded that the Orai application might help to recognize and understand the students' enunciation problems in an objective and consistent way. There is a tendency that some other factors, such as having different background knowledge, tiredness, fatigue, concentration, and the halo effect, might have an impact on the evaluation process. It is perceived that the results have implications for L2 assessment, particularly for nurturing assessment for learning.

REFERENCES

[1] Yano, Y. (2001). World Englishes in 2000 and beyond. *World Englishes, 20*(2), 119–132. doi:10.1111/1467-971x.00204.

[2] Kachru, B.B. (1992). Models for non-native Englishes. In B.B. Kachru (Ed.), *The other tongue: Englishes across cultures* (2nd ed.) (pp. 48–75). Urbana, IL: University of Illinois Press.

[3] Wenfang, C. (2011). Different models of English as an international language and their implications for teaching non-English majors. *Chinese Journal of Applied Linguistics, 34*(2), 5–17. doi:10.1515/CJAL.2011.011.

[4] Jenkins, J. (2002). A sociolinguistically based, empirically researched pronunciation syllabus for English as an international language. *Applied Linguistics, 23*(1), 83–103. doi:10.1093/applin/23.1.83.

[5] Saito, K. (2011). Identifying problematic segmental features to acquire comprehensible pronunciation in EFL settings: The case of Japanese learners of English. *RELC Journal, 42*(3), 363–378. doi:10.1177/0033688211420275.

[6] Khamkien, A. (2010). Thai learners' English pronunciation competence: Lesson learned from word stress assignment. *Journal of Language Teaching and Research, 1*(6), 757–764. doi:10.4304/jltr.1.6.757-764.

[7] Dlaska, A. & Krekeler, C. (2008). Self-assessment of pronunciation. *System, 36*(4), 506–516. doi:10.1016/j.system.2008.03.003.

English Linguistics, Literature, and Language Teaching in a Changing Era – Madya et al. (eds)
© 2020 Taylor & Francis Group, London, ISBN 978-1-03-224160-9

A needs analysis for hearing-impaired students' English writing materials

Wikandari M. Puspasari & Ashadi
English Education Department, Yogyakarta State University, Yogyakarta, Indonesia

ABSTRACT: English is one of the compulsory subjects for junior and senior high school students in Indonesia regardless of their capability. The problems arise when this policy is applied to students with special needs such as hearing-impaired students. One of the problems is that materials development for students with special needs has not been addressed widely in the literature. This article, therefore, identifies the learning and target needs of students with hearing problems and explains the impliations of these on their writing development. To analyze the students' needs in writing materials, the study employs a descriptive approach by means of interview guideline, questionnaire, and observation sheets in order to find out information about the specific students' problems and the teachers' problems in teaching writing. In this study, there are three research sites and a total subject of 12 students and three teachers in the academic year 2016/2017 in West Java, Indonesia. The findings show that the students still have difficulties in finding appropriate materials for the students that meet their level and needs to achieve the core and basic competences in the 2013 curriculum. Materials in the form of visual materials are also needed to assist teachers and students the teaching process. Further implications for materials development for students with specific needs are discussed.

Keywords: needs analysis, hearing-impaired students, materials development, teaching writing

1 INTRODUCTION

English is one of the compulsory subjects for junior and senior high school students in Indonesia regardless of their capability. Students with special needs such as hearing-impaired students must also learn English. However, they usually have difficulty in learning English, particularly in writing English. They have problems not only in generating ideas but also in translating their ideas into texts [1]. The teachers also face some challenges in teaching the students because of the limited existing materials for such students.

Writing is one of the skills that has to be mastered by the students. It is a productive skill so the students have to produce written language. Writing is the stage in which the writer has to produce the written form. The process has four main stages: planning, drafting, editing and final draft [2]. Writing pedagogy focuses on how the students generate and organize their ideas, use discourse markers cohesively, and revise and edit the text to produce the final draft [3]. Writing is a complex activity that has many stages and students must produce written text as the final product. Because of its complexities, many students have difficulties in learning writing. In order students write successfuly, the teacher should consider things such as genre, the writing process, and helping students to build a writing habit. Genre refers to the different types of writing; analyzing the genre of the texts helps the students to construct appropriate text. In the writing process, the teacher will need to encourage students to plan, draft and edit their written product. Encouraging students to write, help them to be better writers. To help students build a writing habit, the teacher needs to engage them, with activities that are easy and interesting [4]. It is important to help the students to learn to write so that they can write properly and overcome assist their difficulties.

Materials play an important role in teaching and learning. Materials are defined as anything that can be used to assist the teaching and learning process of the language [5]. Materials help students to improve their knowledge and develop their writing skills. To assist the teachers and students, materials that meet their needs must be developed. Materials development is defined as the process used by the practitioners who produce or use the materials for language learning [5] (p, 144). The framework for writing materials needs to be considered by the practitioners in order to make materials appropriate for the students this consist of things such as identifying the problem to solve, exploring the problem in term of the language and skills involved, contextual realization of the proposed materials; pedagogical realization of the materials by finding suitable activities and exercises for the students, and physical production of materials such as layout, visuals, etc [6]. However, materials development for hearing impaired has not been addressed widely in the literature and teachers have problems finding materials for the students. Some English textbooks are provided by the government, but these are not available for all grades and there is a lack in particular of resources for eight grade hearing-impaired students. Therefore, the teachers said that they often adapt materials from the internet or use textbooks designed for regular students.

Students with the special needs, such as hearing impaired students, need more attention from the teachers. Hearing-impaired students, for example may get the limited information in learning because one of their senses does not work fully. Hearing loss will not influence the cognitive abilities of the children, but it will impact their developmental experience [7]. The primary consequence for children of having hearing-impairement is that it prevents the development of their spoken language- both speaking and comprehension [8]. Hearing-impaired students have a more limited experience of learning then normal students so their teachers must consider many aspects when teaching them. The the teachers should keep in mind the following points when teaching: clear instructions, building students' motivation, sharing students' ideas in sign language and interpreting them into English, as well as allowing students to translate [9]. Clear communication between teachers and students in the classroom is also important to avoid misunderstanding and misinterpretation. There are five methods of clear communication that the teacher can use in the classroom: repetition, re-phrasing, explaining, simplifying, and clarifying. Repetition gives children the opportunity to hear the whole message while re-phrasing something gives students another chance to comprehend the message. Explanation give students more information and context and a second opportunity to comprehend the messages, while using simple language and a more basic structure can make it easier for students. Clarifying the communication also checks that the students have understood the messages [10]. In addition, teachers must consider using the appropriate materials for the students, so writing materials for hearing impaired students need to be developed.

To assist the teachers and the students, developing materials for hearing-impaired students needs to be encouraged by practitioners. And in developing the materials, needs analysis should be carried out to understand the students' needs. This study aims to identify the learning and target needs of students with hearing problems and to explain the problems they have in writing and the challenges teachers have in teaching writing to these students. The results of this study can be used to develop writing materials for hearing-impaired students.

Needs analysis plays an important role in materials development for students. Needs analysis is the procedure to obtain information about the students' needs [11]. When conducting needs analysis, there are two aspects that practitioners need to consider: target needs and learning needs. Target needs refer to what the students need to do in the target situation and cover necessities, lacks, and wants. Learning needs refer to what the students need to do in order to learn [12]. Needs analysis can be used to discover information about language skills, the language proficiency of the students, the activities in learning English, the difficulties that students face, the prior language learning experience, and the students' perspective about English [13]. This information is needed to make the appropriate materials for the students. Therefore, this article identifies the learning and target needs of students with hearing problems and explains the implications of these problems on their writing development.

2 RESEARCH METHOD

Descriptive methods were used to describe and analyze the students' needs in writing materials. This study identifies the learning and target needs of students with hearing problems and explains the problems they have in writing and the teachers' challenges in teaching writing to these students. The participants of this study were the teachers and the eighth-grade hearing-impaired students in Subang, West Java, Indonesia. In total, the subjects were 12 (seven males and five fimales) students and three teachers in the three research sites.

The study used interview guidelines, a questionnaire and an observation sheet to obtain information from the students and teachers. Teachers in each school were interviewed in order to find out the information about the students' problems and the teacher's problems in teaching writing. The teachers were asked several questions in the interview about points such as students' attitudes to learning English and writing in particular, the writing activities that they usually do, and about the material and media that students use in learning writing. The questionnaires were distributed to the students to find out about their needs in writing. The questionnaire consisted of 11 questions and was divided into six parts: necessities, lacks, wants, input, the students' role, and the teachers' role. The participants can check the appropriate column according to their aspirations and needs. The observation sheet was used as a guideline for the researcher to take into account the general characteristics, the number of students, students' activities and specific students' attitudes in the teaching and learning process. The data from the questionnaire were presented in the form of a pie chart and a table. The data from the interviews and observations were analyzed using descriptive qualitative methods by reducing, displaying and summarizing the data [14]. The result of observations and interviews were reduced into a small number of categories to make the data simpler, then the data were organized and the conclusions from the data were drawn.

3 FINDINGS AND DISCUSSION

3.1 Findings

1) Description of the participants

The participants of this study were of eighth-grade hearing-impaired students at three research sites and the three teachers who teach them. The teachers teach all the subjects to their students, including English. The total numbers of the students in the schools were 12 students as presented in the Table 1.

2) Description of the target needs

The data for the target needs were obtained from the interviews, questionnaires and observations. This covers necessities, lacks(or deficiencies), and wants. The data are explained below.

a. Necessities

For the necessities, the data were obtained from the interview with the teachers, the questionnaire from the students, and observation. There were some aspects related to the necessities which were about the students' purpose in learning writing, their attitudes in learning English and particularly writing, writing activities that they usually do, and the materials and media that students use in learning writing. The aspects and the results are as follows:

Table 1. Numbers of students.

SLB A		Name of Schools SLB B		SLB C	
Male	Female	Male	Female	Male	Female
4	2	1	2	2	1

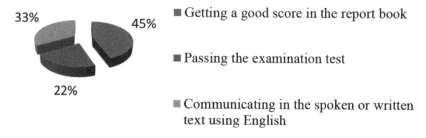

Figure 1. The purpose of the students in learning writing.

    i. The purpose of the students in learning writing. The results from the questionnaire show that the majority of students about 45% said that getting a good score in the report book is their purpose in learning English, particularly writing. (see Figure 1)
   ii. The student's attitudes in learning writing. In the interviews, teachers were asked about students' attitude to learning and observation was also gathered from the observations in the class. The results show that some of the students are enthusiastic about learning English but that others are not too enthusiastic about learning English, particularly writing. Some of the teachers said that the students who are not enthusiastic about learning assume that writing English is difficult to learn.
  iii. Writing activities. According to the teachers and the observations, the students usually wrote imitativewriting for their activities, such as writing English vocabulary, rewriting short conversations, matching the vocabulary with the correct pictures, and completing the short conversation with the correct answers.
  vi. The materials that students use in learning writing. The question about the materials that students use in learning was asked in the interview with the teacher and questionnaire. On the basis of interviews and observations, the students usually use an English textbook for junior high school students. The teachers also said that they adapted materials from the internet for the students. In addition, based on the questionnaire, 69% of the students mostly use an English textbook as their learning materials (see Figure 2).
   v. The media that students use in learning writing. From the results of the interviews and observations in the class, the principle media used by the students are pictures. The teachers stated that they usually print out pictures from the internet that are related to the materials. They also use real things to facilitate the students' learning. The students mostly used pictures as their media in learning; about 50% of the students chose pictures in the questionnaire (see Figure 3).

b. Lacks

The aim of the questions about lacks was to discover the performance gap of the students in the target situation. Some aspects related to the lacks of the students were covered,

Figure 2. Materials that students use in learning writing.

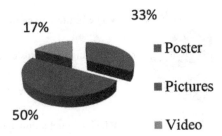

Figure 3. Media that students use in learning writing.

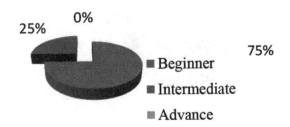

Figure 4. The level of the students in learning writing.

such as the students' lavel in writing, the students' problems in writing, and the teachers' challenges in teaching writing.

i. Students' level in writing. Based on the interviews and observations in the class, the predominant level of the students in writing terms was that of novice writer. The teacher said that most of the students still make error in writing vocabulary, and they still write in simple sentences for their writing. Based on the questionnaire, about 75% of the students are still beginners in writing (see Figure 4).

ii. Students' problems in writing. The results of the students' problems in writing in the questionnaire show that many students still face difficulties in writing such as having a limited range of vocabulary, difficulties in writing words correctly, constructing correct sentences, and determining the generic structure of the texts. The results are as follows (see Figure 5): 17% of students have a limited range of vocabulary; 17% find it difficult to write the words correctly; 17% find it difficult to construct the sentences correctly; 9% still have difficulties in using punctuation correctly; 12% find it difficult to determine the structure of a paragraph, such as opening, content, and closing; 11% have difficulties in mastering the purpose of the texts; and 17% find it difficult to determine the generic structure of the text. In addition, in the interviews with the teachers, they said that students have many difficulties in writing particularly in constructing sentences, and that they have a limited range of vocabulary (see Figure 5).

iii. Teachers' challenges in teaching writing. The teachers said in the interviews that they have some challenges in teaching students. The level of the students is one of the challenges that the teachers face in the teaching and learning process. The teachers said that they have to make the materials as simple as possible so that the students can comprehend them. The limited resources of the materials and media such as textbooks and pictures are also a problem for the teachers. Textbooks that are appropriate for students' needs are difficult to find, and existing media that can assist the students in learning is limited in the schools.

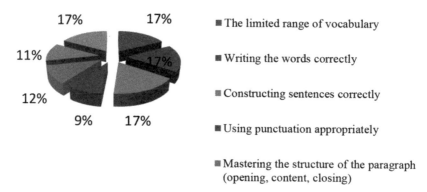

Figure 5. Students' problems in writing.

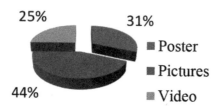

Figure 6. The expected media in learning writing.

c. Wants

The teachers and students are asked some questions in the interview and questionnaire relating to the students wants. The aspects of concern were: the expected media in learning, the expected topics in writing, and the writing skill that they wish to acquire.

i. The expected media in learning. In the interviews, the teachers said that media can facilitate the students in learning and assist the teacher in delivering the materials to the students. Visual media such as pictures, posters, or videos are helpful to facilitate students in their learning. Moreover, from the results of the questionnaire, the largest proportion of the students also expect visual media such as pictures as (see Figure 6).

ii. The expected topics in writing. The question relating to the topics in writing was asked of the students on the basis that they might be more motivated if the writing topics are based on their wants. 67% of the students want topics related to daily activities, 13% would like topics related to cultures and animals, and 7% of the students want topics about sports (see Figure 7).

3) Descriptions of learning needs

The data for the learning needs covered the expected inputs and the teachers' role. The data were as follow:

i. The input for the students. In interviews, the teachers said that they usually use inputs in teaching such as pictures, and short conversational texts. They also bring the real things into the class. The results of the questionnaire show that the greatest proportion of the students (about 44%) chose pictures as their preferred input in learning writing (see Figure 8).

ii. Teachers' role. According to the questionnaire, the students expected that the teachers should present an example first before assigning tasks to the students. It shows in the chart below (as shown in the Figure 9).

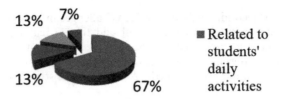

Figure 7. The expected topics in writing.

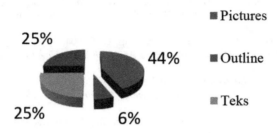

Figure 8. The expected input.

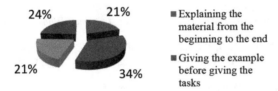

Figure 9. Teachers' role.

3.2 Discussion

In this needs analysis study, the result of the target needs and learning needs of the students show that the students and teachers face many challanges in learning and teaching English writing. The students face difficulties in learning writing such as having a limited range of vocabulary, being unable to construct sentences correctly, and struggling to generate ideas. The hearing-impaired students usually make the same mistakes in reading and writing as those made by second language learners [15]. Hearing-impaired students also have difficulties in using syntax appropriately [16]. These problems affect to their writing skills. In addition, the teachers have difficulties in finding the appropriate materials for the students.

The study also showed that the students need visual materials and media to assist them in learning writing. The visual materials and media will assist them in learning because most of them are visual learners. Visual teaching methods, and the use of pictures can also assist them in learning [17]. In addition, the teachers must also pay more attention to the students when teaching and ensure that they give clear instructions and provide examples to the students beforeassigning them tasks.

4 CONCLUSIONS AND SUGGESTIONS

Based on the results, this study draws the following conclusions. First that hearing-impaired students face many difficulties in learning writing. They have difficulties in mastering the range of vocabulary, in constructing sentences, and in mastering the purpose of generic structure of written texts/Second, teachers also face challenges in teaching such students, such as the limitation of existing media in the school and the difficulty in finding appropriate materials that matchs the students' levels and needs. One suggestion is to engage professional practicioners to develop materials to assist hearing-impaired students in learning; another is that schools and teachers should provide media to facilitate the students' learning.

REFERENCES

[1] J. Richard and W. Renandya, *Teaching Writing*, in *Methodology in language teaching: An anthology of current practice*, J. Richards and W. Renandya, eds., Cambridge University Press, Cambridge, 2002.

[2] J. Harmer, *How to Teach Writing*, Longman Group, UK, 2004.

[3] H. Brown, *Teaching by Principles: An Interactive Approach to Language Pedagogy*, Pearson Education, New York, 2001.

[4] J. Harmer, *How to teach English*, Longman Group, UK, 2007.

[5] B. Tomlinson, *Materials development for language learning and teaching*, Cambridge Journals 45 (2012), pp. 143–179.

[6] B. Tomlinson, *Materials development in language teaching*, Cambridge University Press, Cambridge, Book chapter David jolly and Rod Bolitho, 1998.

[7] S. Kirk, J. Gallagher, M. Coleman and N. Anastasiow, *Educating Exceptional Children*, 12th ed. Cengage Learning, USA, 2009.

[8] R.I. Mayberry, *Cognitive Development in Deaf Children: The Interface of Language and Perception in Neuropsychology*, Elsevier, Canada, 2002.

[9] F. Brokop and B. Persall, *Writing Strategies for Learners Who Are Deaf*, NorQuest Collage, Edmonton, 2010.

[10] NDCS, *Deaf Friendly Teaching*, The national deaf children's society, UK, 2004.

[11] J. Richards, *Curriculum Development in Language Teaching*, Cambridge University Press, New York, 2001.

[12] T. Hutchinson and A. Waters, *English for Specific Purposes*, Cambridge University Press, Cambridge, 1987.

[13] J. Richards, *Key Issues in Langauge Teaching*, Cambridge University Press, UK, 2015.

[14] M.B. Miles, A.M. Huberman and J. Saldana, *Qualitative Data Analysis: A Method Sourcebook*, Sage Publication, inc., USA, 2014.

[15] S. Annete, *Teaching Reading and Writing to Deaflearners in Primary Schools in Uganda*, University of Oslo, 2011.

[16] C. Mayer, *Shaping at the Point of Utterance: An Investigation of composing processes of the deaf student writer*, J. Deaf Stud. Deaf Educ. 1 (1999), pp. 37–49.

[17] *A Deaf or Hard of Hearing Students in Classroom*. Available at http://deafchildrenaustralia.org.au /wp-content/uploads/2014/11/Deaf-Child-in-Classroom-2012.pdf.

English Linguistics, Literature, and Language Teaching in a Changing Era – Madya et al. (eds)
© 2020 Taylor & Francis Group, London, ISBN 978-1-03-224160-9

L1 in L2 classroom: How does it truly assist learning?

Zefki O. Feri & Ashadi
Applied Linguistics Department, Graduate School, Yogyakarta State University, Yogyakarta, Indonesia

ABSTRACT: There have been mixed research results on the use of First Language (L1) in Second Language (L2) classroom. Most of them point out the danger of L1 use that may risk and give negative effects on L2 learning. However, the use of L1 has been a common occurrence in L2 classroom. L1 still has its place in teaching and learning L2 although teachers and students are strongly acclaimed to maximize the L2 use. Hence, by focusing on its significant contributions to L2 learning and teaching, this paper aims at discussing the issue of L1 use in L2 classroom within the existing literature. It tries to elaborate arguments to support the L1 use in L2 classroom by exploring its significances. The arguments are addressed in three main concerns: the purposeful use of L1, functions of L1 use, and strategies for integrating L1 use in L2 classroom. Suggestions and recommendations are also provided.

Keywords: L1 use, L2 Classroom, L2 Learning

1 INTRODUCTION

The use of L1 in L2 classroom has long been debated and becomes a controversy that has attracted a lot of parties to study this area further. Research in this area has shown advances progressively, in which both positive and negative effects of L1 use in L2 classroom are explored. The results of such research have given more insights on the status of L1 use. In general, there are two sides in respect to the use L1 in L2 classroom, one opposes and for the other supports. The opposing party to the L1 use is under monolingual principle, which claims that no L1 interference is allowed in L2 classroom. L2 classroom should be totally conducted in L2. As classroom is considered as the main single L2 source of frequent exposure, it must be used exclusively to support students in learning and acquisition L2 [1,2,3,4].

On the other hand, proponents of L1 use, under the bilingual principle, argue that there are some strong reasons to include L1 in L2 classroom. L1 use is claimed to significantly contribute to L2 learning [5]. The use of L1 is believed to be a significant way to improve students' comprehension particularly in explaining difficult materials of L2 [6,7,8]. L1 is shown to be effective in explaining difficult grammar points/concepts and conveying meaning of L2 [9,10, 11]. Moreover, L1 use also functions as a classroom management tool considering its effectiveness compared to L2 [10]. The use of L1 gives advantage to students with lower proficiency [12].

Despite the possible effects of L1 use, there is no clear cut position of the ideal amount of L1 use in l2 classroom. Most of language teachers are confused to alternate using L1 in their teaching. In common practices, L1 is often overused causing dominance and interference in L2 classroom. It tends to drive the instructional language use in teaching and learning which consequently limits the use of the target language (L2). As a result, it influences the availability and quality of L2 exposure which is absolutely important for students in their L2 learning and acquisition development. Moreover, by the strong emphasis on the maximal L2 use, teachers tend to feel mortified in using L1 in teaching, so that itis not effectively used and explored as an assisting tool in their teaching.

349

Considering its significances to L2 learning, there is a need for a new look on how L1 should be ideally used and organized in L2 classrooms. Teachers who play important roles in the classroom have to be aware of the status of L1 in L2 classroom, so that they could organize the use of L1 by considering its advantages and disadvantages. Therefore, this paper aims at discussing the issue of L1 use in L2 classrooms within the existing literature to specifically explore the benefits of L1 use, and tries to find out in what way L1 is best used. This is to provide teachers the alternative use of L1 and L2 in the classroom. Focusing on the benefits of L1 use, it first explores the functional use of L1 in the classroom to analyse the case of L1 use occurrence. Then, it explores the functions of L1 use in respect to assisting learning. After that, it provides measured ways of using L1 in L2 classroom along with guidance and principles. Further suggestions and recommendations are also provided.

2 THE USE OF L1

The use of L1 in L2 classroom has been discouraged by those who advocate monolingual approach [2]. They believe that students will learn better by providing much exposure of the L2, as the exclusive L2 use in the classroom enriches students' experience in L2. However, it does not mean that teachers cannot alternate using L1 in their teaching [6]. Those who support bilingualism agree that L1 plays significant roles particularly in which L2 use does not work in a particular case. As it has become a part of language teaching, L1 use exists in some common practices as seen through the following use.

Generally, teachers apply L1 in L2 settings for five main purposes. *First*, L1 is mostly used in grammar instruction over other language skills. It is considered as an effective tool to explain grammatical concepts [19]. Grammar is often considered difficult for L2 learners, and L1 use is considered to be an effective way to achieve understanding. Generally, the whole utterances used by teacher in this particular teaching are in L1 [10]. *Second,* L1 is used to explain vocabulary to students [14,15]. Newly introduced vocabulary and specific terms are often explained by teachers through L1. Typically, teachers use code-mixing and code-switching betweenL1 and L2. L1 use is also common in translating L2 to achieve understanding and building student translation skill. *Third*, L1 is used to manage the classroom, where L1 is considered to be more effective particularly in setting up learning activities [16,17,18]. *Fourth,* L1 is used as classroom administrative language. When teachers review sections, mid-terms, or homework, L1 is used in order to build students' understanding towards the review points. *Last* but not least, L1 is used in maintaining solidarity and giving empathy[16]. In such cases, students are best treated in L1 rather than in L2 because they easily understand what teachers say and want in their own language.

For students, L1 use serves several functions in their learning activities. *First,* they use their L1 as a strategy to make social interaction with other students who also have limited foreign language proficiency. *Second,* L1 is considered as a good cognitive resource. Studies show that ideas are better produced in L1rather than in L2 for essay writing[19]in which planning in L1 can give more elaborated content and organization than in L2 [20]. In oral task performance, students using L1 can lead to more interactional coherence and collaborative talks. *Third*, L1 is commonly used as metatalk (21). It is a talk or discussion on how students should employ in building up an activity. It allows students to talk with themselves. Thus, it can possibly mean that students use L1 as an aid to increase their performance, such as in writing and oral task. Allowing students to use their L1, therefore, will contribute in building confidence in performance tasks.

3 FUNCTIONS OF L1 USE

Studies have shown that using L1 alternatively in L2 classroom serves pedagogical functions and plays significant roles in both learning and acquisition. As an alternative language, the use of L1 purposively gives benefits to teachers and students as it facilitates teaching and learning [22]. *First*, L1 improves comprehension/understanding. Comprehension/understanding becomes a goal of teaching and learning. Teaching basically aims to promote students comprehension/understanding on the targeted objectives. Successful teaching is achieved when teachers are able to build students comprehension. For this purpose, L1 is used by teachers in explaining difficult materials such as difficult grammatical concepts and other difficult materials [10]. L1 is used as an effective method to comprehend and analyse the structure of L2 [23]. The goal is to effectively build students' grammatical competence.

Second, L1 can be a source of positive transfer. Unlike those who support monolingual approach with their fear of interference, bilingualism supporters believed that L1 can, to some extent, be considered as positive source [21]. The concept of transfer in language should not always be perceived as a negative one. L1 may have positive impacts on one's L2 development when the two languages are used accordingly in the classroom. In learning L2, students tend to look for linguistic similarities rather than differences, wherever they can find them [24]. These similarities can occur at lexical, phrasal, and even clausal levels.

Third, L1 may function as a communicative strategy which is commonly used to help students to engage themselves in L2 communication [21]. Less fluent students may opt to use L1 as a communication aid. This strategy is used to overcome the crisis in communication where students cannot share ideas in L2. In communicative competence, such strategy is an important aspect of strategic competence [25]. *Fourth,* L1 is an *affect.* The exclusive use of L2 in the classroom can be harmful for students with limited proficiency as it can be a main source of embarrassment for introvert students and those who are less proficient in using L2 [26]. L1 can be used as a means to reduce student anxiety and to create good rapport. Talking in L1 with students who have difficulties and problems becomes an effective way to understand them. L1 is also effective when teachers want to ensure the favourable classroom environment.

4 STRATEGIES FOR L1 USE

L1 must be used carefully in L2 classroom to benefit and bring impacts on L2 learning. Teachers as the key actor have to design the course accordingly by considering the use appropriate language to assist learning and conduct effective teaching, without neglecting the amount and quality of L2 exposure. There are, at least, four points for teachers to consider in integrating L1 into L2 classroom [1]. The first point is efficiency. L1 is better used to present meanings of complicated vocabulary items. It is considered to be more effective and simple for that purpose. Students may, at a certain degree, get frustrated if they are exposed only to full L2 [27]. The second point is learning. Teachers can facilitate students in learning complex grammar concepts, for example, or other learning contents by using L1. There is a strong recommendation to explain grammar in L1 particularly to students of lower proficiency. As grammatical competence is crucial [28], L1 must be considered well to help students achieve this know-how. The third factor is genuineness for the teacher in building rapport with students and setting up good atmosphere of learning environment. The fourth factor is external relevance. It denotes the awareness of when, where, and how to use both L1 and L2 appropriately that helps students to be more successful in their future. For instance, students who are able to do code-mixing and code-switching appropriately can be a successful language user when they are facing a condition where a mix language use is required.

Considering its pedagogical significances to L2 teaching and learning, L1 can be used wisely by teachers mainly as a tool and strategy to achieve the core learning goals. The following are three strategies in using L1 to achieve the learning goals [16]. They lie in three stages: presentation, practice, and production. In order to aid student progress more quickly, teachers can take benefits of L1 use as an efficient way to clarify meanings of words, structures or utterances at the presentation stage. Commonly, students having low proficiency are difficult to understand the main concept of L2 particularly on complex grammar. They also find difficulties in understanding meanings of such difficult vocabularies. For these cases, teachers can help students in understanding those concepts and meanings through L1.

At the practice stage, L1 is used as stimuli for students in practicing L2. At this stage, teachers present the target structures of L2, then L1 is used to stimulate students' understanding through equivalent meaning, which is not only on the structure level but also on the whole meaning level. In dialogue practice, for example, teachers can use L1 in guiding students in constructing a dialogue. After several repetitions, students are hopefully able to produce it well in L2. The same principle is also applied to Grammar Translation Method. L1 is used as a means to produce the texts in L2. This is also as way to develop students' translation skills [23]. At the production stage, teachers may put L1 as a starting point in several designed activities. L1 can be used as stimuli for students in using L2. In its practice, one of the most common activities which L1 use can be alternated is speaking activity particularly for low proficient students. In oral presentation, for example, students can collect and elaborate ideas in L1 by interviewing friends to get some data to be presented later in L2. This is considered as a good strategy for students in preparing good presentation.

5 CONCLUSION

The use of L1 in L2 classroom remains debatable on whether it should be allowed or not, but there is no danger to integrate it in L2 classroom as it supports and brings impacts on teaching and learning. Recent studies have shown that L1 can truly assist learning if it is used appropriately in the proper ways [29]. At least, there are three pedagogical implications of L1 use in L2 classroom. First, usingL1 assists students in learning complex and difficult materials. It helps students in building up understanding in which L1 use eases them in comprehending the concepts. Second, L1 functions as cognitive resource. Students can easily access L2 by exploring what they have in their L1. In this case, the concept of crosslinguistic influence [30] plays a vital role. Third, L1 use facilitates teachers in organizing the classroom. It helps teachers in explaining the course instructions and some other related rules. All of these implications highlight that bi/multilingual teachers sharing the same L1 with students have their own advantages and superiority in assisting students learn L2. As research has shown, local teachers/non-native speaker teachers are good in developing students' language competence particularly in grammar and more effective in facilitating students than native ones because of their ability to make use of their mother tongue appropriately [31,32,33]. In a nutshell, L1 use has the potential to bring significant impacts on L2 learning if it is used in appropriate and measured ways.

REFERENCES

[1] Cook, V. (2001). Using the first language in the classroom. *The Canadian Modern Language Review, 57*(3), 402–423.

[2] Krashen, S. (1982). *Principles and practice in second language acquisition.* New York: Pergamon Press.

[3] Pennycook, A. (1994). *The cultural politics of English as an international language.* London & New York: Longman.

[4] Madrinan, M.S. (2014). The use of first language in second-language classroom: A support for second language acquisition. *Gist Research and Learning Research Journal, 9*, 50–66.

[5] Iswati, L., & Hadimulyo, A.O. (2018). The role of l1 in l2 class. *Journal of English Education, Literature and Culture, 3*(2), 125–134.

[6] Turnbull, M. (2001). There is a role for the L1 in second and foreign language teaching, but.... *Canadian Modern Language Review, 57*(4), 531–540.

[7] de Oliveira, L.C., Gilmetdinova, A., & Pelaez-Morales, C. (2016). The use of Spanish by a monolingual kindergarten teacher to support English language learners. *Language and Education, 30*(1), 22–42.

[8] Tian, L., & Hennebry, M. (2016). Chinese learners' perceptions towards teachers' language use in lexical explanations: A comparison between Chinese-only and English-only instructions. *System, 63*, 77–78.

[9] Mitchell, R. (1988). *Communicative language teaching in practice.* London: CILT.

[10] Polio, C., & Duff, P. (1994). Teachers' language use in university foreign language classroom: a qualitative analysis of English and target language alternation. *Modern Language Journal, 78*(3), 313–326.

[11] Mohebbi, H., & Alavi, S.M. (2014). teachers' first language use in second language learning classroom context: a questionnaire-based study. *Bellaterra Journal of Teaching & Learning Language & Literature*, *7*(4), 57–73.

[12] Seng, G.H., & Hashim, F. (2006). Use of L1 in L2 reading comprehension among tertiary ESL learners. *Reading in a Foreign Language*, *18*(1).

[13] Macdonald, C. (1993). *Using the target language*. Cheltenham, England: Mary Glasgow.

[14] Alshehri, E. (2017). Using learner's first language in EFL classroom. *IAFOR Journal of Language Learning*, *3*(1), 20–33.

[15] Khetaguri, T., Zangladze, M., & Albay, M. (2016). The benefits of using l1 in foreign language learning process. *International Journal of Social Sciences & Educational Studies*, *2*(3), 24–26.

[16] Littlewood, W., & Yu, B. (2011). First language and target language in foreign language classroom. *Lang. Teach.*, *44*(1), 64–77.

[17] Choi, T., & Leung, C. (2017). Uses of first and foreign languages as learning resources in foreign language classroom. *The Journal of Asia TEFL*, *14*(1), 587–604.

[18] Hidyati, I.N. (2012). Evaluating the role of l1 in teaching receptive skills and grammar in EFL classes. *Indonesian Journal of Applied Linguistics*, *1*(2), 17–32.

[19] Stapa, S. & Majid, A. (2009). The use of English in Limited English proficiency classes: good, bad or ugly? *Journal e-Bangi*, *1*(1), 1–12.

[20] Lally, C. (2000). First language influences in second language composition: The effect of pre-writing. *Foreign language Annals*, *33*, 428–432.

[21] Ellis, R. & Shintani, N. (2014). *Exploring Language Pedagogy through Second Language Acquisition Research*. New York: Routledge.

[22] Miles, R. (2004). *Evaluating the Use of L1 in the English Language Classroom* (Master Thesis, University of Birmingham, 2004). 5 September 2018.

[23] Husain, K. (1995). Assessing the role of translation as a learning strategy in ESL. *International Journal of Translation*, *1*(2), 59–84.

[24] Ringbom, H. (2007). *The importance of cross-linguistic similarity in foreign language learning: comprehension, learning and production.* Clevedon: Multilingual Matters.

[25] Faerch C., & Kasper G. (1980). Processes and strategies in foreign language learning and communication. *Interlanguage Studies Bulletin*, *5*(1), 47–118.

[26] Nation, I.S.P. (2003). The role of first language in foreign language learning. *Asian EFL Journal*, *5*(2), 1–8.

[27] Atkinson, D. (1993). Teaching in the target language: A problem in the current orthodoxy. *Language Learning Journal*, *8*(1), 2–5.

[28] Canale, M., & Swain, M. (1980). Theoretical bases of communicative approaches to second language teaching and testing. *Applied Linguistics*, *1*, 1–47.

[29] Karimian, Z., & Mohammadi, S. (2015). Teacher's use of first language in EFL classroom. *Journal of Applied Linguistics and Language Research*, *2*(03), 61–71.

[30] Ortega, L. (2009). *Understanding Second Language Acquisition*. New York: Routledge.

[31] Walkinshaw, I., & Oanh, D.H. (2014). Native and non-native English language teachers: student perceptions in Vietnam and Japan. *SAGE Open*, April-June 2014: 1–9.

[32] Ma, L.P.F. (2012). Advantages and disadvantages of native- and nonnative-English-speaking teachers: student perceptions in Hong Kong. *TESOL QUARTERLY*, *46*(2). 280–305.

[33] Gurkan, S., & Yuksel, Y. (2012). Evaluating the contributions of native and non-native teachers to an English language teaching program. *Procedia - Social and Behavioral Sciences*, *46*, 2951–2958.

English Linguistics, Literature, and Language Teaching in a Changing Era – Madya et al. (eds)
© 2020 Taylor & Francis Group, London, ISBN 978-1-03-224160-9

Author Index

Aceng 283
Andayani, A.T. 44
Andriyanti, E. 187, 227, 243, 251
Ardiani, R. 264
Ashadi 214, 220, 341, 349
Asmara, R. 335
Asmarani, R. 63
Azizah, S.M. 271

Barkhuizen, G. 3
Basikin 44, 108
Budiman, M. 9

Cahyadin, W. 328
Cahyaningrum, D. 130, 165
Ciptaningrum, D.S. 115, 150, 271, 308

Emeral 150, 308
Emzir 57, 283

Fauziati, E. 209
Feri, Z.O. 349
Floriasti, T.W. 315

Galuhwardani, C. 123

Hendriwanto 172
Herawati, O. 235
Hidayah, Y.N. 214
Hidayat, N. 193

Kartikarini, T. 150, 308

Kasse, T. 300
Kiswaga, G. 158
Koso, H. 328
Kuncahya, A.O. 108
Kurniati, U. 172
Kustini, S. 276
Kusumaningrum, W.R. 335

Lestari, H.P. 178
Lestari, S. 193

Madya, S. 20
Marahati, E.M. 150, 308
Marlisa, N. 220
Marmanto, S. 209
Mayasari, I. 214
Maykasari, D. 137
Miqawati, A.H. 94
Muamaroh 193
Muslim, N.I. 214

Ngadiso 130
Nofandi, F. 144
Nurcahyani, D. 199

Oda, M. 14

Permatasari, I. 187, 315
Pratolo, B.W. 123, 178, 264
Purba, D. 144
Purbani, W. 137
Purnawarman, P. 76
Puspasari, W.M. 341

Rachmawati, U. 320
Rahmawati, N. 209
Rahmawati, S.R. 283
Ratnaningsih, D. 144
Rayshata, C.E. 115
Risna, S. 69
Rizqiana, A. 100

Sa'adah, N. 227
Saifuddin, M. 199
Sarjiyati, S. 89
Setyaningrum, S.W. 308
Setyaningsih, A. 289
Shara, R.A. 251
Soidi, O. 57
Stockton, R.J. 257
Sudartini, S. 289
Sugirin 289
Suherdi, D. 76

Tamboto, J.H. 57
Triastuti, A. 100, 158, 300

Utami, W.H. 76

Widodo, P. 69
Wijayanti, F. 94
Wijayati, P. 243
Wiratno, D. 144

Zaid, A. 89
Zainnuri, H. 130